In the Labyrinth of the KGB

In the Labyrinth of the KGB

Ukraine's Intelligentsia in the 1960s–1970s

Olga Bertelsen

LEXINGTON BOOKS
Lanham • Boulder • New York • London

"Crossing Ethnic Barriers Enforced by the KGB: Kharkiv Writers' Lives in the 1960s-1970s," *East/West: Journal of Ukrainian Studies* 7, no. 1 (2020): 7–54.

Bertelsen, Olga. "Rethinking Psychiatric Terror Against Nationalists in Ukraine: Spatial Dimensions of Post-Stalinist State Violence." *Kyiv-Mohyla Humanities Journal* 1 (2014): 27–76.

Published by Lexington Books
An imprint of The Rowman & Littlefield Publishing Group, Inc.
4501 Forbes Boulevard, Suite 200, Lanham, Maryland 20706
www.rowman.com

86-90 Paul Street, London EC2A 4NE

Copyright © 2022 by The Rowman & Littlefield Publishing Group, Inc.

All rights reserved. No part of this book may be reproduced in any form or by any electronic or mechanical means, including information storage and retrieval systems, without written permission from the publisher, except by a reviewer who may quote passages in a review.

British Library Cataloguing in Publication Information Available

Library of Congress Cataloging-in-Publication Data

Names: Bertelsen, Olga, author.
Title: In the labyrinth of the KGB : Ukraine's intelligentsia in the 1960s–1970s / Olga Bertelsen.
Description: Lanham : Lexington Books, [2022] | Includes bibliographical references and index. | Summary: "This book focuses on the writers who lived through the processes of de-Stalinization and re-Stalinization during the 1960s and 1970s in Soviet Ukraine. The author argues that the KGB unintentionally facilitated the transnational and intercultural links among the Kharkiv multiethnic community of writers"—Provided by publisher.
Identifiers: LCCN 2021054894 (print) | LCCN 2021054895 (ebook) | ISBN 9781793608925 (cloth) | ISBN 9781793608949 (paperback) | ISBN 9781793608932 (ebook)
Subjects: LCSH: Authors, Ukrainian—20th century. | Authors, Ukrainian—Ukraine—Kharkiv. | Politics and literature—Ukraine. | Ukraine—Intellectual life—20th century. | LCGFT: Literary criticism.
Classification: LCC PG3916.2 .B47 2022 (print) | LCC PG3916.2 (ebook) | DDC 891.7/9090034—dc23/eng/20211216
LC record available at https://lccn.loc.gov/2021054894
LC ebook record available at https://lccn.loc.gov/2021054895

For Katia—to remember

For Village of Columbus

Contents

Acknowledgments		ix
Introduction		xiii
1	"The Revolution of Poets" and Re-Stalinization	1
2	Petro Shelest, the Literati, and the "Jewish Question"	55
3	The Writers, the Dissent, and the Human Rights Movement in the West	111
4	The Labyrinths of Silence and Psychiatric Abuse	161
5	The Writers and the *Chekists*' Discourse about the Holodomor	203
6	The Years of Timelessness	241
Conclusion		275
Bibliography		283
Index		321
About the Author		343

Acknowledgments

Almost a decade has passed since I began working on this book. During that time, I had come to realize how deeply my early years have influenced my thinking. I would like to thank my parents, posthumously, for inspiring me to learn more about their uneasy, turbulent lives, and about the lives of their friends and colleagues who resided in Soviet Ukraine and their home city Kharkiv. For the first time, I am writing about my parents and their milieu, and I would like to thank their close friends and colleagues for their sincerity and courage in discussing with me the most painful memories and experiences associated with authoritarian Kharkiv of the 1960s–1970s and the dangers they navigated in their lives.

Volodymyr Briuggen, a brilliant literary critic and writer, was especially helpful and generous with his time and insights that found their way into this narrative. I would also like to thank many other Kharkivites, writers, publishers, editors, actors, and painters who contributed greatly to my understanding of the two dramatic decades after the Holodomor and the Second World War, Ukraine of the 1960s and 1970s. Through their oral accounts, published memoirs, and scholarship, as well as in our conversations, they recreated the atmosphere of chronic terror associated with the intellectual elites' suffering and deaths at the hands of Kharkiv's authorities and the KGB. Among them are Radii Polonskyi and Arkadii Filatov, Leonid Osmolovskyi (Osadchuk) and Yurii Stadnychenko, Serhii Boltryk and Yevdokiia Kudakova, Anatolii Starodub and Svitlana Klebanova, Viacheslav Romanovskyi and Olha Ulishchenko, Anatolii Miroshnychenko and Ivan Kulyk, Iryna Myronenko and Tetiana Shamrai, Anatolii Pererva and Ihor Mykhailyn, Pavlo Shihimaha and Viktor Polianetskyi, Oleksa Marchenko and Mykola Kursin, Oleksandr Vasyl'iev and Zinovii Valshonok, Leonid Toma and Olena Kalnytska, Valerii D'iachenko and Anatolii Kazakov, Nelli Epelman and Volodymyr

Mislavskyi, Irena Hryhorenko and Tetiana Pylypchuk, Olha Riznychenko and Rostyslav Melnykiv, Oleksii and Olha Muratovy, Valerii Zamesov and Oleksii Aulov, Tetiana Honcharova and Bohdan Ivchenko. Their contributions to this book are diverse and invaluable. My father's close friend, Sviatoslav Maksymchuk, who has been part of Lviv's Mariia Zankovetska drama theater since 1964, shared with me his experiences in Kharkiv and its atmosphere in the 1960s–1970s. Importantly, his performances and readings of poetry unveiled new senses and emotions imbedded in the texts produced by Kharkiv writers.

I am grateful to Mark von Hagen, Alexander J. Motyl, George O. Liber, Yohanan Petrovsky-Shtern, Norman M. Naimark, Myroslav Shkandrij, Serhii Plokhy, Lynne Viola, Michael C. Hickey, Gennady Estraikh, Svitlana Krys, Marta Baziuk, Frank Sysyn, Anna Procyk, and the anonymous reviewers of this book for their insightful suggestions and comments. Some read the earlier drafts of several chapters from this book, others—the entire manuscript. I would also like to thank Marco Carynnyk and Paul Robert Magocsi whose research and scholarship inspired me to explore in depth the history of the Ukrainian-Jewish encounter.

I also extend my words of gratitude to Yevgenii Yevtushenko who read parts of this manuscript about his trips to Kharkiv as a People's Deputy before the collapse of the Soviet Union. I owe him an apology for not including the details about our shared interactions with Radii Polonskyi, Kharkiv writer and head of the Writers' Union (Kharkiv chapter), and Valerii Meshcheriakov, politician, historian, and professor at the Karazin State University, interactions that would serve as an example of what Yevtushenko identified as the continuity of intellectual traditions of the ethnically diverse Soviet intelligentsia who "were brave enough to ignore the all-arching presence of KGB officers and their tape recorders." Although symptomatic and interesting, an analysis of Kharkiv KGB officers' conspicuous behavior at the Kharkiv hotel "Inturist" and its restaurant where we met on a number of occasions in 1989 and 1990 goes beyond the chronological framework of this study.

I am grateful to the Harriman Institute of Columbia University and to the Robert Schuman Centre for Advanced Studies at the European University Institute (Florence, Italy) that sponsored my archival trips to Kharkiv and Kyiv, Ukraine, in 2015 and 2019. I would also like to thank the SEFER International Center for Research on the History and Culture of Russian Jewry in Different Historical Periods, the Russian Academy of Sciences, Moscow, the program "Academic Jewish Studies in the FSU," and the "Genesis Philanthropy Group" whose support helped me complete my research at the former KGB archives in Ukraine in 2019 and 2020. Special thanks go to the archivists of the Ukrainian archives

Acknowledgments

(DAKhO, TsDAMLIMU, HDA SBU, AU SBUKhO, TsDAHOU, and the Pshenychnyi archive of kino- and photo-documents, Kyiv, Ukraine), the Kharkiv Literary Museum, and the librarians of the Korolenko State Scientific Library (Kharkiv, Ukraine), particularly Nadiia Firsova, for their support of this research. I greatly appreciate the generosity of Viktor Polianetskyi, Kharkiv's prose writer who kindly returned part of my father Robert Tretyakov's private archive that was in Viktor's possession after my father's death. I thank my late mother, Lidiya Tretyakova, who provoked my interest in the Thaw, citing parts of her diaries to me, texts that I could not bring myself to touch for a year after she passed away. Thoughts and texts shared with me by Tretyakov's Kyiv colleagues and friends from his youth, Borys Oliinyk and Valerii Huzhva, were of great assistance that helped me better understand the Thaw generation.

I also wish to thank Svitlana Krys, the editor-in-chief of the scholarly journal *East/West: Journal of Ukrainian Studies*, and Olha Poliukhovych, managing editor of the scholarly journal *Kyiv-Mohyla Humanities Journal*, for kindly granting me permission to include parts of two of my articles published earlier in these journals. I am also grateful to Robert van Voren, Maria Zulim, and Semen Gluzman who helped me clarify biographical details about the Soviet dissident Victor Borovsky, sharing with me valuable sources about political psychiatry in the Soviet Union. Prolific authors and scholars Sergei Zhuk and Taras Kuzio generously shared with me their scholarship and views on the topic that helped me polish the text.

I was fortunate to have close friends residing in Kyiv and Kharkiv who created a comfortable and friendly atmosphere for me in Ukraine while I was conducting archival and library research there. Among them are Serhii Krasnokutskyi, Viktoriia Kas'ianova, Olena Varetska, Vadym Diukanov, and Liudmyla Shalaieva, Ukrainian citizens of various ethnic backgrounds whose intellectual generosity provoked vigorous discussions, intellectual exchange, and memorable experiences.

My students at the College of Security and Intelligence, Embry-Riddle Aeronautical University, Prescott, AZ, were extremely helpful in the process of preparing the manuscript for publication. I am especially thankful to Elizabeth MacManus who helped me create the index for the book and thoroughly proofread the text.

I received tremendous help from Victoria A. Malko, a friend, a scholar, a poet, and a person of many talents. A thorough editor and a formatting genius, she saw errors and typos that my tired eyes had missed in the process of writing and editing. She helped me improve the text grammatically and semantically, and I am indebted to her for her time and valuable suggestions. I would also like to express my gratitude to Eric Kuntzman, acquisitions editor of the History, Asian Studies, and Slavic Studies series, and Jasper Mislak, assistant editor, Lexington Books, for their support, patience, thoughtful suggestions, and faith in the project.

Finally, my husband and scholar Dale A. Bertelsen accompanied me on all of my research trips, helping me make photocopies of thousands of archival documents in the archives and libraries, including the Crimean ones, while Crimea was still not occupied. I am grateful to him for patiently reading the early drafts of this book and for offering me constructive suggestions, comments, and criticisms, and the manuscript became better because of him.

Introduction

The idea for writing a book focusing on the Kharkiv writers of the 1960s and 1970s came from Volodymyr Briuggen, one of the most brilliant Kharkiv writers who belonged to the generation of the sixties. He first mentioned the possibility in a casual way, as request. In the years that have passed since our first discussion, I have gradually come to understand it as an imperative of a somewhat unusual nature. Briuggen told me: "Many history books are miserably wrong and written badly. Many memoirs are mere lies. In contrast to them, many fictions are factual and exciting to read. Can you write a novel about our generation of Kharkiv writers, blatantly honest and factual, using the style you chose for your letters to me?" Briuggen is one of the most celebrated literary critics in Ukraine. I am a historian. Despite the differences in our foci, and my reservations about being able to meet his professional perfection or linguistic sophistication, he referred to me as a "colleague," so I felt deeply obliged to meet his expectations, promising him to attempt the project.[1]

Jill Lepore, professor of American History at Harvard University and a staff writer at the *New Yorker*, has argued that "history is the anti-novel, the novel's twin, though which is Cain and which is Abel depends on your point of view,"[2] and in this context, it was not easy to follow Briuggen's advice. She has aptly noted that history has been transformed into an empirical science since the sixteenth century and, beginning in the nineteenth century, historians emphasized a clear distinction between truth supported by evidence and invention.[3] Yet some scholars, and literary critics and theorists, including Briuggen, have questioned this notion, arguing that the subjectivity and the interpretative nature of historical narratives are a given, and that many postmodern historical narratives deteriorated to "pseudo-philosophical mumbo-jumbo" and, generally speaking, postmodernism that so dramatically influenced historical writings is "nonsense" and the "intellectual equivalent of crack."[4] They are convinced that, to a significant extent, histories are a product of historians' imagination. For instance, James Robins has argued that "[f]or historians, documenting the past without imagination is impossible"; more frequently than not, historians "have neither seen nor heard the catastrophes [or events of other nature] they study—they've reached them through imagination and immersion."[5] Moreover, historians are taught to maintain a distance between people they study and themselves. Sadly, this neutrality or dissociation results in "only a partial understanding" of their research subjects and a narrative that shows that.[6] Thus, many scholars and, importantly, their readers crave histories written in violation of this principle of neutrality and even in violation of the discipline's conventions, desiring a story that would not be constrained by them but rather revealed through personal and emotional involvement of the author and his or her ability to adopt a novel's style and structure. They care about the manner in which a history is written. Even still, all historical narratives are incomplete, regardless of the style historians choose. They do the best they can, relying on what seems to be unreliable—people's words, people's memories, and "documents written by people who were not under oath and cannot be cross-examined."[7]

With these thoughts in mind and Briuggen's will and his valuable suggestions in hand, I began writing this book in an attempt to reconstruct his and his colleagues' lives during the intense and certainly tragic decades of the Soviet era, the 1960s and 1970s, grounded in broken fragments of told and retold stories, scattered archival evidence, and personal recollections. I hope that my readers will read this book as a novel, in which they discover a grain of historical truth, rather than a conventional history book, a sample of scholarship that typically denies partiality, errors, prejudices, and the misreading of evidence. This text abounds with unequivocal evidence and facts that have been arranged in a certain order, analyzed and explained, and its goal is modest—to provide a glimpse into the Kharkiv writers' private and social lives, their worries and interactions with the KGB, and their transnational connections under the Soviets. These writers lived under Stalin, Khrushchev, and Brezhnev, and were the cultural descendants of Kharkiv writers known as the representatives of the Red and later Executed Renaissance. One might identify this study as cultural history, social history, transnational history, or microhistory, but what is important is that every reader will find here what he or she is looking for, evidence, dates, facts, and what Briuggen was concerned about—storytelling and insight into the KGB's deep penetration into the cultural life of Soviet Ukraine and into the very psyche of writers whom they wanted to convert, pacify, recruit, or eliminate.

The emergence of narratives that included opposing portraits of the first secretary of the Communist Party of the Ukrainian Soviet Socialist Republic Petro Shelest,[8] his successor Volodymyr Shcherbytskyi (1972–1989), and the first secretary of the Kharkiv *obkom* Hryhorii Vashchenko (1964–1972), and the panegyrics to some "classics" of Ukrainian literature who closely collaborated with the KGB was another powerful inspiration to complete this project. Briuggen and the former Kharkivite and writer Mykola Shatylov were perplexed while reading narratives or watching documentaries that celebrated Soviet Ukrainian achievements in literature, stripped of the historical context and individual motives behind these achievements which were associated with *chekists*' sadism and violence, and the writers' individual compromises and tragedies.[9] This study pursued an important objective—to tell the story told by the Kharkiv writers themselves about their forced compliance and the enslavement of their minds that largely left no space for artistic or creative achievement during the two decades of terror and mental abuse.

More specifically, this story focuses on how writers of various ethnicities interacted with one another, how they coped with the harassment and terror by the local KGB, what they learned from their experiences, and how this knowledge influenced their ability to observe, perceive, and create. There are many different ways in which people experience space in general, and the political and social environment in particular.[10] Spaces provoke different feelings in different people—of being happy, being intimidated, being cramped, or being delusional. This narrative illuminates most typical human reactions to a space of violence and terror where the concepts of the "other" and "enemy" were manipulated and exploited to control the creative intelligentsia. Crucially, the writers' own perceptions about how they reacted to authoritarian Kharkiv, told in the 1970s and decades later, are part of this analysis.

Soviet Kharkiv seems a perfect place for investigating a community of writers, the most vulnerable group among Kharkivites in the 1960s and 1970s, suspected of dissent, separatism, and treason. The city has a rich intellectual history, and has been historically populated with various ethnic groups contributing to its diverse cultural traditions. The Soviet authoritarian Kharkiv was also linguistically diverse and, as this book will show, language chosen by the writers or inherited by them by birth largely shaped their relationships with the local authorities and the KGB. Knowing little about Benjamin Lee Whorf who in the 1930s began to study with the American anthropologist Edward Sapir, as well as about other outstanding linguists working on the issue of human communication, KGB officers intuitively sensed that language was a major element that shaped the writers' thinking, perceptions, views, and ideologies.[11] The knowledge of Russian, the lingua franca and the means of communication for all Soviet citizen, was "increasingly required for admission to all leadership appointments, even rather low-level ones."[12] Ukrainians who spoke Ukrainian and Jews who spoke Yiddish immediately fell under suspicion. Although literally Yiddish was almost nonexistent among the Kharkiv literati, some Yiddish writers continued to speak Yiddish in their private lives, behavior that was thoroughly scrutinized by the Kharkiv KGB. Writers who wrote in Ukrainian were encouraged to attend festivals of Ukrainian culture in Moscow, but the authorities' reports about the flowering of national languages were accompanied by clandestine surveillance operations and persecution of those who spoke languages other than Russian. Bonds and friendships developed among Ukrainians and Jews were perceived by the KGB as conspiracies. Yet the writers' stories reveal that this cultural terror and their different cultural backgrounds did not prevent them from developing friendships and professional cooperation. Shared experiences of violence and fear instilled by the KGB pushed them closer to one another. Bypassing cultural stereotypes, they collectively disobeyed the authorities and resisted the system of ethnic segregation designed to manipulate and exacerbate their cultural differences.[13]

Ultimately, this study analyzes the foundations of unity developed by the Kharkiv multiethnic community of writers, and explores post-Khrushchev Kharkiv as a political space and a place of state violence aimed at combating Ukrainian nationalism and Zionism, two major targets in the 1960s and 1970s. Despite their various cultural and social backgrounds, the Kharkiv literati might be identified as a distinct bohemian group possessing shared aesthetic and political values and experiences that emerged as the result of de-Stalinization, a process of political relaxation under Nikita Khrushchev. The writers' interviews, diaries, memoirs, and archival documents suggest that the 1960s and 1970s were a period of intense covert KGB operations, "active measures" designed to disrupt a community of intellectuals and to fragment their friendships and bonds along ethnic lines, also curtailing the support of their counterparts in North America, the Ukrainian, Russian, and Jewish diasporas. The history of the literati residing in Kharkiv in the 1960s and 1970s, their formal and informal practices and rituals, and their strategies of coping with state antisemitism, anti-Ukrainianism, terror, and waves of repression demonstrate that the immutability of ethnic barriers, often attributed to Ukrainian-Russian-Jewish encounters and systematically reinforced by the KGB, seems to be a myth and a stereotype. The writers negated these barriers, inevitably augmenting the politics of the place. Their spatial and social practices and habits helped them create a cohesive community grounded in shared experiences of threats and uncertainties, and shared interests in literature and dedication to it. They transcended ethnic and transnational boundaries constructed by the authorities, striving for freedom and unity and walking their own labyrinths, a journey in which writers are often ahead of others.[14]

Several Kharkiv writers referred to their journey during these two decades as the labyrinth they willingly entered. Some of them were lost in it; others had a more positive experience, claiming that fear and terror transformed them and made them realize their true mission and purpose for living. Many scholars attempted to investigate the symbolic meaning of the labyrinth, defining it as a path to ourselves and a path inviting us to explore the world, to learn and to serve.[15] Labyrinths have been known to humans for 4,000 years, the oldest form of which is the Cretan labyrinth known as the classical seven-circuit labyrinth.[16] They were all created for some unknown purpose, and the metaphors associated with the labyrinth are numerous. The labyrinth that is entered is perceived by an individual as a symbol representing the whole. Human intuition helps navigate the labyrinth, and this experience facilitates people's thinking and enhances their knowledge acquired from within. This knowledge helps replace inner chaos with order and certainty, and to "see the infinite in the context of the finite."[17] Scholars do not fully understand the creative intelligence that designed a labyrinth but most of them are certain that the labyrinth is "truly a tool for transformation."[18] Entering together the labyrinth and holding together as a group transformed each Kharkiv writer. As one of them has stated, "beyond literature, we had another shared interest—we were trying to protect ourselves from 'predators,' and sticking together as a group helped us survive."[19] Brought by the writers themselves, the metaphor of the labyrinth will reemerge throughout this book, and the significance of this metaphor might become more transparent in the context of their individual histories and personal choices.

A discussion of post-Khrushchev Kharkiv would be inconceivable without a close look at the Khrushchev Thaw, and some chapters analyze the transformations it triggered in the Kharkiv creative intelligentsia. Many scholars have emphasized the Thaw's fundamental role in reconfiguring the relationship between the state and Soviet society.[20] The Thaw signaled national emancipation and cultural revival that became most evident among students and the creative intelligentsia. The Ukrainians took the Thaw and de-Stalinization at face value, reviving Ukrainian national culture and national consciousness which threatened the cohesion of the Soviet state and Soviet identity.[21] The crippling re-Stalinization began in the second half of 1958, becoming most pronounced in the non-Russian republics, especially in Ukraine. The resistance of the Ukrainian intelligentsia to eventual backward changes in Khrushchev's course and re-Stalinization took aggressive and passive forms, and the KGB immediately reacted to it by launching an operation under the code name "Blok," arresting activists and intellectuals. Local party organizations were instructed to act relentlessly against "bourgeois nationalism" and separatist tendencies. Khrushchev's promises about a more tolerant nationalities policy were abandoned, thus encouraging the KGB to proceed at full speed into purging Ukraine from nationalists of all sorts. In 1958–1959, publicly denying that there was any "Jewish problem" in Ukraine, Khrushchev went further, launching in the late 1950s and early 1960s anti-Zionist and anti-Judaic propaganda that triggered arrests among Zionists, mostly young Jewish activists who demanded freedom of speech, travel, and emigration. Even Yevgenii Yevtushenko, a Russian poet-celebrity and *shestidesiatnik* (member of the sixties generation), was chastised by Khrushchev for his "immaturity" after Yevtushenko published his poem "Babii Yar" in *Literaturnaia gazeta*.[22]

Some scholars continue to argue that during this period the state moved "from mass violence in the Stalin years to the sporadic episodes of political repression."[23] This lopsided view of Soviet history, grounded in research conducted exclusively in Moscow archives, reflects a trend symptomatic of Western scholarship which largely adopted a Russo-centric view of realities in a multinational, multicultural, and multiethnic entity such as the USSR. This view is inconsistent with documents located in the former KGB archives (central and local) in Ukraine and other states, former Soviet republics. The numbers of KGB covert operations, imprisonments, and tried individuals who were sentenced to various terms in labor camps from the late 1950s suggest that political repression in one of the largest Soviet republics, Ukraine, was hardly episodic but rather extensive and systematic. Worse, an analysis of the lives of ordinary people and the creative intelligentsia in Ukraine, as well as its intelligence history, suggests that it was much more difficult and dangerous to live in any Ukrainian city, a place of suspected nationalism, than in other cities of the RSFSR (the Russian Federation). That is why a number of writers, Ukrainians and Jews, moved from Kharkiv to Moscow, Leningrad, Vladivostok, Murmansk, and other Russian cities in search of a safe haven and fame. In this respect, the consistency of the Kremlin's attitudes toward Ukraine and the KGB's spatial practices in the 1960s and 1970s echoed the days of Stalinism. The archival evidence confirms that the scale of violence against national minorities, Ukrainians and Jews in particular, remained quite substantial, rather than episodic, escalating every year from the late 1950s. Rehabilitation campaigns, reevaluating criminal cases against Stalin's political prisoners, were gradually curtailed, and by early 1963, it became clear that re-Stalinization was on the march. The regime continued to lobotomize the national and the creative from Ukraine's intelligentsia, sentencing writers, artists, and teachers to the highest terms in labor camps, and between 1962 and 1963 the Soviets executed more than 250 people for "economic crimes," 60 percent of whom were Jews. The authorities and the KGB used these cases to further stigmatize the republic as a place of nationalism and antisemitism, denying anti-Ukrainian and antisemitic state policies.[24] The discrepancy between the Russo-centric view and a more inclusive view of Soviet history that offers a narrative about re-Stalinization in places other than Moscow, thus illuminating the difference between Moscow's nationalities policy in Ukraine and that in the RSFSR, served as an inspiration for this book.

Introduction

The latter perspective became possible and was substantiated by analyses of KGB operational documents that became available to researchers in the central (Kyiv) and local Security Services archives (former KGB archives) in Ukraine. A common complaint about these documents and general skepticism about them typically come from people who never conducted research in these archives and are unfamiliar with the KGB's patterns of record keeping. The information contained in these documents can be verified, juxtaposed with, and compared against other documents, scattered in various Ukrainian archives, including the former party archive (Kyiv, Ukraine), and with detailed histories of individuals, the subjects of these records. All it requires is patience and time. Knowledge in Soviet intelligence studies is certainly helpful, facilitating understandings of KGB documents. It is undeniable that without this documentation historians lacked a nuanced understanding of how the Soviet system operated, and any generalizations were difficult, if not impossible. The ethnographic part of this research, personal meetings and conversations with Kharkiv writers, helped clarify some crucial information discovered in the Security Services archives. Although various "truths" have been recovered from those who collaborated with the regime and from those who did not, they should not be discarded or viewed as limitations that constrain generalizations.[25] Just the opposite, they did not exclude but enhanced one another, highlighting the complexity of personalities and the influence of the Soviet system that shaped them. The late emeritus professor of sociology at the University of Massachusetts, Amherst, Paul Hollander, has argued that

> even if one agrees with the idea that every society has a certain proportion of human beings with a deformed psyche who can become promising recruits [or informers] for a brutal police force, it does not follow that these individuals always find opportunities to indulge their propensities. Intolerant, vindictive, resentful, and authoritarian human beings have to be brought together in an appropriate organization and given a sense of entitlement by some ideology or "great leader" to act out their impulses.[26]

Documents collected for this book helped examine the ideology and the ethics of the Soviet system, and the writers' and KGB officers' group and individual behavior that manipulated, challenged, consolidated, weakened, and secured its robustness. The narrative elucidated the difference between those who relished their power over others, volunteering to faithfully serve the regime and denouncing their friends, and those who found themselves in an environment hostile to creativity and innovation, experiencing a tremendous pressure to compromise and negotiate with the regime. People's motives are always difficult to pinpoint with certainty, and thus they have been analyzed in the context of dozens of sources, opinions, and views.

To challenge somewhat disfiguring assumptions by some scholars about the institutional and intellectual channels established in the 1950s and 1960s as a result of the Thaw, that, according to them, remained "unchanged in the subsequent two decades"[27] in the Soviet Union, this study adopted historical and ethnographic methods of research that helped hear the voices of writers from Soviet Ukraine, for whom statements characterizing the re-Stalinization period as one without substantial changes ("novels continued to be published; exhibitions continued to be hosted . . .")[28] sound egregiously uniformed, superficial, and even irritating. In the 1960s and 1970s, the Kharkivite and outstanding poet Boris Chichibabin was ashamed to make an inscription, giving his newly published books to his fellow colleagues as a gift. He apologized every time for the censored content, suggesting that his censored poems were like mutilated trees, lifeless and disfigured. Beyond archival KGB institutional documents, the ethnography of the diverse community of Kharkiv writers and close personal interactions with a great many of them, including KGB officers whose responsibility was to supervise the arts, allowed me to better understand the constraints of the professional and private lives of the intelligentsia and the political realities of Kharkiv under late socialism, as well as the KGB and its practices. This story and the analysis behind it would be incomplete without seeing Kharkiv of the 1960s and 1970s through institutional and state lenses, through the writers' eyes and their invaluable insights they shared with me over the years, and through my personal experiences. Most importantly, these interactions were particularly enlightening because they helped me observe and understand people's psychological "shields" protecting them from the KGB, bonds, and behavioral tactics that transcended time and the city boundaries, forcing the powerful agency to fight them on all fronts, including the transnational one. KGB operational materials served as supplemental sources that informed an analysis of the KGB's covert action, domestic and overseas operations of ideological subversion designed to curtail transnational and interethnic bonds developed by human rights activists domestically and overseas. This analysis reveals the KGB's limitations of power and its institutional boundaries, as well as its successes. The KGB's reproduction of its messages, rhetoric, and discourses targeting people's minds and consciences has been an old *chekist* practice, and it is very much alive today. This book might help readers observe parallels and links with modern Russian intelligence tactics, and, most importantly, detect and trace the continuity of *chekism* assisting the Russian Federation in its contemporary information warfare against Ukraine and the West.

Crucially, Kharkiv writers help us observe trends shared by all authoritarian regimes: first, the secret police internalized communist ethics which obliged its officers to act immorally and violently;[29] and second, unrelenting control and punishment from centralizing power institutions met with little active resistance over time but intellectuals extended the boundaries between different communities, including ethnic ones, behavior that is typically in conflict with power structures that try to sow chaos, disarray, and discord among those communities to more effectively control them. In the Kharkiv case, both trends were causally interdependent, amplified due to the peripheral dependent status of the Kharkiv KGB that was subject to the central KGB's inspections, often serving as a scapegoat to justify institutional failures in curtailing the dissent. The contribution of the ethnographic and archival research to understandings of these dynamics is tremendous, although some names of confidential sources listed in the footnotes had to be withheld at the request of the sources. Nevertheless, the majority of the sources have been identified under their real names. Some of them have passed away; many are still alive. The main task was not to psychoanalyze them but rather give them an opportunity to be heard and to include their self-identifications and stories about their coping tactics with the Soviet system.

In addition, this narrative relies on diaries, fascinating documents that open a window into the intimate world of the authors and the era in which they lived. Among several theories of why people keep diaries (the theory of the ego, of the id, and of the superego), the id theory is particularly interesting. According to this theory, people keep diaries because they want to "record wishes and desires that they need to keep secret, and to list failures and disappointments that they cannot admit publicly," which are hurtful, painful, and often destructive.[30] Some people view diary-keeping as a neurotic activity because it seems irrational when people want to leave their traumatic feelings of humiliation, anger, and envy for posterity, even if this posterity would be likely represented by a narrow group of their descendants. Most people are eager to forget those feelings and experiences; they "don't confess; they repress."[31] In the context of Stalinism and Soviet authoritarianism, the application of these theories seems questionable, especially the superego theory which suggests that people write diaries "for the eyes of others."[32]

The Soviet history, however, knows a great number of examples when people wrote diaries, trusting paper more than face-to-face communication.[33] Diaries that have been used for this book seem to be an expression of unconsummated desires and thoughts, negative and positive, that had no listeners to be shared with. In several cases, diaries served as indispensable sources of chronology and factual data, as well as testimonies of human weakness, loneliness, fears, and concerns. They facilitated an analysis of self-representation and introspection that offered an intimate sense of who their authors were and how they perceived the political and cultural landscape and their surroundings. Importantly, these texts provide valuable insight into the world of an intellectual and a writer, which ultimately emerged as historical texts, highlighting people's desire to "control the day" and to "have the last word" in the atmosphere of violence and regimentation when they had control over nothing, even over their own lives.[34] These texts are populated with many people, the Kharkiv, Kyiv, and Moscow intelligentsia of the 1960s and 1970s, Kharkiv party leaders, KGB officers, and representatives of the central authorities who have been described, evaluated, criticized, and praised, and the literary skills of their authors gave these figures a tremendous magical presence, helping me reconstruct various historical events.

These assets combined with my own experiences of living among the writers and KGB informers allowed me to write a book about how the Kharkiv intelligentsia helped open the closed Soviet system, inviting like-minded individuals in Moscow and other Soviet cities into the space of literature, ethnic tolerance, and plurality that ultimately disrupted the KGB's plans and surpassed its institutional organization of space, full of hostilities, instilled with ethnic hatred and regimentation. Although the *chekists'* control and violence had enormously destructive effects on the community of Kharkiv writers as a whole, especially on their mentality, some individuals among the creative intelligentsia of the 1960s and 1970s managed to ignore or bypass this control. These individuals walked their own labyrinths, stopping, zigzagging, and making detours in trying to cheat the system, but their rhythms, behavioral patterns, and social habits inevitably accelerated the Soviet regime's end. I believe my position as an insider is not a shortcoming but rather a privilege that allowed me to take a closer look at the realities of the 1960s and 1970s, as well as to participate in some events that were illegal from the regime's perspective. Comparing my personal notes, experiences, and perceptions of this period with that of other participants who were a generation or two older than I enhanced my understanding of the post-Khrushchev era. Importantly, this perspective prevented me from treating the subjects of my narrative as mere victims or devils who lacked stoicism and courage. I remember them as good friends, mentors, and predecessors who, to a significant extent, shaped me as a human being, and who, through their personal examples, their originality, and at times provocative behavior, enlightened me about the limitations of state power and the infinite power of creativity.

The individual histories of the Kharkiv writers, their cultural resurgence during the Thaw, and their quest for their identities inspire one to think about the roots of violence and authoritarian ideologies that enslaved so many peoples and states. One of the most prominent historians Norman Cohn offered insights into the origin of authoritarian thought, roots that went back to medieval Europe. These insights were inspired by his own experiences in losing his relatives in the Holocaust and in serving as an officer of the Intelligence Corps in postwar Vienna, where he interrogated SS members and spoke with refugees from Eastern Europe who told him about the horrors of the Soviet regime. Since the medieval era, people wanted to purify their communities through the elimination of individuals imagined as "agents of corruption and incarnations of evil."[35] In his book *The Pursuit of the Millennium*, Cohn argued that the majority of revolutionary medieval movements were clearly influenced by the Bible's book of Revelation, and, because of this apocalyptic tradition, the Flagellants massacred Frankfurt Jews in 1349 and the instigators of the German peasants' war were urged to spiritually purify the Earth. According to Cohn, these purification campaigns and traditions survived throughout the twentieth century and materialized in the Holocaust and antisemitism, becoming resurgent during the periods of social upheaval and change.[36] Similarly, another scholar and psychologist, Rauf R. Garagozov, has argued that in Russia, ancient cultural and political traditions and a "schematic narrative template" inspired the Russians to routinely purify their society and to fight external enemies: "this template was constantly reinforced and shaped by history itself in Russia. The interaction of many factors played a role in its creation and in writing a new historical narrative . . . which still directs people to search for enemies and to make war against 'hostile forces.'"[37] The precursors of Soviet state violence and systemic purges were indeed established much earlier, and their secular nature prevented many from recognizing and analyzing their roots. The Russians' proclivity toward authoritarianism and violence became firmly imbedded in the Soviet system that purged their own dissent and "outsiders," the national minorities they subverted.

This book illuminates the consequences of this "schematic narrative template" in Soviet Ukraine in the 1960s and 1970s, a period of short-lived cultural upheaval in a place where the KGB continued to search for enemies and hunt them down. Ukrainian nationalists and Zionists were marked as forces hostile to the Soviet system, and the KGB, politically motivated executionists armed with state anti-Ukrainianism and antisemitism, unknowingly embraced the medieval "schematic narrative template" where the ancient religious traditions and myths coalesced with secular modern philosophies and ideologies, contributing greatly to Soviet genocidal practices that never ceased in Soviet Ukraine until its very end. National humiliation, and the physical and psychological destruction of the brightest, Ukrainian and Jewish intellectuals, continued in labor camps and psychiatric wards to the very last day of the Soviet Union, and this process did not begin with the Holodomor, as many claim. These practices pushed Ukrainians and Jews to one another, in camps and outside the camps, ultimately shaping their group defensive mechanisms against the KGB's harassment and brutality.

Routinized violence and sadism make people mad, and the Jewish historian who observed the horrors of the 1932–1933 famine in Ukraine Mendel Osherowitch might be right, arguing that the *chekists* impressed him as being "not entirely normal": "You get the feeling something is troubling [their] conscience, is bothering [them], won't allow [them] to find any peace." Some of them, indeed, ended up in psychiatric clinics. Osherowitch wrote:

> Every man has a conscience, a moral compass. If he does wrong it doesn't allow him to rest. It troubles him. So this made sense, it was a logical progression: from the GPU—to a madhouse! I am sure if a Dostoyevsky were alive today in Soviet Russia, a writer who wanted to pen a great novel but one free of the "ideology" imposed on writers, all he would need do is visit a *GPU* sanatorium and there record, word for word, what insane *GPU* men sputter on about whenever their consciences plague them, that don't let them rest. After such a visit one could write a great book, a work to evoke a reader's horror and let the world know just how much fear the *GPU* inspire in the population of Soviet Russia.[38]

Fear, denunciations, hostility, ethnic hatred, envy, revenge—these attitudes, feelings, and actions were encouraged to regiment the intelligentsia and the *chekists* themselves at the highest level, a societal environment in which it was extremely difficult to live, work, and create. This book offers a glimpse into this world.

NOTES

1. Volodymyr Briuggen (interview by Yurii Virchenko), *Slobozhanshchyna Slovo*, vyp. 6 (Robert Tretyakov), *YouTube*, 8 May 2012, https://www.youtube.com/watch?v=QIfMn_o0Ow0&t=419s (accessed 11 October 2020).

2. Jill Lepore, "Just the Facts, Ma'am: Fake Memoirs, Factual Fictions, and the History of History," *The New Yorker*, 24 March 2008, p. 80.

3. Ibid., 80–81.

4. In 1990, Sir Geoffrey Elton defined post-modern literary theory as the "intellectual equivalent of crack" (quoted in Lepore, "Just the Facts, Ma'am," 80); in 2005, Donald Kagan delivered a lecture entitled "In Defense of History," here he complained about the quality of historical texts (quoted in Lepore, "Just the Facts, Ma'am," 80); and in 2009, the distinguished professor of Modern History at Penn State Garry Cross identified postmodernism as "nonsense" (class notes, Penn State).

5. James Robins, "Can Historians Be Traumatized by History?," *TNR/The New Republic*, 16 February 2021, https://newrepublic.com/article/161127/can-historians-traumatized-history?fbclid=IwAR1WhvBHwTgnrwQGyENXztkoxrGCtHN5caBfNxS11EIHuhQ-OEmxt5gF0-g (accessed 20 February 2021).

6. Ibid.

7. Lepore, "Just the Facts, Ma'am," 81.

8. Shelest also served as a member of the Politburo of the Communist Party of the Soviet Union and a deputy of the Supreme Soviet of the Ukrainian SSR (1963–1972).

9. See, for instance, Mykola Shatylov's interview with Liutsyna Khvorost "Kozhen mii virsh—shchodennykovyi zapys . . ." *Vsesvit*, 2020, http://www.vsesvit-journal.com /old/content/view/1028/41/ (accessed 11 October 2020). The term *chekists* refers to those who worked for the Soviet secret police. The term originated from the first Soviet abbreviation for the secret agency—Cheka (Chrezvychainaia komissiia po borbe s kontrrevolutsiiei i sabotazhem), Extraordinary (or Emergency) Commission for Combating Counter-Revolution and Sabotage. Sometimes, the VChK term is used which means the All-Russian Extraordinary Commission (Vserossiskaia Chrezvychainaia Komissiia).

10. Edward T. Hall, *The Hidden Dimension* (New York: Anchor Books/ Doubleday, 1990), 51.

11. For more on communication as the core of culture and life, see Hall, *The Hidden Dimension*, 1–6.

12. Helene Carrere d'Encausse, *Decline of An Empire: The Soviet Socialist Republics in Revolt*, trans. Martin Sokolinsky and Henry A. La Farge (New York, NY: Newsweek Books, 1978), 185.

13. On the significance of shared experiences in human communication, see Hall, *The Hidden Dimension*, 2.

14. See Briuggen's aphorism in the eulogy "Pomer Volodymyr Briuggen," *Natsionalna spilka pysmennykiv Ukrainy: Kharkivska oblasna orhanizatsiia*, 19 July 2018, https://kharkiv-nspu.org.ua/archives/5969 (accessed 12 October 2020).

15. Lauren Artress, *Walking a Sacred Path: Rediscovering the Labyrinth as a Spiritual Tool* (New York: Riverhead Books, 1995), 24.

16. Ibid., 40.

17. Ibid., 96–97.

18. Ibid., 170.

19. Interview with Serhii Boltryk, 10 November 1996, Kharkiv, Ukraine. On people's group and individual behavior, see Jonathan L. Freedman, *Crowding and Behavior* (San Francisco: W. H. Freeman and Company, 1975), 1–11.

20. Kenneth Farmer, *Ukrainian Nationalism in the Post-Stalin Era* (The Hague/ Boston/London: Martinus Nijhoff, 1980); Borys Lewytzkyi, *Politics and Society in Soviet Ukraine, 1953–1980* (Edmonton, Canada: CIUS/University of Alberta, 1984); Bohdan Nahaylo and Victor Swoboda, *Soviet Disunion: A History of the Nationalities Problem in the USSR* (New York: The Free Press, 1989); Heorhii Kas'ianov, *Nezhodni: Ukrainska intelihentsiia v rusi oporu 1960-80-kh rokiv* (Kyiv: Lybid, 1995); Martin Mccauley, *The Khrushchev Era, 1953–1964* (London: Routledge, 1995); Miriam Dobson, *Khrushchev's Cold Summer: Gulag Returnees, Crime, and the Fate of Reform After Stalin* (Ithaca/London: Cornell University Press, 2009); Sergei I. Zhuk, *Rock and Roll in the Rocket City: The West, Identity, and Ideology in Soviet Dniepropetrovsk, 1960–1985* (Washington, DC/Baltimore: Woodrow Wilson Center Press/The Johns Hopkins University Press, 2010); Sergei I. Zhuk, *Nikolai Bolkhovitinov and American Studies in the USSR: People's Diplomacy in the Cold War* (New York: Lexington Books, 2017).

21. Nahaylo and Swoboda, *Soviet Disunion*, 130.

22. Ibid., 139–40; private conversation with Yevgenii Yevtushenko, 27 May 1989, Kharkiv, Ukraine. For more on Babyn Yar (Ukr.), see Vladyslav Hrynevych and Paul Robert Magosci, eds., *Babyn Yar: Istoriia i pam'iat* (Kyiv: Dukh i litera, 2016).

23. See, for instance, one of the most recent publications: Eleonory Gilburd, *To See Paris and Die: The Soviet Lives of Western Culture* (Cambridge, MA and London, England: The Belknap Press of Harvard University Press, 2018), 6.

24. Nahaylo and Swoboda, *Soviet Disunion*, 146.

25. For a discussion about anthropological methodological approaches in scholarly studies about the intelligentsia, see Eleonora Narvselius, *Ukrainian Intelligentsia in Post-Soviet L'viv: Narratives, Identity, and Power* (New York: Lexington Books, 2012), 6.

26. Paul Hollander, *Political Will and Personal Belief: The Decline and Fall of Soviet Communism* (New Haven/London: Yale University Press, 1999), 218.

27. Gilburd, *To See Paris and Die*, 8.

28. Ibid., 7.

29. For this insight, see Hollander, *Political Will and Personal Belief*, 220–21.

30. Louis Menand, "Woke Up This Morning: Why Do We read Diaries?" *The New Yorker*, 10 December 2007, p. 106.

31. Ibid.

32. Ibid.

33. Veronique Garros, Natalia Korenevskaya, and Thomas Lahusen, eds., *Intimacy and Terror: Soviet Diaries of the 1930s*, trans. Carol A. Flath (New York: The New Press, 1997).

34. Menand, "Woke Up This Morning," 107.

35. Paul Lay, "Norman Cohn," *The Guardian*, 8 August 2007, https://www.theguardian.com/news/2007/aug/09/guardianobituaries.obituaries (accessed 11 October 2020). See also Douglas Martin, "Norman Cohn, Historian, Dies at 92," *The New York Times*, 27 August 2007, https://www.nytimes.com/2007/08/27/world/europe/27cohn.html (accessed 11 October 2020).

36. Norman Cohn, *The Pursuit of the Millennium*, rev. ed. (Oxford, UK: Oxford University Press; 1970). It does not seem accidental that Cohn was married twice to women that held unorthodox political views. In 1941, he adopted his first wife's dissident views (the historian Vera Broido was the daughter of Menshevik revolutionaries), and in 2004, he supported the views of his second wife, the former Soviet psychiatrist Marina Voikhanskaia, who managed to emigrate from the Soviet Union after she withstood the KGB's pressure and refused to declare one of her patients, a Soviet dissident, insane.

37. R. R. Garagozov, "Collective Memory and the Russian 'Schematic Narrative Template,'" *Journal of Russian and East European Psychology* 40, no. 5 (2002): 87.

38. Mendel Osherowitch, "The Fear of the GPU across the Country," in Mendel Osherowitch, *How People Live in Soviet Russia: Impressions from a Journey*, ed. Lubomyr Y. Luciuk, trans. Sharon Power (Toronto: University of Toronto/Chair of Ukrainian Studies/Kashtan Press, 2020), 196.

Chapter 1

"The Revolution of Poets" and Re-Stalinization

FROM DE-STALINIZATION TO RE-STALINIZATION

Three years before the Twentieth Congress of the Communist Party and several months after Stalin's death, Soviet writer Vladimir Pomerantsev published an article in the monthly literary journal *Novyi Mir* entitled "About Sincerity in Literature," in which he expressed the increasing anxiety of Soviet writers about their "unfreedom." He argued that "Soviet literature lacked honesty and sincerity, that most contemporary works resembled gramophone records and repeated worn-out slogans *ad infinitum* without ever trying to represent truth and real life. 'Even about love they talk as if they were making speeches in a public meeting.'"[1] The Twentieth Congress, held in Moscow in 1956, and Nikita Khrushchev's "secret" speech delivered at the Congress liberated the writers, marking the beginning of de-Stalinization and social, economic, political, and cultural reforms in the Soviet Union. Khrushchev condemned and dethroned Stalin's cult, claiming that the term "enemy of the people" was Stalin's construct that helped eliminate his opposition.[2]

The return to legality and freedom of speech facilitated the emergence of a new atmosphere in Soviet society, free of fear and suspicion.[3] In Ukraine, embracing new approaches to Soviet culture and creativity, the intelligentsia "placed the suffering thinker concerned about his land and culture at the epicenter of their imaginary realm, thereby openly rejecting what they considered the colonialist conditions of their contemporary Ukrainian homeland."[4] This cultural emancipation deeply influenced the style and the form of writers' literary expression.

The 1960s were characterized by the rise of lyric confessional poetry, evidence of the emergence of a new type of subjectivity, openness, and intimacy. Poetry seemed to help overcome the individual and collective tragedy of cultural disruption caused by Stalin's terror. The unprecedented popularity of poetry under Khrushchev is remembered by many who attended large concert halls, public squares, and even stadiums where poets, the "sixties generation" (*shistdesiatnyky*), read their poetry. In Ukraine, Kyiv, Lviv, and Kharkiv became cultural centers where thousands of people stood in lines for hours to acquire tickets for poetry evenings.[5] Crowds of people packed lecture halls to hear poets reading their verses. The chief editor of the Kharkiv literary journal *Prapor* (The Banner), Yurii Makhnenko, recalled that Kharkiv halls could not accommodate all those who tried to get in.[6]

Yet this period was short-lived because in the severe struggle between revisionists and Stalinists the latter prevailed. Lacking serious restructuring of the Soviet system, cautious reforms, and insignificant concessions contributed to the victory of Stalinists. Khrushchev, his successor Leonid Brezhnev, and chairman of the Council of Ministers of the USSR from 1964 to 1980 Aleksei Kosygin themselves never renounced their control over cultural affairs in the Soviet Union, but they were not sure what to build, "a prison or an academy of sciences,"[7] which contributed to the victory of Stalinists. Both groups differed in their views about the methods of control over cultural production but they all shared the idea of its vital necessity for preserving the party's integrity and the Soviet ideological doctrine.[8] Thus, the anticolonial writings of Ukraine's intellectuals and their cultural reaction to the Khrushchev Thaw quickly became a political challenge for Moscow.[9] The writers' hopes and expectations for freedom evaporated with the Soviet invasion of Hungary in 1956, confirming the fragility of these expectations.[10] The unfreezing of Ukraine's literary landscape was replaced with a new freeze, which meant the end of artistic independence for the writers, and a return to strict censorship and control by the KGB. One Kremlin official stated: "We opened the door a little to let in some fresh air, but such a stormy wind came through the aperture that we have to take protective measures."[11]

The "stormy wind" materialized in the form of *shistdesiatnytstvo*, a cultural movement embraced by the sixties generation, which emerged as an all-Union phenomenon, also known as "the Revolution of Poets." The revolution liberated the writers from their fears, awakening their dormant gravitation toward freedom and creativity. This period was marked by literary experimentation and civic bravery, when the poets came boldly to the fore, advocating cultural and political changes in the Soviet Union and accentuating their right and entitlement to their intimate selves. In Ukraine, *shistdesiatnytstvo* has been traditionally associated with Kyiv and Lviv. This might be a reason why most cultural historians turned their attention to Soviet Kyiv and Lviv where this movement carried by *shistdesiatnyky* was particularly vibrant, valiant, and flamboyant.[12] Yet Kharkiv (the first capital of Soviet Ukraine until 1934), that in the 1920s was celebrated for its rich literary traditions and was even named "the capital of arts," nurtured its own sixties generation, and their individual histories reveal a complex nexus of creativity, state control, KGB violence, and conformism. Importantly, literary Kharkiv of the 1960s–1970s is relevant to one of the most important scholarly discourses—multiethnic cross-cultural dialogues in twentieth-century Ukraine, a place where the Soviet secret police (the KGB) complicated these dialogues, and aggravated ethnic stereotypes and hostilities among various ethnic groups.

These KGB practices and the party's attempts to transform Kharkiv into a cultural province frustrated the Kharkiv literati. Cultural centers were associated with dissent, and it was more comforting and safer for city party officials to craft a new image of Kharkiv as an industrial city that produced tanks and ball bearings. For them, the history of Kharkiv as the first capital of Soviet Ukraine and a cultural center in the 1920s was a distant and possibly unknown past, and they invested a great deal of effort into solidifying the image of Kharkiv as a city of workers and factories.[13] The Kharkiv creative intelligentsia was treated by *obkom* functionaries and the KGB as a potential problem rather than a valuable intellectual asset of the city.[14] In the late 1950s, in an attempt to rectify its past mistakes under Stalin, the party failed to anticipate a larger problem—the emergence of a Ukrainian liberation and dissident movement that challenged the legitimacy of communist rule in Ukraine. Ukraine's creative elite experienced a gradual internal evolution, awakening the dissent and often becoming part of the dissent themselves. They hoped to rejuvenate high-brow Ukrainian-language literature and to liberate Ukraine from Moscow's control, saving the nation from its cultural death and linguicide. The writers' aspirations made the party realize the Thaw's consequences in Ukraine—the nationally conscious intelligentsia challenging the Soviet system. Open mass violent repression under Stalin was transformed into clandestine terror against the intelligentsia who, in the state's view, were capable of leading a national liberation movement.

This realization provoked quite rapid political shifts in Ukraine, helping the KGB regroup and conceptualize new approaches to solving the problem of nationalism in the republic. Designed to level the Ukrainian cultural landscape, new forms of terror, such as "prophylactic talks," psychiatric terror, intimidation through beating and assassinations, became common in the 1960s and 1970s, renewing fear among the literati. A younger generation of Moscow writers, who "had not been corrupted in Stalin's school of fear,"[15] also sensed a cultural freeze. The Russian poet Yevgenii Yevtushenko remembered that fear of arrest was characteristic of the sixties generation: "I did not experience fear during the Stalin era, because I was rescued by my young age and foolishness. But I saw this fear in others, and they exhaled it into my lungs, and similar to the predisposition to tuberculosis, our entire generation had a predisposition to fear. The 'sixties' is a generation of people predisposed to fear but the one that began to overcome it [in the 1960s]."[16]

Although the spirit of the Thaw still carried many Kharkiv writers in 1961–1962, and they contested the old world of conformism and dogmatism, by early 1963, they realized that Ukraine's literary renaissance was curtailed. Inspired by Khrushchev's ideological pogrom at the 7 March meeting with the intelligentsia in Moscow,[17] the local authorities and censors delayed the October 1962 issue of *Prapor* for four months. At the time, the Ukrainian literary journal *Prapor* became the podium for many *shistdesiatnyky*.[18] The intellectual hunger of *Prapor*'s readers, developed during the Thaw, was satisfied when, after the delay, an issue was finally published: every single copy of *Prapor*'s circulation of 7,800 was sold immediately. But beginning in February, the content of *Prapor* dramatically changed: new literature of young promising writers was replaced by works resembling that of the Stalinist era.[19] As Feliks Rakhlin, a former Kharkivite, journalist, and educator, has metaphorically stated, censored poems evoked an image of stumps, trees that had been mercilessly mutilated.[20] To appear in the press, they had to be unrecognizably distorted and purified of seditious and national allusions.[21] Many writers exiled their conscience and their shame deeply into their subconscious for their own civic cowardice. Optimism and hope were replaced by inner artistic crises and depression. Confined by the limited cultural space allowed by local bureaucrats and constrained by the financial opportunities prescribed by the authorities, the Kharkiv intellectual elite was isolated from the broader cultural, and most importantly, political movement for the national and cultural liberation of Ukraine.

By early 1963, the Kharkiv *obkom*, with the KGB's assistance, left few opportunities for the writers' creative and stylistic experimentation, and national self-expression and authenticity. The bureaucrats realized that *shistdesiatnytstvo* ceased being a purely literary phenomenon but rather grew into a social-political movement.[22] The KGB intensified its recruitment activities among the literati, intimidating and blackmailing them. The arbitrary, illegal, and ruthless practices of Kharkiv KGB officers even became the subject of routine investigations by the KGB leadership in Kyiv.[23]

After Khrushchev's visit to an exhibition of paintings and sculptures in late 1962 in Moscow, he launched a vicious campaign against Soviet "modernists," which marked a return to regimentation and rigid control in literature. Disobedience, resistance, and opposition to the system became a conscious choice only for a few.[24] In Kharkiv, the Writers' Union engaged in systematic criticism of young poets who exhibited signs of liberal thinking and originality in their writings. One scholar identified the period between November 1962 and May 1963 as a "new freeze" that would last for two decades, a term that was adopted by CIA experts on Soviet culture who wrote extensive reports on the "literary thermometer" in the Soviet Union, including Ukraine.[25] The waves of repression in Ukraine, which peaked in 1965–1966, 1972–1973, and the late 1970s, and the Kharkiv authorities' continuous efforts at provincializing the literati's works further complicated their social and private lives, precipitating the moral and physical decline of many and ruining their professional and familial ties.

WHAT WE KNOW ABOUT UKRAINIAN *SHISTDESIATNYKY*

In Ukrainian historiography, *shistdesiatnytstvo* has been analyzed in the context of anticolonial discourse. The Ukrainian literary scholar Mykola Zhulynskyi, for instance, has argued that *shistdesiatnytstvo* was a cultural and anticolonial movement, a phenomenon that invigorated popular interest in Ukrainian history and culture that was long suppressed by the Soviet regime.[26] In the 1960s, the Ukrainians began to define themselves as a nation because of the Ukrainian language and literature published by the *shistdesiatnyky*. Their frustration with the imposition of imperial practices to politically and psychologically provincialize the Ukrainian culture was reflected in their art and civic activities, placing them squarely in the cultural anticolonial movement which could be curbed only by state repressions. Some scholars see this movement as an attempt to "de-infantilize Ukrainian society" which had been seduced into submission by communist lullabies.[27]

Others have shown that a split occurred among the members of the "sixties generation." One group identified with and gravitated toward the communist regime being part of the *nomenklatura*; the other followed their moral and artistic principles and beliefs that led to their persecution, imprisonment, and labor camps. Liudmyla Tarnashynska has noted that it is important to acknowledge and to examine these two streams within *shistdesiatnytstvo* "not for ostracism but for a deeper understanding of the nature of artistic talent and its vulnerability to changes in the social [and political] climate."[28] Heorhii Kas'ianov has analyzed the political aspect of *shistdesiatnytstvo*, including the dissident activities of Ukrainian intellectuals. His nuanced study revealed the complexities and the ambiguity of the dissident and resistance movement in Ukraine, and has demonstrated that, through its philosophy of "merging nations" and state violence, the Soviet regime itself accelerated the emergence of the national consciousness of many *shistdesiatnyky*.[29] Importantly, he has analyzed the Thaw and post-Thaw periods as the time that produced a constellation of bright and courageous men and women with strong, albeit conflicting, personalities who eventually became the spiritual leaders of the nation.[30]

Ukrainian scholars seem to be unanimous in underscoring the deep ideological inner evolution that happened to most writers under the influence of the Thaw and *shistdesiatnytstvo*.³¹ Vira Aheieva has argued that socialist realism problematized any national and cultural identity of writers, annihilating their Ukrainianness and artistic tradition, and forcing them to reject and disrespect what they were just yesterday.³² "Neurotic cheerfulness and bureaucratic uncontested optimism of Soviet socialist realism" jeopardized the writers' faith in their existential goal, destiny, and cultural traditions, making them "adjust to the timelessness of the sinister victors."³³ *Shistdesiatnytstvo* managed to alleviate the fear and the "neurotic epidemics" of the entire generation of Ukraine's writers who had been traumatized by several wars and revolutions. They became acutely aware of their own artistic deterioration and the deterioration of their national pride which encouraged them to rebel against cultural amnesia cultivated in them by the regime. The *shistdesiatnyk* Ivan Dziuba wrote that it was a national-cultural movement that spurred the national and political awakening and rejuvenation of Ukrainian society.³⁴ Importantly, through an analysis of Leonid Kyseliov's literary legacy, Dziuba has illuminated the fortunate unity and amalgamation of different languages and cultures in each writer being born and living in Ukraine, a phenomenon that enriched Ukraine's cultural production and people's national awakening in the 1960s.³⁵ In 1961, another *shistdesiatnyk* Ivan Svitlychnyi called his colleagues to live up to the highest literary standards, avoiding compromises and embracing the best examples of world literature, yet preserving and remaining true to their unique cultural and national voices.³⁶ The late Ukrainian scholar, cultural historian, and literary critic Volodymyr Panchenko read Svitlychnyi's words as the aesthetic and moral program that conveyed the very spirit of *shistdesiatnytstvo*.³⁷ Similarly, Mykhailo Naienko highlighted the unique poetic voice and originality of the *shistdesiatnyky*, as well as their ability to illuminate and populate the irrational and almost mystical world of human existence, features that symbolized the philosophy of the sixties generation.³⁸

Western scholarship on Soviet intellectuals and *shistdesiatnytstvo* reveals some insightful observations. One of the earliest studies referencing the social, cultural, and political trends among the Soviet intelligentsia in the 1960s attempted to assess their ethnic representation on the all-Union level. According to this study, among "overrepresented" groups were Jews, Georgians, Armenians, and Russians. Kirgiz, Turkmen, Tajik, Uzbek, and Kazakh constituted the "underrepresented" group within the intelligentsia. A special status among "underrepresented" groups was allocated to Ukrainians, Estonians, Tatars, and Azerbaijanis because of their "nationalistic" cultural inclinations and struggle against Russification.³⁹ Such studies, however, should be treated with caution, because the cultural movement in the 1960s also promoted Russian, Jewish, and other nationalisms which decreased educational opportunities for almost all ethnic groups other than Russian in the Soviet Union, thus depriving them of opportunities for social mobility. What is indeed true is that the KGB treated Ukraine as a threatening and dangerous place, a place of "bourgeois nationalism" and dissent. Ukraine's KGB leadership alerted Moscow about attempts by the *shistdesiatnyky* to read and disseminate through *samvydav* texts written by Ukrainian writers of the nineteenth and twentieth centuries who were associated with the national liberation movement.[40] Branded as *banderovtsy*[41] fomenting nationalism among the Ukrainians, the intelligentsia together with dissidents and ex-prisoners (returnees from the Gulag) became a target for KGB operatives.[42]

Among Western scholars, a perception persists that the artistic merit and cultural innovation of the Ukrainian *shistdesiatnyky* were limited. For instance, the British scholar Andrew Wilson has argued that they revived "old cultural icons and cultural styles," neglecting to develop "the conceptual bases of the 'national idea.'"[43] According to Wilson, with some exceptions, many poets (among them Ivan Drach) merely "revisited the modernism of the 1920s."[44] Yet, it would be fairer to say that they reinvented rather than revisited the modernism of the 1920s for a simple reason: the works written by Ukraine's writers of the 1920s, known as the Executed Renaissance, were generally inaccessible, hidden in special repositories (*spetskhrany*) from the public eye.[45] The continuity of the literary tradition in Ukraine was interrupted because of the methodical elimination of writers who wrote in Ukrainian during the interwar period and the physical destruction of their works. Most of those works were burned in the internal yards of the GPU headquarters to never be recovered.[46] Only a few of the *shistdesiatnyky* were aware of their predecessors' rich legacy, and therefore it would be more appropriate to analyze the degree of their cultural and linguistic innovations in the context of the enormous cultural disruption in Ukraine caused by Stalin's terror, repressions, and famines, as well as the strategic and ubiquitous Russification of the republic. Thus, Western perceptions of the derivative nature of the *shistdesiatnyky*'s writings, especially of their poetry, seem to be questionable: the writers of the sixties generation reinvented modernism in their own idiom, transcending the local and rediscovering the importance of personal dignity and the individual intimate voice.

The most insightful studies on Soviet cultural politics and the *shistdesiatnyky* in Ukraine have been published by George S. N. Luckyj, Ivan L. Rudnytskyi, Borys Lewytzkyi, Roman Szporluk, Myroslav Shkandrij, Marko Pavlyshyn, Yohanan Petrovsky-Shtern, and George O. Liber.[47] They have analyzed the *shistdesiatnyky*'s quest for authenticity, the rejection of mass culture, and Ukraine's anticolonial struggle through individual histories and works of people like Vasyl Stus, Yevhen Hutsalo, Leonid Pervomaiskyi, and

Ivan Dziuba. The aforementioned scholars agreed that the polarization of cultural forces and their discourses about modernity and tradition, universalism and parochialism, and modernism and populism has been a noticeable trend in Ukraine, but they also illuminated the features that the *shistdesiatnyky* shared—their deep intellectualism, national sentiment, and gravitation toward universal humanity and freedom.

Remarkably, the movement grew out of conflicts, paradoxes, disharmony, and insecurity. The Thaw created a tiny space of freedom for the generation of the sixties that they expanded in a quite unique way. Nationally committed, they transcended locality through their work, contributing to world culture, aesthetically and intellectually. The Canadian scholar Serhy Yekelchyk has identified Ukraine's *shistdesiatnyky* as "cultural rebels" who existed in a "semiautonomous place of cultural expression" allowed by the state, being part of both mainstream Soviet Ukrainian culture and innovative, nonconformist, and vibrant new Ukrainian culture, provoking ideological conflict with the authorities.[48]

Indeed, ideological constraints and cultural disruption Sovietized even the most liberal and independent-thinking literati. The American scholar Sergei I. Zhuk has noted that the *shistdesiatnyky*, although experimenting with national ideas, still traditionally expressed them in Marxist terms and "referred to Marxism and old Leninist concepts about nationalities" while appealing to Soviet ideologues.[49] Similarly, another American historian, Benjamin Tromly, has suggested that "the 'sixtiers' did not view their boisterous cultural activities as being in fundamental conflict with the party-state."[50] But as George Luckyj has noted, underground poetry and prose that could not be published in Soviet Ukraine and instead was transmitted through *samvydav* best expressed the spirit of *shistdesiatnytstvo*:

> Underground poetry in the Ukraine is predominantly lyrical, although there is some interest in a return to civic and historical themes. Its main achievement is its revitalization of the poetic language and the enrichment of human sensitivity. Both are dangerous commodities under a totalitarian regime, and are therefore especially banned in a country whose cultural policy is geared to mediocrity.[51]

Crucially, Western scholars have recognized the multifacetedness and the ambiguity of this phenomenon, pointing out that, undoubtedly, the Thaw and de-Stalinization renewed a national sentiment among Ukrainians and shaped their new identities, including a Soviet Ukrainian one.[52] Taras Shevchenko, as well as new national (not Soviet) historical interpretations of the poet's role and the role of events, such as the Ukrainian famine referred to as the Holodomor-genocide, in shaping new identities in Ukraine, became the anticolonial and anti-imperial symbols that the generation of the sixties embraced.[53]

The American scholar William Jay Risch has illuminated the contribution of the Lviv intellectual elite (who moved in the 1960s to Kyiv) to the formation of a new identity and national consciousness among the Kyiv *shistdesiatnyky*, a "Soviet Western Ukrainian identity."[54] Moreover, by supporting young and talented writers, Risch has argued, Lviviany like Rostyslav Bratun, Roman Ivanychuk, and Roman Kudlyk, facilitated the process of Ukrainian literature being "more oriented toward the wider world" and Central Europe.[55] Yet, the cynicism and consumerism among the intelligentsia began to dominate during the post-Thaw period, making them complacent. Risch writes: "While some of them flirted with national dissent, others turned to acts of leisure and collective fun that posed no real threat to the Soviet state."[56]

The most recent study on *shistdesiatnyky* by the Italian scholar Simone Attilio Belleza is an attempt to understand who these brave men and women were, and to decipher the factors that shaped their national self-identification and the roots of their cultural and political engagements. Belleza has emphasized that the "shistdesiatnyky did not denounce the Soviet Union as a fallacy and were reluctant to condemn the society that had engendered them."[57] Their identities were fluid, including multiple loyalties and considerations that were largely contingent on temporal and spatial factors, associated with their places of birth, education, professional training, and friendships. Importantly, Belleza's study recognizes the irrationality of a human being and the behavioral inconsistencies and contradictions, generated by a space of violence in which the *shistdesiatnyky* existed. He explains their legacies as being grounded in their rare literary gift, humanity, and the willingness to defend their national culture and basic human rights.

More generally, the historiography of the Khrushchev era has depicted it as the period of brief de-Stalinization and rapid re-Stalinization of Soviet society, although "without relying on excessive use of violence."[58] Literature, journalism, and the creative art of poets, artists, and actors were employed as the vehicle for the ideological mobilization of the masses.[59] Regimented by the Communist Party, cultural production in the 1960s was part of a colossal propaganda machine that helped sustain the regime that, in the eyes of Stalinists, had begun to fall apart. Writers and their texts once again became the center of the party's attention and subject to vigorous censorship.[60] Fear, social passivity, and "whispering" generated an unhealthy atmosphere in various chapters of the Writers' Union, transforming many members into collaborators of the KGB.[61] Some scholars, however, have contended that in the 1960s discussions about state violence and Stalin's crimes against humanity "took place in considerable openness, in and around legitimate publications."[62] Under the influence of these relatively open conversations, the foundations of the Soviet political language and rhetoric were undermined, and this changed the face of the Soviet press: "the images of 'enemies' began to disintegrate."[63] Similarly, others suggested that the 1960s and the 1970s "evidenced the rebirth of the liberal subject, who rediscovered his personal dignity and self-consciously aligned himself with the liberal agenda."[64] There is some truth in these observations. However, the realities in Ukraine during this time were much gloomier, and a more nuanced analysis is required if one hopes to better understand the writers' psyche, and to what extent the Thaw and the subsequent freeze affected the Ukrainian cultural landscape.

It would not be an exaggeration to suggest that these discourses and the phenomenon of *shistdesiatnytstvo*, especially its complexities in Ukraine, remain virtually unknown to many Western researchers and students of Soviet history. In addition, the majority are unaware of the three waves of repression in Ukraine, an operation under the code name "Blok" launched by the KGB in the mid-1960s that lasted throughout the early and late 1970s until the end of the USSR. This campaign was designed to neutralize Ukraine's most prominent and active part of intellectual elites or drive them into submission. Therefore, there seems to be a pressing need to explicate the continuity of Soviet nationalities policy in Ukraine, de jure promoting national cultures and encouraging interethnic dialogues but de facto curtailing them. In addition, a close look at the writers of various ethnic backgrounds representing the cultural movement in Kharkiv in the early 1960s will reveal yet another aspect of Ukraine's *shistdesiatnyky*, an interethnic encounter among the Ukrainian, Russian, and Jewish literati in the space of antisemitism and anti-Ukrainianism, carefully constructed by the KGB. An under-examined place of intercultural and interethnic communication, Kharkiv of the 1960s and 1970s produced a group of writers, highly cultivated and broadly read men and women, whose lives and possibly deaths were shaped by their experiences in authoritarian Soviet Kharkiv. Their stories have not been told, and an analysis of their interactions with one another and with the state might enrich our understanding about Ukrainian *shistdesiatnytstvo* which, beyond artistic achievements, flamboyancy, and hope, was associated with tragic personal experiences, such as the systematic escort of KGB officers, chronic poverty, antiquated clothes, chronically leaking shoes, and ethnic tensions instilled by the KGB. These individual experiences might add incremental changes to a generally known narrative about *shistdesiatnytstvo* in Ukraine, unearthing the voices of those who deserve to be remembered.

There is also another important rationale for examining *shistdesiatnytstvo* in Kharkiv. Extending their knowledge about the relationship between the state and the Russian intelligentsia and applying it to the Ukrainian case, some Western historians define the 1960s and 1970's repressions in Ukraine as "persecution of single individuals," who could be characterized as dissidents. They believe that the notion of terror should not be applied in the Ukrainian context, and particularly regarding the *shistdesiatnyky*, because this term has been historically linked to Stalin's mass repression and the great numbers of victims of Stalin's terror, a phenomenon that largely receded into the past with Stalin's death.[65] A moral challenge to this approach was raised by the Slovenian philosopher Slavoj Žižek and the American linguist and philosopher Noam Chomsky. They lamented that the "abstract-anonymous" victims and their "minimal" numbers somehow become more tolerable, being targets of "less criminal" behavior than millions of Stalin's victims, and thus deserving less attention and scholarly scrutiny. Historians who claim that terror by intimidation and repression becomes a theoretically flawed term when it is applied to the post-Stalinist period overlook a totalizing fear in which the state kept a significant part of the Soviet population, the intelligentsia.[66] In this context, Ukraine was a special case because, beyond the authorities' distrust of the writers, in Ukraine this group was deemed to be susceptible to nationalistic influences. In fact, a priori they were nationalists until the KGB proved they were not. The approach that excludes the term "terror" from the analytical equation with regards to Ukraine becomes especially problematic in light of most recent studies based on KGB archival documents. They reveal that "minimal" numbers of the regime's victims in post-Stalin Ukraine ("singular" victims, as one scholar suggested) actually constitute hundreds, if not thousands, of intellectuals, whose names are no longer anonymous, thanks to archives and oral histories. These men and women were intimidated, arrested, tortured, placed in psychiatric clinics, murdered or died under mysterious circumstances, and went missing without a trace. The official statistics of Ukraine's intellectuals who suffered under Khrushchev and Brezhnev are by no means accurate, yet the Soviet era's statistics offer us some general idea about the numbers of Ukraine's citizens of various ethnic backgrounds who were exterminated by the Soviet regime. From 1927 to 1990, approximately a million of Ukraine's citizens were arrested (more than 50 percent of them were ethnic Ukrainians), of which 545,000 were sentenced to various prison terms and approximately 140,000 were shot.[67]

The 1960s and the 1970s terror and repressions in Ukraine aimed at lobotomizing the national and the creative from the mental worlds of writers. Ideas that seemed seditious to the state appeared almost exclusively in *samvydav* which blossomed in the 1960s. Secret and private "kitchen talks" were inhibited by the popular awareness of intrusive technological innovations broadly used by the KGB. The suppression of social initiatives and political passivity were sustained by routine intimidation tactics employed by those who stood above each individual, people (a chain of chief editors, censors, and party leaders), and entire institutions (boards of directors, primary party cells, *obkomy, gorkomy*, the Central Committee, and the like). However, there were individuals, including Kharkivites, who refused to conform. They made their thoughts and criticism of the regime public, perfectly understanding the consequences of the paths they chose. As one writer has stated, "Salvatore Quasimodo's path, self-sacrificial and altruistic, is more attractive to me than Aleksei Surkov's path, treacherous and perfidious."[68]

Drunk with freedom allowed by the Khrushchev Thaw, the writers wrote what they were not supposed to write, gathered where they were not supposed to gather, and spoke non-Soviet (paraphrasing Stephen Kotkin's metaphor)[69] in literary clubs that mushroomed in Kharkiv in the late 1950s. They organized themselves on the basis of shared aesthetic interests and political views, and began to express themselves in ethno-cultural terms. They established interethnic alliances and bonds, a serious concern for the KGB that designed a set of "active measures" to disband the congregations of the writers and to compromise their friendships that began to form within the Writers' Union and within formal and informal multicultural literary clubs.[70] According to KGB professionals, cultural Kharkiv presented a complex and dangerous network of connections among literati, artists, and actors which transcended ethnic boundaries, covertly erected by the authorities. These interethnic bonds ultimately negated ethnic stereotypes reinforced by KGB operatives during their "prophylactic" private talks with the writers. In the KGB's analyses, the desired ideological and propaganda flair began to disappear from Kharkiv prose, poetry, and art. Instead, romantic, intimate, national, and ethnically patriotic motifs emerged, a phenomenon that was inconsistent with the notions of undeviating fidelity to communist doctrines demanded by the party. As one Kharkiv party leader stated in the 1960s, "it seems quixotic—there is too much of Shevchenko in the writers' and artists' works; it obscures the Leninist international principles of art."[71]

Re-Stalinization and psychological warfare launched by the Kharkiv KGB against the literati confused and disoriented many Kharkivites. Covert and sophisticated, state pressure transformed some of them into nervous and depressed individuals, changes that shaped the culture and social practices of the entire cultural milieu of Soviet literary Kharkiv in the 1960s and 1970s. The individual history of Robert Tretyakov, a *shistdesiatnyk* and a subtle Ukrainian poet, was emblematic of literary Kharkiv of the 1960s.

Robert Tretyakov and His Labyrinths

The Thaw provoked a cultural and national revival in Ukraine, which was led by the Soviet Ukrainian intelligentsia.[72] It would be equally true to suggest that the Ukrainian national liberation movement that emerged in the Gulag provoked the Thaw. The Ukrainians continued the struggle for their right to productive lives and national culture in the labor camps. The Norilsk rebellion that broke out in late May 1953 marked the beginning of a chain reaction of uprisings in the Gulag, events that frightened the Kremlin and

Khrushchev.⁷³ Ukrainian poets, such as Ivan Drach, Lina Kostenko, Mykola Vinhranovskyi, Vasyl Symonenko, and Ivan Dziuba, played a crucial role in the societal transformation associated with civic consciousness, and national and cultural identity. However, as Andrew Wilson has suggested, this was not "a specifically Ukrainian rhythm."⁷⁴ They were influenced by the liberal trends in Moscow and the all-Soviet dissident movement.⁷⁵ Yevtushenko, Andrei Voznesenskii, Robert Rozhdestvenskii, Bella Akhmadulina, and Bulat Okudzhava gathered crowds at stadiums, publicly reading their poetry in the Politechnical Museum and near Vladimir Mayakovskii's monument in Moscow.⁷⁶ The *samvydav* literature, the first liberating prose by the Russian writers Aleksandr Solzhenitsyn, Vladimir Dudintsev, Grigorii Baklanov, and Yurii Bondarev, as well as Aleksandr Tvardovskii's bravery as the editor of the journal *Novyi mir*, inspired the Ukrainian writers to contest the literary stereotypes established by the party. They attempted to extend the spaces accidentally left under-supervised by the censorship and control of central and local party organs under the Thaw.

At first glance, de-Stalinization was characterized by the desire of the center to promote nationalist cultures. Grandiose forums and *dekady* of national cultures (art festivals) were frequently organized in Moscow, but as the German scholar Karl Eimermacher has noted, these events were permeated by Stalinist traditions.⁷⁷ Albeit a chimera and illusion, the values such as truth and openness, advocated in 1956 by Khrushchev at the Twentieth Party Congress, were a breakthrough for Ukrainian intellectuals that inspired a spirit of freethinking. The Ukrainian dissident Leonid Pliushch testified that a variety of underground and semi-underground dissident organizations emerged in Moscow, Leningrad, and Kyiv universities at the time.⁷⁸ The change, however, was short-lived, and with the retreat of the Thaw, these organizations were crushed, and most of their leaders were imprisoned.

Robert Tretyakov, a student of the Shevchenko State University's School of Journalism, was a product of the Thaw, contributing to and shaping the cultural space of Kyiv in 1956–1958 that rapidly was becoming the center of Ukrainian *shistdesiatnytstvo*. Ukrainian poetry became the main means of cultural understanding among people, a "certain communicative currency" and a "symbol of faith and conviction," as Oksana Zabuzhko has characterized it.⁷⁹ The aesthetic and moral upbringing of the nation occurred through poetry and the ideas of the poets—*shistdesiatnyky*. Indeed, the literary talent of Mykola Vinhranovskyi and Lina Kostenko, Borys Oliinyk and Tretyakov made poetry central for many ordinary Ukrainians who for the first time over the last several decades began to write thousands of letters not to film celebrities (the idols of millions), but to the poets, expressing their gratitude for the sincere, almost confessional, tone of their poetry. By 1961, *shistdesiatnytstvo* became a truly cultural (literary) phenomenon rather than a dissident or political movement, albeit some elements of dissent were firmly imbedded in it from the very beginning.

By late 1956, a galaxy of talented poets who would become known as the *shistdesiatnyky* began to form in Ukraine. Among them were Vasyl Symonenko, Mykola Som, Tamara Kolomiets, Vasyl Didenko, Volodymyr Kolomiets, Borys Oliinyk, Valerii Huzhva, and Tretyakov. Tretyakov's young poetic voice, unique and recognizable, emerged in 1955, announcing the arrival of an original Ukrainian poet.[80] His poetry had a sensational effect in Kyiv while he was still a university student. His poetic techniques gravitated toward the classical canon, but what distinguished him from other poets was his intellectualism. His poetry was not simple; it encouraged readers to think. His thinking on paper in a poetic form was multilayered and complex.[81] In 1958, after graduating from the School of Journalism at Shevchenko State University, Tretyakov moved from Kyiv to Kharkiv, stirring the community of Kharkiv literati by his talent, charisma, and intellect. Resuscitating his voice among other voices of the *shistdesiatnyky* and tracing his professional and intellectual journey throughout the most regimented and difficult decades for Ukrainian writers might help us better understand the distinct features of *shistdesiatnytstvo* in Kharkiv as part of a broader cultural movement in Ukraine. Importantly, through his individual history, the Kharkiv intelligentsia's communication and social patterns, including the relationship among writers of various ethnic origins, might become clearer.

A look not *inside the poet* (although his poetry allows this to some degree) but rather an attempt of *looking outside* (at his background, professional career, and interactions, a story told by his colleagues, friends, and relatives) might help "objectivize" the study and approach a more nuanced understanding of Kharkiv's literary space and the authorities' attempts to provincialize it. The Slovenian philosopher and scholar Slavoj Žižek has pertinently noted that "the experience that we have of our lives from within, the story we tell ourselves about ourselves in order to account for what we are doing, is fundamentally a lie—the truth lies outside, in what we do."[82] Tretyakov's intellectual labyrinths and the thematic zigzags of his poetry imply an enormously complicated human existence, and deciphering it through his deeds and the voices of other people might enhance our understanding about how Ukrainian intellectuals coped with the failure of Khrushchev's reforms, the regimentation of their lives and professional activities, and the subsequent escalation of terror and violence in Ukraine.

The film director Sergei Paradzhanov once stated that an artist is born during his childhood.[83] It is certainly true of Tretyakov's poetry and personality that were largely shaped by his childhood years and the Second World War. He was born in Perm (the RSFSR) in 1936. His father was a commander-in-chief in the Red Army, serving as a frontier guard (in Ukr.

prykordonnyk) at an outpost located near the Sluch River. Tretyakov was only five years old, when on 22 June, 1941, under the Nazi bombardment his mother dragged him and his newly born sister Lara for miles through the fields and forests to the rear.[84] The family survived, together with the family of the party chief (*politruk*) Yevhen Tiutiunnyk, who many years after the war told Tretyakov that his father was missing in action defending the outpost.[85] Tretyakov's family was evacuated to the village of Luk'ianivka (Ukrainians took even the names of their villages with them to Siberia) in Omskaia oblast in Siberia that was populated mostly with Ukrainians, where they lost little Lara.[86] She died from the famine, and Robert and his mother were near death. To survive, his mother collected ears of wheat in the fields covered with snow where packs of wolves were searching for food.[87] Sick, with swelling extremities, they were saved by the three potatoes given in aid by their neighbors, and a sack of cinnamon that was accidentally dropped on the road by a delivery truck. For the rest of his life, Tretyakov was unable to tolerate the smell of cinnamon. That was "the smell of woe" that haunted him to his death bed: Kharkiv bakeries, which his children associated with a cornucopia of joyous culinary treats, provoked nausea and dizziness in him.[88] The hardships of war and the loss of his sister determined in many ways his perspective as a human being, a citizen, and a writer.

In 1944, Tretyakov's family moved to the town of Smila (Cherkaska oblast), Ukraine. That same year at Skvyra in Kyiv oblast, Tretyakov, an eight-year-old boy, met Maksym Rylskyi, the famous Ukrainian poet. This meeting was deeply etched in Tretyakov's memory, although at the time he could not imagine the dramatic circumstances of Rylskyi's escape to Skvyra: the poet was hiding there from Stalin's repression in the home of his best friend Yosyp Mahomet, a Ukrainian biologist and recipient of the Stalin Prize.[89] Unmistakably, Rylskyi felt that the NKVD would not take the risk to arrest him in the home of a Stalin Prize winner. Later, among his friends, Tretyakov famously theorized this episode as a sign from a "poetic Olympus" and as an event that determined his aesthetic path.[90]

His poetic journey drew him toward the center of Ukrainian culture, Kyiv, and in 1953 he was accepted as a student at the Shevchenko State University's School of Journalism (Fig. 1.1). His professors were famous scholars Oleksandr Biletskyi, Andrii Vvedenskyi, and Leonid Bulakhovskyi.[91] In 1955, the journal *Dnipro* published his first poem, and he gained fame as a promising Ukrainian poet. Yet personal reasons overpowered his decision to settle in Kyiv. Tretyakov fell in love with Lidiya Trufanova whose parents lived in Kharkiv.[92] The staff of the Kharkiv newspaper *Leninska zmina* was delighted with him as a poet and a journalist and offered him a job. After Lidiya's and Robert's graduation from the Kyiv State University in 1958, the

Figure 1.1 Robert Tretyakov (on the right), a Third Year Student of the Shevchenko State University with a Friend. Kyiv, 1955. *Source*: Lidiya Tretyakova's Private Archive (hereafter: LTPA); a copy is located in the Central State Archive-Museum of Literature and Art (hereafter: TsDAMLIMU) Kyiv, Ukraine, fond 712, opys 1, sprava 18, arkush 1.

two young journalists moved to Kharkiv as a married couple where their son Serhii was born (Fig. 1.2).

Tretyakov befriended the talented young Kharkiv writers Stanislav Shumytskyi, Oleksandr Cherevchenko, Leonid Osadchuk (Osmolovskyi), Volodymyr Briuggen, Arkadii Filatov, Zinovii Valshonok, and Oleksa Marchenko, and an ethnically diverse community of writers, Ukrainians, Russians, and Jews, enthusiastically welcomed a new talent to Kharkiv.

The first two years in Kharkiv the young family had to share a one-room apartment with Lidiya's parents, but Tretyakov's fame as a young gifted poet helped him improve his poor material conditions. In 1960, the Writers' Union provided him with a one-room apartment in Sumska Street in downtown Kharkiv, and Tretyakov's family moved to their own home.[93] This was an unusual move for the Writers' Union because Tretyakov did not become a member until 1962. However, the oldest generation of writers made an exception for him, a sign of their recognition of a new star in the Ukrainian literary landscape.

In 1961, Tretyakov published his first collection of poetry *The Galaxy* (Zorianist),[94] in which the poem "The Core of Happiness" (Sil shchastia), an emotional and an intellectually provocative confession of a young romantic, evoked delight among the established Ukrainian poets, such as Maksym Rylskyi, Platon Voronko, Andrii Malyshko, and Pavlo Tychyna. They began to speak of Tretyakov as a mature poet despite his young age. Pavlo Tychyna noted that the epithet "young" seemed to be inappropriate

Figure 1.2   Lidiya and Robert Tretyakov. Kyiv, 1958. *Source*: LTPA.

when characterizing Tretyakov as a poet: his metaphors, intense emotional expression, and linguistic beauty were powerful and innovative.[95] Indeed, his poetry, saturated with extraordinary and paradoxical poetic metaphors, singled him out of the great majority of the Ukrainian poets at the time:

I won't fall. I won't weep.
I won't hide my
Lifeless eyes in the knotweed and dole.[96]
I will bury her quietly, neatly
In the serene suburbs of my soul.
I knew nothing before, not a thing,
But I know this now, I do—
What hurts more is what's never discovered,
More than losses I ever came through.[97]

His verses absorbed and sublated the emotional gravity and the tragic note shaped by his war experiences and his love of a single woman. For many, Tretyakov entered Ukrainian literature as a "poet of love," remaining true to his call and credo to the very end. Surviving attacks of the party and KGB, as well as an attempted suicide or possibly murder, he published the last collection of his lyrical poems entitled *Tobi* (To you) shortly before his death.[98]

Figure 1.3 Robert Tretyakov, The Mid-1960s. *Source*: LTPA; a copy is located in TsDAMLIMU, f. 712, op. 1, spr. 5, ark. 1.

In 1962, Tretyakov's star continued to rise. On 20 March, 1962, he became a member of the Writers' Union. On this day in Kyiv the Presidium of the Writers' Union chaired by Oles Honchar accepted seven writers into the Union's ranks. This was a cohort of poets and prose writers who shaped the subsequent literary process in Ukraine: Mykola Vinhranovskyi, Yevhen Hutsalo, Volodymyr Drozd, Ivan Drach, Petro Skunts, Mykola Synhaiivskyi, and Robert Tretyakov. His older colleagues, the established Ukrainian poets and writers Ihor Muratov, Vasyl Mysyk, Ivan Vyrhan, and Ivan Bahmut, spoke highly about his poetry and treated him tenderly, as their own son. They recognized his vulnerability and emotionality, and expressed a father-like anxiety when Robert got in trouble. The head of the Union's Kharkiv chapter in the 1980s Radii Polonskyi wrote: "Robert Tretyakov had a rare poetic gift. But his personality was complex, and in some respects even unexplainable."[99] He was open to communication with friends, had a subtle sense of humor, and his sharp mind generated immediate witty and sophisticated responses in poetic form. However, in moments of depression, Tretyakov was unrecognizable: he became gloomy, suspicious, silent, abstruse, and even aggressive.[100]

According to many accounts, Tretyakov was classically old-fashioned and sentimental. His deep respect for women manifested itself in firm responses to men who spoke of women in a denigrating fashion and his habit of greeting women by kissing their hands. He rarely used profanity. His statements were never indolent or primitive. He cried and was embarrassed of it. No one was allowed into this mysterious place, the land of his tears, using Antoine de Saint-Exupéry's metaphor.[101] Apparently, he routinely returned to his childhood and the suffering that he began to experience at the age of six. Cherished and regularly praised by the Kharkiv bohemian community of writers for his poetic gift and physical attractiveness, his shyness and tragic stance persisted, appearing to be almost atavistic. Because of his mass of blond hair that darkened with age and his doomed sky-blue eyes, he looked like the young Sergei Yesenin, a Russian poet of the Silver Age whose poetry was banned in the Soviet Union (Fig. 1.3). However, the resemblance was not only visual. Tretyakov unconsciously followed Yesenin's steps, having a weakness for alcohol which complicated his family life. His translation of Yesenin's lengthy lyrical poem *Anna Snegina* from Russian into Ukrainian remains the only translation of Yesenin into Ukrainian.[102] Its publication in 1967 remains a mystery of censors' limitations and an aberration in the space of rigid literary control. Handsome, flamboyant, easy-going, and opinionated, Tretyakov attracted many. His Yesenin-like look provoked the interest of many artists. The most talented portraits of the poet were painted by the Ukrainian artists Antin Komashka[103] and Mykola Kursin,[104] and the Russian artist Ivan Khristichev.[105]

The process of re-Stalinization in Kharkiv quickly sobered Tretyakov's mind. In December 1963, he was invited to the Kharkiv *obkom* where he had a conversation with a bureaucrat:

Bureaucrat: We heard you got a daughter. Congratulations. So you have two children now, correct?
Tretyakov: That's correct.
Bureaucrat: You see, the thing is that you have to be more careful. Who will raise them, if something happens to you?[106]

Bewildered, Tretyakov returned home where he shared this with his wife Lidiya. Both realized that the days of de-Stalinization and freedom were coming to an end.

The first signs of a new war against intellectuals appeared in late 1956, when the Central Committee criticized the Soviet intelligentsia for ideological errors in their art and anti-Soviet behavioral patterns.[107] The interactions among Soviet writers and the intelligentsia from Poland and Czechoslovakia, as well as political turbulence in Poland and Hungary, made the center visibly nervous. The return to the Stalinist rhetoric of "enemy" was amazingly swift: through the mass media it was effectively reanimated and emphasized. Khrushchev's brutal intervention in Hungary and the Boris Pasternak crisis frightened both the international community and Soviet society.[108] Inspired by the 25 August 1956 KGB report about Pasternak's intention to publish his novel *Doctor Zhivago* in Italy, the Soviet minister of foreign affairs Dmitrii

Shepilov launched a campaign of harassment against Pasternak. Pasternak was identified as a "traitor" and "double-dealer" in the media and was invited to leave the USSR "to personally experience the charms of the capitalist paradise."[109]

Attacks on Pasternak reverberated all over Ukraine, and in all major Ukrainian universities the Komsomol meetings chastised their local "literary geniuses," editors of university journals and newspapers unauthorized by the authorities, for supporting Pasternak and for other ideological heresies.[110] The day of 8 January 1957 became memorable for Robert and Lidiya. In lecture hall no. 361 at the Shevchenko State University their fellow students Borys Mar'ian, Volodymyr Hubanov, and Volodymyr Damaskin were expelled from the Komsomol ranks. On the KGB's order, the rector Ivan Shvets also expelled Mar'ian and Hubanov from the university. The same fate awaited Damaskin because the Komsomol organization of the School of Journalism unanimously supported his expulsion.[111] In addition, approximately 150 students, future journalists and poets, voted for this decision, but not Tretyakov. He refused to give a speech condemning Mar'ian, Hubanov, and Damaskin.[112] Yet the power of one individual in the Soviet Union was quite limited. For Robert, who experienced extreme starvation, it was incomprehensible that among the reasons for expelling one of the students was the famine of 1932–1933 that he incautiously raised in public. Lidiya and Robert realized that Stalinism was back, and as in the past, "the entire state apparatus wielded its power to crush one individual."[113]

Indeed, despite his "revolution" at the Twentieth Party Congress, Khrushchev never broke with party principles or Stalin's tradition of employing police power. Through his close subordinates, the Second Secretary of the KPSS Mikhail Suslov, the Head of the TsK Culture Department Dmitrii Polikarpov, and the Chairman of the KGB Vladimir Semichastnyi, Khrushchev also revived Stalin's practices of repressing families and associates of "transgressors."[114] Arguably, Khrushchev opened the era of "soft" violence and repressions, isolating dissent and intellectuals and reintroducing the concept of enemy. In Ukraine, the party and the KGB identified two main enemies, Ukrainian nationalists and Zionists who attempted to revive their cultural traditions and language, and affirm their individual rights.[115]

For the Kharkiv literati, in the early 1960s the ghost of freedom was sustained through close communication with the older generation of Ukrainian writers, the returnees who survived the Gulag. Tretyakov befriended the Ukrainian writers Vasyl Mysyk, Ivan Vyrhan, and Vasyl Borovyi who had miraculously survived the Holodomor and Stalin's camps. He was aware of their past but never believed in their guilt.[116] The former prisoners enjoyed a brief period of political rehabilitation and toleration by the regime until early 1957 when they once again became members of a politically unreliable group in the eyes of the authorities.[117] Despite re-Stalinization, the Kharkiv chapter of the Writers' Union and the Litfond continued to financially aid the returnees and their families.[118] The contacts between them and a younger generation of writers amplified the KGB's obsession with Ukrainian nationalism, and Tretyakov's gravitation toward Mysyk, Vyrhan, and Borovyi became a subject of close scrutiny by KGB operatives. He never repudiated these deep emotional links, but the powerful agency found a way to co-opt a young and promising poet. Tretyakov was asked to make an appearance in the *obkom* headquarters where he was offered one of the leading positions in the literary journal *Prapor* and a substantial raise under one condition: he had to apply for party membership. He took the bait, and on 9 April 1960, the Bureau of the Regional Party Committee (*raikom*) admitted him into the ranks of candidates to the KPSS.[119]

At that time, the signals from above were extremely contradictory and the political atmosphere appeared to be quite unstable. On 30 October 1961, the Twenty-Second Party Congress issued a resolution about the removal of Stalin's body from the Mausoleum. De-Stalinization would be illusory, its supporters believed, if the body of a terrorist remained untouched.[120] Robert and Lidiya fully supported the resolution of the Congress, as did the majority of their colleagues in Kharkiv.[121] However, the non-transparent and even secret procedure of the burial of Stalin's body before the Anniversary of the October Revolution, the silence in the periodicals about Stalin's repressions, and the reversal of democratic reforms confused the young couple. Several "truths" came out as a result of Khrushchev's Secret Speech, and they struggled to understand which "truth" to believe in. The Gulag again came to life, and during the period from 1960 to 1962 the number of prisoners almost doubled.[122] Soviet citizens observed the "extension of the death penalty, lengthening of prison sentences," and the reintroduction of show trials against social parasites and idlers.[123]

Tretyakov's move to join the party ranks proved to be timely. In March 1962, the Central Committee (TsK) of the Komsomol invited him to Kyiv and offered him a position as chief censor of the press for the TsK KPSS. He was hesitant but Lidiya insisted on staying in Kharkiv. As her diary reveals, Robert never forgave her for this imposition on their lives not because of career considerations but because of his deep and emotional attachment to the city of his youth, Kyiv.[124] After lengthy discussions with Lidiya about the options, he politely rejected the offer, which in hindsight seemed a fatal mistake to both of them. Their decision predetermined his career as a writer and his premature death. In a way, he had voluntarily entered the morbid circle of the system, a labyrinth from which he never escaped. Soon the Writers' Union in Kharkiv offered him an opportunity to move to the legendary House of Writers (*Budynok "Slovo"*).[125] Lidiya was pregnant with their second child, and a two-room apartment in the prestigious building seemed to be a clear improvement of their financial and social status. The process of co-optation continued.

From the early 1960s, the Kharkiv *obkom* and the KGB played a crucial role in controlling cultural affairs in Kharkiv. Its secretary Mykola Siroshtan, whose nickname was Sunduk or Siryi among the intelligentsia, "smelled" Ukrainian nationalism everywhere. A Russian-speaking Ukrainian (Russophone), Siroshtan announced: "The language of the Bolshevik Party is Russian. Everyone must know it and understand it."[126] It was him who in 1978, after Yurii Shovkoplias's death, finally managed to appoint his protégé Colonel Volodymyr Petrov, a former professor of the Kharkiv Military Academy, to one of the most powerful positions at the Kharkiv chapter of the Writers' Union. Through the manipulation of votes, Petrov became the Head of the Presidium of the Writer's Union. In Siroshtan's view, the Russian-speaking Petrov would govern the Union in the proper ideological mode.[127] Unsurprisingly, the members of the Kharkiv *obkom* enthusiastically supported Siroshtan's appointment.

The Kharkiv *obkom* gained fame as an antisemitic and chauvinistic group of people. This institution became a workshop that generated Russian-leaning chauvinist cadres for the center, such as Mykola Pidhornyi and Andrii Skaba.[128] In the 1960s, combating Ukrainian nationalism, Skaba called the *shistdesiatnyky* "literary prostitutes,"[129] and claimed that rehabilitation of former prisoners meant little. "We rehabilitated people but not their ideas!" Skaba announced.[130] Through the *obkom*'s supervision, the cultural institutions in Kharkiv became once again, as under Stalin, miniature replicas of the secret service office. The affiliation and the nature of activities KGB people conducted in each institution were an open secret, and typically the entire staff knew who these people were and what they were doing. Their very presence constrained the creative work and cultural initiatives of the literati. The KGB associates' primary task was to observe the most active and nationally conscious editors and writers, and inform their supervisors about their potential transgressions. Those who spoke exclusively Ukrainian (among them were writers and journalists Andrii Chernyshov, Yurii Stadnychenko, and Vasyl Borovyi) provoked a special interest of the agents.[131]

Tretyakov was no exception. An ethnic Russian, he chose Ukrainian as the language of his writings which became a subject of later "prophylactic" meetings in the *obkom* and *gorkom*, where the local party bosses taught Tretyakov how and what to write. In light of political developments in Moscow that heralded neither comfort nor security for the intelligentsia, these meetings destabilized his nervous system.[132] Khrushchev's 1964 dismissal and Leonid Brezhnev's appointment as the general secretary, who openly praised Stalin's merits during the Second World War, were soon followed by the sensational show trial of Yulii Daniel, writer and a former Kharkivite, and

Andrei Siniavskii, writer and a Moscovite.[133] Brezhnev empowered the KGB, strengthening the re-Stalinization course, and Moscow's political winds were highly perceptible in Ukraine. In the circle of his friends, Tretyakov revealed that he intended to add his signature to the 23 March 1966 collective letter signed by sixty-three writers. The members of the Writers' Union asked the Presidium of the Twenty-Third Party Congress and the Russian and Supreme Soviets to release Daniel and Siniavskii on bail. Tretyakov's friend and a Kharkivite, the Russian-speaking poet Arkadii Filatov, who was close to Daniel, argued that this move would not only be unsuccessful but would also have negative consequences for many who signed the letter.[134] Tretyakov reconsidered and never signed the document.[135]

Constant party harassment and fear for his family affected Tretyakov's social behavior and inhibited his poetic voice.[136] He fully understood that the ears of the KGB were everywhere. He often panicked when someone told a political anecdote in his office or in his home. He interrupted any conversation with his friends or with his family when there was the slightest criticism of the regime or the authorities. He typically switched from Ukrainian to Russian and said: "Change the tracks" or "Let's forget it for clarity" (*zamniom dlia yasnosti*), immediately unplugging the telephone and turning on the radio.[137] His politically correct behavior became almost manic, but it was rewarded. In the late 1960s, Tretyakov became the poet-laureate of the Komsomol Prize named after the Hero of the Soviet Union Oleksandr Zubarev.[138] His politically guarded public speeches and the favorable attitudes of the party establishment toward him distanced him from the dissident movement in Kharkiv and paralyzed his creativity and poetic spirit.[139]

In 1965, Tretyakov worked on his new book *Portrety* (Portraits) which was destined to be published only in 1967, once the turmoil of the 1965–1966 arrests of the Ukrainian intelligentsia settled down. On 4 August 1965, in the theater "Ukraina" in Kyiv, Paradzhanov presented his new film *Tini zabytykh predkiv* (Shadows of Forgotten Ancestors). After the premiere, the Ukrainian writer and scholar Ivan Dziuba (in its documentation the KGB gave him the code name "literator"; he was also referred to as "the ideologist of nationalist elements of the republic")[140] appealed to the audience and announced that twenty cultural figures had recently been arrested by the KGB, and that the shadows of 1937 were again resuscitated.[141] His behavior was viewed as an act of heroism, which was engraved in the annals of the Ukrainian resistance movement. Dziuba's 1965 *samvydav* text *Internationalism or Russification* in which he criticized Soviet nationalities policy and argued that Ukrainian culture was erased by forcible Russification shook intellectuals and the KGB on the all-Union level. The incident in "Ukraina" reenergized the efforts of the KGB, and on Moscow's orders, in the middle of the 1960s, Ukraine erupted with new arrests of the Ukrainian intelligentsia. Among them were Ivan

Svitlychnyi, Mykhailo Kosiv, Panas Zalyvakha, Mykhailo and Bohdan Horyn, and Mykhailo Osadchyi.[142] Their trials were held secretly behind closed doors. The arrested were labeled as *banderovtsy* and Ukrainian nationalists, and were accused of anti-Soviet propaganda and agitation according to Article 62 (part 1) of the Criminal Code of the Ukrainian SSR. Many were psychologically broken and intimidated, betraying their friends and colleagues. Their marginalization and the KGB's rhetoric about the enemies of the Soviet state provoked reaction from Ukraine's Russophones who wrote letters to newspapers, demanding punishment for Ukrainian nationalists who "inflamed national differences" in the republic.[143] No record of Tretyakov's engagement in political activism linked to this period has been located thus far.

The Ukrainian scholar Larysa Masenko suggested that in the 1960s–1970s the anti-Soviet attitudes among the older generation of Ukrainian writers and the educated youth were not a rarity, but only a few among the *shistdesiatnyky* had the courage to fight the regime openly.[144] Many were terrified by the KGB campaign targeting the intelligentsia; some were hiding behind humorous attitudes toward their unfortunate colleagues; others quietly sympathized with them. Various accounts described Tretyakov's extreme mood swings during this period which could be attributed to a confused personality puzzled by political instability and the persistent feeling of uncertainty and fear for his family.[145] The critique of his poetry published in the press contributed to his anxieties. Some literary critics, praising his tireless search for a moral compass and self-purification, accused him of excessive nonproductive self-examination.[146]

Yet, according to the prose writer Radii Polonskyi, in 1966, the peak of repression, Polonskyi, together with two poets, Vasyl Bondar and Tretyakov, created a "literary brigade" and traveled with poetry concerts all over Ukraine. Among other regions, they visited Western Ukraine where they came in contact with the Galician intelligentsia. Polonskyi claimed that at nonofficial and rather private meetings in local hotels after the concerts, the Kharkivites ("*slobozhany*") and Galicians primarily discussed whether Galicia was capable of leading the struggle for the national liberation of Ukraine. Polonskyi and Galician writers believed that historically Galicia played a role as Ukraine's Piedmont, and that the Galician intelligentsia could potentially become the vanguard of the movement.[147] The ethnically Russian Tretyakov was convinced that Kyiv and Slobozhanshchyna (Sloboda Ukraine)[148] would play a decisive role in the struggle. Importantly, Polonskyi suggested that in early 1966, there was no doubt among the critically thinking Ukrainian intelligentsia about the inevitability of the national liberation of Ukraine from Soviet hegemony.[149]

Polonskyi's optimistic view drastically contradicted the feelings and observations of the Kharkiv creative elite. Many considered escaping from

Kharkiv. By 1966 there was an overwhelming feeling of doom and provincial decay among the Ukrainian intelligentsia. All significant publishing houses were in Kyiv ("Dnipro," "Radianskyi pysmennyk," "Molod"). Rigid control of the local authorities and the KGB created a feeling of intellectual isolation.[150] After a cascade of trials in Kharkiv, Leonid Pliushch shared his perception about the city and its atmosphere: "After show trials of my friends, the city [Kharkiv] became a symbol of abomination: ugly, architecturally 'sotsrealistic,' chauvinist, with some mediocre faceless people. Perhaps it is not sensible to blame the entire city, but I saw only a handful of beautiful people . . . the police department, and the court house."[151]

Alcohol helped the Kharkivites subdue their worries and frustration. A store on Sumska Street in Kharkiv (*p'iatyi hastronom*) where one could purchase alcohol by the glassful became quite popular among Kharkiv writers.[152] Indeed, literary Kharkiv of the 1960s became famous for its drinking culture and for places such as the *p'iatyi hastronom* or the restaurant "Kryshtal" (Crystal) that are engraved in the memory of Kharkivites and Kharkiv's guests.[153] For Tretyakov, alcohol lubricated and soothed his anxieties about chronic poverty and political uncertainties. On 22 December 1963, in her diary, the Ukrainian writer Iryna Zhylenko wrote:

> We went to visit Kharkiv. I remember a vigorous discussion at the Kharkiv University, where we read our poetry. What is left in memory is how the Kharkiv poets were irrepressibly drinking, showing up at our hotel with a bag of alcoholic beverages. Tretyakov, Shumytskyi, and someone else. In the morning, I was cleaning the bathroom for a long time to avoid being embarrassed before the janitor. Quite poetic reminiscences.[154]

In another diary entry, she added: "Oh God, how much the boys are drinking here [in Kharkiv]! Horrible. . . . For some reason Tretyakov was ordered to come to Kyiv. . . . There is an acute and musty smell of a war in the air."[155] Her fears were confirmed when she heard a literary dignitary yelling at a meeting: "The Thaw is over."[156]

Kharkiv Writers and Their "Ritual Vice"

Escalated by Moscow ideologues, the rhetoric of fighting Ukrainian nationalism disenchanted Kharkiv writers. Many among the members of the Writers' Union could not handle the stress of surveillance that became quite noticeable and abusive by late 1964.[157] They fell into the abyss of alcoholism and conformism.

The 1964 Brezhnev coup, ousting Nikita Khrushchev as general secretary of the KPSS, entailed significant changes in the Kremlin's political course, particularly in the nationalities policy. Like Khrushchev, Brezhnev established a team of faithful assistants to control the population and nationalist tendencies in the republics. His closest circle included the aforementioned Suslov, Chairman of the KGB Yurii Andropov, and Nikolai Tikhonov, a member of the TsK and later of the Politburo who supervised cultural and economic affairs under Brezhnev. They helped the new General Secretary refine Stalinist methods of governing, reintroducing an effective mechanism of control in the republics over unruly nationalists. Surveillance, intimidation, "prophylactic talks," harassment, arrest, imprisonment, and physical elimination of Ukrainian and Jewish nationalists were among frequently employed KGB practices. In August and September of 1965, some twenty individuals were arrested for possession of *samvydav*. Among them were Ivan Svitlychnyi, Sviatoslav Karavanskii, Valentyn Moroz, Mykhailo and Bohdan Horyn, Mykhailo Osadchii, and Ivan Hel. The Dziuba and Chornovil affairs and the subsequent 1968–1969 arrests of the Ukrainian intelligentsia confirmed the Kharkivites' worst fears: the regime had rolled back to violence.[158]

The censors followed the trend. The secret 31 May 1968 report to the Central Committee, produced by the head of the Administration of the Preservation of State Secrets in the Press M. Pozdniakov, revealed that the Holovlit, Ukraine's main censorship institution, managed to thoroughly monitor 1,600 republican, oblast, city, district, and institutional newspapers; 71 literary and thematic journals; and 234 scholarly and popular journals published in Ukraine.[159] The editor of *Prapor* and heads of its main departments were carefully watched by the KGB and the Holovlit, and were chastised for the slightest unintentional errors that seemed political to the Holovlit inspectors.[160] Precisely during this time the Holovlit was ordered to create a new department that should monitor and control literary and artistic production in Ukraine,[161] a move that was followed by the 7 January 1969 directive issued by the Central Committee in Moscow that ordered an increase in party bureaucrats' personal responsibility for ideological deviations in media, in cultural institutions, and in every publication printed in the USSR.[162]

Moreover, by 1970, state antisemitism and anti-Zionism had regained its militant contours from the Stalinist era. Jewish nationalism, inspired by Israel's victory in the 1967 Six-Day War against the neighboring states of Egypt, Jordan, and Syria, and the Soviet Jews' desire to assert their cultural rights in the USSR or to emigrate to Israel, drove the KGB into their active mode. In Ukraine, the main concerns were the attempt of the Jewish youth to reach out to Jewish intellectuals for the purpose of revitalizing Jewish culture and the rapprochement of Ukrainians and Jews among the intellectual elite. KGB operatives intensified surveillance, investigated people's connections and habits, and conducted interviews with ideological deviationists in KGB headquarters.[163] During individual conversations, through intimidation, they turned Jewish wives against their Ukrainian husbands, writers of Ukrainian or Russian origins against writers of Jewish descent, and vice versa.[164]

Disillusioned and depressed, the writers gathered daily at the headquarters of *Prapor* and the Writers' Union, discussing politics, reading poetry, and drinking (Fig. 1.4). Soon it became clear that the KGB had bugged the building, and the Kharkiv writers ceased talking politics. Guests and writers from Lviv and other Ukrainian cities did not quite understand this behavior, attributing it to the Kharkivites' pro-Soviet position.[165] To be safe, the writers moved their gatherings to cafés and private apartments, but the spatial relocation did not change the routine and their habits. Alcohol made them talkative, liberating their thoughts, otherwise trapped inside their cautious minds. An escape from reality, this became a "ritual vice" (*ritualnyi porok*) of many, using the Russian scholar Yurii Lotman's term.[166] Lotman has argued that, from a semiotic perspective, poetry transformed alcohol consumption from a physiochemical process into a fact of culture, where a poetic masterpiece was a sublimation-product. Many Kharkiv writers were sinners of this vice. "Everyone drank—Ukrainians, Russians, and Jews. What varied was the length of time each of us managed to stay sober," stated Serhii Boltryk, the administrator of the Writers' Union.[167]

The writers' all-pervasive alcoholism became a concern for the KGB. The pernicious habit was associated with too much freedom. The Russian writer Andrei Bitov most accurately explained this connection. He was convinced that a writer needs a drink to write—to liberate his characters and make them talk: "Under the influence, I am giving them freedom to talk about anything; or possibly I acquire freedom from them to write."[168] The problem of Kharkiv writers' drinking habits reached Kyiv, and in May 1971, the head of Ukraine's KGB Vitalii Fedorchuk wrote a report to Ukraine's party boss Petro Shelest, in which several Kharkiv writers were blacklisted: Radii Polonskyi, Robert Tretyakov, Oleksandr Cherevchenko, Boris Silaiev, Lev Galkin, and Vasilii Omelchenko. The KGB leader also expressed his doubts about their ideological fitness and ability to represent the Kharkiv chapter at the Sixth Congress of the Writers' Union. Fedorchuk admitted that the Kharkiv chapter, in contrast to the Kyiv chapter, seemed to be less divided, but nevertheless, in his view, the symptoms of stagnation and ideological unorthodoxy were there. Beyond the writers' alcoholism, Fedorchuk was also concerned about the poet Roman Levin who systematically slandered the Soviet system, Boris Chichibabin whose poems were permeated with anti-Sovietism, and Polonskyi who adopted a nationalistic stance. According to KGB operational documents, Polonskyi privately stated: "We should treat Russians as colonizers. . . . The writers' mouths are tightened up, and they cannot write what they want."[169] Decades later, another Ukrainian intellectual who closely communicated with Kharkiv writers, the director at the theater

"Berezil" Anatolii Starodub, confessed: "We drank too much and talked too freely, and one day we might say too much to a wrong person or to a foreign guest . . . our alcohol consumption was for sure a problem for the KGB."[170]

The writers' gatherings and their ritual vice united Ukrainians, Russians, and Jews in the face of danger that emanated from the KGB. These rituals enabled them to write, secretly read their unpublishable work to one another, and to collectively write ironic, sarcastic, and "difficult" poetry.[171] Kharkiv writers Aleksandr Basiuk, Vladimir Motrich, Leonid Osmolovskyi (Osadchuk), and Stanislav Shumytskyi, among others, became an inseparable part of the writers' memoirs about their pernicious habit[172] and subjects of KGB reports. The KGB pressed the leadership of the Writers' Union to break this union and to punish those who most frequently were seen drunk.[173]

The early 1960s protocols of the Kharkiv chapter of the Writers' Union reveal that attempts by its leadership to alter their members' habits had limited success. For instance, Vladimir Dobrovolskii and Vasyl Bondar, both talented writers of rare literary gift and innovative style, were frequently chastised for their alcoholism.[174] For KGB literary experts, both wrote an ideologically questionable prose and poetry. In his novels *I dukh nash molod* (Our Spirit Is Young) and *Za nedeliu do otpuska* (A Week Before Vacation) Dobrovolskii, a 1949 laureate of the Stalin Prize, slandered the Soviet system, depicting the insufficient optimism of Soviet youth and nepotism, "gloomy and untrue realities of Soviet life." As a former prisoner of war and a survivor of the Dachau concentration camp, Bondar had no prospects

Figure 1.4 The Members of the Kharkiv Chapter of the Writers' Union in the 1960s. *Source*: Robert Tretyakov Private Archive (hereafter: RTPA); a copy is located in TsDAMLIMU, f. 783, op. 1, spr. 26, ark. 4.

for publishing his work, yet those few poems that he did publish before his death were interpreted as ones that "glorified the suffering and the struggle of World War II prisoners, offering metaphors evoking parallels between the Nazis' and the Soviets' violence" (i.e., "The Black Sky Violently Tortures"/ Chorne nebo zhorstoko katuie).[175] Dobrovolskii was constantly reprimanded (Fig. 1.5); Bondar's membership in the Union was questioned.

Despite the stigma perpetuated by the KGB, Bondar was respected and admired by his fellow writers and gathered around himself people of various ethnic backgrounds. Together with other prisoners, he was liberated from Dachau by American troops. He went through the American DPs (displaced persons) camp and the Soviet filtration camp in Eastern Germany. After his return to Ukraine, he shared his knowledge and experiences of the Holocaust and the Nazis' brutality with the younger writers. Being a perpetual suspect and incessantly guilty because of his imprisonment experience, Bondar was also a person of tragic individual history. He met a woman he loved but she, having learned that Vasyl was arrested, married his brother and bore two children with him. Vasyl's brother died at the front, and Vasyl married the widow. Difficult memories about Dachau and routine persecution by the KGB prompted Vasyl to seek relaxation in alcohol which complicated the couple's life. During a quarrel, his wife confessed that his brother betrayed Vasyl, surrendering him to the Nazis. Thereafter, the couple divorced.[176] In the early 1960s, even Yurii Zbanatskyi, head of the republican chapter of the Writers' Union, made a special trip from Kyiv to Kharkiv to defend Bondar.[177]

The writers tried to grasp what was happening *around* them and *within* them, continuing to gather in downtown Kharkiv. The most frequent places

Figure 1.5 **Vladimir Dobrovolskii with the Workers at the Kharkiv Tractor Factory.** The date is unknown. *Source*: RTPA; a copy is located in TsDAMLIMU, f. 816, op. 1, spr. 350, ark. 1.

for their meetings were inexpensive cafés and restaurants, the legendary bookstore "Poeziia" (Poetry) on Poetry Square,[178] and Chichibabin's apartment on Rymarska Street.[179] In the 1960s–1970s, the House of Writers "Slovo," a cultural marker of the 1930s and the Kharkiv writers' place of residence and gatherings, lost its significance. The Writers' Union no longer had control over the building, and few writers resided there. Yet this place, as any other place of congregation of the Kharkiv intelligentsia, was under close KGB surveillance. The close proximity of these places to the KGB headquarters on Radnarkomivska Street facilitated the task of surveillance. Ultimately, Kharkiv's political space delineated and absorbed the cultural space the Kharkiv literati created for themselves, threatening to abrogate their existential values, imaginations, and practices.

The KGB and the Kharkiv Literati

In July 1967, the KGB created special counterintelligence departments to combat the ideological sabotage created by the opposition. In the cities, including Kharkiv, the Fifth Directorate and its subordinate departments were in charge of this mission, conducting surveillance of the most active dissidents or individuals who attracted the KGB's attention by their nonconformist behavior.[180] Under Moscow's close supervision, the KGB launched an operation "Blok" designed to isolate Ukrainian nationalists and dissidents.[181] The operational methods were rather traditional but, by the late 1960s, the KGB resorted to a more assertive method of intimidation. The main idea was to make surveillance and the presence of KGB officers among Ukrainian intellectuals apparent and perceptible. Many *seksoty* did not even try to hide their identity.[182] On the contrary, they bragged about their affiliation with the powerful agency. One of them was Viktor Deineko who was rather conspicuous in provoking Kharkiv writers to "speak anti-Soviet."[183]

KGB agents were patient and persistent, breaking an individual for months. They subjected their surveilled victim to chronic stress, infiltrating the circle of his or her closest friends and attending the victim's parties and formal professional meetings.[184] The KGB preferred to recruit ambitious philologists who dreamed of becoming writers and poets, students of the Kharkiv State University. KGB officers trained them to befriend established writers, members of the Writers' Union, and report on their mood and talks. Frequently KGB operatives themselves penetrated the literary circles, creating their own clubs, groups of writers with whom they spent time together, partying, reading poems, and discussing the news. Oleksandr Kasha, a stout man with a kind face, who was traditionally introduced by his friends as a KGB agent, infiltrated Tretyakov's company which in the early 1960s consisted of literati, artists, and actors. Tretyakov's relatives remembered a joyful Kasha for decades as Tretyakov's shadow and an inseparable part of each gathering.[185]

By 1967, the tension between the Ukrainian intelligentsia and the authorities grew substantially. In 1967, the Ukrainian writer and dissident Viacheslav Chornovil was arrested for his book *Gore ot uma* (Woe from Wit). The same year the militia and the KGB forcibly dispersed a gathering in Kyiv near the monument to Shevchenko, characterizing the commemorative event as an anti-Soviet demonstration. Five people were arrested and those who protested the arrests were dispersed with water cannons.[186] Some individuals were ready to sacrifice themselves for Ukraine's liberation from Moscow's and the KGB's control. On 5 December 1968, and 10 February 1969, in Kyiv, two former prisoners of the Gulag, Vasyl Makukha and Mykola Beryslavskyi, publicly immolated themselves in protest against anti-Ukrainian policies, Russification, and repressions in Ukraine.[187]

Similarly, in 1968, Kharkiv was shaken because of the protest of a group of activists who signed letters addressed to the authorities against persecution of national minorities in the Soviet Union, including Crimean Tatars. The most active were Arkadii Levin, Genrikh Altunian, Aleksandr Paritskii, Vladislav Nedobora, Yurii Tarnapolskii, and Itskhak Moshkovich. The same year Altunian was expelled from the party and was dismissed from the Military Academy after the KGB found *samvydav* in his possession written by Aleksandr Solzhenitsyn and Andrei Sakharov.[188] Soon, the entire Kharkiv group, which was referred to as *pidpysanty* (signatories) by the state, was arrested and charged with libel against the state, a charge stipulated by Article 187 of the Criminal Code of the Ukrainian SSR.[189]

According to Leonid Pliushch, the chief mistake of the Kharkivites was that they tried to reason with the authorities, attempting to prove that the law was on their side. In fact, the law had been violated even procedurally: criminal cases of individuals who were investigated within Article 187 should have been under the jurisdiction of the Prosecutor's Office. Instead, the KGB conducted the preliminary investigation, and only after it was completed, was the case transferred to the Kharkiv Prosecutor's Office. The Soviet dissident Itskhak Moshkovich remembered that KGB agents constantly played these games to demonstrate their power over human life. Most of them had no ideological motivations, and as one of them stated, "this was only a job for me."[190] Preparing the trials, they worked hard, yet, as Moshkovich has noted, "the machine worked ninety percent ineffectively, because only ten percent of 'actors-witnesses' (I believe even this estimation is inflated) agreed to testify in show trials against the accused."[191] The trials against Kharkiv dissidents were transparently scripted, ultimately becoming engraved in the memories of those who attended them. Yet, the chief deputy of the Ministry of Internal Affairs in the Kharkiv oblast confessed that the dissidents and human rights activists were a minor concern for him; Ukrainian nationalists (*nezalezhnyky* or independents) were a constant headache, and this problem was to be taken care of urgently.[192]

By 1969, Ukrainian *samvydav* became a serious problem for the KGB. Surveillance was a solution to this problem and the key to state power.[193] Surveillance and the subsequent illegal searches of the writers' apartments were frequently crowned with success because many homes of Ukrainian writers were the repositories of illegal literature. A wave of arrests in 1969 harvested Ukrainian journalists, teachers, and writers who were accused of Ukrainian nationalism and anti-Soviet propaganda. KGB documentation suggests that the agency eschewed any enlightening purpose, and its lieutenants had no interest in reforging their clients or forgiving their transgressions. The "nationalists" were always reminded about the possibility of a harsher punishment than they had already experienced.

On 17 June 1969, the Kharkiv literati were informed that Ivan Sokulskyi, a young promising poet from the neighboring city of Dnipropetrovsk, was arrested. During the search of his apartment, the KGB found *samvydav*, works written by Valentyn Moroz and Ivan Dziuba.[194] In January 1970, Sokulskyi received four-and-a-half years in prison. Before his release in 1973, he was found psychiatrically unstable which complicated his life after the camps. Radii Polonskyi who headed the Kharkiv chapter of the Writers' Union during the last Soviet years remembered that the arrest of Sokulskyi, his colleague and friend, devastated him. Polonskyi identified the late 1960s and early 1970s as the time when

> the shcherbytskyis [pl. of Shcherbytskyi, Ukraine's party boss] and the malanchuks [pl. of Malanchuk, Ukraine's chief ideologue] deployed repression, torture, and violence all over Ukraine, closing the last Ukrainian schools in the cities and towns of eastern and southern Ukraine. They could not wait to destroy the sixtiers as a phenomenon, to beat out of the freedom-loving minds any resemblance of a thought about Ukraine's revival, and to trample even the sparks of liberal thinking, national dignity, and consciousness. The rampaging censorship transformed the newspaper and journal editors into a frenzied police force under the threat of punishment for their failure to be ideologically vigilant; they reduced Ukraine to a geographical notion, forcing the Ukrainian culture and language to disappear.[195]

Polonskyi was convinced that under these circumstances, the spring 1964 fire in the Kyiv Public Library that raged in the center of the city for three days was a KGB operation designed to excoriate the Ukrainian culture together with its artifacts (Fig. 1.6).[196] The authorities did not even try to extinguish the fire which destroyed 600,000 volumes of the Ukrainian rare book collection, archives, and ancient publications.[197]

To purge the nationalist heresy in Ukraine, the KGB employed perlustration, an old method of surveillance utilized since the reign of Catherine II in imperial Russia.[198] The practice was reliable but consumed a great deal of resources. According to the Soviet data of the 1960s–1970s, approximately 8 billion letters and 170 million parcels were mailed annually in the Soviet Union. An army of 1 million postal workers (*sviazisty*) sorted the mail by hand.[199] Most of them worked for the secret organs. Perlustration helped the KGB identify those who expressed "nationalist sentiment" or frustration with the Soviet system in their letters. Being aware of this KGB tactic, the writers stopped using official channels of communication, and the epistolary genre among them gradually dried out being replaced with oral communications.

In the late 1960s, after the first wave of arrests, Moscow realized that it was time to replace the republic's party chief Petro Shelest (1963–1972) with Brezhnev's protégé Volodymyr Shcherbytskyi who eagerly awaited his new appointment. Vitalii Fedorchuk, who in July 1970 became the new chairman of the KGB in Ukraine, seemed to have played a crucial role in Shelest's dismissal. Fedorchuk believed that Shelest ingratiated himself with Ukrainian nationalists.[200] Moscow demanded the resolution of the Ukrainian question once and for all.

In response, the KGB radicalized their approach to nationalists. The agency was not averse to the use of violence. Similar to the prewar period, the secret police began to beat the disobedient and politically active intellectuals in the streets, bludgeoning them with blunt, heavy objects (*kastety*). Cases of murder were disguised as street hooliganism, and the "guilty" were never found.[201] In Kharkiv, the chain of tragic and mysterious deaths commenced in October 1969 when the Ukrainian writer Vasyl Bondar died in the hospital after being thrown under a tram. He was found on the tram tracks with a fractured skull (Fig. 1.6).[202] Before his death, Bondar was harassed by the KGB that distrusted him because of his experiences at the Dachau concentration camp and Soviet labor camps during the postwar period. In 1962, he was dismissed from his position as a contributing journalist in *Literaturna Ukraina*.[203] Oleksa Marchenko who visited the dying Bondar in the hospital stated that before his death Bondar revealed that the KGB agents had pushed him under the tram.[204]

Frightened by Bondar's death, the Kharkiv literati maintained a low profile. They realized that they were not only mortal but "suddenly mortal" (*vnezapno smertny*), as the Russian writer Bulgakov's character Woland famously stated.[205] The KGB's use of "tram accidents" as a method of killing persisted. In 1972, Tretyakov, together with a writer whose name he preferred not to reveal, was almost murdered near his home. A group of men approached the two and without saying a word began to beat the writers. The target of their attack was Tretyakov's neck area; the weapons were heavy boots. When the

Figure 1.6   Vasyl Bondar (Left) and Radii Polonskyi (Right), 1966. *Source*: RTPA; a copy is located in TsDAMLIMU, f. 781, op. 1, spr. 72, ark. 6.

job was finished and Tretyakov and his colleague were unconscious, the men dragged them to the tram tracks and left them there so that an early morning tram would cut them in half. Nothing valuable was taken from them. Tretyakov regained consciousness first and helped his friend get to the hospital. The circumstances of this incident suggest a premeditated murder attempt rather than a random case of hooliganism. He survived the attack, but he lost his voice for a long time. The vocal ligaments were permanently damaged. For a poet, this could be tragic. Kharkiv throat specialists gave up on him, but his voice was gradually partially restored. It remained low-pitched and subdued to his last days.[206] The overpowering horror of violence terrified Tretyakov, and his poetry, like his voice, became insipid, low-pitched, and subdued.

In 1974 in Kharkiv, Tretyakov's friend, the talented Ukrainian poet Stanislav Shumytskyi, also fell victim to the KGB's and militia's violence.[207] Shumytskyi, when it came to the use of the Ukrainian language, was uncompromising which irritated the Russian-speaking militia and the KGB for quite some time. In a Russified city such as Kharkiv, where the Ukrainian language was an aberration rather than a language of public communication, speaking Ukrainian and writing in Ukrainian aggravated the authorities. In early January 1974, Shumytskyi's body was found in a deep ravine near Kharkiv with two identification cards in his pocket, membership in the Writers' Union and the Journalists' Union. Surprisingly, the authorities asked several Kharkiv writers to identify the body in Kharkiv's central morgue three weeks after Shumytskyi was found. Volodymyr Briuggen remembered that Shumytskyi was recognizable, although his body had been disfigured by severe beatings.[208] The militia (MVS) secretly kept Shumytskyi's passport, claiming that they took him into custody shortly before he "disappeared" because he was drunk but noted that they had released him. The militia rejected accusations that they had beaten Shumytskyi to death. The investigation of the homicide was ended by a phone call from the *obkom*. The authorities ordered Shumytskyi's burial to be quick and quiet.[209] Many writers did not attend the funeral, fearing they might violate the *obkom*'s order to avoid speeches. Tretyakov was among the few who attended Shumytskyi's funeral.[210] The rumors about the KGB having something to do with Shumytskyi's death circulated for years, but what heated the speculations among his fellow writers was information that Shumytskyi's name was purged from future publications, and his poetry was banned.

Shumytskyi was among a few who fought for the right of the Ukrainian language to exist against the aggressive Russification of eastern Ukraine. The literary journal *Prapor*, where Tretyakov had been invited to lead the poetry section in the early 1970s, was arguably the only Ukrainian journal in Ukraine's Left Bank. *Prapor*'s circulation in the 1960s was approximately 7,400 copies, and this journal was akin to a bone in the throat of Kharkiv KGB officials.[211] At a meeting of the Writers' Union, one writer shared with his colleagues the details of a conversation he held with a KGB general. The general stated that "it [was] time to finish here the Ukrainian language." The writer expressed some hope that the Ukrainian language would "outlive the 'theoreticians' of the liquidation of this language."[212] The content of this discussion was immediately delivered to the KGB headquarters on Radnarkomivska Street, and the KGB leadership ordered stronger measures against the writers.

Tretyakov joined *Prapor*'s staff when the journal was permeated with the *chekist* spirit due to two women—Natalia Cherchenko (the chief editor) and Olha Muzhytska (the head of the prose section) whose husbands worked for the KGB.[213] In the headquarters of *Prapor*, everyone avoided discussing the 1972 pogrom among the Ukrainian intellectual elite. The 1970 appointment of Fedorchuk as the chief of the KGB and the 1972 appointment of Valentyn Malanchuk as the party secretary and the chief ideologue in Ukraine marked this period by "the most rigorous censorship of national self-expression" and the arrest of intellectuals.[214] In 1972, a total of 100 people were arrested; eighty-nine of them were charged with anti-Soviet activities. Among the arrested were the most prominent representatives of the Ukrainian creative intelligentsia Iryna Kalynets, Ihor Kalynets, Ivan Dziuba, Ivan Svitlychnyi (second arrest), Nadiia Svitlychna, Vasyl Stus, Yevhen Sverstiuk, Nina Strokata-Karavanska, Zinovii Antoniuk, Mykola Plakhotniuk, Oleksandr Serhienko, Danylo Shumuk (third arrest), Leonid Pliushch, Viacheslav Chornovil (second arrest), Ivan Hel (second arrest), Mykhailo Osadchyi (second arrest), and Stefaniia Shabatura.[215] The Ukrainian writer Oksana

Zabuzhko remembered that a high-ranking KGB official explained to her parents the necessary isolation of the Ukrainian intelligentsia in labor camps in a manner that was typical of the Soviet era: "In order to eliminate the base for growth . . ."[216] By the mid-1970s, some Kharkiv writers were imprisoned; many were broken and recruited by the KGB; a few escaped to Moscow; others were ostracized.

At the height of the Cold War, the Soviet Union failed to conceal a new terror targeting the intelligentsia in Ukraine. The "elimination of the base for growth" of nationalism, including the sensational case of Ivan Dziuba and other cases of persecuting Ukraine's intellectuals, transcended the Iron Curtain, offering the American intelligence agencies an opportunity to closely observe and analyze the political situation, the dissident movement, and the changes in the literary landscape in the republic. As mentioned earlier, CIA analysts identified the period following 1963 as "A New Freeze" in Ukraine. In their reports, they wrote: "Poets and writers are not only asked to write according to the 'New' Party line, they must also discard and castigate what they have written before. Some of them refuse and answer new challenges with a proved argument: silence."[217] In 1968, the CIA launched a covert operation code named "Project QRDYNAMIC." It was designed to support Ukrainian writers and dissidents politically and financially, bringing the international community's attention to Soviet repression in Ukraine and Moscow's attempts to erase Ukrainian culture and language. Among other tactics, the operation aimed at publishing literature unpublishable in Ukraine, smuggling it to Ukraine, and making it available to Western intellectuals, "concerned about the entire problem of human rights in the USSR."[218] CIA analysts realized that despite the fact that there were many supporters of the Soviet regime among party functionaries, the government, and the intelligentsia, there was also a significant minority of intellectuals who did not succumb to the regime's pressure. CIA analysts concluded: "Even among those who apparently conform, there may be hidden nationalist sentiments." Their assessment seemed to be quite accurate.[219]

Tretyakov persisted in his use of Ukrainian and shared stories with his fellow writers that irritated KGB agents who accurately attended each working meeting at the headquarters of *Prapor* and the Writers' Union. He repeated the words of his closest friend Ivan Vyrhan, a subtle Ukrainian poet of the older generation and a former prisoner of the Gulag, which Vyrhan uttered on his death bed in 1975: "Everything is a lie" (*Vse brekhnia*).[220] Soon the entire community of the Kharkiv literati whispered those words to one another. Mykola Shatylov, writer and a former Kharkivite, wrote about Tretyakov: "they [the KGB] were trying to bend him—he did, but he was never broken."[221] He simply could not write anything under the KGB's supervision. This transformation was accelerated after he was called to attend a meeting at

"The Revolution of Poets" and Re-Stalinization

the Kharkiv *obkom* where the Kharkiv cultural ideologue Yurii Skliarov chastised him for publishing Ivan Drach's poem in *Prapor*. According to Skliarov, as the head of the poetry section and as a member of the Communist Party, Tretyakov "failed to recognize" the anti-Soviet essence of Ivan Drach's poem (Fig. 1.7).[222] Drach experienced similar pressure but some of his colleagues were kind enough and had been protecting him over the years from the authorities' attacks. For example, one of Drach's fellow students wrote a letter to the Writers' Union characterizing Drach's new poem "Nizh u sontsi" (A Knife in the Sun) as anti-Soviet. Oles Honchar who was the head of the Union then told Stanislav Telniuk: "Call Ivan, let him read it, and then destroy it."[223]

After the "tram" and "Drach" incidents, Tretyakov seemed to undergo a galvanizing transformation of his consciousness. Ideological motifs prevailed in his poetry, and the melodies of his lyrics became more melancholic, often becoming lost in the debris of Leninist rhetoric. At the peak of the arrests, in 1971–1972, Tretyakov published an article which was dedicated to the 100th birthday of the Ukrainian poetess Lesia Ukrainka. In this article, he used the term "Ukrainian bourgeois nationalism" in a negative connotation. The politically correct text praised Ukrainka's internationalism and revolutionary spirit. Not surprisingly, Tretyakov chose to write the article in the Russian language and to publish it in the Kharkiv Russian newspaper *Krasnoie znamia*.[224] The date of publication does not seem accidental either, 25 February, a day before Tretyakov's birthday. Traditionally, he hosted parties for his friends

Figure 1.7 Kyiv and Kharkiv Writers with Their Families in Koktebel, Crimea, 1966: Ivan Drach (Second on the Left, Standing); Radii Polonskyi (Second on the Right, Sitting). *Source*: RTPA; a copy is located in TsDAMLIMU, f. 781, op. 1, spr. 71, ark. 3.

and colleagues on 26 February. He carefully prepared them, and it appears that in 1971 he wanted nothing to overshadow the celebration, either a prophylactic conversation at the *obkom* headquarters or an unexpected visit of KGB agents. Yet, as the literary critic Volodymyr Briuggen argued, "this was a temporary eclipse of his consciousness. We all tried to avoid being cast as nationalists, which in the spatial context of Ukraine connoted and presaged a crime against the Soviet state. Tretyakov never abandoned his language, his culture, or rejected his Ukrainianness."[225]

Moreover, Tretyakov clearly ignored the attempts of narrow-minded ideological *apparatchiki* to segregate Ukrainians, Jews, and Russians, maintaining friendships with the brightest, regardless of their ethnic self-identification. Hence, the political violence against "cultural nationalists," the Kharkivites like Tretyakov, Bondar, and Shumytskyi, was undoubtedly calculated and premeditated. Further unearthing and analyzing the major—cultural—factor of the state political violence in Kharkiv would allow us to better understand the subsequent developments in Ukraine, and ultimately the reasons for the disintegration of the Soviet system that devoured itself through cultural and information wars.

NOTES

1. Vladimir Pomerantsev, "Ob iskrennosti v literature," *Novyi Mir* 12 (1953): 218. Also quoted in Marc Slonim, *Soviet Russian Literature: Writers and Problems, 1917–1977*, 2nd ed. (New York: Oxford University Press, 1977), 321.

2. See Khrushchev's Secret Speech, "'On the Cult of Personality and Its Consequences,' delivered at the Twentieth Congress of the Communist Party of the Soviet Union" on 25 February 1956, *Wilson Center/History and Public Policy Program Digital Archive* (from the Congressional Record: Proceedings and Debates of the 84th Congress, 2nd Session, 22 May 1956–11 June 1956, C11, Part 7, 4 June 1956, pp. 9389–9403), http://digitalarchive.wilsoncenter.org/document/115995 (accessed 25 August 2021); Miriam Dobson, *Khrushchev's Cold Summer: Gulag Returnees, Crime, and the Fate of Reform after Stalin* (Ithaca and London: Cornell University Press, 2009), 3.

3. Slonim, *Soviet Russian Literature*, 320.

4. Paul Robert Magocsi and Yohanan Petrovsky-Shtern, *Jews and Ukrainians: A Millennium of Co-Existence* (Toronto: University of Toronto Press, 2016), 170.

5. On the popularity of poetry under Khrushchev, see Emily Lygo, "The Need for New Voices: Writers' Union Policy towards Young Writers, 1953–1964," in *The Dilemmas of De-Stalinization: Negotiating Cultural and Social Change in the Khrushchev Era*, ed. Polly Jones (London: Routledge, 2006), 193–208; Anatoly Pinsky, "The Diatristic Form and Subjectivity under Khrushchev," *Slavic Review* 73, no. 4 (2014): 806–07.

6. Osyp Zinkevych, "Rozhrom molodoi literatury v Ukraini," *Dysydentskyi rukh v Ukraini*, 4 March 2016, http://archive.khpg.org/index.php?id=1457121207 (accessed 6 July 2020). Zinkevych's essay was initially published in *Smoloskyp* (July–August 1963) and republished in *Literaturna Ukraina*, no. 14 (5302), 9 April 2009.

7. Grigorii Pomerants, "Without Repentance," *Russian Studies in Literature* 34, no. 3 (1998): 74.

8. Slonim, *Soviet Russian Literature*, 338.

9. Mark Von Hagen, "Wartime Occupation and Peacetime Alien Rule: 'Notes and Materials' toward a(n) (Anti-) (Post-) Colonial History of Ukraine," in *The Future of the Past: New Perspectives on Ukrainian History*, ed. Serhii Plokhy (Cambridge, MA: Ukrainian Research Institute, Harvard University, Harvard University Press, 2016), 170–71.

10. Slonim, *Soviet Russian Literature*, 321.

11. Quoted in ibid., 339.

12. Simone A. Bellezza, "Wings to Lift the Truth Up High: The Role of Language for the *Shistdesiatnyky*," *Harvard Ukrainian Studies* 35, no. 1–4 (2017–2018): 213–32; Serhy Yekelchyk, "The Early 1960s as a Cultural Space: A Microhistory of Ukraine's Generation of Cultural Rebels," *Nationalities Papers* 43, no. 1 (2015): 45–62; Tarik Cyril Amar, *The Paradox of Ukrainian Lviv: A Borderland City between Stalinists, Nazis, and Nationalists* (Ithaca, NY: Cornell University Press, 2015); William Jay Risch, *The Ukrainian West: Culture and the Fate of Empire in Soviet Lviv* (Cambridge, MA: Harvard University Press, 2011); Liudmyla Tarnashynska, *Ukrainske shistdesiatnytstvo: profili na tli pokolinnia (Istoryko-literaturnyi ta poetykalnyi aspekty)* (Kyiv: "Smoloskyp," 2010); Benjamin Tromly, "An Unlikely National Revival: Soviet Higher Learning and the Ukrainian 'Sixtiers,' 1953–1965," *Russian Review* 68, no. 4 (2009): 607–22.

13. On the spatial history of Kharkiv, see Tatiana Zhurzhenko, *Borderlands into Bordered Lands: Geopolitics of Identity in Post-Soviet Ukraine* (Stuttgart: ibidem-Verlag, 2010); Volodymyr Kravchenko, "Stolytsia dlia Ukrainy," in *Ukraina, Imperiia, Rosiia: Vybrani statti z modernoi istorii ta istoriohrafii*, ed. Volodymyr Kravchenko (Kyiv: Krytyka, 2011), 45–85.

14. *Obkom* refers to *obslasnyi komitet partii* (regional party committee).

15. Slonim, *Soviet Russian Literature*, 350.

16. Yevgenii Yevtushenko, "Igra v poddavki: Istoriia odnoi verbovki," *Sovershenno Sekretno*, no. 4 (51) (2012): 20.

17. Listen to Khrushchev's shameful attack against Andrei Voznesenskii at this meeting on *YouTube*, 1 June 2010, https://www.youtube.com/watch?v=3f9izHJGIoo (accessed 6 July 2020).

18. The first issues of *Prapor* appeared in 1956. In 1991, it was renamed *Berezil*. At different times the chief editors were Yurii Shovkoplias, Yurii Barabash, Yurii Makhnenko, Natalia Cherchenko, Ivan Maslov, and Yurii Stadnychenko. Since 2000, Volodymyr Naumenko serves as *Berezil*'s editor. See Ihor Mykhailyn, *Literaturna Kharkivshchyna. Poeziia* (Kharkiv: "Maidan," 2007), 19.

19. Zinkevych, "Rozhrom molodoi literatury v Ukraini."

20. Feliks Rakhlin, *O Borise Chichibabine i iego vremeni: Strochka iz zhizni* (Kharkov: Folio, 2004), 65.

21. Paul A. Goble, "Readers, Writers, and Republics: The Structural Basis of Non-Russian Literary Politics," in *The Nationalities Factors in Soviet Politics and Society*, eds. Lubomyr Hajda and Mark Beissinger (Boulder, San Francisco, and Oxford: Westview Press, 1990), 131–47.

22. Slonim, *Soviet Russian Literature*, 383.

23. Haluzevyi Derzhavnyi Arkhiv Sluzhby Bezpeky Ukrainy (The Sectoral State Archive of Security Services in Ukraine; hereafter: HDA SBU), f. 16, op. 1, spr. 1060, ark. 135–39.

24. L. G. Churchward, *The Soviet Intelligentsia: An Essay on the Social Structure and Roles of the Soviet Intellectuals during the 1960s* (London/Boston: Routledge & Kegan Paul, 1973), 11; for a discussion about the Ukrainian cultural revival during and after the Thaw period, see Kenneth C. Farmer, *Ukrainian Nationalism in the Post-Stalin Era: Myth, Symbols and Ideology in Soviet Nationalities Policy* (The Hague, Boston, London: Martinus Nijhoff Publishers, 1980), 80–89, 97, 105.

25. Slonim, *Soviet Russian Literature*, 394; Central Intelligence Agency, "A New Freeze: A Collection of Material on Recent Developments in Ukrainian Soviet Literature," *CIA Archive*, 28 August 1963 (declassified and released in 2007), https://www.cia.gov/library/readingroom/docs/AERODYNAMIC%20%20%20VOL.%2026%20%20%28OPERATIONS%29_0071.pdf (accessed 11 July 2020).

26. Mykola Zhulynskyi, *Natsiia. Kultura. Literatura: Natsionalno-kulturni mify ta ideino-estetychni poshuky Ukrainskoi literatury* (Kyiv: Naukova dumka, 2011).

27. Stefania Andrusiv, "Shistdesiatnytstvo iak iavyshche, ioho vytoky i naslidky," *Slovo i chas* 8 (1997): 50–52.

28. Tarnashynska, *Ukrainske shistdesiatnytstvo*, 571.

29. Heorhii Kas'ianov, *Nezhodni: Ukrainska intelihentsiia v rusi oporu 1960–80-kh rokiv* (Kyiv: Lybid, 1995), 185.

30. Ibid., 186.

31. Volodymyr Panchenko, *Kiltsia na drevi* (Kyiv: TOV "Vydavnytstvo 'Klio,'" 2015), 358–59; Oles Obertas, *Ukrainskyi samvydav: Literaturna krytyka ta publitsystyka (1960-i – pochatok 1970-kh rokiv)* (Kyiv: Smoloskyp, 2010).

32. Vira Aheieva, *Mystetstvo rivnovahy: Maksym Rylskyi na tli epokhy* (Kyiv: Vydavnytstvo "Knyha," 2012), 243.

33. Ibid., 261–62.

34. Ivan Dziuba, *Z krynytsi lit*, vol. 1 (Kyiv: Vydavnychyi dim "Kyievo-Mohylianska akademiia," 2006), 623.

35. Dziuba, *Z krynytsi lit*, vol. 1, 624.

36. Ivan Svitlychnyi, "Mriiaty vysokoiu metoiu," *Literaturna hazeta*, 24 November 1961.

37. Panchenko, *Kiltsia na drevi*, 358.

38. Mykhailo Naienko, "Shistdesiatnyky," in *Khudozhnia literatura Ukrainy: Vid mifiv do modernoi realnosti* (Kyiv: Vydavnychyi tsentr "Prosvita," 2008), 1016.

39. Churchward, *The Soviet Intelligentsia*, 12, 30.

40. *Samvydav* (Ukr.) or *samizdat* (Rus.) refers to texts that did not pass a censorship examination, and which were reproduced by hand (typing) and secretly distributed among trustworthy liberal thinking individuals. In Ukraine in the 1960s, the scale of *samvydav* impressed its authors, its readers, and the KGB itself. The KGB tasked the Institute of the History of the Party which was established under the umbrella of the TsK KPSS (the Central Committee of the Communist Party of the Soviet Union; thereafter: TsK KPSS) to analyze *samvydav* texts. The Institute's scholars identified the texts as "anti-Soviet literature" and constructed its first classification. For details, see Obertas, *Ukrainskyi samvydav*, 118.

41. This term originated from Stepan Bandera (1909–1959), a Ukrainian politician and the leader and organizer of the Ukrainian liberation movement in Western Ukraine. For an enlightening analysis of Bandera's legacies, see Alexander J. Motyl, "Ukraine, Europe, and Bandera," *The Cicero Foundation Great Debate Paper* 10, no. 5 (2010): 1–14.

42. Sergei I. Zhuk, "'Cultural Wars' in the Closed City of Soviet Ukraine, 1959–1982," in *Soviet Society in the Era of Late Socialism, 1964–1985*, eds. Neringa Klumbyte and Gulnaz Sharafutdinova (New York: Lexington Books, 2013), 73.

43. Andrew Wilson, *The Ukrainians: Unexpected Nation*, 2nd ed. (New Haven and London: Yale University Press, 2002), 155.

44. Ibid.

45. This term (in Ukr. *Rozstriliane vidrodzhennia*) is associated with the generation of Soviet Ukrainian writers and artists of 1920s and early 1930s who were repressed by Stalin and perished in the Gulag. The term was first suggested by Polish publicist Jerzy Giedroyc in his letter to the Ukrainian literature researcher Yurii Lavrynenko. Lavrynenko published a collection of literary works written by these writers under the same title. I would like to thank N. K. Firsova, assistant director of the Korolenko State Scientific Library in Kharkiv for her help in accessing the rare book collection.

46. AU SBUKhO, file no. 017800 (Yurii Vukhnal's criminal case).

47. George S. N. Luckyj, "Polarity in Ukrainian Intellectual Dissent," *Canadian Slavonic Papers* 14, no. 2 (1972): 269–79; George S. N. Luckyj, "The Ukrainian Literary Scene Today," *Slavic Review* 31, no. 4 (1972): 863–69; Ivan L. Rudnytskyi, "The Political Thought of Soviet Ukrainian Dissidents," in *Essays in Modern Ukrainian History*, ed. Peter L. Rudnytsky (Edmonton: Canadian Institute of Ukrainian Studies, 1987), 477–89; Borys Lewytzkyi, *Politics and Society in Ukraine, 1953–1980* (Edmonton: Canadian Institute of Ukrainian Studies, 1984); Roman Szporluk, "The Press and Soviet Nationalities: The Party Resolution of 1975 and Its Implementation," in *Russia, Ukraine, and the Breakup of the Soviet Union*, ed. Roman Szporluk (Stanford, CA: Hoover Institution Press, 2000), 277–97; Myroslav Shkandrij, "Poet of Dissent: Vasyl Stus," in *Russia and Ukraine: Literature and Discourse of Empire from Napoleonic to Postcolonial Times* (London: McGill-Queen's University Press, 2001), 249–58; Marko Pavlyshyn, "Martyrology and Literary Scholarship: The Case of Vasyl Stus," *The Slavic and East European Journal* 54, no. 4 (2010): 585–606; Yohanan Petrovsky-Shtern, "Being for the Victims: Leonid Pervomais'kyi's Ethical Responses to Violence," in *The Anti-Imperial Choice: The Making of the Ukrainian*

Jew, ed. Yohanan Petrovsky-Shtern (New Haven & London: Yale University Press, 2009), 165–227; George O. Liber, "The Thaw," in *Alexander Dovzhenko: A Life in Soviet Film*, ed. George O. Liber (London: British Film Institute Publishing, 2002), 246–74.

48. Yekelchyk, "The Early 1960s as a Cultural Space," 45–46, 59.

49. Sergei I. Zhuk, *Rock and Roll in the Rocket City: The West, Identity, and Ideology in Soviet Dniepropetrovsk, 1960–1985* (Washington, DC/Baltimore: Woodrow Wilson Center Press/The John Hopkins University Press, 2010), 64.

50. Tromly, "An Unlikely National Revival," 616.

51. Luckyj, "The Ukrainian Literary Scene Today," 868–69.

52. Benjamin Tromly, *Making the Soviet Intelligentsia: Universities and Intellectual Life under Stalin and Khrushchev* (Cambridge, UK: Cambridge University Press, 2014), 226.

53. Ibid., 228.

54. William Jay Risch, *The Ukrainian West* (Cambridge, MA: Harvard University Press, 2012), 255–56.

55. Ibid., 131–33.

56. Ibid., 256.

57. Simone Attilio Belleza, *The Shore of Expectations: A Cultural Study of the Shistdesiatnyky* (Edmonton/Toronto: Canadian Institute of Ukrainian Studies Press, 2019), 323.

58. Dobson, *Khrushchev's Cold Summer*, 240.

59. Thomas C. Wolfe, *Governing Soviet Journalism: The Press and the Socialist Person after Stalin* (Bloomington and Indianapolis: Indiana University Press, 2005); Oksana Zabushko, *Khroniky vid Fortinbrasa: Vybrana eseistyka* (Kyiv: Fakt, 2006), and *Z mapy knyh i liudei* (Kamianets-Podilskyi: Meridian Czernowits, 2012); Max Hayward and Edward L. Crowley, eds., *Soviet Literature in the Sixties: An International Symposium* (New York: Frederick A. Praeger, Publisher, 1964).

60. For a discussion about the party's control over the literary process in Western Ukraine (Lviv), see Mykola Ilnytskyi, *Na perekhrestiakh viku*, vol. II (Kyiv: KMA, 2008), 524–80.

61. Orlando Figes, *Whisperers: Private Life in Stalin's Russia* (New York: Metropolitan Books, 2007); for various perspectives on the issue of collaboration, see Lynne Viola, "The Question of the Perpetrator in Soviet History," *Slavic Review* 72, no. 1 (2013): 1–23; Wendy Z. Goldman, "Comment: Twin Pyramids—Perpetrators and Victims," *Slavic Review* 72, no. 1 (2013): 24–27; Peter Fritzsche, "Comment: Making Perpetrators," *Slavic Review* 72, no. 1 (2013): 28–31.

62. Denis Kozlov, *The Readers of Novyi Mir: Coming to Terms with the Stalinist Past* (Cambridge, MA: Harvard University Press, 2013), 7.

63. Ibid., 8.

64. Neringa Klumbyte and Gulnaz Sharafutdinova, eds., *Soviet Society in the Era of Late Socialism, 1964–1985* (New York: Lexington Books, 2013), 10. The authors have argued that "in late socialism Soviet citizens were liberal individuals, not because they resisted the state or consciously aligned themselves with an anti-Soviet

agenda, but because they lived self-fulfilling, free, and happy lives during the late Soviet era."

65. Personal conversations with Nick Baron in 2010, the author of *Soviet Karelia: Politics, Planning and Terror in Stalin's Russia, 1920–39* (New York: Routledge, 2007); see also the introduction to Kevin McDermott, and Matthew Stibbe, eds., *Stalinist Terror in Eastern Europe: Elite Purges and Mass Repression* (Manchester and New York: Manchester University Press, 2010).

66. Slavoj Žižek, *Violence: Six Sideways Reflections* (New York: Picador, 2008), 44–45.

67. Dmytro Vedenieiev, "Nezakonni politychni represii 1920–1980-kh rokiv v Ukraini ta problemy formuvannia natsionalnoi pam'iati," *Istorychna Pravda*, 26 December 2012, https://www.istpravda.com.ua/research/50db659307b77/ (accessed 7 July 2020).

68. Salvatore Quasimodo (1901–1968) was an Italian poet, the 1959 Nobel Prize Laureate in Literature who protested against fascism, supported the participants in the resistance movement, and defended the repressed and persecuted writers. For a discussion about Quasimodo's life and poetry, see Oksana Pakhliovska, "Poeziia liubovi i strazhdannia," *Literaturna Ukraina*, 11 December 1981, p. 4. Aleksei Surkov (1899–1983) was a Russian writer who from 1954 to 1959 was the secretary of the Writers' Union Administration. From 1956 to 1966, he was a candidate for membership in the TsK KPSS. He is also remembered by his harassment of Boris Pasternak. A collection of documents, edited by V. I. Afiani and N. G. Tomilina, *"A za mnoiu shum pogoni . . ." Boris Pasternak i vlast': Dokumenty, 1956–1972* (Moskva: ROSSPEN, 2001), will provide readers with a sense of who Surkov was as a writer and as a human being.

69. A broadly quoted term "speaking Bolshevik" came from Stephen Kotkin, *Magnetic Mountain: Stalinism as a Civilization* (Los Angeles/London: University of California Press Berkeley, 1995).

70. Similar tendencies could be observed in other Soviet republics, including the RSFSR. See Serhii Plokhy, *Lost Kingdom: The Quest for Empire and the Making of the Russian Nation* (New York: Basic Books, 2017), 290–94. "Active measures" (or covert operations of ideological subversion) is a KGB term that emerged in the early 1950s and implied domestic actions and transnational special operations designed to change the oppositionists' and the rivals' ideology, their perception of reality, and ultimately the course of world events to the advantage of the USSR. On active measures, see Tomas Schuman, *Black Is Beautiful. Communism Is Not* (Los Angeles, CA: Almanac, 1985); Olga Bertelsen, ed., *Russian Active Measures: Yesterday, Today, Tomorrow* (Stuttgart/New York: ibidem-Verlag/Columbia University Press, 2021).

71. Interview with Volodymyr Briuggen, 16 July 2015, Kharkiv, Ukraine; V. S. Yarova, "Shevchenkivska tema v drukovanii hrafitsi Kharkova 1960-kh rokiv," *Visnyk Lvivskoi natsionalnoi akademii mystetstv* 25 (2014): 228–37.

72. Andrew Wilson, *Ukrainian Nationalism in the 1990s: A Minority Faith* (Cambridge: Cambridge University Press, 1997), 19, 53–55.

73. Yevhen Hrytsiak, *Korotkyi zapys spohadiv: Norylske povstannia. Pislia povstannia* (Kyiv: Smoloskyp, 2013), 6; Yevhen Sverstiuk, "Povist pro nemozhlyve,"

in Hrytsiak, 11–12; Oleksandr Hladkykh, "My podolaly strakh," *Literaturna Ukraina*, 13 June 2013, pp. 13–14. In 1953, Norilsk was a settlement in the tundra where 26,000 free volunteers worked, and approximately 30,000 political prisoners labored in the camps, according to the memoirs of the chief and commandant— NKVD colonel Zverev. In the network of camps there was a camp called Gorlag no. 3 where 80 percent of the prisoners were Ukrainians. Among 3,500 people 500 were invalids who, physically destroyed by hard labor, hunger, and cold, were simply lying, awaiting their deaths. The two months of non-violent strike and resistance brought moral and political victory over the camp authorities. According to one of the leaders of the Norilsk rebellion Yevhen Hrytsiak, this victory helped the imprisoned people overcome fear once and forever (see Hladkykh, "My podolaly strakh," 13–14).

74. Wilson, *Ukrainian Nationalism*, 54.

75. Ibid., 53.

76. On the "newcomers," Moscow poets, and their meetings in Moscow public squares, see Slonim, *Soviet Russian Literature*, 342–43, 383–93.

77. Karl Eimermacher, "Predislovie," in *Apparat TsK KPSS i kultura. 1953–1957: Dokumenty*, eds. V. I. Afiani et al. (Moskva: ROSSPEN, 2001), 6. On Stalinist *dekady* of Ukrainian art, see Serhy Yekelchyk, *Stalin's Empire of Memory: Russian-Ukrainian Relations in the Soviet Historical Imaginations* (Toronto: University of Toronto Press, 2004), 129–30, 143, 146, 157.

78. Leonid Pliushch, *Na karnavale istorii* London: Overseas Publications Interchange Ltd., 1979), 26–27. On the liberal trends in Soviet universities after the Twentieth Party Congress, see Vladislav M. Zubok, *A Failed Empire: The Soviet Union in the Cold War from Stalin to Gorbachev* (Chapel Hill: The University of North Carolina Press, 2007), 168–70.

79. Zabuzhko, *Z mapy knyh*, 42.

80. Borys Oliinyk, "Robertu Tretyakovu – 50," *Literaturna Ukraina*, 27 February 1986, p. 5.

81. "Moloda literatura v Ukraini," *Smoloskyp*, January/February 1962, p. 8.

82. Žižek, *Violence*, 47.

83. Sergei Paradzhanov, "Kak ia zavidoval Fellini," in *Kollazh na fone avtoportreta: Zhyzn – igra*, ed. K. D. Tsereteli (Nizhnii Novgorod: Dekom, 2005), 96.

84. Yurii Gerasimenko, "Glaza v glaza," *Krasnoe znamia*, 18 February 1982, p. 3.

85. Ibid., 3. There is a striking similarity between Tretyakov's and Leonid Pliushch's childhood years: fathers missing in action, mothers saving them from the Nazi's bombs, evacuation, the war and post-war famine, stealing wheat ears from the *kolhosp's* fields collective farms.

86. See the interview of Robert Tretyakov in *Leninska zmina*, 3 March 1984, p. 4.

87. Robert Tretyakov's private archive (hereafter: RTPA), handwritten notes. I am grateful to the Ukrainian prose writer Viktor Polianetskyi who returned a part of Tretyakov's private archive to me after Tretyakov's death.

88. Personal conversations with Tretyakov, 27 June 1982, Kharkiv, Ukraine.

89. RTPA, handwritten notes.

90. Ibid.

91. Ibid. On the literary scholar Biletskyi, see O. Matviichuk and N. Struk, eds., *Kyivskyi natsionalnyi universytet imeni Tarasa Shevchenka: Nezabutni postati* (Kyiv: Svit uspikhu, 2005), 336; on the historian Vvedenskyi, see V. M. Danylenko, ed., *Entsyklopedia istorii Ukrainy*, t. 1 (Kyiv: NAN Ukrainy; Instytut istorii Ukrainy, "Naukova dumka," 2003), 688; on the Ukrainian and Russian linguist Bulakhovskyi, see Maryna Navalna, ed., *Vydatni osobystosti z ukrainskoho movoznavstva. Khrestomatiia* (Pereiaslav-Khmelnytskyi: V-vo KSV, 2016), 20–21.

92. RTPA, handwritten notes; Lidiya Tretyakova's diary (hereafter: LTD), vol. 2, the 23 January 1957 entry; Aleksandr Malis, "Nash 'Robertino,'" *Sloboda*, 20 May 1997, p. 2. In the late 1950s, A. Dykan was the chief editor of *Leninska Zmina*.

93. The State Archive of the Kharkiv Oblast (hereafter: DAKhO), f. R-6165, op. 1, spr. 118, ark. 11.

94. Robert Tretyakov, *Zorianist: Poezii* (Kharkiv: Kharkivske knyzhkove vydavnytstvo, 1961).

95. RTPA, handwritten notes.

96. Dole is grief or sorrow (archaic).

97. Translations from Ukrainian throughout the text are the author's unless specified otherwise.

98. Ihor Mykhailyn, *Literaturna Kharkivshchyna: Poeziia* (Kharkiv: "Maidan," 2007), 172–90; Leonid Toma, "Ty uiavy sobi . . ." *Slobozhanskyi kruh* 5 (2011): 62; Olga Bertelsen, "Robert Tretyakov—'poet kokhannia,'" *Literaturna Ukraina* 7, no. 5636 (2016): 6–7.

99. Radii Polonskyi, "Nepoiasnymyi Robert," *Vechernii Kharkov*, 18 July 1998, p. 3.

100. Ibid., 23 July 1998, p. 7.

101. Antoine de Saint-Exupéry, *The Little Prince*, trans. Katherine Woods (New York: Harcourt Brace Jovanovich, 1971); see ch. 7.

102. See Yesenin's "Anna Snegina" in Tretyakov's translation in Robert Tretyakov, *Portrety* (Kharkiv: Vydavnytstvo "Prapor," 1967), 73–98.

103. Antin Mykhailovych Komashka (1897–1970) was a Ukrainian artist and a student of Il'ia Repin in 1915–1918. The portrait is dated 22 May 1964.

104. Mykola Nykyforovych Kursin (b. 1939) is an artist-monumentalist. He lives and works in Kharkiv.

105. Ivan Ignatievich Khristichev (b. 1940) is a Russian artist, one of the most talented representatives of neo-sentimentalism in art. He lives and works in Moscow.

106. Private conversation with Robert Tretyakov, 2 July 1986, Kharkiv, Ukraine. See also Bertelsen, "Robert Tretyakov—'poet kokhannia,'" p. 7.

107. See the text of the 1 December 1956 report of the Department of Culture of the TsK KPSS in E.S. Afanasieva, V. I. Afiani, Z. K. Vodop'ianova, T. A. Dzhalilov, T. I. Dzhalilova, and M. I. Prozumenshikov, eds., *Apparat TsK KPSS i kultura, 1953–1957: Dokumenty* (Moskva: ROSSPEN, 2001), 570–80.

108. See the text of Shepilov's letter to the Department of Culture in the Central Committee in the KPSS in V. I. Afiani and N. G. Tomilina, eds., *"A za mnoiu shum pogoni . . .": Boris Pasternak i vlast: Dokumenty, 1956–1972* (Moskva: ROSSPEN, 2001), 63.

109. *Pravda*, 2 November 1956. On the expulsion of Pasternak from the Writers' Union, see the 28 October 1958 note by the Head of the Department of Culture of the TsK KPSS Dmitrii Polikarpov to the TsK KPSS in "Boris Pasternak i vlast, 1956–1960 gg.," *The Aleksandr N. Yakovlev Archive*, http://www.alexanderyakovlev.org/almanah/inside/almanah-doc/149 (accessed 9 July 2020).

110. Pliushch, *Na karnavale istorii*, 27.

111. LTD, vol. 5. Mar'ian, Hubanov and Damaskin wrote a "political program" that they distributed among the students. The program consisted of thirty points, in which the authors demanded the freedom of movement within and outside the Soviet Union, the elimination of the collective farms, the distribution of land among the peasants (1–3 hectares to each household), the elimination of the Soviet Army as a state institution, and free speech.

112. Ibid. Borys Mar'ian was arrested in 1957 and was sentenced to five years in labor camps in Mordovia. The regime accused him of supporting the 1956 Hungarian revolution and of writing a "program-minimum" designed to optimize the agricultural sector in the USSR, which would help change the political system in the USSR as a whole. The fates of Hubanov and Damaskin remain unknown. For more details about Mar'ian, see Stanislav Bondarenko, "Odyn iz tvortsiv sprotyvu," *Literaturna Ukraina*, 18 October 2012, p. 5.

113. Zubok, *A Failed Empire*, 171.

114. For example, on 30 May 1960, people close to Pasternak were immediately arrested after his death, Olga Ivinskaia and her daughter Irina Yemel'ianova. In 1960, the American journalist Frank Gibney noted that "if Khrushchev's Russia was more relaxed and confident-seeming than Stalin's, exactly the same apparatus of police controls remained at the ruling Party's disposal. They had merely been loosened." Yet he also noted that "the extent of the loosening was highly debatable." See Frank Gibney, *The Khrushchev Pattern* (New York: Duell, Sloan and Pearce, 1960), 7.

115. For a typical Soviet propaganda publication with a Marxist critique of Zionism branding it as a "tool of the most reactionary, anti-Soviet and anti-communist forces of imperialism," see Sergei Sergeyev, comp., *Zionism – Enemy of Peace and Social Progress*, trans. Barry Jones (Moscow: Progress Publishers, 1984).

116. LTD, vol. 6, the 7 April 1960 entry. See also Oliinyk, "Robertu Tretyakovu – 50."

117. Dobson, *Khrushchev's Cold Summer*, 104.

118. DAKhO, f. R-6164, op. 1, spr. 44, ark. 1–3; DAKhO, f. R-6164, op. 1, spr. 48, ark. 19, 24; DAKhO, f. R-6164, op. 1, spr. 50, ark. 1.

119. LTD, vol. 8.

120. Dobson, *Khrushchev's Cold Summer*, 239. For more details about this procedure, see "Vynos tela Stalina iz Mavzoleia," *YouTube*, 1 January 2012, http://www.youtube.com/watch?v=YR9o6A3Nfl0 (accessed 9 July 2020). On the symbolic meaning of Stalin's body, see Dobson, *Khrushchev's Cold Summer*, 97.

121. Private conversation with Lidiya Tretyakova, 8 September 2013, Bloomsburg, PA, U.S.A.

122. Dobson, *Khrushchev's Cold Summer*, 185. It grew from 550,882 to 968,080.

123. Ibid., 177, 185, 218.

124. LTD, vol. 10.

125. On the history of *Budynok "Slovo"*, see Olga Bertelsen, "The House of Writers in Ukraine, the 1930s: Conceived, Lived, Perceived," *Carl Beck Papers* 2302 (August 2013): 4–72.

126. Mykola Shatylov, *Kliati simdesiati . . . Na pam'iati stalo, na pam'iati staly* (Kharkiv: Vydavnytstvo "Apostrof," 2011), 100–2.

127. For more details about Siroshtan, see Vasyl Sokil, *Zdaleka do blyzkoho: spohady, rozdumy* (Edmonton: Canadian Institute of Ukrainian Studies, 1987), 278–83.

128. Shatylov, *Kliati simdesiati*, 70–72. In 1950–1953, Mykola Pidhornyi was the first secretary of the Kharkiv *obkom*; from 1965 to 1977 he served as chairman of the Presidium of the Supreme Soviet in the USSR. In 1951–1959, Andrii Skaba was a secretary of the Kharkiv *obkom* (the ideological sector); in 1959–1968 he served as a secretary of the TsK KPSS in Ukraine (the ideological sector).

129. Iryna Zhylenko, *Homo Feriens: Spohady* (Kyiv: Smoloskyp, 2011), 245.

130. Les Taniuk, *Talan i talant Lesia Kurbasa* (Kyiv: Derzhavnyi tsentr teatralnoho mystetstva imeni Lesia Kurbasa, 2007), 6.

131. Shatylov, *Kliati simdesiati*, 86. Chernyshov's literary activity was obstructed once and forever, he became a mailman, ultimately retiring in that position. Borovyi spent years in Soviet camps and was viewed by the KGB as a Ukrainian nationalist. Stadnychenko managed to retain his position in the literary journal *Prapor* which was later renamed *Berezil*. From 1974, he served as the deputy of *Prapor*'s chief editor, and from 1990 to 1999 as the chief editor of *Berezil*.

132. LTD, vol. 8–9.

133. The show trial lasted from the autumn of 1965 to February 1966. Daniel and Siniavskii were convicted for publishing their works abroad and for criticizing the Soviet regime. See the archival copy of the resolution on the completion of the preliminary investigation of Daniel's and Siniavskii's case and suggestions on the trial procedures made by the Secretariat of the Party Central Committee, the 23 December 1965 note from the KGB and the Prosecutor Office no. 2843c, and the February 1966 note from the Department of Culture, Propaganda and Agitation (the TsK) in *Vladimir Bukovsky Archive* (hereafter: VBA), http://www.bukovsky-archives.net/pdfs/dis60/ct132-66.pdf (accessed 9 July 2020).

134. The text of the letter can be found in Diane P. Koenker and Ronald D. Bachman, eds., *Revelations from the Russian Archives: Documents in English Translation* (Washington, DC: Library of Congress, 1997), 276–77.

135. Private conversation with Robert Tretyakov, 2 July 1986, Kharkiv, Ukraine.

136. Bertelsen, "Robert Tretyakov – 'poet kokhannia,'" p. 7.

137. LTD, vol. 7; Shatylov, *Kliati simdesiati*, 161.

138. Vasyl Horovyi, "Ia prahnu v svit . . ." *Leninskyi shliakh*, 16 November 1971, p. 3.

139. Tretyakov's second collection of poetry entitled *Palitra* (The Pallete): *Virshi* published by *Prapor* in 1965 and its constrained tone disappointed many. See Bohdan Horyn, *Ne tilky pro sebe: Knyha druha (1965–1985)* (Kyiv: Pulsary, 2008), 294–95. On the dissident movement in the 1960s in Kharkiv and the political climate in

Kharkiv during the post-Khrushchev period, see Genrikh Altunian, *Tsena svobody: Vospominaniia dissidenta* (Kharkov: Folio, 2000).

140. Yurii Shapoval, "Ideolog natsionalisticheskikh elementov respubliki . . ." *Gazeta ZN, UA*, 22 July 2011, http://gazeta.zn.ua/SOCIETY/ideolog_natsionalis ticheskih_elementov_respubliki_.html (accessed 9 July 2020).

141. Pliushch, *Na karnavale istorii*, 144–45.

142. Ibid., 145, 150–51. In August–September 1965, twenty-four "nationalists" and "dissidents" were arrested by the KGB. See TsDAHOU, f. 1, op. 24, spr. 5991, ark. 116.

143. For a discussion about similar moods in the capital, Kyiv, see Risch, *The Ukrainian West*, 256.

144. Larysa Masenko, "Lyst Vasylia Stusa do Andriia Malyshka: Istoriia nezdiisnymoi sproby dialohu," *Literaturna Ukraina*, 12 September 2013, p. 6.

145. LTD, vol. 7.

146. Polonskyi, "Nepoiasnymyi Robert," *Vechernii Kharkov*, 23 July 1998, p. 7.

147. For a discussion about Galicia as Ukraine's Piedmont, see Paul Robert Magocsi, *The Roots of Ukrainian Nationalism: Galicia as Ukraine's Piedmont* (Toronto: University of Toronto Press, 2002).

148. Sloboda Ukraine refers to the "free-settlement frontier just north of what is today Kharkiv and the Russian-Ukrainian border." See Paul Robert Magocsi, *A History of Ukraine* (Seattle: University of Washington Press, 1998), 211, 265–67.

149. Polonskyi, "Nepoiasnymyi Robert," *Vechernii Kharkov*, 23 July 1998, p. 7. The 1 December 1991 national referendum demonstrated that both parties, the Slobozhany and Galicians, were correct, and Ukraine was born as an independent state due to the common efforts of Ukrainian intellectuals of eastern and western parts of Ukraine.

150. Shatylov, *Kliati simdesiati*, 8.

151. Pliushch, *Na karnavale istorii*, 302.

152. Shatylov, *Kliati simdesiati*, 10.

153. For a discussion about the drinking culture in Kharkiv, Ukraine, and the Soviet Union, see Eduard Limonov, *Molodoi negodiai* (Kostroma: Zhurnal "Glagol," 1992); Eduard Limonov, *U nas byla velikaia epokha; Podrostok Savenko* (Moscow: Literaturno-khudozhestvennyi zhurnal "Glagol," 1994); Vitalii Korotich, *Zhili-byli—eli-pili* (Kharkov: Folio, 2005).

154. Zhylenko, *Homo Feriens*, 166. A bottle of port wine "Primorskii" that cost one ruble and ten kopeks and a bottle of vodka "Russkaia" that could be purchased for three rubles and sixty-two kopeks were quite affordable for the Kharkiv literati.

155. Ibid., 352.

156. Ibid., 166.

157. Kas'ianov, *Nezhodni*, 47.

158. Jaroslaw Bilocerkowycz, *Soviet Ukrainian Dissent: A Study of Political Alienation* (Boulder and London: Westview Press, 1988); Kas'ianov, *Nezhodni*; Olga Bertelsen, "Political Affinities and Maneuvering of Soviet Political Elites: Heorhii Shevel and Ukraine's Ministry of Strange Affairs in the 1970s," *Nationalities Papers: The Journal of Nationalism and Ethnicity* 47, no. 3 (2019): 394–411.

159. TsDAHOU, f. 1, op. 25, spr. 17, ark. 68–77.
160. TsDAHOU, f. 1, op. 25, spr. 17, ark. 75.
161. TsDAHOU, f. 1, op. 25, spr. 17, ark. 77.
162. Kas'ianov, *Nezhodni*, 80.
163. HDA SBU, f. 16, op.1, sp. 1034, ark. 176–77.
164. Interviews with Aleksandr Kasha, 5 July 1985; Anatolii Starodub, 12 August 2008 (all interviews were conducted in Kharkiv, Ukraine); private conversation with Lidiya Tretyakova, 19 July 2005.
165. Horyn, *Ne tilky pro sebe*, 294.
166. Y. M. Lotman, *Stat'ii po semiotike kultury i iskusstva*, edited by R. G. Grigor'ieva (Moskva: Akademicheskii proekt, 2002).
167. Interview with Serhii Boltryk, 11 November 1996, Kharkiv, Ukraine.
168. Andrei Bitov, "Pisatel sam ne p'iet . . . ," *Moskovskie novosti*, 21 October 2011, http://www.mn.ru/friday/74757 (accessed 9 July 2020); Mikhail Zolotonosov, "Kak pisateli borolis s p'ianstvom . . . ," *812 Online*, 30 December 2010, http://www.online812.ru/2010/12/29/003/ (accessed 9 July 2020).
169. HDA SBU, f. 16, op. 1, spr. 1017, ark. 6–8.
170. Interview with Anatolii Starodub, 12 August 2008, Kharkiv, Ukraine.
171. Aleksandr Cherevchenko, "Bunt bessmyslennyi i besposhchadnyi?," *Press Latviia*, 6 February 2014, http://press.lv/post/bunt-bessmyslennyj-i-besposhhadnyj/ (accessed 9 July 2020).
172. Aleksandr Vernik, "Boris A. Chichibabin," in *The Blue Lagoon: Anthology of Modern Russian Poetry*, eds. Konstantin Kuzminsky and Grigorii Kovalev (Newtonville, MA: Oriental Research Partners, 1982).
173. Interview with Radii Polonskyi, 16 May 1988, Kharkiv, Ukraine.
174. DAKhO, f. R-6165, op. 1, spr. 134, ark. 70–71, 93, 99; f. R-6165, op. 1, spr. 144, ark. 12; T. M. Sharova, "Vasyl Bondar: Osoblyvosti biohrafichnoi prozy ta ideino-khudozhni poshuky pysmennyka," *Visnyk Luhanskoho Natsionalnoho Universytetu imeni Tarasa Shevchenka* 3, no. 166 (2009): 179–85.
175. Interview with Aleksandr Kasha, 5 July 1985, Kharkiv, Ukraine.
176. Interview with Oleksa Marchenko, 19 July 2004, Kharkiv, Ukraine; Valentyna Kryvcheniuk, "Stanislav Shumytskyi ta ioho seredovyshche," *Official site of Liubotynska miska rada*, 20 March 2015, http://lubotin.kharkov.ua/main/5669-do-dnya-narodzhennya-s-shumickogo.html (accessed 10 July 2020).
177. DAKhO, f. R-6165, op. 1, spr. 134, ark. 70–71, 93, 99; f. R-6165, op. 1, spr. 144, ark. 12.
178. In the 1960s, on Poetry Square, Yevgenii Yevtushenko, hoarse from reading his poetry outside the doors of the bookstore, received a bottle of warm milk tied on a rope and dangling from some caring fan's balcony; in the late 1980s, on the same Poetry Square, Yevtushenko, tasked by the Writers' Union in Moscow to give a new membership card to Boris Chichibabin whose membership was restored due to Gorbachev's perestroika, did it in the presence of thousands of Kharkivites. Interview with Yevgenii Yevtushenko, 6 May 1988, Kharkiv, Ukraine.
179. Vitalii Orlov, "Akh, Zhenia, Zhenia, Zhenechka, s nim sluchai byl takoi . . . ," *Elegant New York*, 27 January 2017, http://elegantnewyork.com/evtushenko

-orlov/ (accessed 10 July 2020); "Yevtushenko i Kharkov," *Kharkovskiie Izvestiia*, 7 April 2017, http://izvestia.kharkov.ua/on-line/18/1237277.html (accessed 10 July 2020); Limonov, *Molodoi negodiai*, 31, 104, 155; Vasilii Omelchenko, "Tam zhili poety . . . ," *Prostranstvo literatury*, 5 May 2016, www.kpi.kharkov.ua - /archive/ Conferences/Пространство литературы, искусства и образования – путь к миру, согласию и сотрудничеству между славянскими народами/2013/ (accessed 10 July 2020), 199–205.

180. Shapoval, "Ideolog natsionalisticheskikh elementov respubliki . . . ." See also Yurii Shapoval, "Sprava Ivana Dziuby," *Z arkhiviv VUChK/GPU/NKVD/KGB* no. 1 (36) (2011): 260; Volodymyr V'iatrovych, "Operatsiia 'Blok.' Diia persha," in *Istoriia z hryfom "Sekretno"* (Lviv/Kyiv: Tsentr doslidzhen vyzvolnoho rukhu, 2011), 204–12.

181. On the subordination of the *chekists* to the center and the party, see V. A. Zolotariov and Y. I. Shapoval, "'Kolyvan u provedenni linii partii ne bulo' (Storinky biohrafii K. M. Karlsona)," *Ukrainskyi istorychnyi zhurnal* 1 (1996): 91–105; Yu. Shapoval and V. Panchenko, eds., *Poliuvannia na Valdshnepa: Rozsekrechenyi Mykola Khvyliovyi* (Kyiv: Tempora, 2009); Vadym Zolotariov, *Sekretno-politychnyi viddil DPU USRR: Spavy ta liudy* (Kharkiv: Folio, 2007); Shapoval, "Ideolog natsionalisticheskikh elementov respubliki . . . ."

182. *Seksot* refers to *sekretnyi sotrudnik* (in Rus.), or an agent recruited by the KGB.

183. Shatylov, *Kliati simdesiati*, 60–61.

184. A. Korotenko and N. Alikina, *Sovetskaia psikhiatriia: Zabluzhdeniia i umysel* (Kiev: Sphera, 2002), 166.

185. LTD, vol. 7.

186. Pliushch, *Na karnavale istorii*, 221.

187. Ibid., 289.

188. In July 1969, Altunian (an Armenian) was arrested and accused of Ukrainian nationalism. He received seven plus five years in labor camps. Altunian, *Tsena svobody*, 34–42, 278–94.

189. Pliushch, *Na karnavale istorii*, 300–2. See also Itskhak Moshkovich's memoirs "Dissidenty i otkazniki," *World.lib.ru*, 26 October 2004, http://world.lib.ru/m/moshkowich_i/dissidentsrefusniks.shtml (accessed 10 July 2020).

190. Interview with Oleksandr Kasha, 5 July 1985, Kharkiv, Ukraine.

191. Moshkovich, "Dissidenty i otkazniki."

192. Ibid.

193. On surveillance, see Peter Holquist, "'Information Is the Alpha and Omega of Our Work': Bolshevik Surveillance in Its Pan-European Context," *The Journal of Modern History* 69, no. 3 (1997): 415–50; Olga Velikanova, *Popular Perceptions of Soviet Politics in the 1920s: Disenchantment of the Dreamers* (New York: Palgrave Macmillan, 2013), 17; David L. Hoffmann, *Cultivating the Masses: Modern State Practices and Soviet Socialism, 1914–1939* (Ithaca, NY: Cornell University Press, 2011). The collection of documents on the harassment of Pasternak published by Afiani and Tomilina confirms that the KGB broadly used tape-recorders in dachas and private apartments of the intelligentsia. Aleksandr Shelepin's report revealed that this

method was used by the KGB in Olga Ivinskaiia's dacha before her arrest in 1949. See Yevgenii Pasternak, "V osade," in Afiani and Tomilina, 49.

194. Pliushch, *Na karnavale istorii*, 304–5; Zhuk, *Rock and Roll in the Rocket City*, 37–40, 48–52, 57–64.

195. Polonskyi, "Nepoiasnymyi Robert," *Vechernii Kharkov*, 23 July 1998, p. 7. Since 1961, Volodymyr Shcherbytskyi was a member of the TsK KPSS. In 1972, he replaced Petro Shelest as the first secretary of the TsK of the Communist Party in Ukraine. In 1967, Valentyn Malanchuk was the deputy minister of Higher Education in the UkrSSR. From 1972 to 1979, he served as the secretary of the TsK of the Communist Party in Ukraine.

196. Private conversation with Radii Polonsky, 16 May 1988, Kharkiv, Ukraine.

197. Zabuzhko, *Z mapy knyh*, 47. This KGB operation is the subject of another study. For more details about the fire and the arsonist Pohruzhalsky and his trial, see Central Intelligence Agency, "On Occasion of Pohruzhalsky's Trial," *CIA Archive*, 1964 (declassified in 2007), https://www.cia.gov/library/readingroom/docs/AERODYNAMIC%20%20%20VOL.%2030%20%20(OPERATIONS)_0029.pdf (accessed 11 July 2020).

198. Perlustration means the examination of people's intercepted correspondence passing through the post office for surveillance purposes. For more on perlustration, see A. G. Brikner, "Vskrytie chuzhykh pisem i depesh pri Ekaterine II (Perliustratsiia)," *Russkaia starina* 7, no. 1 (1873), *Bibliotekar.ru/Reprinty starinnykh knig*, 2021, http://www.bibliotekar.ru/reprint-133/ (accessed 10 July 2020). For a comparative analysis of surveillance and perlustration in the Soviet Union, see Holquist, "'Information.'"

199. I. Yakimov, "Chtoby pisma shli bystree," *Krasnoe znamia*, 25 February 1971, p. 4. Compare the number of 1 million workers during the Soviet era with 10,000 trained officials who were reading and analyzing people's mail during the Civil War. For details, see Holquist, "Information," 422.

200. Shapoval, "Sprava Ivana Dziuby," 262; Yurii Shapoval, "Petro Shelest: zhyttia ta polityczna dolia," in *Petro Shelest: "Spravzhnii sud istorii shche poperedu,"* ed. Yurii Shapoval (Kyiv: ADEF-Ukraina, 2011), 19–44.

201. Pliushch, *Na karnavale istorii*, 260.

202. Ivan Babenko, "Poryv," *Slobozhanskyi kruh* 5 (2011): 59.

203. DAKhO, f. R-6165, op. 1, spr. 134, ark. 80; DAKhO, f. R-6165, op. 1, spr. 144, ark. 8.

204. Shatylov, *Kliati simdesiati*, 31; Sokil, *Zdaleka do blyzkoho*, 276.

205. Mikhail Bulgakov, *The Master and Margarita*, trans. Diana Burgin and Katherine Tiernan O'Connor (New York: Vintage International, 1995).

206. LTD, vol. 8. Having exhausted all local resources, Lidiya Tretyakova wrote to the Moscow actress Iia Savvina who experienced a similar problem with her vocal ligaments. A Moscow professor helped her restore her voice. In her response to Tretyakova, Savvina regretted that the professor was old and had died soon after he helped her. Tretyakov's treatment was put on hold.

207. Tretyakov and Shumytskyi had a great deal in common. Both were born during the Great Terror (Tretyakov was born on 26 February 1936, and Shumytskyi

on 20 March 1937) in the Russian Federation. Shumytskyi grew up in Saratov on the Volga River. Their fathers died during the Second World War. In 1944–1945, together with their mothers, both teachers, they moved to Ukraine. The Shumytskyi moved to the town of Liubotyn (Bohodukhivskyi district), where Stanislav went to school. In 1946, Stanislav and his mother moved to Kolomyia (Valkivskyi district) and later to Karavan (Kharkivskyi district) where Stanislav graduated from high school. He published three volumes of poetry, *Features of Faithfulness* (Oznaky virnosti) (1963), *Forty Beatings of the Heart* (Sorok udariv sertsia) (1966), and *The Heroes Are Entering the Song* (Heroi prykhodiat u pisniu) (1971). On Stanislav's biography, see his mother's handwritten narrative at http://karavan-school.edu.kh.ua/gallery/stanislav_shumicjkij/, *Karavanska Shkola*, 2020 (accessed 11 July 2020).

208. Private conversation with Volodymyr Briuggen, Kharkiv, Ukraine, 10 August 2013.

209. Shatylov, *Kliati simdesiati*, 14; Sokil, *Zdaleka do blyzkoho*, 276–77; Valerii Zamesov, "Dlia nas vin buv klasykom," *Slobozhanskyi kruh* 5 (2011): 68.

210. Anatolii Miroshnichenko, "Zapiski inzhenera-poeta," *Slobozhanskyi kruh* 5 (2011): 74.

211. DAKhO, f. R-6165, op. 1, spr. 122, ark. 90, 93. The Right Bank of Ukraine was the location of seven (together with *Perets*) venues that published literary works in Ukrainian.

212. DAKhO, f. R-6165, op. 1, spr. 122, ark. 121.

213. Shatylov, *Kliati simdesiati*, 96–97.

214. Risch, *The Ukrainian West*, 136.

215. Most of them were human rights activists and members of the Ukrainian Helsinki Group. For more on the history of the UHG and biographies of its members, see Osyp Zinkewych, ed., *Ukrainska Helsinska Hrupa, 1978–1982: Dokumenty i materiialy* (Toronto: V. Symonenko Smoloskyp Publishers, 1983) and *Persecution of the Ukrainian Helsinki Group* (Toronto: Human Rights Commission of the World Congress of Free Ukrainians, 1985). For more details, see V'iatrovych, *Istoriia z hryfom "Sekretno,"* 208–10. Ihor and Iryna Kalynets were arrested for anti-Soviet agitation and propaganda, and distribution of *samvydav*, depriving their little daughter of her parents for nine years. They were sentenced to six years in severe regime camps and three years of exile. The *shistdesiatnyky* in Kyiv, Ivan Drach, Dmytro Pavlychko, and others became quieter. Ivan Dziuba wrote a repentant article. The Ukrainian dissident Valentyn Moroz, who was arrested twice in 1965 and 1970, considered such compromises with the state immoral. Moroz criticized Drach and Pavlychko, who, as he stated, wrote "90 percent of their poems for the KGB, and 10 percent—for the people." See Pliushch, *Na karnavale istorii*, 406–7.

216. Zabuzhko, *Z mapy knyh*, 48. In Russian, it reads: "Chtob ne bylo bazy rosta."

217. CIA, "A New Freeze," 48.

218. Central Intelligence Agency, "Project Action: QRDYNAMIC," *CIA Archive*, 5 April 1973 (declassified and released in 2007), https://www.cia.gov/library/readingroom/docs/QRPLUMB%20%20%20VOL.%202%20%20(DEVELOPMENT%20AND%20PLANS,%201970-78)_0018.pdf (accessed 11 July 2020), 1.

219. Central Intelligence Agency, "Project Action: QRDYNAMIC" (see 8 May 1973, secret Memorandum "RDYNAMIC Project Renewal Comment").

220. In an article in *Encounter* in July 1969, Hugh Seton-Watson defined the Soviet regime as a "pseudocracy" (government by lie). Quoted in *Ferment in the Ukraine: Documents by V. Chornovil, I. Kandyba, L. Lukyanenko, V. Moroz, and Others*, foreword by Max Hayward, ed. Michael Browne (Woodhaven, NY: Crisis Press, 1973), ix.

221. Shatylov, *Kliati simdesiati*, 164.

222. Ibid., 159–60.

223. See Ivan Drach's interview in *Literaturna Ukraina*, 15 August 2013, p. 7. On 18 July 1961, *Literaturna Hazeta* (since 1962—*Literaturna Ukraina*) published Drach's poem "Nizh u sontsi" that gave fame to a twenty-five-year-old man as a uniquely talented Ukrainian poet. For more on Drach, see L. B. Tarnashynska, "Ivan Drach: 'Narodzhuite sebe, dopoky svitu . . . ,'" in *Ivan Drach: Literatura. Kinematohraf. Polityka* (Kyiv: Natsionalna parlamentska biblioteka Ukrainy, 2011), 5–32.

224. Robert Tretyakov, "Stal i nezhnost ee poezii," *Krasnoe znamia*, 25 February 1971, p. 3.

225. Interview with Volodymyr Briuggen, 15 July 2011, Kharkiv, Ukraine.

Chapter 2

Petro Shelest, the Literati, and the "Jewish Question"

THE ATMOSPHERE OF CONTROLLED FREEDOM AND JEWISH *SHISTDESIATNYTSTVO*

The Twentieth Party Congress, Khrushchev's not-so-secret speech, and official de-Stalinization inspired change and creativity in Ukrainian society, and invited Ukrainians and Jews to reassess their identities and their past, promoting their cultural and political activism. The subsequent nonofficial re-Stalinization achieved results quite opposite from what was expected by the party and the KGB. Soviet antisemitic practices, ethnic politics, the renewed terror against intellectuals, and political maneuverings of Petro Shelest, first secretary of the Central Committee of the Communist Party in Ukraine (TsK KPU), inspired nationalist sentiments among various ethnic groups and the formation of trans-ethnic bonds, literary alliances, and friendships among the literati, amplifying their gravitation toward their cultural traditions and heritage.[1] Writers of various ethnic backgrounds, even the most apolitical of them, began to secretly, if not openly, support and engage in national and dissident movements in Ukraine. Importantly, they realized the scale of cultural disruption that occurred under Stalin.[2] Encouraged by the Russian and Ukrainian *shistdesiatnytstvo*, the Jewish intelligentsia experienced cultural awakening, searching for their national identities.

Kharkiv of the 1960s and 1970s produced a constellation of brilliant poets and prose writers who enriched national and world literature. Understanding what was special about this place, and what prompted and nurtured these men's and women's persistence in their literary paths is not an easy task. After all, they found themselves amid renewed state violence. Moreover, being a writer in the 1960s and 1970s meant being an ultimate suspect for the authorities. For Kharkiv writers of Jewish descent, this period transpired as a time of danger and insecurity. Being identified as "Zionists" by the KGB because of being Jewish, regardless of their willingness or unwillingness to emigrate from the Soviet Union, made them face some difficult choices. Their choices varied, but they all were engaged in undoing the concepts of fixed identities prescribed by the state, unsettling the boundaries imposed on them and reinventing their selfhood, their nationhood, their cultural roots, and the literary community they were part of. An analysis of their own statements and perceptions might be of great value for those who want to understand how places of violence and regimentation invigorate creativity and awaken people's cultural roots. Most importantly, the stories of the Kharkiv Jewish generation of the sixties and their intellectual and ideological evolutions and transformations reveal a feature characteristic of all authoritarian regimes—their propensity to generate a chorus of chattering, compliant, and mediocre voices. Simultaneously, through the cacophony of mediocrity, these regimes nourish truly original poets who manage to identify their "root-voice," uncompromising and imaginative.

The quest for their "root-voice" was devastating for some and rewarding for others. Like many other writers, they dreamed about "drink[ing] from the well of origin; to write the poem that has not yet been written."[3] The Irish poet John O'Donohue is right arguing that "the poet must reach deeper inward; go deeper than the private hoard of voices down to the root-voice. It is here that individuality has the taste of danger, vitality, and vulnerability. Here the creative has the necessity of inevitability; this is the threshold where imagination engages raw, unformed experience. This is the sense you have when you read a true poem."[4] This existential understanding of poets' paths and their life choices was challenged by the authorities, clandestinely and openly.

In Ukraine, with the rise of the human rights and dissident movements after the mid-1960s, both Ukrainians and Jews engaged in a search for national identity, and constituted symbols of nationalism and anti-Soviet forces for the KGB. Both had powerful and wealthy protectors, the Western "imperialists," and both had to be unmasked and neutralized. In fact, the KGB and Soviet propagandists linked Zionism to Ukrainian bourgeois nationalism, and both phenomena were described in negative connotations and in terms used interchangeably.[5] Shelest emphasized this link in his public speeches and private conversations: "All forces of reaction have joined hands, beginning with aggressive American imperialism and rabid Zionism, and ending with the White Guard remnants, the bourgeois nationalist riff-raff, and all sorts of opportunists and traitors."[6] For him, leniency toward the Ukrainian intelligentsia would be as dangerous as toleration of Jewish intellectuals. Moscow would accuse him of acceptance of Ukrainian nationalism and softness toward Zionism. In his polemical remarks, Shelest condemned both Western Ukrainian and Jewish diasporas for having been collaborators with the Nazis, masterminding a conspiracy against the USSR, and spreading lies about Soviet nationalities policies.

Like many other Ukrainian party functionaries, Shelest was neither prepared to discard his Soviet identity and communist values, nor to fully assert the national and multicultural distinctiveness of Ukraine. The persistence of national communism that had dominated Ukraine's intellectual landscape since the 1920s, albeit in a modified form, shaped Shelest's position "in between."[7] This happenstance is no surprise because the worldviews of Ukrainian leaders developed under severe ideological pressure from Moscow during the Stalin era and after Stalin's death. Their memories about the installation of Soviet power in Ukraine, their participation in it, and their individual backgrounds contributed to the intellectual and ideological foundations of their political behaviors and practices.

Ukrainian officials of substantial rank and power understood very well the de-facto status of Ukraine: its state sovereignty was an illusion, and its subordinate status was sustained by the systematic elimination of the nationalist movements.[8] The destruction of native noncommunist leadership and the subsequent indoctrination of the masses with communist ideas produced a cohort of national communists who were intrinsically toothless before Moscow's dictatorship. This cohort exhibited some leniency toward Ukrainian nationalism and national culture, articulated by their desires for more autonomy for themselves and for Ukraine, but it was anemic and often led to their dismissal or their destruction by the Kremlin. Their communist beliefs were of little help to them. This position "in between" shared by a great many party officials in Ukraine won them little support in Moscow and limited respect among the multiethnic people of Ukraine. This is true especially of Shelest. For the Moscow leadership, he was a person who sided with Ukrainian nationalists, yet for systematically persecuted and prosecuted Ukrainians, Jews, and other "national minorities" of Ukraine, he embodied state violence and antisemitism. His political maneuvering inevitably tarnished his political image and humanity. Yet, precisely because of Shelest's oscillation and his position "in between," Ukrainian and Jewish cultural revival gained strength in the 1960s, an argument that it seems difficult to accept by both students of Ukrainian and Jewish histories.

Although the liberal reforms launched by Nikita Khrushchev were centered in Moscow, the Thaw and the cultural movement of the 1960s that followed engaged intellectuals of most Soviet republics, signifying their aspiration for cultural freedom and creativity that had been subdued by Stalinism and state violence.[9] A pan-Soviet phenomenon, the movement, however, had its distinct features in Ukraine. In contrast to their Russian counterparts in the RSFSR, Ukrainian and Jewish writers who were natives of Ukraine became part of the national cultural revival in which the national and political elements became rather pronounced.[10] But this was not a clear-cut paradigm. *Shistdesiatnytstvo* was multifaceted, and the mental worlds and ideologies of its members were extremely diverse. In the RSFSR, there were also individuals like Vasilii Aksionov who identified himself as a "fiftier" (*piatidesiatnik*), because his visit to his mother's place of exile (Yevgeniia Ginzburg) fully transformed him at a very early age, before the sixties movement was formed. By the early 1950s, he was a staunch *antisovetchik*.[11]

The era of Stalin's cult and its antisemitism sharply contrasted with the Thaw's reforms and promises. Closing Jewish schools, newspapers, theaters, and publishing houses, as well as physically eliminating the Jewish intelligentsia combined with discrimination against Jews in the sphere of educational and professional opportunities, devastated Ukraine's Jewish community under Stalin. Khrushchev rehabilitated the most prominent Jewish cultural figures, but his democratic reforms were stalled as abruptly as they had begun. As one observer has stated, antisemitic rules, albeit often unwritten, remained in place. In the early 1960s, in Odesa, for instance, out of its 150,000 Jews (25 percent of its population), only from 3 to 5 percent were students of universities because of the secret party injunction about the Jewish quotas for acceptance to the institutions of higher education.[12] Ukraine's military academies had even lower numbers of students (as well as faculty) of Jewish descent, and their opportunities for promotion were significantly limited.[13] As one Jewish colonel from Kharkiv has posited, the progression of antisemitism from 1941 was "extraordinary," and "it would have been even worse if Stalin had lived longer."[14]

Despite Khrushchev's rhetoric of internationalism, brotherly friendship among various Soviet ethnic groups, and supranational Soviet identity, "Line five" (ethnicity) stayed in Soviet passports untouched, signaling and prescribing for the bureaucrats a certain restrictive mode of behavior and attitudes toward the passport holder. Both Khrushchev and Shelest were reluctant to address the Jewish question in Ukraine. They governed in silence about the fact that under Stalin, Jews suffered disproportionally from persecution and prosecution for their "otherness," perceptions that led to their oppression during the Great Terror and postwar period, and to the obliteration of major Yiddish institutions.[15]

During the rehabilitation campaign in the late 1950s and 1960s, Stalin's infamous anti-Ukrainian stance and antisemitism were questioned by both communities. Ukrainian writers pressured the authorities to rehabilitate the writers of the "Red Renaissance" (*Rozstriliane Vidrodzhennia*), and Jewish intellectuals demanded the restoration of justice and the rehabilitation of the members of the Jewish Anti-Fascist Committee. Yet in the early 1960s, the state became increasingly selective about who among nationals deserved the right to be identified as victims, the first signs of the emerging process of re-Stalinization. Hypocritically, the regime romanticized the bravery and the resurrection of the victims of Stalin's terror, but significantly downplayed state violence and obscured the identification of agencies and participants in Stalin's terror.[16] Nevertheless, this hypocrisy and the de-evolution of liberal reforms were unable to curtail the creative impulse and the feeling of liberation from the regime's ideological constraints among writers.

Yevgenii Yevtushenko's poem "Babii Yar" published in the *Literaturnaia gazeta* on 19 September 1961, and Dmitrii Shostakovich's Thirteenth Symphony broke the public silence about the taboo subjects of the Holocaust and antisemitism, becoming a turning point for many Jews.[17] In addition, the threat of antisemitic Russian nationalism was publicly addressed by the filmmaker Mikhail Romm and the writer and leading Ukrainian intellectual Ivan Dziuba. In his *Internationalism or Russification?* Dziuba criticized the Soviet nationalities policy and its principles that severely departed from Lenin's ideas. He insisted that one's membership in humanity was possible only through "one's own nation" and was among other Ukrainian writers (i.e., Ivan Svitlychnyi and Yevhen Sverstiuk) who ardently supported Ukraine's Jewish community.[18]

Yevtushenko's and Dziuba's support was very much needed and appreciated by the Jewish intelligentsia. Their courage emboldened the Jewish literati who began to produce texts that illuminated a break with the canons of socialist realism. But the post-Holocaust generation of Jews had been assimilated into Russian culture, and the majority of writers in Ukraine wrote in Russian.[19] Literary Kyiv and Kharkiv included a few who wrote in Yiddish. Their creativity, innovative thinking, and civic gallantry were inspired by the Thaw and relaxed censorship. The Jewish literati, however, quickly realized that Khrushchev's antisemitism and his negative attitude toward the revival of Yiddish institutions and periodicals would significantly limit their opportunities for national revival and fundamental freedoms.[20]

In Kharkiv (an important center of Yiddish culture in the late 1920s and the first part of the 1930s),[21] Jewish cultural institutions, including Yiddish schools that were eliminated under Stalin, were not restored after the war, thus further jeopardizing the survival of the Yiddish language and culture. Indeed, the process of their destruction continued. As a result of an antireligious campaign, from 1953 to 1963, only one-fifth of USSR synagogues survived.[22] Kharkiv had only two writers writing in Yiddish—playwright Oizer Goldesgeim whose pen name was Goldes, and Hana Levina who wrote prose and poetry.

After 1945, the community of ethnic Jews in Kharkiv revived, and by 1959 it constituted 84,000 people which was approximately 9 percent of the Kharkiv population.[23] The former Kharkivite, writer, and Russian politician Eduard Limonov (Savenko) once shared with his readers a much broader observation about a small but noticeable and flamboyant part of Kharkiv: "If there were no Jews in Kharkiv, the city would be so boring . . . Jews animate Kharkiv, making it a market place and representing the East in it."[24] Limonov became a successful professional writer decades after he left Kharkiv for Moscow, and later for New York City. But he was among the first Kharkiv writers who offered readers a "taste" of bohemian literary Kharkiv, conceived, lived, and perceived as an island of controlled freedom in the re-Stalinized Soviet Ukraine of the early 1960s.[25] Like many other literati, Limonov has been contradictory in his treatment of Kharkiv that simultaneously seemed to him a bohemian paradise, a cultural backwater, and a politically stifling place from where one needs to escape to Moscow or abroad.

Yet there was another annoying element that disoriented and perplexed many writers. The KGB skillfully exploited a lingering historical hostility between Ukrainians and Jews and camouflaged traditional state antisemitism with the necessity to fight "Jewish reactionary Zionism" and "inherent Ukrainian antisemitism," a strategy that disturbed both Ukrainians and Jews.[26] Everyone sensed the disingenuousness of the authorities' rhetoric but largely ignored it. One of the most prominent Kharkiv poets Marlena Rakhlina, who wrote her poems and memoirs in Russian, once stated: "Certainly, I always felt myself a Jew. Taking turns, Hitler and then Stalin took care of this [perception]. These worries, however, had never been dominant in my life."[27] Anatolii Brusilovskii, famous artist and a son of the Russian writer of Jewish origin Rafail Brusilovskii (both were residents of the House of Writers "Slovo" in Kharkiv), also affirmed that the 1960s was the time of artists and writers, and for him, nation, ethnicity, or the Jewish question instilled by the authorities were not his concerns, instead his focus was culture and art.[28] Rakhlina spent her entire life in Kharkiv; Brusilovskii moved to Moscow, and later to Europe. Both were repulsed by KGB tactics, but paradoxically both preserved affinities with the Kharkiv culture of the 1960s and the imperial culture that for them always had been centered in Moscow.[29]

The political instability of the 1960s–1970s and the escalation of terror against Ukraine's intellectuals contributed to people's mental confusion and ambivalence. The official Soviet discourse focused on the new unity paradigm, advocating the "friendship of peoples" concept that was supposed to replace the old imperial pan-Russian idea,[30] and simultaneously fighting against and "unmasking" Ukrainian nationalists and Zionists. An effective tool of control, inflaming ethnic stereotypes and segregating intellectuals on the basis of their cultural and ethnic backgrounds helped the KGB prevent national separatism and attempts at secession. Passively resisting KGB efforts, the Kharkiv intelligentsia chose to be surrounded by like-minded individuals, regardless of their ethnic belonging or identity, and to live a life of the mind.[31] They built a community of supporters to resist conformism and state violence. Their existence was essentially a life tied to a tiny space of freedom they created for themselves, a remnant of the Thaw. They valued independent thinking and admired the literary gift in others, an ability that shaped their collective identity. The search for their identity also included the national: their mental maps and work were populated with images imbedded in their ethnicity, cultural memories, and experiences. Kharkiv's political space systematically adjusted it but what survived unchanged over decades was their sense of spatial belonging. Without thinking about it, they traversed ethnic barriers, reinforced by the KGB, yet were constantly reminded of the fallacy of both—their supranational existence and their sagaciously national literature in which they advanced national themes. Subsequently, the "cursed seventies" (*kliati simdesiati*), a term that the Kharkiv writer Mykola Shatylov offered to describe the political space of Kharkiv, shaped their ambivalent attitudes toward the city, yet also fashioned an unforgettable Kharkiv of the 1960s–1970s, a place of hope and creativity.

AMBIGUITY IN ACTION: PETRO SHELEST

Shelest was Mykola Pidhornyi's and Nikita Khrushchev's protégé. In 1961, Khrushchev was trying to improve his relationships with the Ukrainian political leadership and the intelligentsia. In May, he even interrupted his trip to Vienna and stopped in Kyiv with his wife to "kneel at the grave of Taras Shevchenko in Kaniv."[32] He planted an oak tree and attended the Shevchenko Museum. Decades later, in his book about his father Nikita Khrushchev, Sergei Khrushchev wrote:

> The conflicts that poets and artists had with the authorities, including with Khrushchev himself, although they resounded very loudly, had results that differed from those in preceding periods of Soviet history. In the end, they only stirred the air, with serious consequences no more. The first dissidents made their appearance. The authorities did not know how to proceed and began making mistakes. They were adjusting themselves to the new situation. Their opponents were also adjusting.[33]

An eager critic would deconstruct and easily dismiss every statement of this brief description by Sergei Khrushchev as, at the very least, a naïve and poorly informed view of a loving son. Sergei Khrushchev attempted to assess positive changes and reforms implemented by his father, as well as the mistakes he made during his tenure as the first secretary of the Communist Party of the USSR (KPSS), but he avoided discussing his father's treatment of either Jews or Ukrainians during the prewar or postwar periods.

Ukraine's literati, including those of Jewish descent, had mixed feelings regarding their tormentors. Shelest was feared, detested, hated, respected, admired, and accepted by the citizens of Ukraine and was treated as any other political leader, something that was given and inevitable. Because of the most recent exhaustive studies that shed light on Shelest's ideology and subjectivity, one can safely suggest that when he said that "a people does not exist without culture," he indeed meant it.[34] Yet, in the Soviet Union the incongruities between the beliefs, words, and deeds of people in power were enormous, behavior for which they were held accountable generations later. Today in Ukraine, Shelest's power politics shaped by his ideological views and fear has been criminalized. His name appears in the list associated with the de-communization laws, and streets named after him were to have been renamed before 21 November 2015.[35]

The information about Khrushchev's antisemitic practices and the restriction of movements of Jews who wanted to join their families in Israel transcended the Iron Curtain. This happened partially because Khrushchev, eager to democratize Soviet society, allowed Soviet citizens, including Jews, to reinstate contact with relatives abroad, a practice that had been nearly abolished under Stalin. The privilege to travel abroad, however, was only granted to a few celebrities.[36] In 1968, emigration became an official policy but because of the intricate procedure established by the Soviets, only a small number of Soviet Jews could leave. Between 1965 and 1970, less than 9,000 Soviet Jews managed to emigrate.[37] They became not only a "lifeline that grew into a huge bridge," but also a source of information for the West about state antisemitism in the USSR.[38] In addition, Trokhym Kychko's antisemitic publications in Ukraine alerted the international community. The president of the Zionist Organization of America Abraham A. Redelheim, reelected on 13 September 1959, called on Khrushchev to assure Soviet Jews equal treatment and permit them to join their families in Israel.[39] Redelheim's appeal was also inspired by the Society for the Propaganda of Political and Scientific Knowledge's move to republish a 43,000-copy second edition of Trokhym Kychko's antisemitic booklet *The Jewish Religion: Its Origin and Nature* in 1959.[40] In 1957, the *New York Times* viciously criticized the text, and the United Press agency published a series of materials about Kychko's defamatory texts that had been pouring out of Ukraine. Having understood that he could cash in on this topic, Kychko, a former militia man who was arrested by the MGB for apparent criminal activity before the war, systematically published his work from 1957 to 1963, even defending his dissertation entitled "Contemporary Judaism and Its Reactionary Role."[41] He gained fame as the leading "expert" and as a critic of Judaism and later Zionism not only in Ukraine but in the entire Soviet Union. In 1963, Kychko published his infamous work *Judaism without Embellishment* that declared an enduring link between Judaism and Zionism.⁴² He suggested that Jews and Zionists sided with American imperialists and reactionary anti-Soviet forces, arguing that the fascist essence of Zionists had become clear during the Second World War when Zionists had collaborated with the Gestapo and antisemitic parties in Hungary. The Nazis' role in the Holocaust was completely omitted from Kychko's book.⁴³ This work solidified the Soviet Union's reputation as an antisemitic state.

Systematically employing the notion of internationalism in his speeches, Khrushchev failed to openly address either Kychko's activities or the issue of popular antisemitism in the USSR and the reasons for KGB operations targeting Jewish believers and Zionists in the USSR, something that ironically was revealed in Kychko's works. *Judaism without Embellishment* was clearly an attempt to rejuvenate the anti-Jewish campaign pursued by Stalin, offering a rationale for Jewish believers, "anti-Soviet Zionists," and Jewish dissent being forced underground.⁴⁴

Although Kychko was not Shelest's project (Shelest was appointed the first secretary of the KPU on 2 July, 1963, and the peak of Kychko's career was from 1957 to 1963), Shelest's attitude toward Kychko's activities is telling. Leonid Iliichiov, secretary of the TsK KPSS and head of the Propaganda and Agitation Department supervising Soviet republics (1958–1965), called Shelest, asking him to take care of the issue of Kychko's *Judaism without Embellishment*, Shelest wrote in his diary (the 21–31 March 1964, entry): "I did not find anything seditious [in this book]. I do not understand why there is such a noise around this brochure. Why is it allowed to criticize all religions except Judaism, and why is it prohibited to take a close look at Zionists' actions? Well, we will provide explanations."⁴⁵ The "noise" was raised at the highest international level, when on 6 March 1964, the U.S. representative at the United Nations and president of the American Jewish Committee (AJC) Morris B. Abram wrote about this matter to the Soviet representative Boris Ivanov. After Iliichiov's phone call, on 24 March, Shelest was also contacted by Luka Palamarchuk, Ukraine's minister of foreign affairs, who explained to him the seriousness of the situation. The leading Communist parties in the West, including American, French, British, and Italian, protested against the Soviet politics of antisemitism, and forced the Soviet government to criticize and ostracize the "expert." Shelest must have done something, because Kychko disappeared for a while, and the Soviets were forced to place critical articles about Kychko's antisemitism in the leading Soviet newspapers *Pravda* and *Izvestiia*.⁴⁶ In the late 1960s, however, Kychko's service was again in demand because of the KGB covert operation "Vozmezdiie" (Retribution or Payback), which has been discussed elsewhere.⁴⁷

Shelest's dual loyalties, expressed in his obedience to the center and his affinity for Ukrainian culture, fostered popular perceptions of apparent freedom among Ukrainians, or an "atmosphere of controlled freedom."[48] This atmosphere stimulated the Ukrainians' "proactive drive to inhabit, redefine, and expand the national cultural space they shared with the cultural establishment,"[49] which in turn created an ever-widening space for their intellectual interaction with like-minded individuals of various ethnicities, including Jewish writers. Importantly, this space was saturated with politics, radicalizing the ethnically diverse cultural movement. Its participants began to emphasize social, cultural, and economic problems in the republic that needed to be addressed. Like the Ukrainian literati, the Jewish intelligentsia attempted to establish themselves within the official cultural space, extending and often transcending its boundaries.

The issue of Shelest's subjectivity and his attitudes toward Jews is not as simple as it might seem. Was he a racist or an organic antisemite with paranoid hatred of Jews, similar to that of the Russian anarchist and revolutionary Mikhail Bakunin, the French politician and philosopher Pierre-Joseph Proudhon, or the Russian poet Boris Pasternak? Bakunin characterized the Jewish people as leeches. Proudhon wrote in his diary in 1847: "The Jew is the enemy of humankind. They must be sent back to Asia or be exterminated. By steel or by fire or by expulsion the Jew must disappear."[50] Pasternak suffered from a "passionate, almost obsessive, desire to be thought a Russian writer with roots deep in Russian soil."[51] According to Isaiah Berlin, this was "particular evident in his negative feelings towards his Jewish origins. He was unwilling to discuss the subject—he was not embarrassed by it, but he disliked it: he wished the Jews to assimilate, to disappear as a people. Apart from his immediate family, he had no interest in relatives, past or present. . . . If I mentioned Jews or Palestine, this, I observed, caused him visible distress."[52] If one seeks these sorts of sentiments in Shelest's diary, his writings will be a complete and utter disappointment. Instead, we learn that Shelest's best friends were Jews—the army artist Sasha Shorokh and Yevhen Kaplun, head of production at the Kharkiv factory "Serp i molot" (Hammer and Sickle) where Shelest worked as the chief engineer in 1939.[53] In 1989 in his interview with the journal *Kyiv*, Shelest stated:

> Throughout my long life I worked with representatives of many nationalities—Bulgarians, Georgians, Jews, Armenians, and Tatars. I have never had any conflicts based on national grounds—I simply could not imagine that I can respect a worker or an engineer more, simply because he is a Ukrainian, and to depreciate one because he is a Jew or a Tatar. In communication, there is no place for a national question among toiling people. . . . I similarly despise and despised antisemitism, chauvinism, and nationalism . . . [which] humiliate any people and blemish their dignity.[54]

Shelest's career and promotions seem to have been shaped by his educational background and professional experiences. He was born in 1908 in the village of Andriivka of today's Kharkiv oblast, and received his degree in engineering at the Mariupol Metallurgical Institute. After the war in 1948, he directed factories in Leningrad and later in Kyiv. The party appreciated his leadership skills and style, and after Stalin's death in 1954 he was invited to join the ranks of Ukrainian party bureaucrats.[55] There is little doubt that, as a Ukrainian official, Shelest guarded his political behavior and statements to stay in tune with the leadership in the Kremlin, and he might have done this at the end of his life. His personal affinities and friendships with Jews do not prove or disprove anything. Rather, testimonies of those who worked closely with Shelest provide us with some level of certainty about his intolerance toward antisemites. He constrained those who made antisemitic remarks in his presence and detested practices of discrimination against Jews at universities and in the party establishment. Shelest insisted that nationality was secondary in the context of humanity. "There are simply good and bad people," he argued.[56] It is likely that, apart from other factors, this disposition and his leniency toward dissent and the intelligentsia, regardless of their ethnicity, served as reasons for his dismissal in 1972.

Shelest's alternative vision of the Soviet nationalities policy was shaped by his experiences in the Kyiv, Vinnytsia, and Cherkasy oblasts, while he worked as the head of the Rehabilitation Commission established by the Presidium of the Supreme Council of the USSR in 1956. The Commission often worked 12–14 hours a day, reading up to fifty criminal files daily. This was a transformative experience for Shelest. For the first time, he had an opportunity to learn about the intimate mechanisms of Stalin's terror. Unquestionably, Shelest expedited and facilitated the process of rehabilitation and the liberation of thousands of innocent victims of Stalin's terror, among whom there were Ukrainians, Jews, Russians, and people of other ethnicities.[57]

The Ukrainian Komsomol leader Aleksandr Kapto has argued that there were two Shelests. One was a staunch communist and fighter against any sort of bourgeois nationalism. The other was a sentimental human being with a distinct Ukrainian consciousness.[58] Indeed, Shelest's Ukrainophilia, although of Soviet nature, has been well documented.[59] Shelest supported young talented Ukrainian poets, writers, artists, and historians, protecting them from local and Moscow ideological dogmatists, like Mikhail Suslov. In his diary, referring to Suslov, Shelest wrote: "such people are a frightening phenomenon in our party."[60] Under Shelest's supervision, the highest literary award named after Taras Shevchenko was established in Ukraine, and he defended individuals such as film directors Yurii Illienko and Serhii Paradzhanov, and the right of their creative art to exist.[61] Shelest also insisted on the legitimacy of the Ukrainian language. In 1966, at the Fifth Congress of the Union of Ukrainian Writers he stated: "We must approach our beautiful Ukrainian language with care and respect, it is our treasure, a great heritage which each of us, and primarily you writers, should cherish and develop."[62]

Yet his appreciation of Ukrainian culture and language did not obscure his broader vision of Ukraine as a land of multicultural and multiethnic traditions. Shelest supported the writer of Jewish origin David Vishnevskii whose work was viciously criticized by Kharkiv antisemitic party functionaries, and he was able to decipher the literary talent of the Jewish satirist Mikhail Zhvanetskii from Odesa, offering him an apartment in Kyiv, as well as to Roman Kartsev and Viktor Ilchenko, Jewish actors who from the stage popularized Zhvanetskii's texts critical of the Soviet system.[63] In March 1971, in a personal conversation with Brezhnev, Shelest dismissed Brezhnev's concerns about the rise of nationalism in the republic by arguing that the national question was artificially created by excessively ideological functionaries. He reminded Brezhnev that Ukraine was a multinational, multiethnic, and multicultural entity, and for ordinary people the national question, either Ukrainian or Jewish, did not exist. This was an overall optimistic interpretation of interactions among various ethnic groups in Ukraine, designed perhaps to ameliorate the center's anxieties about nationalistic tendencies in Ukraine. In a domestic format, Shelest was more honest, expressing his concerns about the antisemitic stance of party leaders in the localities. Typically, these discussions occurred at the meetings with the Ukrainian intelligentsia, whom Shelest trusted. It is noteworthy that in his 10 April 1966, letter of protest against discriminatory practices and the persecution of Soviet Jews addressed to the head of the Nationalities Council of the Supreme Council of the USSR Yan Peive, the Ukrainian poet and dissident Sviatoslav Karavanskyi blamed Khrushchev for curtailing Jewish culture and institutions.[64] Karavanskyi was aware of Shelest's position on antisemitic practices in the republic, and for that reason, he left Shelest out of his discussion.

Despite Shelest's ideological limitations and political constraints, he seemed to create an alternative informal space where the literati learned the art of coexistence with the system and with one another. The emergence of Ukrainian literary, theater and cinema clubs, such as "Suputnyk" in Kyiv and "Prolisok" in Lviv,[65] invited Jewish writers to create similar informal groups. People began to gather in private apartments, coffee houses, and cafes to read poetry and discuss new political developments in Ukraine. Importantly, these groups were not ethnically segregated. For instance, in Kharkiv, the Russian poet Boris Chichibabin's apartment became a gathering place for young Jewish, Ukrainian, and Russian writers. Among them were Russian poets of Jewish origin Mark Bogoslavskii and Marlena Rakhlina. A younger generation of Jews joined Chichibabin's "club" later, after Chichibabin discovered them through his formal literary studio, organized under the umbrella of the Writers' Union. Not surprisingly, many exhibited political and cultural

Russophilism, a phenomenon about which Lew Shankowsky insightfully wrote sixty years ago.[66] Assimilated and urbanized Jews, they were indifferent to the idea of the restoration of Yiddish cultural institutions and language.[67] Similarly, they were far from being enthusiastic about supporting the idea of Ukraine's de-Russification advocated by their Ukrainian colleagues. Although sympathizing with the Ukrainian liberation movement, people like Rakhlina, the Jewish poet Liliia Karas (Chichibabin's wife), and Chichibabin himself rejected the anti-Russian stance, associating themselves with Russian culture and literature. They defended the one and indivisible Russia in the form of the Soviet Union even after Ukraine became independent.[68]

Volodymyr Briuggen's Labyrinths

One Kharkiv journalist remembered that many Kharkiv poets dreamed of escaping from Kharkiv because it seemed to them provincial. "'To Moscow, to Moscow!' Only in Moscow there is a real [literary] life."[69] The party constraints and the framework they prescribed were disturbing and irritating to the Kharkiv literati. Half a century later, renowned literary critic Volodymyr Briuggen assertively claimed that Kharkiv had never been provincial.[70] He continued: "Literary talent is a rare gift and commodity. Some preferred to use it where they were; the position of the body means little, you know. Some preferred to sell it in the Soviet capital. By moving there, those literary slaves did not make it less provincial, authoritarian, or imperial. I've always felt sorry for them."[71] Other writers shared similar observations: many returned home from Moscow "with burned wings, or without wings, to die quietly in a hospital with a pancreas deteriorating from drinking."[72]

In 2013, with his subtle sense of humor, Briuggen ruminated about his ethnic origin:

> It all might be that Jews in the Netherlands, Dutch-German Jews, were my predecessors on one side, but I feel affinity with two men that I believe my distant relatives (although the family history tells me otherwise): Adolph Cornelis "Dolf" van Bruggen (1929–2016), known as A. Bruggen, a Dutch botanist and entomologist, and Kees van Bruggen, born Cornelis Johannes Antonius van Bruggen (1874–1960), a Dutch writer and journalist.[73] I inherited talents from both men, and that's why every summer I escape to the Biological Station in Crimea (Biostantsiia), where I write.[74]

This frivolous interpretation of his background had never occurred in public, because he said, "I simply did not want to raise this topic. For 'them,' I was Jewish. Period. And, god knows, who else."[75] According to his family history, Aleksandr Fiodorovich Briggen, a Decemberist, was one of

Briuggen's father's predecessors, who belonged to the family of Baron von Brüggen from Westphalia and the Duchy of Courland and Semigallia in the Baltic region.[76] Briuggen's parents met and married in Siberia, in Tiumen, moving to Ukraine before the war.[77]

Briuggen was born in 1932 in Kharkiv. He and his family survived the famine and the Second World War by being evacuated to the Urals. The Briuggens returned to the city after the war. After high school, Briuggen became a student at the Kharkiv Polytechnical Institute but after two years of studies there he realized that literature was his true calling. He joined the School of Journalism at the Kharkiv State University, later transferring to the School of Journalism at the Kyiv State University. He graduated in 1956 and worked as a journalist for small newspapers in the Kharkiv oblast and for Kharkiv television. The beginning of his professional career was traditional, but he chose an extremely radical path for a Soviet writer, which arguably saved him from trouble and persecution. For two decades, the 1960s and 1970s, he was head of the criticism section in the journal *Prapor*, a period when he built a reputation as an intellectual, a translator, and a writer with rare literary gifts and critical skills. He befriended Tretyakov, and their friendship was grounded in the intellectualism of their creative work. As readers, they consumed thousands of pages per week, at work and at home. For both, nights were the most productive time when they read and wrote. "We were both nocturnal, and the rhythms of our daily activities coincided. At work, we together escaped from graphomaniacs, running to Poetry Square. Parked on 'our' bench, we were reading to each other what we wrote over the night" (Fig. 2.1).[78] But Briuggen's favorite time was twilight, "the time of expectations and silence, memory and forgiveness. It is so quiet that one can hear how the seconds are being dropped in the hourglass."[79] A Russian, writing in Ukrainian, and a Jew, writing in both Ukrainian and Russian, Tretyakov and Briuggen were not only friends but they represented a constellation of talented Kharkiv *shistdesiatnyky*, and together with Vasyl Bondar and Oleksa Marchenko, were selected to represent the Kharkiv delegation at the festival of Ukrainian culture and literature in Moscow (*dekada ukrainskoi literatury ta mystetstva*) in 1960.[80]

An innovative literary critic, Briuggen also established high standards of translation from languages with which few writers worked in Ukraine—English, French, and German. He translated the poetry of the Nobel Prize Laureate and French poet Saint-John Perse and the novels of Louis Henri Boussenard, Jules Gabriel Verne, René Fallet, Pascal Lainé, Agatha Christie, James Hadley Chase, Leicester Hemingway, and Bernard Malamud into Russian and Ukrainian. He was extremely proud of his translation of the ethnographic works by Volodymyr Hnatiuk (from German and old Galician into Russian). His work as a translator also brought him additional income that allowed him to build a decent library. Those who visited Briuggen's apartment were struck by the association of its environment with "The Library of Babel," a short story written by the Argentine writer Jorge Luis Borges, imagining a universe as a vast library that simultaneously embodies order, chaos, and infinity.[81] Borges's imagined library contained all the books that had ever been written, including the translations of each book in all world languages. Beyond practical consideration, Briuggen's efforts at translating the masterpieces of world literature seemed to be an apparent subconscious impulse to contribute to the construction of such a library. When he ran out of space on the bookshelves, he began to create stacks of books, wrapping the walls of his small one-room apartment from the floor to the ceiling. In this seemingly chaotic space and random arrangement of books, Briuggen could unerringly find a newspaper, a journal, or a book that he needed at the moment. The insignificance of the external visual chaos to Briuggen was a manifestation of his general attitude toward the brutalities of re-Stalinization. He learned how to live and not notice the authorities. Like Borges, Briuggen understood the labyrinths of his own library and thoughts which were erected to help cope with and structure his experiences of reality, saturated with politics and illogical state violence. In fact, Briuggen himself jokingly compared himself with the legendary architect Daedalus who built a labyrinth for King Minos of Crete at Knossos to hold the Minotaur, the monster who was eventually killed by Theseus. In Briuggen's world, the "deliberately confusing structure he built in the form of his lifestyle" worked perfectly for him, permitting him to establish his own rules of reality: by containing himself in the limited space of his library, he constrained the state in pursuing him as the "other," and a foreign and anti-Soviet element. When asked about the analogy and Daedalus who barely escaped the labyrinth after he finished building it, Briuggen answered: "I've never attempted to escape it. That was my home."[82]

Indeed, literature and his library were Briuggen's home for the rest of his life. At a very early age, he realized that literature requires sacrifices and freedom, and his published translations granted him a degree of freedom. In keeping with this mindset, he made one of the most uncommon and important decisions in his life: in the mid-1970s he quit his job at *Prapor*, whose atmosphere was suffocating, in hopes of surviving as an independent writer ("pishov na tvorchi khliba," as Briuggen stated). This decision had been ripening since 1967, when Briuggen began to recognize the fatal effect of ideological masters on literary Kharkiv. A conversation with an *obkom* functionary, in which he reminded Briuggen of his "briuggenness," was a point of no return. He consciously isolated himself from the nonsense of bureaucracy and the danger of literary freedom, carefully constructing a space of his intellectual solitude and productivity. He wanted to be invisible for the authorities and concentrate on something that he liked the most—literature. Briuggen

Figure 2.1　Volodymyr Briuggen and Robert Tretyakov. Kharkiv, 1966. *Source*: LTPA.

wrote: "[Anatolii] Mariengof shows that [Sergei] Yesenin feared solitude the most. For me, solitude is the only good that I actually possess."[83] He constructed an intellectual bubble for himself, reading and "working like a dog," in which he existed until his death in 2018. "I realized that I could develop my talent only if I became free," he posited, "internally and spiritually."[84]

Unsurprisingly, Briuggen began to plan his departure from *Prapor* in 1967, the year when the subtle balance of informal space of controlled freedom maintained by Shelest in the 1960s was disrupted. Yurii Andropov, newly appointed head of the KGB who was highly recommended for this position by Suslov, intensified repressions against nationalists, "Zionists," and dissent. These measures had an effect polar opposite from what the authorities tried to achieve in Ukraine. Writers of various ethnic backgrounds began to write non-Soviet poetry and texts, politically and nationally charged, distributing them through *samvydav* that quickly transcended Ukraine's borders. This was not only political resistance but also a "struggle for self-respect, a break with the internalized inferiority complex that [was] the result of cultural colonization."[85]

For ethnic Jews, this year also marked an identity crisis and cultural awakening. The state's refusal to allow Jews to emigrate provoked the formation of a Jewish national movement that gained distinct contours by the early 1970s.[86] This movement relied on and was strengthened by the support of other national movements in the Soviet Union, but the 1967 Arab–Israeli

Six-Day War exacerbated the disillusionment of the Jewish intelligentsia with the Soviet nationalities policy and discrimination, further fostering their Zionism. Importantly, the war revived the idea of a Jewish community and made Jews conscious and proud of their ethnic origin, connecting them with the global Jewish community, regardless of their geographic location or status.[87] Some individuals, like Mikhail Kheifets who in 1974 was arrested for anti-Soviet propaganda, described this feeling as enduring and prevailing, a state of mind that many Jews carried with them into Soviet camps. Even there, they behaved as victors: Israel existed, a reality that served as the foundation for "national comfort and tranquility" for Soviet Jews, making the Soviet empire nervous and weak.[88]

Outside the camp gates, after Israel's victory, Kharkiv Jews lived national lives previously unknown to them. Many young Jewish poets, like Yurii Miloslavskii and Aleksandr Vernik, dreamed about emigration. Lev Frukhtman, son of the Jewish poet Iosif Kotliar who in the 1930s resided in "Slovo," the Writers' House, remembered how the war changed his habits and social behavior. Every day he sneaked to the radio to listen to the news broadcast by "Col Israel" which was persistently jammed by the Soviets.[89] The state of Israel encouraged Soviet Jews to emigrate but its strategy was to advise them "to avoid alliances with the dissidents."[90] Cooperation with dissidents would have certainly made it easier for the authorities to portray Jews, willing to emigrate from the Soviet Union, as anti-Soviet.[91] Ironically, many Soviet Jews, including Ukrainian Jews, had already cooperated with dissidents, having become dissidents themselves before 1967, and some had already served terms in the Soviet camps.[92] The Soviet authorities had already branded the human rights movement a Zionist conspiracy because of the overwhelming number of Jews among its activists.[93] The Soviet invasion of Czechoslovakia in 1968 and the crackdown on liberal reforms in Prague further radicalized Jewish cultural and political dissidence, amplifying the Jewish intelligentsia's gravitation toward Zionism. Because of the media attack on Zionists (for the Soviet authorities all Jews were identified as Zionists) and the state's persecution and discrimination against Jews, Zionism became an increasingly attractive solution and a communal refuge for many. These transformative experiences made Ukrainian-Jewish writers realize the tragedy of Soviet Jewry's cultural and internal colonization. They constituted both a persecuted national minority and a political and professional elite, or a "discriminated elite."[94] This phenomenon shaped their identities and loyalties which in turn determined the vector of their political affinities and cultural activism in the 1960s and the 1970s.[95]

Briuggen had never been apolitical. He engaged in these developments mentally and intellectually, although he seemed to avoid any direct political engagement or entanglement. He considered active protests against the authorities ineffective, arguing that his front is a "literary front," and his residence simply signified the physical position of his body in a space of literature. Answering a question about his potential emigration to Israel or the United States, he said: "Why should I go to Israel or the United States? They come to me through their writers."[96] He added in writing: "One should die in his own country. Let alone live."[97] In addition, by the late 1960s, Briuggen belonged to the same space of literary criticism and perfection that had been created by Ivan Svitlychnyi, Ivan Dziuba, Vitalii Donchyk, Mykola Ilnytskyi, and Hryhorii Syvokin. A friend and a thorough student of Mykola Lukash, a Ukrainian genius at translation, Briuggen inherited Lukash's philosophy and attitudes toward the material which was irrelevant to both of them.[98] Literature led him through the labyrinths of life. He read, translated, and published his own books exclusively in Kyiv in the 1960s and 1970s, the city of his youth to which he had a special emotional attachment.[99] Decades later, Briuggen summarized his life choice: "Life is a complex labyrinth, but nevertheless one has to remain within it instead of searching for an exit. People lose the sense of direction, searching for an exit."[100] However, his "briuggenness" that he was warned against by an antisemitic Kharkiv official bothered him, and in 1977, reporting to the director of the Bureau of Propaganda of the Writers' Union T. Petrovska about his travel plans and the thematic agenda of his public readings, a duty of any member of the Writers' Union, he included ideologically and politically correct themes that guaranteed him approval of both the party and the Writers' Union: "the historical role of Soviet literature in the process of ideological upbringing of the masses," "the international reputation of Soviet literature," "a vigorous development of national cultures in the USSR," "the significance of party resolutions about literary criticism and the work with the creative youth," and the like.[101]

Yet Briuggen as a cultural phenomenon will be remembered not for that. He wrote for Ukrainians, Jews, Russians, and, as some claimed, for God. Petro Soroka, for instance, believed that "Briuggen would write even when he would know that there are only two hours left before the apocalypse. This means that he writes also for God."[102] Beyond the works of literary criticism and translations, Briuggen had been writing his most intimate thoughts in the form of aphorisms or maxims over half of a century without any intention of ever publishing them. Untouched by censorship, the first collections of his brief thoughts under the laconic title *From the Notepads* appeared in journals of post-Soviet Ukraine such as *Vitchyzna*, *Berezil*, *Dzvon*, and *Tiomnyie alei*. The Ukrainian literary critic Yevhen Baran identified Briuggen's genre as philosophical meditations.[103] Briuggen began to write *The Notepads* in the 1960s. This was spontaneous occasional writing which he identified as purposeless. This was his need to liberate himself from thoughts that populated his busy brain. After Ukraine's independence, Briuggen reconsidered the meaning and the significance of his exercises, stating that the notes had become his main and most engaging activity. He published several *Notepads*, and, without exaggeration, each of them contributed to world literature, alongside virtuosos of the brief literary form, such as François VI, Duc de La Rochefoucauld, Hryhorii Skovoroda, Blaise Pascal, Pierre-Jules Renard, Jean de La Bruyère, and Vasilii Rozanov. The late Ukrainian writer Svitlana Yovenko identified Briuggen as the Kharkiv Montaigne, and the intellectual path to his writings as difficult and winding.[104] Importantly, his notes organized and shaped his behaviors and worldviews. Because of them, Briuggen became a rare example of a Soviet writer who remained free during the Soviet era. He stated that

> freedom [was] an ability (and readiness) to accept any change. Freedom [was] an opportunity to forget. Nature is savvy having deprived a human to repeat his or her life. The unfreedom of thought comes from the unfreedom of behavior. . . . Free movement is possible only in a free space that we create for ourselves. I engage in literature which means I am not involved in the bureaucracy of the making of my career, in discussing rumors, and in worrying about money.[105]

Briuggen was certain that no one can grant someone freedom. One should take it to pursue his or her call: "We have to cherish our dignity and humor. And freedom. The dead end that one observes in the course of his life is being typically transformed into a tunnel [and a trap]."[106]

However, truth should be told: the destructive inner workings of the Soviet system and its ideological terrain effected even independent Briuggen with his brilliant analytical skills. The Soviet anti-Jewish and anti-Zionist campaigns nurtured ethnic stereotypes and mistrust of everything non-Russian in many. Briuggen's mode of thinking was far from stereotypical. While Soviet popular antisemitism thrived on ignorance and trust in the authorities, Briuggen's critical remarks about Jews were grounded in personal observations and comparative analyses. Yet apparently, the feature ascribed to him by the authorities, while he was young (his "briuggenness"), frightened him in the 1960s, being internalized, deeply hidden, and submerged over the years, but not forgotten. Perhaps, that fear from which he consciously separated himself was still irritating and offensive to him as a writer and as an intellectual. Like the material, the issue of ethnicity excited Briuggen exclusively from a cultural and historical point of view but inspired little interest on the scale of moral-ethical values and literary achievements. He was not a Jew who fought Jews, Ukrainians, or Russians but rather he was a person of supra-ethnic views, writing negatively about ethnocentrism and ultra-patriotism, regardless of their ethnic origin. Jewish ethnocentrism also became a subject of Briuggen's criticism on a number of occasions. To an extent, he was a fanatic of the craft of writing, and his egocentric nature as a writer coexisted with universal altruism and an acute feeling of justice and impartiality.[107]

Among Briuggen's close friends were ethnic Jews (Ihor Muratov), Russians (Robert Tretyakov), Ukrainians (Ivan Dziuba), Poles (Stanisław Supłatowicz), and Americans (Dale A. Bertelsen). Yet some writers claimed that "literary antisemitism" was symptomatic of Briuggen.[108] He criticized self-promotion and self-aggrandizement of certain Jewish initiatives, and commercial activities around the tragedy of the Holocaust. Briuggen argued that genocide cannot and should not be commercialized. He criticized the rhetorical overuse of antisemitism: "If I criticize a man for his immorality and he happened to be a Jew, is it antisemitism?" he wondered.[109] As an opinionated man, he denied Joseph Brodsky's literary genius and the artistic value of Steven Spielberg's *Schindler's List*, a 1993 American historical drama about the Holocaust.[110] Similarly, he rejected the greatness and the genius of the Ukrainian poet Lina Kostenko that was "grossly exaggerated," according to Briuggen, and viciously criticized the Ukrainian government.[111] Several representatives of the Jewish intellectual elite in Kharkiv accused Briuggen of antisemitism.

When thinking about Briuggen's "literary antisemitism," another intellectual comes to mind. The American literary theorist Kenneth Burke was also accused of antisemitism by his colleagues, American scholars. In his insightful essay, one American rhetorical critic and scholar explored Burke's ethnocentric tendencies with regard to the Jewish community, arguing that "staunchly independent Burke could not escape the formative nature of the ideas he encountered."[112] Burke himself admitted his ethnocentrism and antisemitic rhetoric, and offered an apologia about his depreciatory stereotypes. The difference between Burke and Briuggen lays in their self-evaluations. Briuggen insisted that his criticism had nothing to do with ethnicity or his allegedly negative attitudes toward the Jews as a nation. "I am critical not of certain ethnic groups or nations, but rather of human vices, ignorance, and stupidity."[113]

Negotiating the Labyrinth: Jewish *Shistdesiatnytstvo* and the "Jewish Question"

Other Kharkiv literati also had to navigate the labyrinth of politics and choices. Re-Stalinization, combined with renewed repressions against Ukrainian nationalists and Zionists and KGB efforts at deepening the rift between them, pushed Kharkiv writers closer to one another. The degree of cultural and social segregation among Ukraine's intellectuals on the basis of ethnicity had been dramatically reduced during the Shelest era. The dangerous climate of renewed state terror created, boosted, and sustained a common cultural space that attracted the most talented writers, artists, composers, and historians of Ukrainian, Russian, and Jewish backgrounds. Moreover, they were eager to keep their membership in it.[114] The disruption of national traditions and assimilation implemented through violence was the common tragedy that united them in articulating similar existential goals of individual and cultural survival.

Yet despite their consolidating capacities, neither the Thaw nor de-Stalinization were able to erase the generational gap that accentuated differences in ideological dispositions among writers. The majority of the older generation of Jewish writers, such as Natan Rybak, Grigorii Gelfandbein, and Leonid Yukhvid, were committed to both communism and cultural nationalism. The literature they produced during the Thaw represented the "culture of builders of Communism, a culture of grandiose political, social, industrial, agricultural and scientific projects."[115] The younger generation despised their double-speak and often mocked them behind their backs. They were highly skeptical about the bright communist future promised by the Soviet authorities and were increasingly frustrated with their hypocrisy and antisemitism. However, young Kharkiv Jews, the literati who predominantly were not members of the Writers' Union, were not a homogenous group. The Jewish cultural and political movement was divided along strategic and spatial lines. Some advocated emigration, and others believed that Jewish culture and literature could be developed in the Soviet Union.[116]

Despite these differences, some representatives of both generations entered the history of literary Kharkiv as part of the sixties' movement who rebelled against the Soviet practices of reducing "national" literatures to the status of provincial literatures. Anthony Adamovych has noted that "not only the central but also the centralizing position in the complex of the 'multinational literature' was given to Soviet Russian literature."[117] Although most of the *shistdesiatnyky* were engaged in cultural production, their texts embodied the struggle for national self-preservation and the revival of national literary traditions. Interestingly, Jews writing in Ukrainian or Russian who had no knowledge of Yiddish were profoundly "national" and touched on exceptionally novel and important Jewish themes, such as the Holocaust. The works by Kharkiv Yiddish writers, experienced and talented, faded against the younger generation's original and innovative poetry and prose written in languages other than Yiddish. Moreover, their works were written through tears, pain, and despair caused by their guilt for losing their ancestors' language and cultural traditions. In this respect, they produced perceptively national literature, being more Jewish than that of their Jewish colleagues, writing in Yiddish and publishing their politically correct works in the bimonthly periodical *Sovetish Heymland* that emerged in Moscow in 1961.[118]

The cultural and linguistic logic behind people's identities that informed their creative work was obscured and often lost, as was the logic and consistency of Khrushchev's political reforms. Yet Jewish *shistdesiatnytstvo* existed and survived in Kharkiv, represented by a few rather than by many. Among them were Zinovii Valshonok, Marlena Rakhlina, Zelman Kats, Leonid Osmolovskyi (Osadchuk), Lev Galkin, Vadim Levin, and Volodymyr Briuggen. Young Jewish poets, such as Yurii Miloslavskii, Aleksandr Vernik, Eduard Siganevich, and Genrikh Shmerkin, were still learning the art of verse, having published their first books abroad only in the 1970s and 1980s after they emigrated from Ukraine.

What inspired the emergence of the Jewish cultural and "poetic" space in Kharkiv in the 1960s, in which an alternative literature and national themes blossomed? In his assessment of this phenomenon, Briuggen has posited that this was first and foremost a phenomenon of youth that was fortunately integrated into a societal need for moral and literary rejuvenation, and a return to people's cultural and familial roots, enthused by political and aesthetic conditions that matured under the influence of the Khrushchev Thaw.[119] The thirst for freedom and the birth of civic gallantry produced new literature and new behaviors conscious of people's ethnic roots.

Cross-cultural insemination, fostered by writers of various cultural backgrounds, and friendships developed as a result of intellectual exchange among them, created a need for individual expression. In the post-Thaw period of tightened censorship, writers' communications inspired their activities as translators which had a dual purpose: their original work had little chance to be published, and their published translations helped them survive financially. For post-Thaw Yiddish writers, their translations of works written by Ukrainian writers helped them express their inner suffering, and themes of alienation and national subversion. That is what inspired Dovid Hofshteyn who in the 1930s translated the Ukrainian Romantic poet Taras Shevchenko (1814–1861) into Yiddish.[120] Kharkiv Yiddish writers also welcomed the opportunity to be translated into Russian or Ukrainian. These publications satisfied the cultural needs of Russian-speaking Soviet Jews who were indifferent to Yiddish and the idea of restoring Yiddish cultural institutions.[121] For the local authorities and censors, translations were deemed safer, serving as evidence of Soviet internationalism.

The Khrushchev era brought relative relaxation on Yiddish literature, and Yiddish writers were quite productive, publishing their work in Ukraine, Israel, and the Russian Federation.[122] Their poetry and prose became less predictable and more saturated with national flavor. Tragedy as a literary genre for which there was no room in Stalinist Soviet literature occupied a significant space in post-Thaw literature. Departing from their previous thematic scope and aesthetics, some writers, especially the returnees from the labor camps, turned to Jewish historical topics, and the Bible or Talmud motifs. Yet the space of controlled freedom allowed by Khrushchev had limitations, being routinely sanitized of "tragic" texts. As Lucjan Dobroszycki and Jeffery S. Gurock have noted, "Yiddish literature, translated or not translated, had to comply with certain demands, shun certain themes, and beware of any shadow of nationalism or Zionism."[123] Nevertheless, in the 1960s, attempts at transcending the boundaries established by censorship were sometimes crowned with success, being published even in heavily censored *Sovetish Heymland.*

These successes and errors of censors were strictly monitored and punished by the authorities. One of the most effective levers of control over the writers was Litfond. At the dawn of the Soviet era, economic provisions were made for the Soviet cultural elite, including composers, artists, theater directors, filmmakers, and architects, constituting a form of bribery and manipulation.[124] Created under the umbrella of the Writers' Union, Litfond took care of the writers' financial needs, heavily subsidizing their professional trips and leisure time at various resorts that had been created specifically for the writers to rest and work there. These places had their own infrastructure, allotting the best spots at the sea beaches for the Union's members. Litfond had the liberty of including or excluding writers from the circle of the privileged who could use the Litfond's services and special offers. In 1970, a subtle poet and a Kharkivite of Jewish descent, Zinovii Valshonok was removed from the list of privileged members of Litfond in 1970.[125] A 1956 graduate of the Philology Department of Kharkiv State University, Valshonok absorbed the free spirit of the Thaw. A poet writing in Russian, he began to publish his poems in 1957 in *Novyi mir*, *Zvezda*, *Druzhba narodov*, *Ogoniok*, *Smena*, *Sovetskii ekran*, and *Raduga*. He published his first two volumes of poetry in Kharkiv in 1964 and 1967. For the authorities, these two volumes announced the birth of a poet who broke the unwritten rules, producing a passionate and national poetry. His membership in the sixtiers' movement exacerbated his difficulty in publishing his poetry in Kharkiv and coping with the KGB's and *obkom*'s attacks: "We are the sixtiers . . . we emerged to become messiahs . . . but we, the navy seals of the future who were shot from the land, did not manage to break the era."[126] The tragedy of the Drobytskyi Yar near Kharkiv where thousands of Kharkiv Jews were shot by the Nazis was tattooed on Valshonok's heart, awakening in him the shoemaker Mendel, the rabbi Yankel, the librarian Revekka, and the little barefoot girl Rakhil. They were pushed into the mass grave but survived in Valshonok's poetry: "I am that kid," he writes, "laying with the killed and hugging them in the bloody hole."[127]

A moral and suffering character has always been at the center of Valshonok's poems, a character victimized by violence, indifference, and oblivion. Internalizing other people's experiences and suffering from the rhetorical incongruity between the Thaw and the period that followed it, Valshonok's poetry written in Russian is intrinsically Jewish and philosophical. The experiences of war, evacuation in the Altai,[128] and the Kharkiv anti-semitic authorities' terror against intellectuals in the 1960s and 1970s neither exhausted his creative and emotional reserves nor annihilated his premonition of his new ethnic identity, absorbing the creative, the intellectual, and the national, everything that the Kharkiv party bosses tried to erase. Although with some degree of Soviet cliché, Valshonok's early poetry was intensely disturbing, emotional, and intellectually rich. In 1970, persecution (*goneniia*) against him reached its apogee. The Kharkiv authorities ordered the destruction of a volume of poetry ready for publication. From thousands of poems received by *Novyi mir*, Aleksandr Tvardovskii chose Valshonok's several poems that were published in the ninth issue of the journal in 1962. These memories encouraged Valshonok to make an important decision to leave Kharkiv for Moscow, hoping to pursue his literary career. He moved there in 1976, although he remained silent for a decade. He survived there through the support of Arsenii Tarkovskii, Pavel Antokolskii, David Samoilov, and Stepan Shchipachiov. Over the years, he has published more than fifty volumes of poetry, prose, and memoirs but Kharkiv remained a special place for Valshonok due to his close links to the circle of Kharkiv *shistdesiatnyky*, Robert Tretyakov who he lovingly called "Robertino," Volodymyr Briuggen, and Boris Chichibabin (Fig. 2.2). Valshonok writes:

I am searching for my roots in Kharkov,
Where there are shadows
Of a sorrowful catastrophe,
Where I was coughing up
With blood at night
Still immature stanza
Of my songs.[129]

In his foreword to Valshonok's five-volume selected writings, Chichibabin who held a high opinion of Valshonok's poetry wrote that the highest praise for a poet was when another poet lamented that those verses he read had not been written by him.[130] That was Chichibabin's feeling, while he was reading Valshonok's verses.

Only a few were fortunate like Valshonok. Those who stayed in Kharkiv were routinely harassed by the KGB and *obkom* leaders and published little during the 1960s and 1970s. Identified as "Zionists," many were investigated by the authorities or invited to KGB headquarters for discussions about their potential disloyalty as Soviet citizens.

Figure 2.2 Boris Chichibabin and Zinovii Valshonok, Kharkiv, the 1970s. *Source*: Courtesy of Zinovii Valshonok (private archive), 23 July 2020.

The trends of state and popular antisemitism seem to be similar. In his article, "Glasnost, Perestroika and Antisemitism," Zvi Gitelman revealed that "in 1980-81 a group of 1,161 ex-Soviet citizens was interviewed. All had left the U.S.S.R. between 1977 and 1980 and resettled in Israel or the United States. Respondents were asked whether they 'had personally experienced antisemitism in the Soviet Union.'"[131] Among all Soviet republics, Ukraine had the highest percentage of frequency of antisemitic encounter (38 percent against 33.2 percent in Russia, 26.8 percent in the Baltic republics, 25.2 percent in Moldova, 6.3 percent in Georgia, and 13.1 percent in Central Asia republics).[132] However, according to the Kharkiv literati, antisemitic manifestations were rare among them. For instance, Leonid Kurokhta, a talented writer of Jewish descent who in the mid-1990s left Kharkiv for Israel, remembered that Kharkiv was a special city where he had never been insulted or offended because he was Jewish. Kurokhta argued that popular ethnic stereotypes existed but he was fortunate: only once over the course of his life, he heard a comment behind his back made by his colleague, not a writer but a militia man, when Kurokhta was young working for the militia: "Unbelievable, he is a Jew but a normal fellow."[133]

Indeed, the general atmosphere in the world of the literati in which Kurokhta existed was kind, and the relationships among the members of the Kharkiv chapter of the Writers' Union appeared to be peaceful and free of serious conflicts,[134] in contrast to the constant tensions that could be observed among Moscow literati. An antisemite and Stalinist, the Russian writer from Moscow Vladimir Bushin was shocked by how freely Viktor Koptylov, a Kyivite, and Andrii Chernyshov, a Kharkivite, discussed the Jewish question in Koktebel (Crimea) in front of Briuggen, a person with Jewish-German roots.[135] According to many memoirs, the Jewish question has never been a forbidden topic for Kharkiv writers. As noted earlier, the KGB used it as a divisive tool, and encouraged the Union's members who cooperated with the KGB to bring it occasionally to the surface in their private conversations to identify the position of the writers on this sensitive topic.[136] A historically diverse community of Kharkiv writers, they passively resisted to participate in KGB games. Yet Briuggen was convinced that by making Jews vulnerable through its antisemitic practices, the authorities instilled paranoia in many of them who became more sensitive than Ukrainians or Russians to any type of jokes, suspecting antisemitism.[137] But typically, ironic remarks that were often grounded in the interplay of words and stereotypes were taken with ease by writers. For instance, the satirical gift of Aleksandr Khazin helped him produce a statement memorable among many Kharkiv literati. In his view, the talented poet Boris Sukhorukov had a unique phenotype, possessing both Slavic and Jewish features. This somatic phenomenon provoked Khazin's joke: "From the front, Sukhorukov looks like the organizer of the Jewish pogrom, and from behind—like its victim."[138] Everyone was aware of Sukhorukov's rejection of antisemitism. He, like many of his Russian and Ukrainian colleagues, had a Jewish wife, the poet Anna Fisheleva. Khazin's joke was greatly appreciated by Sukhorukov and his Jewish friends, and has been reiterated by three generations of Kharkiv literati.

In the 1960s, two Ukrainians and a Jew served as heads of the Writers' Union: Viktor Kochevskyi, Yaroslav Hrymailo, and Ihor Muratov (Fig. 2.3).[139] The Union's administration included nine people—five ethnic Ukrainians, two ethnic Russians, and two ethnic Jews.[140] Among the forty-eight members of the Union, there were seventeen ethnic Jews who wrote mostly in Russian. Muratov and Briuggen used both languages, Ukrainian and Russian, and only two writers of the older generation, Levina and Goldes, wrote in Yiddish. Three decades of Soviet Russification and assimilation practices resulted in a dramatic reduction of Yiddish speakers. Levina's and Goldes's colleagues called them "the last of the Mohicans," using the title of one of James Fennimore Cooper's books.

The Yiddish-language literary journal *Sovetish Heymland*, based in Moscow, was the only outlet for Levina and Goldes to publish their work. The journal was quite popular among Yiddish speakers, but over the years that followed the 1967 Six-Day War, when the journal was populated with texts of anti-Zionist propaganda, the number of its subscribers fell dramatically. With a population of 2 million, Kharkiv received only sixty-eight copies of the journal for retail sales through the Soiuzpechat network.[141] As a person who spent four years in prison, from 1951 to 1955, Goldes remained an "enemy" and was treated with suspicion by the authorities. He had to beg the Litfond and the Writers' Union to restore his rights to continue to work.[142]

Figure 2.3 Viktor Kochevskyi (Fourth from the Right), Yaroslav Hrymailo (Second from the Left), and Ihor Muratov (Second from the Right), the 1950s. *Source*: RTPA; a copy is located in TsDAMLIMU, f. 783, op. 1, spr. 24, ark. 1.

With the death of Goldes in 1966 and Levina in 1969, the Writers' Union in Kharkiv had no Yiddish-language writers.

Ultimately, by 1970, the cultural space of Kharkiv, a crossroads of multiple cultures and languages that nurtured the literary talents of Ukrainians, Russians, and Jews, had been narrowed to two languages—Russian and Ukrainian. Vladimir Zhabotinskii has argued that "to write in Russian does not exactly mean to abandon Jewish literature . . . the 'nationality' of a literary product is not defined by the language in which it was written."[143] He further suggested that the ethnic origin of the writer means little, and that it is the writer's attitude and intended audience that is important. One who does not know Yiddish but who writes for Jewish people and appeals to them does not desert the Jewish literature. Similarly, Chichibabin has posited that "[t]he place of a Jew is in a culture, in which he discovered himself."[144] Despite the fluidity of languages and identities Kharkiv *shistdesiatnyky* embraced, they contributed greatly to many cultures, writing for and about the peoples of these cultures. An ethnic Russian, Chichibabin was famous for his Jewdophilia, discovering and falling in love with Israel and Jewish culture which found reflection in his poetry.[145] A German Jew, Briuggen wrote equally gracefully and eloquently in Ukrainian and Russian, and translated from French, Polish, and English. He was surprised when asked whether he gravitated more to Ukrainian, Russian, Jewish, or any other culture, replying, "You are trying to fill in the blanks, and there are no blanks in my life. They are all culturally filled in a variety of linguistic and intellectual ways."[146] An ethnic Russian and a Jew both writing in Ukrainian, Tretyakov and Muratov translated Levina's Yiddish poems, helping Jewish culture reach out to Ukrainian-speaking audiences.[147]

Importantly, Jewish *shistdesiatnyky* represented a small sample of the remarkable talent assembled in the Kharkiv of the 1960s, an ethnically diverse community of writers with distinct and pronounced cultural and regional affinities, amalgamated and overlapping multiple identities, intense intellectualism, and inimitable poetic styles. Ihor Muratov was respected by all Kharkiv writers, regardless of their ethnic or cultural backgrounds. Born in 1912 in Paris to the family of an engineer and professional revolutionist, Levant Maksudovych Muratov (Leontii Maksymovych Muratov, according to his Soviet passport), and the young Kharkivite from a wealthy Jewish family Yevheniia Yosypivna Rosenbaum (she was a relative of Charlotte Embden [Rosenbaum] or Charlotte Heine, sister of the German poet Heinrich Heine), Muratov belonged to an older generation of Kharkiv writers who participated in the Russo-Finish war where he, wounded, was saved by Aron Kopshtein, a soldier and a poet, and miraculously survived a number of German concentration camps under the fake name of Pavlo Stetsenko.[148] After liberation from the concentration camps, for some unknown reason, Muratov was returned to the army as a soldier, a nontypical solution for the Soviets who treated war prisoners as criminals.[149] After the war, in the 1950s, he was sent to Berlin to work for the infamous Committee entitled "For Return to the Motherland," a KGB front organization located in East Berlin, as the chief editor of the Ukrainian newspaper *For Return to the Motherland*.[150] The Committee was established by Soviet intelligence organs (the MGB) to lure or kidnap former Soviet citizens living in Europe who did not wish to return to the Soviet Union.[151] Needless to say, they were doomed to end up as prisoners in the Soviet Gulag upon their return to the USSR. An ideologically reliable Soviet citizen and a famous Ukrainian writer who in 1951 was awarded the Stalin Prize for his *Bukovyna Novels*, he was a perfect candidate for this position.

After completing his assignment in the late 1950s, Muratov returned to Ukraine as a new person. Possibly, the diagnosis of cancer liberated him from fear and ideological constraints. The aesthetics of his poetry, as well as his social and political behavior, honest and principled, were inconvenient for the authorities.[152] His fellow writers remembered how *Prapor* was pressured by the *obkom* to reject Lina Kostenko's poem "Berestechko" and how Muratov wholeheartedly fought for it to be published.[153] His self-discipline and broad intellectual horizons were legendary, and what Muratov should be remembered for is what he wrote during the last ten years of his life—poetry, novels, plays, and critical essays. He strove for philosophical and intellectual depth in his works, no matter what genre he was writing in.[154] His tragic war experiences and constant intellectual labor shaped him as a professional subtle writer who had never repeated himself either in his poetry or in his prose.[155]

His poetry was "galactic," his critical essays were original and sophisticated, and his public speaking skills were unique and legendary.[156] In 1971, Muratov published his "Brocken," alluding to the Holocaust tragedy:

Oh, my kind guides, Faust's grandchildren,
Take me to the observation towers,
And help me live in a fairy tale,
So that I forget about Ravensbrück's gas chambers
And Dachau's hand-made wires.[157]

Yet his poem about Stalin written on 24 October 1954, was published only in 2012, almost forty years after Muratov's death:

The dictator could live
Until he was a hundred years old,
As his blinded children-lambs were wishing him,
The slaves, kneeling in the darkness.
While one was waiting secretly for his death,
The dictator might not have died,
And might have finished his devilish farce
To turn our prison into a paradise.
The cut off heads could still be
Displayed on the tower bells,
When the only savior was
A hundred-faced death . . .
But everyone is silent.[158]

Being of Jewish origin, Muratov chose to write in Ukrainian and to support the talented Ukrainian and Jewish youth in an anti-Ukrainian and anti-Jewish space, a courageous path for a man whose spirit was liberated by his knowledge about the little time that was left for him on earth. Although he planned every day to the last second, he was generous with his time with everyone who reached out to him for help and advice. A brilliant conversationalist, he was humble and elegant, never condescendingly bragging about his fluency in four languages.

For Kharkiv writers, Muratov set an example of professionalism and humanity, and their friendships seemed to blossom precisely out of the diversity of their community—differences in their ethnic and social backgrounds, cultural gravitations, bilingualism, and trilingualism. They shared the existential feeling of togetherness that was so much needed in the space of terror and state violence. Governed by antisemitic and anti-Ukrainian Communist Party bosses, Kharkiv of the "cursed seventies" taught them to appreciate "literary brotherhood, talent, and professional competence."[159] The affiliation with the Writers' Union was not what Briuggen meant by brotherhood. The elitist club had many extremely gifted writers who elevated the standards of literary product for others. Most belonged to the Kharkiv prewar generation (Muratov, Ivan Vyrhan, Ivan Bahmut, Yurii Shovkoplias), and the caliber of their intelligence and literary gift was indisputable. Their reputation, "organic culture, intelligence, and talent" left minimal room for moral compromise for others,[160] and thus not ethnic solidarity but principles and respect for the literary gift shaped the writers' behavior and the ways they voted at the Union's meetings. At the root of these practices was brotherhood, nurtured by their commitment to literature.

The writers felt privileged to learn and to advance their skills in the company of the best, regardless of their cultural backgrounds. They instantly diagnosed graphomaniacs and developed a subtle understanding and appreciation of rare talents. In 1962, the Ukrainian poet Vasyl Mysyk published a new volume of his poems entitled *Borozny* (The Grooves). It became clear to all members that Mysyk's book was an outstanding literary phenomenon that deserved to be nominated for Ukraine's highest literary award—the Shevchenko Award. The literary critic of Jewish descent Grigorii Geldfandbein enthusiastically supported the nomination, suggesting that Mysyk's poetry was innovative, powerfully metaphoric, humanistic, and subtle.[161] The Shevchenko Committee granted the 1963 award posthumously to a former Kharkivite, the Lviv prose writer Hryhorii Tiutiunnyk for his novel *Vyr*, but the unanimous support of Ukrainians, Jews, and Russians for Mysyk's nomination is telling.[162] The appreciation of literature rose above possible ethnic pride or cultural affinities.

David Vishnevskii's case, reflected in the minutes of the Writers' Union meetings, appears to be rare. A discussion of his new book entitled *The 72nd Day* (*72-i den*) turned into a 4-hour battle at the prose section meeting. The members were divided along ethnic lines on whether the book deserved to be nominated for the Lenin Award, which was no less prestigious than the Shevchenko Award. Writers of Jewish descent argued that the novel was excellent while Ukrainian writers believed its literary value was modest. Yet the majority were adamant: the book seemed weak and did not deserve the nomination. Vishnevskii realized that he had overestimated the value of his novel and withdrew his self-nomination for this award.[163]

The writers, however, exhibited astonishing unity in their responses to graphomaniacs, regardless of their cultural identity, who routinely showed up at the Union's headquarters to corner the members and read their work to them. The members collectively hid from "prodigies," and their schemes of escape were strategically planned in advance. Assisted by his colleagues, the head of *Prapor*'s poetry section Tretyakov and the head of the criticism section Briuggen habitually escaped from a group of graphomaniacs who were determined to conquer this invincible fortress, the Parnassus, and to persuade them to publish their works.[164]

Despite the KGB's persistent efforts to provoke hostilities between Ukrainians and Jews, the protocols of the Union reveal no signs of antisemitism or discrimination against Jews. Along with Ukrainians and Russians, they chaired various thematic commissions and committees and were provided opportunities to take advantage of financial opportunities available in the Litfond for research purposes and for vacations that the writers typically used for completing a new book.[165] The writers were generously rewarded for reading poetry before large audiences, including those at Kharkiv factories. From the Soviet point of view, their compensation for one concert (7–8 rubles) was a rare opportunity to earn additional income. Monetarily, two concerts often given by writers in one day provided 15–20 percent of the monthly salary of a Soviet white-collar worker. The writers created teams and preferred to travel to factories in groups. Drained emotionally, they typically celebrated together, relaxing after such concerts. The groups were ethnically mixed. Personal affinities and friendships played a huge role in these arrangements, and the Union's secretary Olena Lukashova scheduled these trips according to the writers' requests. For instance, Aleksandr Kravtsov enjoyed the company of Geldfandbein, Tretyakov preferred to join Zelman Kats and Leonid Osmolovskyi, and Yurii Barabash traveled with Lev Galkin.[166]

Ethnic origin meant little in the hierarchy of the writers' values. But the absence of literary gift or basic humanity provoked tensions in the community, as Kravtsov's case demonstrates. Kravtsov was despised by many, and apparently Gelfandbein was the only person who could somewhat tolerate him. On several occasions, Kravtsov became the main point of discussion at the Writers' Union meetings. His graphomaniac poetry was appreciated by few. Worse, Kravtsov, out of professional jealousy of his talented colleagues, slandered many, spreading insinuations about anti-Soviet and immoral poems allegedly written by some members of the Union. Eventually, Kravtsov's antisemitic rants put an end to the Union administration's patience. Kravtsov was reprimanded for his black deeds and was obliged to publish an apology in the local press to all he had offended.[167] Moreover, Kravtsov's case illuminated the writers' small victory over the KGB. According to some testimonies, Kravtsov had close connections with this powerful agency, and the writers' solid unity and intransigence toward Kravtsov's boorishness and poetic mediocrity was a personal insult to his supervisors. Kravtsov's apologies were accepted but his humiliation was forgotten neither by Kravtsov, nor by the KGB.[168]

Roman Levin (b. 1939) and Vadim Levin (b. 1933), two poets of Jewish descent, exemplified the writers' gravitation toward and support for literary talent, cases where considerations of ethnic solidarity were not part of the equation. Roman was a writer with modest literary talent; Vadim established a reputation as an extremely gifted poet and thinker, writing poems for children that are read as philosophical parables and are much appreciated by adults.[169] Roman was systematically criticized for his mediocre work and "long speeches about nothing" at Writers' Union meetings.[170] In contrast, Vadim was praised for his subtle ironic poetry and protected by his talented colleagues from unsubstantiated attacks. For instance, at the 23 January 1961 Writers' Union meeting, Tretyakov appealed to some individuals in the older generation of Ukrainian writers who doubted Vadim's ability to grow into a serious writer. These members even questioned Vadim's maturity, and his ability to read his work before large audiences, let alone his qualifications to be a member of the Union: "What kind of poetry can a person write without life experience?" Tretyakov mocked this sort of logic, claiming that age never defined the artistic and intellectual magnitude of poetry: "[Vadim] Levin is thirty-years-old . . . and it would be incorrect to think that he cannot write something [that you want him to write] because he is not yet fifty."[171] Aleksandr Cherevchenko, a young poet of Ukrainian background writing in Russian, was a vivid example of Tretyakov's argument: in 1967, endorsed by the Union for his literary talent, Cherevchenko received the prestigious Lenin Komsomol Award, becoming a leading journalist (*spetskor*) of the Kyiv newspaper *Pravda Ukrainy* (its Kharkiv chapter), an important outlet at the time. He was only twenty-six years old.[172]

The absence of major quarrels and antisemitism among the Kharkiv literati that the KGB tried to provoke through the assistance of people like Kravtsov made the Kharkiv KGB worry that they did not follow the party line, lagging behind Kyiv. Prominent victims of state antisemitic and anti-Zionist campaigns in Kyiv that gained widespread popular support in Ukraine were Leonid Pervomaiskyi, Savva Holovanivskyi, and Illia Stebun.[173] To instigate a rift between Ukrainians and Jews in the Kharkiv Writers' Union, the KGB spread rumors that ethnic Jews voted for excluding Vasyl Bondar, an ethnic Ukrainian, from the Union at the April 1961 meeting. A former DP, Bondar, who had no prospects for publishing his work and had family problems, got progressively worse. He was rarely seen sober, ultimately frightening the Union's administration who could be accused of violations of party discipline. In the party's eyes, the Union's leadership were responsible for the morale of their colleagues. Pressured by the *obkom* to expel Bondar from the Union, Muratov, the Union's chief secretary at the time, found a compromise, suggesting that Bondar should be expelled from the Union only for a year and agree to check into a rehabilitation clinic. Kats supported Muratov's proposition. Two highly regarded members of the Union, the Ukrainian writers Ivan Vyrhan and Vasyl Mysyk interceded on Bondar's behalf, asking the Union to grant Bondar another chance. The majority of the members supported Vyrhan's and Mysyk's request. The Union's resolution even included a clause obliging the Litfond to finance Bondar's retreat at a rehabilitation clinic.[174] The tone of speeches given at the meeting suggests that all members, irrespective of their status and ethnicity, sincerely sympathized with Bondar's problems and genuinely wanted to help. They respected and admired Bondar's literary gift, and difficulty in publishing was familiar to most writers.[175]

KGB backroom schemes and *obkom* officials' personal attitudes toward the Jews drastically differed from the official Communist Party position of internationalism and "brotherly friendship among all nationalities." The most notorious case was the harassment of Vishnevskii whose work was viciously criticized by party functionaries. In 1977, the first secretary of the Kharkiv *obkom* Mykola Antonovych Siroshtan accused Vishnevskii of tarnishing the heroism of Soviet soldiers during the Second World War in his new novel. Siroshtan suggested that for Vishnevskii Leonid Brezhnev's memoirs *Malaia Zemlia* (The Small Land) should have served as an example of literary excellence and historical truth with which Vishnevskii was supposed to align his novel. Vishnevskii constantly redrafted the text but Siroshtan was adamant: "It won't fly."[176] Kharkiv's suffocating atmosphere of the 1970s was unkind not only to Jews. Control and persecution constrained the creativity of all writers and, beyond alcoholism and conformism, it propelled a chain of suicides and mysterious deaths. Among them were the tragedies experienced by Bondar, Shumytskyi, Ukrainian prose writer and a graduate of Kharkiv University Hryhir Tiutiunnyk, and the satire writer Osmolovskyi.[177]

Figure 2.4 Lev Galkin (In the Middle) with Ivan Bahmut (On the Left) and Yurii Shovkoplias (On the Right). *Source*: RTPA; a copy is located in TsDAMLIMU, f. 783, op. 1, spr. 24, ark. 7.

Officially, the party supported Jews, approving their leading positions in the Writers' Union, newspapers, and primary party cells of cultural institutions. For instance, in the 1960s Galkin was the trusted assistant of the secretary of the Union's primary party cell, a *nomenklatura* appointment made by the Kharkiv *obkom* (Fig. 2.4).[178] Geldfandbein led one of the largest literary studios in Kharkiv despite his past. After the Second World War, he was chastised for "cosmopolitanism," falling out of the Communist Party's favor because of his panegyrics to Leonid Pasternak and Anna Akhmatova. His literary studio was founded under the umbrella of the Writers' Union and located at the Kharkiv factory "Serp i Molot" (Hammer and Sickle).[179] For decades, Geldfandbein was also the chief editor of the Kharkiv newspaper *Krasnoie znamia* (The Red Banner). Yet to break friendly relationships among the members of the Union and disrupt their unity, the Jews were badmouthed before the Ukrainians and vice versa in the KGB and party headquarters.

High posts in the Writers' Union came not only with privileges but with great responsibilities of ideological flexibility. The political maneuvers of Boris Kotliarov, who in the 1960s was the secretary of the Union's primary party cell, were shameful. At a meeting at one of the Kharkiv factories, he explained the Communist Party's critique of Yevtushenko's poem "Babii Yar" to the audience as follows: "Friends, please understand, we all sympathize with Jews who were killed by the fascists. But according to Yevtushenko, the fascists killed only them [the Jews], and this is not true."[180] Kotliarov knew that Yevtushenko's poem denounced a very specific kind of killing—genocide, and an enduring tradition of state antisemitism that denied a monument to the victims of this genocide at Babii Yar. Yet Kotliarov chose to follow the party's talking points and accused Yevtushenko of political shortsightedness.

The extent of antisemitism among the literati in Kharkiv was incomparable with that in Moscow, Kyiv, or Lviv.[181] Nevertheless, those few members of the Union in Kharkiv who were insensitive toward the Jews made some young writers of Jewish descent feel vulnerable. This feeling was exacerbated by Khrushchev's antireligious campaign and the assault on Judaism.[182] Many of them were Chichibabin's students, members of his literary studio.

New Pathways for "Young Zionists"

Young Jewish literati searched other ways to get through the labyrinth of Kharkiv politics. Most of them were Chichibabin's students. Carefully watched by the KGB, the Kharkiv Puppet Theater was a workplace for two of them who graduated from the Philological Department of Kharkiv State University, Vitalii Svirskii and Yurii Miloslavskii. Due to Svirskii who stayed in Kharkiv, this theater remained the mecca for all Kharkiv literati to the very end of the USSR.

According to the writer Raisa Beliaieva (Gurina), Miloslavskii was a noticeable figure among Kharkiv writers and the leader of "Europeanized boys," very well educated, talented, and flamboyant individuals.[183] Limonov remembered that most members of Miloslavskii's circle were Jewish literati who were jokingly referred to as "Zionists." Arkadii Filatov and other Kharkiv writers routinely greeted them: "Hello, Zionists! How are you?"[184] More frequently than others, "Zionists" gathered near a little fountain in the Park of Victory in Sumska Street, where they read their poetry and discussed new trends in literature. They were unforgivably young for their remarkable literary talent that was greatly appreciated by Chichibabin. They attended his literary studio which was also quite popular among official writers, *shistdesiatnyky*, who were already members of the Writers' Union. Among frequent guests of Chichibabin's studio were Aleksandr Cherevchenko, an ethnic Ukrainian writing in Russian and Tretyakov, an ethnic Russian writing in Ukrainian. The two closely communicated with "Zionists," and Chichibabin's studio was a place of intellectual exchange where enduring friendships and links emerged.

Miloslavskii was one of the most remarkable students of Chichibabin, yet his studio produced other gifted poets who ended up in Israel, the United States, and Germany. Located in the heart of Kharkiv, in the Palace of Culture affiliated with the workers' union of communication and highways (*DK rabotnikov sviazi i avtoshoseinykh dorog*), Chichibabin's literary studio existed only two years, from 1964 to 1966, but it became a gathering place and a playground for the most promising and rebellious poets, a factor that played a role in the studio's closure. Importantly, Chichibabin's discussions of Marina Tsvetaieva's and Boris Pasternak's poetry at the studio's sessions contributed to the authorities' frustration with the leader, and in 1966 they closed the studio.[185]

Yet beyond Chichibabin's profound influence, the Kharkiv Jews were exposed to the stories of the older generation of returnees who awakened the young literati's interest in their culture and history.[186] Because of the returnees' revelations about Stalin's brutalities, the faith of Chichibabin's literary students in socialism and communism disappeared almost entirely.[187] At the very least, it was seriously undermined and tarnished. In the 1960s, on his visit to Kharkiv (in the late 1950s, he moved to Moscow), the former Kharkivite, artist, and a son of the writer of Jewish descent Rafail Brusilovskii, Anatolii Brusilovskii sensed immediately that there was a "complex, developed, and intellectual environment" in Kharkiv.[188] Most did not actively oppose the Soviet regime, but they did create non-Soviet literature, although not fully aware of it. Several decades later, Brusilovskii wrote about *shistdesiatnyky*—his generation of writers and artists—in this fashion: "One should not identify them as heroes—they did not fight; they did not scream. . . . Often they were very scared when the flames licked their heels. They did not always understand what they did, what they achieved. Their goals were not always clear. . . . These blessed people were not eager to decipher either the surroundings or the future. Some other passion possessed them—they were Artists."[189] They just lived in the space of poetry and creativity, committing their whole beings, minds, and bodies to them. Being *shistdesiatnyky* in the 1960s, they were uncertain of who they were. Their identity was undetermined and fluid, and they could not imagine then that in the future their voices and art would contribute greatly to Russian, Ukrainian, Jewish, and world literature and art.

Kharkiv also produced tandems such as Miloslavskii and Konstantin Skoblinskii who, coping with re-Stalinization and "dying from laughter" in 1966–1967, produced short kitsch stories and fairy tales filled with black humor, vulgarity, and profanity.[190] Another Jewish tandem was established in the early 1960s when Leonid Osmolovskyi and Arkadii Inin published short satirical stories, brilliant and subtle. The tandem seemed to be stable and productive until the moment Inin escaped to Moscow, leaving his much more gifted coauthor behind. Chichibabin's students who in the 1970s and 1980s emigrated to Israel and Germany, Kharkiv poets Aleksandr Vernik, Eduard Siganevich, and Genrikh Shmerkin (he joined their group later) also became part of the Kharkiv Jewish elite, shaping the unforgettable literary Kharkiv of the 1960s and being shaped as poets by the quality time spent with people like Chichibabin, Rakhlina, Briuggen, Tretyakov, and Muratov.[191]

Interestingly enough, the friendships of these individuals were formed in their childhood. For instance, Shmerkin began his "literary career" at the age of nine in the company of the future poets Olga Landman, Siganevich, and the prose writer Nelli Epelman-Sterkis. They all attended a literary studio (*kruzhok*) in the Kharkiv Palace of Pioneers led by Kats. Kats, however, was soon fired for his gravitation toward the pessimistic poetry of Sergei Yesenin and Aleksandr Blok. Katz was replaced by the Jewish historian and literati Yurii Finkelshtein but for unknown reasons he did not keep the job. The same fate awaited the journalist Valentina Yezhenkova who replaced Finkelshtein. Vernik and Miloslavskii joined the *kruzhok* under her leadership. Yet Yezhenkova's independent critical thinking skills became a problem for the Palace's administration: at the end of the Khrushchev Thaw, she was dismissed for immoral behavior. The writer Vadim Levin, Hana Levina's nephew, took over and continued to raise and nurture new literary talents. Within a decade they all became part of Kharkiv's diverse literary community.[192] In several decades Vladimir Maksimov, Russian writer and chief editor of the journal *Kontinent* who in 1974 left the USSR for Paris and was stripped of Soviet citizenship, suggested that the entire Russian émigré literature was sustained due to three people—Miloslavskii, Vasilii Aksionov, and Limonov.[193] Two of them were ex-Kharkivites.[194]

Beyond state antisemitism and censorship, however, there was a combination of factors that awakened nationalism and ethnic pride among Kharkiv "Zionists." The post–Israeli Six-Day War spirit inspired Yasha Kazakov, a twenty-year-old Moscow university student, to publicly renounce his Soviet citizenship on 13 June 1967, and the next summer Soviet tanks invaded Czechoslovakia to curtail the Prague Spring.[195] The true character of Khrushchev's reforms was exposed, and the "Zionists" began to seriously think about emigration. Marlena Rakhlina's brother Feliks, who was part of Chichibabin's circle, attempted to explain this phenomenon by the emergence of double identities among his friends: many Jewish literati vacillated between two identities—of an "assimilated Russian Jew" and an "authentic" Jew. The former kept them in beloved "Russia" and the latter called them to leave for their "historical Motherland."[196]

Their inner transformations were exacerbated by renewed KGB repressions against human rights activists and Ukrainian intellectuals. Discussions about the Holocaust and Soviet antisemitism contributed to the "ethnicization" of consciousness among Jewish intellectuals. Re-Stalinization of the Soviet system intensified their fears of potential repetition of the tragedies, such as Stalin's anti-Jewish terror and the Holocaust.[197] Intellectually and emotionally, the majority no longer supported the Soviet regime, gravitating instead toward dissent and opposition.[198] Sovietized and Russified, the Jewish intelligentsia felt a pressing need to return to their cultural roots and to acquire individual and collective stability in a democratic state. Neither the Soviet Union nor Ukraine could offer it, but Israel could. These perceptions were especially noticeable among Chichibabin's students, young poets of Jewish descent whose prospects to be productive and to be published in Ukraine were murky.

Knowledge about the Holocaust and the Soviets' role in it through the Molotov-Ribbentrop Pact strengthened their faith in Zionism. They realized that just a few celebrities, such as Yevtushenko and Andrei Voznesenskii, were allowed to publish anything about this. In 1965, Voznesenskii wrote a poem "Zov ozera" (The Call of the Lake). He was devastated by the discovery that Vladimir Kostrov and he were fishing in the lake near Stanislaviv (today Ivano-Frankivsk, Ukraine) which was created by the Soviets on the spot where the Nazis exterminated the Jewish ghetto, barely covering the corpses with soil.[199] Young Kharkivites understood very well that Kharkiv censors would bury their texts before they saw the light of day.

Miloslavskii and others always felt the support of Chichibabin, whose Jewdophilia and internationalism in a true humanistic sense bled through his poetic lines:

While antisemitic cretins
And state boors, groomed like khans,
Are still around, incessantly lying,
While a briber is arrogant
And bureaucrat is joyful,
While the denouncer is waiting for his prey,
Stalin has not died yet.[200]

The vulgarity of Soviet definitions of internationalism and antisemitism was organically disgusting to Chichibabin. A Russian poet living in Ukraine, he felt the pain of all nationalities, Jews, Crimean Tatars, Lithuanians, and Armenians. His strong anti-antisemitic stance, support for Ukrainian dissidents, and condemnation of Russian chauvinism permeate many of his poems. His Jewish friends, colleagues, and students highly regarded his civic position, celebrating it in their memoirs.[201] Because of Chichibabin's affinity with Jews, his Jewish students gave him two nicknames—Chichman and Chichibabel.[202] Miloslavskii's friend who occasionally attended Chichibabin's studio sessions, Limonov, was convinced that his cultural and literary development, including his miraculous transformation from a worker and a criminal into a poet, was nurtured by and occurred because of Jewish "surroundings," the Jews' creativity, and the Jewish family of which he was part.[203]

The continuity and distribution of knowledge about the horrors of Nazism and the Holocaust occurred through people like the Russian Chichibabin and the Ukrainian Bondar, and the ethnicity of the narrators mattered little for Jewish listeners. Later Limonov confirmed that these themes were vigorously discussed by the Kharkiv literati. They were aware of the horrific scene in the center of Kharkiv liberated from the Nazis in August 1943: retreating, the Nazi troops hung a Jew on each tree of Kharkiv's central streets, a site that was witnessed by the local population and the Soviet troops that liberated the city.[204]

Kharkiv's tragic past, frightening present, and murky future created a supra-ethnic community of intellectuals who reached out to each other for professional advice, support, and protection. The older generation of Kharkiv literati celebrated the success of the beginners, regardless of their ethnicity, learning of them and from them. Several times Muratov recommended the Union grant the brilliant Rakhlina membership. Together with Gelfandbein and the poet Mark Cherniakov, Muratov immediately sensed the emergence of an extremely gifted poet and praised her at every opportunity.[205] Galkin and Kats enthusiastically welcomed Tretyakov to the Kharkiv chapter, who at the age of twenty-two became a Kyiv celebrity, a journalist, and a sixtier, willing to relocate to Kharkiv after graduating from the Shevchenko State University in Kyiv.[206] Jews fell in love with Ukrainians and Russians, and vice versa. The Ukrainian poet Yurii Gerasimenko fell in love with Rakhlina and, trying to win her heart, was bringing her huge bouquets of fresh lilac.[207] The Russian Limonov had a lasting relationship with the Jewish artist Anna Rubinshtein, and Chichibabin married the Jewish poet, an attendee of his literary studio, Lilia Karas. These personal relationships help us recognize that the Kharkiv space of the Khrushchev era was not only multiethnic but also multidimensional, where Gaston Bachelard's metaphor, the "poetics of space," gains real romantic and historical contours, revealing the nexus of people's identities—cultural, political, ethnic, and intimate.[208]

The cynicism of the re-Stalinization period that began in 1958 changed this space, uniting ethnically and culturally the Writers' Union and the informal community of the Kharkiv literati. During the subsequent three decades, Kharkiv also lost Yurii Barabash, Zinovii Valshonok, and Arkadii Inin to Moscow; Zelman Kats, Aleksandr Vernik, and Irina Ruvinskaia to Israel; Yurii Mislavskii and Nelli Epelman-Sterkis to the United States; and Genrikh Shmerkin to Germany. Limonov also left Kharkiv, and his spatial and ideological zigzags remained unpredictable and striking for the rest of his life.

Bewildered, the Kharkiv *shistdesiatnyky* observed how, with one hand and with unmatched alacrity, Khrushchev and Shelest rehabilitated the victims of Stalin's terror, and with the other they tried to obscure the reasons for why these victims found themselves in the Gulag in the first place. They failed to clearly formulate their attitudes toward Stalin's hangmen and Stalin's state antisemitism, and to remediate the trauma experienced by the Jewish community during the Holocaust and Stalin's postwar anti-Jewish campaign. In Ukraine, as in the entire Soviet Union, Jews continued to suffer from discriminatory practices in educational and cultural spheres. Constantly maneuvering between the centrist and anti-centrist political discourses, Shelest sent contradictory messages to both Ukrainians and Jews.[209] It was Shelest who, living in fear because of the increasing pressure from the center, particularly from Suslov's apparatus, called the KGB to act decisively and to curtail the protest movement, eliminating the "unhealthy manifestations" and nationalism in society.[210] Ukraine's KGB and its head Vitalii Nikitchenko responded to Shelest's call with persecution and arrests of the most active part of Ukraine's intelligentsia.[211] Vitalii Fedorchuk, who in 1970 replaced Nikitchenko as the head of Ukraine's KGB, launched a new wave of repression against writers and dissidents, cleansing the republic of many Ukrainian and Jewish nationalists. Shelest actively supported it, as he correctly suspected that Fedorchuk was dispatched to Kyiv by Brezhnev to prepare the grounds for Shelest's soft removal.

Shortly before Shelest's dismissal, at the 30 March 1972 meeting of the Politburo of TsK KPSS in Moscow, he suggested limiting the entry of foreign tourists into the USSR, the freedom of telephone conversations between Soviet citizens and their relatives abroad, and Jewish emigration to Israel.[212] But this did not help Shelest keep his position. On 10 May 1972, he was dismissed as the First Secretary of the TsK KPU and appointed the Deputy of the Head of the Council of Ministers of the USSR. By April 1973, he was stripped of his membership in the Politburo of the TsK KPSS and granted honorable retirement "due to his poor health." In Brezhnev's view, Shelest exacerbated the nationalist tendencies in Ukraine, where Ukrainian nationalists, Zionists, and dissidents of all types established a solid anti-Soviet network, even reaching out to their counterparts abroad.[213]

When placing Shelest in the context of Brezhnev's clandestine disinformation campaign designed to undermine Shelest's reputation and eventually remove him from his position, it is worthwhile remembering that these sorts of campaigns had been employed by the Soviet secret police since its inception. Before Shelest's dismissal, the KGB prepared defamatory reports about him. Moreover, in March and May 1972, the KGB organized two pogroms against Jews in the vicinity of the Kyiv synagogue, simultaneously spreading rumors that the pogroms were masterminded by Shelest personally.[214] The antisemitic and pro-Ukrainian nationalist Shelest was an excellent justification and excuse for change in Ukraine. One might argue that he was more preoccupied with the growing Ukrainian nationalist movement in the republic rather than with Jewish concerns or Jewish literary dynamics, and there is plenty of evidence to support this thesis. However, in contrast to the extremes of Stalin's politics and his institutionalized anti-Jewish violence that left little or no space at all for many Jewish writers to continue, Shelest's ideological oscillations and power calculations created a breathable space for Ukraine's Jewish intellectuals, "a space of controlled freedom."

In fact, the sense of a new space that emerged under Shelest, at times dangerous, at times tranquil, encouraged Jewish *shistdesiatnytstvo* to persist. In 2009, at the meeting in Kharkiv commemorating the forty-fifth anniversary of Chichibabin's literary studio, Yurii Miloslavskii noted that the 1960s was a remarkable time in Kharkiv when there were so many literary studios led by extraordinary writers, such as Zelman Kats, Grigorii Gelfandbein, Roman Levin, Boris Kotliarov, and Revolt Bunchukov, and everyone could attend their sessions.[215] The Jewish youth were thirsty for creative authentic voices and for the truth about their own culture and history. The late Russian historian, former Soviet Jewish dissident, and a cofounder of the Memorial Arsenii Roginskii has argued that in the 1960s something extraordinary happened in the Soviet Union when people, eager for creativity and truth, immediately occupied a tiny space of freedom which emerged because of the Thaw: "We always had a feeling that we were robbed of our past (in fact, we lived with this feeling for years that our past was stolen from us) but we realized that we are also being robbed of our future."[216]

In 1960, at one of the first large public meetings with his audience in Kharkiv, Boris Slutskii, Russian poet of Jewish origin, stated that the intelligentsia and books guided his life as a poet. For him, his country was good enough, as long as books there were sold cheaper than tobacco or bread.[217] During the Khrushchev Thaw, the intelligentsia who traditionally struggled for personal and political liberty seemed to officially regain their freedom, inviting people like Slutskii and millions of other Soviet citizens to write and enjoy new "brave" books and poetry, and to celebrate the creativity of the human mind.[218] This intellectual journey was a path to internal, if not political, liberty and free thinking. Subsequently, the Six-Day War and the authorities' hostile attitudes toward Jews complicated the matter. The Six-Day War had a dual influence on the Jewish literati: it revived their national consciousness and fanned the fervor of Zionism. They no longer felt like Slutskii. They were looking for a way out. To prevent massive Jewish emigration, nationalism, and dissent, Shelest, unsure of his position's stability, advocated harsher emigration and surveillance policies, which ultimately amplified discriminatory practices of Soviet authorities against Jews. Nevertheless, Brezhnev's covert re-Stalinization and the KGB's renewed terror against Zionists did not paralyze the Jewish literati because of the support of people like Muratov, Chichibabin, Tretyakov, Polonskyi, and Cherevchenko. Many remained sufficiently productive and even joined the ranks of Ukraine's dissidents.

Importantly, the Thaw and de-Stalinization provoked a cultural and political upheaval among Ukrainian and Russian intellectuals, facilitating the rapprochement of Ukrainians and Jews and fundamentally changing the psyche of both communities. As Briuggen has stated, the Thaw seemed to liberate many from the gravity of their own stereotypes and myopic views about cultures other than their own.[219] Moreover, the revival of distinct Jewish themes in literary works in the 1960s, regardless of the language in which they had been written, won their authors enormous popularity among highly urbanized Jews, also reaching out to Ukrainian and Russian readers in their own languages.[220] For the first time they realized that Ukraine was also Jewish, not only Ukrainian or Russian. Yurii Vlodov, Russian Jewish poet born in Kharkiv, has argued that

> an ethnic Armenian, a Jew, or a Tatar, who writes in Russian, will nevertheless remain an Armenian, a Jewish, or a Tatar poet, even if he does not know the language of his ancestors. Because in his genes and poetic mentality, [sustained by suppressed but still distinct family memories and traditions] he remains Armenian, Jewish, or Tatar. Similarly, an ethnic Russian will not become a Jew, if he is relocated to Israel and begins to write in Hebrew.[221]

Vlodov's ruminations and his poetic vision are certainly debatable but what should be added to this equation is the emergent space and place where the talent of Ukrainian-Jewish literati was nurtured and matured. The discrepancy between Soviet ideology and realities fundamentally distorted the moral and aesthetic values of many. At the same time, the place of violence, fear, and antisemitism made the Kharkiv Jewish literati rediscover their Jewishness, although remaining supra-nationalists and humanists. Their humanism grew out of literary studios and teachings of people like Chichibabin who developed in them a love for poetry and a special emotional attachment to multiethnic and multicultural Ukraine where one could write for Jews, Russians, Ukrainians—for people. Interestingly enough, from the early 1960s to the early 1970s when Ukraine experienced three sensational waves of repression against its intellectuals (1964–1965, 1968–1969, and 1972–1973), the Jewish literati reached broader audiences in a variety of ways, from publications in newspapers and journals to public readings of their work. They were people who were writing for people, trying to grasp the meaning of violence, life, and death and to confront their individual labyrinths, having experienced it all and having survived even after their death, through their writings and intellectual legacies.

NOTES

1. Shelest served in this position from 1963 to 1972.
2. Serhy Yekelchyk, *Stalin's Empire of Memory: Russian-Ukrainian Relations in the Soviet Historical Imagination* (Toronto: University of Toronto Press, 2004), 160–61.
3. John O'Donohue, The official site of John O'Donohue, 2020, https://www.johnodonohue.com/works (accessed 1 August 2020).
4. Ibid.
5. Kenneth C. Farmer, *Ukrainian Nationalism in the Post-Stalin Era* (The Hague/Boston/London: Martinus Nijhoff Publishers, 1980), 202.
6. See Shelest's speech in *Radianska Ukraina*, 1 April 1971. Also quoted in Farmer, *Ukrainian Nationalism*, 203.
7. On national communism in Ukraine during the interwar period, see James E. Mace, *Communism and the Dilemmas of National Liberation: National Communism in Soviet Ukraine, 1918–1933* (Cambridge, MA: Harvard University Press, 1983).
8. Ivan Lysiak-Rudnytskyi, "Politychna dumka ukrainskykh pidradianskykh dysydentiv" in *Istorychni ese*, vol. 2 (Kyiv: Osnovy, 1994), 477; William Henry Chamberlin, *The Ukraine: A Submerged Nation* (New York: The Macmillan Company, 1944), 84.
9. Benjamin Tromly, "An Unlikely National Revival: Soviet Higher Learning and the Ukrainian 'Sixtiers,' 1953–65," *Russian Review* 68, no. 4 (2009): 607–22. For a review of various definitions of *shistdesiatnytstvo*, see Serhy Yekelchyk, "The Early 1960s as a Cultural Space: A Microhistory of Ukraine's Generation of Cultural

Rebels," *Nationalities Papers: The Journal of Nationalism and Ethnicity* 43, no. 1 (2015): 45–46.

10. Yohanan Petrovsky-Shtern, "Reconceptualizing the Alien: Jews in Modern Ukrainian Thought," *Ab Imperio* 4 (2003): 557.

11. See Vasilii Aksionov's account in *Shestidesiatniki*, ed. M. Barbakadze (Moskva: Fond "Liberalnaia missiia," 2007), 53.

12. Ivan Maistrenko, *Natsionalnaia politika KPSS* (Munich: Suchasnist, 1978), 199.

13. Michael T. Westrate, *Living Soviet in Ukraine from Stalin to Maidan: Under the Falling Red Star in Kharkiv* (Lanham/Boulder/New York/London, 2016), 78–80.

14. Ibid., 79–80.

15. On the tragic fate of Jewish culture and the Jewish intelligentsia, see Gennady Estraikh, *In Harness: Yiddish Writers' Romance with Communism* (Syracuse, NY: Syracuse University Press, 2005); Gennady Estraikh, *Yiddish in the Cold War* (London: Legenda, 2008), 13–14; Gennady Estraikh, "The Yiddish Kultur-Lige," in *Modernism in Kyiv: Jubilant Experimentation*, eds. Irena R. Makaryk and Virlana Tkacz (Toronto: University of Toronto Press, 2010), 210–12; on Stalin's terror against Ukrainian intellectuals, see Myroslav Shkandrij and Olga Bertelsen, "The Soviet Regime's National Operations in Ukraine, 1929–1934," *Canadian Slavonic Papers* LV 3–4 (2013): 417–47; Olga Bertelsen and Myroslav Shkandrij, "The Secret Police and the Campaign against Galicians in Soviet Ukraine, 1929–34," *Nationalities Papers: The Journal of Nationalism and Ethnicity* 42, no. 1 (2014): 37–62; Olga Bertelsen, "The House of Writers in Ukraine, the 1930s: Conceived, Lived, Perceived," *Carl Beck Papers* 2302 (August 2013): 4–72.

16. Miriam Dobson, *Khrushchev's Cold Summer: Gulag Returnees, Crime, and the Fate of Reforms after Stalin* (Ithaca and London: Cornell University Press, 2009), 200, 207; Vladislav Zubok, *Zhivago's Children: The Last Russian Intelligentsia* (Cambridge, MA: The Belknap Press of Harvard University Press, 2009), 230.

17. Yevtushenko's poem "Babii Yar" condemned the 29–30 September 1941, Kyiv massacre at a place where 33,771 Jews were killed by the Nazis. Khrushchev, however, criticized it, arguing that Jews were not the only victims of the Babii Yar massacre. See "Full Story of Massacre of Jews at Babi Yar Told by Soviet Writer," *Jewish Telegraphic Agency: Daily News Bulletin* XXXIII, no. 164, 26 August 1966, p. 2.

18. On Romm's speech at the November 1962 conference on the art of socialist realism, see Zubok, *Zhivago's Children*, 235; Ivan Dziuba, *Internationalism or Russification? A Study in the Soviet Nationalities Problem*, 2nd ed. (London: Weidenfeld and Nicolson, 1970), 49–50; Petrovsky-Shtern, "Reconceptualizing the Alien," 554–56; Myroslav Shkandrij, *Jews in Ukrainian Literature: Representation and Identity* (New Haven and London, Yale University Press, 2009), 197.

19. Gennady Estraikh, "Literature versus Territory: Soviet Jewish Cultural Life in the 1950s," *East European Jewish Affairs* 33, no. 1 (2008): 41; Judith Deutsch Kornblatt, *Doubly Chosen: Jewish Identity, the Soviet Intelligentsia, and the Russian Orthodox Church* (Madison: The University of Wisconsin Press, 2004), 8.

20. On Khrushchev's "derogatory off-the-cuff remarks about Jews," see Estraikh, *Yiddish in the Cold War*, 25–26, 51.

21. Gennady Estraikh, "Jewish Wards of the Soviet State: Fayvl Sito's *These Are Us*," in *Children and Yiddish Literature: From Early Modernity to Post-Modernity*, eds. Gennady Estraikh, Kerstin Hoge, and Mikhail Krutikov (New York: Legenda, Studies in Yiddish, Modern Humanities Research Association and Routledge, 2016), 142.

22. Viktoria Khiterer, *Dokumenty po ievreiskoi istorii XVI-XX vekov v Kievskikh arkhivakh* (Kyiv: Institut Yudaiki, and Moscow: Mosty kultury, 2001), 146; Shkandrij, *Jews in Ukrainian Literature*, 196.

23. On Kharkiv Jews, see "Kharkiv," *YIVO Encyclopedia of Jews in Eastern Europe*, 2020, https://yivoencyclopedia.org/article.aspx/Kharkiv (accessed 14 July 2020); Zvi Gitelman, "The Social and Political Role of the Jews in Ukraine," in *Ukraine in the Seventies*, ed. Peter J. Potichnyj (Oakville, ON: Mosaic Press, 1975), 173 (167–86); Mordechai Altshuler, *Soviet Jewry on the Eve of the Holocaust: A Social and Demographic Profile* (Jerusalem: Maureen Mack, 1998); Vasilii Grossman and Il'ia Erenburg, eds., *Neizvestnaia chiornaia kniga* (Moskva: Izdatelstvo ACT, 1993), 9–175; Yurii M. Liakhovitskii, *Poprannaia mezuza: Kniga Drobitskogo Yara*, vol. 1 (Kharkiv: Osnova, 1991); Mendel Osherowitch, *Shtet un shtetlekh in Ukraine* (New York: The M. Osherowitch Jubillee-Committee, 1948), 24–35.

24. Eduard Limonov, *Molodoi negodiai* (Kostroma: Zhurnal "Glagol," 1992), 133.

25. For an explanation of the triad "conceived, lived, and perceived," see Henri Lefebvre, *The Production of Space*, trans. Donald Nicholson-Smith (Malden, MA: Blackwell Publishing, 1991).

26. For a discussion about Soviet state antisemitism and anti-Zionism, see Leo Heiman, "Ukrainians and the Jews," in *Ukrainians and Jews: A Symposium* (New York: The Ukrainian Congress Committee of America, Inc., 1966), 57–64; Taras Kuzio, "The Soviet Roots of Anti-Fascism and Antisemitism," *New Eastern Europe* 6 (2016): 93–100; Taras Kuzio, *Putin's War Against Ukraine: Revolution, Nationalism, and Crime* (Toronto: University of Toronto, CreateSpace, 2017), 118–26.

27. Marlena Rakhlina, *Chto bylo—vidali* . . . (Kharkiv: "Prava liudyny," 2006), 90–91.

28. Anatolii Brusilovskii, *Studiia*, Official site of Anatolii Brusilovskii, 2021, https://www.anatolbrusilov.com/тексты/книги/ (accessed 15 July 2020).

29. Rakhlina, *Chto bylo—vidali* . . .; private correspondence with Brusilovskii, 2 September 2017 email. Brusilovskii argued: "smaller peoples are hysterically afraid to be dissolved in a greater people! And thus they are burning with hatred! And black ungratefulness! It is known that during the *sovok* [a slang for the Soviet Union], Ukraine had many advantages in contrast to the Russians. There was the Writers' Union in Ukraine, but not in Russia [*sic*!]! This is only one small example. Yes, I confess—I am an *imperets* [an empire person]. And I congratulate myself with this!"

30. Lowell Tillett, *The Great Friendship: Soviet Historians on the Non-Russian Nationalities* (Chapel Hill: University of North Carolina Press, 1969); Igor Torbakov, "Ukraine and Russia: Entangled Histories, Contested Identities, and a War of Narratives," in *Revolution and War in Contemporary Ukraine: The*

Challenge of Change, ed. Olga Bertelsen (Stuttgart/New York: ibidem-Verlag/Columbia University Press, 2017), 112; Pål Kolstø, "Faulted for the Wrong Reasons: Soviet Institutionalization of Ethnic Diversity and Western (Mis)interpretations," in *Institutional Legacies of Communism: Change and Continuities in Minority Protection*, eds. Karl Cordell, Timofey Agarin, and Alexander Osipov (New York: Routledge, 2013), 31–44.

31. Like elsewhere, here the notion of ethnicity refers to people's backgrounds, associated with their culture and the family patterns of upbringing that include their native language, heritage, religion, and customs. In the writers' world, the language(s), in which they write, think, and communicate most frequently, define their membership in an ethnic group. This notion is closely related to the notion of ethnic identity that implies people's social identity, their affiliation with a cultural or social group, and their knowledge about this group's cultural traditions and history.

32. Borys Lewytzkyj, *Politics and Society in Soviet Ukraine: 1953–1980* (Edmonton: Canadian Institute of Ukrainian Studies, University of Alberta, 1984), 49–50.

33. Sergei Khrushchev, *Khrushchev in Power: Unfinished Reforms, 1961–1964*, trans. George Shriver (Boulder, CO: Lynne Rienner Publishers, 2014), 589. On 18 June 2020, Sergei Khrushchev, a rocket scientist, committed suicide at his home in Rhode Island, United States: "The Rhode Island medical examiner's office said the cause was a gunshot wound to the head, according to The Associated Press. The police said there were no signs of foul play." See Katharine Q. Seelye, "Sergei Khrushchev, Son of Former Soviet Premier, Dies at 84," *The New York Times*, 24 June 2020, https://www.nytimes.com/2020/06/24/us/sergei-khrushchev-dead.html (accessed 16 July 2020).

34. Petro Shelest's interview with the journal *Kyiv* in no. 10, April 1989, 90–110. See also Yurii Shapoval, ed., *Petro Shelest: 'Spravzhnii sud istorii shche poperedu . . .' Spohady, shchodennyky, dokumenty, materialy* (Kyiv: Heneza, 2003), 960.

35. See the list at the official site of the Ukrainian Institute of National Remembrance, "Spysok osib, yaki pidpadaiut pid zakon o dekomunizatsii," *Ukrainskyi Instytut natsionalnoi pam'iati*, http://www.memory.gov.ua/publication/spisok-osib-yaki-pidpadayut-pid-zakon-pro-dekomunizatsiyu (accessed 29 July 2020).

36. Zubok, *Zhivago's Children*, 230, 236.

37. Kornblatt, *Doubly Chosen*, 88–89.

38. Ibid., 89.

39. "Zionists Appeal for Soviet Jews," *The New York Times*, 14 September 1959, p. 6.

40. T. K. Kychko, *Iudeiska relihiia: ii pokhodzhennia i sut* (Kyiv: Radianska Ukraina, 1957).

41. For more information about Kychko, see Mikhail Mitsel's interview with Mikhail Gold "Zasluzhennyi antisemit. Kak Trofim Kichko zvezdoi stal," *Hadashot*, 4 April 2020, http://hadashot.kiev.ua/content/zasluzhennyy-antisemit-kak-trofim-kichko-zvezdoy-antisionizma-stal (accessed 16 July 2020).

42. T. K. Kychko, *Iudaism bez prykras* (Kyiv: V-vo Akademii Nauk URSR, 1963).

43. Lewytzkyj, *Politics and Society in Soviet Ukraine*, 42–43
44. Ibid., 43.
45. Shapoval, *Petro Shelest*, 268 (the 21–31 March 1964 entry in Shelest's diary).
46. See Mikhail Mitsel's interview with Mikhail Gold "Zasluzhennyi antisemit."
47. On Soviet covert operations of ideological subversion and anti-Zionist campaigns in the 1960s and 1970s domestically and abroad, see also Olga Bertelsen, "Ukrainian and Jewish Émigrés as Targets of KGB Active Measures in the 1970s," *International Journal of Intelligence and Counterintelligence* 34, no. 2 (2021): 267–92.
48. For Sverstiuk's notion, "atmosphere of controlled freedom," see Yevhen Sverstiuk, "My obraly zhyttia," in *Bunt pokolinnia: rozmovy z ukrainskymy intelektualamy*, ed. Bogumila Berdykhovska and Olia Hnatiuk, trans. Roksana Kharchuk (Kyiv: Dukh i litera, 2004); on Shelest's dual loyalties, see Olga Bertelsen, "Political Affinities and Maneuvering of Soviet Ukrainian Political Elites: Heorhii Shevel and the Ministry of Strange Affairs in the 1970s," *Nationalities Papers: The Journal of Nationalism and Ethnicity* 47, no. 3 (2019): 394–411.
49. Yekelchyk, "The Early 1960s as a Cultural Space," 47.
50. See Proudhon's diary entry, dated 26 December 1847, in *Carnets*, vol. 2, ed. P. Haubtmann (Paris: Marcel Rivière, 1960), 337 (No VI, 178).
51. Isaiah Berlin, *Personal Impressions*, ed. Henry Hardy (New York: The Viking Press, 1980), 179.
52. Ibid., 179–80.
53. Shapoval, *Petro Shelest*, 118, 963.
54. Ibid., 962 (see also Shelest's 1989 interview to the journal *Kyiv* 10, p. 90–110).
55. Oleh Bazan, "Petro Shelest: Shtrykhy politychnoho portreta," *Instytut Istorii Ukrainy, NANU*, http://resource.history.org.ua/cgi-bin/eiu/history.exe?I21DBN=EJRN&P21DBN=EJRN&S21REF=10&S21CNR=20&S21STN=1&S21FMT=ASP_meta&C21COM=S&2_S21P03=IDP=&2_S21STR=xxx_2011_16_152 (accessed 16 July 2020), 152–61.
56. Shapoval, *Petro Shelest*, 963.
57. Bazan, "Petro Shelest," 154.
58. Leonid Mlechin, *Brezhnev*, in the series "Zhisn zamechatelnykh liudei" (Moskva: Molodaia gvardiia, 2011). Also available at https://www.e-reading.club/chapter.php/91018/25/Mlechin_-_Brezhnev.html (accessed 16 July 2020).
59. Oleh Bazhan, "Do pytannia pro 'ukrainofilstvo' pershoho sekretaria TsK KPU Petra Shelesta," *Arkhiv Sluzhby Natsionalnoi Bezpeky Ukrainy*, http://dspace.nbuv.gov.ua/bitstream/handle/123456789/40456/14-Bazhan.pdf?sequence=1 (accessed 16 July 2020).
60. Yurii Shapoval, "Petro Shelest u konteksti politychnoi istorii Ukrainy XX stolittia," *Ukrainskyi istorychnyi zhurnal* 3 (2008): 134–49.
61. Ibid.
62. Quoted in *Digest of the Soviet Ukrainian Press* 3 (1969): 15. See also Lowell Tillett, "Ukrainian Nationalism and the Fall of Shelest," *Slavic Review* 34,

no. 4 (1975): 766; V. V. Ivanenko, "'Mala vidlyha' P. I. Shelesta: mif chy realnist?," *Hrani* 8 (136) (2016): 185; Hiroaki Kuromiya, "Political Leadership and Ukrainian Nationalism, 1938–1989: The Burden of History," *Problems of Post-Communism* 52, no. 1 (2005): 42.

63. See Mikhail Zhvanetskii's interview with Dmitrii Gordon, *Bulvar Gordona*, 14 November 2006, http://bulvar.com.ua/gazeta/archive/s46_5398/2859.html (accessed 16 July 2020).

64. F. I. Gorovskii et al., *Ievrei Ukrainy (kratkii ocherk istorii)*, part II (Kiev: Ukrainsko-finskii institut menedzhmenta i biznesa, 1999), 199–200.

65. Stanislav Kulchytskyi, *Chervonyi vyklyk: Istoriia komunizmu v Ukraini vid ioho narodzhennia do zahybeli*, vol. 3 (Kyiv: Tempora, 2013), 193.

66. Lew Shankowsky, "Russia, the Jews and the Ukrainian Liberation Movement," in *Ukrainians and Jews: A Symposium* (New York: The Ukrainian Congress Committee of America, Inc. 1966), 90–91. Shankowsky's analysis has been enriched by more recent studies published by Ewa Thompson and Myroslav Shkandrij in the early 2000s: Ewa M. Thompson, *Imperial Knowledge: Russian Literature and Colonialism*, 1st ed. (Westport, CT: Greenwood Press, 2000); Myroslav Shkandrij, *Russia and Ukraine: Literature and the Discourse of Empire from Napoleonic to Postcolonial Times* (Montreal & Kingston: McGill-Queen's University Press, 2001).

67. This was not only a Jewish but also a pan-Soviet trend. See Mikhail Agursky, *Pepel Klaasa: Razryv* (Jerusalem: URA, 1996), 125–59; Zubok, 231.

68. See Benedikt Sarnov's memoirs about his conversations with Chichibabin and Chichibabina (Karas) in Benedikt Sarnov, *Skuki ne bylo. Vtoraia kniga vospominanii*, https://www.e-reading.club/bookreader.php/1053492/Sarnov_-_Skuki_ne _bylo._Vtoraya_kniga_vospominaniy.html (accessed 22 January 2018). See also B. A. Chichibabin, *Ranneie i pozdneie* (Kharkov: Folio, 2002), 263.

69. Tamara Logachiova, *Rozhdionnaia v SSSR* (Kharkov: Maidan, 2012), 54.

70. Interview with Volodymyr Briuggen, 9 August 2013, the restaurant "Kryshtal," Kharkiv, Ukraine.

71. Ibid.

72. Logachiova, *Rozhdionnaia v SSSR*, 55.

73. Kees van Bruggen's wife, Carry van Bruggen (1881–1932), a Dutch writer of Jewish origin born to the Orthodox Jewish family as Caroline Lea de Haan, became more famous than her husband Kees van Bruggen whom she divorced in 1917. Her talent and contribution to Dutch literature were recognized and acknowledge after her death. See J.M.J. Sicking, "Judaism and Literature in Carry van Bruggen and Jacob Israël de Haan," *Studia Rosenthaliana* (Proceedings of the Seventh International Symposium on the History and Culture of the Jews in the Netherlands) 30, no. 1 (1996): 99–108.

74. Interview with Volodymyr Briuggen, 9 August 2013, the restaurant "Kryshtal," Kharkiv, Ukraine. The Biological Station is adjacent to the village of Koktebel and the Karadag Nature Reserve, which is a protected nature reserve of Ukraine that covers a portion of the southeast coast of the Crimean peninsula, currently occupied by the Russians. This is one of the most significant research institutions in southeast

Crimea with a 100-year history. It was founded in 1914 by Terentii Viazemskii. In 1977, on the grounds of the Station, a research institution was established that worked with dolphins and seals. From 1979, the Biological Station has been the headquarters of the Karadag Nature Reserve established under the umbrella of the National Academy of Sciences of Ukraine.

75. Interview with Volodymyr Briuggen, 9 August 2013, the restaurant "Kryshtal," Kharkiv, Ukraine.

76. Later it was known as Livonia that existed from 1561 to 1569 as a vassal state of the Grand Duchy of Lithuania. From 1569 to 1726, it was part of the Crown of the Polish Kingdom, and in 1726 it was incorporated into the Polish-Lithuanian Commonwealth. In 1795, it was annexed by the Russian Empire in the Third Partition of Poland. Under the same name, a short-lived wartime state existed from 8 March to 22 September 1918. It was supposed to become part of the United Baltic Duchy under the German Empire but this did not happen because of Germany's surrender of the Baltic region at the end of the First World War. This area became a part of Latvia at the end of the First World War.

77. Volodymyr Briuggen, *Liudy i knyhy: Statti i spohady* (Kharkiv: Maidan, 2006), 10.

78. Ibid.

79. Tamara Logachiova, "Dialog s pisatelem: realnyi i myslennyi," *Kharkov–350: Gumanitarnyie resursy*, 2020, http://kharkovhumanit.narod.ru/Liki_kult.html (accessed 18 July 2020).

80. TsDAMLIMU, f. 840, op. 1, spr. 83, ar. 1–5.

81. Nikolai Artamonov, "Otshelnik s ulitsy Astronomicheskoi," *Kharkov–350: Gumanitarnyie resursy*, 2020, http://kharkovhumanit.narod.ru/Liki_kult.html (accessed 18 July 2020).

82. Interview with Volodymyr Briuggen, 9 August 2013, the restaurant "Kryshtal," Kharkiv, Ukraine.

83. Vladimir Briuggen, "Iz 'Bloknotov,'" *Tiomnyie alei* 6 (1996): 180.

84. Artamonov, "Otshelnik s ulitsy Astronomicheskoi."

85. Shkandrij, *Russia and Ukraine*, 257. On the politicization of the cultural movement in Ukraine in the 1960s, see Kas'ianov, *Nezhodni*, 224; A. Rusnachenko, *Natsionalno-vyzvolnyi rukh v Ukraini: seredyna 1950–kh–pochatok 1990-kh rokiv* (Kyiv: V-vo imeni Oleny Telihy, 1998); B. Zakharov, *Narys istorii dysydentskoho rukhu v* Ukraini (1956–1987) (Kharkiv: Folio, 2003); O. Bazhan and I. Z. Danyliuk, *Opozytsiia v Ukraini (druha polovyna 50-kh–80-ti rr. XX st.)* (Kyiv: NAN Ukrainy, Instytut istorii Ukrainy, Ridnyi krai, 2000); V. Moroz, *Esei, lysty, dokumenty* (Miunkhen: Suchasnist, 1975); Lysiak-Rudnytskyi, "Politychna dumka," 477–88; Sverstiuk, "My obraly zhyttia," 33–90; Ivan Hel, *Vyklyk systemi: Ukrainskyi vyzvolnyi rukh druhoi polovyny XX stolittia*, ed. I. Yezerska (Lviv: Chasopys, 2013); Osyp Zinkevych, ed., *Rukh oporu v Ukraini: Entsyklopedychnyi dovidnyk* (Kyiv: Smoloskyp, 2010); Vasyl Ovsiienko, *Svitlo liudei: Memuary ta publitsystyka*, 2 vol. (Kharkiv: Kharkivska pravozakhysna hrupa, 2005); Mykola Plakhotniuk, *Kolovorot: Statti, spohady, dokumenty* (Kyiv: Smoloskyp, 2012); Yaroslav Seko, "Rozvytok ukrainskoho shistdesiatnytsva u 1965–1971 rr.," in *Naukovi zapysky Ternopilskoho*

natsionalnoho pedahohichnoho universytetu imeni Volodymyra Hnatiuka, vyp. 2, ch. 1 (Ternopil: Vyd-vo TNPU im. V. Hnatiuka, 2014), 128–34.

86. Yaacov Roi, "Union of Soviet Socialist Republics," *The YIVO Encyclopedia of Jews in Eastern Europe*, 2020, http://www.yivoencyclopedia.org/article.aspx/Union_of_Soviet_Socialist_Republics (accessed 17 July 2020); Samuel Barnai, "Social Trends Among Jews in the Post-Stalin Years," in *Revolution, Repression, and Revival: The Soviet Jewish Experience*, eds. Zvi Gitelman and Yaacov Roi (New York: Rowman & Littlefield Publishers, Inc., 2007), 143.

87. Vladimir (Zeev) Khanin, "The Jewish National Movement and the Struggle for Community in the Late Soviet Period," in *Revolution, Repression, and Revival: The Soviet Jewish Experience*, eds. Zvi Gitelman and Yaacov Roi (New York: Rowman & Littlefield Publishers, Inc., 2007), 225.

88. Mikhail Kheifets, *Ukrainskiie siluety* (Kyiv: Ukrainska pres-hrupa, 2014), 30; Zinkevych, *Rukh oporu v Ukraini*, 687–89.

89. Lev Frukhtman, "Golos zhizni," *My zdes*, no. 561, 14–24 January 2018, http://newswe.com/index.php?go=Pages&in=view&id=1724 (accessed 17 July 2020).

90. Ludmilla Alexeyeva and Paul Goldberg, *The Thaw Generation: Coming of Age in the Post-Stalin Era* (Boston: Little, Brown and Company, 1990), 292.

91. On the official Soviet antisemitism and anti-Zionism of the post-Stalin era and its historiography, see Andreas Umland, "Ofitsialnyi sovetskii antisemitism poslestalinskogo perioda," *Pro et Contra* 7, no. 2 (2002): 158–68.

92. Among them were members of the Ukrainian National Committee (UNK), an underground organization in Lviv. Its members organized an underground "publishing house" that printed anti-Soviet leaflets and proclamations. In 1961, the KGB uncovered the organization; among others, Hryhorii Zelman was sentenced to fifteen years in prison, Oleksii Zelman—to twelve years in prison, Mykola Mashtalier—to ten years in prison. For more on the UNK and its members, see Zinkevych, *Rukh oporu v Ukraini*, 142, 176, 293, 301, 423. See also Olena Herasymiuk, *Rozstrilnyi kalendar* (Kharkiv: Klub simeinoho dozvillia, 2017).

93. Zubok, *Zhivago's Children*, 269.

94. Larissa I. Remennick, *Russian Jews on Three Continents: Identity, Integration, and Conflict* (New Brunswick, NJ: Transaction, 2007), 31; this phenomenon was especially pronounced in the early Soviet period when many Soviet Jews were employed by various Soviet institutions, including the Soviet secret police, and were able to participate in the Soviet construction project as both the subjects and the agents of internal colonization. On the notion of internal colonization, see Alexander Etkind, *Internal Colonization: Russia's Imperial Experience* (Cambridge, UK: The Polity Press, 2011); Sasha Senderovich, "Scenes of Encounter: The 'Soviet Jew' in Fiction by Russian Jewish Writers in America," *Prooftexts* 35, no. 1 (2015): 102. For a discussion about Ukraine's Jews working for the Soviet secret police, see Yuri Slezkine, *The Jewish Century* (Princeton, NJ: Princeton University Press, 2004); Yurii Shapoval and Vadym Zolotariov, "Yevrei v kerivnytstvi orhaniv DPU-NKVS USRR-URSR u 1920-1930-kh rr," *Z arkhiviv VUChK-GPU-NKVD-KGB* 1 (2010): 53–93; Vadym Zolotariov, "Kerivnyi sklad NKVS URSR pid chas 'velykoho teroru' (1936–1938 rr.): sotsialno-statystychnyi analiz," *Z arkhiviv VUChK-GPU-NKVD-KGB* 2

(2009): 86–115; Vadym Zolotariov, "Nachalnytskyi sklad NKVS USRR naperedodni 'yezhovshchyny': sotaialno-statystychnyi analiz," in *Ukraina v dobu "Velykoho teroru", 1936–1938 rr.*, ed. S. Bohunov et al. (Kyiv: Lybid, 2009), 60–80; Vadym Zolotariov and Valerii Stepkin, *Chk-GPU-NKVD v Donbasse: 1919–1941* (Donetsk: Aleks, 2010); Vadym Zolotariov, *Sekretno-politychnyi viddil DPU USRR: Spravy ta liudy* (Kharkiv: "Folio," 2007).

95. On the various channels and factors through which Jewish identity was shaped in the Soviet Union, see Harriet Murav, *Music from a Speeding Train: Soviet Yiddish and Russian-Jewish Literature of the Twentieth Century* (Stanford, CA: Stanford University Press, 2011); Anna Shternshis, *Soviet and Kosher: Jewish Popular Culture in the Soviet Union, 1923–1929* (Bloomington: Indiana University Press, 2013); Jeffrey Veidlinger, *In the Shadow of the Shtetl: Small Town Jewish Life in Soviet Ukraine* (Bloomington: Indiana University Press, 2013).

96. Interview with Volodymyr Briuggen, 9 August 2013, the restaurant "Kryshtal," Kharkiv, Ukraine.

97. Vladimir Briuggen, *Bloknoty* (Kharkov: Maidan, 2007), 147.

98. Briuggen, *Liudy i knyhy*, 2006, 5–11.

99. V. O. Briuggen, *Liudyna tvoryt dobro: Literaturno-krytychni narysy* (Kyiv: Radianskyi pysmennyk, 1966); V. O. Briuggen, *Zvychainyi khlib mystetstva: Literaturno-krytychni statti* (Kyiv: Radianskyi pysmennyk, 1969); V. O. Briuggen, *Pro Ihoria Muratova: Literaturno-krytychni statti* (Kyiv: Radianskyi pysmennyk, 1972); V. O. Briuggen, *Zemlia i liudy* (Kyiv: Radianskyi pysmennyk, 1973).

100. Logachiova, "Dialog s pisatelem."

101. TsDAMLIMU, f. 816, op. 1, spr. 211, ark. 5–6.

102. Quoted in Svitlana Yovenko's foreword "'Omanlyvist velykykh istyn' Volodymyra Briuggena," *Bloknoty* by Vladimir Briuggen (Kharkov: Maidan, 2007), 6.

103. Yevhen Baran, "Volodymyr Briuggen: Ya rozumiiu literaturu peredusim yak sposib zhyttia," *Kharkov–350: Gumanitarnyie resursy*, 2020, http://kharkovhumanit.narod.ru/Liki_kult.html (accessed 18 July 2020).

104. Yovenko, "'Omanlyvist velykykh istyn,'" 6–7.

105. Logachiova, "Dialog s pisatelem."

106. Ibid.

107. Vladimir Briuggen, *Bloknoty: Kniga tret'ia* (Kharkov: Maidan, 2010), 743.

108. Yevhen Baran, "Zradlyva nizhnist 'Bloknotiv' Volodymyra Briuggena," *Berezil* 9–10 (2012): 156–63.

109. Interview with Volodymyr Briuggen, 9 August 2013, the restaurant "Kryshtal," Kharkiv, Ukraine.

110. Briuggen, *Bloknoty*, 2010, 48, 278, 375, 434.

111. Briuggen, *Bloknoty*, 2010, 161, 315, 463.

112. Dale A. Bertelsen, "Kenneth Burke and Multiculturalism: A Voice of Ethnocentrism and Apologia," *Qualitative Research Reports in Communication* 3, no. 4 (2002): 83. For more on Burke's antisemitism, see Janice W. Fernheimer, "Confronting Kenneth Burke's Anti-Semitism," *Journal of Communication & Religion* 39, no. 2 (2016): 36–53.

113. Interview with Volodymyr Briuggen, 9 August 2013, the restaurant "Kryshtal," Kharkiv, Ukraine.

114. Sverstiuk, "My obraly zhyttia," 76; Iryna Zhylenko, *Homo Feriens: Spohady* (Kyiv: Smoloskyp, 2011), 152, 209; Yekelchyk, "The Early 1960s as a Cultural Space," 49–50.

115. Estraikh, *Yiddish in the Cold War*, 88.

116. On the overlapping identities and views (nationalism/socialism/communism) during the Thaw, see John-Paul Himka, "Leonid Plyushch: The Ukrainian Marxist Resurgent," *Journal of Ukrainian Studies* 9 (1980): 61–79; Ludmilla Alexeyeva, *Soviet Dissent: Contemporary Movements for National, Religious, and Human Rights* (Middletown, CT: Wesleyan, 1985), 33; Barnai, "Social Trends Among Jews in the Post-Stalin Years," 137, 143; Yekelchyk, "The Early 1960s as a Cultural Space," 55. See also Alexeyeva and Goldberg, *The Thaw Generation*, 292.

117. Anthony Adamovych, "The Non-Russians," in *Soviet Literature in the Sixties*, eds. Max Hayward and Edward L. Crowley (London: Methuen & Co Ltd., 1964), 100.

118. Estraikh, *Yiddish in the Cold War*, 52. Among them were those who were arrested as Jewish nationalists under Stalin and returned from the labor camps only in 1955–1958. They were educated at universities and some held degrees in Yiddish, working as journalists, scholars, artists, theater directors, and actors.

119. Personal conversation with Volodymyr (Briuggen), 16 July 2015; for Briuggen's views about *shistdesiatnytstvo*, see also Liudmyla Tarnashynska, *Ukrainske shistdesiatnytstvo: profili na tli pokolinnia* (Kyiv: Smoloskyp, 2010), 572.

120. See an analysis of Dovid Hofshteyn's translation of Shevchenko's poetry in Amelia M. Glaser, "Jewish Alienation through a Ukrainian Looking Glass: Dovid Hofshteyn's Translations of Taras Shevchenko," *Prooftexts* 36, no. 1–2 (2017): 83–110.

121. Gennady Estraikh, "Literature Versus Territory: Soviet Jewish Cultural Life in the 1950s," *East European Jewish Affairs* 33, no. 1 (2003): 42.

122. Efraim Sicher, *Jews in Russian Literature after the October Revolution: Writers and Artists Between Hope and Apostasy* (Cambridge: Cambridge University Press, 1995), 215; Elena M. Kats, "The Literary Development of Yekhiel Shraybman: A Jewish Writer in Soviet Clothing," *East European Jewish Affairs* 38, no. 3 (2008): 281–301.

123. Lucjan Dobroszycki and Jeffery S. Gurock, eds., *The Holocaust in the Soviet Union: Studies and Sources on the Destruction of Jews in the Nazi-occupied Territories of the USSR, 1941–1944* (New York: Routledge, 1994).

124. See, for instance, an analysis of Muzfond under the umbrella of the Composers' Union: Kiril Tomoff, "Creative Union: The Professional Organization of Soviet Composers, 1939–1953," vol. 1 (unpublished doctoral dissertation, The University of Chicago, 2001), 395–426; for more on Litfond, see John and Carol Garrard, *Inside the Soviet Writers' Union* (New York: The Free Press, 1990).

125. TsDAMLIMU, f. 500, op. 1, spr. 316, ark. 38–40.

126. Available at *Zolotoie runo*, https://zolotoeruno.org/avtory/zinovij_valshonok/stihotvorenija._chast1_zv.aspx (accessed 23 July 2020).

127. Ibid.

128. TsDAMLIMU, f. 500, op. 1, spr. 316, ark. 40.

129. Eduard Kuznetsov, "Poet krutogo zamesa: Zinoviiu Valshonku – 85," *NG Ex Libris*, 7 March 2019, https://www.ng.ru/ng_exlibris/2019-03-07/13_973_poet.html (accessed 23 July 2020).

130. "Zinovii Valshonok," *Sem iskusstv* 46, edited by Yevgenii Berkovich, http://7iskusstv.com/Avtory/Valshonok.php (accessed 23 July 2020).

131. Zvi Gitelman, "Glasnost, Perestroika and Antisemitism," *Foreign Affairs*, 1 March 1991, p. 144.

132. Ibid.

133. Leonid Kurokhta, "Chomu ia vybrav novu zemliu," *Proza.ru*, 2013, https://proza.ru/2013/04/21/1969?fbclid=IwAR3GDCxjnsl0N8XZ4WxUDKwabEVZQUrnVjSqP_50NWlyiNdzWuiXAWzh850 (accessed 24 July 2020).

134. Vasilii Omelchenko, *Smutnyie gody (zapiski ochevidtsa)* (Kharkiv: Maidan, 2013), 388.

135. Vladimir Bushin, *Ia zhyl vo vremena Sovetov. Dnevniki* (Moskva: Algoritm, 2014); see the 12 June 1984 entry.

136. Interview with Volodymyr Briuggen, 27 July 2011, Kharkiv, Ukraine.

137. Ibid.; Briuggen, *Bloknoty*, 2010, 48.

138. Feliks Rakhlin, *O Borise Chichibabine i iego vremeni: Strochka iz zhizni* (Kharkiv: Folio, 2004), 94.

139. Rostyslav Melnykiv, *Literaturni 1920-ti: Postati (Narysy, obrazky, etiudy)* (Kharkiv: Maidan, 2013), 21; Anatolii Pererva, ed., *Natsionalna spilka pysmennykiv Ukrainy: 75 rokiv* (Kharkiv: Maidan, 2009), 19.

140. DAKhO, f.R-6165, op.1, spr. 134, ark. 116.

141. Estraikh, *Yiddish in the Cold War*, 128.

142. TsDAMLIMU, f. 500, op. 1, spr. 316, ark. 54–54 zv.

143. Vladimir (Zeev) Zhabotinskii, "O 'yevreiakh i russkoi literature,'" an excerpt from *Izbrannoe* (Jerusalem: Biblioteka-Alia, 1978), *YouTube* (read and posted by Mikhail Polskii), 4 May 2019, https://www.youtube.com/watch?v=Li-I0NWdHp0&t=795s (accessed 24 July 2020).

144. Interview with Boris Chichibabin by Svetlana Dudar, "'Da budet volia tvoia, a ne moia, gospodi . . .,'" *Official site of Boris Alekseevich Chichibabin*, 1993, http://chichibabin.narod.ru/interview.html (accessed 24 July 2020).

145. Boris Chichibabin, *Stikhotvoreniia* (TO Ekskliuziv, 2003), 254–57.

146. Briuggen, *Bloknoty*, 2010, 295; interview with Briuggen, 16 July 2015, Kharkiv, Ukraine.

147. Khana Levina, *Ridne* (Kharkiv: Prapor, 1967).

148. Private correspondence with Muratov's daughter Olha Muratova, 13 August 2017, FB; Natalia Zabila, "Pro Zhyttia i tvorchist Ihoria Muratova," a foreword to *Veselo, soniachno, druzhno* by Ihor Muratov (Kyiv: Derzhavne vydavnytstvo dytiachoi literatury URSR, 1960), 4; Natalia Biletska-Muratova, ". . . Ne smiiuchy skazaty: 'Vin pomer,'" in *Na krylakh Litany* by Ihor Muratov (Kharkiv: Maidan, 2012), 31. The fact that Muratov was born in Paris and spent the first six years of his life there was thoroughly hidden from the authorities.

For more on Aron Kopshtein (1915–1940), see Rina Lapidus, *Young Jewish Poets Who Fell as Soviet Soldiers in the Second World War* (London/New York: Routledge, 2014), chapter 8.

149. Ihor Mykhailyn, *Literaturna Kharkivshchyna. Poeziia: Eseistyka, portrety, retsenzii* (Kharkiv: Maidan, 2007), 73.

150. Mykhailyn, *Literaturna Kharkivshchyna*, 77; for more on this Committee, see Lilita Zalkalns, *Back to the Motherland: Repatriation and Latvian Émigrés 1955–1958* (Stockholm, Sweden: Stockholm University, 2014).

151. On forcible repatriation of Soviet citizens, see Donna E. Dismukes, *The Forced Repatriation of Soviet Citizens: A Study in Military Obedience* (Monterey, CA: Department of Defense/Naval Postgraduate School, 1996).

152. Mykhailyn, *Literaturna Kharkivshchyna*, 78.

153. Mykola Kozak, "Maister pershoi ruky," *Gonta Project*, 25 April 2006, http://virchi.narod.ru/poeziya/muratov-biograf2.htm (accessed 25 July 2020).

154. Ihor Muratov, "Prahnuty filosofskoi hlybyny," in *Tvory* by Ihor Muratov, vol. 4 (Kyiv: Dnipro, 1983), 406.

155. Volodymyr Briuggen, "Znaiomyi i neznaiomyi Muratov," *Natsionalna spilka pysmennykiv Ukrainy/Kharkivska oblasna orhanizatsiia*, 20 September 2012, https://kharkiv-nspu.org.ua/archives/549#respond (accessed 24 July 2020).

156. Kozak, "Maister pershoi ruky."

157. Ihor Muratov, *Na krylakh Litany* (Kharkiv: Maidan, 2012), 83.

Ravensbrück was a German concentration camp where the Nazis kept exclusively women from 1939 to 1945. It is located in northern Germany, 90 kilometers north of Berlin, near the village of Ravensbrück. From summer of 1942, the Nazis conducted medical experiments on the Polish political prisoners, fracturing and infecting their leg bones and muscles. The Dachau concentration camp was established 16 kilometers northwest of Munich in the state of Bavaria, Germany, in March 1933 to hold political prisoners. The Nazis practiced forced labor there and kept Jews and people of other nationalities, conducting medical experiments on them and subjecting them to hypothermia and rapid decompression to pressures found at 4,300 meters.

158. Muratov, *Na krylakh Litany*, 87.

159. Interview with Briuggen, 16 July 2015, Kharkiv, Ukraine.

160. Interview with Arkadii Filatov by Nikolai Artamonov "Khrani tebia gospod," *Kharkovhumanit*, 2003, http://kharkovhumanit.narod.ru/Intervu.html (accessed 25 July 2020).

161. DAKhO, f. R-6165, op. 1, spr. 144, ark. 22.

162. Hryhorii Tiutiunnyk was Hryhir Tiutiunnyk's brother. The second part of the novel *Vyr* was published in 1962, after Tiutiunnyk's death. See Olena Bondarenko's sketch about Hryhorii Tiutiunnyk "23 kvitnia 1920 narodyvsia ukrainskyi pysmennyk Hryhorii Tiutiunnyk," *Ridna kraina*, https://ridna.ua/2019/04/23-kvitnya-1920-roku-narodyvsya-ukrajinskyj-pysmennyk-hryhorij-tyutyunnyk/ (accessed 25 July 2020).

163. DAKhO, f. R-6165, op. 1, spr. 144, ark. 27–28.

164. Private conversation with Robert Tretyakov, 17 June 1996, Kharkiv, Ukraine.

165. DAKhO, f. R-6165, op. 1, spr. 144, ark. 11–12.

166. DAKhO, f. R-6165, op. 1, spr. 144, ark. 15.

167. DAKhO, f. R-6165, op. 1, spr. 134.

168. Interview with Anatolii Starodub, 12 August 2008, Kharkiv, Ukraine.

169. Vadim Levin, *Kuda uiekhal tsirk* (Kharkiv: Folio, 2001).

170. Interview with Ivan Perepeliak by Ihor Mykhailyn, "Poet v optytsi svoho chasu," *Official site of the Kharkiv chapter of the Writers' Union (NSPU)*, 2013, https://kharkiv-nspu.org.ua/archives/2644 (accessed 26 July 2020).

171. DAKhO, f. R-6165, op. 1, spr. 134, ark. 48. Some party functionaries and older writers identified Vadim Levin's poems as "muddy and double-meaning" work. See also CIA (Central Intelligence Agency) Archive, Collection: Nazi War Crimes Disclosure Act, "A New Freeze (A Collection of Material on Recent Developments in Ukrainian Soviet Literature)," 28 August 1963 (declassified: 2007), https://www.cia.gov/library/readingroom/docs/AERODYNAMIC%20%20%20VOL.%2026%20%20%28OPERATIONS%29_0071.pdf (accessed 26 July 2020), 22 (1–49).

172. Limonov, *Molodoi negodiai*, 102.

173. Borys Lewytzkyj, *Politics and Society in Soviet Ukraine, 1953–1980* (Edmonton: Canadian Institute of Ukrainian Studies, University of Alberta, 1984), 2.

174. DAKhO, f. R-6165, op. 1, spr. 144, ark. 12.

175. For an in-depth analysis of Bondar's writings, see T. M. Sharova, "Vasyl Bondar: Osoblyvosti biohrafichnoi prozy ta ideino-khudozhni poshuky pysmennyka," *Visnyk Luhanskoho Natsionalnoho Universytetu imeni Tarasa Shevchenka* 3, no. 166 (February 2009): 179–85.

176. Shatylov, *Kliati simdesiati . . . Na pam'iati stalo, na pam'iati staly* (Kharkiv: "Apostrof," 2011), 100–01. Brezhnev's trilogy of memoirs was published in the Moscow journal *Novyi mir* in 1978—*Malaia Zemlia* in the second issue, *Vozrozhdeniie* (Rebirth) in the fifth issue, and *Tselina* (Virgin Lands) in the eleventh issue. The circulation of each issue was approximately 15 million.

177. Shatylov, *Kliati simdesiati*, 158, 173. Both Bondar and Shumytskyi were harassed by the authorities for speaking Ukrainian; also Bondar—for his DP past; Shumytskyi—for his open hostile stance toward the local militia and the KGB. For a subtle analysis of Tiutiunnyk's tragic worldview through the prism of his creative work, see O. V. Chepurna, "Obraz dytyny-dyvaka – kliuch do rozuminnia khudozhnioho svitu Hryhora Tiutiunnyka," *Visnyk Luhanskoho Natsionalnoho Universytetu imeni Tarasa Shevchenka* 3, no. 166 (February 2009): 91–100.

178. DAKhO, f. R-6165, op. 1, spr. 144, ark. 16.

179. Interview with Ivan Perepeliak by Ihor Mykhailyn, "Poet v optytsi svoho chasu."

180. Rakhlin, *O Borise Chichibabine*, 70.

181. On antisemitism in Lviv, see William Jay Risch, The Ukrainian West: *Culture and the Fate of Empire in Soviet Lviv* (Cambridge, MA: Harvard University Press, 2011), 166–67; Benjamin Tromly, *Making the Soviet Intelligentsia: Universities and Intellectual Life under Stalin and Khrushchev* (Cambridge, UK: Cambridge University Press, 2015), 241–42.

182. Gitelman, "Glasnost, Perestroika and Antisemitism," 144.

183. Raisa Beliaieva (Gurina), "Dom dlia druzei," in *Vsemu zhivomu ne chuzhoi: Boris Chichibabin v statiakh i vospominaniiakh*, eds. M. I. Bogoslavskii, L. S. Karas-Chichibabina, and B. Y. Ladenzon (Kharkov: Folio, 1998), 318.

184. Limonov, *Molodoi negodiai*, 138, 140.

185. Mikhail Stasenko, "'... Skachut loshadki Borisa i Gleba...'" in Bogoslavskii, Karas-Chichibabina, and Ladenzon, 327; see also the memoirs of Chichibabin's wife "Liliia Karas-Chichibabina o Borise Chichibabine," *Omiliya* (International Literary Club), 2 March 2009, https://omiliya.org/article/liliya-karas-chichibabina-o-borise-chichibabine.html (accesses 26 July 2020).

186. Limonov, *Molodoi negodiai*, 23, 25.

187. See a similar analysis in Kornblatt, 132.

188. Limonov, *Molodoi negodiai*, 65.

189. Anatolii Brusilovskii, *Studiia*, https://www.unvergessliche-augenblicke.com/download/studija.pdf (accessed 26 July 2020), 6.

190. Yurii Miloslavskii and Konstantin Skoblinskii, "Skazy," in *Antologiia noveishei russkoi poezii "U goluboi laguny,"* eds. Konstantin K. Kuzminskii and Grigorii L. Kovalev, vol. 3a (Newtonville, MA: Oriental Research Partners, 1980–1986), *kkk-bluelagoon.ru*, 2020, http://kkk-bluelagoon.ru/tom3a/miloslavsky2.htm (accessed 26 July 2020).

191. "Aleksandr Vernik," *Art in Process*, 2020, http://art-in-process.com/avtory/literatura/aleksandr-vernik/ (accessed 26 July 2020). Siganevich passed away in 2010. See Tatiana Chekhova, "Umer Eduard Siganevich. Literaturnyi dnevnik," *Proza.ru*, 18 November 2010, https://www.proza.ru/diary/mamlakat0256/2010-11-1 (accessed 26 July 2020).

192. Genrikh Shmerkin, "Boris Chichibabin i russkaia drama," *Sem iskusstv* 11, no. 12 (November 2010), http://7iskusstv.com/2010/Nomer11/Shmerkin1.php (accessed 26 July 2020).

193. Quoted in Shmerkin, "Boris Chichibabin."

194. In February 2009, the poets who were part of Chichibabin's literary studio came to Kharkiv to celebrate its forty-fifth anniversary, a studio that survived only two years before it was closed. See Stanislav Minakov, "Dom dlia druzei," *Nezavisimaia gazeta*, 26 February 2020, https://www.ng.ru/ng_exlibris/2009-02-26/5_home.html (accessed 29 July 2020).

195. Gal Beckerman, *When They Come for Us, We'll Be Gone: The Epic Struggle to Save Soviet Jewry* (Boston/New York: Houghton Mifflin Harcourt, 2010), 10, 110.

196. Rakhlin, *O Borise Chichibabine*, 159–60.

197. Gennadii Kostyrchenko, *Stalin protiv "kosmopolitov": Vlast i yevreiskaia intelligentsia v SSSR* (Moskva: Rosspen, 2010), 298.

198. Kornblatt, 132.

199. "Yevreiskaia tragediia Voznesenskogo," *IsraLove*, 2020, https://isralove.org/load/14-1-0-1462 (accessed 27 July 2020).

200. Boris Chichibabin, "Klianus na znameni veselom," in *Stikhotvoreniia* (Kharkov: TO Ekskliuziv, 2003), 54.

201. On Chichibabin's Jewdophilia, see, for instance, Rakhlin, *O Borise Chichibabine*, 5; Lazar Berenson, "'Napishut nashi imena.' Vospominaniia o Borise

Chichibabine," *Sem iskustv* 2, no. 15 (February 2011), http://7iskusstv.com/2011/Nomer2/Berenson1.php (accessed 27 July 2020).

202. Shmerkin, "Boris Chichibabin."
203. Limonov, *Molodoi negodiai*, 145–46.
204. Ibid., 131.
205. Rakhlin, *O Borise Chichibabine*, 9.
206. LTD, vol. 5, 30 March 1957 entry.
207. Rakhlin, *O Borise Chichibabine*, 9.
208. Gaston Bachelard, *The Poetics of Space: The Classic Look at How We Experience Intimate Places*, trans. Maria Jolas (Boston: Beacon Press, 1994).
209. Yurii Shapoval, "Petro Shelest u konteksti politychnoi istorii Ukrainy XX stolittia," *Bakhmutskyi shliakh* 1–2 (2008): 101–12.
210. Kasianov, *Nezhodni*, 64, 80; Oleh Bazhan, "Petro Shelest i protestnyi rukh v URSR u 1960–1970-kh rr.," *Z arkiviv VUChK-GPU-NKVD-KGB* 2, no. 43 (2014): 443–56, http://resource.history.org.ua/publ/za_2014_2__16.
211. Vasyl Danylenko, ed., *Polityczni protesty i inakodumstvo v Ukraini (1960–1980)* (Kyiv: Smoloskyp, 2013), 87; see also the original of the document in HDA SBU, f. 16, op. 3 (1968), spr. 2, ark. 241–82.
212. Kasianov, 121; Mlechin, *Brezhnev*, https://www.e-reading.club/chapter.php/91018/25/Mlechin_-_Brezhnev.html.
213. Bertelsen, "Ukrainian and Jewish Émigrés."
214. Lewytzkyi, *Politics and Society in Soviet Ukraine*, 142.
215. Minakov, "Dom dlia druzei."
216. Arsenii Roginskii, "KGB reformirovat nevozmozhno," *Radio Svoboda*, 18 December 2017, https://www.svoboda.org/a/28924835.html (accessed 4 March 2021).
217. The poem "Intelligentsiia byla moim narodom" grew out of this sentiment. Boris Slutskii, *Sovremennyie istorii* (Moskva: Molodaiia gvardiia, 1969), 126.
218. For definitions of the intelligentsia, see Isaiah Berlin, *The Soviet Mind: Russian Culture under Communism*, ed. Henry Hardy (Washington, DC: Brookings Institution Press, 2004), 167.
219. Interview with Volodymyr Briuggen, 9 August 2013, the restaurant "Kryshtal," Kharkiv, Ukraine.
220. By 1959 more than 95 percent of Soviet Jews were city dwellers. For more on the process of urbanization among Soviet Jews, see Barnai, "Social Trends Among Jews in the Post-Stalin Years," 136.
221. This stance evoked a storm of protests among Russian Jewish writers after Vlodov publicized his views on the pages of the newspaper *Rossiia*. See Sergei Kniazev's 1995 documentary about Iurii Vlodov (1932–2009) *A genii – sushchii diavol!* (Moscow Studio "Chelovek i vremia"), *Facebook* (placed by Liudmila Osokina), 30 January 2018, https://www.facebook.com/vlodowa/videos/1582318815184098/ (accessed 2 August 2020); see the film's transcript at *InterLit: Mezhdunarodnyi literaturnyi klub*, 2020, http://archive.li/rMD80#selection-1535.11-1535.516 (accessed 2 August 2020).

Chapter 3

The Writers, the Dissent, and the Human Rights Movement in the West

RAPPROCHEMENT

By the early 1960s, re-Stalinization had the unintended effect of facilitating cross-generational and cross-ethnic bonds and friendships among Ukrainians, Russians, and Jews among the Kharkiv literati, based on their mutual feelings of respect, their appreciation for each other's literary gift, and their longing for freedom of expression. The majority of the literati despised the authorities that established rigid control over their private and professional lives, and the divide et impera approach embraced by the Kharkiv party and KGB leadership that aimed at provoking mistrust, suspicion, and polarization between Ukrainians and Jews seemed to have the opposite effect. Briuggen remembered that "Zionists" and "Ukrainian bourgeois nationalists," two major enemies of the Soviet system identified by the KGB, began to frequently see each other in the KGB headquarters in Sovnarkomivska Street in downtown Kharkiv.[1] The officers scheduled meetings with the writers at the same time but in different rooms, and the writers waiting in the halls for their appointments were afraid to ask one another about the purpose of their visits. Stirring distrust and insecurity among them, the KGB assumed that a Jew and a Ukrainian might see an informant in one another. Typically, the officer was extremely polite, inviting one of the writers to his office, and apparently, in the KGB's view, this tactic should have amplified another writer's suspicion about his colleague being a KGB informer and unofficial collaborator, or a "source of operational information," using the KGB term.[2] However, the members and nonmembers of the Writers' Union very quickly figured this scheme out and secretly shared this knowledge.

The KGB and Soviet propagandists were rather persistent, hoping to sow discord among the intelligentsia and to nurture the culture of denunciations and conformity. They regularly published texts in the Soviet press against the "'unholy alliance' between Ukrainian bourgeois nationalists and Jewish Zionists"[3] that was allegedly developed domestically and abroad. In KGB documents, Soviet Ukrainians were routinely referred to as nationalists, and Jews—as *otshchepentsy* ("stateless cosmopolits"), Zionists, or "agents of imperialism." Both were described as anticommunist and anti-Soviet forces. The diaspora Ukrainians were also labeled as "Ukrainian bourgeois nationalists," and the diaspora Jews—as Zionists. In addition, KGB analysts often used a collective term for both diasporas—"imperialists." The Western "imperialists" tried to protect and support Soviet Ukrainians and Jews who resisted co-optation by the Soviet regime in Ukraine, and the diasporas' human rights activism was misrepresented, mocked, and criticized by Soviet ideologues and Soviet cartoonists who perpetuated the image of diaspora groups as enemies of the USSR. Valerii Zelinskii, for instance, depicted anti-Soviet Ukrainian and Jewish émigré as two forces in one harness, dragging the wagon of the Cold War. The journal *Perets* published a great many variations of this cartoon in the 1970s and 1980s (Fig. 3.1).

Compared with the atmosphere and the cultural space of Kyiv, Lviv, and Moscow, poisoned by the KGB, where the literati developed animosities toward each other and where personal attacks and interethnic conflicts became a systemic problem, the Kharkiv community of writers was void of interethnic hatred and serious conflicts. Yohanan Petrovsky-Shtern enlightened audiences about vicious attacks against Kyiv *shistdesiatnyky* by Mykola

Figure 3.1 Valerii Zelinskii's Cartoon for the Cover of the Magazine *Perets* (June 1981). *Source*: Courtesy of *Lekhaim* (*Lekhaim*, no. 271, 30 October 2014, http://old.lechaim.ru/2461).

Sheremet, Ukrainian graphomaniac and the author of more than fifty books. Sheremet included the Ukrainian poet of Jewish origin Leonid Pervomaiskyi (Illia Hurevych) in the list of his targets. Sheremet's comments often went far beyond what could be identified as literary criticism. For instance, he rebuked Pervomaiskyi that Yiddish, not Ukrainian, was his native language, suggesting that Pervomaiskyi was an imposter with dual identity who was not sufficiently patriotic to "eat our Ukrainian bread."[4] The hostility between Sheremet and Pervomaiskyi was rooted in the past, but Sheremet's antisemitic rhetoric was inflamed by and was entirely consistent with anti-Jewish messages emanating from the Kremlin and the anti-Zionist campaigns conceived by the KGB.[5] As a historically multicultural, multiethnic, and borderland city, Kharkiv was more resilient to KGB's divide et impera tactics.

In Kharkiv, amid the cultural and political movement that surfaced in Ukraine in the 1960s, for most Jewish literati, the cultural and the political coalesced, transforming cultural issues into a political agenda, associated with two options—emigration, internal emigration as in Briuggen's case, or the challenge of transforming the regime from inside to rejuvenate Jewish cultural traditions and to restore fundamental human rights for education and self-expression. According to some accounts, most Jews and Russians were indifferent to the Ukrainians' dream of Ukraine as a sovereign country, because the impact of Soviet propaganda was quite strong, making them believe in Ukrainian militant nationalism and Ukrainians' organic antisemitism. Two decades after the collapse of the Soviet Union, the former Soviet dissident Ivan Hel remembered that in 1985 Gleb Pavlovskii, today Russian "political technologist" and chauvinist whom he met in exile in the Komi ARSR, told Ivan: "If you proclaim Ukraine independent and try to secede from Russia, we will eliminate you, physically, within 24 hours."[6] Yet, the leading figure in the Ukrainian-Jewish community and former Soviet dissident Iosyp Zisels suggested that the gradual evolution of views and the reevaluation of attitudes toward the Soviet regime and toward other ethnic groups occurred within each individual who was involved in human rights activism in the 1960s and the 1970s. This transformation was sensed by Kyiv and Moscow officials, including the KGB, who made a decision to excoriate nationalisms by escalating arrests and prosecutions in the republic.[7] Among the arrested were Ukrainian and Jewish intellectuals Ivan Dziuba, Sviatoslav Karavanskyi, Yevhen Sverstiuk, Viacheslav Chornovil, Leonid Pliushch, Vasyl Stus, Petro Hryhorenko, Ar'ie (Yurii) Vudka, Eduard Kuznetsov, Avraam Shifrin, and Semen Gluzman. By 1972, for many, the urban space of human creativity, interactions, and political activism was replaced with the monotonous landscape of Siberian, Mordovian, and Ural camps. Many Ukrainians and Jews learned a great deal about each other's culture and aspirations only in Soviet camps, serving long-term sentences for anti-Soviet propaganda and nationalism. The Soviet and Israeli writer Mikhail Kheifets wrote: "[in camps] Ukrainians taught me that God needs every people . . . there are no unmerited or great peoples . . . due to Ukrainians I realized my national existence as a Jew. I am grateful to them; they opened my eyes at myself."[8] Among his fellow inmates was the Ukrainian poet Vasyl Stus who helped Kheifets realize the degree of his own assimilation and the damage to the Jewish cultural traditions and language under the Soviets.[9]

The bonds between Ukrainians and Jews established in the Gulag encouraged many Soviet Ukrainians and Jews to join Ukraine's dissident movement, and among the members of the Jewish emigration movement were those who gravitated toward dissidence. These connections among human rights activists of various ethnicities and their shared goals shaped the fabric of the dissident movement, and its waves inevitably transcended national borders, involving the largest diaspora groups in North America, Ukrainians and Jews, sympathetic to the cause of their brethren in Ukraine and other Soviet republics. Despite the geography and the ethnic barriers erected by the Soviets, the diverse Kharkiv human rights movement and the Ukrainian and Jewish diaspora groups in North America were connected in numerous ways. Moreover, these connections and cooperation have a rich history. This chapter offers a glimpse into the Kharkiv dynamics and the extent of the interaction between Ukraine's "cultural rebels" and Western diaspora groups, and illuminates the individual histories of several individuals whose courage and stoicism resonated in the West, ultimately bringing two worlds together amid the Cold War.

The removal of Khrushchev in October 1964 was followed by a brief period of relaxation of control over intellectuals, but in late 1965 censorship and control was reestablished in the form of growing pressure, persecutions, and arrests. The writers prematurely celebrated the abolishment of the Ideological Commission and Illichiov's removal from the Party Secretariat. The party intensified control over the writers through their Union, primary party cells, exhausting obligatory congresses, the press, and the KGB—all of which pushed many writers to join the dissident movement.[10]

The Soviet dissident movement gained clear contours by the late 1960s. It is difficult to calculate the exact number of dissidents who were active in Ukraine at the peak of the Cold War. The Canadian scholar Bohdan Kravchenko has compiled a list of 975 individuals who were quite visible and active in the Ukrainian SSR between 1960 and 1972. This number reflects a tiny portion of Ukraine's 50 million population.[11] A similar trend could be observed in Kharkiv. By 1960, among nearly a million of Kharkiv residents, 67.2 percent were Russian-speaking people, 31.2 percent Ukrainian-speaking people, and 1.6 percent of people who spoke other languages,[12] and there were only several dozen nationally conscious individuals among them who by 1972 joined the dissident movement. Most of them were representatives of creative and technical intelligentsia who were carefully watched by the Fifth Directorate of the KGB.

After 1967 when Yurii Andropov became head of the KGB, he proposed setting up a directorate explicitly tasked with countering anti-Soviet propaganda spread by the intelligentsia and "ideological subversion" emanating from abroad. The Central Committee of the Communist Party of the Soviet Union was responsive to Andropov's proposition, issuing resolution no. P 47/97 that ultimately helped establish the Fifth Chief Directorate. From 1971, a special unit managed operations against "Zionists" in the Soviet Union and "foreign subversive Zionist centers," and two years later the Eighth Department was established within the directorate that investigated the "subversive anti-Soviet" activities of Jewish diaspora groups. The directorate grew rapidly, faster than any other Directorate of the KGB. But the more aggressive the KGB became, the more actively the Soviet dissidents resisted control and surveillance.[13]

Cooperation among Soviet dissidents of various ethnic backgrounds emerged as a response to state violence and repression, expanding the space of anti-Soviet sentiment and resistance beyond the borders of the USSR. The links among the dissidents grew domestically, involving broad circles of their counterparts abroad. The West learned about the dissent in Ukraine through the uncensored dissident literature that penetrated the Iron Curtain in the mid-1960s and the activities of Western journalists in the Soviet Union.[14] As a result, the KGB failed to keep secret the clandestine persecution and arrests aimed at isolating human rights activists. To an extent, Soviet party officials themselves contributed to the expansion of Ukrainian-Jewish cooperation in the West, publicly labeling the diaspora's human rights campaign as "anti-Soviet imperialism,"[15] and raging about Ukrainian nationalists and Zionists in Ukraine. These practices invited the Ukrainian and Jewish diasporas to overcome individual and collective stereotypes and hostilities toward each other and invest their efforts in liberating their persecuted and prosecuted brethren in Ukraine.

Many Soviet Jews and Ukrainians benefited from this cooperation, but a great many were psychologically and physically destroyed by their experiences of imprisonment before they received help from the West. Undoubtedly, the sophistication of the Soviet propaganda machine and the anemic bonds between the Ukrainian and Jewish diaspora exacerbated by the KGB played a role in the broken lives and premature deaths of hundreds, if not thousands, of Soviet Jewish and Ukrainian dissidents. In their struggle against human rights abuses in the Soviet Union, the Western Ukrainian and Jewish communities, however, remained divided and even segregated in their activities to a significant degree.

Cooperation, albeit limited, between Ukrainians and Jews within the Western anti-Soviet human rights movement did occur, despite the carefully planned Soviet propaganda campaign designed to discredit Ukrainians in the eyes of the Western Jewish community and vice versa, and to nullify their human rights activities. The Western grassroots human rights movements, Helsinki monitors, and many other diaspora interest groups and associations directly and indirectly fueled significant change in the Soviet Union, and ultimately across Europe. Many observers hold that the end of the Cold War became possible due to the civic gallantry of many human rights activists and the transnational cooperation of various ethnic communities, at times conflicting and difficult and at times enjoyable and fruitful.

Cooperation between Two Diaspora Groups and Its Challenges

The human rights movement in the Soviet Union engaged many ethnic groups in the USSR. Although the grievances of various ethnic communities in the USSR had their distinct character, all members of this movement advocated the rule of law, free speech, the freedom of movement and emigration, and the right for their culture to exist and develop. Within this movement that by the early 1970s became a pan-Soviet phenomenon, there were Ukrainians who protested against Russification, persecution, and imprisonment of the Ukrainian intelligentsia, and Jews, *refusenik* groups and individuals who advocated the rights of Soviet Jewry to develop their culture or to emigrate to Israel.[16] Both groups relied on internal and external sources of support, including diaspora organizations and Western governments, although various Soviet Jewish groups took advantage of the support of "'external' rather than 'internal' resources."[17]

In the early 1960s, the Soviet regime managed to keep the diaspora in the dark for quite some time about arrests of human rights activists and dissidents. Kremlin propaganda and the KGB tried to obscure communicative links that existed between the diaspora and its brethren in the USSR. Persecution and arrests of the opposition were camouflaged by false accusations that portrayed Soviet dissidents as criminals or psychiatrically ill individuals.[18] Despite the fact that by 1963 in the United States, there were approximately 300 Ukrainian periodicals that routinely enlightened their readers about the situation in Ukraine,[19] the first wave of Soviet repressions launched in 1964–1965 against the Ukrainian and Jewish intelligentsia received little international attention. Western outlets, such as *Voice of America*, *Radio Liberty*, *Vatican Radio*, and *BBC*, began to extensively cover the abuse of dissidents in the Soviet Union, including Ukraine, only in the late 1960s, although some degree of popular awareness of violations of human rights in the USSR can be traced to the beginning of the 1960s.[20]

The informational breakthrough occurred during the second part of the 1960s when *samvydav* penetrated through the Iron Curtain, and the United Nations and UNESCO were bombarded by letters of complaint about human rights abuses in Ukraine, authored by Ukrainian and Jewish émigré individuals and organizations. Because of the imprisonment of Ukrainian and Jewish activists, many associations and defense committees were formed in Canada and the United States. They sprang from the political activism of the Ukrainian and Jewish diaspora and their grassroots committees that organized solidarity hunger strikes, appealing to the local press and elected officials for their help. The charity movement on behalf of Soviet prisoners and their families emerged in 1966. Human rights activists donated money, clothes, and food and, by 1972, many unofficial charity funds for Russian, Ukrainian, and Jewish political prisoners were established.[21] These committees also organized rallies and protests in support of political prisoners, and their participants were people of various ethnicities, including Ukrainians and Jews.[22] For instance, in November 1974, approximately eighty people rallied at the Harvard Burr Hall to protest the fourteen-year incarceration of the Ukrainian dissident and historian Valentyn Moroz.[23] He was arrested by the authorities twice, in 1965 and in 1970, for "anti-Soviet agitation and propaganda," and the day of the rally was the 148th day of Moroz's voluntary hunger strike in the infamous Vladimir Prison outside Moscow. The rally was organized by the Harvard chapter of the Committee for the Defense of Soviet Political Prisoners, and speakers at the rally urged supporters to appeal to the U.S. Congress to obtain its support for Moroz.[24] Some committees were named after dissidents and victims of Soviet terror. For instance, Branch 111 of the Ukrainian National Women's League of America was named after Alla Horska, a Ukrainian artist and dissident who in 1970 was violently murdered, likely by the KGB, for her dissident activities. By the late 1970s, many grassroots groups founded in the middle of the 1970s were transformed into fully functioning associations, such as Americans in Defense of Human Rights in Ukraine led by Ihor Olshanivskyi. Its chapters were established in Canadian and American cities, such as Detroit, Rochester, Chicago, and Troy, NY.

The role of civil society was significant in this struggle, because the Cold War left little space for Western governments to be actively engaged in the issue of human rights violations in the Soviet Union during the 1960s–1980s. In addition, Soviet propaganda contributed to the view held by Western policymakers, including the American executive branch, that Ukraine was an integral province of Russia, and defending Ukraine's dissidents was thought of as interference in the internal affairs of the Soviet Union. Thus, various diaspora civil organizations and NGOs quickly filled this space, expanding it significantly through their moral and financial support for Soviet dissidents. As mentioned earlier, in the 1960s, the most active Soviet Ukrainian and

Jewish dissidents found themselves in labor camps, sharing the same cells and learning more about each other, and the process of rapprochement among the Ukrainian and Jewish diaspora was accelerated precisely because of these initial contacts among Ukrainian and Jewish dissidents who were sent to serve their sentences outside Ukraine.

The base for support of human rights activities in the West was substantial. Individual and collective memories and experiences of displacement and terror to which people were subjected in the Soviet Union inspired their political activism. The third wave of forced migration from Ukraine occurred during the Second World War, when approximately 4.2 million people were transported to Western Europe. At the end of the war the majority of the survivors returned to Ukraine. Yet approximately 310,000 remained in Western Europe, 240,000 of whom later migrated to the United States and Canada, 35,000–40,000—to Argentina and Brazil, and 30,000—to Australia. Moreover, in the 1970s–1980s, a group of Soviet nationally conscious individuals joined the Ukrainian and Jewish diaspora. Among them 30,000 Ukrainians found themselves in Canada, and 100,000—in the United States. Well-educated people, they occupied the leading positions in various diaspora organizations, and significantly advanced their infrastructure, moving the center of the Ukrainian diaspora activities from Europe to North America.[25] Between 1970 and 1980, approximately 250,000 Soviet citizens emigrated on Israeli visas. By 1980, however, the Soviet government placed restrictions on Jewish emigration, and in 1981 approximately 40,000 Jews were denied visas.[26]

Jewish-Ukrainian cooperation in North America that began to form in the late 1960s–early 1970s within the Western anti-Soviet human rights movement was built on the extant personal and institutional connections, established during the postwar decades in the United States and Canada. For instance, in the early 1950s, a commission of Jewish-Ukrainian affairs was formed at the Ukrainian Academy of Arts and Science in New York, and the Association to Perpetuate the Memory of Ukrainian Jews and the Support Committee for Ukrainian Jews were founded in New York under the leadership of Mendel Osherowitch, a Jewish writer, translator, historian, and the author of the three-volume publication *Jews in Ukraine* (1961).[27] Personal links and friendships among Ukrainian and Jewish families, members of these associations, survived through generations, serving as a social bond for their political activities in the 1970s. The Ukrainian diaspora in Canada, especially those who were leaders of various Ukrainian diaspora organizations and communities, took an active part in the human rights movement, protesting against the incarceration of intellectuals in Ukraine under Shelest and Brezhnev.[28] The diaspora tried to influence the societal and political developments in Ukraine through several channels, economic, informational, and cultural. However, because the USSR and its authoritarian governing and policymaking were less susceptible to diasporic influence than that of more democratic regimes, the Ukrainian diaspora, as any other interest group, sought support from other ethnic interest groups, including the Jewish diaspora community, and employed its financial resources locally to promote the anti-Soviet human rights grassroots movement exerting direct and indirect influence through donations to various "civil society" projects and lobbying state officials.[29]

The Ukrainian and Jewish diaspora encouraged and supported Western students' human rights initiatives, from rallies to street protests in front of Soviet embassies. Those students who struggled for Soviet Jewry's rights engendered local "action" committees in half a dozen cities in the United States. These activities served as the foundation for establishing an umbrella organization in 1970—the Union of Councils for Soviet Jews (UCSJ). In the 1970s, the Union functioned as the principal grassroots organization that facilitated the effectiveness of the Soviet Jewry Movement. The Union offered moral and financial support for the movement, and its objectives included assistance to Soviet political prisoners and their eventual release from Soviet labor camps and emigration from the USSR. Many other ethnic grassroots groups and NGOs participated in the activities of the UCSJ. They shared general strategies and methods of influence on the Soviet government in human rights matters. Individual contacts among the members of the UCSJ and organizations, such as the Human Rights Commission (HRC) of the World Congress of Free Ukrainians (WCFU), were preserved until the very collapse of the Soviet Union, strengthening Western commitment to human rights that led to revolutionary changes in Eastern Europe at the end of the twentieth century.[30]

Soviet propaganda, however, that reinforced the idea of organic Ukrainian antisemitism discouraged many representatives of Jewish organizations from collaborating with the Ukrainian diaspora. Individual cases of Soviet political prisoners were handled on the basis of "ethnic membership," and cooperation between Ukrainians and Jews remained limited in the 1970s. Individuals like Ivan Bahrianyi, a former Soviet prisoner and a survivor of physical and psychological torture during his incarceration, published widely on antisemitism in the Soviet Union, arguing that antisemitism is "a Russian, not Ukrainian phenomenon."[31] "Antisemitism in the USSR is only a chapter of a greater and more frightening phenomenon, that is [Soviet] national politics," Bahrianyi wrote.[32] He posited that antisemitism in the Soviet Union was a "manifestation of old traditional Russian imperialism," and that no one else but the Soviet authorities employed antisemitism in foreign politics for their imperial interests.[33] In his analysis of Ukrainian-Jewish encounters and the treatment of Jews in Ukrainian thought, including Bahrianyi's writings, Yohanan Petrovsky-Shtern has suggested that even if it could sound self-indulgent, this implication demonstrated a new tendency in Ukrainian thought, namely, to disassociate from anti-Jewish sensibilities and thus purify Ukrainian nationalist logic. In a sense, it was an attempt to disassociate genuine Ukrainian nationalism from the ignominious traces of Dontsov's antisemitism. And the importance of this shift for further Ukrainian-Jewish encounter is difficult to overestimate—especially given the fact that Bahrianyi was not the only one who moved in that direction.[34]

Petrovsky-Shtern recalled the views of Denys Kwitkowskyi [Kwitkowsky] (1909–1979), a diaspora's journalist, the head of the Movement of Ukrainian Nationalists (PUN, stands for *Provid Ukrainskykh Natsionalistiv*), and a lawyer who resided in North America. Kwitkowskyi was impressed by the bravery and approach of the Israeli Jewish leaders to creating an independent state of Israel. He deconstructed the complexity of historical events that prevented the rapprochement of the Jewish and Ukrainian nations, calling for mutual respect, equal partnership, and struggle against "the common enemy—'communist Moscow'—the only entity that benefits from Ukrainian-Jewish discord."[35] According to Kwitkowskyi, the common fate shared by Ukrainians and Jews and shaped by Soviet persecution on the basis of their ethnic origin should unite them in this struggle.

The idea of the historical inevitability of hostilities based on ethnicity is fraught with dogmas that enslave thinking processes, making people "accept whatever happens as irresistible and foolhardy to oppose."[36] Scholars and thinkers challenged this idea in the hope that their arguments and explanations would eventually reach out to a broader public, illuminating popular fallacies, biases, and prejudices that obfuscated productive communication and rapprochement among various ethnic groups. Such an attempt in the realm of Ukrainian-Jewish encounters was undertaken by Jewish and Ukrainian scholars in Canada and the United States in the 1960s and 1970s. Among them were diaspora historians Ivan Lysiak-Rudnytsky (1919–1984) and Omeljan Pritsak (1919–2006), the founder of the Ukrainian Research Institute at Harvard University (HURI) whose ideas were built on Viacheslav Lypynskyi's (1882–1931) multiethnic approach to Ukrainian history. This approach inspired seminal works written by Canadian Ukrainian scholars Orest Subtelny (1941–1916), Paul Robert Magocsi, and Zenon Kohut.[37] They wrote an inclusive history of Ukraine in which Jews played an important role. Moreover, a collaborative effort by the Jewish scholar Howard Aster and the Ukrainian scholar Peter Potichnyj served as the intellectual foundation for rapprochement of two peoples ("two solitudes")—Jews and Ukrainians.[38] These efforts had practical implications and, to a significant degree, were advanced because of state violence in Soviet Ukraine and the growing number of political prisoners in the Soviet Gulag in the 1960s and 1970s. Soviet repressions against dissidents motivated the collaborative work of Ukrainian and Jewish scholars and inspired Ukrainian-Jewish conferences and roundtable workshops, where they discussed the tragic events in the USSR and a shared Ukrainian and Jewish history.[39] In the 1970s, at the height of Soviet terror against dissidents, the Munich-based and later New York-based *Suchasnist* journal and the Israeli-based Ukrainian-language *Dialohy* journal became the platforms for such discussions.[40]

The developments on both sides of the Iron Curtain, as well as Jewish aspirations to emigrate from the USSR, provoked serious concerns among Soviet officials. They took urgent measures to prevent the "spread of global Zionism," as well as the truth about state violence, targeting dissidents and nationalists throughout the Soviet Union.[41] Most importantly, Western alliances that supported Ukraine's dissidents were to be compromised and broken. The major targets of various Soviet institutions, including the KGB, were Ukrainian-Jewish human rights initiatives in the United States and Canada, and the initiatives of support emanating from Israel for *refusenik* and Jewish political prisoners.

The KGB identified "the collaboration of Zionism and Ukrainian bourgeois nationalism" as the priority, and the aforementioned Fifth Directorate got to work, investigating and undermining these interactions (Fig. 3.2).

Figure 3.2 Images of Ukrainian and Jewish Nationalists (a Cartoon in *Perets*). *Source*: Courtesy of *Lekhaim* (*Lekhaim*, no. 271, 30 October 2014, http://old.lechaim.ru/2461).

The objective was to discredit Ukrainian émigrés in the eyes of the Jewish diaspora, Jewish NGOs, and Israel, blemishing the Ukrainians' reputations by facts mixed with half-truths, disinformation, forgeries, and false testimonies.[42] Western Jewish diaspora groups and associations were also subjected to scrutiny, falling under the collective term of "intelligence centers of imperialist states" that were identified by the KGB and Soviet propagandists as agents that undermined the image and reputation of the Soviet Union.[43]

The task of compromising Ukrainians and Jews in each other's eyes was considered feasible by the Soviets because the foundations for mutual hostilities were established centuries ago and were exacerbated at the beginning of the twentieth century and especially during the Second World War.[44] Shimon Redlich has noted that "Poles, Ukrainians, and, most of all, Jews were at the epicenter of suffering. It has been very difficult, nearly impossible, for them to view with empathy and understanding the plight of the others. Decades of communism, with its ideological and manipulative restrictions, made a genuine and honest facing of their common past highly unlikely."[45] Stalin's terror against Ukrainians during the interwar period and his latent pre–Second World War antisemitism incited popular antisemitism among some Ukrainians that was amplified by German propaganda in occupied Ukraine, calling to "avenge the wrongs done them by the 'Judeo-Bolsheviks.'"[46] The participation of Ukrainian radical nationalist groups in the Holocaust inculcated anti-Ukrainian attitudes among Jews. As a result, Ukrainian-Jewish relations in the West have been difficult and were aggravated by several developments in the 1970s and 1980s, including the sensational cases of Dr. Mikhail Stern, a Ukrainian Jew and Soviet political prisoner, and John Demjanjuk, a diaspora Ukrainian who, according to the Soviets, exterminated thousands of Jews, while working at the Nazi concentration camp near Treblinka, Poland.[47]

Formally, Stern was sentenced to prison for receiving bribes from his patients, yet the underlying reason for his trial and his subsequent imprisonment was his refusal to discourage his sons from emigrating to Israel.[48] After his release and emigration to the West, Stern, also a supporter of Ukrainian national aspirations, was warmly welcomed by the Ukrainian diaspora in the United States but was shunned by American Jews. According to various sources, there were a number of reasons for this pattern. First, the Israeli government was frustrated that after doing everything possible to release Stern, he went to the United States instead of Israel. Second, in view of the influential Western Jewish diaspora, Stern's close association with the Ukrainian diaspora in the United States could jeopardize Jewish emigration from the Soviet Union. Third, expressing his gratitude to Ukrainians who refused to testify against him and arguing that "the Ukrainian people are not anti-Semitic people," Stern provoked a protest among American Jews, the majority of whom were firm believers in Ukrainian organic antisemitism.[49]

The Office of Special Investigations (OSI) in the United States was another powerful actor that ultimately undermined the effort of those Ukrainians and Jews who were willing to work together to help Soviet dissidents. In the middle of the 1960s, a special working group was established within the U.S. Immigration and Naturalization Service whose objective was to identify war criminals who committed crimes against humanity by collaborating with the Nazis, and who illegally resided in the United States. In 1977, the U.S. Congress established the OSI under the umbrella of the U.S. Department of Justice, whose officials investigated individual cases of Nazi war criminals, bringing them to justice. The major criticism of the Office's broad prerogatives included the claim that the Office relied heavily on evidence provided by the Soviets which turned out to be forgeries, like in Demjanjuk's case launched by the Department of Justice in 1977.[50] Eager to bring an alleged Nazi criminal to justice and experiencing pressure from the Jewish international community, the OSI withheld the evidence in their possession, prolonging and pursuing this case for decades. The details of the Demjanjuk affair and the OSI's misconduct have been examined in detail elsewhere but what is clear is that this case neatly dovetails the objectives of the Soviet secret campaign launched to break the coalition of Ukrainian ("Ukrainian nationalists") and Jewish ("Zionists") émigrés by perpetuating the image of Ukrainians as organic antisemites and war criminals.[51] Moving against the logic of the Cold War at its height, the Soviet government expressed its eagerness to work with American officials, providing "evidence" of a Ukrainian immigrant's war crimes, evidence that proved to be forged in the process of Demjanjuk's lengthy legal battle in the United States, Israel, and Germany.[52]

More interestingly, recently discovered archival documents about the KGB operation "Retribution" (or Payback) designed to drive a wedge between North America's Ukrainian and Jewish communities and curtail their mutual anti-Soviet activities confirm the argument of Roman Kupchinsky, the director of *Radio Liberty* in Ukraine, that he made several decades ago. According to Kupchinsky, the Russian disinformation campaign in the 1960s and 1970s was organized by the highest echelons of power in the USSR as a response to rapprochement between the Ukrainian and Jewish diaspora and the state of Israel for the purpose of defending the human rights of Soviet dissidents. Indeed, for the Soviets, the consolidation of Western forces that helped release Soviet dissidents and expose human rights abuses and state violence in the Soviet Union meant a blow against the myth about the USSR as the most humane political system.[53] Archival documents discovered in the former KGB archive and the former party archive in Kyiv, Ukraine, fully expose the plans of Soviet authorities to disrupt these activities.

Beyond the KGB, high-ranking Ukrainian officials contributed greatly to this campaign—from the Central Committee (TsK) to most important Soviet institutions, such as Ukraine's Ministry of Foreign Affairs and Ukraine's Academy of Sciences. Their records suggest that, following Moscow's orders, in July 1976, two members of the TsK KPU Anatolii Merkulov, the head of the Department of Foreign Relations, and Yurii Yelchenko, the head of the Department of Propaganda and Agitation, informed Valentyn Malanchuk, Ukraine's key ideologue, about the pressing need to launch a counterpropaganda campaign to neutralize the activities of the Ukrainian diaspora nationalists who seemed to coordinate their efforts with the Western Jewish diaspora, identified by a collective term "Zionists." Their activities, it was reported, aimed to discredit the Soviet Union. Merkulov received information about "reactionary Ukrainian immigration" and the ideological conglomerate they allegedly created with Zionists from Ukrainian diplomats who worked for the UN Secretariat. Merkulov and Yelchenko suggested that in order to break this union, the Central Committee should engage historians from the Institute of History of Ukraine's Academy of Sciences. Scholars would provide the Western and Soviet Jewish community with documents that would compromise Ukrainian nationalists in their eyes. Evidence of Ukrainians' violence against Soviet Jews during the Second World War that "exceeded that of the Nazis" would serve this purpose. Merkulov and Yelchenko posited: "Documents, images, and other factual materials would be especially valuable to uncover the hypocrisy of Ukrainian immigrants who yesterday were killing the Jews and today are involved in ingratiating behavior with Zionists." These documents, they insisted, should be published in Western outlets such as *Visti z Ukrainy* and *News from Ukraine* in Ukrainian and English.[54] As the Demjanjuk affair had shown, historical facts and authentic materials mixed with forgeries created by the KGB constituted the evidential base for this operation.

Furthermore, the Ministry of Foreign Affairs was assigned a similar task to design a set of measures that would neutralize "Ukrainian nationalists" and compromise the Ukrainian community in the West. In August 1979, Minister Heorhii Shevel devised a comprehensive plan that would restrain the activities of Western bourgeois nationalist organizations and the Ukrainian diaspora.[55] He identified four categories of Ukrainian immigrants: reactionary (Ukrainian bourgeois nationalists), progressive, "neutral," and politically indifferent.[56] Shevel suggested that Soviet embassies should invest their efforts in (1) studying the connections between nationalists and the local influential political, business and clerical elites, governments, and secret services; (2) analyzing the extent of interactions between nationalists and other ethnic reactionary circles, such as Zionists, Maoists, and others; and (3) examining the relationship between various factions within nationalist organizations and the role of the Ukrainian Autocephalous Orthodox Church (*Ukrainska avtokefalna pravoslavna tserkva*) and informational centers of nationalist organizations in anti-Soviet propaganda abroad. Shevel also suggested that to curtail the anti-Soviet activities of these organizations, it would be prudent to recruit and convert their youth. It would be especially fruitful, he stressed, to ideologically subvert those who belonged to the "neutral" immigrant category who might become loyal to the Soviet regime. Shevel argued that to reach these goals, the associates of Soviet embassies should organize cultural events and meetings to reach out to those who were undecided in their ideological positions. These individuals should be provided with Soviet propaganda literature which should also be popularized through the local mass media. The Soviet embassies should also facilitate meetings between those ideologically stable individuals who were allowed to travel abroad and the local youth of Ukrainian origin, and to organize various cultural events abroad (i.e., "The Days of the UkrSSR Abroad") that would promote the Soviet way of life in Ukraine. The main objective of these events would be to deliver the message about the humane nature of Soviet nationalities policies and to discredit the claims of Ukrainian bourgeois nationalists that damaged peaceful coexistence and international relations between the Soviet Union and the West. Shevel also suggested that Soviet embassies should regularly inform the Ministry about the subtle dynamics of their missions and promised that the Ministry would provide information and financial support for implementing this goal.[57]

This secret campaign, it was thought, would distract the attention of the world community from the human rights issue in the USSR and would disrupt a concerted effort of various ethnic communities abroad aimed at mobilizing a broader international community to help Soviet dissidents. At the very least, the campaign would obscure Soviet nationalities policies that denied Ukrainians and Jews their right to develop their languages and cultures. To a significant extent, this Soviet covert operation, combined with massive propaganda efforts, was a success, engraving in Jewish memory the image of Ukrainians as antisemites, an image that hampered collaboration between the Ukrainian and Jewish communities in the West for decades to come.

Nevertheless, *samvydav* that kept Western communities informed about the realities in the Soviet Union, and Soviet dissidents' petitions to the Soviet authorities and international organizations created a space for a dialogue between the two ethnic diaspora groups. For the first time since the attempts at a Ukrainian-Jewish dialogue that were curtailed by the Bolsheviks in the postrevolutionary decade,[58] this space became truly transnational, inviting the Ukrainian and Jewish communities to participate in the movement against injustice and terror in the Soviet Union. Importantly, communication among imprisoned Ukrainian and Jewish dissidents created a new intellectual, cultural, and humane context for Ukrainian and Jewish émigrés that made their rapprochement possible.

Unstable Cooperation

During the second half of the 1960s, *samvydav* reached its peak distribution and popularity. The KGB designed special methods that would help destroy the centers of its production and distribution. Before the second wave of arrests of Ukraine's writers and dissidents in 1972, from 1965 to 1971, the secret police detained and arrested approximately 6,000 people in Ukraine who "radicalized" *samvydav* or had anything to do with its production or circulation. The first wave of repression targeted Ukrainian intellectuals. Twenty-five prominent writers and scholars were arrested in 1965. Hundreds of students were expelled from universities, and university professors were fired for their political views.[59] The dissidents were charged with "anti-Soviet propaganda" and "bourgeois nationalism" and sentenced to labor camps for two to seven years. Others were placed in psychiatric clinics. People were held in cells of preliminary imprisonment (KPZ) for months without trial and were subjected to beatings. Most trials were held behind closed doors and without adequate defense. Illegal searches and interrogation, and seizure of manuscripts and private archives "must run into thousands,"[60] and writers, actors, artists, and the technical intelligentsia most of whom were struggling to earn a crust of bread were the primary target of the KGB. For those who were still free, the uncertainty and fear were something that they inhaled daily, unsure of their present and future.

By the late 1960s, the authorities' attention turned to Ukraine's Jews. Ukrainian-Jewish human rights activist and the former Soviet dissident and member of the Ukrainian Helsinki Group Iosyp Zysels has aptly noted that, living in diaspora for 2,000 years, the Jewish people developed a powerful instinct for self-preservation, orienting themselves first and foremost on the strong central power of the state, because only the state could protect the minority against hostile environments in the localities.[61] Yet despite these adjustment strategies, the Jewish experience during the Soviet interwar and postwar period was tragic. Stalin exterminated thousands of Jews working in the highest echelons of the party and the secret organs during the Great Terror, and institutionalized antisemitism as a state policy after the Second World War, executing and imprisoning Jews as "poisoners" and "cosmopolitan traitors." Devastated by the terror and inspired by the national liberation movements in Ukraine, the Jewish community, more often than not, began to align themselves with Ukrainians who in the 1960s–1980s resisted Soviet imperial practices by distributing *samvydav* and creating illegal national unions and clubs, the Helsinki groups in particular.[62] The liberalization of Ukraine during the Khrushchev Thaw and the subsequent re-Stalinization prompted 5,762 Ukrainian Jews to submit immigration papers to the Ministry of Internal Affairs in the second part of the 1960s.[63] The June 1967 Six-Day

War between Israel, Egypt, Syria, and Jordan awakened Jewish consciousness, encouraging Jews to seek external support to emigrate from the USSR. In 1969 and 1970, they signed petitions and wrote letters, addressing them to the United Nations Committee on Human Rights, high-ranking party officials in the USSR, and President Zalman Shazar (1889–1974) of Israel.[64] These activities resulted in restrictions on emigration and persecution and imprisonment of the most active petitioners. Nevertheless, by 1973, the number of Jews who were willing to emigrate from Ukraine almost doubled.[65] Many were denied permission to emigrate to Israel, forming a group of people who were referred to as "immigrationist," "refusenik," or a Zionist group.[66] There was also another group of Jewish activists, "culturalists," who advocated the rejuvenation of Jewish cultural traditions in Ukraine by creating illegal Jewish educational centers (*ulpany*) in Kyiv, Kharkiv, Odesa, and other Ukrainian cities and towns.[67] Distribution of *samvydav*, teaching Hebrew in *ulpany*, and secretly (under pseudonyms) publishing prose and poetry abroad became widespread strategies of protests against the authorities. Kharkiv activists organized seminars on teaching Hebrew in their private apartments, trying to escape the KGB's attention.[68]

The Cold War, the Iron Curtain, and Soviet restrictions on tourism and emigration prevented the Israeli government from openly pursuing a policy of assistance to Soviet Jewry to avoid further harm.[69] Israel tried to recruit American Jewry to assist Soviet Jews in emigrating from the Soviet Union and to invite the American Jewish community to develop their connections with other ethnic communities in the United States. The goal was to find solutions for alleviating the suffering of Soviet Jewry, including Ukrainian Jews. The American Jewish community, however, objected to Israel's insistence on forcible resettlement of Soviet Jews in Israel, a dispute that culminated in a crisis between Israeli and American Jews.[70] The common ground, however, was a shared belief that the Soviet government should be further pressed to grant visas to Soviet Jews. The collective efforts of Western human rights activists bore fruit, and in the early 1970s, the Soviet authorities began to grant visas to Jews. In 1970, of 14,300 Soviet Jews granted exit visas, the majority emigrated to Israel, compared with 4,300 from 1968 to 1970.[71] In 1972, Jewish emigration increased to 31,903 and in 1973 to 34,733. In total, in the 1970s, of almost 250,000 emigrants, 150,000 went to Israel and 64,000 to the United States. Yet the Soviets continued to be extremely selective, and many Jews were denied their visas.[72] The most vocal and persistent Jewish activists were arrested and sent to labor camps.

Throughout three decades of late Soviet socialism, Amnesty International, a London-based NGO founded in 1961 by the lawyer Peter Benenson, was one of the most active organizations that helped Soviet political prisoners. Importantly, under its auspices, many Ukrainian and Jewish scholars and activists worked together to draw international attention to human rights abuses in the Soviet Union. In the late 1960s, only two sections of this organization functioned in the United States—the Washington center and the Riverside Group in New York. In the middle of the 1970s, Amnesty chapters mushroomed throughout the United States, working on individual cases of prisoners and facilitating their release. For instance, the American scholar of Ukrainian descent Anna Procyk joined the Madison Avenue Group led by Yadya Zeltman. Together they began to work on the case of Zenovii Krasivskyj, historian, author of *samvydav*, member of the Ukrainian Helsinki Group (UHG) and of the Ukrainian National Front (UNF), Soviet political prisoner, and victim of Soviet political psychiatry.[73] The former Soviet Jewish prisoners Viktor Fainberg and Anatolii Radygin, who in 1974 managed to emigrate to Israel, brought the name of Krasivskyj to the attention of Amnesty's London headquarters. Both victims of Soviet political psychiatry, Fainberg and Krasivskyj met in Moscow in 1972, at the Serbsky Institute, the infamous psychiatric prison known for its unethical practices, targeting Soviet dissidents.[74] Procyk who was closely involved in Krasivskyj's case wrote:

> The Madison Group's efforts on behalf of Krasivskyj spanned for more than a decade and this perseverance, persistence and ultimate success has been unique in the history of human rights organizations. The Group's activities were largely responsible for keeping the prisoner alive in psychiatric prisons, labor camps and the bleakness of exiles in Siberia until the cracks in the Soviet system surfaced at the end of 1980s.[75]

Amnesty International maintained close ties with human rights activists, representatives of the Ukrainian and Jewish diaspora. Among them was Zbigniew Brzezinski, an American-Polish scholar of Jewish descent who in the 1960s was an adviser to John F. Kennedy, worked for the Johnson Administration, and served as Jimmy Carter's National Security Adviser.[76] Brzezinski was always available for Amnesty leaders and assisted them in human rights matters, including the defense of Jewish rights in the Soviet Union, advocated by the Ukrainian political prisoner Sviatoslav Karavanskyi. Brzezinski also helped publish documents collected by Viacheslav Chornovil, a Ukrainian politician, writer, and Soviet political prisoner, documents known as *The Chornovil Papers*, which first appeared in the American journal *The New Leader*.[77]

By the late 1970s, the geography of the human rights movement concerning Soviet repressive practices in Ukraine extended to European countries. Many of those Ukrainians and Jews who managed to emigrate or escape from Ukraine to Europe joined various human rights groups. For instance, at their 25 September 1978 clandestine meeting, as members of Polish and Czechoslovak human rights groups and the Polish Public Self-Defense Committee and Charter 77, they expressed their solidarity with dissidents in Ukraine, Armenia, Bulgaria, Georgia, Lithuania, East Germany, Russia, and Hungary. They extended their gratitude to the Russian human rights activist and nuclear physicist Yurii Orlov, the Ukrainian dissident and poet Mykola Rudenko, the Ukrainian dissident and teacher Oleksa Tykhyi, the Jewish dissidents and *refuseniks* Natan Sharanskii and Ida Nudel, and the Jewish journalist and poet Aleksandr Ginzburg for their cooperation and assured them that they would support them in their struggle to relieve their suffering. Their open letter reads: "The common fate of all our countries today binds us closer than ever before. It is very important, therefore, that those who seek to ensure a better life unite their efforts."[78]

Former Soviet Ukrainian prisoners who traveled to the West contributed greatly to the cause of Western human rights groups through their speeches and writings. Ukrainian-Jewish friendships established in camps extended to the public space, with no geographical or state borders, finding their reflection in essays, books, and articles published in the West. For instance, Valentyn Moroz who was arrested twice in Ukraine, in 1965 and 1970, for condemning the Soviet regime for its regimentation, censorship, and state violence,[79] admired the resilience of Jews and their ability to build a state. He wrote:

> A nation is something much deeper than language, territory, economy, culture.... I deeply sympathize with the Israeli people. Even more: I am enthralled with the idea of people who spent 2000 years in exile, and nonetheless experienced a rebirth. After 2000 years the Messiah reappeared in the land of Palestine and brought hope to the disheartened and faith to the disbelieving. He gave strength to those who had become weary in the struggle to hold one's own against assimilation and in the process doubted and asked: will we make it?... Yes, a nation is something very deep. It is inexhaustible.[80]

This rhetoric strengthened connections between many representatives of the Ukrainian and Jewish diaspora. Despite the tension between them, aggravated by the poisonous Soviet propaganda campaign, Ukrainian and Jewish human rights activists continued their collaborative work on individual and institutional levels.

Individuals, like Orest Deychakiwsky, served as connecting links among various American ethnic communities and institutions, whose interests were to help their men and women, abused by the Soviet system. Deychakiwsky, who from 1981 to 2017 worked for the Commission on Security and Cooperation in Europe (CSCE) as security officer and policy adviser for Belarus, Bulgaria, Moldova, Romania, and Ukraine, served as a member of

U.S. delegations to numerous OSCE meetings and election observation missions in nine countries.[81] Beyond his work as the commission's author, he participated in many forums, conferences, and meetings, where together with the representatives of various Jewish organizations, he discussed the treatment of Soviet dissidents, including Ukrainians and Jews.[82] The CSCE was founded in 1976 as an independent agency of the U.S. Federal Government. For forty years, the commission has monitored compliance with the Helsinki Accords, promoting democracy, human rights, and multifaceted cooperation in the fifty-seven-nation OSCE region. Most importantly, in monitoring violations of Helsinki human rights provisions, the commission served as a platform for intellectual exchange and cooperation among various diaspora groups across the globe. The organization provided a means to connect with one another and to discuss common approaches to pursuing effective tactics and strategies on influencing governments to comply with the Helsinki Final Act. The USSR and the states of Eastern Europe were the major focus of these discussions.[83] Helsinki activism became a transnational phenomenon and, as some have argued, it "shaped the end of communism in Central and Eastern Europe."[84]

Furthermore, beyond institutional cooperation, individual links continued to expand, and the mutual kindness of both communities made their dialogue more pleasant and productive. The past and present suffering of Ukrainians and Jews inflicted on them by the Soviet regime produced a bond of compassion between the leaders of the Jewish and Ukrainian diaspora groups that often grew into deep respect and friendships. For instance, in 1979, the AJC awarded the vice president of the Ukrainian National Association (UNA)[85] Myron Kuropas a Certificate of Appreciation that recognized him for "respecting diversity of all groups within our society; for helping to bring these groups together for the betterment of mankind; [and] for working together in responding to the needs of these diverse groups."[86] In addition, in 1981, the Consul General of Israel in Chicago invited Kuropas to visit Israel. The trip was sponsored by the AJC in Chicago and organized by David Roth, an official of the Committee and Kuropas's friend. One of Kuropas's objectives in Israel was to meet with Avraham Shifrin, Soviet *refusenik* and former chair of the Public Committee for Jewish-Ukrainian Cooperation founded in 1979 by Ukrainian-Jewish émigrés in Israel, and Yakov Suslenskii, former Soviet dissident and prisoner who in 1981 became head of the Public Committee (in 1981 the Committee became the Society of Jewish-Ukrainian Relations).[87] During his visit, Kuropas recorded interviews with the members of the Society that suggested that the issue of Jewish emigration from the Soviet Union, Soviet Jews' human rights, Ukraine's independence, and cooperation between the Ukrainian and Jewish diasporas were paramount to the Society's activities and aspirations.[88]

Suslenskii was planning a trip to the United States in the coming weeks, and Kuropas was eager to meet him on American soil. In concert with the Ukrainian Democratic Movement, Suslenskii appealed to Ukrainian and Jewish emigrants from the USSR, calling for the creation of a similar organization in North America.[89] He argued that it was time to overcome the antagonism between the two peoples, to normalize their relations on the basis of trust and cooperation, and to help others who lived behind the Iron Curtain. Suslenskii revealed the reasons for creating this Society: "In Soviet prisons the majority of prisoners were so-called Ukrainian nationalists and Zionists. We established normal relationships—we supported each other, and precisely Ukrainians often stood up to defend Jews. I was saved several times by them, and this cannot be forgotten."[90]

Sadly, Suslenskii's mission to the United States to strengthen cooperation between Israeli and American Ukrainians and Jews was not a success. In April 1981, the UNA warmly welcomed Suslenskii in Jersey City, NJ, and organized a series of talks and meetings for the former Soviet dissident. Yet Suslenskii's affiliation with the Ukrainian diaspora provoked skepticism among Jewish groups, and their lack of enthusiasm eventually thwarted his efforts. Some among the American Jewish community openly let Suslenskii know that they did not appreciate the ties. The young editor of the *Sentinel*, a Chicago Jewish newspaper, bluntly asked Suslenskii and Roth, "Why do you associate with such people?", pointing at Kuropas and his wife Lesia present at this meeting.[91] Not surprisingly, the interest in maintaining the Ukrainian-Jewish dialogue advocated by Suslenskii was unevenly covered by the Ukrainian and Jewish diaspora press. The American Jewish community published little on Suslenskii's initiative. Most publications that supported cooperation appeared in the *Ukrainian Weekly*.[92] Moreover, during his subsequent trips to the United States, Suslenskii gathered fewer and fewer people and his support base among American Jews soon became minimal.

The persistence of the Ukrainian community that continued to question the dubious practices of the OSI and the Soviets' deliberately misleading contributions to the OSI's evidentiary base distanced the leaders of the Jewish community from Ukrainians. The Jewish diaspora perceived these activities (*circa* the Demjanjuk affair) as the obstruction of justice and a manifestation of antisemitism. Kuropas wrote: "The Ukrainian-Jewish dialogue faded as both communities adopted a more militant posture toward each other, in the wake of the OSI investigations."[93] The officials of the Department of Justice and the OSI director who were reached out to by the leaders of the American Baltic and Ukrainian communities in hopes of being heard further contributed to mutual hostilities between Ukrainians and Jews. According to Kuropas, American officials were rude and discourteous toward the members of the delegation and dismissed their concerns. The climate of their meeting was described as "adversarial from the beginning."[94]

These attitudes and the general atmosphere of conflict, however, did not discourage either Suslenskii, Kuropas, or Roth. Their shared history of human rights activism inspired them to continue. In April 1985, Roth was presented with a recognition of service award by the Chicago chapter of Americans for Human Rights in Ukraine. Many years of Roth's dedication to Ukrainian-Jewish cooperation, human rights activism, and his testimony on behalf of the Ukraine Famine Commission bill earned him respect among the majority within the Ukrainian and Jewish communities.[95] Roth rejected divisiveness in relations among various ethnic groups, pioneering a multicultural approach to ethnic and minority affairs. Nevertheless, by the early 1980s, the dialogue and cooperation between the Ukrainian and Jewish human rights groups declined. The insights of Christina Isajiw, the former director of the HRC of the WCFU (currently the Ukrainian World Congress) who began her career as a human rights activist in Toronto with Amnesty International in 1973, help illustrate this point.

Over Isajiw's twenty-plus years of work on behalf of human rights and dissidents in the former Soviet Union, she attended numerous forums and conferences that, beyond theoretical and practical tasks of the human rights movement, negotiated the strategies of lobbying Western governments to pressure the USSR and its satellites in Eastern Europe to follow the human rights provisions of the Helsinki Final Act. One such conference of the National Inter-Religious Task Force on Soviet Jewry was held in Washington, D.C., in September 1982. Among speakers at the conference were Spencer Oliver, chief of staff of the CSCE Commission; Richard Pipes, director of Eastern European and Soviet Affairs for the National Security Council; and Elliot Abrams, assistant secretary of state for Human Rights and Humanitarian Affairs. Pipes argued that the USSR used Soviet Jewry as leverage in American-Soviet relations, generally treating them as the "fifth column." Soviet leaders understood very well that by pressuring Jews domestically, they ultimately applied pressure on American Jewry, which would inevitably exert influence over U.S. government officials who would have to make significant concessions to the USSR, considering the level of the Jewish community's power in American politics.[96] Pipes also suggested that "only by building up the armed forces and withholding foreign aid could the West have any leverage over human rights and other policies in the Soviet Union."[97] Abrams seemed to be rather skeptical about the concept of deterrence and the proposition to limit freedoms for Soviet officials while they were on American soil. In contrast, Abrams advocated a softer economic approach, implying manipulation of the sales of wheat that would disadvantage the Soviets, in turn encouraging them to think twice about how they should treat

Soviet Jewry. But the question about how his office was going to react to the Soviet treatment of non-Jewish dissidents in the Soviet Union stunned the majority of the attendees. Abrams stated that this would be the responsibility of other Western ethnic communities to defend the rights of their counterparts in the Soviet Union. He also pointed out that the political feasibility and the present priorities on Capitol Hill (he opined that at the time they were Soviet Jewish emigration) to a larger degree shaped the agenda of his office.[98] In other words, other ethnic diasporas had to have their own Abrams working for the State Department to alleviate the suffering of Ukrainian, Latvian, Estonian, Armenian, and Georgian political prisoners in the Soviet Union. This logic discouraged many but at the same time this reality stimulated activists to work harder and to seek new approaches to alleviating the situation for Soviet political prisoners.

The Kharkiv Dissidents

Several names have been forever engraved in the history of Kharkiv's dissident movement. Vladislav Nedobora, Sofiia Karasik, Genrikh Altunian, Aleksandr Kalinovskii, Lev Kornilov, Vladimir Ponomariov, Arkadii Levin, Ihor Kravtsiv, Anatolii Zdorovyi, Stepan Sapeliak, and Volodymyr Pasichnyk were the representatives of technical and creative intelligentsia whose lives became intertwined with the founders of the human rights movement in the Soviet Union Petro Grigorenko, Andrei Sakharov, Aleksandr Podrabinek, and Kharkiv-born Viktor Fainberg (Fig. 3.3).[99] An ethnically diverse group of people, they bonded together, united by shared moral principles, experiences in prisons and psychiatric clinics, and beliefs in individual freedoms and independent creative activities, unconstrained by party or KGB orders. In the space of state terror and fear, when the dissidents' best friends were frightened to approach their homes and avoided any contacts with them, there were a few brave individuals who offered the "transgressors" their friendship and intellectual support. In Kharkiv, two Borises, a Russian and a Jew, exemplified civic gallantry, spending time with the military engineer and the Ukrainian dissident of Armenian origin Genrikh Altunian and his family, when they needed their support the most. Between Altunian's two arrests, his classmate Boris Ladenzon and his wife Alla who seemed to be immune to fear brought to Genrikh's home that was under constant surveillance two Kharkiv couples, poet Boris Chichibabin and his wife Liliia Karas, and poet Marlena Rakhlina and her husband Yefim Zakharov.[100]

Chichibabin had his own history that was no less tragic than Altunian's. In June 1946, Chichibabin, at the time a student at Kharkiv State University's Philology Department, was arrested for anti-Soviet agitation. Marlena, also a student there, was in love with Boris. Not being married to him, she managed

Figure 3.3 Top Row: Naum Meiman, Sofia Kallistratova, Piotr and Zinaida Grigorenko, Natalia Velikanova, Father Sergei Zheludkov, and Andrei Sakharov. Bottom Row: Genrikh Altunian and Alexander Podrabinek. *Source*: Courtesy of Andrew Grigorenko (private archive).

to visit Chichibabin three times in the town of Kai where the ViatLag was located, earning the reputation as a rebel in the KGB.[101] Unsurprisingly, in Kharkiv officials' view, her poetry was inconsistent with the principles of socialist realism established as the canon for Soviet writers' works. The Third Secretary of the Kharkiv *obkom* characterized one of Rakhlina's poems as follows: "The author is trying to escape from [Soviet] life to the edge of the planet, even to the harem."[102] Chichibabin returned to Kharkiv in summer 1951 and established friendly relationships with many Kharkiv writers. He reconnected with his former fellow students and friends, philologists Yulii Daniel, Russian poet and son of a Jewish writer, and Daniel's first wife Larisa Bogoraz, a graduate of Kharkiv State University's Philology Department and daughter of a Jewish professor at Kharkiv State University. In the late 1950s, Daniel and Bogoraz moved to Moscow, and invited Chichibabin to join them and attempt to establish his literary career in Moscow. In the early 1960s, Chichibabin resided in Daniel's and Bogoraz's apartment, befriending Samuil Marshak, Il'ia Erenburg, Viktor Shklovskii, the former Kharkivite and poet Boris Slutskii, and the Russian poet and the founder of the literary association "Magistral" Grigorii Levin. By the time Chichibabin returned from Moscow to Kharkiv, he was a well-established poet who published his poems in *Novyi mir* and other literary journals in Kharkiv and Kyiv. Marlena, who was more famous among KGB operatives than among her readers, and Boris parted but preserved cordial, albeit complicated, relationships for the rest of Chichibabin's life.

Rakhlina, a poet of amazing breadth and depth, was a constant irritation for Kharkiv KGB operatives who, using the members of the Writers' Union, ethnic Russians and Ukrainians, attempted to intimidate and recruit her on numerous occasions. The KGB was aware that her poems were broadcast by *The Voice of America* and published by the Russian literary journal *Kontinent* in Paris. Moreover, Rakhlina's courage bewildered KGB officers: she persistently wrote letters of support to Altunian when he was in the Gulag.[103] Undoubtedly, her close connections with dissidents was the reason why she experienced difficulty in securing membership in the Writers' Union. Rakhlina remembered the shameless behavior of the Russian prose writer Boris Silaiev at the headquarters of the Writers' Union where she, a non-member, was invited for a conversation. Under the supervision of two individuals who, according to Rakhlina, looked like criminals, Silaiev informed Rakhlina that there was a report about her anti-Soviet poems that she allegedly published in the "anti-Soviet" journal *Kontinental* [sic!].[104] Sitting in the company of Ukrainian writers who like Silaiev were tasked to admonish Rakhlina, frightened Silaiev was constantly looking into his notes. Rakhlina interrupted him, stating that she did not send her poems to *Kontinent*. One of the Ukrainian writers exclaimed: "You take us for fools!" Rakhlina responded: "Even the KGB did not talk to me this way." Years after this conversation, Rakhlina perceived it as a surrealistic absurdity that occurred daily in the authoritarian Kharkiv. She believed this was an awkward attempt to intimidate her and to encourage her to denounce the staff of *Kontinent* in the presence of KGB people. KGB agents were quite persistent, routinely harassing Rakhlina, surveilling her apartment and frequently inviting her to their headquarters for "friendly" conversations. Soon after her conversation with Silaiev, Revolt Bunchukov, a writer with transparent KGB connections, visited her at home, openly asking her to denounce *Kontinent*.[105] Rakhlina rejected the request.

The dissident movement in Kharkiv that began to form in the mid-1960s kept the Kharkiv KGB quite busy. They investigated a myriad of links and friendships that connected the writers with the dissidents. The movement was represented by people of various educational and ethnic backgrounds, but Jews and Ukrainians stood out prominently among them throughout several decades of late socialism. Yet, the most frequently mentioned figure associated with the dissent in Kharkiv was the ethnic Russian Chichibabin who paradoxically, being a member of the Writers' Union, had never become an "official" writer. Moreover, the geography of the dissent's links and bonds extended far beyond Kharkiv because of the former Kharkivites Bogoraz and Daniel.

Bogoraz's marriage to Daniel determined her future as a human rights activist. In September 1965, Daniel, writer and translator of prose and poetry critical of the Soviet regime, and Andrei Siniavskii, literary critic known as the author of books on Picasso and Soviet poetry of the 1920s, were arrested in Moscow and accused of publishing their works abroad under the pseudonyms of Nikolay Arzhak and Abram Tertz. One scholar has argued that "the outcome of the pseudo-legal proceedings had been decided in advance by the Kremlin, and the debates resembled a dialogue of the deaf. The prosecutor, members of the court, and the well-chosen 'witnesses' spoke in strictly political terms, while the two writers referred to their tales as literary works and claimed the freedom of artistic expression—a move that stunned the magistrates with its daring."[106] The 1965–1966 Daniel-Siniavskii trial that coincided with the 1966 trials in Ukraine, including the Moroz-Ivashchenko trial, galvanized the dissident movement, which united the Russian, Jewish, and Ukrainian intelligentsia and helped establish links among dissidents and writers in Moscow and Kharkiv.[107] For Bogoraz, defending human rights and freedom of speech became her life mission.[108]

Common interests (love for the Russian language, poetry, and freedom of expression) and friendships, including romantic engagements among Bogoraz and Daniel, Rakhlina, and Chichibabin became the nucleus and the social glue that bonded the Russian-speaking Kharkiv literati and the dissidents from all over the Soviet Union. After Bogoraz's and Daniel's departure to Moscow, the group was further shaped by "Chichibabin's Wednesdays." By the early 1960s, an ethnically diverse group of Kharkiv poets and writers was formed who regularly visited Chichibabin's 7-square-meter apartment in Rymarska Street to chat and to read poetry. The "literary club" initially included five members: poets Mark Bogoslavskii and Arkadii Filatov, actor and artist Leonid Pugachiov, actress Aleksandra Lesnikova, and Marlena Rakhlina.[109] Later on, a graduate of the Kharkiv State University's Philology Department and Rakhlina's closest friend, poet Iosif Goldenberg joined the club. Goldenberg survived the Holocaust but lost all his relatives in Belarus under the Nazis. In the mid-1960s, he departed for Russia, where he taught Russian language and literature in the Novosibirsk *Akademgorodok*.[110] In 1968, after signing a letter, protesting the arrest of the dissidents Aleksandr Ginsburg, Yurii Galanskov, Aleksei Dobrovolskii, and Vera Lashkova, Goldenberg was fired and deprived of his teaching privileges.[111] Although closely monitored by the KGB, "Chichibabin's Wednesdays" survived as a nonofficial literary club for several years. Beyond reading poetry, the club's attendees discussed the human rights violations in Soviet society, facilitating the emergence of a network of like-minded people and bonds that transcended the ethnic and republican boundaries, far beyond Moscow (RSFSR) and Kharkiv (Ukraine).[112]

In the early 1970s, Chichibabin became acquainted with Ukrainian writers and dissidents Ivan Dziuba, Mykola Rudenko, and the aforementioned

Kharkivites Genrikh Altunian and Volodymyr Pasichnyk. The Soviet legal system criminalized their behavior, identifying them as Ukrainian nationalists and *antisovetchiki*. Dziuba, the author of the "anti-Soviet" pamphlet *Internatsionaliszm chy rusyfikatsiia?* (Internationalism or Russification?), was excluded from the Writers' Union in 1972. In 1975, the Writers' Union deprived Mykola Rudenko of his membership for his relationships with Moscow dissidents and protests against violations of human rights in Ukraine. Chichibabin admired Rudenko's bravery when at the peak of Stalin's antisemitic campaign in 1949, Rudenko refused to negatively characterize Jewish writers who were about to be dismissed from the Union.[113] Altunian signed a collective letter protesting against the authorities' persecution of General Petro Grigorenko and demanded the end of discrimination against the Crimean Tatars.[114] In 1964, the Ukrainian poet and a fifth-year student of the Kharkiv State University's Department of Philology Volodymyr Pasichnyk was expelled from the university for his poetry propagating "bourgeois nationalist ideology."[115] These acquaintances that grew into friendships shaped Chichibabin's affinities with the Ukrainian cause which the KGB identified as nationalism and "Ukrainian fascism," using these terms interchangeably in the press for propaganda purposes.

For Chichibabin, the efforts of the KGB were quite transparent, as well as the danger of his connections. He was respectful of the aspirations of people representing various ethnic groups in the dissident movement. Each group had its own specific goals. Jews united to preserve their Jewish identity and culture, and to assert their right to emigrate to Israel, Crimean Tatars— their right to return to their homeland, Crimea, and the Baltic nations—to preserve their national identities. While Russian dissidents were largely concerned with human rights, freedom of speech, and the democratization of life in the Soviet Union, Ukrainian dissidents defended their civil and national rights. Ukrainian dissidents opposed Russification that presented an "imminent threat to Ukraine's existence as a nation."[116] For instance, at Kharkiv State University, out of 777 lecturers only 104 (13 percent) lectured in Ukrainian, and the language of instruction at the Kharkiv Institute of Law that trained specialists for the Ukrainian legal institutions (typically, 85 percent of its graduates remained to practice in Ukraine) was Russian, realities that contradicted the Constitution of the UkrSSR and its legal code, according to which all judicial proceedings should have been conducted in the Ukrainian language.[117] That is precisely why the KGB applied different standards to criminal cases of Ukrainian and Russian dissidents. For Ukrainians, even the possession of Taras Shevchenko's works fell under the article of the Criminal Code specified as anti-Soviet agitation and propaganda.[118] Moreover, Ukrainian dissidents received harsh sentences and served them outside Ukraine, typically in the RSFSR. According to many accounts, the majority of political prisoners were Ukrainians.[119] Residing in Kharkiv for quite some time, Chichibabin understood these specifics and, indisputably, his "difficult" poetry, his "Jewdophilia," and his affiliations with dissidents, "Zionists" and "Ukrainian nationalists," played a decisive role in the 1973 decision of the Writers' Union to revoke his membership.[120] Chichibabin also understood the gravity of the Writers' Union disobeying the KGB's order to purge him from the Union, and preserved warm relationships even with those who voted him out, those whom he respected not for their cowardice but for their poetry.

Yet there was also a deeper and subtler connection that held the writers together amid state violence: they were nurtured by decades of existence in Kharkiv's cultural space which was not only a space of regimentation and national humiliation for them, but also a space saturated with the intellectualism of the philosopher Hryhorii Skovoroda, the historian Dmytro Bahalii, the ethnographer Mykola Sumtsov, and the linguists Oleksandr Potebnia and George Shevelov.[121] The writers cherished Kharkiv's historical and intellectual traditions and were proud of the fact that Kharkiv was home for the Ukrainian writer and scholar Ivan Franko who in 1906 received a doctorate in Russian linguistics at Kharkiv University, and for Nobel Prize laureates of Jewish origin, physicist Lev Landau, immunologist Il'ia Mechnikov, and economist Simon Kuznets.[122] These memory links were fostered by their collective trips to Skovorodynivka, a village near Kharkiv where the Ukrainian philosopher Skovoroda was buried, the Memorial of Glory, and the Drobytskyi Yar where 20,000 Jews, Ukrainians, and Russians were murdered by the Nazis.[123] Forbidden by the authorities, this cultural space and the space of their memories were guarded, respected, and attended regularly by the writers and by the administration of the Writers' Union who refused to identify the former Gulag and Nazi camps' prisoners as enemies and anti-Soviet elements, supporting them morally and financially. Arkadii Filatov contended that this intellectual space and shared experiences and memories of war were sacred for many writers. Their life paths at times divorced them from the place of their youth, a place of violence and insecurity, but they returned to Kharkiv again and again, intellectually and physically, remembering what they wanted to remember.[124] In his eulogy dedicated to Chichibabin, Filatov identified Kharkiv in the 1960s and 1970s as follows: "It seems like the entire life turned against us . . . punishing us, excommunicating us, and admonishing us. But we ignored it, having taken it easy. Chichibabin cherished and celebrated these minutes of [terror]; they made him feel young and creative . . . we believed our path was righteous and harmonious."[125]

This unorthodox perception of their roles as writers, their cultural and intellectual affinities, and their extensive communication with the representatives of the ethnically diverse dissident movement made the KGB intensify their efforts at curtailing "this cozy circle," as one KGB officer has stated. The KGB leadership considered these trends systemic and disturbing, and their operations designed to eradicate these pernicious trends lasted until the very end of the Soviet Union.[126] The interethnic bonds were meant to be destroyed through propaganda and public campaigns that mobilized the Ukrainian and Russian writers to argue that the "Jewish question" in Ukraine was a construct of Western propaganda.[127] Encouraged by Moscow's orders to disrupt the links and to curtail the cooperation between various ethnic groups, KGB and law enforcement officials no longer refrained from open antisemitic remarks in their offices and courts.[128] In their documentation, they blamed Jews and the "Zionist" intelligentsia for glorifying Jewish poets and writers, such as Osip Mandelshtam, arguing that by praising Jewish writers, they promoted their ethnic exclusivity and national exceptionalism.[129]

In the spring of 1971, the head of the KGB in Ukraine Vitalii Fedorchuk was ordered to analyze the ideological situation in the Writers' Union in Kharkiv. On 11 May 1971, his report was forwarded to the Central Committee, in which Fedorchuk emphasized that Kharkiv writers seemed to be politically and ideologically unstable: they criticized domestic and foreign policy of the Soviet Union and complained about discrimination against Ukrainian writers, the Ukrainian language, and more broadly Ukrainian culture.[130] He noted that despite the prophylactic talks with Chichibabin in the KGB headquarters, he continued to write anti-Soviet poems, praised Aleksandr Solzhenitsyn, and systematically communicated with dissidents, engaging in exchange of *samvydav* with them.[131] According to Fedorchuk's report, Radii Polonskyi went even further and stated: "The entire world knows that the Russians are colonizers and treat them accordingly. Only we, Ukrainians, for some reasons, do not know what to do about them. The writers' mouths are shut."[132] Fedorchuk also included a Jew in the list of "anti-Soviet elements," the writer Roman Levin who allegedly denounced the Soviet system and Soviet realities.[133] In addition, Fedorchuk illuminated a new trend among writers: they learned very well how to use more effectively the Aesopian language and the "language of hints" in their writings,[134] a practice that had been adopted in the process of their communication with dissidents and former political prisoners. The most disturbing aspect for Fedorchuk was the writers' channels that they used to communicate with Ukrainian nationalists abroad.

The informational leaks abroad about persecution of Ukraine's intelligentsia and Ukrainian and Jewish "nationalists" provoked anxiety among Kharkiv *chekists*. Their fear of potential insurrection in Kharkiv was exacerbated by the leaflets that the KGB systematically discovered in Kharkiv and the Kharkiv oblast. The texts of these messages were openly anti-Soviet, calling to rebel against the *chekist* regime and the Russian occupation. Moreover, these leaflets also revealed that there was an underground organization with printing capabilities functioning in Kharkiv.¹³⁵ In late August 1971, on the basis of Soviet intelligence, Fedorchuk offered the Central Committee a fairly detailed report that confirmed the awareness of "Western nationalist centers" about human rights abuses in Soviet Ukraine. Fedorchuk analyzed the dynamics of rapprochement among Western Ukrainian, Jewish, Estonian, and Polish nationalists who together organized anti-Soviet demonstrations in London, New York, Montreal, and many other cities of the United States and Canada.¹³⁶ He emphasized that Ukrainian nationalists were especially active in seeking cooperation with the Western "Zionist" circles for the purpose of helping Ukrainians and Jews persecuted by the KGB, and organizing protests and rallies in the West in their defense. Fedorchuk stated that, according to the most recent intelligence, a large convention had been planned with participation of the leaders (*glavari*) of both Western Ukrainian and Jewish nationalist organizations.¹³⁷ The leaks from Ukraine's Writers' Union abroad about the violations of human and national rights of Ukrainians and Jews, and the political activism of the Jewish intelligentsia who were seeking the support of the Writers' Union, were identified as alarming signals that the KGB had to further investigate and prevent.¹³⁸

The Challenges of the Kharkiv *Chekists*

On 12 January 1972, the KGB launched the second wave of arrests among the Ukrainian intelligentsia, and the most prominent representatives of *shistdesiatnytstvo* received seven years in strict regime prisons and an additional five years of exile. Those who refused to cooperate with the KGB were placed in mental institutions where life was gradually sucked out of them through forcible treatment with psychotropic drugs and sedatives.¹³⁹ In some cases, KGB intelligence strategies and tactics, inciting ethnic hatred among Ukrainians, Russians, and Jews and encouraging Jews to denounce Russians and Ukrainians and vice versa, worked, and Fedorchuk's reports appeared quite optimistic.

For instance, on 2 February 1973, Fedorchuk evaluated the *chekists'* work in 1972 as a success, and assured Shcherbytskyi that Ukrainian *chekists* acted according to Yurii Andropov's orders that he formulated at the joint June 1971 meeting at the KGB headquarters in Moscow. Fedorchuk argued that the KGB managed to stabilize the situation in Ukraine and to significantly improve the intelligence and counterintelligence tactics and strategies abroad.¹⁴⁰ He seemed to be especially proud of the *chekists'* effectiveness in the West: they penetrated a number of Ukrainian and Jewish nationalist centers and the intelligence services in the United States, Canada, Germany (FRG), England, and France; they recruited twenty-seven foreign citizens, three of whom were members of the Western OUN (Organization of Ukrainian Nationalists); they established friendly contacts with forty-five foreigners, eleven of whom agreed to work against Western Ukrainian nationalist centers; they identified twenty-nine communication channels through which information from Ukraine was transmitted to the West and vice versa; they obtained 310 pieces of valuable intelligence that helped the *chekists* identify the plans of Western Ukrainian nationalists in advance and understand the nuances of conflicts between the leaders of Ukrainian and Jewish nationalist organizations; they planted five "moles"/"sleepers" in the United States and Israel with the task to penetrate "Zionist" organizations in the West; in 1972 alone they prepared 177 Soviet citizens to be sent abroad to collect intelligence from 109 Western ideological centers, including eighty OUN chapters and eleven "Zionist" centers.[141] The general tactics designed to paralyze the activities of Western nationalist centers included the co-optation of their members, distribution of false materials that would compromise their leaders, the infiltration of KGB agents in these centers, and the facilitation of a rift between various nationalist centers to thwart their cooperation.[142] Fedorchuk also noted that as a result of effective counterintelligence operations, the KGB identified seventy-one people, members of Ukrainian and Jewish nationalist organizations, who were sent to the USSR to conduct operations of ideological subversion and to locally establish contacts with the Ukrainian and Jewish intelligentsia. In 1972, fourteen members of the OUN and two members of Zionist organizations were extradited from Soviet Ukraine.[143] The report also detailed the arrests of the most politically active individuals in Ukraine among the Ukrainian intelligentsia within an operation under the code name "Blok": in January 1972, the KGB arrested thirty-four people, and later in the year—sixty people; in addition, 731 individuals were questioned by KGB operatives at the KGB headquarters. In addition, Fedorchuk stressed that the KGB launched a massive propaganda campaign, organizing press conferences and TV programs where several individuals, including Zinoviia Franko, Mykola Kholodnyi, Leonid Seleznenko, and Ivan Dziuba, denounced Ukrainian nationalism and their own criminal activities.[144] According to Fedorchuk, the KGB was also quite effective in neutralizing Jewish and "Zionist" activists: in 1972, five Jewish nationalists were arrested; prophylactic talks about their nationalist activities were held with 224 Jews, twenty-nine Jews were subjected to administrative punishment, and 129 operational cases were opened and handled by KGB operatives in Ukraine.[145]

Yet Fedorchuk lamented that, despite the KGB active measures that undoubtedly impeded the process of spreading Ukrainian and Jewish nationalisms in the republic, by 1 January 1973, the KGB registered an additional 1,949 people whose political activities and lifestyles were of a nationalist and anti-Soviet nature. To further investigate these individuals and to combat

Ukrainian nationalists, Ukraine's KGB had at its disposal 7,180 specially trained agents, 1,140 of whom were recruited in 1972 (162 people were recruited through KGB *compromat* documents).[146] Moreover, in the localities, some KGB operatives exhibited incompetence and carelessness in the work with recruits. For instance, in August 1972, the KGB established a special group of inspectors who were supposed to investigate the unprofessional and incompetent behavior of some Kharkiv operatives who worked with recruits.[147] After a month of investigation, the KGB operative of the Fifth Directorate of the Kharkiv KGB V. P. Kazarin was fired for violating *chekist* ethics and discipline, and for serious violations in his work with Jewish recruits. He gathered information about the Jewish nationalist manifestations and the moods among the Kharkiv Jewish community, in the process sharing internal top-secret information with his recruits. On 12 September 1972, Fedorchuk informed Shcherbytskyi in detail about the Kazarin affair, arguing that it would be difficult to prevent leaks of this information to the West. Several secret agents learned from Kazarin that the KGB broadly used surveillance equipment in the apartments of the suspects and possessed a significant number of apartments in downtown Kharkiv for special meetings with recruits. Worse, Kazarin revealed the names of other secret agents to his recruits, offering them complete freedom in decision-making and promising them various perks for their services, including eventual emigration from the Soviet Union.[148] As a result of Kazarin's unprofessionalism and a lack of supervision, his recruits approached their duties from a purely pragmatic perspective: according to Fedorchuk, they were insincere in their relationships with the KGB, trying to take advantage of their close relations to the agency. Moreover, when interrogated by the inspectors from Kyiv, they complained that Kazarin failed to keep his promises to fully employ them as permanent KGB operatives with the subsequent right to emigrate to Israel.[149] The KGB made sure that the Kharkiv KGB leadership were punished: N. M. Terekhin, head of the department, who was supposed to closely supervise the work of Kazarin was forced to retire, and G. I. Dubrava, head of the Fifth Directorate in Kharkiv, was reprimanded.[150] Fedorchuk informed Shcherbytskyi that Dubrava was thoroughly instructed about the importance of work with "Zionsits" and Jewish nationalists. Only extensively trained and experienced cadres, from now on, were allowed to work with Jews.[151] According to several interviews, this internal investigation intensified the zeal of Kharkiv *chekists* who, with more vigor than in the past, continued to terrorize the Kharkiv literati, forcing several of them to leave the city. Poet Aleksandr Cherevchenko "voluntarily" left for Magadan,[152] and Zinovii Valshonok for Moscow.

KGB documents are remarkably consistent with Vladimir Usoltsev's narrative published under the title "The Destructive Symbiosis. The KGB and Jews." Usoltsev (his real name is Levintov) was a KGB operative who specialized in working with and recruiting Jews. His recruits helped him identify destructive social trends and anti-Soviet sentiments among Soviet Jews.[153] Indeed, after fighting the West, neutralizing "Zionists" and Jewish nationalists was the second significant issue that occupied the minds of KGB officials. Usoltsev remembered that entire KGB sub-departments and groups were created that worked exclusively on Soviet Jews. As we have seen earlier, Rakhlina and Briuggen were routinely harassed by KGB agents who frequently invited the writers to attend mandatory meetings with intelligence officers. The KGB pursued two objectives, to intimidate the writers and to possibly recruit them as informers. As Usoltsev has noted, it was astonishingly easy to recruit a Soviet citizen whose dependent status facilitated the task: "the memory inertia, developed during the preceding decades, was firmly entrenched in people's psyche, and the fear of the KGB's revenge was still strong."[154]

Often the KGB sent a written invitation to the writers' home address. The time and the date of the appointment at the KGB headquarters was not discussed; it was assigned. KGB officers also informed writers by phone about the upcoming meeting. In special cases, two KGB associates appeared at the writers' doorstep unannounced and took them immediately for questioning to Sovnarkomivska Street in downtown Kharkiv. Archetypally, the writers were incriminated for writing "anti-Soviet" poems and defending dissidents. Open threats of imprisonment were part of the routine. For instance, the Kharkiv KGB operative Babusenko who threatened to put Altunian in prison (Babusenko kept his word, of course) employed the same strategies in conversation with Rakhlina and Chichibabin.[155]

The party's 1972–1973 attack against dissidents and nationalists silenced the majority of writers. On the national level, many were imprisoned and sent to labor camps. People like Rakhlina and Chichibabin were intimidated, ostracized, and denied publication. In 1973, Chichibabin was expelled from the Writers' Union for "publishing" his poems in *samvydav* and for the public reading of his poem about Aleksandr Tvardovskii's secret funeral (*vorovskiie pokhorony*). What preceded it was an invitation from the poetry section of the Union chaired by Zelman Kats for Chichibabin to read his poems. It would be problematic to establish whose idea it was to invite Chichibabin. Perhaps, the KGB offered Kats the opportunity to finally uncover *antisovetchik* Chichibabin who could not keep himself from reading the most provocative poems in front of any audience. On 9 January 1973 (Chichibabin's fiftieth birthday), he read his "seditious" poems that were recorded. At the Union's meeting, when its members discussed Chichibabin's behavior, Kats was the most vocal accuser. The only writer who supported Chichibabin was the Jewish writer Lev Boleslavskii, but his voice was lost in the chorus of perturbed literati.[156] The Kharkiv chapter voted almost unanimously to excommunicate Chichibabin with two abstentions—Tretyakov and Boleslavskii. Privately, the critic Grigorii Gelfandbein told Marlena Rakhlina's brother, Feliks, that Chichibabin was a fool: "Who would allow this and forgive him these poems?"[157]

On the same day, the Union also got rid of another member, the Ukrainian poet Vasyl Borovyi. Like Chichibabin, a former political prisoner, Borovyi inspired no trust among KGB officers and the *obkom* functionaries in Kharkiv.[158] The Jewish writer from Uzhhorod (later a citizen of Israel) Feliks Krivin has noted with bitter irony that a new category of writers emerged in the 1970s—former members of the Writers' Union who were expelled as dissidents all over Ukraine, an identification that became no less honorable than membership in the Union.[159]

The Soviet state violence and KGB arrests of intellectuals and nationalists in the early 1970s seemed to break the ice between the "two solitudes," Ukrainians and Jews, who helped promote a similar change and cooperation between the Ukrainian and Jewish diasporas. The peaks of their rapprochement and cooperation appear to coincide with the periods of crises and political violence in Ukraine. The Soviet dissident and the Jewish national movements in the 1960s and 1970s initiated an unstoppable social and political process that mobilized the efforts of the diaspora, inciting its human rights movement, which in turn perpetuated and strengthened the human rights movement in Ukraine. In the 1970s, it was only "muffled" but was never silenced.[160] During the two decades, the KGB sponsored and published dozens of anti-Ukrainian books and pamphlets. Their leitmotif was a condemnation of Ukrainian nationalists.[161] However, these efforts could not complete the process of cultural amnesia among Ukraine's citizens. In Kharkiv, in the 1980s, a new generation of political activists emerged—Volodymyr Pasichnyk, Valerii Bondar, Petro Cheremskyi, Andrii Cheremskyi, Yevhen Zakharov, and Stepan Sapeliak who established Kharkiv national organizations, such as the Ukrainian Helsinki Human Rights Union, the Union of Ukrainian Youth (*Spilka Ukrainskoi Molodi*), and the People's Movement of Ukraine (*Narodnyi Rukh Ukrainy*).[162]

The persistence of diaspora groups in promoting change in the Soviet Union and the subsequent Gorbachev's perestroika and glasnost in the 1980s facilitated mass Jewish emigration from the Soviet Union and the independence movement in Ukraine. The diaspora groups continued to smuggle anti-Soviet literature to the USSR, and secret channels were established, through which *samvydav* and other important documents were transported to the West. Polish Solidarity greatly contributed to this exchange and expanded the contacts between Soviet dissidents and Western human rights groups, smuggling Ukrainian émigré publications such as *Suchasnist* and distributing illegal newspapers and leaflets in Ukraine.[163]

However, the KGB's detrimental influence in shaping Ukrainian-Jewish relations was enormous during the 1960s and 1970s. It would certainly be myopic to make one side (or the KGB) accountable for the deceleration of dialogue between Ukrainians and Jews. Throughout history both "solitudes" were unkind to one another. Levko Luk'ianenko, a Ukrainian dissident and former Soviet political prisoner, published his notorious antisemitic text, which prompted Yakov Suslenskii to send Luk'ianenko a letter, notifying him that their friendship had ended.[164] Similarly, in his 23 October 1994 CBS TV's 60 Minutes broadcast *The Ugly Face of Freedom*, Morley Safer, a Canadian-American broadcast journalist, reporter, and correspondent for CBS News, claimed that all Ukrainians were "genetically anti-Semitic."[165] This episode was watched by approximately 17.5 million households. Despite the firm position of the AJC who in their letter to CBS rejected Safer's superficial view of Ukraine and Ukrainians, Safer's program strengthened the beliefs of many American Jews regarding the chronic nature of Ukrainian antisemitism.[166] Many individuals on both sides let their stereotypical thinking prevail, complicating the relations between two ethnic groups for generations to come.

Words, as much as violence, were a powerful weapon that was employed by Soviet propagandists, KGB and party officials, and their hostages—Soviet citizens. When chosen unwisely, they destroyed bonds, trust, and faith in the possibility of change and kind relationships among various ethnic groups. Juan Gelman, an accomplished Argentine poet, whose literary talent and moral position as a political activist and journalist serve as a model to which many writers all over the world aspire, once illuminated the overarching power of words:

> Look, words are like the air: they belong to everybody. Words are not the problem; it's the tone, the context, where those words are aimed, and in whose company they are uttered. Of course murderers and victims use the same words, but I never read the words utopia, or beauty, or tenderness in police descriptions. Do you know that the Argentinean dictatorship burnt *The Little Prince*? And I think they were right to do so, not because I do not love *The Little Prince*, but because the book is so full of tenderness that it would harm any dictatorship.[167]

Yet, beyond militant and threatening rhetoric, the Soviet space of violence also included another sophisticated torture designed to silence the literati, the dissent, and thinking individuals in Ukraine. The medicalization of terror frightened even most experienced dissidents who often chose to cooperate with the regime rather than find themselves in psychiatric clinics, being locked and forcibly treated with psychotic drugs.[168] The Kharkiv psychiatric clinic, known as the Saburova Dacha, became a place of such torture, where many representatives of the Kharkiv creative intelligentsia were isolated from the rest of society in the 1960s and the 1970s.

NOTES

1. Interview with Volodymyr Briuggen, 9 August 2013, the restaurant "Kryshtal," Kharkiv, Ukraine.
2. Ibid.
3. Ivan L. Rudnytsky, "Comments on Professor Zvi Gitelman: The Social and Political Role of the Jews in Ukraine," in *Ukraine in the Seventies*, ed. Peter J. Potichnyi (Oakville, Ontario: Mosaic Press, 1975), 188.
4. Yohanan Petrovsky-Shtern, *The Anti-Imperial Choice: The Making of the Ukrainian Jew* (New Haven & London: Yale University Press, 2009), 213.
5. Ibid., 216.
6. Ivan Hel, *Vyklyk systemi: Ukrainskyi vyzvolnyi rukh druhoi polovyny XX stolittia* (Lviv: Chasopys, 2013), 38. Andrei Sakharov's wife and Soviet dissident Yelena Bonner wrote that she fully understood who Pavlovskii was in 1980 and 1981 when he began to cooperate with the KGB, denouncing Russian human rights activists from Sumy, Ukraine, and a biophysicist Ivan Kovaliov and his wife Tatiana Osipova.
7. Private conversation with Iosyp Zisels (3 October 2017) at the roundtable "Ukrainian-Jewish Encounter in Postwar Soviet Ukraine," held at the Pocantico Conference Center (Sleepy Hollow, NY; the estate of John D. Rockefeller) from 1 October to 4 October 2017; see also Zysels's report "Ukrainski ta yevreiski dysydenty: vid spilnoi borotby do samorealizatsii v natsionalnykh derzhavakh," delivered at this event, at *Madan*, 6 October 2017, http://madan.org.il/ru/news/iosif-zisels-ob-ukrainskih-i-evreyskih-dissidentah (accessed 18 July 2020); Vladimir Khanin, "Introduction," in *Documents on Ukrainian-Jewish Identity and Emigration, 1944–1990*, ed. Vladimir Khanin (New York: Frank Cass Publishers, 2003), 21; Danylenko, *Politychni protesty*, 334.
8. Mikhail Kheifets, *Ukrainskiie siluety* (Kyiv: Ukrainska pres-hrupa, 2014), 4. See also Osyp Zinkevych, ed., *Rukh oporu v Ukraini. 1960–1990: Entsyklopedychnyi dovidnyk* (Kyiv: Smoloskyp, 2010), 126; "Arie Vudka," *Berkovich*, 2020, http://berkovich-zametki.com/Avtory/Vudka.htm (accessed 28 January 2018); S. F. Gluzman, *Risunki po pamiati, ili vospominaniia otsidenta* (Kiev: Izdatelskii dom Dmitriia Burago, 2012).
9. Vasyl Stus (1938–1985) was a Ukrainian poet, thinker, dissident, and human rights activist. He was arrested twice by the KGB for anti-Soviet agitation and propaganda. In 1972, he was sentenced to five years in labor camps and three years of exile, and in 1980 to ten years in labor camps and five years of exile. Stus died in a solitary confinement cell on 4 September 1985. Vasyl Ovsiienko suggested that Stus was possibly killed in his prison cell in the VS-389/36-1 camp in the village of Kuchino (which is today in the Chusovskii district of the Perm region, the Russian Federation) for being "rebellious," protesting against the sadism and

violence of the camp guards and authorities. See Vasyl Ovsiienko, *Svitlo liudei: Memuary ta publitsystyka*, 2 ed., Knyha I (Kharkiv: "Prava liudyny," 2007), 211, 213, 214, 282, 289.

10. L. G. Churchward, *The Soviet Intelligentsia: An Essay on the Social Structure and Roles of the Soviet Intellectuals during the 1960s* (London/Boston: Routledge & Kegan Paul, 1973), 141–45.

11. Referenced in Ivan L. Rudnytsky, "The Political Thought of Soviet Ukrainian Dissidents," in *Essays in Modern Ukrainian History* by Ivan L. Rudnytsky, ed. Peter L. Rudnytsky (Edmonton: Canadian Institute of Ukrainian Studies, 1987), 486.

12. Roman Szporluk, "Russians in Ukraine and Problems of Ukrainian Identity in the USSR," in *Ukraine in the Seventies*, ed. Peter J. Potichnyj (Oakville, Ontario: Mosaic Press, 1975), 203.

13. Christopher Andrew and Vasili Mitrokhin, *The World Was Going Our Way: The KGB and the Battle for the Third World* (New York: Basic Books, 2005), 222–45; Churchward, *The Soviet Intelligentsia*, 131.

14. Lesya Jones and Bohdan Yasen, "Preface," in *Dissent in Ukraine: The Ukrainian Herald: An Underground Journal from Soviet Ukraine*, trans. Lesya Jones and Bohdan Yasen (Baltimore/Paris/Toronto: Smoloskyp Publisher, 1977), 5.

15. Kenneth C. Farmer, *Ukrainian Nationalism in the Post-Stalin Era: Myth, Symbols and Ideology in Soviet Nationalities Policy* (The Hague, Boston, and London: Martinus Nijhoff Publisher, 1980), 203.

16. *Refuseniks* were those Soviet Jews whose requests to emigrate and visas were denied by the Soviet authorities.

17. On the phenomenon of refuseniks, see Vladimir (Ze'ev) Khanin, "The Refusenik Community in Moscow: Social Networks and Models of Identification," *East European Jewish Affairs* 41, nos. 1–2 (2011): 78.

18. On Soviet punitive psychiatry, see Alexander Podrabinek, *Punitive Medicine*, 1st ed. (Ann Arbor: Karoma Publishers, Inc., 1980); Rebecca Reich, *State of Madness: Psychiatry, Literature, and Dissent After Stalin* (DeKalb, IL: Northern Illinois University Press, 2018); Olga Bertelsen, "Rethinking Psychiatric Terror against Nationalists in Ukraine," *Kyiv-Mohyla Arts and Humanities* 1 (2014): 27–76.

19. Y. S. Bukhtoiarova, *Obraz UPA u svitskii presi ukrainskoi diaspory SShA (1950–1980-ti rr.)* (unpublished thesis), (Lviv: Ukrainskyi katolytskyi universytet, 2014).

20. Olena Zashko, *Pidtrymka uv'iaznenykh dysydentiv diasporoiu SShA (za materialamy vydan "Ameryka" ta "Svoboda")* (unpublished thesis) (Lviv: Ukrainskyi katolytskyi universytet, 2017), 48–49; Christina Isajiw, *Negotiating Human Rights: In Defence of Dissidents during the Soviet Era* (Edmonton and Toronto: Canadian Institute of Ukrainian Studies, 2014), xxiii.

21. For a discussion about the charity movement, see Barbara Walker, "Pollution and Purification in the Moscow Human Rights Networks of the 1960s and 1970s," *Slavic Review* 68, no. 2 (2009): 376–95.

22. Zashko, "Pidtrymka uv'iaznenykh dysydentiv," 32.

23. Valentyn Moroz (1936–2019) was a Ukrainian historian, scholar, and dissident. He was arrested twice for anti-Soviet agitation and propaganda. In 1965, he was

sentenced to five years in labor camps. In 1970, he was again arrested and sentenced to six years in a special prison, three years in labor camps, and five years of exile. Under pressure from the international community, Moroz and four other dissidents were exchanged for two KGB agents at Kennedy Airport, New York.

24. Monique L. Burns, "Committee Rallies to Support Soviet Dissident Writer Moroz," *The Harvard Crimson*, 26 November 1974, http://www.thecrimson.com/article/1974/11/26/committee-rallies-to-support-soviet-dissident/ (accessed 15 August 2020).

25. Bukhtoiarova, "Obraz UPA"; see also V. Kubiiovych and V. Markus, "Emihratsiia," in *Entsyklopediia Ukrainoznavstva*, T. 2, ed. V. Kubiiovych (Paris/New York: "Molode zhyttia," 1955–1957), 629–37 (after the Second World War, 635–37); B. D. Lanovyk, M. V. Traf'iak, R. M. Mateiko, and Z. M. Matysiakevych, *Ukrainska emihratsiia vid mynuvshchyny do siohodennia* (Ternopil: Charivnytsia, 1999).

26. "Jews," *Encyclopedia of Ukraine*, vol. II, ed. Volodymyr Kubijovyc (Toronto: University of Toronto Press, 1988), 390.

27. Ibid.; "Osherowitch Mendel," *Entsyklopediia Ukrainskoi diaspory: Spolucheni Shtaty Ameryky*, vol. 1, kn. 2, eds. Vasyl Markus and Dariia Markus (New York and Chicago: Naukove Tovarystvo im. Shevchenka v Amerytsi, 2012), 222. See also the recently published book by Mendel Osherowitch, *How People Live in Soviet Russia: Impressions from a Journey*, ed. Lubomyr Y. Luciuk, trans. from the original Yiddish edition by Sharon Power (Kingston, Ontario: Kashtan Press, 2020).

28. On various groups of the Ukrainian diaspora in Canada, see Denis Horelov, "Vplyv orhanizatsii ukrainskoi diaspory na rozvytok hromadianskoho suspilstva v Ukraini," *Stratehichni priorytety* 3, no. 20 (2011): 34.

29. On how diasporas operate, see Yossi Shain and Aharon Barth, "Diasporas and International Relations Theory," *International Organization* 57, no. 3 (2003): 449–79.

30. Isajiw, *Negotiating Human Rights*, 294–95, 320–22.

31. Ivan Bahrianyi, *Publitsystyka: Dopovidi, statti, pamflety, refleksii, ese*, 2nd ed., ed. Oleksii Konoval (Kyiv: Smoloskyp, 2006), 632–35; see also Yohanan Petrovsky-Shtern, "Reconceptualizing the Alien: Jews in Modern Ukrainian Thought," *Ab Imperio* 4 (2003): 539.

32. Bahrianyi, *Publitsystyka*, 634.

33. Ibid., 635.

34. Petrovsky-Shtern, "Reconceptualizing the Alien," 539.

35. Ibid., 539–41.

36. On historical inevitability, see Bernard Berenson, *Rumour and Reflection: 1941–1944* (London: Constable, 1952), 116.

37. Serhii Plokhii, "Quo Vadis Ukrainian History?" *Harvard Ukrainian Studies* 34, no. 1–4 (2015–2016): 16–17.

38. Howard Aster and Peter J. Potichnyj, *Jewish-Ukrainian Relations: Two Solitudes* (Oakville, Ontario: Mosaic Press, 1983).

39. Walter Dushnyck, ed., *Ukrainians and Jews: A Symposium* (New York, NY: The Ukrainian Congress Committee of America, Inc., 1966); see also papers

and proceedings of the October 1974 McMaster Conference on Contemporary Ukraine; Peter J. Potichnyi, ed., *Ukraine in the Seventies* (Oakville, ON: Mosaic Press, 1975).

40. On some aspects of *Suchasnist*, see Simone Attilio Bellezza, "Making Soviet Ukraine Ukrainian: The Debate on Ukrainian Statehood in the Journal Suchasnist (1961–1971)," *Nationalities Papers* 47, no. 3 (2019): 379–93.

41. Anatoliy Kruglashov, "Chernivtsi: A City with Mysterious Flavor of Tolerance," *Eurolimes* 19 (2015): 151–52.

42. Myron B. Kuropas, *Ukrainian-American Citadel: The First One Hundred Years of the Ukrainian National Association* (Boulder, CO: East European Monographs, 1996), 574. Forgeries were the most popular method employed by the KGB. Thirty years ago Yaroslav Bilinsky warned the scholarly community that information that had emanated from the Soviet Union and was given to the American government should not be taken at face value, as it was concocted by the KGB. From 1960 to the late 1980s, forged documents became an inseparable part of Soviet covert activities, designed to discredit Soviet opponents. Soviet forgeries were "formulated and executed through Service A of the KGB's First Chief Directorate." See also Richard H. Shultz and Roy Godson, *Dezinformatsia: The Strategy of Soviet Disinformation* (New York: Berkley Books, 1986), 149.

43. See, for instance, Anatolii Belov and Andrei Shilkin, *Diversii bez dinamita* (Moskva: Izdatelstvo politicheskoi literatury, 1972).

44. Joshua Shanes and Yohanan Petrovsky-Shtern, "An Unlikely Alliance: The 1907 Ukrainian–Jewish Electoral Coalition," *Nations and Nationalism* 15, no. 3 (2009): 483–505; Shimon Redlich, *Together and Apart in Brzezany: Poles, Jews, and Ukrainians, 1919–1945* (Bloomington and Indianapolis, IN: Indiana University Press, 2002); John-Paul Himka, "The Lviv Pogrom of 1941: The Germans, Ukrainian Nationalists, and the Carnival Crow," *Canadian Slavonic Papers* LUI, nos. 2–4 (2011): 209–43; John-Paul Himka, "Interventions: Challenging the Myths of Twentieth-Century Ukrainian History," in *Convolutions of Historical Politics*, eds. Alexei Miller and Maria Lipman (Budapest: Central European University Press, 2012), 211–38; John-Paul Himka, "Ukrainian Memories of the Holocaust: The Destruction of Jews as Reflected in Memoirs Collected in 1947," *Canadian Slavonic Papers* LIV, nos. 3–4 (2012): 427–42.

45. Redlich, *Together and Apart in Brzezany*, 163.

46. Alexander V. Prusin, "A 'Zone of Violence': The Anti-Jewish Pogroms in Eastern Galicia in 1914–1915 and 1941," in *Shatterzone of Empires: Coexistence and Violence in the German, Habsburg, Russian, and Ottoman Borderlands*, eds. Omer Bartov and Eric D. Weitz (Bloomington and Indianapolis, IN: Indiana University Press, 2013), 371; Peter Klein, ed., *Die Einsatzgruppen in der besetzten Sowjetunion, 1941/42: Die Tätigkeitsund Lageberichte des Chefs der Sicherheitspolizei und des SD* (Berlin: Edition Hentrich, 1997), 319.

47. For a discussion about Demjanjuk's case, the KGB operation "Retribution," and the role of the U.S. OSI in this case, see Olga Bertelsen, "Ukrainian and Jewish Émigrés as Targets of KGB Active Measures in the 1970s," *International Journal of Intelligence and Counterintelligence* 34, no. 2 (2021): 267–92.

48. For the tape recording of the Soviet trial against Stern, see August Stern, ed., *The USSR vs. Dr. Mikhail Stern: The Only Tape Recording of a Trial Smuggled Out of the Soviet Union*, trans. Marko Carynnyk (New York: Urizen Books, 1977).

49. Kuropas, *Ukrainian-American Citadel*, 575.

50. For more details on Demjanjuk's case, see Yoram Sheftel, *The Demjanjuk Affair: The Rise and Fall of a Show-Trial*, revised ed. (London: Victor Gollancz, 1994). On Soviet forgeries during the late 1950s, the early 1960s, and the mid-1970s, see Shultz and Godson, *Dezinformatsia*, 148–57.

51. To better understand the failure of the U.S. government to protect an innocent U.S. citizen, unearthing of the government conspiracy in this case, and the unethical behavior of the OSI's leadership and some of its lawyers, see Mark Burdman, "British Documentary Exposes OSI Fraud in Demjanjuk Trial," *Executive Intelligence Review* 17, no. 24 (1990): 45–48; Nigel Jackson, "John Demjanjuk: The Man More Sinned Against," *Inconvenient History* 4, no. 2 (2012), https://codoh.com/library/document/3177/?lang=en (accessed 4 September 2020); Bertelsen, "Ukrainian and Jewish Émigrés as Targets of KGB Active Measures in the 1970s"; D. Stephen Voss, "The Story of the Two Ivans: Portrait of a Government Conspiracy," *University of Kentucky*, 2020, http://www.uky.edu/~dsvoss/docs/ps101/twoivans.htm (accessed 4 September 2020); and documents pertaining to the Demjanjuk deportation case at: *United States Citizenship and Immigration Services* (USCIS), www.uscis.gov› foia › PRD2014000534-John_Demjanjuk (accessed 4 September 2020).

52. Vic Satzewich, *The Ukrainian Diaspora* (London and New York: Routledge, 2003), 173–74. For more details about the dialogue between American officials and the Ukrainian diaspora who were concerned about Soviet forgeries in Demjanjuk's case, see Myron B. Kuropas, "Fighting Moscow from Afar: Ukrainian Americans and the Evil Empire," in *Anti-Communist Minorities in the U.S.: Political Activism of Ethnic Refugees*, ed. Ieva Zake (New York: Palgrave Macmillan, 2009), 60–61 (43–66); Kuropas, *Ukrainian-American Citadel*, 567–74, 624–27. For details about the Demjanjuk affair, see Sheftel, *The Demjanjuk Affair*.

53. Roman Kupchinsky, "Nazi War Criminals: The Role of Soviet Disinformation," in *Ukraine During World War II: History and its Aftermath*, ed. Yury Boshyk (Edmonton: Canadian Institute of Ukrainian Studies Press, 1986), 143; Myron Kuropas, "Ukrainian Americans and the Search for War Criminals," in *Ukraine During World War II: History and Its Aftermath*, ed. Yury Boshyk (Edmonton: Canadian Institute of Ukrainian Studies Press, 1986), 151; Satzewich, *The Ukrainian Diaspora*, 174.

54. TsDAHOU, f. 1, op. 25, spr. 1362, ark. 1, 2, 8.

55. TsDAHOU, f. 1, op. 25, spr. 1891, ark. 55. See also Olga Bertelsen, "Political Affinities and Maneuvering of Soviet Ukrainian Political Elites: Heorhii Shevel and the Ministry of Strange Affairs in the 1970s," *Nationalities Papers: The Journal of Nationalism and Ethnicity* 47, no. 3 (2019): 394–411.

56. According to Shevel, approximately 3 million ethnic Ukrainians resided in the countries of Europe, North and South Americas, and Australia.

57. TsDAHOU, f. 1, op. 25, spr. 1891, ark. 69–71.

58. On the Jewish-Ukrainian dialogue in the twentieth century's second decade, see Henry Abramson, *A Prayer for the Government: Ukrainians and Jews in Revolutionary Times, 1917–1920* (Cambridge, MA: Harvard University Press, 1999); on the literary representation of Jews in Ukrainian authors' writings, see Myroslav Shkandrij, *Jews in Ukrainian Literature: Representation and Identity* (New Haven and London: Yale University Press, 2009), 92–106.

59. Oles Obertas, *Ukrainskyi samvydav: Literaturna krytyka ta publitsystyka (1960-i – pochatok 1970-kh rokiv)* (Kyiv: Smoloskyp, 2010), 118–19.

60. Churchward, *The Soviet Intelligentsia*, 143–44.

61. Iosyp Zysels (interview by Mykhailo Shterngel), "Prymyrennia ne pochynaietsia zi spyskiv vzaiemnykh zvynuvachen,'" *Ukrainska Helsinska Spilka z prav liudyny*, 18 January 2010, For Iosyp Zysels's biography, see Zinkevych, *Rukh oporu v Ukraini*, 255–56. On Zysels's human rights activities and imprisonment, see Hel, *Vyklyk systemi*, 35, 180, 336, 346.

62. Iosyp Zysels (interview by Mykhailo Shterngel), "Prymyrennia ne pochynaietsia." See also O. H. Bazhan, "Diialnist klubiv tvorchoi molodi v Ukrainiv 1960-kh rokahk u pershodzherelakh," *Kraieznavstvo* 1–4 (2006): 80–82.

63. Haluzevyi derzhavnyi arkhiv MVS Ukrainy (hereafter: HDAMVSU), f. 54, op. 1, spr. 288, ark. 56.

64. Zalman Shazar, an Israeli politician, author and poet, served as the third president of Israel from 1963 to 1973.

65. HDAMVSU, f. 54, op. 1, spr. 379, ark. 18.

66. For many, the ideology of Zionism was less important than the right of Jewish spatial existence in an independent Jewish state. See, for instance, Aleksandr Ioffe (interview by Yulii Kosharovskii), *Kosharovskii*, 29 April 2004, http://kosharovsky.com/интервью/александр-иоффе/ (accessed 4 September 2020).

67. O. H. Bazhan, "Dysydentski (opozytsiini) rukhy 1960–1980-kh rokiv v Ukraini," in *Entsyklopediia istorii Ukrainy*, t. 2, eds. V. A. Smolii et al. (Kyiv: Instytut Istorii Ukrainy NANU/"Naukova dumka," 2004), 688; Oleh Bazhan, "Represyvni zakhody Radianskoi vlady shchodo hromadian ievreiskoi natsionalnosti v URSR (1960-ti–1980-ti rr.)," *Z arkhiviv VUChK-GPU-NKVD-KGB* 22 (2004): 117; also available at http://history.org.ua/JournALL/gpu/gpu_2004_22_1/6.pdf.

68. Bazhan, "Represyvni zakhody Radianskoi vlady shchodo hromadian ievreiskoi natsionalnosti."

69. Yossi Yonah, "Reclaiming Diaspora: The Israeli State, Migration, and Ethnonationalism in the Global Era," *Diaspora: A Journal of Transnational Studies* 16, no. 1/2 (2007): 203.

70. Yonah, "Reclaiming Diaspora," 211. See also Zvi Gitelman, "Soviet Jews: Creating a Cause and a Movement," in *A Second Exodus: The American Movement to Free Soviet Jews*, ed. M. Friedman and A. D. Chernin (Hanover, NH: Brandeis University Press, 1999): 84–96; Fred A. Lazin, *The Struggle for Soviet Jewry in American Politics* (New York: Lexington Books, 2005); Walter Ruby, "The Role of Non-establishment Groups," in *A Second Exodus: The American Movement to Free Soviet Jews*, ed. M. Friedman and A. D. Chernin (Hanover, NH: Brandeis University Press, 1999), 200–23; Nehemiah Levanon, "Israel's Role in the Campaign," in *A*

Second Exodus: The American Movement to Free Soviet Jews, ed. M. Friedman and A. D. Chernin (Hanover, NH: Brandeis University Press, 1999), 70–83.

71. Victor Rosenberg, "Refugee Status for Soviet Jewish Immigrants to the United States," *Touro Law Review* 19, no. 2, Art. 22 (2014): 422.

72. This approach to Jewish emigration prompted the United States to act, and in 1980 the American Congress passed the Refugee Act, according to which all Jewish immigrants were granted refugee status. This reversed the pattern of Jewish immigration. In the 1980s, the majority of Jews left the Soviet Union for the United States—79,000 out of the 117,000 emigrants, while only 29,000 went to Israel. See Yonah, "Reclaiming Diaspora," 213; Rosenberg, "Refugee Status for Soviet Jewish Immigrants to the United States," 425.

73. Krasivskyj was arrested three times and served his sentences in the Soviet Gulag from 1949 to 1953, from 1967 to 1972, and from 1980 to 1985. See Zinkevych, *Rukh oporu v Ukraini*, 350–52.

74. Anna Procyk, "Dissent in Ukraine through the Prism of Amnesty International," *Human Rights in Ukraine*: The Kharkiv Human Rights Protection Group, 1 November 2012, http://khpg.org/en/index.php?id=1326302237 (accessed 4 September 2020).

75. Procyk, "Dissent in Ukraine."

76. Ibid."; "Zbigniew Brzezinski . . . ," *Telegraph*, 27 May 2017, https://www.telegraph.co.uk/news/2017/05/27/zbigniew-brzezinski-jimmy-carters-national-security-adviser/ (accessed 4 September 2020).

77. Procyk, "Dissent in Ukraine"; Vyacheslav Chornovil, ed., *The Chornovil Papers* (New York: McGraw-Hill, 1968).

78. See the letter of the Polish Self-Defense Committee and Charter 77 in *Smoloskyp* 1, no. 1 (1978): 6 (1–12).

79. On American campaigns for Moroz's release, see Andrew Fedynsky, "Perspectives: Valentyn Moroz – 25 Years Later," *The Ukrainian Weekly* LXXII, no. 4 (25 January 2004), http://www.ukrweekly.com/old/archive/2004/040418.shtml.

80. See an excerpt from Valentyn Moroz's essay "Moses and Dathan," trans. Olenka Hanushevska, *Smoloskyp*, 1, no. 1 (1978): 4.

81. The CSCE is also known as the U.S. Helsinki Commission.

82. "Deychakiwsky Orest," *Entsyklopedia Ukrainskoi Diaspory: Spolucheni Shtaty Ameryky*, vol. 1, kn. I, eds. Vasyl Markus and Dariia Markus (New York and Chicago: Naukove Tovarystvo im. Shevchenka v Amerytsi, 2009), 224. Orest Deychakiwsky, "Helsinki Review Process: Making Progress Slowly, but Surely," *Ukrainian Weekly*, 18 January 1987, pp. 7, 13.

83. For a discussion about the Helsinki network and its influence, see Sarah B. Snyder, "'Promising Everything Under the Sun': Helsinki Activism and Human Rights in Eastern Europe," in *The Establishment Responds: Power, Politics, and Protest since 1945*, eds. Kathrin Fahlenbrach, Martin Klimke, Joachim Scharloth, and Laura Wong (New York: Palgrave Macmillan, 2012), 91–102.

84. Snyder, "'Promising Everything Under the Sun,'" 98.

85. The UNA was founded in 1894 as a non-profit fraternal benefit society in Shamokin, Pennsylvania.

86. Myron B. Kuropas, *Lesia and I: A Progress Report and a Ukrainian-American Love Story* (Bloomington, IN: Xlibris, 2014), 229.
87. "Jews," *Encyclopedia of Ukraine*, 390.
88. Kuropas, *Ukrainian-American Citadel*, 576–77.
89. See the text of his open letter in Zynovii Knysh, *"Yevrei" chy "zhydy"* (Toronto: Sribna Surma, 1984), 9–10.
90. Quoted in Reznik, "Zhydobanderovtsy. Pokoleniie 1.0."
91. Kuropas, *Lesia and I*, 230. Sadly, these stereotypical attitudes, inherent in both communities, can be traced to the distant and recent past. For instance, see accusations of antisemitism against Kuropas in Chris Rickert, "Kuropas Maintains He Is Not an Anti-Semite," *Daily Chronicle*, 3 February 2005, http://www.daily-chronicle.com/2005/02/03/kuropas-maintains-he-is-not-an-anti-semite/aqriqsz/news01.txt (accessed 15 August 2020).
92. See articles in the *Ukrainian Weekly*: "Cleveland Historian Discusses Ukrainian-Jewish Relations" (29 March 1981); "Top Jewish, Ukrainian Spiritual Leaders Meet in Philadelphia" (18 May 1981); "Anti-Semitism and Ukrainophobia: Roadblocks to Progress" by George Woloshyn (7 February 1982); "Panel Discusses Ukrainian-Jewish Relations" (21 March 1982); "How to Achieve Ukrainian-Jewish Cooperation" by Drs. Myron Kuropas and Israel Kleiner (31 October 1982); and "Modernization and Its Impact on Jewish-Ukrainian Relations" by Drs. Howard Aster and Peter J. Potichnyj (30 January 1983).
93. Kuropas, *Ukrainian-American Citadel*, 579.
94. Ibid.
95. Kuropas, *Ukrainian-American Citadel*, 578.
96. Isajiw, *Negotiating Human Rights*, 72–73.
97. Ibid., 74.
98. Ibid., 74–75.
99. The text of the letter, a protest against the arrest in Tashkent of the former General-Major of the Soviet Army Petro Grigorenko that was signed by fifty-five Soviet citizens, was broadcast by *The Voice of America* and *BBC* in late May 1969. The KGB opened a criminal case against several Kharkivites, the signatories of the letter: Nedobora, his wife Karasik, Altunian, Kalinovskii, Kornilov, Ponomariov, and Levin. See HDA SBU, f. 16, op. 1, spr. 985, ark. 333–35.
100. G. O. Altunian, *Tsena svobody: Vospominaniia dissidenta* (Kharkov: Folio, 2000), 69; available at *The Sakharov Center*, https://www.sakharov-center.ru/asfcd/auth/?t=page&num=7447 (accessed 15 August 2020). Altunian was a human rights activist from Kharkiv who was one of the founders of the Initiative Group on Human Rights in the USSR. He was a political prisoner in 1969–1972 and 1981–1987.
101. ViatLag refers to one of the largest labor camps within the Gulag system, known under the number K-231. Located nearly 370 kilometers from the city of Kirov, the camp functioned from 5 February 1938, until the 1990s. Its capacity was estimated at approximately 15,000–20,000 prisoners.
102. David Rakhlin and Feliks Rakhlin, *Rukopis* (Kharkov: "Prava liudyny," 2007); see also "Umerla Marlena Rakhlina" (Feliks Rakhlin), http://old.memo.ru/2010/06/06/marlena_rakhlina.htm (accessed 16 August 2020).

103. Altunian, *Tsena svobody*, 71.

104. Boris Silaiev was the head of the Kharkiv chapter from 1979 to 1986. He clearly made a mistake. The title of the leading literary journal of the third wave of the Russian immigration was *Kontinent*. It was founded and edited by the Russian writer Vladimir Maksimov in Paris from 1974 to 1992 (later the journal was published in Moscow under Igor Vinogradov's editorship—from 1992 to 2013). Since 2013 *Kontinent* is an online journal. For more on Silaiev, see Piotr Chalyi, "Zemkiaki, ili Kharkovchanin iz moiei Rossoshi," *Den literatury*, 11 October 2016, https://denliteraturi.ru/article/2083 (accessed 15 August 2020); Anatolii Pererva, ed., *Natsionalna spilka pysmennykiv Ukrainy: 75 rokiv* (Kharkiv: Maidan, 2009), 19.

105. Marlena Rakhlina, *Chto bylo—vidali* . . . (Kharkov: "Prava liudyny," 2006), 105.

106. Mark Slonim, *Soviet Russian Literature: Writers and Problems, 1917–1977*, 2nd ed. (New York: Oxford University Press, 1977), 397–98.

107. Galina Medvedeva, "'Sushchestvovan'ia svetloe usilie' (Yulii Daniel)," *Znamia* 2 (2001); also available in *Zhurnalnyi zal*, http://magazines.russ.ru/znamia/2001/2/medvedeva.html (accessed 15 August 2020).

108. Daniel, although having served his term in the Gulag, did not become an active participant in the dissident movement after his return. He remained a very private person, resisting the assertive environment created by Soviet dissidents. Unlike many Jewish literati, he stayed in Russia. He stated: "I am indifferent to the call of blood. Moreover, I cannot imagine myself in any environment other than [Russian]. . . . My pedigree is Russian, and it is no shorter or poorer than that of the Golitsyn, the Murav'iov and others. . . . This is my position, and everyone has the right to decide for himself." Like Chichibabin who lived the quiet life of an accountant, Daniel after his release, being on a black list of "unpublishable" writers, survived due to ghostwriting translations, some of which were published under Bulat Okudzhava's name. See Medvedeva, "Sushchestvovan'ia svetloe usilie."

109. Arkadii Filatov, "Vdogonku," *Chichibabin.narod.ru*, 1995, http://chichibabin.narod.ru/filatov.html (accessed 15 August 2020).

110. On the Siberian Science-City known as *Akademgorodok*, a city built in the vicinity of Novosibirsk approximately 3,000 kilometers from Moscow, see Ksenia Tatarchenko, "Calculating a Showcase: Mikhail Lavrentiev, the Politics of Expertise, and the International Life of the Siberian Science-City," *Historical Studies in the Natural Sciences* 46, no. 5 (2016): 592–632. The Siberian Branch of the Russian Academy of Sciences is located there, which provided the name for this city.

111. "Iosif Goldenberg," *Sviaz vremen*, 2020, http://www.thetimejoint.com/taxonomy/term/3893 (accessed 16 August 2020); Feliks Rakhlin, *O Borise Chichibabine i iego vremeni: Strochki iz zhizni* (Kharkov: Folio, 2004), 42.

112. Yevhen Zakharkov, Marlena Rakhlina's son and the head of the Kharkiv human rights group (interview by Mykola Kniazhytskyi), "Yak reformuvaty sudovu systemu" (Kharkivska pravozakhysna hrupa), *Espreso*, 24 July 2016, http://espreso.tv/article/2016/07/24/zakharov (accessed 16 August 2020).

113. Rudenko was a Ukrainian writer, human rights activist, and the founder of the UHG. In February 1977 he was arrested for anti-Soviet propaganda and agitation

and sentenced to seven years in camps and three years of exile. In December 1987 he was released and emigrated to Germany. Rudenko returned to Ukraine in 1990. For more on Rudenko's biography and his political activism, see Raisa Rudenko, ed., *Mykola Rudenko: "Naibilshe dyvo – zhyttia." Spohady* (Kyiv: "Smoloskyp," 2013).

114. HDA SBU, f. 16, op. 1, spr. 985, ark. 333–35; Altunian, *Tsena* svobody; Hel, *Vyklyk systemi*, 324–25; Rakhlin, *O Borise Chichibabine*, 131. For more on Grigorenko, see Petro G. Grigorenko, *Memoirs*, trans. Thomas P. Whitney (New York & London: W.W. Norton and Company, 1982).

115. Volodymyr Kalynychenko, "Volodymyr Pasichnyk – poet-protestant, borets-orhanizator," in *Zona*, no. 27, ed. Oleksa Riznykiv (Odesa: Simeks-prynt, 2011), 126–34.

116. Jones and Yasen, "Preface," 6.

117. Ibid., 34–35.

118. Ibid., 7.

119. Ibid., 8. See also Anna Procyk, ed., *Two Worlds. One Idea* (New York/Kyiv: Smoloskyp Publisher, 2013), 9. For instance, the Ukrainian poet and the leading member of a clandestine organization, the UNF, Zinovii Krasivskyj received a seventeen-year sentence that included prison, labor camp, and exile. He was not the only one who received such a lengthy sentence. There were some who languished for twenty or more years in these camps.

120. Rakhlin, *O Borise Chichibabine*, 112–16, 131–45, 148–54, 178–206.

121. Hryhorii Skovoroda (1722–1794) was a Ukrainian philosopher, poet, and teacher, known to his contemporaries and to the subsequent generations as a contemporary Socrates because of his philosophical concepts, worldview, and lifestyle. He was buried in the village of Pan-Ivanivka (today Skovorodynivka) in the Zolochivskyi district of the Kharkiv oblast.

Dmytro Bahalii (1857–1932) was a Ukrainian philosopher, historian, and civil servant. From 1906 to 1910, he was Rector of Kharkiv University, and one of the founders of the Ukrainian Academy of Sciences. From 1914 to 1917 he was Kharkiv's governor, and from 1917 he was Head of Kharkiv's "Prosvita." He died from pneumonia and was buried in Kharkiv.

Mykola Sumtsov (1854–1922) was a Ukrainian ethnographer, folklorist, literary scholar, art historian, and educator. He graduated from Kharkiv University's History and Philology department in 1875 and continued his education at Heidelberg University, Germany. Supported by his mentor Oleksandr Potebnia, he returned to Kharkiv University in 1878 as a lecturer in Russian literature. He defended his PhD thesis in ethnography, becoming a professor at Kharkiv University. In 1917, Sumtsov signed an appeal to the government, requesting the free use of the Ukrainian language in all Kharkiv institutions. Buried in Kharkiv.

Oleksandr Potebnia (1835–1891) was a prominent Ukrainian philologist, philosopher, ethnographer, folklorist, educator, and a member of the St. Petersburg Academy of Science since 1875. From 1875, he was a professor of Russian literature and language at Kharkiv University. He was one of the founders of the Kharkiv Historical and Philological Association. Buried in Kharkiv.

George Shevelov (name at birth: George Yurii Schneider; also known under his Ukrainian names and pen names: Yurii Volodymyrovych Sheveliov and Yurii Sherekh) (1908–2002) was a Ukrainian-American professor, linguist, philologist, literary historian, and literary critic. In 1939, he became assistant professor and deputy chair of the Kharkiv Pedagogical Institute's philology department, and in 1941 he became a research fellow at the Linguistic Institute of the Academy of Sciences of the UkrSSR. After the Second World War, he and his mother fled the Red Army's advance on Kharkiv in February 1943, and eventually settled in the United States. From 1952, he was teaching Russian and Ukrainian languages at Harvard University and Columbia University. Buried in New York.

122. Ivan Franko (1856–1916) was a Ukrainian poet, writer, journalist, doctor of philosophy, and ethnographer. He was one of the founders of the socialist and national movement in Western Ukraine. Beyond his own literary work, he also translated the works of Dante Alighieri, Victor Hugo, Adam Mickiewicz, Johann Wolfgang Goethe, Friedrich Schiller, William Shakespeare, and Lord Byron into Ukrainian. Buried in Lviv.

Lev Landau (1908–1968) was a Soviet physicist who made fundamental contributions to theoretical physics. Between 1932 and 1937, he headed the Department of Theoretical Physics at the National Scientific Center of the Kharkiv Institute of Physics and Technology, and taught at Kharkiv University and the Kharkiv Polytechnical Institute. His research established the foundation of what is referred to as the Landau School. Together with his former student Yevgenii Lifshitz, he wrote ten volumes of the Course of Theoretical Physics that are used by graduate students today. During the Great Terror, he was investigated by the GPU in Kharkiv, but he managed to leave for Moscow. In 1962, he barely survived a car accident and could not accept in person the Nobel Prize in physics that he was awarded the same year. Buried in Moscow.

Il'ia Mechnikov (1845–1916) was a zoologist by training of Moldavian, Ukrainian, and Jewish origin who became famous for his pioneering research in immunology. At Kharkiv University, he completed his four-year degree in natural science in two years, and continued his education in Germany and Italy, and returned to Russia in 1867. He defended his doctorate at the University of St. Petersburg, and taught and conducted his research at Odesa University. In 1888, he left for Paris to work together with Louis Pasteur, who offered him a position at the Pasteur Institute, where he remained for the rest of his life. Mechnikov's discovery of phagocytes won him the Nobel Prize in Physiology or Medicine in 1908. He shared the Prize with Paul Ehrlich. His cinerary urn has been placed in the Pasteur Institute library, Paris, France.

Simon Kuznets (1901–1985) was an American economist and statistician who received the Nobel Prize in Economic Sciences in 1971 for his empirical research on economic growth and social structure. He facilitated the transformation of economics into an empirical science and the formation of quantitative economic history. He graduated from the Kharkiv Institute of Commerce, and in 1922 he emigrated to the United States. He defended his PhD thesis at Columbia University and taught at Harvard University, John Hopkins University, the University of Pennsylvania, and Columbia University. Buried in Cambridge, MA.

123. For a discussion about the influence of Ukrainian culture and history on Chichibabin, see Ivan Dziuba, "Slovo sovisne i dobre," in *Vsemu zhivomu ne chuzhoi: Boris Chichibabin v stat'iakh i vospominaniiakh*, eds. M. I. Bogoslavskii, L. S. Karas-Chichibabina, and B. Y. Ladenzon (Kharkov: Folio, 1998), 200–208; Natalia Peleshenko, "Dukhovnyi podvyh kniaziv Borysa i Hliba v ukrainskii literaturi XX st. (na materiali poezii Borysa Chychybabina)," *Ukrainska Mohylianska akademiia*, 2020, http://ekmair.ukma.edu.ua/bitstream/handle/123456789/11556/Peleshenko_Dukhovnyi_podvyh_kniaziv.pdf?sequence=1&isAllowed=y (accessed 16 July 2020).

124. Private conversation with Arkadii Filatov, 14 July 2005, Kharkiv, Ukraine; Filatov, "Vdogonku."

125. Arkadii Filatov, "Vdogonku."

126. See photocopies of KGB reports to the Central Committee of the Communist Party of Ukraine from 1987 to 1991 in Oles Shevchenko, ed., *Ukrainska Helsinska Spilka u spohadakh i dokumentakh* (Kyiv: "Yaroslaviv Val," 2012), 441–811; and texts of KGB reports to the Central Committee of the Communist Party of Ukraine from 1960 to 1990 in Vasyl Danylenko, ed., *Politychni protesty i inakodumstvo v Ukraini (1960–1990)* (Kyiv: "Smoloskyp," 2013).

127. See a statement of the Kharkiv writer Boris Kotliarov in HDA SBU, f. 16, op. 1, spr. 994, ark. 93.

128. HDA SBU, f. 16, op. 1, spr. 1001, ark. 77.

129. See, for instance, HDA SBU, f. 16, op. 1, spr. 1005, ark. 253–55.

130. HDA SBU, f. 16, op. 1, spr. 1017, ark. 7.

131. HDA SBU, f. 16, op. 1, spr. 1017, ark. 8.

132. Ibid.

133. Ibid.

134. HDA SBU, f. 16, op. 1, spr. 1017, ark. 13.

135. See a text of one of those leaflets circulated in the town of Balakliia of the Kharkiv oblast, included in the 9 November 1972 KGB report in HDA SBU, f. 16, op. 1, spr. 1056, ark. 269.

136. HDA SBU, f. 16, op. 1, spr. 1024, ark. 255.

137. HDA SBU, f. 16, op. 1, spr. 1024, ark. 256.

138. HDA SBU, f. 16, op. 1, spr. 1030, ark. 223–24.

139. Vasyl Ovsiienko, "Druha khvylia areshtiv, 1972–73 rr.," *Kharkivska pravozakhysna hrupa*, 1 November 2006, http://museum.khpg.org/index.php?id=1162386564 (accessed 29 August 2020); Bertelsen, "Rethinking Psychiatric Terror against Nationalists in Ukraine."

140. HDA SBU, f. 16, op. 1, spr. 1064, ark. 5–22.

141. HDA SBU, f. 16, op. 1, spr. 1064, ark. 6–7.

142. HDA SBU, f. 16, op. 1, spr. 1064, ark. 12.

143. Ibid.

144. HDA SBU, f. 16, op. 1, spr. 1064, ark. 13–14.

145. HDA SBU, f. 16, op. 1, spr. 1064, ark. 15.

146. HDA SBU, f. 16, op. 1, spr. 1064, ark. 14.

147. HDA SBU, f. 16, op. 1, spr. 1064, ark. 21.

148. HDA SBU, f. 16, op. 1, spr. 1060, ark. 135–36.

149. HDA SBU, f. 16, op. 1, spr. 1060, ark. 137–38.
150. HDA SBU, f. 16, op. 1, spr. 1060, ark. 136.
151. HDA SBU, f. 16, op. 1, spr. 1060, ark. 139.
152. On Cherevchenko's story, see Ivan Babenko, "Neskolko strok o bylom," in *Slobozhanskii krug*, ed. Pavel Gulakov et al. (Kharkov: TAL "Slobozhanshchyna," 2006), 38.
153. Vladimir Usoltsev, "Gubitelnyi simbioz. KGB i yevrei," http://berkovich-zametki.com/Nomer35/Usolcev1.htm. This text was removed from this site on demand of the Roskomnadzor (the Russian Federal Service for Supervision of Communications, Information Technology, and Mass Media). See some quotations from this text in duel_gazeta, *Livejournal*, 31 July 2007, https://duel-gazeta.livejournal.com/97147.html (accessed 19 August 2020). See also Vladimir Usoltsev (interview by Andrei Sharogradskii about Vladimir Putin), *Radio Svoboda*, 11 November 2003, https://www.svoboda.org/a/24187711.html (accessed 29 August 2020).
154. Usoltsev, "Gubitelnyi simbioz."
155. Rakhlin, *O Borise Chichibabine*, 140–41.
156. Ibid., 128.
157. Ibid., 129.
158. Liliia Karas-Chichibabina, "Ty i sama b do smerti ne zabyla," in *Vsemu zhivomu ne chuzhoi: Boris Chichibabin v stat'iakh i vospominaniiakh*, eds. M. I. Bogoslavskii, L. S. Karas-Chichibabina, and B. Y. Ladenzon (Kharkov: Folio, 1998), 137–38; see also Vasyl Borovyi (interview by Serhii Shelkovyi), "No On-to darom sroka ne daiot...," *Kharkivska oblasna orhanizatsiia: Natsionalna spilka pysmennykiv Ukrainy*, 15 November 2014, http://kharkiv-nspu.org.ua/archives/3444 (accessed 29 August 2020); Vasyl Borovyi (interview by Liutsyna Khvorost and Larysa Vyrovets), "Vasyl Borovyi: 'Mene blahoslovyv do druku Svidzinskyi,'" *Official site of Liutsyna Khvorost*, 14 March 2012, https://dobrolucina.wordpress.com/2012/03/14/василь-боровий-мене-благословив-до-д/ (accessed 29 August 2020).
159. Feliks Krivin, "Druz'ia moi, prekrasen nash soiuz!" in *Vsemu zhivomu ne chuzhoi: Boris Chichibabin v stat'iakh i vospominaniiakh*, eds. M. I. Bogoslavskii, L. S. Karas-Chichibabina, and B. Y. Ladenzon (Kharkov: Folio, 1998), 151. Both Chichibabin and Borovyi have always existed outside the Union as nationally and internationally recognized poets, and their membership in the Union has never enhanced their fame or influence as writers. Both Chichibabin and Borovyi left "official" literature in 1973 without any intention to return, but during perestroika in 1987 and 1990, respectively, their membership in the Union was restored. The Union's invitation for Chichibabin to restore his membership was preceded by Yevgenii Yevtushenko's phone call to the Union's leadership in Kyiv. Bulat Okudzhava, Grigorii Pozhenian, Sergei Zalygin, and a group of writers from the editorial board of *Novyi Mir* sent telegrams to the Kharkiv chapter of the Writers' Union, demanding its administration restore Chichibabin's membership. The Union's meeting occurred on 30 October 1987, and those who excluded Chichibabin fourteen years ago voted for his "return."
160. Farmer, *Ukrainian Nationalism*, 206.

161. Myron B. Kuropas, *Scourging of a Nation: CBS and the Defamation of Ukraine* (Kingston and Kyiv: The Kashtan Press, 1995), 28.

162. Andrii Cheremskyi, "Tribute to Valer Bondar," *Ukrainskyi Kharkiv/FB*, 31 October 2016, https://www.facebook.com/openkharkiv/posts/1305232809510237/ (accessed 5 March 2021); Kostyantyn Cheremskyi, "'Spohady pro pochatok . . . ,'" *Spilka Ukrainskoi molodi*, 14 March 2013, http://cym.org.ua/2015.03/spogady-pro-pochatok/ (accessed 29 August 2020); Maks Podorozhnii, "Pam'iati Petra Cheremskoho (1942–2006)," *Spilka Ukrainskoi molodi*, 10 July 2016, http://cym.org.ua/2016.07/pam-yati-petra-cheremskogo-1942-2006/ (accessed 29 August 2020).

163. Solidarity refers to a Polish labor union that was founded in September 1980 at the Lenin Shipyard under the leadership of Lech Walesa. This trade union became the first non-communist union in a Warsaw Pact country. See Yurii Zaitsev, "Polska oposytsiia 1970–1980-kh rokiv pro zasady ukrainsko-polskoho porozuminnia," in *Deportatsii ukraintsiv ta poliakiv: kinets 1939–pochatok 50-kh rokiv*, ed. Yurii Slyvka (Lviv: NAN Ukrainy, Instytut ukrainoznavstva im. Kryp'iakevycha, 1998) 57; Zbigniew Wojnowski, *The Near Abroad: Socialist Eastern Europe and Soviet Patriotism in Ukraine, 1956–1985* (Toronto: University of Toronto Press, 2017), 177.

164. Levko Luk'ianenko, *Neznyshchennist* (Kyiv: Diokor, 2003); On Luk'ianenko's antisemitism, see Iosif Zisels (interview by Maksim Sukhanov), "Yevrei Ukrainy ili ukrainskiie yevrei?" *Association of Jewish Organizations and Communities of Ukraine*, May 2015, http://vaadua.org/news/iosif-zisels-evrei-ukrainy-ili-ukrainskie-evrei (accessed 29 August 2020); see also Semen Gluzman (interview by Mikhail Gold), "V SSSR byli eshche odni yevrei – ukraintsy," *Lekhaim* 5772 – 2(238) (February 2012), https://lechaim.ru/ARHIV/238/gold.htm (accessed 29 August 2020).

165. Kuropas, *Scourging of a Nation*, 20.

166. Ibid., 25, 26.

167. Juan Gelman (1930–2014) authored more than twenty books of poetry, and received the Argentine National Poetry Prize and the Cervantes Prize, most important prizes for Spanish-language writers. He was also an accomplished journalist writing for the Argentinian newspaper *Pagina/12* until 2014.

168. Vasyl Ovsiienko, "Vidkrytyi lyst dysydenta Ovsiienka dysydentu (i fantazeru) Sapeliaku," *Istorychna Pravda*, 29 August 2011, https://www.istpravda.com.ua/articles/2011/08/29/53451/ (accessed 29 August 2020).

Chapter 4

The Labyrinths of Silence and Psychiatric Abuse

SILENCE AS STATE PRACTICE

Leonid Osmolovskyi was a uniquely gifted Russian-speaking Jewish satirist. A 1962 graduate of the Kharkiv State University's Philology Department, he began to publish short satirical essays in the early 1960s. Most of them were coauthored with his friend Arkadii Inin, a student at the Kharkiv Polytechnical Institute. They quickly became famous as a result of their publications in the celebrated Soviet satirical magazine *Krokodil* (*The Crocodile*).[1] The magazine was extremely popular among Soviet citizens and enjoyed the largest circulation among Soviet periodicals, nearly 5.3 million copies. Their first texts, funny and witty, were tested on the stage of the Kharkiv State University's theater that was led by Osmolovskyi.[2] From the very beginning, Osmolovskyi published his texts under the pen name Osadchuk. His decision to adopt a Ukrainian last name did not seem unusual for either the Kharkiv authorities or for his colleagues: the KGB campaign against Zionism made Osmolovskyi appreciate that his literary career would be more successful if he erased the traces of Jewishness at least on paper.[3]

Yet Osmolovskyi's literary career and his private life became more tragic than he ever imagined. The influence of Hryhir Tiutiunnyk who studied with him in the Philology Department, Tiutiunnyk's uncompromised nature, literary gift, and suicide in 1980[4] shaped Osmolovskyi's path and the circle of writers whom he considered his friends and whose literary talents and worldviews helped him navigate the ideological seas of authoritarian Kharkiv. Robert Tretyakov was one of his closest friends. In the 1960s, they were inseparable but, according to some accounts, the KGB managed to break the bond between the writers.[5] During the last two decades of the Soviet Union, they no longer saw each other socially and celebrated their birthdays separately, an odd practice inconsistent with their tradition established early in the 1960s.

Osmolovskyi's fellow students who later became his colleagues remember him as a "tender soul," and a vulnerable and lonely person.[6] In the 1970s, they noticed a dramatic change in him: he began to drink heavily. Some attributed this to his unhappy private life: being in love with the same woman for his entire life, he failed to maintain this relationship.[7] Some argued that Osmolovskyi felt betrayed by his coauthor Inin who, as soon as he became successful in Moscow in the mid-1980s, abandoned his friend and colleague, allegedly publishing texts written together with Osmolovskyi under his own name.[8] Inin rarely mentioned his collaboration with Osmolovskyi, referring to his former coauthor as simply a "talented journalist."[9] Osmolovskyi's morale and visual appearance continued to deteriorate. After the collapse of the Soviet Union, in the early 1990s, he complained to his colleagues that he lived from honorarium to honorarium, having no means to buy even clothes for himself and freezing to death in his apartment during the cold winter months.[10]

However, there was also another reason for Osmolovskyi's misfortunes: he revealed that in the late 1970s, the KGB approached him with a handsome proposition to become an informer. He politely rejected the offer but was placed in the Saburova Dacha, Kharkiv's infamous psychiatric clinic, for being recalcitrant. Local psychiatrists quickly diagnosed him with schizophrenia, and he was imprisoned there for several months being treated as a patient potentially dangerous to society. Eventually, the doctors released him, but he was forced to return there for "prophylactic" treatment to "prolong the remissions."[11] Under Ukraine's independence, he lived a quiet life, surviving the poverty and coping with enduring memories of Soviet medicalized terror. He died as quietly as he lived, and attempts at establishing the details of his last days, and his literary activities, have been largely unsuccessful.[12]

Osmolovskii's story, unclear and incomplete, provided a powerful impetus to further examine the space of silence and state power that managed to stifle so many voices and to erase the legacies of so many Kharkiv writers, voices that may never be recovered or heard. This chapter focuses on a person whose literary talent began to blossom in the 1970s, nurtured by Kharkiv's professional writers. His name was Victor Borovsky.[13] The Soviet system and the KGB did not allow him the opportunity to develop his literary gift, dramatically changing his life. During the "cursed seventies," they silenced him, announcing that he was mentally ill and needed the professional intervention of psychiatrists.

Silence might be therapeutic and may be thought of as a desirable state for peaceful existence, a momentary respite from the doldrums of daily living, a prerequisite condition where intellectual contemplation might occur. For

Boris Pasternak, silence was a space of comfort, and "the best thing that he had ever heard."[14] However, for those who forcibly interned mentally healthy people in psychiatric clinics for seditious thinking, silence was a method of control, and for their victims—oblivion and void, and eventual death. From the mid-1950s to the late 1980s, Soviet psychiatry was used as a political means to control and intimidate dissenters, and its abuse was endemic in all former Soviet republics without exception. Instead of imprisonment which could resonate internationally and "entail serious political costs,"[15] Moscow silenced much of the opposition through involuntary mental hospitalization, "the fig-leaf of medical expertise,"[16] that has been characterized by many doctors and scholars as a crime against humanity. Internally, the state's task was to compromise the ideas and demands of oppositionists, and to instigate fear among their adherents.[17]

KGB top-secret documents suggest that roughly half of Soviet dissidents were interned in psychiatric clinics which required the development of a specific construction industry—building more psychiatric hospitals.[18] The 1971–1975 Five-Year Plan included the construction of 114 psychiatric clinics where 43,800 patients could be hospitalized simultaneously.[19] According to the statistics of the Soviet Ministry of Health, by 1971, the number of those who were on the psychiatric register grew from 2.1 million (1966) to 3.7 million, and 290,000 individuals were treated in psychiatric clinics.[20] Hundreds, if not thousands, of these people were isolated for their political views. In 1989, the journal *Ogoniok*, which became famous for its liberal views during perestroika under the editorship of Vitalii Korotych, published the number of Soviet citizens who were on the psychiatric register—10.2 million.[21] The vagueness and subjectivity of psychiatric diagnoses and the imperfection of psychiatric classifications conveniently contributed to the industry of fear that held the Soviet Union together. Psychiatric clinics (*psikhushki*) became a secret tool of social and political control, and they were feared even more than prison or exile.

In the 1960s–1980s, psychiatric terror was effectively applied to nationalists who constituted approximately one-tenth of those who fell victim to political psychiatry.[22] Some were not willing to speak Russian, preferring instead their native languages, which provoked a hostile reaction from the authorities. Others advocated national sovereignty and even political autonomy, a right that was guaranteed to the Soviet republics by the Constitution. Many wanted the revision of national cultural and educational policies.[23] Through the case of the student Victor Borovsky, this chapter will analyze the effectiveness of silence as state practice that surrounded the cases of "psychiatric patients" in the context of increasing discontent in the republic and the national liberation movement. The medicalization of social control, psychiatric abuses, state violence, and brutality exacerbated nonviolent popular resistance in

Ukraine, which culminated in the political activism of Ukrainian patriots in the late 1980s, contributing greatly to the collapse of the Soviet Union and the emergence of independent Ukraine. Despite these ultimate outcomes, forced silence through psychiatric terror was an effective tool in the Soviet arsenal of suppression.

Recognizing Medical Power

Michel Foucault responded to a crisis of progress in the twentieth century, a century of violence, by writing a history of the birth of psychiatric clinics and modern prisons. He traced the methodological transformations in medicine through time and illuminated the paths that led to a scientifically structured discourse about an individual. But besides the temporal factors, Foucault also discussed the important role of spatial factors and places such as hospitals that played a crucial role in understanding a patient. The clinic prescribed a "group gaze" at a patient. In Foucault's view, medical perception should be freed from the hospital experience: "hospital practice . . . kills the capacity for observation and stifles the talents of the observer by sheer number of things to observe."[24] Moreover, according to Foucault, the spatialization of medical practices conditions their abuses, which are institutionalized by a group that tries to protect itself in its drive for power and recognition. This group shapes a social space, in which laws stipulate human behavior not only in "gated" places, such as hospitals and asylums, but also in society as a whole.

The emergence of civilization and complex social forms inevitably resulted in the creation of hospitals, and medicine gained a political status: individual medical care was replaced by collective care which was marked by a new set of rules and dimensions. Such an approach to medicine required the state's assistance which of course entailed considerable control and supervision of doctors to prevent abuses of their privileged position: "medicine bec[ame] a task for the nation," as Foucault aptly noted.[25] Authoritarian regimes and their leaders, being themselves in a privileged position, immediately took advantage of their role as chief managers and financiers of state clinics: they exploited and perverted the original idea of the clinic to separate sick people from the rest of society, and utilized it as a justification for the physical isolation of the regime's critics. The healthy were proclaimed mentally ill and oppositional thinking was portrayed as a psychiatric pathology. Interestingly, the medical problem of contagion and transmission of a disease from one individual to another, a fundamental rationale for isolating sick people in hospitals to prevent an epidemic, became the model for the state's ideological applications. The state's early intervention in "the treatment" of "sick people" was crucial, and the transmission of "societally harmful" ideas was prevented through the clinic and diagnoses prescribed by the state. In a police state, such as the Soviet Union, control of information, supervision, and constraint transcended the field of medicine and governed the thinking of not only psychiatrists, the state's employees, but also of all Soviet citizens, even those who were close to the inner circle of party bosses in Moscow.

The ambiguity of knowledge that informed psychiatry became a very convenient basis for the Soviet authorities to achieve conceptual transformation of psychiatric science into an ideological weapon against dissent. The accumulation of empirical data based on multiplicities and similarities of individual cases was pushed into the background. Instead, individual exceptionality was emphasized and was made the vehicle of establishing new psychiatric topologies. In other words, a certain qualitative density of symptoms across many individual cases became a secondary consideration for deciding on individual diagnoses. Doctors were advised to pay scrupulous attention to "unique" cases and nontypical social behavior which became confirmation of a psychiatric pathology. Although in the past the extraordinary cases had been equally outside and inside the boundaries of pathology, now they were claimed to be a guarantee of mental malfunction. The uncertainty and the arbitrariness intrinsic to psychiatry solidified the basis for diagnostic practices which employed a new theoretical premise supported by the authorities. Largely, these practices were prescribed by the state, and doctors' efforts in observing and describing patients' symptoms became rather modest. The language of patients' files (*istoriia khvoroby*) became formal and opaque, and doctors' everyday observations were often reduced to a couple of sentences. This helped to institutionalize a new tradition of the Soviet clinic—deficient medical practice, abbreviated to a diagnosis which in many cases was fabricated. Importantly, no one could challenge this practice but the party and the KGB, and information about it, as well as about "patients," was strictly secret.

The diagnosis of mental sickness became an effective tool of camouflage which bolstered the legal means of fighting against the opposition: conveniently for the state, critically thinking individuals were forcibly hospitalized for indefinite terms. Instead of popularizing medical knowledge and awareness of mentally sick people in society, the state limited the space of popular medical consciousness to conceal its deceit. By the late 1950s, psychiatry became a branch of Soviet medicine fully controlled and heavily subsidized by the state, a field of political application and manipulation. The state not only authorized the "correct" psychiatric diagnoses but also dictated the course of treatment and hospitalization. In Ukraine in the late 1950s and the early 1960s, when the dissident movement gained momentum during the Khrushchev Thaw, the spatial restructuring of psychiatry as a medical practice and as a theoretical discipline became especially important for the state. Very quickly, sadistic practices of political psychiatry were fully established, and they went beyond Foucault's notion about state control through spatial isolation and abuses.

The elimination of political opposition through coercion and violence undermined the professional integrity of psychiatrists, constrained the scientific progress of psychiatry as a medical discipline, and perpetuated crimes against humanity. Multiple accounts of the "mentally ill" have been written about psychiatric misdiagnoses, such as sluggish schizophrenia that helped lock political activists in special and ordinary psychiatric hospitals (SPHs or OPHs).[26] In his book *Punitive Medicine*, Alexander Podrabinek has noted that a psychiatric diagnosis for a dissenter was predetermined after the KGB chose the psychiatric scenario for his or her punishment: "For an experienced Soviet psychiatrist, it does not matter *how* the prisoner behaves; the charming advantage of Soviet psychiatry consists precisely in the fact that any form of behavior can be interpreted as 'clearly abnormal.' . . . The officials experienced in these procedures do not chase after symptoms but instead cleverly twist the interpretation of any gesture in the direction needed. . . . 'The Serbsky guys' will certainly know how to process them [prisoners] correctly."[27]

The documents of the Central Committee of the Communist Party of the USSR copied by the Soviet dissident and human rights activist Vladimir Bukovsky in the early 1990s reveal that some of the central objectives of the regime during late socialism were the isolation of the dissidents in psychiatric clinics, the production of psychotropic drugs to immobilize and to silence them, and the reliable security system in clinics that would prevent the leak of information about their forcible treatment.[28] Importantly, SPHs were under the jurisdiction of the Ministry of Internal Affairs (MVD), while OPHs were subordinated to the Ministry of Health. The surveillance and a strict prison regime were enforced in both types of psychiatric hospitals making it extremely difficult for the victims of political psychiatry to resist or escape.

The accounts of victims of political psychiatry (Vladimir Bukovsky, Valery Tarsis, Petro Grigorenko, Leonid Pliushch, Victor Borovsky, and many others), as well as the testimonies of Soviet psychiatrists (Anatoly Koriagin, Semen Gluzman, and Aleksandr Voloshanovich) helped several scholars in the West recognize medical power in the Soviet Union.[29] Sidney Bloch, Peter Reddaway, Robert van Voren, Harvey Fireside, Teresa Smith, Thomas Oleszczuk, and Dan Healey have thoroughly examined the punitive aspect of Soviet psychiatry and the state's cover-up tactics to hide the truth.[30]

Bloch's and Reddaway's extensive research on Soviet political psychiatry provided a better understanding of the mechanisms of psychiatric terror in the Soviet Union, and the efforts of international organizations to intervene on behalf of dissenters, "prisoners of conscience." They explained the foundations for psychiatric ethics and stressed that psychiatrists were uniquely empowered by society to hospitalize patients in a psychiatric institution without their consent.[31] The KGB pressured Soviet psychiatrists to manipulate diagnoses for political purposes because there were no objective criteria that would with certainty prove a person's psychiatric "abnormality." Bloch and Reddaway discussed Professor Andrei Snezhnevsky's all-inclusive theories that extended the boundaries of mental illness, extending in turn the application of political psychiatry.[32] The diagnosis of "sluggish schizophrenia" was conveniently applied to dissenters and to those who the regime felt were socially maladjusted and suspicious. They explained that, of course, the interconnectedness between people's mental health and their social adjustment existed. However, compulsory hospitalization was not to be used as a measure of punishment for social maladjustment but rather should be considered as a therapeutic measure to alleviate human suffering. In case of the Soviet Union, deviant political behavior was "treated" by social isolation, and mental, physical, and drug abuse became the methods that corrupted the entire psychiatric system, engaging psychiatrists, nurses, and orderlies in nonmedical schemes designed by the state.[33]

One of the most active scholars in this area, Robert van Voren, continues to investigate the legacies of Soviet punitive psychiatry in Ukraine, Russia, and other former Soviet republics. In the context of rich scholarship on the subject, statements by some scholars who suggested that discussions about the extent of psychiatric malpractice in repressing dissidents were largely of a speculative nature, a trend also evident in the post-Soviet period, seem at least surprising.[34] They argued that the implications and legacies of Soviet political psychiatry and its influences on post-Soviet psychiatry have been neglected by scholars, and posited that some "are quick to conclude" that history repeats itself when observing cases of political psychiatry in contemporary Russia.[35] In defense of competent and thorough scholars, such as van Voren, it should be mentioned here that these scholars did not distinguish between the Russian Association of Independent Psychiatrists and the Russian Association of Psychiatrists, nor did they recognize the difference in what these organizations stand for. Moreover, some have identified the Serbsky Institute as "*allegedly* [italics mine] one of the major centres of 'punitive psychiatry,'" and has spoken highly of Tatiana Dmitrieva, the apologist of Soviet punitive psychiatry, and characterized her as a person who "has been on the front lines in this internal professional struggle."[36] To interrogate these views and position that seem at great odds with the preponderance of research, a discussion about Soviet psychiatric practices, key agencies, and individuals who participated in them seems appropriate.

Soviet Psychiatric Practices

During the 1950s–1980s, the Serbsky Central Scientific Research Institute of Forensic Psychiatry in Moscow[37] became the chief psychiatric institution which decided the fates of Soviet dissidents and human rights activists. The Institute became a psychiatric subsidiary of the KGB. The director of the Serbsky Institute was Georgy Morozov (1957–1990), who, as van Voren noted, was "one of the main architects of Soviet systemic political abuse of psychiatry."[38] The special fourth department of the Serbsky Institute that was fully subordinated to the KGB became a place of captivity for many dissidents, and those psychiatrists who worked there never shared the details of their work with their colleagues.[39] However, those who were sent to the Serbsky Institute constituted only a small portion of those who were forcibly interned in regional psychiatric facilities in the Soviet republics.[40] The advantage to the state of this particular approach to silencing dissenters was transparent: they were quietly removed from the public eye for indefinite terms, and often for life.[41] The legal means of defense were unavailable to those who were "diagnosed" with schizophrenia, and trials were held in the absence of the "patients."

Political psychiatry as a method for dealing with dissent gained popularity under the patronage of the KGB chairman Yurii Andropov. He became a key figure who accelerated psychiatric terror against Soviet dissidents.[42] The avalanche of KGB resolutions facilitated the *chekizatsiia* of psychiatry.[43] The accretion of the state, secret organs, and the core psychiatrists who occupied leading positions occurred rather quickly: doctors were deprived of any opportunity to act independently; *chekists* were thoroughly educated in issues related to psychiatric pathologies. For instance, students of the Counterintelligence Department No. 2 of the School of Advanced Studies of the KGB (*Vysshaia shkola KGB*) were regularly taken to the Serbsky Institute to attend "practical sessions" where they observed psychiatric patients.[44] The cooperation between the punitive organs and psychiatrists was rather productive. According to the 1976 statistical data of the Moscow Helsinki Group, the Moscow militia sent on average twelve people per day to mental institutions. Among them were those who visited the Supreme Soviet of the USSR to deliver their grievances, individuals who attempted to penetrate foreign embassies to ask for political asylum, and those who were arrested in the streets for various violations.[45]

In the 1960s–1980s, national grievances were registered mostly in Ukraine and the Baltic Soviet republics, where the share of "mentally ill" people who advocated national and cultural autonomy was rather large.[46] Psychiatric terror was broadly employed as an intimidation tactic during the waves of mass arrests of Ukrainians (in 1965–1966, 1969–1972, and the early 1980s) for their membership in the dissident movement. The separatist tendencies among Ukrainian dissidents were more perceptible in Western Ukraine, while people from Eastern Ukraine gravitated more toward cultural and intellectual opposition to the Soviet regime.[47] Either view was perceived by the Soviet authorities as anti-Soviet, which had to be addressed.

As Kenneth C. Farmer has noted, it would be impossible to establish a distinction between human rights activists and "nationalist dissenters" during these decades in Ukraine.[48] The KGB ignored the distinction and referred to all political activists in the republic as "Ukrainian nationalists," a term that had a pejorative connotation. Leonid Pliushch, a Ukrainian human rights activist, preferred to be identified as a "patriot" to avoid accusations of national exceptionalism and condescending attitudes toward other nationalities. He argued that an identification of Ukrainian dissenters as nationalists would be inaccurate and would simply reduce them to the all-embracing Soviet police definition.[49]

Employing Pliushch's definition, the majority of Ukrainian patriots were young people between twenty and twenty-nine years old, who were born before or during the Second World War, and whose memories of Stalin's terror and the genocidal famine of 1932–1933 in Ukraine were fresh and reinforced by their parents and grandparents. Most were university graduates who held advanced degrees in arts and humanities, and those who were professional writers, artists, historians, philologists, and scientists.[50] Later they were grouped under the collective term of *shistdesiatnyky* whose romantic nationalist orientation manifested itself in their art and social activities in the 1960s. Farmer characterized them as "the first kernel of a deliberate, committed, and self-identified nucleus of opposition among the mobilized and Soviet-educated generation."[51] A considerable portion of them were interned in mental institutions; some experienced both the camps and psychiatric clinics.

The most recalcitrant individuals were incarcerated in SPHs. The widespread diagnoses for the dissidents were "sluggish schizophrenia," "reformist delusions," "reformational paranoia," "nervous exhaustion caused by justice-seeking," and the like.[52] In Ukraine, the Dnipropetrovsk special psychiatric hospital gained fame as the cruelest mental institution in the territory of the USSR. Bloch and Reddaway have characterized the conditions in SPHs as a "highly disturbed environment," saturated with the insanity of severely ill patients, and the cruelty of the staff, the orderlies who usually were criminals-trusties.[53]

Scholars identified several methods of nontherapeutic "treatment" which were punitive in essence: beatings, sexual abuse, the "wet pack," electro-convulsive therapy or electric shock therapy, and drug misuse (Sulphazin, *skipidar* [turpentine oil], various neuroleptics/anti-psychotics (Haloperidol), sedatives and tranquilizers, and insulin shock "treatment").[54] The drugs served as a chemical straitjacket that helped control people's behavior and mind and, including other methods, such a "therapy" was also a form of intimidation and encouragement to recant. Recanting was a sign of "recovery" and a condition for release.

Neuroleptics quickly demoralized people: they became deranged and indifferent to their surroundings, refraining from any activities and generally losing their grip on reality. Viktor Rafalsky wrote:

> When I got to prison, which was often enough, this was a resort for me, believe it or not. . . . There are things that are difficult to imagine. This is merely unimaginable, when a person is kept under the influence of neuroleptics for years. Only uncertainty is ahead of you. This incapacitates and kills you. Weak people fail to tolerate it and hang themselves. Neuroleptics break your spirit, and people lose their human dignity and integrity. They kneel before their executioners and beg for mercy, as it happened to the journalist Lavrov.[55]

Significantly, the KGB supervised the use of drug torture for recalcitrant individuals, prescribing the injection of neuroleptics and other drugs, and even the dosage. The KGB told Leonid Pliushch's wife that if she behaved herself and stopped complaining about the violation of human rights in the Soviet Union, the dosage of neuroleptics prescribed to her husband would be decreased.[56] A number of secret laboratories worked at creating new drugs, and the interned dissidents served as guinea pigs, involuntarily participating in drug experiments. Slavoj Žižek made it clear that at the notorious Serbsky Institute, a drug was invented to torture dissidents. The drug provoked bradycardia when injected into the prisoner's heart zone, which caused a feeling of horror and terrifying anxiety. "Viewed from the outside, the prisoner seemed just to be dozing, while in fact he was living a nightmare," Žižek noted.[57]

Physical and mental torture was accompanied with everyday inconveniences, such as showers that were allowed once a week, collective trips to the toilet allowed every 4 hours, and so on. Moreover, the infrastructure of most psychiatric clinics literally fell apart (many had not seen renovation since prerevolutionary times), and doctors were engaged in solving plumbing, catering, and other economic problems.[58] "Open door policies" were proclaimed by luminaries of Soviet psychiatry as a progressive approach to treating psychiatric patients. However, bars on the windows, locked doors, cages, and everyday prison-like practices were the norm in psychiatric wards.[59] In the atmosphere of total disregard for human dignity and deteriorating material conditions of the clinics, the majority of psychiatrists were concerned about their personal well-being, privileges, salaries, and promotion.[60]

People's physical isolation in psychiatric wards from their relatives and from the rest of society ensured absolute secrecy and prevented leaks of information. Typically, neither the "patients" nor their relatives requested help. Those who challenged the regime were isolated in a psychiatric clinic "by force or by deception,"⁶¹ and the Soviet authorities did their best to hide them from foreigners and especially from foreign journalists to keep the numbers of those who were dissatisfied with the regime secret from the outside world. For instance, many people were interned in psychiatric clinics before and during Richard Nixon's 1972 visit to Moscow and the 1980 Olympic Games in the USSR. They were diagnosed as psychopaths (70 percent) or schizophrenics (30 percent) who allegedly suffered from various paranoiac symptoms. Often the interned did not receive any treatment, and the "wall therapy" (containment in a cell) was the only method applied to them. Paradoxically, despite the all-pervasive mode of secrecy, the KGB's interventions became so normal and obvious that neither psychiatrists nor their "patients" concealed the fact of the secret police's active participation in medical procedures.⁶² But this information circulated inside the walls of psychiatric clinics and did not very often travel outside. Podrabinek has argued that the corruption and venality of the core group of psychiatrists at the Serbsky Institute who worked together with the secret police (some of them were secret police) was so obvious that they even "stopped pretending that they [were] interested in finding the truth. The conscience of an SPH physician has been replaced with the cynicism of a Chekist."⁶³ Many psychiatrists of the Kharkiv Psychiatric Hospital (Saburova Dacha) exhibited similar behavior.

Kharkiv Psychiatrists and the Saburova Dacha

The Soviet socialist system of medicine and its total control by the party shaped psychiatry, its ethical principles, and the mode of functioning, employing the principles of "naked coercion" and violence.⁶⁴ The career of rank-and-file psychiatrists and their professional behavior were under complete control of chief psychiatrists and heads of psychiatric clinics who were a part of the party *nomenklatura*. The working schedule of psychiatrists, especially in the peripheries, was rather hectic. Normally, they had to see approximately 25–30 patients per day, which, as the former Soviet psychiatrist and dissident Anatoly Koryagin argued, "precluded a deep, thoughtful approach to the patients, and medical skill was reduced to routine form-filling and stamping."⁶⁵

Micro supervision by head doctors, the deplorable material conditions of psychiatric clinics, and more serious problems, such as professional forgery and deception, demanded by the party and the KGB, became obstacles to personal moral adjustments for some psychiatrists. Their testimonies revealed the mechanisms of cleansing dissent through the use of political psychiatry. Sadly, the majority of doctors were aware of psychiatric abuse; moreover, they were actively engaged in perpetuating the system.⁶⁶

Ordinary Soviet psychiatrists faced a dilemma: by the order of the KGB they had to abuse the ethics of psychiatry and medicine, or, if they disobeyed, be themselves interned into psychiatric clinics and treated as schizophrenics. Views about Soviet psychiatrists' professionalism differ. Van Voren believes that the majority of psychiatrists had no idea what they were doing, and psychiatric diagnoses for dissent seemed plausible to them.[67] The Ukrainian psychiatrist and human rights activist Gluzman argues that ordinary psychiatrists "saw it all, understood it all, but were afraid to protest."[68] The Ukrainian psychiatrists Ada Korotenko and Nataliia Alikina posit that Soviet psychiatrists' conformism and cowardice perpetuated psychiatric abuse.[69] Podrabinek has emphasized that psychiatric care, as medicine in general, was built vertically, and "psychiatrists always act[ed] on orders from above."[70] Yet corruption blossomed, and many psychiatrists were not squeamish about taking bribes from "patients"—who wanted them to reduce the dose of drugs or to relax the hospital regimen.[71] What was worse is that the power and the influence of the core psychiatrists at the Serbsky Institute, such as Morozov, Snezhnevsky, and Lunts, on their colleagues in regional mental institutions was tremendous. In a sense, for them power became a more substantial asset than money, a pledge for personal enrichment and professional self-aggrandizement. Yet the *saburianyn* and neurologist V. I. Taitslin insisted that deep professionalism, decency, liberalism, and faithfulness to science and patients were intrinsic features of the Kharkiv school of psychiatry and the Saburova Dacha.[72] However, accounts by Saburova Dacha's patients and psychiatrists who worked in Kharkiv during the Soviet era do not support this claim. The solid reputation of the Kharkiv school of psychiatry was tainted when the evidence of psychiatric abuse and even sadism exercised by the staff of the Saburova Dacha in the 1960s–1980s emerged.

In his book *Madness and Civilization*, Michel Foucault has demonstrated that confinement in psychiatric hospitals had been historically a method of exclusion. He has traced this phenomenon to the late Middle Ages, but certainly people's fear of the mad and their attempts to control or to isolate them goes back to pre-biblical times. "Confinement did seek to suppress madness, to eliminate from the social order a figure which did not find its place within it," he wrote.[73] Moreover, he argued that sadism, not accidentally, "was born of confinement and, within confinement."[74] In this context, the Soviet regime was neither innovative, nor pioneering. However, at the end of the eighteenth century, European psychiatric practices began to change. Doctors became salient figures in the asylums, and because of their concerns for humanity and knowledge, these places were transformed into a "medical space."[75] Juridical places of confinement where abuses were institutionalized and considered normal were converted into places of medical realms where observation became a step toward understanding mental illness, and medical knowledge, not emotions, guided human activities.

But the Soviet situation seems to be reversed: as a part of the international space of humane and progressive forms of new social and medical arrangements for quite some time,[76] the state experienced a tremendous regression of humanity, and returned to the norms of the Middle Ages. Careful investigations conducted by Western scholars have demonstrated the depth of the immoral abyss into which Soviet psychiatry had fallen. These regressive trends and individual animalistic sadism, which were miraculously "transmitted intact" through space and time[77] and which reigned at the top of the Soviet power structure and in psychiatric clinics, were exacerbated by the triumph of Soviet Communist ideology, utopia, and illusions, which elevated violence to the rank of normal state practices and traditions. Soviet psychiatric hospitals became not only institutions of correction and punishment for nonconformity and non-complicity but also theaters of sadism and brutality where they were practiced, perfected, and enjoyed by those in power.

However, not all Soviet psychiatrists participated in psychiatric abuse. The first attempt to resist psychiatric terror was undertaken in 1977, when a group of human rights activists formed the Working Commission to Investigate the Use of Psychiatry for Political Purposes. Aleksandr Voloshanovich became its main consulting psychiatrist and helped the commission collect and evaluate cases of psychiatric abuse. Importantly, the Working Commission contributed to our understanding of the "nature and extent of the interlocking psychiatric, legal and police systems, as applied to victims of 'punitive medicine.'"[78] Moreover, its conclusions help identify the motivations for why the state resorted to political psychiatry. Despite the fact that a number of punitive options were available, including imprisonment and exile, political psychiatry became the simplest way for the state to handle Soviet dissidents. Psychiatric "treatment" of oppositionists "took less effort and was less time-consuming and more economical for the authorities."[79] Conveniently, the KGB transferred a great share of responsibility to the shoulders of psychiatrists who not only guarded the oppositionists, physically locking them in psychiatric wards, but also controlled them mentally through drug abuse and violence. After the collapse of the Soviet Union, the Soviet psychiatrist Yakov Landau, who worked in the Serbsky Institute, publicized his point of view about abuses of psychiatry: "the organs [KGB] burdened us with very responsible work. . . . They expected us to do what they asked us to do, and we knew what they expected."[80] Understandably, being aware of the control mechanisms that could be easily redirected and aimed at them, the majority of Soviet psychiatrists failed to resist manipulation by the authorities. Those who were members of the Moscow Working Commission functioned for four years but were crushed by the KGB. By 1981, all six members but Voloshanovich had been imprisoned.[81]

Koryagin, who worked in Kharkiv, continued Voloshanovich's work and became one of the most vocal advocates of Soviet psychiatry's purification. Until his arrest, he gathered information for the Working Commission about psychiatric abuse and those political activists who were identified as schizophrenics.[82] Not surprisingly, Koryagin was aware of psychiatric abuses at the Saburova Dacha where a great number of dissidents were interned in the 1950s–1980s.

By the mid-1970s, the Saburova Dacha, a territorial behemoth that occupied 30 hectares, had thirty various departments and could accommodate 3,000 patients. However, all departments were incredibly overcrowded. Each patient had approximately 1.8–2.0 square meters instead of 7.0 square meters per person, identified by the authorities as a sanitary norm. It was common for two people with a psychiatrically chronic pathology to share a bed; many slept on the floor. Epidemic infections erupted systematically, and the lethality among the patients was tremendous. The kitchen facilities that provided food for the hospitalized worked intermittently because the sanitary inspection constantly sealed it for violations of sanitary norms. The infrastructure of all buildings was incredibly poor and chronic crises, such as leaking pipes and sewage system failure, disrupted the normal functioning of the clinic.[83]

According to Ivan Sosin, who was the deputy chief and manager of the clinic from 1976 to 1978, at that time psychiatry was one of the most prestigious clinical disciplines, and to be hired for a position at the Saburova Dacha was deemed extremely difficult. Vacancies were a rare opportunity. Saburova Dacha's personnel, including psychiatrists, numbered 2,500 people divided into clans. The Soviet system of privileges and the supervision of the *obkom*, *gorkom*, and the KGB contributed to inner clashes.[84]

Orders from the KGB reached the clinic directly, or through the chief oblast psychiatrist who usually made a phone call and clarified the details of the diagnosis. "Patients" dangerous to the regime were supposed to be kept in the clinic for an indeterminate duration; psychiatrists who disobeyed the authorities were supposed to be condemned at a party meeting as anti-Soviet propagandists. For instance, before Koryagin's arrest, on 5 February 1981, the chief doctor at the Kharkiv Psycho-Neurological Clinic (a part of the Saburova Dacha) was ordered by the Kharkiv Regional Prosecutor General to analyze Koryagin's activities as a member of the Working Commission at a collective meeting. The Prosecutor General provided a working definition that would determine his activities as "anti-Soviet" and "criminal." Koryagin's fate was sealed: the collective proceeded according to the prescribed scenario, and the verdict of the meeting mirrored the authorities' injunctions.[85]

The majority of psychiatrists of the Saburova Dacha were actively involved in various illegal activities. They simultaneously murdered and saved people, although not for altruistic or humanitarian reasons. As we have seen, the protracted murder of the minds of mentally healthy and vigorous intellectuals and dissidents by drugs prescribed by psychiatrists is notorious and well-documented. Yet there was another widespread practice among psychiatrists which still survives today, as Peter Pomerantsev has suggested. Many young men did not and still do not mind spending a month in a psychiatric clinic to receive a medical certificate that would help them avoid military service. "The mad are not trusted with guns," and the youth preferred and prefer to be "mad" rather than to be drafted and possibly killed in the army. Historically, political psychiatry and long periods of deception by both psychiatrists and their patients made them a part of the system, *sistema*, in which illegal (political) arrangements and agreements between the parties transformed both into semi-legal individuals and transgressors. To be saved or to be wealthy, one should cheat *sistema* which immediately co-opts or entraps the cheater, firmly and permanently.[86] The mechanism of such entrapment will be analyzed further through the individual history of the Ukrainian student and the neophyte writer Victor Borovsky.

Ukrainian Nationalists as Mentally Ill

On a December morning in 1974, Victor Borovsky who was born in a small Ukrainian town of Lozova near Kharkiv knocked at the door of the editor of *Prapor*'s poetry section Robert Tretyakov. "Another young prodigy," thought Tretyakov, and invited Borovsky to sit in a comfortable chair. Borovsky brought his poems written in Ukrainian to get Tretyakov's professional opinion: "Just let me know if I should continue to write," Borovsky asked timidly. They agreed that he would come in a week to hear Tretyakov's verdict. Tretyakov warned Borovsky that he would be brutally honest but assured the young man that there would be another poet who would also take a look at his verses. They parted. Tretyakov remembered that when he began to read Borovsky's poetry, he could not stop: "A fresh breeze filled the room, and I could not grasp where this boy's freedom and a delicate and subtle feeling for harmony and language came from. He was just a boy."[87] Borovsky never showed up again, and Tretyakov had no way of knowing what happened to him. In 1975, at the age of nineteen, Borovsky was expelled from the Sloviansk Pedagogical Institute, arrested, and spent five months in psychiatric clinics, first being confined in the Sloviansk psychiatric hospital (Donetsk oblast), and later in the Saburova Dacha (Kharkiv). He lived a short life, passing away on 11 May 2009 from cancer at the age of fifty-two, far from Ukraine—in the City of New York, the United States, and was buried at Hallandale Beach, Florida. Having abandoned his poetic gift, he became a priest, and Tretyakov's message prepared for a young poet in the mid-1970s had never reached him.

Much has been written about punitive psychiatry in the Soviet Union, yet the fate of its youngest victim, Victor Borovsky, was overlooked by scholars. Scholarly literature and archival data that have been analyzed over the last decade suggest that political psychiatry and other sorts of repression targeted very specific groups of dissenters. Nationalists occupied a special place among those who ran a high risk of finding themselves in psychiatric wards. Thomas A. Oleszczuk aptly noted that this tendency was "rooted in the implicit challenge of nationalism to the integrity of the USSR," and nationalists' social and political behavior was perceived as threatening to the state.[88]

In the atmosphere of totalizing Russification in Ukraine, those who spoke Ukrainian were an immediate target for the authorities. Borovsky was one of them. Many were accused of anti-Soviet propaganda and sent to camps. The indictment was usually based on Paragraph 62, point 1 of the Ukrainian SSR Criminal Code, the charge of antagonism to Soviet authorities, aimed at destabilizing the Soviet regime and "fomenting nationalistic sentiments."[89] Semen Gluzman has noted that in the early 1970s when he served his prison sentence in the camps, the majority of prisoners were Ukrainians.[90] He "ha[d] not met a single Belorussian, Uzbek, Tadzhik, or Kirgiz, despite the fact that the KGB existed in all Soviet republics. Here in Ukraine there is a ferment of resistance," he posited.[91] The most recalcitrant were sent to psychiatric clinics. As a psychiatrist and as a person who closely communicated with dissidents who went through psychiatric clinics, Gluzman is also convinced that political psychiatry was more terrifying than prison.[92]

Ukrainian patriots who were "diagnosed" as mentally ill constituted a majority among those who were interned in various psychiatric clinics all over Ukraine. They were inspired by people, such as the Ukrainian poets Ivan Sokulskyi and Mykola Kulchynskyi who were concerned not with the fact that "not everyone spoke Ukrainian" but rather that "no one spoke Ukrainian" in their home city of Dnipropetrovsk because of totalizing Russification.[93] They dreamed of a free Ukraine and supported the Ukrainian students Lidiia Piven (Huk), Vil'iamin Mykhalchuk, and Yaroslav Hevrych who became known for defending the right of Ukrainians to use their native language.[94] Yet some did not clearly understand what kind of Ukraine they were fighting for. Similar to the Ukrainian writer Mykola Khvyliovyi, they felt they had to get "away from Moscow," which was abusive toward their language and culture.[95] Having found themselves in an abusive environment where they were not only proclaimed to be psychiatrically ill but where they were routinely tortured physically and mentally, they were confused and began to doubt their identity. The orderlies influenced by Soviet propaganda were especially cruel to "nationalists." They took a special pleasure in humiliating and beating them until they were unconscious. Doctors knew about this but turned a blind eye toward this situation. In his memoirs, Vladimir Bukovsky stated that he knew a few instances when orderlies in hospitals chose political prisoners who were Ukrainians as their victims: they beat them severely, and, as a result, several people died from complications.[96]

The Scottish psychiatrist Ronald David Laing discussed in detail the vulnerability of psychiatric patients whose insecurity was constantly challenged by any new relationships, even harmless and pleasant ones, which often triggered psychoses in them. Their identity was jeopardized and often distorted.[97] One can imagine what mentally healthy people experienced, being routinely tortured in psychiatric wards by abusive orderlies, psychiatrists, and aggressive mental patients. Their identity was threatened to the point of inner mental crisis and even insanity.

The pretext for internment differed in each individual case. For instance, an unidentified person from Ivano-Frankivsk (a patient of the Saburova Dacha) was trying to change the title of the Kharkiv metro station from "Soviet Ukraine" to "Free Ukraine";[98] some individuals were interned in various psychiatric clinics because they were protesting against Soviet cultural policies in Ukraine near Taras Shevchenko's monument in Kyiv;[99] others were members of civil organizations fighting against Russification of Ukraine.[100]

The most persuasive evidence of punitive medicine in the cases of "Ukrainian nationalists" was the fact that they began to receive "treatment" for mental illness before the conclusion of the forensic examination commission, as happened in Borovsky's case.[101]

Growing up in a Ukrainian-speaking town, he could not speak Russian in college. He used Ukrainian, and everyone teased him about it, Borovsky recalled.[102] He mentioned Aleksandr Solzhenitsyn's name during a Party History seminar which cost him his freedom. Like other "patients," Borovsky had no idea about the duration of his hospitalization or the methods of "treatment." He recalled that a nurse who greeted him upon his arrival in the clinic stated after briefly studying his file: "Don't worry, we'll fix your way of thinking; medicine is capable of miracles."[103] Borovsky began to receive Sulphazin during the very first week in the hospital for being recalcitrant. The observational period that usually precedes a forensic examination by a group of specialists and a diagnostic conclusion were skipped, and the insulin shock therapy and neuroleptics were administered to Borovsky to validate his alleged insanity before his mother came to visit him.

In the KGB's view, he behaved insanely, discussing Stalinism and Solzhenitsyn's works in class. His attempt to visit the writer Viktor Nekrasov in Kyiv, who was persecuted by the authorities for his support of Solzhenitsyn, was evaluated as anti-Soviet activity and as a psychiatric pathology.[104] But most importantly, as the head of the psychiatric ward Anatoly Bezuhly stated, Borovsky's insanity manifested itself in using a "dialect" (meaning the Ukrainian language) instead of Russian.[105]

In the drama that unraveled around a nineteen-year-old man, one detail seems particularly interesting. The new tactics of the KGB were more subtle than during the Stalin era. The secret agency acted behind the scenes, using intermediaries to persecute Borovsky. The rector of the university, professors, the party and Komsomol functionaries, and doctors were those individuals who directly came into contact with Borovsky and, ultimately, they were held accountable for anything they said or did. The leak of information about Borovsky abroad or anything that might have run counter to the KGB's scenario was an ultimate responsibility of these people, not of the KGB. Borovsky understood this: "The times when the blood of honest people could not dry on the hands of the NKVD and when the chekists themselves beat, choked, shot and tortured, receded into the past. Now the KGB estranges itself from this, and gives orders to others without any deep concerns about how it may appear."[106]

The *chekists* revealed themselves only before his release from the Sloviansk hospital. They made direct threats and gave orders for him to make regular appearances at KGB headquarters for "conversations." Later, having published his memoirs in the West, Borovsky described in detail the sadistic nature of these "conversations."

It seems that sadistic inclinations were also an important criterion in the selection of orderlies for psychiatric clinics. According to many patients' accounts, they humiliated the "patients," beating them, exploiting them as slaves, and forcing them to dance or sing.[107] There were also a great number of sadists among psychiatrists. Arkady Zhuravsky, a psychiatrist at the Sloviansk psychiatric clinic, personally administered injections of turpentine into the periosteal part of the bone to inflict an excruciating pain that escalated every hour.[108] The injections provoked neurological symptoms and caused spasms of the airways. A high dose could be lethal, causing renal and pulmonary failure. Zhuravsky's routine question was: "Do you like Soviet power better after the injection?"[109] Occasional deaths provoked by the overdose of turpentine did not disturb the staff or the executioner who perceived them as part of the norm.[110]

Again, secrecy and confidentiality played an important role in political psychiatry. Conveniently for the Soviet regime, patients' files, as well as reports of forensic psychiatric examinations, have always been considered confidential, because secrecy and privacy are those necessary elements that help protect psychiatric patients from publicity about their mental condition and prevent their embarrassment and trauma. Feelings of embarrassment, humiliation, or guilt contribute little to therapy and to the efforts of psychiatrists to stabilize the mental state of their patients.[111] In the Soviet Union, only a limited number of people had access to the files of "Ukrainian nationalists," "patients" of psychiatric clinics. Moreover, they are still locked in psychiatric hospitals' archives under the pretext of preserving patients' privacy.

However, Borovsky managed to secretly examine his 200-page file because of the kindness of a nurse who sympathized with him. According to his testimony, his file contained no evidence of chronic abuses and the actual "therapy" he received in the Sloviansk psychiatric hospital. In other words, Zhuravsky falsified information about Borovsky's treatment and never put his prescriptions in writing. Borovsky claimed he was routinely tortured by Sulphazin injections, but his everyday prescription reports demonstrated that he was injected with Sulphazin only once, and that he was systematically given vitamins and other useful supplements.[112]

After three months of torture, Borovsky was released from the Sloviansk psychiatric clinic. The KGB forced him to sign a document in which he promised to work for the benefit of the Motherland and to refrain from using Ukrainian in public offices.[113] The *chekists* quite cynically advised him that he should forget everything that he saw or heard in the clinic. Borovsky was instructed that if someone questioned his long absence in Lozova, he was supposed to tell them that he was resting at a resort.[114]

After his release, Borovsky unsuccessfully tried to enter the Odesa Spiritual Seminary. The KGB also used its power to facilitate Borovsky's permanent unemployment.[115] Disillusioned, he sent a telegram to the Head of the KGB of the USSR Yurii Andropov. It read:

> The violation of human rights by the KGB you chair is a shameful page in the history of our state which was built on the bones of honest people. The violation of human rights, the trampling of human dignity and integrity, and an attempt to destroy anything national, transforming it into a common Soviet, is a Nazi-like crime. I demand the end of the repression against me for my free thinking, and to restore me at the university so that I might receive a higher education guaranteed by the Constitution.[116]

These sorts of letters that Borovsky wrote to various organizations and high party organs, and his continuous contacts with Ukrainian dissidents, such as Oleksa Tykhyi[117] and Mykola Rudenko,[118] could not be tolerated by the KGB for very long. Not surprisingly in spring 1977, he was detained in the Saburova Dacha.

The condescending explanations of the psychiatrist Ivan Sosin, at that time the deputy chief of the Saburova Dacha, given to Borovsky's mother shed light on his perception of mental illness:

Psychiatry is a very complex thing. As an uneducated woman, you are unable to comprehend all the subtleties of this complex science. We treat people's acts that cannot be characterized as normal human behavior as a mental illness. For instance, your son's acquaintance with Rudenko is an illness. Your son wanted to meet him without any reason. Millions of citizens live and have no desire to meet Rudenko and people like Rudenko. Yet your son wanted to meet him—this is an unhealthy phenomenon. You are a normal person, and you did not want to meet Rudenko, but your son did. Why did he? There is no answer to this question. Thus, psychiatry deems unexplainable behavior as abnormal, and accordingly those who exhibit this behavior—as psychiatrically ill people.[119]

Was he sincere in his beliefs, or was he co-opted by the KGB to an extent that fear obscured his mind and muddled his professional principles and ethics that were nurtured in him when he was a student of a medical university? According to witnesses' accounts, Sosin received his orders directly from KGB officials or through the chief psychiatrist of Kharkiv oblast G. A. Nikitin who decided the fates of the Ukrainian dissidents.[120] After the collapse of the Soviet Union, Sosin himself stated that his October 1976 appointment as the deputy chief of the Saburova Dacha was facilitated by Nikitin, obviously for his diligent service.[121] Sosin's attempt to silence Borovsky's mother reveals his full awareness of ongoing psychiatric abuse that became so normal for him: "Today your son might be healthy, but tomorrow he might be found ill. Psychiatry is such a thing that behavior might be interpreted in a variety of ways. Thus, your son can be diagnosed as mentally ill at any moment, and no one will help him . . . you simply have to behave yourself and be quiet and, perhaps, your son will be released soon."[122]

Borovsky's mother's threat that she would send a telegram of complaint to the General Secretary Leonid Brezhnev, Andropov, and the Minister of Health Boris Petrovsky had little effect on Sosin. "Who needs them and who reads them?" he responded.[123] The intellectual and moral divide in Sosin obviously occurred under pressure from the authorities: political psychiatry became a norm for him, and like many psychiatrists, he ceased to conceal its power before the powerless relatives of his victims.

Under pressure from the hospital's administration, Borovsky's doctor Liubov Hrytsenko demanded his recantation, as did Mykola Shevchenko who was the party chief (*partorh*) of the Saburova Dacha and the head of the second psychiatric department where Borovsky was placed. Shevchenko insisted that the first sign of the restoration of Borovsky's mental health would be "his condemnation of his own behavior and an honest account about all his friends."[124] Shevchenko also emphasized that Borovsky should perceive this as friendly advice about the conditions for his release. It seems appropriate to mention here that in 1996, Sosin characterized Shevchenko as a most energetic psychiatrist and organizer, a patriot of the Saburova Dacha, and a decent human being. Moreover, Sosin recommended the authorities promote Shevchenko, and in 1978 Shevchenko became the chief of the Saburova Dacha serving as such until 1988.[125] It would be very tempting to characterize this recommendation as not only a professional collegiality but also as a common bond of guilt, the guilt of the criminal past that linked these two individuals together forever.

Yet the Saburova Dacha employed not only doctors, such as Sosin and Shevchenko, but also those few who had the courage to say, at least informally, that Borovsky was absolutely healthy. Liubov Hrytsenko was rather open with Borovsky's friend Genrikh Altunian and, according to Altunian, she even prepared Borovsky for his forensic examination, advising him to answer doctors' provocative questions in a certain way to avoid being diagnosed with schizophrenia. However, the KGB quickly silenced Hrytsenko, and even forced her to provide a false deposition against Altunian that helped later sentence him to a prison term.[126]

Constant physical and mental abuse, amplified by the abrogation of basic constitutional and human rights, dehumanized some and made others more resilient. For many, recanting was morally impossible. So it was for Borovsky. The violence and brutality he experienced in the Sloviansk psychiatric clinic and in the Saburova Dacha merely strengthened his principles. Repentance for him was impossible on an almost biological level.[127] Zhuravsky's words "the treatment is designed so that you see the society the way we want you to see it, not the way you see it in your imagination" made Borovsky resilient: he never admitted his guilt despite torture and humiliation.[128]

As mentioned earlier, the torture in psychiatric clinics was prolonged and sophisticated. Political prisoners experienced beatings, rapes, heavy doses of neuroleptics, and were even forced to swallow live frogs and foreign objects.[129] Surveillance and censorship in psychiatric clinics were no less torturous and painful. "Patients" were allowed to write letters only to their relatives at the discretion of their psychiatrists or nurses: the censors' task was to identify anti-Soviet statements that would ultimately confirm a psychiatric pathology that had been previously "diagnosed." The orderlies especially enjoyed standing behind "patients" and reading while they were writing their letters. This was perceived by many as a sophisticated torture that suppressed and ruined them morally and intellectually.[130] Borovsky was not permitted to write letters.

Those "patients" who wrote their letters in Ukrainian and used the Ukrainian language during forensic psychiatric examinations at the Serbsky Institute were diagnosed with an "acute psychosis provoked by nationalism."[131] The psychiatrist of the infamous Dnipropetrovsk special psychiatric clinic Ella Kamenetska, when hearing Mykola Plakhotniuk's Ukrainian word *sil* (salt), asked the orderly: "Slavik, take the patient for your training. Teach him to speak Russian. We use here 'sol.'" Slavik responded: "No problem. I will teach him."[132] To be sure, psychiatric abuse and beatings were designed to excoriate "Ukrainian nationalism" and to have corporal effects, prolonging pain and suffering to infinity, and punishing the recalcitrant every day by a "thousand deaths" they experienced in horror.[133] It was designed to leave a permanent scar in the souls of oppositionists who were supposed to live for the rest of their lives with the memory of horror and fear which would substantiate psychiatrists' claims about their insanity: the horror would mark them as "sick" and as the "others," which would doom them for isolation even when they would be "free"—outside the fence of a psychiatric clinic.

Similar to Borovsky, many Ukrainian patriots resisted Soviet anti-Ukrainian policies and terror. Two waves of repression in the late 1960s and early 1970s that were designed to curtail the nationalist movement in Ukraine intensified popular resistance to terror, especially among the Ukrainian intelligentsia. At the peak of psychiatric abuses, in 1976 in Kyiv the Ukrainian intelligentsia organized a human rights organization—the Ukrainian Helsinki Group (*Ukrainska Helsinska Hrupa*, UHH) to promote compliance with the Helsinki Accords, a group that maintained close links with similar groups in Moscow, Georgia, Armenia, and Lithuania.[134] The UHH was conceived to defend human rights and to fight for the national survival of Ukraine. Today it is a documented fact that repressions that specifically targeted the members of this organization (the earliest arrests began in early 1977 and the latest occurred in 1984) did not break them. Over eight years, only one person repented out of the forty-one individuals who were repressed. Thirty-nine members experienced the entire arsenal of torture practiced by the regime, in camps and psychiatric clinics. Mykhailo Melnyk committed suicide before he was arrested. As a Jew, Volodomyr Malynkovych was allowed to emigrate. Valerii Marchenko, Oleksa Tykhyi, Yurko Lytvyn, and Vasyl Stus were tortured to death in the camps.[135] Those who survived renewed the organization in 1988 under the title the Ukrainian Helsinki Union (*Ukrainska Helsinska Spilka*) and played a crucial role in establishing an independent Ukraine.

Because of the efforts of former political prisoners to renew the Ukrainian liberation movement, in March 1987, in his report to Volodymyr Shcherbytsky, the head of the KGB in Ukraine Stepan Mukha (1982–1987) suggested that the famous representatives of the Ukrainian intelligentsia, among them Oles Honchar and Borys Oliinyk, should be pushed to publish articles which would condemn the anti-Soviet activities of Ukrainian nationalists who returned from the camps.[136] Mukha insisted that this approach would once again demonstrate the humanity of the Soviet regime that allowed criminals charged with anti-Soviet agitation and propaganda to integrate into the social fabric of Soviet life. As in the late 1920s and the early 1930s, having received orders from on high, periodicals were sprinkled with scathing articles that condemned Ukrainian nationalists.

The terms, such as "accomplices," "nationalists," and "extremists" that were applied by the *chekists* to Viacheslav Chornovil, Levko Luk'ianenko, Pavlo Skochok, Yevhen Sverstiuk, Ivan Svitlychnyi, and Bohdan and Mykhailo Horyn, traveled from the KGB's reports directly to newspaper articles.[137] Gorbachev's perestroika had little effect on the reconceptualization of the KGB's terms for Ukrainian nationalists. In his 1988 reports to the Central Committee, Mykola Holushko who replaced Mukha as the head of the KGB in Ukraine (1987–1991) continued to identify Viktor Rafalsky and other Ukrainian patriots as mentally sick individuals.[138] The "nationalistic manifestations," such as the signs on buildings and fences "Live long free Ukraine" and the drawings of the *Tryzub* (trident, the state coat of arms of Ukraine that features the Ukrainian flag's colors, blue and yellow) that began to appear more and more frequently in various Ukrainian cities and towns made the KGB nervous. As a result, their operational work and surveillance intensified, and they sought more effective methods for neutralization of nationalists.[139] KGB reports to the highest party organs issued in 1988–1989 are quite revealing and demonstrate serious concerns of the secret police about the radicalization of "nationalistic groups." They characterized the Ukrainian Helsinki Union as an "anti-socialist" organization and its members as individuals who led anti-social lifestyles, participating in seminars about democracy and humanism and spreading negative information and "rumors" about the Chernobyl tragedy. Moreover, they dared, it was said, to belittle regional party secretaries, and even the founder of the Communist Party and the Soviet state. Further, the reports casually state that consequently they were forcibly interned in regional psychiatric hospitals for forensic psychiatric examination, as if this sort of human behavior was a certain sign of mental illness.[140] The KGB's reports in the capital were mirrored by similar reports written in Kharkiv. In 1989, the Head of the KGB Administration in the Kharkiv oblast N. G. Gibadulov routinely referred to the activities of the Ukrainian Helsinki Union as manifestations of Ukrainian bourgeois nationalism, a rhetorical echo from the Stalin era.[141]

Borovsky was no longer in Ukraine during perestroika. In late May 1977, after five months of "treatment," the forensic commission at the Kharkiv psychiatric hospital wrote a verdict: mentally healthy. His case resonated not only among Ukrainian dissidents but also internationally. However, even after the verdict, on Nikitin's order, Borovsky was kept in the Saburova Dacha for another week.[142] The KGB told Borovsky he could cease communication with Ukrainian dissidents or be interned in a psychiatric clinic for the rest of his life, or he could be exiled from the Soviet Union. Borovsky was released from the Saburova Dacha on the condition that he would immigrate to Israel, although he was not Jewish.¹⁴³ He was only twenty-one years old when he was exiled from the USSR which granted him a Jewish visa.¹⁴⁴ He resided in Canada and later in New York, and worked for the radio station "Svoboda" (PC, Radio Liberty) which was routinely "jammed" by the Soviets to prevent Soviet citizens from listening to "foreign propaganda."¹⁴⁵ But he remained actively involved in the human rights movement. He protested against the invasion of Soviet troops in Afghanistan and demanded freedom for political prisoners in the Soviet Union. On 24 November 1984, together with Mykola Movchan, Borovsky wrote an open letter to Raisa Gorbacheva in defense of political prisoners and victims of political psychiatry.¹⁴⁶ Borovsky was among many who realized at a very early stage of his resistance to Soviet repressions and terror that the more coercive the system became, the more courageously people behaved. Opposition in Ukraine grew in numbers, and silencing the dissent became a daunting task and another delusory utopia of the state.¹⁴⁷

The Writers' Paths in the Labyrinths of Medical Power

The labyrinths of the Saburova Dacha were tricky, becoming a place where Kharkiv writers were intimidated, sedated, and ultimately silenced in the 1970s and 1980s. Tretyakov was placed there in 1972 and 1979, two years after Borovsky was exiled from the USSR. Two poets might have shared the same bed that had been rarely changed in the Saburova Dacha but had never learned about one another's subsequent lives. Nevertheless, like in the Austrian-British philosopher Ludwig Wittgenstein's labyrinth-imagery, both made a linguistic order from the existing chaos and violence, eventually having discovered the meaning of their lives, one in post-Soviet Ukraine and the other in the United States. Scholars have written about Wittgenstein's philosophy as being centered in the labyrinth-imagery, a notion that was grounded in the "analogy with Theseus' perilous journey into the center of an immensely confusing structure to win his freedom."¹⁴⁸ They have argued that there was, however, a major difference between the ancient Theseus's meaning of his labyrinth and Wittgenstein's conception, as well as the conceptions of two other innovative thinkers, the Argentine poet Jorge Luis Borges and the Bohemian writer of German-Jewish origin Franz Kafka. They all adopted more pessimistic conceptions of the labyrinth, a sign of modernity and a perception provoked by external chaos and inner psychological imbalance. Through their creative writings, they all suggested that people "must learn to live in the Labyrinth."¹⁴⁹

Like some of their predecessors in the 1920s and 1930s, Volodymyr Sosiura and Andrii Holovko who were patients of the Saburova Dacha and the Poltava psychiatric clinic,¹⁵⁰ Tretyakov and Osmolovskyi went through similar labyrinths of mental instability and abuse in the Saburova Dacha. Yet no one asked them, while they were still alive, whether they learned the art of living in the labyrinth of cruelty and state violence. Borovsky managed to escape from this labyrinth. Yet, they all seem to learn how to write in the language of the labyrinth story, following the steps of Wittgenstein and his pessimistic modern conception of the labyrinth. They suffered enormously while living, and they underwent agonizing deaths, remembered by a few. Tretyakov passed away first in Kharkiv in 1996, suffering from pulmonary edema. His body was lost in the labyrinths of a Kharkiv hospital's morgue, and his daughter was invited to identify it among other corpses.[151] Osmolovskyi's place and date of death remain unknown, and thus far any attempts at establishing them have failed, a situation suggesting a tragedy. While in emigration, Borovsky never had an opportunity to visit his elderly mother who lived in a village in the Kharkiv oblast. During the last year of his life, Borovsky suffered from cancer. He passed away far away from Ukraine and was buried by his friends in Florida, survived by his mother in independent Ukraine.[152] The author of this book was late in identifying Borovsky's whereabouts, depriving him of an opportunity to hear Tretyakov's flattering message about his poetic gift, albeit through an intermediary.[153] In the KGB's view, the Saburova Dacha was the right place for the ethnic Jew (Osmolovskyi), the ethnic Russian (Tretyakov), and the ethnic Ukrainian (Borovsky), where they had to be treated and purified of their "mental instabilities." Not so much their ethnicity but rather their literary talent, unorthodox views, and their Ukrainianness presented a threat to the system.

The Soviet labyrinths of punitive psychiatry seemed to survive the transitional period after the collapse of the Soviet Union. The recent trends in Russia—the remilitarization of political culture and power and a return to Soviet psychiatric persecution of the opposition—point in this direction.[154] One of the Russian protesters in the so-called Bolotnoe delo Mikhail Kosenko was condemned to forced psychiatric treatment and became another victim of punitive psychiatry, a practice that has been rejuvenated under Putin.[155] Claims of Kosenko's mental incompetence and government silence about his criticism of Putin's regime exemplify the restoration of political psychiatry, practices that better contextualize the neo-totalitarian regime in Russia.[156] The "medicalization" of social behavior and politics are also noticeable in Ukraine,[157] and further potential importation of abusive practices from Russia to Ukrainian territories, influenced, infiltrated, or invaded by Putin, is a concern that should be taken seriously. Complacency with the status quo in psychiatry as a discipline and as a branch of medicine, and a lack of professional engagement and scholarly research in this area might result in the rejuvenation of pernicious practices of political psychiatry in this part of the world.

The nineteenth-century American writer Ralph Waldo Emerson argued that words devalued and distorted truth and reality. He has posited that the age of words should be followed by "an age of silence, when men shall speak only through facts" to restore the "health" and the value of words.[158] If applied to the political, cultural, and social practices of the Communist regime in the Soviet Union, Emerson's idea appears to be reversed: silence about the crimes against humanity committed by the Soviet state necessitated the invention of new words, notions, and concepts that were nothing but lies which delayed the emergence of a new age of words, politically meaningful and transparent. Psychiatric terror was concealed by placing it in the realm of new idioms of confidentiality, inaccessible for popular discussions or debates.

Yet, an attempt to hide and, at the same time, to intensify psychiatric terror was a gross error of Soviet leaders. The overdose of violence and lies had drastic repercussions for the regime. As embarrassing as it was, internationally the truth about post-Stalinist brutality and savagery in the USSR eventually emerged, and in January 1983, in anticipation of shameful expulsion from the World Psychiatric Association (WPA), the All-Union Society of Psychiatrists withdrew from the WPA, claiming that the accusations of psychiatric abuses in the USSR were unfounded.[159]

However, the arbitrariness of punishments and everyday heinous crimes against humanity committed in Soviet psychiatric hospitals became visible and obvious for observers inside and outside the Soviet Union. The Soviet authorities' boundless certainty of the illegibility of these crimes and their presumed unprovability had an unintended effect. Punitive psychiatry cultivated and tempered people like Vladimir Bukovsky, Leonid Pliushch, Petro Grigorenko, and Victor Borovsky.[160] Their alleged madness and suffering made them famous all over the world and respected for their courage to resist state violence. In a sense, the Soviet state immortalized them in people's memory, undermining its own foundations and ideology.

During the decades of the 1960s–1980s, the suppression of the autonomist strivings of nationals, including Ukrainians and Jews, was the primary task of the Soviet party leaders. The efforts of Brezhnev and Andropov were rather effective: by the late 1970s most activists were imprisoned and interned in psychiatric wards. The cadre rotation in Ukraine (the Ukrainian party boss Petro Shelest was replaced by Volodymyr Shcherbytskyi, and the Ukrainian KGB head Vitalii Nikitchenko—by Vitalii Fedorchuk) solidified centralized control over nationalities policy. Silence about the state's crimes and lies were institutionalized, and as Edward Crankshaw has noted, they became "an instrument of policy, cherished, burnished."[161]

The KGB Chairman of the USSR Andropov played a decisive role in installing the practices of psychiatric terror and designing cover-up operations to hide from the West the fact that the state was murderously destroying the minds of sane people by drugging them and isolating them from the rest of society. This task seemed to present few difficulties or moral concerns for Andropov, who was tempered in the re-Sovietization of Hungary and Czechoslovakia that was implemented through terror and blood. Crankshaw has posited that Andropov, unable to beat the system, joined it, and "what he will be remembered for has been the systematic elimination of dissidents wherever they showed their heads."[162] Psychiatric clinics "curing" oppositionists to the Soviet regime became a major industry under Andropov.[163]

The medicalization of social behavior appears to be one of the symptoms of authoritarian regimes which employ it as a method of social control. Using medical terms, the acute stage of the Soviet authoritarian regime, Stalinism, made little use of political psychiatry. Its emergence coincided with the chronic stage of authoritarianism which required more subtle and less radical means of destruction of the opposition, and mirrored the emergence of stable hierarchical structures in society. This inevitably led to the expansion of psychiatric clinics, psychiatrists' power, and state laws that allowed forcible hospitalization, abuse, and neglect. Pseudo-medical interventions, ordered by the state, were perfect tools for silencing the opposition. Hiding behind pseudo-medical concepts and diagnoses, such as "sluggish schizophrenia," "the paranoid reformist delusion," "mania of justice-seeking," "Marxismomania," and the like, the state, through the psychiatrists it had co-opted, made verdicts and executed them. What was extremely valuable for the regime was that this occurred in psychiatric wards which were much better guarded than prisons and camps. Silence triumphed there.

Koryagin, a psychiatrist who used to work in the Saburova Dacha, believed that Snezhnevsky's theory of sluggish schizophrenia did not produce the phenomenon of political psychiatry but on the contrary, the Soviet system built on principles of coercion and violence generated Snezhnevsky and his theory.[164] This facilitated the creation of more subtle forms of violence that supposedly helped stabilize the regime and prevent it from inner crises. However, as Žižek argues, coercive systems that are grounded in more subtle forms of violence, which are experienced on a subconscious level, often lead to catastrophic consequences. The seemingly smooth functioning of economic and political systems suddenly collapses. He identified this phenomenon as "systemic violence."[165] Žižek claims that this form of violence constitutes the "invisible background" and the very fabric of people's everyday lives.[166] In the Soviet Union, a similar "background" exacerbated by the fear of punishment produced Snezhnevsky and psychiatrists like him. In a sense, the emergence of his theory and its catastrophic consequences for humanity were inevitable, given the steady and monotonous functioning of the system that relied on systemic violence.

Fear, "an essential presence in the asylum" and in any place of confinement,[167] became a desirable final result of the pseudo-treatment of dissenters, and a long-lasting self-reinforcing element of people's psyches. As the Soviet dissident, journalist, and the author of the book *Punitive Medicine* Alexander Podrabinek has suggested, the authorities preferred to "drive them ['patients'] to degradation and intimidate them permanently."[168] The ruthlessness of the state that employed intimidation, repression, and political psychiatry in the 1960s–1980s left a permanent scar in people's memory, and precisely this factor played a role in Ukraine's national revival in the late 1980s and the early 1990s. The deplorable state of Ukrainian culture, but most importantly, the old wounds of humiliated dignity and pride, dehumanization, and the amputated wholeness of people's mental and moral inner core reactivated resistance in the late 1980s when the Soviet system took the first steps in its restructuring.[169]

The point made by Dmitry Gorenburg, a political scientist and a commentator on the Russian military, about the alleged oscillation of Soviet nationalities policy between Russification and ethnophilia is highly debatable. However, he has rightly noted that Soviet assimilation policies and Russification defined the character of the nationalist movements during Gorbachev's perestroika.[170] In the context of state practices in the 1960s–1980s, assimilation was merely a euphemism for the limited choice the majority of Ukrainians had: assimilation or repression. Therefore, Gorenburg's observation should be further clarified: not assimilation policies per se but sadism and violence, through which assimilation policies were implemented in Ukraine, precipitated the political climax in the republic in the late 1980s and the early 1990s. Political psychiatry and its practices further antagonized the Ukrainian intelligentsia, fostering its desperation to free Ukraine from the ties of the Union, and predisposing their sense of urgency to call for the national referendum for Ukrainian sovereignty in 1991.

In 1987, Gorbachev's perestroika brought release to sixty-four political prisoners from psychiatric clinics.[171] Subsequently, approximately 800,000 patients who were charged with anti-Soviet agitation and propaganda were removed from the psychiatric registry list.[172] An additional investigation should be conducted to identify how many Ukrainians, Jews, and other nationals were on this list. Tragically, those who were released from psychiatric clinics never recovered in a neurological sense. Those who were tortured by haloperidol injections developed a chronic extra-pyramidal syndrome and experienced chronic nightmares.[173] It is equally tragic that we will never know how many people had been murdered in psychiatric clinics by injections and torture, and how many people had been shot by the guards when they were trying to escape from special psychiatric clinics. These sorts of statistics are completely missing from the picture. The case of the talented Kharkiv writer Osmolovskyi about which we know next to nothing attests to this.

The issue of lustration remains one of the most salient questions that relates to psychiatric terror. Although it is beyond the scope of this study, a brief discussion might clarify the problems related to the former Soviet psychiatrists' lustration. Generally speaking, lustration of those who were directly involved in psychiatric abuse has never been implemented, and those doctors who collaborated with the KGB have never repented. For instance, Sosin, who was personally involved in Borovsky's torture in the Saburova Dacha, today chairs the Narcology Department at the Ukrainian Institute of Doctors' Advancement and advises the Private Narcology Center "Avitsenna" in Kharkiv.[174] A former expert in schizophrenia, he cures people from alcoholism in Ukraine today. He writes memoirs about the Saburova Dacha, where he discusses everything but Soviet political psychiatry. In 2010, Sosin's biography was included in the publication entitled *Prominent Representatives of the Kharkiv Medical School of Higher Education*. According to this volume, Sosin's creed is to lead a "healthy lifestyle" and to "learn more."[175]

In 1991, the Ukrainian Ministry of Health conducted a survey which revealed that among 568 psychiatrists who participated in the survey only 50 percent advocated publicizing psychiatric abuse in Ukraine. Every fourth person rejected informational leaks about political psychiatry, and every tenth person considered those who publicized the knowledge about it the enemies of psychiatry.[176] In 1989, Rafalsky who spent more than twenty years in prisons and psychiatric clinics praised honest psychiatrists and lamented that the majority of Soviet psychiatrists still kept silent about psychiatric abuse and the crimes the Soviet state committed against humanity.[177]

Koryagin reminded us that one can judge a society by the way it treats its mentally ill.[178] He supported the idea of Soviet psychiatrists' lustration.[179] In contrast, Gluzman, president of the Ukrainian Psychiatric Association, prefers to focus on the problems of contemporary psychiatry and psychiatric care in Ukraine. He believes that the positive effects of this project might be very limited. Although lustration laws remain a highly debatable issue, they would undoubtedly facilitate democratic reforms in the states throughout Eastern Europe. Mark S. Ellis, an international criminal law expert and the executive director of the International Bar Association, has demonstrated that lustration laws in Russia, Ukraine, and other states that once belonged to the former Communist bloc were never enforced and, in fact, were counterbalanced by other laws that made it possible to classify information about individuals who used to work for the Communist Party and the secret police, and who were engaged in operations that could be qualified as crimes against humanity.[180]

Gluzman's and van Voren's rejection of the narratives about political psychiatry that are depicted in black and white and their calls to decipher the "shades" of the past and present realities deserve attention. Narratives that exploit a binary concept lack analytical depth. Binaries as an analytical tool have recently become a warning for scholars, a sign of superficiality and limited vision. However, for many, binary oppositions are "useful, indeed unavoidable," as it was for Fredric Jameson, an American literary critic and philosopher who is best known for his analyses of cultural trends in contemporary society such as postmodernism and capitalism. In his review of Jameson's *The Antinomies of Realism*, Michael Wood, an English historian and broadcaster, has posited that the most important thing is to see the binary oppositions' parts "as entangled in each other": their relation is more significant than their difference.[181] In the case of political psychiatry, binaries, such as the state and psychiatrists, and psychiatrists and their "patients," should be considered in the context of the political system that functioned rather smoothly for decades in a mode of systemic violence but eventually fractured as a result of the extreme imbalance of violence. Ironically, it is unavoidable to consider this imbalance without considering a binary: violence and nonviolence.

As many scholars have argued, including Foucault, detention in prisons and the state's abuse of power there led to recidivism.[182] In a similar fashion, detention in mental institutions and the "excesses" of torture provoked a "relapse" to nationalism and political activism among the "patients." The fear instigated by the KGB that penetrated the depths of society generated a state of latent resistance that was temporarily subdued by terror and state violence. Psychiatric methods designed to dehumanize dissenters undermined the "carceral texture of society." The nationalists' isolation and incarceration inside the psychiatric clinic resulted in their greater presence outside, internationally, inciting new discourses and the romanticizing and mythologizing of their suffering. Their feeling of injustice was inflamed by state violence and became "untamable."[183]

Foucault has argued that "power and knowledge directly imply one another," and "knowledge extends and reinforces the effects of this power."[184] Naturally, conflicts, struggles, and social turmoil constantly "traversed" the domains of power and knowledge. But it is equally true that knowledge when it is resistant to power generates a domain of silence which assists power to preserve its political investments. Silencing the public and obfuscating undesirable knowledge about abuses of power are vital to state control and ideological conquests.

In a sense, political psychiatry was a secret political operation inscribed in silence, which was a significant factor in consolidating and centralizing power in the Soviet Union. The three decades of silence about psychiatric abuse applied to Ukrainian dissent is an incredible example of the power silence is capable of. Through the press and mass media, people's alleged psychiatric disorders were made visible and serious, and their national strivings and grievances disappeared in obscurity through propaganda and misinformation. The techniques of discipline, such as repression and psychiatric terror, required cover-up operations and silence, because the space within silence is usually devoid of diverse voices and therefore permits little dissent. Without dissent, there is little resistance, thereby guaranteeing maintenance of the existing power structure.

In the context of barbaric applications of political psychiatry in the Soviet Union, the statements by the German-Jewish cultural critic and philosopher Walter Benjamin do not appear too radical. On one occasion he argued that "there is no document of culture which [was] not at the same time a document of barbarism"; on another, he posited that "it is virtually impossible to write a history of information separately from a history of the corruption of the press."[185] During the era of late socialism, the state controlled information about its dissidents through several channels, including the press and its opposite—silence. The Saburova Dacha in Soviet Kharkiv became a place of silence which was commanded by the KGB through an army of obedient psychiatrists. The history of psychiatric abuse applied to the literati in this place awaits further investigation, as people's simple stories and their travels through the labyrinths of state and bureaucratic power allude to complicated broader political contexts that we need to understand. The knowledge of this history would open the window into the past to reveal the power of both silence and discourse in the hands of the Soviet *chekists* that emboldened them and let them rule for more than seventy years.

NOTES

1. For more on *Krokodil*, see John Etty, *Graphic Satire in the Soviet Union: Krokodil's Political Cartoons*, 1st ed. (Jackson, MS: University Press of Mississippi, 2019); on the use of satire in official Soviet art and propaganda, see Annie Gérin, *Devastation and Laughter: Satire, Power, and Culture in the Early Soviet State (1920s–1930s)* (Toronto: University of Toronto Press, 2018); for cartoons published in *Krokodil*, see Aleksey Pyanov, ed., *Soviet Humor: The Best of Krokodil* (Kansas City/New York: Andrews and McMeel/A University Press Syndicate Company, 1989).

2. "Kharkovskiie filologi otlichaiutsia chuvstvom iumora i priamotoi," *Vechernii Kharkov*, 23 April 2012, https://vecherniy.kharkov.ua/news/62847/ (accessed 12 September 2020).

3. Private conversation with Leonid Osadchuk, 20 November 1996, Kharkiv, Ukraine.

4. Like Osmolovskyi, Tiutiunnyk studied at the Kharkiv State University (Philology Department) from 1957 to 1962. See Hryhir Tiutiunnyk, *Buty pysmennykom: shchodennyky, zapysnyky, lysty*, ed. O. Nezhyvyi (Kyiv: Yaroslaviv Val, 2011); O. Nezhyvyi, *Hryhir Tiutiunnyk: tekstolohichna ta dzhereloznavcha problematyka zhyttia i tvorchosti* (Luhansk: Vyd-vo "Luhanskyi natsionalnyi universytet imeni Tarasa Shevchenka," 2010).

5. Interview with Aleksandr Kasha, 5 July 1985, Kharkiv, Ukraine; interview with Anatolii Starodub, 12 August 2008, Kharkiv, Ukraine.

6. Private correspondence with Olha Ulishchenko who together with Leonid graduated from the Kharkiv State University's Philology Department, later working as an editor of the Publishing House "Prapor," 25 April 2019, FB.

7. Mykola Shatylov, *Kliati simdesiati . . . Na pam'iati stalo, na pam'iati staly* (Kharkiv: Vydavnytstvo "Apostrof," 2011).

8. Private conversation with Yurii Stadnychenko, 3 July 2007, Kharkiv, Ukraine. The last book by the tandem (Inin and Osadchuk) was published in Moscow in 1985: A. Y Inin and L. V. Osadchuk, *V ozhidanii chuda* (Moskva: Iskusstvo, 1985). Inin is a pen name of Arkadii Gurevich.

9. Arkadii Inin, "'Vybiraiu sovetskuiu vlast . . .'" (interview by Grigorii Kroshin), *Partner* 5, no. 188 (2013), https://www.partner-inform.de/partner/detail/2013/5/237/5959/arkadij-inin-vybiraju-sovetskuju-vlast?lang=ru (accessed 12 September 2020); Arkadii Inin, "'Vsia Ukraina – russkoiazychnaia'" (interview by Konstantin Kevorkian), *Ukraina.ru*, 22 August 2020, https://ukraina.ru/interview/20200822/1028627200.html?fbclid=IwAR3pxpW3y7OTEwqVqyMZigv53si1vb_bwAwnPukcmlFBNFMXaeMJA5es4N4 (accessed 12 September 2020).

10. Private correspondence with Olha Ulishchenko, 25 April 2019, FB.

11. Private conversation with Leonid Osadchuk, 20 March 1996, Kharkiv, Ukraine. I saw Osadchuk the last time in March 1996, accidentally bumping into him in Sumska Street, near the theater "Berezil." His appearance was horrid, resembling a person from Holodomor images. His body seemed emaciated, and he was moving in slow motion. But what struck me was his shoes with many holes in them that seemed to be completely dysfunctional. I approached him, and we had an opportunity to exchange a few sentences. He was clearly ashamed because of his appearance and rushed to end our brief encounter. There were tears in the eyes of "Uncle Lionia" who knew me as a little girl. He found a hard candy in his pocket wrapped in tobacco and bread crumbs. He gave it to me, as this was a tradition he established in the 1960s (he always had a hard candy for me since I was five years old), and we parted.

12. Private correspondence with Olha Ulishchenko, 25 April 2019, FB.

13. Throughout the text, the first and the last names of Victor Borovsky are spelled as Borovsky himself spelled them after he resided in the United States. A similar approach has been used in Vladimir Bukovsky's case.

14. From Pasternak's poem "Zvezdy letom" (The Stars in Summer) (1917). In Rus.: "Tishina, ty – luchshee iz vsego, chto slyshal." See Boris Pasternak, *Izbrannoe v dvukh tomakh: Stikhotvoreniia i poemy* (Moscow: Khudozhestvennaia literatura, 1985), 86.

15. For a discussion about Soviet policies toward dissidents during the post-Stalin era, see Peter Reddaway, "Soviet Policies Toward Dissent, 1953–1986," *Journal of Interdisciplinary Studies* 24, nos. 1–2 (2012): 67; see also Thomas S. Szasz, *Ideology and Insanity: Essays on the Psychiatric Dehumanization of Man* (New York: Anchor Books, 1970), 113.

16. Dan Healey, "Russian and Soviet Forensic Psychiatry: Troubled and Troubling," *International Journal of Law and Psychiatry* 37, no. 1 (2014): 77.

17. Reddaway, "Soviet Policies Toward Dissent," 68.

18. Robert van Voren's statement (information is based on the KGB archival documents found at the Stasi archives) from: Semen Gluzman's and Robert van Voren's micro-lectures, *Volyn Media*, 7 June 2013, http://www.youtube.com/watch?v=zjt8jQ-qies (accessed 12 September 2020).

19. Robert van Voren, *Cold War in Psychiatry: Human Factors, Secret Actors* (Amsterdam and New York: Rodopi, 2010), 119.

20. The Vladimir Bukovsky Archive, Document 0202 (CT31/19) "About Psychiatric Care in the USSR" (18 February 1972), http://www.bukovsky-archives.net/pdfs/psychiat/psy-rus.html (accessed 12 September 2020), 164. See also van Voren, *Cold War in Psychiatry*, 120.

21. The State Statistics Committee, *Ogoniok*, no. 16 (15–22 April 1989): 24. For details, see also van Voren, *Cold War*, 322.

22. Sidney Bloch and Peter Reddaway, *Soviet Psychiatric Abuse: The Shadow over World Psychiatry* (Boulder, CO: Westview Press, 1985), 31.

23. Ibid.

24. Michel Foucault, *The Birth of the Clinic: An Archaeology of Medical Perception* (New York: Vintage Books, 1994), 15.

25. Ibid., 19.

26. For more details about the procedural routine of placing a patient in these institutions, see Bloch and Reddaway, *Soviet Psychiatric Abuse*, 22–23.

27. Alexander Podrabinek, *Punitive Medicine*, trans. Alexander Lehrman (Ann Arbor: Karoma Publishers, Inc., 1980), 9, 12.

28. On the goals of the Central Committee, see the Vladimir Bukovsky Archive, Document 0202 (CT31/19) "About Psychiatric Care in the USSR" (18 February 1972), http://www.bukovsky-archives.net/pdfs/psychiat/psy-rus.html (accessed 12 September 2020), 166.

29. Vladimir Bukovsky, *To Build a Castle – My Life as a Dissenter*, trans. Michael Scammell (New York: The Viking Press, 1979); Valeriy Tarsis, *Ward 7: An Autobiographical Novel*, trans. Katya Brown (New York: E. P. Dutton & Co., Inc., 1966); Petro G. Grigorenko, *Memoirs*, trans. Thomas P. Whitney (New York & London: W. W. Norton and Company, 1982); Leonid Pliushch, *U karnavali istorii: Svidchennia* (Kyiv: Fakt, 2002); Victor Borovsky, *Potsilunok satany: Spohady* (New York: Meta Publishing Company, 1981); Anatoly Koryagin, "Autobiographical Notes," in *Koryagin: A Man Struggling for Human Dignity*, ed. Robert van Voren (Amsterdam: Second World Press, Vladimir Bukovsky Foundation, 1987); S. F. Gluzman, *Risunki po pamiati ili vospominaniia otsidenta* (Kyiv: Izdatelskii dom Dmitriia Burago, 2012); The Royal College of Psychiatrists, "Dr. Alexander Voloshanovich: A Critic of the Political Misuse of Psychiatry in the USSR," *The Psychiatric Bulletin* 4 (1980): 70–71, http://pb.rcpsych.org/content/4/5/70.full.pdf (accessed 12 September 2020).

30. Bloch and Reddaway, *Soviet Psychiatric Abuse*; van Voren, *Cold War in Psychiatry*; Harvey Fireside, *Soviet Psychoprisons* (New York: W. W. Norton & Co., 1979); T. C. Smith and T. A. Oleszczuk, *No Asylum: State Psychiatric Repression in the Former USSR* (New York: New York University Press, 1996); Thomas A.

Oleszczuk, *Political Justice in the USSR: Dissent and Repression in Lithuania, 1969–1987* (New York: Columbia University Press, 1988); Dan Healey, "Russian and Soviet Forensic Psychiatry."

31. Bloch and Reddaway, *Soviet Psychiatric Abuse*, 13.

32. For details about Snezhnevsky's Moscow School, see Bloch and Reddaway, *Soviet Psychiatric Abuse*, 40–41; van Voren, *Cold War in Psychiatry*, 96–104; A. Korotenko and N. Alikina, *Sovetskaia psikhiatriia: Zabluzhdeniia i umysel* (Kyiv: Sfera, 2002), 50. Andrei Snezhnevsky was a Soviet psychiatrist, professor, academic of the Soviet Academy of Sciences, and the founder of one of psychiatric schools in the Soviet Union. He was the key person responsible for the use of psychiatry for political purposes and was personally involved in cases of dissidents, such as Petro Grigorenko, Vladimir Bukovsky, Zhores Medvedev, and Leonid Pliushch.

33. Bloch and Reddaway, *Soviet Psychiatric Abuse*, 14–15.

34. See Julie V. Brown's "Afterword" in *Madness and the Mad in Russian Culture*, ed. Angela Brintlinger and Ilya Vinitsky (Toronto: University of Toronto Press, 2007), 292.

35. Ibid., 292, 294.

36. Ibid., 294–95.

37. This translation of the Serbsky Institute has been broadly used in secondary sources.

38. Van Voren, *Cold War in Psychiatry*, 257. Morozov was personally involved in the cases of Vladimir Bukovsky, Viktor Fainberg, Natalia Gorbanevskaia, Petro Grigorenko, and Leonid Pliushch.

39. Korotenko and Alikina, *Sovetskaia psikhiatriia*, 42; Viktor Rafalsky, "Reportazh niotkuda," in Korotenko and Alikina, 222, 233–34. For many years, Daniil Lunts, the KGB colonel and psychiatrist, was the head of the fourth department, who implemented the orders of the KGB and instructed his subordinates about the prescribed fates of political prisoners, patients of the Serbsky Institute.

40. Van Voren, *Cold War in Psychiatry*, 115.

41. Bloch and Reddaway, *Soviet Psychiatric Abuse*, 20, 29. This concept was not new. Mirabeau, the eighteenth-century French economist, characterized the category of people who had to be interned in houses of confinement as "prisoners of State whose crimes must not be revealed." Secrecy helped the state save face and conceal the deception. See Michel Foucault, *Madness and Civilization: A History of Insanity in the Age of Reason* (New York: Vintage Books, 1988), 226.

42. Van Voren, *Cold War in Psychiatry*, 115. See the Vladimir Bukovsky Archive, Document 0200 (P151), the 22 January 1970 Decree of the Politburo TsK KPSS about identifying and isolating mentally ill individuals with terrorist and politically harmful inclinations, http://www.bukovsky-archives.net/pdfs/psychiat/psy-rus.html (accessed 12 September 2020). According to the 15 December 1969 report by the KGB head of the Krasnodar region S. Smorodinsky, from 1967 to 1969, 180 "mentally ill" individuals were identified who made anti-Soviet statements, wrote letters of complaint to authorities, and made attempts to escape from the Soviet Union. Smorodinsky lamented that psychiatric hospitals were designed to accommodate only 3,785 patients, while approximately 11,000–12,000 needed psychiatric treatment.

See the Vladimir Bukovsky Archive, Document 0200 (P151), http://www.bukovsky-archives.net/pdfs/psychiat/psy-rus.html (accessed 12 September 2020), 11–13.

43. The term *chekizatsiia* is related to the term *chekist*, an agent of the Soviet secret police.

44. Van Voren, *Cold War in Psychiatry*, 247, 256; Leonid Mlechin, "Pochti ezhednevno...," *Novaia gazeta*, 18 October 2013, p. 17. I am grateful to Robert van Voren for providing me with Mlechin's article.

45. *Moskovskaia Helsinskaia Gruppa* [*Moscow Helsinki Group*], Document 8, "O zloupotrebleniiakh psikhiatriei" (Nomer AC: 2818. Том СДС: 30. 1977 g.), http://samizdat.memo.ru/samizdat/sdspage/tom/30/page/2 (accessed 12 September 2020). The Moscow Helsinki Group is a Russian organization that defends human rights. Initially, it was founded in 1976 to monitor Soviet compliance with the Helsinki Accords and to report Soviet human rights abuses to the West. It was forcibly dissolved in the early 1980s, but revived in 1989 and continues to operate in Russia today.

46. Van Voren, *Cold War in Psychiatry*, 147.

47. For more details about the demographic breakdown of dissidents in Soviet Ukraine in the 1960s–1970s, see Kenneth C. Farmer, *Ukrainian Nationalism in the Post-Stalin Era: Myth, Symbols and Ideology in Soviet Nationalities Policy* (The Hague, Boston, London: Martinus Nijhoff Publishers, 1980), 176–84.

48. Farmer, *Ukrainian Nationalism*, 161.

49. Ibid., 168.

50. Ibid., 181–83.

51. Ibid., 100.

52. Van Voren, *Cold War in Psychiatry*, 142, 213; Podrabinek, *Punitive Medicine*, 78.

53. Bloch and Reddaway, *Soviet Psychiatric Abuse*, 26.

54. Ibid., 27; Petro Grigorenko, "Zvychaina psykholikarnia," in Borovsky, 5. The "wet pack" means wet canvas or linen that was tightly bound around the "patient's" body. While drying, the canvas prevented the person from breathing freely, causing hypoxia and unimaginable suffering.

55. Rafalsky, "Reportazh niotkuda," 228. Viktor Rafalsky is a human rights activist and a victim of political psychiatry. He spent twenty-three years in various psychiatric clinics. For more details about Rafalsky, see Osyp Zinkevych, ed., *Rukh oporu v Ukraini 1960–1990: Entsyklopedychnyi dovidnyk* (Kyiv: Smoloskyp, 2010), 531.

56. Pliushch, *U karnavali istorii*, 550.

57. Slavoj Žižek, *Violence: Six Sideways Reflections* (New York: Picador, 2008), 44.

58. Koryagin, "Autobiographical Notes," 19; I. K. Sosin, "Dva goda iz dvukh stoletii...," *Novosti Ukrainskoi psikhiatrii*, 2003, http://www.psychiatry.ua/books/saburka/paper034.htm (accessed 12 September 2020).

59. Koryagin, "Autobiographical Notes," 19.

60. Ibid., 24.

61. Anatolii Koryagin, "Unwilling Patients," *The Lancet*, 11 April 1981, p. 822.

62. Koryagin, "Unwilling Patients," 822–23.
63. Podrabinek, *Punitive Medicine*, 13, 123–24.
64. Koryagin, "Autobiographical Notes," 25.
65. Ibid., 18. In 1979, Koryagin joined the Working Commission that investigated the abuse of psychiatry. On 13 May 1981, he was accused of anti-Soviet agitation and propaganda according to Article 62 (1) of the Ukrainian Criminal Code and of illegal possession of firearms according to Article 218 (1) of the RSFSR Criminal Code, and sentenced to seven years in prison and five years of exile. For details about Koryagin's trial, see van Voren, *Koryagin*, 57.
66. Ibid., 36.
67. van Voren, *Cold War in Psychiatry*, 106. See also his micro-lecture for *Volyn Media*, http://www.youtube.com/watch?v=zjt8jQ-qies (accessed 12 September 2020).
68. van Voren, *Cold War in Psychiatry*, 414.
69. Korotenko and Alikina, *Sovetskaia psikhiatriia*, 77.
70. Podrabinek, *Punitive Medicine*, 38, 51.
71. Ibid., 15.
72. V. I. Taitslin, "O Saburovoi Dache," *Novosti Ukrainskoi psikhiatrii*, 2003, http://www.psychiatry.ua/books/saburka/paper038.htm (accessed 12 September 2020). Those doctors and staff who work at the Saburova Dacha call themselves *saburiany* (pl.) or *saburianyn* (sin.).
73. Foucault, *Madness and Civilization*, 115.
74. Ibid., 210.
75. Ibid., 270. See also Angela Brintlinger, "Russian Attitudes toward Psyche and Psychiatry, 1887–1907," in *Madness and the Mad in Russian Culture*, ed. Angela Brintlinger and Ilya Vinitsky (Toronto: University of Toronto Press, 2007), 175.
76. Brintlinger, "Russian Attitudes toward Psyche and Psychiatry," 177.
77. Foucault, *Madness and Civilization*, 209.
78. Bloch and Reddaway, *Soviet Psychiatric Abuse*, 81.
79. van Voren, *Koryagin*, 26.
80. Quoted in van Voren, *Cold War in Psychiatry*, 99.
81. Anatoliy Koryagin, "Compulsion in Psychiatry: Blessing or Curse?" *Psychiatric Bulletin* 14 (1990): 396; see also van Voren, *Cold War in Psychiatry*, 170. The authorities let Voloshanovich emigrate because he drew too much attention to political psychiatry in the West. One member, Irina Kaplun, died in a car accident under mysterious circumstances days before she was to immigrate to Israel.
82. van Voren, *Koryagin*, 35.
83. Sosin, "Dva goda iz dvukh stoletii . . ." A similar situation existed in many other Soviet psychiatric clinics. See van Voren, *Cold War in Psychiatry*, 120.
84. Sosin, "Dva goda iz dvukh stoletii . . ." In 1973, Sosin defended his thesis (*kandidat nauk*) on schizophrenia. Interestingly, in 2007 at the International Congress on Schizophrenia Research (28 March–1 April), the majority of psychiatrists voted to ban this pseudo-diagnosis from the American psychiatric topology. In 1988, Sosin defended his doctoral dissertation in narcology. In the Soviet era, he received numerous rewards, medals, and honors from the government.

85. van Voren, *Koryagin*, 42.
86. Peter Pomerantsev, "Diary," *London Review of Books*, 5 December 2013, p. 42. See also van Voren, *Cold War in Psychiatry*, 319.
87. Private conversation with Robert Tretyakov, 25 July 1996, Kharkiv, Ukraine.
88. Oleszczuk, *Political Justice in the USSR*, 95, 102. Some scholars argued that Lithuanian and Ukrainian nationalists were usually sentenced to the longest terms possible under the Criminal Code. See Ludmilla Thorne, "Three Years of Repression in the Soviet Union: A Statistical Study," *Freedom Appeals* 9 (March–April 1981): 30.
89. See a discussion about routine charges against the Ukrainians in the memoirs of the psychiatric "patient" of many years Josyp Terelya (with Michael H. Brown), *Witness to Apparitions and Persecution in the USSR: An Autobiography* (Milford, OH: Faith Publishing Company, 1991), 193–94.
90. In 1972, Gluzman was sentenced to seven years in camps and three years in exile for anti-Soviet agitation and propaganda.
91. See the interview with Semen Gluzman "Semen Gluzman: Mne stydno, chto ia grazhdanin Ukrainy," *Glavred*, 11 April 2012, http://glavred.info/archive/2012/04/11/084510-1.html (accessed 13 September 2020).
92. Semen Gluzman and Robert van Voren (interview by Oleksii Bukhalo, RTB), *YouTube*, 11 June 2013, http://www.youtube.com/watch?v=iz04k1hWNgI (accessed 13 September 2020); see also Semen Gluzman's "Posobie po psikhiatrii dlia inakomysliashchikh," written together with Vladimir Bukovsky, in Korotenko and Alikina, *Sovetskaia psikhiatriia*, 197–218.
93. Mykola Plakhotniuk, *Kolovorot: Statti, spohady, dokumenty* (Kyiv: Smoloskyp, 2012), 145.
94. Plakhotniuk, *Kolovorot*, 228–29.
95. Korotenko and Alikina, *Sovetskaia psikhiatriia*, 31, 111.
96. Bukovsky has been quoted in Podrabinek, *Punitive Medicine*, 31.
97. R. D. Laing, *The Divided Self: An Existential Study of Sanity and Madness* (New York: Penguin Books, 1990), 43–45. Laing suggested analyzing people's psychological equilibrium, and social and personal circumstances, in which they developed psychoses. Laing represented the anti-psychiatry movement, although he never subscribed to the term or its premise.
98. Borovsky, *Potsilunok satany*, 152.
99. For details about the fate of Anatoly Lupynis who spent twelve years in camps and five years in psychiatric clinics, see Rafalsky, "Reportazh niotkuda," 234–35, and Zinkevych, *Rukh oporu v Ukraini*, 387–88.
100. Oles Shevchenko, ed., *Ukrainska Helsinska Spilka u spohadakh i dokumentakh* (Kyiv: Yaroslaviv Val, 2012).
101. See also a discussion about this particular practice in Podrabinek, *Punitive Medicine*, 126. For Borovsky's brief biography, see Zinkevych, *Rukh oporu v Ukraini*, 85.
102. *Post-Gazette*, 7 December 1981, p. 7. See also *Observer-Reporter*, Washington, PA, 8 December 1981, A-5.
103. Borovsky, *Potsilunok satany*, 30.

104. For his human rights activities and literary work, Nekrasov who wrote in Russian was cast as *antisovetchik* (an anti-Soviet element) by the Soviet authorities. In May 1974, Nekrasov was expelled from the party, and in 1974 he was allowed to emigrate. For more details about Nekrasov, see Zinkevych, *Rukh oporu v Ukraini*, 458–59.

105. Borovsky, *Potsilunok satany*, 69.

106. Ibid., 24.

107. Ibid., 38.

108. Ibid., 52. This was normally the nurses' responsibility but Zhuravsky preferred to do it himself.

109. Ibid., 53, 64.

110. Ibid., 53–54.

111. Thomas S. Szasz, *The Myth of Mental Illness: Foundations of a Theory of Personal Conduct* (New York: Harper & Row Publishers, 1974), 52.

112. Borovsky, *Potsilunok satany*, 68.

113. Ibid., 73.

114. Ibid., 70.

115. Zinkevych, *Rukh oporu v Ukraini*, 85.

116. Borovsky, *Potsilunok satany*, 74.

117. Oleksa Tykhyi (1927–1984) was a teacher and writer from the Donbas, and a Soviet dissident and political prisoner. Charged with Ukrainian nationalism, he was first arrested in February 1957 and sentenced to seven years in labor camps and five years' exile. He returned to Ukraine in 1964, and in 1976 he became a founding member of the Ukrainian Helsinki Group. The KGB arrested him in February 1977, and sentenced him to ten years in labor camps and five years' exile. He died in a Mordovian camp and his remains, together with the remains of two other dissidents, poets Vasyl Stus and Yurii Lytvyn, were transferred to Kyiv in 1989. Their interment at the Baikove cemetery turned into a mass procession of people, carrying blue and yellow Ukrainian flags. For more details about the reburial of these three writers, see Iryna Shtohrin, "Iak vyvozyly ostanky Stusa, Lytvyna, i Tykhoho z Gulagu," *Radio Svoboda*, 19 November 2019, https://www.radiosvoboda.org/a/perepohovannya-stusa-lytvyna-tyhoho/30278986.html (accessed 18 September 2020).

118. Mykola Rudenko (1920–2004) was a Ukrainian writer, human rights activist, and the founder of the Ukrainian Helsinki Group (UHH). In February 1977, he was arrested for anti-Soviet propaganda and agitation and sentenced to seven years in camps and three years of exile. In December 1987, he was released and emigrated to Germany. Later, like Borovsky, he worked for radio "Svoboda" (Radio Liberty) in New York (1988–1990). Rudenko returned to Ukraine in 1990. For details about Rudenko, see Zinkevych, *Rukh oporu v Ukraini*, 543–46.

119. Borovsky, *Potsilunok satany*, 146–47.

120. Ibid., 154.

121. Sosin, "Dva goda iz dvukh stoletii . . ."

122. Borovsky, *Potsilunok satany*, 155.

123. Ibid.

124. Borovsky, *Potsilunok satany*, 149.

125. Sosin, "Dva goda iz dvukh stoletii . . ."
126. Genrikh Altunian, *Tsena svobody: Vospominaniia dissidenta* (Kharkiv: Folio, 2000), 132–34.
127. Borovsky, *Potsilunok satany*, 64.
128. Ibid., 66–67.
129. For more details, see Terelya, *Witness to Apparitions and Persecution in the USSR*, 152.
130. Plakhotniuk, *Kolovorot*, 168.
131. Ibid., 169. Mykola Plakhotniuk (1936–2015) was a Ukrainian doctor and a victim of punitive psychiatry. For his biography, see Zinkevych, *Rukh oporu v Ukraini*, 499–500.
132. Plakhotniuk, *Kolovorot*, 170.
133. Michel Foucault, *Discipline and Punish: The Birth of the Prison* (New York: Vintage Books, 1995), 33–34.
134. Farmer, *Ukrainian Nationalism*, 165–66.
135. Levko Luk'ianenko, "Do istorii Ukrainskoi Helsinskoi Spilky," in *Ukrainska Helsinska Spilka u spohadakh i dokumentakh*, ed. Oles Shevchenko (Kyiv: "Iaroslaviv Val," 2012), 12. According to the KGB report to the Central Committee of the Communist Party in Ukraine and Volodymyr Shcherbytskyi, forty-eight UHH members were sentenced to various terms in prison. See the photocopy of the document in Shevchenko, 441. For more details about Melnyk, Malynkovych, Marchenko, Tykhyi, Lytvyn, and Stus, see Zinkevych, *Rukh oporu v Ukraini*, 372–74, 399–400, 412–14, 426, 648–50, 630–35.
136. See the photocopy of the document in Shevchenko, *Ukrainska Helsinska Spilka*, 445.
137. For more details on these Ukrainian intellectuals, see Zinkevych, *Rukh oporu v Ukraini*, 158–62, 383–87, 559–62, 566–70, 599–600, 706–10.
138. See the photocopy of the document in Shevchenko, *Ukrainska Helsinska Spilka*, 517. On Rafalskyi, see Natalia Karpenkova, "Viktor Rafalskyi – maiak, svitlo iakoho klyche do novykh zvershen," *Fortuna*, 1 March 2018.
139. See the photocopy of the August 1988 KGB report signed by the Deputy Head of the KGB in Ukraine V. Yevtushenko in Shevchenko, 542. See also the 1 December 1988 KGB report signed by Holushko about the rejuvenation of Ukrainian national symbols advocated by the Ukrainian intelligentsia in Shevchenko, 593–95.
140. See, for instance, the 10 May 1989 KGB report to the Secretary of the Kherson *obkom* of the Communist Party of Ukraine about the activities of the member of the Ukrainian Helsinki Union in Shevchenko, 613–14. The report was signed by the Head of the KGB Administration in Kherson I. V. Taranenko.
141. See, for instance, the 19 October 1989 KGB report to the first secretary of the Kharkiv *obkom* V. P. Mysnychenko signed by Gibadulov in Shevchenko, 703–7. The Kharkiv KGB was especially concerned with the "anti-Soviet nationalist activity" of the Ukrainian poet Stepan Sapeliak. In June–October 1989, the KGB organized and orchestrated an attack against Sapeliak in the press.
142. Amnesty International Publications, *A Chronicle of Current Events: Journal of the Human Rights Movement in the USSR* 46 (1977) (New York: Khronika Press, 1978): 85.

143. "Borovsky Tells Rutgers Students of Life Behind Iron Curtain," *The Ukrainian Weekly* 68 (23 March 1980), p. 5.

144. United States Congressional Serial Set, vol. 8000 (Washington, DC: U.S. Government Printing Office, 1980), 122.

145. Altunian, *Tsena svobody*, 129, 135. In the mid-1970s, besides Borovsky, many Ukrainian dissidents worked for Radio Liberty, such as Leonid Pliushch, Nadia Svitlychna, and Moisei Fishbein. Using pseudonyms, the Ukrainians Emma Andievska, Ihor Kachurovsky, Ihor Hordievsky, Bohdan Osadchuk, Ivan Maistrenko, and Borys Levytsky participated in various activities initiated by Radio Liberty.

146. *The Ukrainian Weekly*, 47 (24 November 1985), pp. 1, 11. Borovsky and Movchan asked Raisa Gorbacheva to intervene with her husband Mikhail Gorbachev on behalf of two Ukrainians, the political prisoner Petro Ruban and the English teacher Anna Mykhailenko from Odesa whose crime was that she used the Ukrainian language for communicating with her students, and "suggested to them that they read more Ukrainian books than Russian." The KGB fabricated criminal cases against both. Mykhailenko, on false charges, was sentenced to camps but later was transferred to the Serbsky Institute of Forensic Psychiatry.

147. Borovsky, *Potsilunok satany*, 76.

148. Richard McDonough, "Wittgenstein's and Borges' Labyrinth-Imagery," *Athens Journal of Humanities & Arts* 5, no. 4 (2018): 425–26.

149. McDonough, "Wittgenstein's and Borges' Labyrinth-Imagery," 425.

150. Iryna Antypova, "Volodymyr Sosiura: Vriatovanyi bozhevilliam," *Druh Chytacha*, 25 June 2009, https://vsiknygy.net.ua/review/1011/ (accessed 18 September 2020); Vita Levytska, "Andrii Holovko: Ubyvtsi – Shevchenkivsku premiiu," *Druh Chytacha*, 7 July 2008, https://vsiknygy.net.ua/person/424/ (accessed 18 September 2020).

151. Olga Bertelsen, "Robert Tretyakov – 'poet kokhannia,'" *Literaturna Ukraina* 7, no. 5636 (25 February 2016), p. 7.

152. A telephone conversation with Borovskyi's friend, Maria Zulim, 12 October 2013.

153. I discovered Borovsky's trace and identified people who knew him in New York in 2013, while continuing my research on political psychiatry as a post-doctoral fellow at Columbia University. Sadly, I was four years too late to deliver the message.

154. "Psych Ward Verdict for Russian Protester 'A Return to Soviet Psychiatric Persecution of Dissidents,'" *CCHR InternationalThe Mental Health Watchdog* (by Agence France-Presse), 10 October 2013, https://www.cchrint.org/2013/10/11/psych-ward-verdict-for-russian-protester-a-return-to-soviet-psychiatric-persecution-of-dissidents/ (accessed 5 March 2021).

155. The NGO Amnesty International that is focused on human rights attributed the status of prisoners of conscience to several peaceful protesters, including Mikhail Kosenko, who participated in the 6 May 2012 peaceful protest demonstration "The March of the Millions" against Putin's presidential inauguration. See "Amnesty International priznala triokh figurantov Bolotnogo dela uznikami sovesti," *Bolotnoe delo*, 3 October 2013, http://bolotnoedelo.info/news/3975/amnesty-international-priznala-trex-figurantov-bolotnogo-dela-uznikami-sovesti (accessed 18 September

2020). For more details about Kosenko who was declared insane and "diagnosed" with paranoid schizophrenia by psychiatrists at the Serbsky Institute in Moscow, see "Psych Ward Verdict"; "Russia: Withdraw Charges Against Protesters; No Compulsory Psychiatric Treatment," *Human Rights Watch*, 4 October 2013 (updated 8 October 2013, 26 March 2014, 11 June 2014), http://www.hrw.org/news/2013/10/04/russia-withdraw-charges-against-protester (accessed 18 September 2020); Sergei L. Loiko, "Activist to Get Mental Treatment," *Los Angeles Times*, 9 October 2013, p. A3. For details about the earlier case of the Russian poet Yulia Privedyonnaya who was prescribed a month-long psychiatric examination at the Serbsky Institute for organizing the Poetic Association that seemed problematic to the authorities, see Peter Leonard, "Russian Faces Soviet-Style Treatment in Psychiatric Ward," *Waterloo Region Record* (Ontario, Canada), 22 January 2010.

156. Between 1998 and 2004, psychiatrists at the Serbsky Institute, possibly encouraged by the Russian security services, pressed the Duma to return to Soviet law on psychiatric care that would allow specialists to detain and forcibly treat people who exhibited signs of opposition to the regime. For details, see "Russia Considering Restoring Soviet-Era Law on Psychiatry, Opening Door to Political Abuse," *The Jamestown Foundation*, 15 November 2012, (reprinted by *United Nations High Commissioner for Refugees*) http://www.refworld.org/docid/50a4d26f2.html (accessed 18 September 2020); see also the interview of the President of the Independent Psychiatric Association of Russia Yuri Savenko "In Russia, the Mental Health System May be Used to Silence Political Dissent," *Mental Illness* (2013): 124–30.

157. See Robert van Voren, "Yanukovych Victim of Soviet Psychiatric Abuse?" *Euromaidan PR*, 2 February 2014, https://euromaidanpr.wordpress.com/2014/02/02/yanukovych-victim-of-soviet-psychiatric-abuse/ (accessed 18 September 2020).

158. R. W. Emerson, *Basic Selections from Emerson: Essays, Poems, Apothegms*, ed. Eduard C. Lindeman (New York: Mentor Books, 1960), 173.

159. Robert van Voren, *On Dissidents and Madness: From the Soviet Union of Leonid Brezhnev to the "Soviet Union" of Vladimir Putin* (New York: Rodopi, 2009), 63; see also Bloch and Reddaway, *Soviet Psychiatric Abuse*, 9.

160. For the individual history of Petro G. Grigorenko, see his *Memoirs*, ed. Greg Eghigian (with Gail Hornstein's contribution), *From Madness to Mental Health: Psychiatric Disorder and Its Treatment in Western Civilization* (New Brunswick, N.J.: Rutgers University Press, 2010), 317–28; for a discussion of Leonid Pliushch's case, see Tatyana Khodorovich, ed., *The Case of Leonid Plyushch*, trans. Marite Sapiets, Peter Reddaway and Caryl Emerson (Boulder, CO: Westview Press, 1976).

161. Edward Crankshaw, "Yury Andropov: Prisoner of His Country's Lies," in *Putting Up with the Russians: Commentary and Criticism, 1947–84* (New York: Elisabeth Sifton Books, Viking, 1984), 156. Edward Crankshaw (1909–1984) was a British writer and translator who is best known for his work on the Soviet Union and the Nazi secret police (Gestapo).

162. Crankshaw, "Yury Andropov," 157–58.

163. Ibid., 158.

164. van Voren, *Koryagin*, 37.

165. Žižek, *Violence*, 2, 9.
166. Ibid., 10.
167. Foucault, *Madness and Civilization*, 245.
168. Podrabinek, *Punitive Medicine*, 137.
169. Yurii Shcherbak reminded us that mass awakening of peoples usually occurred under the influence of dramatic events and shocking human experiences. See Yurii Shcherbak, *Ukraina v zoni turbulentnosti: demony mynuloho i tryvohy XXI stolittia* (Kyiv: Ukrainskyi pysmennyk, 2010), 315.
170. Dmitry Gorenburg, "Soviet Nationalities Policy and Assimilation," in *Rebounding Identities: The Politics of Identity in Russia and Ukraine*, ed. Dominique Arel and Blair A. Ruble (Washington, DC: Woodrow Wilson Center Press, 2006), 299.
171. van Voren, *Cold War in Psychiatry*, 318.
172. Mlechin, "Pochti ezhednevno . . . ," 17.
173. Podrabinek, *Punitive Medicine*, 91, 92.
174. See the official website of the Private Narcology Center "Avitsenna," and a brief biography of Professor Ivan Sosin, one of the founders and main advisers of "Avitsenna": Narkotsentr "Avitsenna," 2020, http://narkocentr.com.ua/kafedra-narkologii/sotrudniki-kafedry/sosin-ivan-kuzmich/; see also http://narkocentr.com.ua/?id=44 (accessed 19 September 2020).
175. "Sosin Ivan Kuzmich," *Narkotsentr "Avitsenna,"* 2020, http://narkocentr.com.ua/kafedra-narkologii/sotrudniki-kafedry/sosin-ivan-kuzmich/ (accessed 19 September 2020).
176. Korotenko and Alikina, *Sovetskaia psikhiatriia*, 10.
177. Rafalsky, "Reportazh niotkuda," 219.
178. Koryagin, "Autobiographical Notes," 24.
179. Koryagin, "Compulsion in Psychiatry," 398.
180. Mark S. Ellis, "Purging the Past: The Current State of Lustration Laws in the Former Communist Bloc," *Law and Contemporary Problems* 59, no. 4 (1996): 195–96.
181. Michael Wood, "Report from the Interior," *London Review of Books* 36, no. 1 (9 January 2014), p 30.
182. Foucault, *Discipline and Punish*, 265–66.
183. See Bigot de Préameneu's discussion about the arbitrary power of administration in prison and prisoners' recidivism in Foucault, *Discipline and Punish*, 266.
184. Foucault, *Discipline and Punish*, 27–29.
185. Quoted in Leland de la Durantaye, "Sedan Chairs and Turtles," *London Review of Books* 35, no. 22 (21 November 2013), p. 22.

Chapter 5

The Writers and the *Chekists'* Discourse about the Holodomor

THE HOLODOMOR AS A DISCURSIVE FORMATION

In 1977, Volodymyr Myliukha, head of the Culture Department of the Kharkiv *obkom*, invited a graduate of the Kharkiv Institute of Arts and successful actor and director Leonid Bykov to lead the famous Shevchenko Ukrainian Drama Theater in Kharkiv known in the 1920s and 1930s as "Berezil." Established in 1922 in Kyiv by the Ukrainian theater and film director Oleksandr (Les) Kurbas, "Berezil" moved to Kharkiv in 1926 but was ultimately disbanded after Kurbas's arrest in 1933. *Bereziltsi* (actors of "Berezil") found themselves under the leadership of the actor and theater director Mar'ian Krushelnytskyi in the Shevchenko Ukrainian Drama Theater which became an heir of Kurbas's traditions and legacies.[1]

Bykov's career began in the Shevchenko Ukrainian Drama Theater. From 1950 to 1961, he was a promising Kharkiv actor who played twenty roles on its stage. However, unpleasant memories about the political atmosphere in Kharkiv during the period of re-Stalinization and the Kharkiv *obkom*'s decision to prevent him from staging Aleksandr Galich's play-poem *Pokhodnyi marsh* (Marching Song) (1957) there played a role in Bykov's polite decline of Myliukha's offer. Bykov stated: "It is better to live standing straight in Kryshopil rather than to live standing on my knees in Kharkiv."[2] Born in 1928 in the village of Znam'ianka in the Donbas, Bykov survived the Holodomor, and this psychological trauma shaped his future career and love for Ukraine. In 1977, when he learned about Myliukha's invitation, he asked Tretyakov who visited Kyiv a rhetorical question: "In 1971, they expelled Galich from the Writers' Union and in 1972 from the Screenwriters' Union. Three years ago, they forced him to emigrate to Western Europe. Do you believe Myliukha will let me stage his 1957 play today or a play about the Holodomor for that matter?"³

The 1932–1933 famine in Ukraine was a forbidden topic for the intelligentsia. They were constantly reminded of this taboo in the *obkom* and at the KGB headquarters during their "prophylactic" talks. Many of those who survived the genocidal famine tried to forget the horrors of mass starvation and the Bolsheviks' violence that accompanied it, but the *chekists*' fixation on the "rumors" about the famine did not let them excoriate it from their memories. In their vigor to deny the tragedy, to depoliticize it, and to lobotomize it from the Ukrainians' psyche, the *chekists* achieved the opposite effect: "the politics knocked at the doors and crawled in through all cracks [of people's mental worlds]," as Yevhen Sverstiuk has stated.⁴ The *shistdesiatnyk* and Ukrainian dissident Sverstiuk who personally did not experience the famine realized that he, like other people such as Robert Conquest and James Mace who knew of the famine or studied it, vehemently reacted to "a lie and attempts to hide a serious crime and subversion of the people. They were shocked by the unbelievable cynicism [of the state]: to take all the bread from those who fed the entire country."⁵ Sverstiuk has argued that the systematic attempts of the authorities to hide the crime from its victims and the absurdities of these attempts opened the window into the past of discursive formations created by the Soviet regime, prompting his own broader realization of other crimes committed by the Soviet regime that went far beyond the famine. It was an attempt to take away a "spiritual bread" from the Ukrainian people and erase their language and cultural traditions.⁶ In the anonymous document that was circulated in the USSR as *samvydav* from 1964 entitled "On the Pohruzhalskyi's trial," beyond the 24 May 1964 arson and destruction of a rare Ukrainian manuscript collection preserved in the Kyiv Public Library of the Academy of Sciences of the UkrSSR by its associate Viktor Pohruzhalskyi, the author discussed the Kremlin's systemic politics of "memorycide" in Ukraine and the deliberate destruction of Ukrainian artifacts and culture.⁷ On this tragic day, approximately 600,000 volumes of ancient prints, rare books, and manuscripts were burned. This document was written by Sverstiuk and edited by Ivan Svitlychnyi, two Ukrainian scholars and writers who appealed to their fellow citizens: "Ukrainians! Do you know what they burned? They burned part of your mind and soul."⁸

Most recently, in 2020, the editors of the scholarly journal *Gender & History* based in Canada planned to publish a special issue that would discuss the connection between sovereignty and food. In their call for proposals they pinpointed this connection as follows: "Sovereignty and food are intimately entwined. Food has been an instrument of both power and empowerment, a site of negotiation for control of bodies, spaces, states, institutions, identities and the self."⁹ In the Ukrainian case, control over resources such as food was indeed a powerful political weapon that was used by Stalin to subvert the nation. The famine, however, was part of a larger crime of genocide, targeting everyone who resisted violence and the elimination of Ukrainian cultural traditions—its intellectuals, the clergy, and the farming population.[10] Roman Serbyn has pertinently identified this genocide as the Holodo*more*, implying that there was much more to what the Kremlin and its servants did, beyond the intentional mass killings of Ukraine's citizens by hunger, to pacify the rebellious nation in the late 1920s and the early 1930s.[11] Control over this discourse, associated with genocide, has been a building block of memorycide by the perpetrators and their descendants, a tactic designed to finish the job, inducing cultural and historical amnesia among the victims of genocide that would reign in posterity. The examination of the Ukrainian famine discourses shaped by the *chekists* throughout Soviet history might help us trace GPU/NKVD/MGB/KGB officers' persistence and patterns in returning to the topic of the 1932–1933 famine in their daily activities as torturers and interrogators. This exercise sheds light not only on Soviet writers' perceptions of the tragedy but also illuminates the continuity of KGB operations of ideological subversion domestically and abroad during the Cold War, in which KGB operatives manipulated the Holodomor discourse and tried to curtail commemorative events organized by Ukraine's intelligentsia and the Ukrainian diaspora in North America.

Ultimately, this chapter will help us observe the significance of the Holodomor as a discursive formation and as a diagnostic test for the *chekists* that assisted them in identifying and isolating "nationalists" and in provoking discord among writers of various ethnic groups to control their memories and behavior. The vitality and continuity of this discourse controlled by the *chekists* become abundantly clear when it is explored throughout several decades, beginning in the early 1930s. This discourse shaped social, political, and cultural realities in Soviet Ukraine and far beyond, transcending space and time and producing a phenomenon, known as post-genocidal society that lost its sense of purpose and direction. The *chekists*' deep penetration into Ukraine's cultural sphere through a variety of methods and discourses made many writers walk their labyrinths with caution.[12] For many, these journeys to the center of their being became chaotic and torturous, forcing them to hide or erase their memories and feelings. The *chekist* idiom compromised and largely destroyed the idea of labyrinth, the "universal symbol for unity and wholeness" that was supposed to inspire human imagination and a sense of community, as well as people's "longing for connectedness and the remembrance of purpose for living."[13] Directly or indirectly, the *chekists* were deeply involved in the crime, the killing of millions through starvation, and those who survived in Ukraine were perpetually on probation, suspected of potential crimes against the regime. Their attitudes, moods, views, and memories were studied and repetitively tested through a single discursive formation of the Holodomor, an effective tactic for identifying the "others."

CARRIERS, GUARDIANS, AND GUARDS OF THE HOLODOMOR RHETORIC

Spatial and ritual fluidity has been stressed in numerous philosophical and historical studies. Places change and so does everything that makes them distinct—their social, political, and cultural landscapes; architecture; and people who populate them, especially their rituals, ideals, beliefs, and rhetoric.[14] Yet despite the fact that change is inevitable and permanent, some behaviors and rituals resist change, persistently following the patterns shaped by history and politics. The Soviet era and its ideologues left a permanent inscription on institutional practices, and on the mentality and behavior of generations of people. This mark has shaped people's language, rhetoric, discourses, and ultimately worldviews, perpetuating historical clichés, beliefs, and stereotypes, and making it difficult to distinguish between appearances and realities.

One of the examples of such persistence is the *chekists'* discourse and rhetoric pertaining to the Holodomor, a man-made famine that resulted in the deaths of millions in Ukraine and beyond.[15] Faithful intelligence servants of the Soviet regime, the *chekists* recurrently reproduced the Soviet discourse of the 1932–1933 famine during the Soviet and post-Soviet era, equipping the contemporary Russian secret services with rhetorical tools, effectively tested over the decades of Soviet rule.[16] Archaic, yet enduring, these tools are employed even today in lecture halls and courtrooms in the Russian Federation, identifying new scholarship that abandoned the Soviet rhetoric and adopted the term "the Holodomor" as narratives committed to a Ukrainian national perspective. Crucially, grounded in archival research conducted in the former KGB archives and published by Ukrainian scholars, these studies have been included in the list of extremist materials in keeping with Russia's anti-extremism legislation.[17]

A substantial body of scholarly literature, discussing the nexus of Soviet ideology, language, and rhetoric, has highlighted their vitality and their interlocking relationships which significantly influenced state and institutional practices in Soviet and post-Soviet space.[18] According to many studies, the rhetoric of the Cold War amplified and perpetuated these relationships, producing a stable mnemonic and temporal connection embraced by subsequent generations, the heirs of former Soviet citizens.[19] The Soviet rhetoric, vocabulary, and the ideological paradigms and imaginings survived the collapse of the Soviet Union, foreshadowing their revival in post-Soviet Russia.

Having adopted and employed the language and rhetoric of the Soviet historical narrative, the *chekists* had become their carriers, guardians, and guards, obscuring the gap between historical reality and its falsified Soviet version. They accepted the claims emanating from their supervisors and the party about a connection between the famine discourse and Ukrainian nationalism, which was allegedly the template for anti-Soviet activities, especially among the Ukrainian intelligentsia. To a significant extent, the *chekists* advanced and shaped the Soviet narrative, sharpening the language of Soviet ideologues and party leaders, an exercise evident in fabricated individual and collective criminal cases against Ukrainian nationalists and intellectuals.[20] They discovered the power of language, discourse, and rhetoric, employing them in interrogation cells to break the accused. Language became a tool of control and psychological torture. Especially gifted *chekists* effectively combined it with physical torture, meeting statistical quotas for arrests and executions prescribed by the state. One scholar has posited that "in every society the production of discourse is at once controlled, selected, organized and redistributed by a certain number of procedures whose role is to ward off its powers and dangers,"[21] further arguing that the regimentation of discourse helps the state implement "mass slaughter and individual control [that] are two deep characteristics of all modern totalitarian societies."[22]

Soviet intelligence officers have been the main focus of numerous studies examining their methods, institutional culture, and traditions.[23] Yet very little has been written about the *chekists*' discursive tools, and how powerful they were in the space of authoritarianism and regimentation.[24] Even less is known about how they addressed the topic of the Holodomor in their daily practices, and how sensitive the issue of food shortages and mass starvation was to the Soviet government in general, and Soviet intelligence in particular. In this light, it seems prudent not to psychoanalyze the *chekists* or to explain why they acted the way they did but rather to trace the persistence of the famine discourse in their practices and communications, reflected in the documents they created over the decades of Soviet rule. The topic of the famine was forbidden in public discussions, but it was routinely raised in interrogation rooms and reflected in top secret documents, spaces which were hidden from the public eye.

Many thinkers, including Sigmund Freud and Michel Foucault, have insisted that discourses and their recurrent rhetorical themes highlight their interlocutors' hidden desires, needs, and intentions and reveal their objectives and priorities, "exemplifying power which is to be seized."[25] Like any discourse which is inherently rhetorical and is designed to influence the audience by changing its perceptions of reality, the *chekists*' discourse about the famine reinforced their power, suppressing and marginalizing other voices and truths that were inadmissible for the Soviet regime. Moreover, these voices were criminalized by the Soviet courts and laws, because for the state the famine did not exist, and the narratives contrary to state officials' truth were considered anti-Soviet propaganda.[26] Tracing the evolution of the Holodomor discourse in the Soviet Union and decoding the meaning of the famine that had been constructed in Soviet police documents from the early 1930s until the very end of the Soviet era might help us better understand contemporary Russia that continues to follow these discursive practices, issuing new laws to sustain the Soviet historical narrative about the 1932–1933 famine in Ukraine.[27] To a significant degree, these practices deeply embedded in the Russian security services, which limited Russian democrats' attempts to reorganize Russian society and Russian political and social institutions, foreshadowed cultural realignment in the Russian Federation, where open violence has been replaced with its more subtle forms, more sophisticated yet no less destructive.[28]

In the *chekist* traditions and practices pertaining to the Holodomor, two themes seem to stand prominently—the attitudes of the intelligentsia toward the 1932–1933 mass starvation in Ukraine, and *chekist* operations designed to obscure the knowledge of Western inspectors about food shortages and grain production in the USSR. The 1932–1933 famine in Ukraine indeed made the issue of food in the Soviet Union extremely sensitive. For the international community, its absence, shortages, and the Holodomor were largely associated with the loss of Ukraine's sovereignty; domestically, the tragic memories of survivors haunted them, spilling out onto the pages of their diaries and creative work. The Kharkiv writer Briuggen argued that the *chekists* were "sniffing around" constantly, searching for transgressors who wrote about or mentioned the Holodomor.[29] Moreover, they themselves raised questions about the famine over and over again in an attempt to provoke the writers' revelations and memories. These provocations helped the *chekists* identify and criminalize the *holodomornyky*'s creative work and social activities.[30] Importantly, KGB officers reactualized the discourse about the Holodomor in the 1960s, casting "Holodomor talks" and complaints about food shortages as manifestations of Ukrainian nationalism. Yet the formation of the *chekist* discourse, terminology, and the modus operandi in processing *holodomornyky* can rightfully be traced to 1932–1933 when Ukraine's intellectuals were arrested and prosecuted en masse for their "counterrevolutionary" activities and participation in alleged Ukrainian nationalist organizations.

The *Chekists* and Ukraine's Intellectual Elites in the 1930s

The initial knowledge about the *chekist* rhetoric of the Holodomor comes from analyses of their interrogation protocols and operational documentation. Undoubtedly, these sources leave some room for imagination: they are stripped of speech, tones, gestures, emotions, and people's live reactions and behaviors. Nevertheless, juxtaposed with other sources, including the *chekists*' accounts and memoirs, and the scholarship on the topic, these documents help us recognize the recurrent themes of the famine that the *chekists* linked to nationalist ideology, and their persistent attempts to conceal food shortages and famines in the USSR. In contrast to many other studies that assessed the responses of the accused, most of which were fabricated by the *chekists*, this research includes an analysis of the *chekists*' contribution to interrogation, and their own assessments of the Ukrainian famine. Their extensive discussions of the famine with the arrested suggest their absolute certainty that this state secret was not going to be shared with broader audiences due to the eventual and inevitable isolation or death of the accused. References to the famine functioned as a discursive formation, an interpretative framework that implied the predetermined distribution of roles in this encounter: the interrogator meant to be the survivor; the accused was doomed to isolation or extermination because of his (her) nationalist stance and affiliations.[31] The diagnostic and interpretive power of this discourse perpetuated itself, reiterated by the *chekists* over decades, shaping cultural and historical discourses about the Holodomor until the present day, as well as the cultural and collective memory of those who reside in Ukraine and beyond. The first capital of Soviet Ukraine, Kharkiv, and the Kharkiv and Kyiv intellectual elite of the 1920s and 1930s are central to this discussion.

According to American literary theorist and rhetorical critic Kenneth Burke, certain rhetorical tools and strategies (i.e., language and symbols) are capable of inducing actions in other people and influencing their perceptions and changing their identities.[32] The *chekists* pursued the aforementioned goals and influences, but the scenarios for those who found themselves in the *chekists*' interrogation rooms were quite limited: to be silenced and comply, or to be isolated or killed. Those who insisted that the Soviet regime used the famine as a political weapon against the opposition were doomed.

In the *chekists*' practices, there was an intrinsic connection between their rhetoric and deception, a reflection of a vicious cycle of lies, initiated, institutionalized, and perpetuated by the state. The state goal was to overcome, to convert, to dispossess the intended audience of their own opinion or identification, saturating society with uncertainties that resulted in people's loss of critical perspectives. Soviet citizens had to accept the proposed description of reality and state ideology voluntarily or through coercion. The *chekists* never trusted them, nor believed in their conversion. Importantly, the *chekists* had state and institutional support, a machine of power that rationalized and valorized their coercive practices.

Ukraine's writers, actors, and artists, the representatives of the Red Renaissance known as the Executed Renaissance, were openly confronted about what they knew or thought of the famine only after their arrest. Some were drawn into these discussions by provocative questions about their experiences and their shared and individual practices of reflecting on mass starvation and deaths in Ukraine in 1932–1933. Others were induced to situate the famine in the context of Soviet forcible Russification and subversion of Ukraine. For instance, in his confession, the actor and leading director of the Ukrainian theater "Berezil" Les Kurbas identified the year 1932 as the most crucial period in the activities of the Ukrainian Military Organization, a "counterrevolutionary organization" in which he was allegedly a member. Its "members" (among them were also the director of "Berezil" Mykhailo Datskiv, the leading actor Yosyp Hirniak, and the playwright Myroslav Irchan) confirmed Kurbas's deposition, allegedly stating that the famine, Mykola Khvyliovyi's suicide, and political repression that beheaded intellectual Ukraine encouraged them to pursue the strategies of individual terror and assassinations of party and GPU leaders in Ukraine. According to their depositions, among those who organized the famine in Ukraine and had to be eliminated were Vsevolod Balytskyi, Stanislav Kosior, and Pavlo Postyshev.[33] Whether these statements were authentic or fabricated by the interrogators remains a subject for conjecture. Yet the appropriation of the famine discourse by the *chekists* and its very appearance in interrogation protocols demonstrate that real or imagined acknowledgment of the famine served as incriminating evidence of crimes against the state. On 17 March 1934, answering the interrogator's question about his counterrevolutionary activities at the peak of the famine, Kurbas stated:

> In February of 1933, I renewed my activities, and because of even more severe famine, I began to notice new popular moods. They can be characterized as a longing for a united national front. . . . Especially after Khvyliovyi's suicide, I used every opportunity to discredit party policies . . . and employed the example of the famine in Ukraine to incite nationalistic and anti-Soviet sentiments among the actors in the theater.[34]

Interestingly enough, Kurbas's self-incriminating answers appear to be a reiteration of his interrogator's questions, and a confirmation of the interrogator's suppositions, formulated as questions.

The interrogators' persistent interest in identifying the connection between the famine discourse, Ukrainian nationalism, and anti-Soviet activities can be traced in hundreds of criminal files. The depositions, made under duress by the most prominent cultural figures in Ukraine, appear to be strikingly formulaic and linguistically similar, as if an invisible force orchestrated the procedures, shaped their language, and conceptualized the evidence of state treason. The interrogators' strategies and the vector of their questions in various cases suggest the existence of a thematic script and injunctions that they followed, which were supposed to link the attitudes of the intelligentsia toward the state policies of collectivization and their "rabid Ukrainian nationalism" and separatism.[35] Using various methodologies, scholars have already established that Soviet interrogation techniques were arbitrary and unethical. The goal was not to discover the truth but rather to arrange a confession to imagined crimes, and this goal was achieved through intimidation, coercion, and violence.[36] Sensing an unmistakable nationalist spirit in the accused, GPU associates engaged them in a discussion about the famine. This probe was deemed truly successful when the accused began to criticize Stalin's collectivization campaign, expressing support and sympathy for the starving peasants who resisted it. Peasant resistance presented a serious threat to Soviet power. In 1932 in several regions of Ukraine, Soviet power was challenged and ceased to exist for a brief period of time.[37] The sympathetic attitudes of the accused toward the rebels and his or her criticisms of high party officials were discursively connected to the famine and to "anti-Soviet rebellions," and the template for a portrait of a Ukrainian nationalist was thus considered by the interrogator firmly established. Further embellished with his or her alleged membership in a Ukrainian "nationalist fascist" organization, this image ultimately served as the foundation for the future verdict. The inevitable extraction of confession was a routine technical matter and typically did not require much time. A week or two weeks of torture and severe beatings provided the necessary signatures of the accused that he or she had to place on every page of the interrogation protocols.[38]

The multivolume criminal file of Ukrainian intellectuals Mykola Zerov, Anannii Lebid, Pavlo Fylypovych, Marko Voronyi, Leonid Mytkevych, and Borys Pylypenko includes a myriad of interrogation protocols completed by more than a dozen intelligence officers, but what they have in common are similar, almost identical, rhetorical tools employed over and over again, suggestive of a top-down script and regimentation in place.[39] The 1935 depositions of the young writer Serhii Zhyhalko and the engineer Ivan Kozub echo Kurbas's, Zerov's, and Fylypovych's words, as well as other statements made by many other intellectuals in interrogation rooms. They were shaped by the interrogators' questions and reveal these individuals' "anti-Soviet" attitudes. In response to the interrogator's suggestive question, Zhyhalko, for instance, explicitly made a connection between the famine and the persecution of the Ukrainian intelligentsia,[40] and Kozub supposedly argued in front of his interrogator Rapoport that people were dying from the famine in Ukraine because Moscow persecuted Ukrainians with the same vigor as in imperial Russia.[41]

The archival documents reveal that those under investigation included their views on the 1932–1933 famine in their testimonies as responses to the *chekists'* persistent requests to elaborate on their counterrevolutionary activities.

Allegedly, the prisoners' discussions about mass deaths in the Ukrainian countryside and cities, held with their colleagues and friends prior to their arrest, were part of those counterrevolutionary activities. According to GPU interrogation protocols, extreme starvation of the peasants and their mass rebellions registered since 1928 allegedly served as a justification for the Ukrainian intellectual elite to organize "nationalistic forces" to resist the Kremlin's domination and violence in Ukraine. The interrogators persisted, requiring explanations from the accused about their radicalism and terrorist operations targeting the party and GPU leadership. All the arrested had to do was to confirm a supposition embedded in his interrogator's question: "Did you participate in organizing an operation designed to eliminate Moscow's abusive power, liberate Ukraine from it, and promote Ukraine's national revival that might save Ukraine from national humiliation and demise?" With few exceptions, the protocols included the affirmative answers allegedly given by the accused.[42]

There is no way of knowing whether the accused actually described their plans in these particular terms or affirmatively answered such detailed questions. Thousands of cases that were reopened during the first rehabilitation campaign in the Soviet Union in 1956–1958 revealed that the stories of the accused were extracted under torture, which led to false confessions and miscarriages of justice. The unlawful police practices also included fabrication of interrogation protocols, interrogations that had never taken place. According to many memoirs of those who happened to have been in custody at least once during the Stalin era and survived the experience, entire cases were fabricated by the *chekists* from start to finish, including the paperwork involved. But what is important here is that the *chekists*, the record compilers and proprietors, made sure that their documents revealed an explicit connection between the "lies" about the famine in Ukraine, counterrevolutionary and terrorist activities, such as the assassinations of the Soviet political and administrative elites, and the Ukrainians' intellectual gravitation toward the nationalist and fascist philosophy emerging in Germany at the time.[43] Thus, typically, *holodomornyky* and sympathizers with the farmers dispossessed of land and property were identified as members of "Ukrainian nationalist fascist organizations," fabricated by GPU associates.

This ideological scheme of the alleged connection between Ukrainian nationalism and fascism was effectively exploited by the GPU/NKVD/KGB for decades, a strategy that shaped Soviet/Russian covert operations of ideological subversion conducted in Soviet Ukraine and in the West during the entire Cold War period, and Russia's transnational disinformation campaigns during the post-Soviet era.[44] The tone was set in the early 1930s, when interrogators and the GPU leadership constructed the plots of the alleged united nationalistic front in Ukraine, Moscow, and abroad, aimed to prepare the cadre and support for Nazi Germany in case it attacked the USSR.[45] The

Ukrainian painter Mykhailo Boichuk, for instance, was accused of being a member of the Ukrainian counterrevolutionary nationalist fascist organization that prepared a coup in Soviet Ukraine, collaborating with foreign "fascists" such as the Metropolitan Archbishop of the Ukrainian Greek Catholic Church Andrey Sheptytsky, residing in Poland. Moreover, supposedly Sheptytsky and other Ukrainian nationalists and fascists in Lviv, Prague, Vienna, and Paris helped Boichuk conceive and move forward with the plan of Ukraine's separation from the USSR.[46] On invitation from Mykola Skrypnyk, the People's Commissar of Education in Ukraine, Boichuk returned to Soviet Ukraine from Europe in 1933, the peak of the famine. Apparently, Boichuk's interrogator Khaet believed this was no coincidence. His questions were quite suggestive: "The investigative team has information that you collaborated with the Metropolitan Archbishop Sheptytsky in Poland, scheming about how to conduct counterrevolutionary subversive activities in Soviet Ukraine. Please elaborate on that";[47] "We expect that you should finally begin to give us truthful depositions. We know that since 1927 when the People's Commissariat of Education sent you abroad [for professional advancement], you communicated with the Metropolitan Archbishop Sheptytsky. We are waiting for your honest depositions."[48] Khaet informed Boichuk that he was accused of active participation in a nationalist conspiracy. The evidence suggested that Skrypnyk, a "Ukrainian national leader," encouraged Boichuk to return to Ukraine and join the resistance movement against the state political course that led to the famine of 1933 and the arrests of the Ukrainian nationally conscious intelligentsia.[49]

The leitmotif of the majority of confessions included the opinion allegedly expressed by the accused that, devastated by the famine, Ukraine was in the process of "perishing" as an independent political entity.[50] The very fact that the *chekists* considered this supposition seditious suggests that, for the Soviet government, Ukraine de jure independent was not and should not have been independent from Moscow, a legal contradiction that had not seemed to register with the *chekists*. They defined the Ukrainians' struggle for Ukraine's de facto sovereignty and people's resistance to Soviet collectivization as anti-Soviet, counterrevolutionary, and fascist activity. These references ultimately connote a secret discrepancy between the Soviet government's public discourse structured for foreign consumption and the *chekists*' practices ordered by Soviet leaders.

To further criminalize the transgressors' behavior, the *chekists* created special documentation, known as Summary Reference (*obzornaia spravka*) that offered a brief overview of the case, key evidence, and conclusions in a given case. Strategically, the operatives also included a summary of depositions by the intelligentsia recruited by the GPU who denounced their colleagues and friends. The theme of the famine was skillfully interwoven into the narrative.

For instance, through intimidation and blackmailing tactics, the Ukrainian artist and sculptor and a 1930 graduate of the Kyiv Art Institute Akim Mekhed agreed to cooperate with the GPU and to closely observe the political behavior of Okhrim Kravchenko, a brilliant artist and a student of Mykhailo Boichuk. Trained by the GPU, Mekhed engaged Kravchenko in discussions of sensitive topics, such as collectivization and the increasing famine in Ukraine. Mekhed presented himself as a Ukrainian nationalist-petliurite and invited Kravchenko to create an organization that would liberate Ukraine from Soviet power. Mekhed's revelations about Kravchenko's counterrevolutionary essence shared with the *chekists* ultimately resulted in Kravchenko's two arrests, in March 1930 and February 1935.[51] The *chekists*' chronicle reveals that discussions about the famine with Kravchenko during his two arrests, and Kravchenko's horrid experiences in the village of Kyshyntsi, where he returned in 1933 after his first prison term, were forever engrained into his memory. Kravchenko's famine-related statements and Mekhed's denunciations found their way into Kravchenko's Summary Reference.[52]

During their interrogations, the *chekists* routinely dwelled on the issue of collectivization, requesting information about how the Ukrainian intelligentsia assessed Soviet practices in their private conversations. Their questions included the quotations obtained from their informers who allegedly overheard phrases, such as the "destructive force of collectivization," "the famine that suppresses the Ukrainian nation," and the like. These questions shaped a certain direction and context of the discussion to which the accused were supposed to contribute. Combined with humiliation tactics and physical torture, these tactics were effectively used against the Ukrainian poet, scholar, and literary critic Mykola Zerov who, succumbing to the *chekists*' pressure, expressed his negative attitudes toward Soviet collectivization that "disoriented" him and shaped his nationalistic views.[53] Inevitably, many others who were similarly "disoriented" by collectivization produced a narrative in which the suicides of Skrypnyk and the prominent Ukrainian writer Mykola Khvyliovyi drained them emotionally. The *chekists* typically drew a conclusion themselves, asking the accused to confirm a supposition: "So, because of the famine, frustrated and disillusioned, you decided to act and organized an anti-Soviet nationalist fascist organization, correct?"

According to these narratives, the peak of the famine (the spring of 1933) and changes in the party leadership that struck against Ukrainian nationalism provoked severe depression in people like Zerov, the Ukrainian poet and scholar Maksym Rylskyi, and the Ukrainian professor and writer Ananii Lebid. During their interrogation, they were forced to admit that they wholeheartedly shared Zerov's feelings and views.[54] The *chekists* allocated the role of the "leader" of this counterrevolutionary organization to Zerov. His confession about a larger plot discussed with other Ukrainian intellectuals—Ukraine's break from the USSR with the help of fascist states—became the logical culmination of his depositions.[55]

The Ukrainian writers' discussions about the countryside devastated by the famine and their alleged gravitation toward fascism as a solution to saving Ukraine from the Soviets stand prominently in the Ukrainian poet and translator Marko Voronyi's interrogation protocols. Steering Voronyi's in the "right" direction, the *chekists* forced him to argue that the assistance of fascist states might help Ukraine and its youth survive.[56] Similarly, the Ukrainian writer Mykola Bazhan was directed to agree with Voronyi. Frightened and delusional, Bazhan stated that Ukrainian writers should promote fascist ideas in Ukraine and form a Ukrainian national-socialist party with a fascist nucleus that would include himself and other renowned writers, such as Yurii Yanovskyi, Rylskyi, Zerov, Pavlo Fylypovych, Mykhailo Drai-Khmara, Lebid, Marko Voronyi, and Marko's father Mykola Voronyi. Leading Bazhan through the stages of the interrogation process, the GPU interrogators finally secured the evidence that illuminated the writers' hostile attitudes toward Soviet collectivization that allegedly prompted them to organize party chapters in Kyiv, Moscow, and Kharkiv for the purpose of "tearing Ukraine and the Caucasus from the USSR."[57] More profoundly, according to their depositions, the writers allegedly planned to recruit and involve broad masses of the rebellious farmers, who would help them demolish Soviet power and assassinate the head of the GPU Vsevolod Balytskyi and Ukraine's party boss Pavlo Postyshev who organized the terror-famine in Ukraine.[58]

Fabricated or forcefully extracted, these statements accentuated the worst fears of the Soviet government about the powerful ideological inspiration and leadership of the Ukrainian intelligentsia who were potentially capable of mobilizing millions of Ukrainian farmers against Soviet rule. The closely linked famine discourse, alleged nationalist and fascist tendencies, and anti-Soviet views had to be exposed and eliminated in Ukraine. GPU interrogators made sure that those links were thoroughly documented and reported up the chain of command to legitimize the reasons for prosecuting as many Ukrainian intellectuals as needed to eradicate potential separatist tendencies in Ukraine.

It is important to keep in mind that the Soviet politics of silencing discourses, inconvenient and dangerous to the regime, naturally excluded the calamity of 1932–1933 in Ukraine from public discourse. At the same time this discourse was institutionalized and made routine and legal behind the closed doors of GPU interrogation rooms, practices that ultimately elevated the *chekists* to the status of the elite exclusive group of trustworthy untouchables who could keep a secret and be rewarded for that. They could use the famine discourse as a testing ground and often a point of departure for interrogation where the views and attitudes toward the famine expressed by the arrested decided their fates.

The *chekist* tactics helped break many Ukrainian intellectuals who denounced their friends and cried and begged their tormentors for forgiveness. Ananii Lebid, part of the case fabricated against Mykola Zerov, was among the few who withstood the *chekists'* tortures and refused to agree to scenarios proposed by his interrogators about a counterrevolutionary organization that allegedly existed in Ukraine. Yet, when pressured about his talks with the writers Rylskyi and Zhyhalko about the famine and mass deaths in Ukraine, Lebid admitted that such discussions indeed took place in 1932. His naiveté and admission to the very fact of the encounter inevitably criminalized Rylskyi's and Zhyhalko's behavior as listeners, despite Lebid's attempt to speak only about his views. He allegedly told his interrogator that the Soviet regime was responsible for the famine and highlighted the dramatic differences between the methods and the dynamics of collectivization in Ukraine and the Russian SFSR, a confession that sealed his fate.[59] Like many other criminal files of the Stalin era, Zerov's file abounds with the *chekists'* references to the famine and talks about it among prominent Ukrainian writers, scholars, editors, and painters. For the *chekists*, this discourse functioned as a system of exclusion. Shaped and controlled by them, this discourse was detrimental to those, on whom it was imposed.[60]

The *Chekists na cheku* (Are Alert): The Domestic Postwar Famine Discourse

The technology of terror and the famine as a discursive formation worked hand in hand in Ukraine, acting as an interpretive framework and a filtering system for the *chekists* that included those few who could be used by the regime and excluded many more who were to disappear. The *chekists* continued to prosecute the witnesses of the famine after 1945, writers and artists who dared to write about the tragedy or paint the horrors of the devastated villages and semi-alive famished people. Those who survived the famine and the Nazi occupation in Ukraine were doubly guilty.[61] The Ukrainian poet from Kharkiv Vasyl Borovyi was arrested in 1947 for his memoirs and poems about the Holodomor that he published in *Nova Ukraina*,[62] a newspaper that was printed from 1941 to 1943 in Nazi-occupied Kharkiv:

I ponykly sela vid naruhy
Pid tiazhkym iarmom pechali i bid.
Navit z ruk dytiachykh zli katiuhy
Vyryvaly ukrainskyi khlib.[63]

After an onslaught, the villages have fallen
Under the heavy yoke of misery and troubles.

The vicious torturers snatched Ukraine's bread
from little children's hands.⁶⁴

Borovyi remembered a conversation that occurred between him and his interrogators:

*MGB*⁶⁵ *officers:* We will hang you from the windowsill for this poem.
Borovyi: All right, hang me.
MGB officers: You are arrogant. You should not have written this.
Borovyi: It was written by itself.

Borovyi's poem about the famine and his survival in Nazi-occupied Kharkiv shaped and preconditioned his future. In 1947, the MGB sentenced Borovyi to death but later the verdict was changed to twenty-five years in exile. He was exiled to Norilsk, Russia, where he participated in the famous 1953 prison uprising.⁶⁶ After Stalin's death his sentence was reduced to ten years. He returned to Kharkiv and even joined the Kharkiv chapter of the Writers' Union, but in 1973, the time of the second wave of repression in Ukraine, he was excluded from the Writers' Union and was able to publish his poems only under a pseudonym. These experiences prevented him from being nominated for the highest literary award in independent Ukraine—the Shevchenko Prize. According to Borovyi, his friends and supporters, Ivan Dziuba and Anatolii Pohribnyi, encountered resistance from Mykola Zhulynskyi who made sure that Borovyi's name did not appear among the nominees. Zhulynskyi rationalized and explained his position, allegedly stating: "If Vasyl was at the front during the Second World War, or at least was part of the guerilla fighters' movement—we would gild him. But not under these circumstances."⁶⁷ The space of violence created by the Soviet police seemed to transcend time and persisted in independent Ukraine, as did the Soviet mentality, taking a variety of shapes and forms.

The end of the war brought no symbolic or ideological closure, rather reopening a new war between the USSR and the West and creating a space for warriors to identify new enemies and to formulate new goals and values. The Cold War incited the KGB to conceptualize new anti-Western rhetoric and strategies, and to reinforce the rationality of old discursive formations, established in the 1930s for domestic and foreign consumption.

In the 1960s, disturbed by the rise of the dissident movement in the USSR and the formation of the anti-Soviet human rights movement in the West, the KGB reiterated, reinforced, and communicated the old discursive formations and Soviet historical interpretations, including that of the Holodomor, to broader audiences. Moreover, in cooperation with intelligence services in the Eastern bloc such as Stasi, the KGB leadership designed a series of disinformation campaigns to fight ideological enemies. Their goal was to perpetuate the feelings of danger that emanated from the noncommunist world and from the "fifth column" domestically, and to mobilize Soviet citizens and Soviet-friendly nations to win this ideological war.[68] These initiatives ultimately shaped and sustained Soviet cultural trends, people's behavioral patterns, and memory in the post-Stalin Soviet Union.[69] The rationality of these initiatives was communicated through Soviet propaganda and special operations, provoking the emergence of "fractured mnemonic regimes" in post-Soviet space that engaged (and continue to engage) in symbolic violence and distortions of historical records.[70] Foucault has argued that "[w]hat is most dangerous in violence is its rationality . . . the deepest root of violence and its permanence come out of the form of the rationality we use."[71]

In the mid-1960s to early 1970s, the KGB launched a series of criminal cases in Ukraine to curb nationalism and the dissident movement. Ivan Suk who produced and distributed *samvydav* in Ukraine was among many who was arrested in 1970.[72] He was accused of keeping, producing, and distributing literature that defamed the Soviet state and spread lies about Soviet nationalities policy. The KGB paid special attention to a manuscript entitled *The Famine*, in which Suk identified the 1932–1933 famine in Ukraine as a tool of subversion and control over its citizens. Suk's conclusions sealed his fate: he argued that a careful examination of the Soviet press suggested that the Soviet regime thoroughly organized the 1932–1933 famine and subsequently blamed Ukrainian nationalists and *petliurites* for it. In a brief summary of Suk's manuscript written by KGB analysts, they noted that it contained anti-Soviet rhetoric and arguments: Suk claimed that it was a man-made famine, the result of deliberate expropriation of all foodstuffs from Ukrainians, events that the regime tried to conceal from the international community. To offer additional evidence of Suk's treason, they also included Suk's calculations of the casualties of these policies, according to which from 1926 to 1939 more than 8 million people died in Ukraine, which constituted one-fifth of Ukraine's entire population.[73] This information contradicted the official version of the failure of Stalin's collectivization, supported and distributed by Soviet mnemonic warriors since 1933. To prevent the manuscript from finding its way to the West, this text disappeared in the cellar of the KGB, and attempts to learn more about Suk's life and possible death in Soviet camps have been unsuccessful.

The intense KGB operational activities in the 1970s resulted in a substantial paper trail that included reports, assessments, recommendations, and analyses. Among them were documents that analyzed the nature of anonymous letters sent to the press, Ukraine's party leadership, and various Soviet institutions. The Soviets' genocidal practices in Ukraine in the 1930s, including the 1932–1933 famine, was the most frequent topic discussed in these letters.

KGB analysts identified their content as "manifestations of Ukrainian nationalism" and suggested that the intelligence work should be intensified to establish the anonymous authors' identities and places of residence. Protective of chief editors who were accused by anonymous authors of being the regime's accomplices helping the Soviet regime camouflage its crimes and silence about the Holodomor discourse, the KGB awarded them with valuable watches and certificates, further encouraging them to forward anonymous letters of "nationalist" content to the KGB headquarters. Because many letters included quite graphic and frightening narratives of personal experiences during the Holodomor (i.e., cannibalism and the like), revealing the leading role of the Kremlin in organizing the famine, the KGB established special teams that were working on intelligence gathering, trying to identify the transgressors and bring them to justice.[74] Guarding the "true" version of the past, the KGB succeeded on several occasions.

For instance, on 15 January 1974, Ukraine's party leader Volodymyr Shcherbytskyi received a KGB report, together with the text of a letter sent to the magazine *Perets*. Its anonymous author accused *Perets*'s journalists (*perchany*) of cowardice and lies, putting them to shame for their failure to publish the truth about Soviet power that murdered millions of Ukrainians and dehumanized other millions, many of whom survived the famine by eating human flesh. The author sarcastically reminded *perchany* of safe topics that they systematically raised in their publications that glorified the "most democratic" system in the world—Soviet socialism: "Of course, how can you write about cannibalism during this historical and beautiful time?"[75] Within a week, the anonymous writer was identified and put on trial for anti-Soviet activities and treason.

As in the 1930s, during the 1960s–1970s, Ukrainian writers who wrote or spoke about the Holodomor were featured prominently in KGB documents. The evidence of the writers' treason (their creative writings) were obtained through searches of their homes. KGB analysts reported that many of their works narrated the suffering of the Ukrainian people in 1932–1933, anti-Soviet propaganda that the writers shared with their relatives, colleagues, and friends. They criticized the current Soviet government for violence, grain export from Ukraine, and economic plunder in Ukraine leading to chronic food shortages. The operatives suggested that Ukrainian nationalism was again on the rise, and the Holodomor defenders had to be carefully monitored and subsequently isolated from the rest of society to prevent leaks abroad.

The majority of these writers became subjects of the KGB operation code-named "Blok" that was concluded with the arrest of hundreds of Ukrainian intellectuals. Among them were Mykola Rudenko, Mykhailyna Kotsiubynska, and Yevhen Cherednychenko, poets, scholars, and dissidents whose crimes and nationalist activities found their way into the 3 January

1977 report written by the head of Ukraine's KGB Vitalii Fedorchuk to Shcherbytskyi. Fedorchuk informed his party boss that Rudenko systematically spread rumors about the "headless Soviet agricultural policies," arguing that grain imports in 1977 helped little, and could not possibly alleviate people's impoverishment, hunger, and suffering. Fedorchuk labeled Rudenko an anti-Soviet ideologue who suggested that the issue of food shortages persisted in Ukraine and might lead to another famine, similar to that of 1932–1933. This information resulted in KGB agents showing up at the doorstep of Rudenko's apartment. They thoroughly searched it and discovered texts, discussing the possibility of a new famine in Ukraine, as well as poems about the Holodomor. The seized materials helped KGB operatives build a case against Rudenko who was accused of anti-Soviet agitation and propaganda and was sentenced to seven years in a labor camp and five years of exile.[76]

The KGB considered the mention of the Holodomor in any shape or form a sign of "counterrevolutionary activity" and the influence of subversive activities conducted by "Western nationalistic centers." Fedorchuk believed that the scholar Mykhailyna Kotsiubynska's worldview was shaped by the "Polish anti-Soviet centers" and the events of 1977 in Warsaw when the Polish opposition challenged the leadership of Edward Gierek who formalized Poland's commitment to socialism and the Soviet-Polish alliance through constitutional changes. Fedorchuk also emphasized Kotsiubynska's concerns about the food shortages in Ukraine. She shared her thoughts with her colleague, a KGB agent, suggesting that the Ukrainian people's patience could not be endless. Ukraine did not need another Holodomor, and if the government did not address this question, the situation might result in protests similar to the Polish events in the summer of 1977. Her colleague immediately denounced Kotsiubynska.[77] Harassed by the KGB since 1966 for her participation in the sixtiers' movement, Kotsiubynska was discriminated against in her workplace, systematically humiliated as a scholar, and deprived of an opportunity to create a family, recovering her title and job at the Shevchenko Institute of Literature of Ukraine's Academy of Sciences only during Gorbachev's perestroika.

Similarly, the KGB identified the Ukrainian poet Yevhen Cherednychenko as an anti-Soviet element and recidivist. On a number of occasions, he revealed his thoughts about food shortages in Ukraine and people's suffering during the Holodomor. Cherednychenko, a former prisoner of Stalin's Gulag, and his wife Vira Nechyporivna, a teacher of Ukrainian language and literature, were openly harassed by the KGB for their political activism, living for months without jobs and simple means of survival. Followed by KGB secret operatives (*seksot*), they happened to reveal their knowledge and attitudes toward the famine in front of several of them.[78] As one KGB officer stated, "that's all right. We will make sure that they are 'unhirable.'"[79]

Ironically, Fedorchuk's report fully confirmed Rudenko's, Kotsiubynska's, and Cherednychenko's concerns and fears, informing Shcherbytskyi about critical shortages of meat, eggs, milk, bread, and other foodstuffs in Ukraine. According to Fedorchuk, among regions and cities that suffered greatly were the Donbas, Crimea, Lviv, Zhytomyr, Chernihiv, Poltava, Kharkiv, Zaporizhzhia, Rivne, and Lutsk. People's concerns, however, about a lack of food on their tables and their truthful description of realities were unwelcome and punishable. In Fedorchuk's inconsistent conclusions, they were identified as "provocations" and "rumors."[80]

Furthermore, the strategic silencing of public discourse about the Holodomor and the KGB's persecution of the intelligentsia who wrote or spoke, albeit secretly, about the famine had another aspect that seems to be under-investigated. The Holodomor discourse and the denial of the tragedy also served the *chekists* as a tactic to divide the writers of Ukrainian and Jewish backgrounds. This tactic was especially effective when applied to the members of the Writers' Union. As one KGB officer stated: "They have something to lose. We are not interested in unity among them; just the opposite, we need chaos. In this case, they will not have time to think about nationalism."[81] With the Jews, KGB associates tried to appear open and sincere, throwing some rhetorical questions at them: "Do you think that those *holodomornyky* care about your relatives that were burned in the Nazi gas chambers? Give me a break."[82] Savvy people like Briuggen ignored those questions; others fell into the trap, accepting the rhetoric and sharing *compromat* about those "antisemitic *holodomornyky*." These fishing expeditions occurred daily in Kharkiv, and the initiative to discuss this painful topic emanated from a person who either was a KGB agent or a KGB informer. The irony of this situation can be observed on several levels, but the major logical inconsistencies are these: first, Kharkiv KGB agents worked for a notoriously antisemitic institution that from 1967 to 1982 was headed by an ethnic Jew, Andropov, and which systematically purged the Jews in its administration since the Great Terror.[83] Second, following the manual of active measures, KGB recruiters, most of whom were antisemites, pretended to be the best friends of Jews with whom they sided against Ukrainians. In reality, the KGB considered both groups of writers dangerous, suspecting nationalism and disloyalty in them. The recruitment scenario, however, was never rejected, and the recruiter's trustworthiness, good nature, and the sympathy for the recruited often bore fruit. As the former major of the KGB Yuri Shvets has stated, domestically, the extent of recruitment operations was mindboggling: "We recruited everything that was moving."[84] The manipulation of the Holodomor discourse, which was played against unsuspected victims, was an inseparable part of these active measures.

Michel Foucault has argued that the production of discourse in all societies is "at once controlled, selected, organized and redistributed according to a certain number of procedures."[85] There is no doubt that the Holodomor discourse was shaped at the very top of the Soviet security services and was creatively employed and advanced as KGB associates, mnemonic warriors, saw fit. Ultimately, in the 1960s and the 1970s, they, who had never starved and who internalized the Soviet narrative about the 1932–1933 famine, continued to thoroughly control and manipulate the discourses about the Holodomor and food shortages, multifunctional tools that helped them surveil, control, and isolate, if needed, those who documented or referenced the history of the famine. The power over these discourses allowed the *chekists* to subdue alternative discourses that were promoted by the "unruly Ukrainian nationalists," thus thoroughly guarding the Soviet version of the past and the space, void of challenges to Soviet rule and power.

Reinforcing the Famine Discursive Formation Abroad

By late 1976, thirteen of every twenty male political prisoners and one-fourth of all female political prisoners in the USSR were Ukrainians.[86] Many of them criticized the hypocrisy of the Soviet system, forcible Russification, and Soviet ideologues' attempts at falsifying historical records. The food crises in Ukraine and references to the Holodomor increasingly became a concern for the KGB at the peak of the Cold War. The critics' isolation, however, did not silence them. Their appeals and criticisms reached Western human rights activists who in the late 1960s began to organize.

The Holodomor was among the most sensitive topics that prompted the Ukrainian diaspora in North America and Western Europe to launch several initiatives designed to bring the attention of the international community to the Soviet state's crimes committed in Ukraine in 1932–1933.[87] Major irritants, various Ukrainian émigré organizations involved in political activism became the focal point of Soviet covert operations known as active measures, aimed at undermining national narratives of the Holodomor abroad and obscuring the discourse about chronic food shortages in Ukraine.[88]

The strategic planning and the objectives of these operations are reflected in KGB operational documents available today for researchers. The use of emotionally charged semantic tools and metaphors transforms otherwise monotonous and dry KGB reports into an astonishing read. The repeated mockeries of Western initiatives to correct the historical record of the famine give meaning to the *chekists*' creativity and their use of language, which in the mid-1970s became the language of war, consistent with the general atmosphere of the time. The détente began to deteriorate because of the Soviets' treatment of Jews and a horrible human rights record, and anti-Western rhetoric became pronounced, making its way into official documents. Promoted in the West, the concept of a man-made famine that constituted Ukraine's national tragedy was identified as an "insinuation," and the Ukrainian diaspora organizations, such as the World Congress of Free Ukrainians (*Svitovyi Konhres Vilnykh Ukraintsiv*, hereafter SKVU), were categorized as "hostile nationalist centers" that spread "lies and anti-Soviet propaganda."[89] Semantic additions, such as "so-called," "alleged," and "as if," permeate KGB reports to the Central Committee, signed by Fedorchuk.

Fedorchuk, a corrupt KGB official loyal to Brezhnev, consistently referred to the leaders of the diaspora associations and groups as "gang leaders" (*glavari*), arguing that in the battle between the KGB and Western Ukrainian nationalists the KGB would prevail and destroy them ideologically and financially.[90] In his 5 February 1973 secret letter to the Central Committee, Fedorchuk included a special section under the rubric "Hostile Activities of Ukrainian Nationalists Overseas," informing the Central Committee that Ukrainian nationalists in the United States published two books about the "so-called 'artificial famine in Ukraine,'" *Pravda pro sovetsku vladu v Ukraini* (The Truth About Soviet Power in Ukraine) by Petro Stradnyk, and *Organizovannyi golod v Ukraine 1932–1933 gg.* (The Organized Famine in Ukraine, 1932–1933) by Nikolai Gallii.[91] Fedorchuk also emphasized the danger of the 1 January 1973 open letter produced by the SKVU Secretariat that claimed that the crop collected in 1932 in the Soviet Union, as well as in Ukraine, was good and could not have possibly led to the disastrous famine that killed people by the millions. The SKVU Secretariat placed the blame for mass murder on the Soviet government that ordered the transport of grain from Ukraine and the Kuban to Russia, as well as to export it overseas. Fedorchuk rejected these allegations and ridiculed the accusations of the Ukrainian diaspora that Moscow had committed a genocide against the Ukrainian people. He stressed that this was a typical example of anti-Soviet propaganda organized by the militant thugs—Ukrainian nationalists, designed to persuade the "free world that Moscow supposedly (*iakoby*) engaged in colonial politics against Ukraine."[92]

The Ukrainian Congress Committee of America (*Ukrainskyi Konhresovyi Komitet Ameryky*, hereafter UKKA) was also featured prominently in KGB documents. Fedorchuk informed the Central Committee that this organization designed anti-Soviet campaigns, including the events commemorating the fortieth anniversary of the artificial famine in Ukraine. He assured the party leadership that KGB countermeasures would prevent the "anti-Soviet" and "nationalistic" campaign and the dissemination of knowledge about the Soviet genocidal practices in Ukraine, reinforcing the narrative about the incidental and climatic nature of the 1932–1933 famine. Fedorchuk also emphasized that since May 1967, the American authorities exempted the

UKKA from paying federal taxes which positioned it to "advance its subversive activities against the Soviet Union."[93] Yet he was confident that, through active measures, the KGB would effectively compromise the Ukrainian "thugs" in the eyes of the Western community, forcing them to spend every single penny for legal defense in American courts.

Similar rhetoric was used in Fedorchuk's 9 April 1973 report to Ukraine's Central Committee and the Politburo. According to KGB intelligence, "foreign anti-Soviet centers" planned to spoil the celebrations of International Workers' Day (1 May) and upset the spirit of the upcoming meetings of Soviet party leaders with American and German officials. Fedorchuk blamed "Ukrainian nationalists" in Toronto who were especially active in preparing this operation, those who also organized commemoration events dedicated to the fortieth anniversary of the famine.[94] He continued that the topic of the famine and Soviet repressions against Ukrainian intellectuals was prominent at several gatherings of Western nationalists, including the second meeting of the SKVU where *glavari* gave speeches in defense of Ukrainian political prisoners.[95] Fedorchuk posited that covert operations in North America would disrupt and counter this ideological threat to the USSR.

Shcherbytskyi was systematically briefed about the Western Holodomor discourse. As KGB documents demonstrated, the KGB was aware of the Ukrainian diaspora's planned activities at least a month in advance. They had penetrated almost all Ukrainian diaspora organizations, systematically delivering intelligence about these organizations' activities, plans, and their internal and financial dynamics. Frequently, the intelligence gathered through KGB agents overseas preceded information obtained by the KGB from open sources. Various types of intelligence provided the KGB with an opportunity to mobilize local propaganda resources to reinforce the state narrative of the Holodomor and to compromise that of "Ukrainian nationalists." The KGB thoroughly pursued the topic of the famine and researched it domestically and abroad.[96] Importantly, the *chekists* emphasized the danger of the context in which this issue was raised in the West: the Holodomor was seen as evidence of Ukraine's colonial status and the ethnic component of Soviet genocide. The "inflammatory" texts published in the Ukrainian newspaper *Svoboda* (Liberty) that discussed the famine as Moscow's subversive tool in Ukraine received special attention in Fedorchuk's reports.[97]

Throughout the decades following the 1932–1933 famine, the KGB tried to prevent information leaks to the West about the famines and wheat deficits in the USSR (regardless of its nature), an attempt to impede the emergence of discursive analogies and patterns, suggestive of economic deficiencies of the Soviet system, and the profound connection between food shortages and state regimentation.[98] The Soviet government never admitted or accepted its responsibility for the millions of victims who died of extreme starvation during the Holodomor, the direct result of political will and state violence. In their reports, the KGB leadership routinely placed the famine in quotation marks, an expression of irony and sarcasm over the definitions employed by Ukrainian intellectuals or "foreign Ukrainian bourgeois nationalist centers." In the 1970s, the sensitivity of the Holodomor discourse extended to any discussions about food shortages or agricultural failures in the USSR. The potential allusions to or associations with the Holodomor seemed inevitable, a situation which, in the KGB's view, might undermine the durability of the uniformed historical narrative promoted by the regime, and damage the USSR's prestige during the Cold War.

To inhibit the associative links among mass starvation, state violence, and subversion, the KGB worked diligently to thwart any historical or semantic parallels between the sequence of famines in the USSR (1921–1922, 1932–1933, 1946–1947) that damaged Ukraine the most, and chronic and serious food shortages that systematically shook the Soviet command economy during the period of late socialism.[99]

Secrecy, the foundational principle of Stalin's command economy, became imperative during the Cold War. As some commentators have argued, "the reality of social and economic injustice had been among the Soviet Union's darkest secrets . . . [because] there was clear evidence of profound national and even racial inequalities at the core of daily Soviet life."[100] The sensitive data on economic disparities, droughts, hunger, grain balance, food production, and food reserves were classified, being available only to the top party leadership and ministries of agriculture.[101] The leaks abroad, however, were inevitable. On 20 August 1975, the deputy head of Ukraine's KGB Stepan Mukha informed Shcherbytskyi that according to foreign Ukrainian nationalist newspapers, such as *Svoboda* and *Shliakh Peremohy*, the drought in several strategic Soviet regions resulted in a significant wheat deficit of approximately 20 million tons in 1975. Mukha continued that the authors who wrote for these newspapers were aware of the Soviets' plans to purchase 7–10 million tons of wheat from the United States and 3 million tons from Canada, and according to them, the Soviet government tried to conceal the shortages from the West and secretly purchase the wheat from third countries.[102]

The preceding famines during the Stalin era and their secrecy undermined the trust of the Westerners in Soviet domestic and foreign policies. In their letters and articles published in *Svoboda*, the authors suggested that the United States and Canada should carefully investigate the real situation with food shortages in the USSR. For humanitarian reasons, the leading Western countries might agree to sell the wheat to the Soviets but, in the authors' views, there was a possibility that the USSR would exploit the threat of a new famine, purchasing the wheat for nothing from the West, and reselling it or giving it as a gift to developing countries to win their support and to ensure their pro-communist allegiance.[103]

Mukha emphasized that the authors of these "reactionary" texts offered a solution to Washington and Ottawa in case they were approached by Soviet leaders about the wheat sales: in exchange for their positive decision to sell their wheat to the USSR, the United States and Canada should demand that Soviet leaders reconsider their emigration policies and release political prisoners.[104] Mukha identified these texts as "provocations" that damaged the prestige of the USSR. Food shortages and the suffering of ordinary Soviet citizens seemed to be less disturbing to the *chekist* than the failure of his agency to effectively maintain a secret about domestic economic problems. Even more troubling was the fact that the food shortages in Brezhnev's Ukraine evoked memories, comparisons, and allusions to the Holodomor among the Ukrainian diaspora, many of whom survived and remembered the famine. These considerations encouraged the KGB to reconceptualize counterintelligence and mobilize professionals of several Soviet institutions, including Ukraine's Ministry of Foreign Affairs and Ukraine's Academy of Sciences, to help the KGB design and implement secret operations abroad to sustain and strengthen the Soviet historical narrative about the 1932–1933 famine.[105]

Grain and wheat were commodities that were employed as tools of control in domestic and foreign policies by all political regimes, but several man-made famines and the infamous Soviet practices of concealment and manipulations encouraged the United States to pursue more transparent trade policies. As a result, the Soviet government grew anxious about grain and wheat sales and Western requests to subject the USSR to various inspections. These initiatives emanated from the West, first and foremost from the U.S. government, which aggravated American-Russian relations. Despite the fact that the Soviet Union was one of the largest producers of wheat, the Soviet government had regularly purchased grain and wheat overseas since the early 1960s, mostly from Australia, Western Germany, and Canada. The domestic shortages became chronic and were caused by wheat exports to the countries of the Communist bloc, such as Cuba, and developing countries of Africa and South America to win and control their loyalty and support. Because of John F. Kennedy's initiatives and pressure from American grain producers, in late 1963 the Soviet Union finally signed multiple contracts with the American Continental Grain Company that was granted a license by the U.S. government, allowing it to sell wheat to the USSR. The Soviets paid for wheat with gold and oil.[106]

For the two most powerful rivals, the United States and the Soviet Union, the 1970s presented a number of economic challenges. If conducted thoughtlessly, the Cold War trade wars and wheat sales could have potentially weakened their economies, which was ultimately a serious threat to their national security designs. In 1972 and 1975, the USSR purchased large amounts of grain, and the U.S. government felt bewildered and threatened by these unexpected purchases, known as "Great Grain Robberies," leading to "inflationary pressures" in the United States.[107] Besides the price impact, the U.S. government felt threatened by the unknown, mobilizing the efforts of the U.S. Department of Agriculture. Its tasks were multifaceted, including a supply-demand analysis on a country in an effort to evaluate its normal import levels to make decisions that would ensure that U.S. foreign food aid programs did not interfere with normal American commercial trade, and did not damage economic interests and the expansion of exports by other competing states, such as Canada, Australia, and Argentina.[108] Donald J. Novotny, a leading figure in the U.S. Foreign Agricultural Service and director of the Grain Division Office within the U.S. Department of Agriculture in 1976, revealed that in 1972 their office learned about a bad freeze in the USSR.[109] The Americans made a counter-offer in the form of a short-term credit to the USSR. Instead, the Soviets began to secretly approach grain producers to make deals, favorable to the Soviets, on large purchases of wheat and feed grain.[110] These tactics resulted in the 1973 and 1974 moratoriums on further sales of grain to the USSR, followed by issuing a long-term grain trade agreement in 1975. But in 1975 the story repeated itself, which brought about a bilateral grain agreement signed by both countries.

This history inspired no trust among the U.S. Agricultural Attachés to the U.S. Embassy in Moscow who performed frequent inspections (spring crop surveys) to avoid information blindness and to accurately evaluate the USSR's import needs and the United States' export capacities. Stipulated by the bilateral agreement, these surveys were also accompanied by thorough CIA satellite monitoring of the grain fields. The mistrust was mutual, and American Attachés and their assistants were followed everywhere by KGB people. The Americans' reports typically went beyond assessing crop capacities, also including the social dimensions of food shortages in the USSR. KGB surveillance was thorough, allowing KGB operatives to review even the Attachés' private notes about the condition of Soviet fields, crops, and the availability of foodstuffs in Soviet food shops. For example, the assistant agricultural attaché to the U.S. Embassy in Moscow, Larry Panasuk, who from 29 June to 1 July 1976 traveled to Kharkiv, Dnipropetrovsk, and Zaporizhzhia oblasts, and Crimea, was carefully watched by KGB officers who tried to obscure Panasuk's observations about severe food shortages in Ukraine at that time.[111] In June 1977, the *chekists* went even further, stealing survey notes from the representative of the U.S. Department of Agriculture D. Hickman, the U.S. Agricultural Attaché to the U.S. Embassy in Moscow Alan Trick, and several of his associates, an operation about which Fedorchuk reported in detail to Shcherbytskyi.[112]

Economic considerations were closely linked to ideological ones. The political rhetoric of the Cold War combined with intelligence and counterintelligence produced a situation, in which silencing the realities of economic disparities and food shortages, as well as related discourses about the chronic nature of hunger used as a political tool in the USSR, made the deployment of alternative discourses and ideologies of democracy difficult. Concerns about the Western diasporas building bridges with the Soviet opposition forced the KGB to prevent the Iron Curtain from becoming more porous than it had already been. Diaspora politics and "foreign hostile voices," enforcing the memory of the Holodomor, had to be subdued and erased.

However, the 1986 Gorbachev glasnost and national movements in the USSR that facilitated the ties of Soviet "national minorities" with the diasporas engendered the tipping point, when the grip of the KGB began to slip, together with the Soviet discursive formation of the 1932–1933 famine. The diaspora used all means possible to publicize knowledge about the Holodomor. Shown at various international film festivals, the documentary *Harvest of Despair* (1985), sponsored by the Ukrainian Famine Research Committee (today the Ukrainian Canadian Research & Documentation Center) and made by the Canadian filmmakers Slavko Nowytskj and Yurij Luhovy, as well as the creation of the Commission on Ukraine Famine by the U.S. Congress in 1986 that laid responsibility for the Holodomor on the Soviet government, drew international attention to the atrocity.[113] In March 1985, Ukraine's head of the KGB Mukha expressed his concerns about preventing the film from being smuggled into Ukraine. In his view, the documentary might have inspired commemorative events dedicated to the "50th anniversary of the so-called artificial famine in Ukraine."[114] Mobilized by the KGB, journalists, historians, and some Canadian researchers characterized the documentary as a fabrication and falsification.[115] Mukha assured the Central Committee that the KGB would certainly prevent the film's appearance on Soviet soil.[116] *Harvest of Despair*, however, was widely shown and won a number of awards and honors at international film festivals.[117] Despite intense operations, the KGB failed to marginalize the alternative famine discourse that over the last two decades contributed to the growing awareness about the anti-Ukrainian component of Stalin's genocide.

A Battle over Meaning

Any discourse is intentional, designed to shape people's understandings of the past and promote their political action. Equally so, any discourse shapes people's resistance to its meaning and domination. Many have agreed that the success or failure of discourse depends on ideologies and cultural and political trends that shape this discourse and its ability to be heard and to be embraced. Others have posited that new technologies of communication aggressively shape discourses, making them pervasive and dominant, in turn changing social and cultural contexts, and people's intellectual and emotional spaces in which they exist.[118] The Holodomor became one of the most sensitive topics the *chekists* addressed in their documents. Its discourse, informed by Soviet ideology and shaped by the truncated Soviet historical narrative, transcended institutional borders, influencing audiences much broader than a circle of high-ranking party officials, intelligence officers, or Ukraine's intellectuals. The Holodomor discursive formation, reinforced by the *chekists* over several decades, illuminates how the famine discourse was appropriated and buttressed in Soviet Ukraine and beyond—through terror domestically and active measures abroad, silencing other alternative discourses.

Moreover, the *chekist* discourse silenced most writers, including those who survived the Holodomor or other famines in the USSR. As a result, Soviet *leniniana* (literature focused on Lenin and his legacies) significantly exceeds (numerically) Soviet *holodomoriana*. Most prose and poetry reflecting on the Soviet genocide and human tragic experiences in 1932–1933 only saw the light of day overseas and in independent Ukraine. The writers' psychological healing began to occur after 1991, and many began to live fully when they liberated themselves, telling stories about their traumas and wounds, caused by hunger, the loss of their parents and relatives, and human cruelty. Their aching hearts seemed like desolate places because of what they had lost, but their souls they invested in their creative work appeared to be rejuvenated because of what they had found—freedom of thinking and writing.[119]

The Soviet culture of terror, institutionalized by Vladimir Lenin, who in 1922 suggested establishing it through legal means by using clear and broad definitions,[120] helped the Soviet myth of the famine survive and infiltrate Soviet domestic and foreign policies. Following Lenin's advice to neutralize those who spread anticommunist agitation and propaganda with death sentences or lengthy prison sentences and exile, the *chekists* focused, among other things, on the Holodomor, shaping the collective memory and eliminating in the process those who challenged its Soviet interpretation. As one scholar has pointed out, managed collective memory can make the task of managing the present and the future much easier.[121] Reframing political questions in society and shaping collective memory is an art that helps the elites avoid dealing with challenges to their power. The *chekists*' discursive strategies help us observe how the Soviet myth about the famine was produced and reproduced in the KGB's practices, substantiating the Soviet ideology and empowering its adherents to perpetuate it. The overarching power of this ideology and hijacking of collective memory have been evident during the Soviet era and the early post-Soviet period, the time when the Ukrainians' attitudes toward their own country's future, under Moscow or independent of it, remained ambiguous,[122] and the meaning of the Holodomor was contested. Today the Russian Parliament regiments the work of state archives and historians to fortify the Soviet myth about the famine as the all-Union phenomenon, a narrative stripped of evidence of the Holodomor's ethnic component.[123] The most recent social and political realities in post-Soviet space threatened the survival of the *chekists*' discursive formation in Ukraine, but strengthened its grip over Russian society, a phenomenon that invites further scrutiny.

NOTES

1. On the Kharkiv period of "Berezil," see Olga Bertelsen, ed., *Les Kurbas i teatr "Berezil": Arkhivni dokumenty (1927–1988)* (Kyiv: "Smoloskyp," 2016).

2. For correspondence between the Kharkiv actor Mykola Borysenko, who in 1973 became the Kharkiv Institute of Arts' Dean, and Leonid Bykov, see Oleksandr Rudiachenko, "Leonid Bykov: Prybulets, shcho vidbuv," *Ukrinform*, 12 December 2018, https://www.ukrinform.ua/rubric-culture/2598839-leonid-bikov-pribulec-so-pisov.html (accessed 19 September 2020).

3. Private conversation with Robert Tretyakov, 17 July 1996, Kharkiv, Ukraine.

4. Yevhen Sverstiuk, *Na poli chesti: Nevzhe to ya?*, ed. Oleksii Sinchenko (knyha I) (Kyiv: TOV "Vydavnytstvo 'Klio,'" 2015), 35–36.

5. Sverstiuk, *Na poli chesti*, kn. I, 89–90.

6. Sverstiuk, *Na poli chesti*, kn. I, 90.

7. Oksana Zabuzhko "Z neznyshchennoho," in *Na poli chesti: Nash suchasnyk Yevhen Sverstiuk*, ed. Vasyl Ovsiienko (knyha II) (Kyiv: TOV "Vydavnytstvo 'Klio,'" 2015), 143; see the text of the document at *Ukrainske zhyttia v Sevastopoli*, 2020, http://ukrlife.org/main/evshan/kdb.htm (accessed 21 September 2020). The document was also published in *Suchasnist*, rik V, ch. 2, November 1965, pp. 78–84; see also "1964 – vid pidpalu Derzhavnoi biblioteky Akademii nauk URSR zhoriv viddil ukrainiky," *Ukrainskyi Instytut Natsionalnoi Pam'iati*, 22 May 2019, https://uinp.gov.ua/istorychnyy-kalendar/traven/24/1964-vid-pidpalu-derzhavnoyi-biblioteky-akademiyi-nauk-ursr-zgoriv-viddil-ukrayiniky (accessed 3 October 2020). Readers may note similar phenomena in the "cancel culture" perpetrated in the Middle East, and also evident in contemporary Europe and the United States.

8. Quoted in Vasyl Ovsiienko, "Z pryvodu procesu nad Pohruzhalskym," *Dysydentskyi rukh v Ukraini/Kharkivska pravozakhysna hrupa*, 6 November 2006, http://museum.khpg.org/index.php?id=1162802785 (accessed 21 September 2020).

9. "CfP (Journal): Gender & History Special Issue on Food and Sovereignty," *H-Net: Humanities and Social Sciences Online*, 20 August 2020, https://networks.h-net.org/node/35008/discussions/6351728/cfp-journal-gender-history-special-issue-food-and-sovereignty (accessed 12 October 2020).

10. On the genocidal nature of the Holodomor from international law perspective, see Volodymyr Vasylenko and Myroslava Antonovych, eds., *Holodomor*

1932–1933 rokiv v Ukraini yak zlochyn henotsydu zhidno z mizhnarodnym pravom, 4th ed. (Kyiv: Kyievo-Mohylianska akademiia, 2016).

11. Roman Serbyn, 17 September 2020, FB.

12. On the KGB's deep penetration into the cultural realm of Soviet society, see the retired KGB lieutenant colonel Vladimir Popov (interview by Dmytro Gordon), *YouTube*, 28 July 2020, https://www.youtube.com/watch?v=oFcrn7w57TU (accessed 3 October 2020); and Boris Gulko, Vladimir Popov, Yuri Felshtinsky, and Viktor Kortschnoi, *The KGB Plays Chess: The Soviet Secret Police and the Fight for the World Chess Crown* (Milford, CT: Russell Enterprises, Inc., 2010).

13. For a symbolic meaning of the labyrinth, see Lauren Artress, *Walking a Sacred Path: Rediscovering the Labyrinth as a Spiritual Tool* (New York: Riverhead Books, 1995), esp. xii.

14. Kenneth Burke, *Permanence and Change: The Anatomy of Purpose*, 3rd ed. (Berkeley, CA: University of California Press, 1984).

15. The Soviet secret police is abbreviated in the text as GPU/NKVD/MGB/ KGB. For the most recent literature on the 1932–1933 famine in Ukraine, known as the Holodomor-genocide (official term used in the name of the National Museum of Holodomor-Genocide), see Stanislav Kulchytsky, *The Famine of 1932–1933 in Ukraine: An Anatomy of the Holodomor*, trans. Ali Kinsella (Edmonton/Toronto: CIUS Press, 2018); Victoria A. Malko, ed., *Women and the Holodomor-Genocide: Victims, Survivors, Perpetrators* (Fresno: The Press of California State University, 2019); Anne Applebaum, *Red Famine: Stalin's War on Ukraine* (Anchor, 2018; New York: Doubleday, 2017); Andrea Graziosi and Frank E. Sysyn, eds., *Communism and Hunger: The Ukrainian, Chinese, Kazakh, and Soviet Famines in Comparative Perspective* (Edmonton/Toronto: CIUS Press, 2016); Andrij Makuch and Frank E. Sysyn, eds., *Contextualizing the Holodomor: The Impact of Thirty Years of Ukrainian Famine Studies* (Edmonton/Toronto: CIUS Press, 2015); Omelian Rudnytskyi, Nataliia Levchuk, Oleh Wolowyna, Pavlo Shevchuk, and Alla Kovbasiuk, "Demography of a Man-Made Human Catastrophe: The Case of Massive Famine in Ukraine 1932–1933," *Canadian Studies in Population* 42, no. 1–2 (2015): 53–80; Bohdan Klid and Alexander J. Motyl, eds., *The Holodomor Reader: A Sourcebook on the Famine of 1932–1933 in Ukraine* (Edmonton and Toronto: CIUS Press, 2012); Liudmyla Hrynevych, *Khronika kolektyvizatsii ta Holodomoru v Ukraini: 1927–1933* (Kyiv: Krytyka, 2008–2012); Timothy Snyder, *Bloodlands: Europe Between Hitler and Stalin* (New York: Basic Books: 2012); Norman M. Naimark, *Stalin's Genocides* (Princeton, NJ: Princeton University Press, 2010).

16. On more recent *chekist* practices during the post-Soviet time, see Victoria A. Malko, "Russian (Dis)information Warfare vis-à-vis the Holodomor-Genocide," in *Russian Active Measures: Yesterday, Today, Tomorrow*, ed. Olga Bertelsen (Stuttgart and New York: ibidem-Verlag/Columbia University Press, 2021), 215–62; Tatiana Zhurzhenko, "'Capital of Despair': Holodomor Memory and Political Conflicts in Kharkiv after the Orange Revolution," *East European Politics and Societies* 25, no. 3 (2011): 597–639.

17. Yurii Shapoval, Volodymyr Prystaiko, and Vadym Zolotariov, *ChK-GPU-NKVD v Ukraini: Osoby, Fakty, Dokumenty* (Kyiv: Abris, 1997); Vadym Zolotariov,

ChK-DPU-NKVS na Kharkivshchyni: liudy ta doli. 1919–1941 (Kharkiv: Folio, 2003); Serhii Bilokin, *Masovyi teror iak zasib derzhavnoho upravlinnia v SRSR (1917–1941): dzhereloznavche doslidzhennia* (Kyiv: Fundatsiia "Volia," 1999); Vasyl Danylenko, ed., *Ukrainska intelihentsiia i vlada: Zvedennia sekretnoho viddilu DPU USSR, 1927–1929 rr.* (Kyiv: Tempora, 2012); "Holodomor: What is the Kremlin Afraid Of?" *The Kharkiv Human Rights Protection Group*, 4 July 2012, http://khpg.org/en/index.php?id=1341237033&w=holodomor (accessed 19 December 2019); Vasyl Marochko, "'Russkii Mir' u Feodosii: zaborona slova pro Holodomor," *Istorychna Pravda*, 28 January 2015, http://www.istpravda.com.ua/columns/2015/01/28/146975/ (accessed 23 May 2020). On Russia's anti-extremism legislation, see Emily B. Baran and Zoe Knox, "The 2002 Russian Anti-Extremism Law: An Introduction," *The Soviet and Post-Soviet Review* 46, no. 2 (2019): 97–104; Olga Bertelsen, "A Trial *in Absentia*: Purifying National Historical Narratives in Russia," *Kyiv-Mohyla Humanities Journal* 3 (2016): 57–87. As some scholars have argued, the word "Holodomor" was used in print for the first time in 1926 in the Lviv newspaper *Dilo*, but the word has existed in the Ukrainian language since ancient times when people died of plague and hunger. Considering a cascade of man-made famines in Soviet Russia, the use of this term in Ukrainian seems organic and natural ("holod" means hunger; "mor" means mass deaths). The Ukrainian scholar Vasyl Marochko has argued that the term was first used to refer specifically to the Holodomor on 17 August 1933 in a news article entitled "Hladomor v SSSR," published by *Večerník P.L.* in Prague. See Vasyl Marochko, "Holodomor – henotsyd," in *Entsyklopediia Holodomoru 1932–1933 rokiv v Ukraïni* (Drohobych: "Kolo," 2018), 91–93. On the origin of the term, see also Yaroslav Hrytsak, "Khto i koly vpershe vzhyv slovo 'Holodomor?,'" *Ukraina Moderna*, 24 November 2017, https://uamoderna.com/blogy/yaroslav-griczak/etymology-holodomor (accessed 3 October 2020).

18. Among others, see Richard Pipes, *The Formation of the Soviet Union: Communism and Nationalism, 1917–1923* (New York: Harvard university Press/Atheneum, 1968); Robert Tucker, *The Soviet Political Mind* (London: George Allen and Unwin, 1972); Martin J. Medhurst et al., *Cold War Rhetoric: Strategy, Metaphor, and Ideology* (East Lansing, MI: Michigan State University Press, 1997); Michael Gorham, *Speaking in Soviet Tongues: Language Culture and the Politics of Voice in Revolutionary Russia* (DeKalb, IL: Northern Illinois University Press, 2003); Sarah Davies and James Harris, eds., *Stalin: A New History* (Cambridge, UK: Cambridge University Press, 2005), 181–201; Yuri Slezkine, *The Jewish Century* (Princeton, NJ: Princeton University Press, 2004); Alexander J. Motyl, *Ukraine vs. Russia* (Washington, DC: Westphalia Press, 2017); Armin Krishnan, "The Neglected Dimension of Ideology in Russia's Political Warfare Against the West," *Global Security and Intelligence Studies* 4, no. 2 (2019): 25–46. On the politics of silence, see Cheryl Glenn, *Unspoken: A Rhetoric of Silence* (Carbondale: Southern Illinois UP, 2004); Jahmese M. Fort, "Politics of Silence: Theorizing Silence as Altered Participation," *Kinesis: Graduate Journal of Philosophy* 40, no. 2 (2015): 65–74; Barry Brummett, "Towards a Theory of Silence as a Political Strategy," *Quarterly Journal of Speech* 66, no. 3 (1980): 289–303; William Forrest Harlow, "The Rhetoric of Silence and the Collapse of the Soviet Empire," *American Communication Journal*

16, no. 2 (2014): 52–66; Olga Bertelsen, "Starvation and Violence amid the Soviet Politics of Silence 1928–1929," *Genocide Studies International* 11, no. 1 (2018): 38–67.

19. On this phenomenon studied in various geographical and cultural contexts, see David James Tietge, *Post-World War II Rhetoric of Science and Its Impact on Civic Ideology in a Nuclear Age* (Carbondale: IL: Southern Illinois University; ProQuest Dissertations Publishing), 1997; Ira Chernus, *General Eisenhower: Ideology and Discourse* (East Lansing, MI: Michigan State University Press, 2002); Bob Mileke, "Rhetoric and Ideology in the Nuclear Test Documentary," *Film Quarterly; Berkeley* 58, no. 3 (2005): 28–37; Michael Bernhard and Jan Kubik, eds., *Twenty Years After Communism: The Politics of Memory and Commemoration* (New York: Oxford University Press, 2014); Konstantin Sheiko and Stephen Brown, *History as Therapy: Alternative History and Nationalist Imaginings in Russia, 1991–2014* (Stuttgart: ibidem-Verlag, 2014); Jie-Hyun Lim, Barbara Walker, and Peter Lambert, eds., *Mass Dictatorship and Memory as Ever Present Past* (New York: Palgrave Macmillan, 2014).

20. As some observers have noted, the counterrevolutionary plots and conspiracies of Ukrainian nationalists were formulated and commissioned from above. On the subordination of the *chekists* to the party and the narratives that emanated from the Kremlin, see V. A. Zolotariov and Y. I. Shapoval, "'Kolyvan u provedenni linii partii ne bulo' (Storinky biohrafii K. M. Karlsona)," *Ukrainskyi istorychnyi zhurnal* 1 (1996): 91–105; Yu. Shapoval and V. Panchenko, eds., *Poliuvannia na Valdshnepa: Rozsekrechenyi Mykola Khvyliovyi* (Kyiv: Tempora, 2009); Vadym Zolotariov, *Sekretno-politychnyi viddil DPU USRR: Spavy ta liudy* (Kharkiv: Folio, 2007). On the regime's attitudes (i.e., Stalin's and his circle) toward the famine in Ukraine, see Robert Conquest, *Harvest of Sorrow: Soviet Collectivization and the Terror-Famine* (New York: Oxford University Press, 1986); R. W. Davies, Oleg V. Khlevniuk, and E. A. Rees, eds., *The Stalin-Kaganovich Correspondence: 1931–1936* (New Haven/London: Yale University Press, 2003); James E. Mace, *Communism and the Dilemmas of National Liberation: National Communism in Soviet Ukraine, 1918–1933* (Cambridge, MA: Harvard University Press, 1983).

21. Michel Foucault, "The Order of Discourse," in *Untying the Text: A Post-Structuralist Reader*, ed. Robert Young (Boston: Routledge, 1981), 52.

22. Millicent Dillon and Michel Foucault, "Conversation with Michel Foucault," *The Threepenny Review* 1 (1980): 4.

23. George Legget, *The Cheka: Lenin's Political Police* (Oxford, Clarendon Press, 1981); Robert Conquest, *Inside Stalin's Secret Police: NKVD Politics, 1936–39* (London: Macmillan Press LTD, 1985); Amy Knight, *Beria: Stalin's First Lieutenant* (Princeton, NJ: Princeton University Press, 1993); V. I. Prystaiko, and Yu. I. Shapoval, *Sprava "Spilky Vyzvolennia Ukrainy": nevidomi dokumenty i fakty* (Kyiv: Intel, 1995); Christopher Andrew, *The Sword and the Shield: The Mitrokhin Archive and the Secret History of the KGB* (New York: Basic Books, 1999); Paul Hollander, "Leading Specialists in 'State Security' (Political Police)," in *Political Will and Personal Belief: The Decline and Fall of Soviet Communism* by Paul Hollander (New Haven and London, 1999), 209–74; J. Arch Getty & Oleg

V. Naumov, *Yezhov: The Rise of Stalin's "Iron Fist"* (New Haven and London: Yale University Press, 2008); Niels Erik Rosenfeldt, *The "Special" World*, 1–2 vols. (Copenhagen: Museum Tusculanum Press, 2009); Yurii Shapoval and Hiroaki Kuromiya, eds., *Ukraina v dobu "Velykoho Teroru": 1936–1938 roky* (Kyiv: Lybid, 2009); Julie Fedor, *Russia and the Cult of State Security* (New York: Routledge, 2011); Olga Bertelsen and Myroslav Shkandrij, "The Secret Police and the Campaign against Galicians in Soviet Ukraine, 1929–34," *Nationalities Papers* 42, no. 1 (2014): 37–62; Lynne Viola, *Stalinist Perpetrators on Trial: Scenes from the Great Terror in Ukraine* (Oxford, UK: Oxford University Press, 2017); Immo Reblitschek, "Lessons from the Terror: Soviet Prosecutors and Police Violence in Molotov Province, 1942 to 1949," *Slavic Review* 78, no. 3 (2019): 738–57.

24. Hiroaki Kuromiya, *The Voices of the Dead: Stalin's Great Terror in the 1930s* (New Haven: Yale University Press, 2007); Igal Halfin, *Language and Revolution: Making Modern Political Identities* (London: Routledge, 2004), and *Stalinist Confessions: Messianism and Terror at the Leningrad Communist University* (University of Pittsburgh Press, 2009); Wendy Z. Goldman, *Inventing the Enemy: Denunciations and Terror in Stalin's Russia* (New York: Cambridge University Press, 2011); Mykola Riabchuk, "Vid VChK do SBU: Tiahlist i mody-fikatsiia 'antynatsionalistychnykh' dyskursiv i polityk," *Historians*, 14 March 2013, http://www.historians.in.ua/index.php/en/dyskusiya/618-mykola-riabchuk-vid-vchk-do-sbu-tiahlist-ta-modyfikatsiia-antynatsionalistychnykh-dyskursiv-i-polityk (accessed 2 July 2020).

25. Foucault, "The Order of Discourse," 52–53.

26. Bertelsen, "Starvation and Violence," 38–67.

27. Bertelsen, "A Trial *in Absentia*," 64.

28. For Russia's contemporary Holodomor discourse and *chekist* practices, see Malko, "Russian (Dis)information Warfare"; Zhurzhenko, "'Capital of Despair'"; and Pavlo Solodko, "Yak pysaty pro Holodomor," *Istorychna pravda*, 26 November 2012, http://www.istpravda.com.ua/artefacts/2012/11/26/101572/ (accessed 4 July 2020).

29. Interview with Volodymyr Briuggen, 9 August 2013, the restaurant "Kryshtal," Kharkiv, Ukraine.

30. Ibid. In Kharkiv, some *chekists* referred to those who discussed or wrote about the Holodomor as *holodomornyky*.

31. On the notion of discursive formation, see Michel Foucault, *The Archeology of Knowledge and the Discourse on Language*, trans. A. M. Sheridan Smith (New York: Pantheon Books, 1972).

32. Kenneth Burke, *A Rhetoric of Motives* (New York: Prentice-Hall, 1950) and *Language as Symbolic Action* (Berkeley: University of California Press, 1966); on rhetoric, see Aristotle, *Rhetoric*, ed. C. D. C. Reeve (Indianapolis, IN: Hackett Publishing Company, Inc., 2018); Martin Heidegger, *Being and Time*, trans. John Macquarrie and Edward Robinson (New York: Harper and Row, 1962).

33. HDA SBU, f. 6, spr. 75608-FP, ark. 8–12, 22, 28, 49.

34. HDA SBU, f. 6, spr. 75608-FP, ark. 49, 51.

35. For documents that reveal this "thematic script," identifying specific enemies, and their links and connections, see J. Arch Getty and Oleg V. Naumov, *The Road to*

Terror: Stalin and the Self-Destruction of the Bolsheviks, 1932–1939 (New Haven/ London: Yale University Press, 1999); Danylenko, *Ukrainska intelihentsiia i vlada*.

36. Myroslav Shkandrij and Olga Bertelsen, "The Soviet Regime's National Operations in Ukraine, 1929–1934," *Canadian Slavonic Papers* LV, nos. 3–4 (2013): 417–47.

37. DAKhO, f. R-846, op. 4, spr. 44, ark. 124.

38. Shkandrij and Bertelsen, "The Soviet Regime's National Operations in Ukraine."

39. On brief sketches of Zerov's biography, see Lada Kolomiiets, *Ukrainskyi khudozhnii pereklad ta perekladachi 1920-30-kh rokiv* (Vinnytsia: Nova Knyha, 2015), 128–34; Viacheslav Briukhovetskyi, "Mykola Zerov," *Literaturna Ukraina* 32, no. 4441, 8 August 1991, available at http://poetyka.uazone.net/default/pages.pht ml?place=zerov&page=bio&alist=skip (accessed 12 December 2021).

40. HDA SBU, f. 6, spr. 48570-FP, vol. 5, ark. 10, 47, 56.

41. HDA SBU, f. 6, spr. 48570-FP, vol. 5, ark. 48; on Kozub, see also Liudmyla Totska, "Na perekhrestiakh doli. Ivan Kozub," *Trudova slava* 37–40 (16 March 2018), http://raybori.gov.ua/2018/03/16/na-perehrestyah-doli-ivan-kozub/(accessed 5 July 2020).

42. HDA SBU, f. 6, spr. 48570-FP, vol. 5, ark. 48–52.

43. HDA SBU, f. 6, spr. 48570-FP, vol. 5, ark. 46, 48–49, 60, 63–64.

44. Olga Bertelsen, "Ukrainian and Jewish Émigrés as Targets of KGB Active Measures in the 1970s," *The International Journal of Intelligence and Counterintelligence* 34, no. 2 (2021): 267–92.

45. HDA SBU, f. 6, spr. 48570-FP, vol. 5, ark. 57–60. For an analysis of how these plots were constructed, see Shkandrij and Bertelsen, "The Soviet Regime's National Operations," 417–47.

46. HDA SBU, f. 6, spr. 46293-FP, ark. 15–20.

47. HDA SBU, f. 6, spr. 46293-FP, ark. 15.

48. HDA SBU, f. 6, spr. 46293-FP, ark. 17–20.

49. Ibid.

50. HDA SBU, f. 6, spr. 48570-FP, vol. 5, ark. 56.

51. HDA SBU, f. 6, spr. 48570-FP, vol. 5, ark. 29–32, 33–36; for an analysis of Kravchenko's art and survival during the Stalin era, see Yaroslav Kravchenko, "Okhrim Kravchenko. Kriz zhyttia. Virnist tradytsiiam shkoly Mykhaila Boichuka," *Tekst i obraz: Aktualni problemy istorii mystetstva* 1 (2017): 39–54.

52. Kravchenko's interactions with the GPU and his experiences in Kyshyntsi helped him produce several masterpieces in the early 1970s, including "Holod na Ukraini. Skorbota" (The Famine in Ukraine. Despair) (1972).

53. HDA SBU, f. 6, spr. 48570-FP, vol. 1, ark. 164–65.

54. HDA SBU, f. 6, spr. 48570-FP, vol. 1, ark. 165–71,176, 200.

55. HDA SBU, f. 6, spr. 48570-FP, vol. 1, ark. 232.

56. HDA SBU, f. 6, spr. 48570-FP, vol. 2, ark. 87.

57. HDA SBU, f. 6, spr. 48570-FP, vol. 2, ark. 99.

58. HDA SBU, f. 6, spr. 48570-FP, vol. 2, ark. 66, 101–02.

59. HDA SBU, f. 6, sp. 48570-FP, vol. 3, ark. 199, 246–47; Tamara Andriichuk, "Ananii Lebid (1898–1937): trahediia liudyny i naukovtsia," in *Reabilitovani istoriieiu. Chernihivska oblast*, vol. 4 (Chernihiv: Vydavets V. M. Lozovyi, 2012), 207.

60. HDA SBU, f. 6, sp. 48570-FP, vol. 3, ark. 196, 136–47; f. 6, sp. 48570-FP, vol. 5, ark. 10, 47, 113; f. 6, spr. 40213-FP, ark. 15; on the functions of discourse, see Foucault, "The Order of Discourse," 56; on its characteristics, see Douglas R. Bruce, "Silence, Rhetoric, and Freedom: Explicating Foucault through Augustine," in *Visions of Rhetoric: History, Theory and Criticism*, ed. Charles W. Kneupper (Arlington, TX: Rhetoric Society of America, 1987), 166.

61. Iryna Reva, *Po toi bik sebe: sotsialno-psyholohichni i kulturni naslidky Holodomoru ta stalinskykh represii* (Dnipro: A. L. Svidler, 2013).

62. The first issue of *Nova Ukraina* was published in December 1941. In April 1942, its editor Petro Sahaidachnyi was replaced by Vsevolod Carynnyk. See Yurii Sheveliov (Yurii Sherekh), *Ia, meni, mene (i dovkruhy). Spohady* (Kharkiv/New York: Vydavnytstvo M. P. Kots, 2001).

63. This is transliteration of Borovyi's original poem included in Vasyl Borovyi (interview by Liutsyna Khvorost and Larysa Vyrovets), "Mene blahoslovyv do druku Svidzinskyi," *Kharkivska spilka pysmennykiv Ukrainy*, 3 January 2014, https://kharkiv-nspu.org.ua/archives/2794 (accessed 3 October 2020).

64. Victoria Malko's translation.

65. The MGB is an abbreviation for the Ministry of State Security of the USSR, dealing with foreign and domestic intelligence/counterintelligence from 1946 to 1953.

66. For details about the 1953 prisoners' uprising in Norilsk, see Yevhen Hrytsiak, *Korotkyi zapys spohadiv: Norylske povstannia. Pislia povstannia* (Kyiv: "Smoloskyp," 2013).

67. Borovyi, "Mene blahoslovyv do druku Svidzinskyi."

68. Thomas Rid, *Active Measures: The Secret History of Disinformation and Political Warfare* (New York: Farrar, Straus, and Giroux, 2020), 145–66; Vladimir O. Pechatnov and C. Earl Edmondson, "The Russian Perspective," in *Debating the Origins of the Cold War*, eds. Ralph B. Levering et al. (New York: Rowman & Littlefield Publishers, Inc., 2001), 85–151; on the Soviet dissident movement, see Ludmilla Alexeyeva, *Soviet Dissent: Contemporary Movements for National, Religious, and Human Rights* (Middletown, CT: Wesleyan University Press, 1985); Renee Baigell and Matthew Baigell, eds., *Soviet Dissident Artists: Interviews After Perestroika* (New Brunswick, NJ: Rutgers University Press, 1995).

69. Lim, Walker, and Lambert, *Mass Dictatorship*.

70. According to Jan Kubik and Michael Bernhard, fractured memory regimes emerge when "mnemonic warriors" reinforce debates or discourse on a particular issue with an "intention of drawing a sharp line between its authors, the guardians of the 'true' version of the past and 'them'—the prevaricators or opportunists who do not know or care about the 'proper' shape of collective memory." See Jan Kubik and Michael Bernhard, "A Theory of the Politics of Memory," in Bernhard and Kubik, 17; on symbolic violence, see Pierre Bourdieu and Richard Passeron, *Reproduction in Education, Society, and Culture*, trans. Richard Nice (Los Angeles, CA: Sage, 1990).

71. Dillon and Foucault, "Conversation with Michel Foucault," 4.

72. On political changes in Ukraine in the 1970s, see Olga Bertelsen, "Political Affinities and Maneuvering of Soviet Political Elites: Heorhii Shevel and Ukraine's Ministry of Strange Affairs in the 1970s," *Nationalities Papers* 47, no. 3 (2019): 401.

73. HDA SBU, f. 6, spr. 32571-FP; see the document in V. M. Danylenko, L. L. Aulova, and V. V. Lavreniuk, eds., *Holodomor 1932–1933 rr. v Ukraini za dokumentamy HDA SBU: Anatovanyi dovidnyk* (Kyiv: Tsentr doslidzhen vyzvolnoho rukhu, 2010), 334.

74. TsDAHOU, f. 1, op. 20, spr. 5255, ark. 26–29; on cannibalism in Ukraine in 1932–1933, see Olga Bertelsen "Women at Sites of Mass Starvation: Ukraine, 1932–1933," in *Women and the Holodomor-Genocide: Victims, Survivors, Perpetrators*, ed. Victoria A Malko (Fresno: The Press at California State University, 2019), 46–47.

75. HDA SBU, f. 16, op. 1, spr. 1084, ark. 139.

76. HDA SBU, f. 16, op. 1, spr. 1128, ark. 11. Rudenko had been arrested in April 1975 on the same charges but was released on amnesty as a Second World War veteran. In 1976, Rudenko wrote a collection of poems about the Holodomor, entitled *The Cross*. Listen to these poems, performed by Ihor Murashko, on *YouTube*, 21 November 2015, https://www.youtube.com/watch?v=f96u05qz7G0 (accessed 23 April 2019).

77. HDA SBU, f. 16, op. 1, spr. 1128, ark. 13.

78. Ibid.

79. "Unhirable" means unsuitable for hiring. The author's interview with the Ukrainian writer Volodymyr Briuggen, 2 July 2011, Kharkiv, Ukraine.

80. HDA SBU, f. 16, op. 1, spr. 1128, ark. 14.

81. Aleksandr Kasha, private conversation, 27 July 1989, Kharkiv, Ukraine.

82. Interview with Volodymyr Briuggen, 2 July 2011, Kharkiv, Ukraine.

83. On the antisemitic nature of the KGB, see the former KGB lieutenant colonel Vladimir Popov (interview by Dmytro Gordon), *YouTube*, 28 July 2020, https://www.youtube.com/watch?v=oFcrn7w57TU (accessed 3 October 2020). Yurii Andropov's mother, the music teacher Yevgeniia Karlovna Flekenshtein, was a daughter of Karl and Yevdokiia Flekenshtein, a wealthy Finnish-Jewish family of proprietors of a jewelry store in Moscow located in 26 Bolshaia Lubianka Street. Not coincidentally, Andropov's nick name was "Jeweler." See *Vsia Moskva: Adresnaia i spravochnaia kniga na 1914 god* (Moskva: T-vo A. V. Suvorina "Novoie Vriemia"/Gorodskaia Tipografiia, 1914), *Gosudarstvennaia publichnaia biblioteka Rossii*, 2020, http://elib.shpl.ru/ru/nodes/2923-na-1914-god-m-1914#mode/inspect/page/1541/zoom/4 (accessed 4 October 2020).

84. See Yuri Shvets (interview by Dmytro Gordon), *YouTube*, 2 March 2019, https://www.youtube.com/watch?v=M4YFeXr031E; *YouTube*, 18 August 2020, https://www.youtube.com/watch?v=wjMJIUZLJVs (accessed 3 October 2020).

85. Michel Foucault, *Power Knowledge: Selected Interviews and Other Writings, 1972–1977*, ed. Colin Gordon, trans. Colin Gordon, Leo Marshall, John Mepham, Kate Sopher (New York: Vintage, 1980), 216.

86. Alexeyeva, *Soviet Dissent*, 46; Ilya Prizel, *National Identity and Foreign Policy: Nationalism and Leadership in Poland, Russia, and Ukraine* (Cambridge, UK: Cambridge University Press, 1998), 352.

87. Olga Andriewsky, "Towards a Decentered History: The Study of the Holodomor and Ukrainian Historiography," in *Contextualizing the Holodomor: The Impact of Thirty Years of Ukrainian Famine Studies*, eds. Andrij Makuch and Frank E. Sysyn (Edmonton/Toronto: The CIUS Press, 2015).

88. On Soviet/Russian active measures in the realms of politics, culture, and memory, see Bertelsen, *Russian Active Measures*.

89. On the history of the World Congress of Ukrainians (SKU), prior to 1993 the SKVU, see O. H. Bazhan and O. O. Kovalchuk, "Svitovyi Konhres Ukraintsiv," *Entsyklopediia istorii Ukrainy*, t. 9 (Kyiv: "Naukova dumka," Instytut istorii Ukrainy, NANU, 2009), 479; also available at http://www.history.org.ua/?termin=Svitovyj_Konhres (accessed 3 July 2020).

90. On Fedorchuk's corruption and anti-Western stance, see Oleg Kalugin, *Spymaster: My Thirty-Two Years in Intelligence and Espionage against the West* (New York: Basic Books, 2009), 248–49, 353. Kalugin writes: "a Brezhnev hack, Vitaly Fedorchuk . . . was a rude, conceited bone crusher, bent on smashing internal dissent and tightening discipline within the KGB. He peppered KGB offices at home and abroad with ridiculous warnings of impending Western aggression, imperialist plots, and CIA efforts to destroy the Soviet economy."

91. HDA SBU, f. 16, op. 1, spr. 1063, ark. 226. For a reprinted edition, see Petro Stradnyk, *Pravda pro sovetsku vladu v Ukraini* (Kyiv: Tsentr navchalnoi literatury, 2019); Nikolai Gallii, *Organizovannyi golod v Ukraine 1932–1933 gg* (Chicago/New York: Ukrainskii publitsysticheskii institut, 1968).

92. HDA SBU, f. 16, op. 1, spr. 1063, ark. 227.

93. Ibid.; HDA SBU, f. 16, op. 1, spr. 1064, ark. 39.

94. On 23 September 1973, the Ukrainian Congress Committee of America organized major demonstrations to commemorate the Holodomor victims in Ukraine in 1932–1933. The commemorative events took place in major American and Canadian cities. See "Holodomor Remembrance Day," *The Holodomor Museum*, https://holodomormuseum.org.ua/en/holodomor-remembrance-day/ (accessed 7 November 2020); see also Ihor Dlaboha, "Thousands Rally in New York To Commemorate Kremlin-Made Famine in Ukraine," *Svoboda: The Ukrainian Weekly*, 29 September 1973, pp. 1, 3; also available at *The Ukrainian Weekly Archive*, 2020, http://ukrweekly.com/archive/pdf2/1973/The_Ukrainian_Weekly_1973-37.pdf (accessed 7 November 2020).

95. HDA SBU, f. 16, op. 1, spr. 1067, ark. 275.

96. HDA SBU, f. 16, op. 1, spr. 1106, ark. 51.

97. *Svoboda* was founded in New Jersey in 1893 by Father Hryhorii Hrushka. In 1894, the UNA adopted the newspaper as its organ.

98. Bertelsen, "Starvation and Violence," 38–67.

99. Some of the sources that discuss all three famines: *Holod v Ukraini u pershii polovyni XX stolittya: prychyny ta naslidky (1921–1923, 1932–1933, 1946–1947): Materialy Mizhnarodnoi naukovoi konferentsii, Kyiv, 20–21 lystopada 2013 r.* (Kyiv,

2013); O. M. Veselova, V. I. Marochko, and O. M. Movchan, eds., *Holodomory v Ukraini. 1921–1923, 1932–1933, 1946–1947: Zlochyny proty narodu* (Kyiv: Vyd-vo MP Kots, 2000). I am grateful to Victoria Malko for introducing these collections to me.

100. Nadia Diuk and Adrian Karatnycky, *The Hidden Nations: The People Challenge the Soviet Union* (New York: William Morrow and Company, Inc., 1990), 47.

101. Mark Harrison, "Why Secrets? The Uses of Secrecy in Stalin's Command Economy," *University of Warwick*, 10 October 2003, https://www.academia.edu/2865010/Why_secrets_The_uses_of_secrecy_in_Stalin_s_command_economy; and "Secrecy, Fear, and Transaction Costs," *University of Warwick*, 8 October 2010, https://www.academia.edu/2864919/Secrecy_Fear_and_Transaction_Costs_The_Business_of_Soviet_Forced_Labour_in_the_Early_Cold_War (accessed 5 July 2020); John Barber, Mark Harrison, Nikolai Simonov, and Boris Starkov, "The Structure and Development of the Soviet Defense-Industry Complex," in *The Soviet Defense-Industry Complex from Stalin to Khrushchev*, eds. John Barber and Mark Harrison (London: Macmillan, 2000), 3–32.

102. HDA SBU, f. 16, op. 1, spr. 1108, ark. 287–88.

103. HDA SBU, f. 16, op. 1, spr. 1108, ark. 287.

104. Ibid.

105. Bertelsen, "Political Affinities," 394–411.

106. On the Soviet gold trade, see Nikolai Krotov, "Gonka na zolotykh teltsakh," *Neprikosnovennyi zapas* 2, no. 52 (2007), http://magazines.russ.ru/nz/2007/2/kro13.html (accessed 22 April 2019).

107. Donald J. Novotny (interview by Allan Mustard), *The Association for Diplomatic Studies and Training*, 1 April 2009, https://www.adst.org/OH%20TOCs/Novotny,%20Donald.toc.pdf (accessed 21 April 2019), 10.

108. Novotny, *The Association for Diplomatic*, 3, 10–12.

109. This information came from Nikolai Patolichev, Minister of Foreign Trade and his First Deputy Mikhail Kuzmin who offered the United States an exchange of Soviet oil for grain.

110. Daniel Morgan, *Merchants of Grain: The Power and Profits of the Five Giant Companies at the Center of the World's Food Supply* (New York: Viking Adult, 1979).

111. HDA SBU, f. 16, op. 1, ark. 1119, ark. 164–65.

112. HDA SBU, f. 16, op. 1, ark. 1138, ark. 91–92. These notes were made by the Americans during their working trips to Kharkiv, Zaporizhzhia, Simferopol, Kyiv, Odesa, Chernivtsi, and Vinnytsia.

113. The full title of the film is *Harvest of Despair: The Man-Made Famine of 1932–1933 in Ukraine* (1985) by Slavko Nowytskj and Yurij Luhovy (Toronto, ON, Canada); the video available at *Ukrainian Canadian Research and Documentation Center*, http://www.ucrdc.org/Film-Harvest_of_Despair.html (accessed 18 December 2019); James E. Mace and Leonid Heretz, eds., *Investigation of the Ukrainian Famine, 1932–1933: Oral History Project of the Commission on the Ukraine Famine* (Washington, DC: U.S. Government Printing Office, 1990); *International*

Commission of Inquiry Into the 1932–33 Famine in Ukraine: The Final Report, Stockholm, Sweden/Stockholm Institute of Public and International Law, no. 109, 1990, *The Wayback Machine Internet Archive*, 2020, https://web.archive.org/web/20081001225745/http://www.ukrainianworldcongress.org/Holodomor/Holodomor-Commission.pdf (accessed 7 November 2020).

114. HDA SBU, f. 16, op. 1, spr. 1225, ark. 193–94.

115. Ibid.

116. Ibid.

117. For the specific prizes awarded to the documentary, see *Harvest of Despair, Ukrainian Canadian Research and Documentation Center*, http://www.ucrdc.org/Film-Harvest_of_Despair.html (accessed 18 December 2019).

118. Paul N. Edwards, *The Closed World: Computers and the Politics of Discourse in Cold War America* (Cambridge, MA: The MIT Press, 1997).

119. For an allusion to these experiences and psychological healing, see Artress, *Walking a Sacred Path*, 36–37.

120. See Lenin's 17 May 1922 letter to Dmitrii Kurskii, the first Soviet prosecutor, in V. I. Lenin, *Polnoie sobraniie sochinenii*, vol. 45 (Moskva: IPL, 1970), 190.

121. Jill A. Edy, "The Presence of the Past in Public Discourse," in *Politics, Discourse, and American Society*, eds. Roderick P. Hart and Bartholomew H. Sparrow (New York: Rowman & Littlefield Publishers, Inc., 2001), 62–63.

122. Oxana Shevel, "Memories of the Past and Visions of the Future Remembering the Soviet Era and Its End in Ukraine," in Bernhard and Kubik, 147; Taras Kuzio and Andrew Wilson, *Ukraine: Perestroika to Independence* (New York: Palgrave Macmillan, 1994), 161.

123. Solodko, "Yak pysaty pro Holodomor."

Chapter 6

The Years of Timelessness

"THE JEWISH QUESTION" UNDER ANDROPOV

In October 1964, on holiday away from Moscow, Khrushchev, whose Thaw loosened political and cultural controls, was toppled by a Presidium coup. For the next decade, observing the rise of dissent and nationalist sentiment, Khrushchev's conservative colleagues tried to reverse his partial de-Stalinization. Alexander J. Motyl has aptly noted that the Thaw had a side effect: "[n]ot only did it create the dissidents, it also politicized them. . . . Many Ukrainians and other non-Russians not unreasonably concluded that republican rights were inauthentic, that the Soviet state was in fact a Russian state, and that political independence was the only guarantee of their nations' cultural and political development."[1] Khrushchev's anti-Jewish policies, including a *numerus clausus*[2] that was introduced in all Soviet universities, were reinforced under Brezhnev who replaced Khrushchev as the general secretary of the Communist Party of the USSR and returned to a "watered-down version of Stalinism," granting special powers to the KGB.[3]

Because of enduring traditions of state antisemitism and the anti-Zionist campaign launched in the 1960s, the Jews were persecuted and prosecuted, suspected of alleged links with Israel (often fictitious) and nationalist conspiracies.[4] The intelligentsia was especially vulnerable. In 2002 in his memoirs, Vladimir Semichastnyi, head of the KGB from 1961 to 1967 and a deputy prime minister in the UkrSSR from 1967 to 1981, suggested that Moscow had always been suspicious of the intelligentsia in Ukraine, and the nationalist question was so sensitive that Kremlin officials preferred to exaggerate the threat of nationalism and separatism emanating from Ukraine, rather than underestimate it.[5] Jews were the main focus of the KGB Second Chief Directorate that dealt with the *refuseniks*, and the First Chief Directorate was in charge of covert operations abroad designed to create a rift among major world Jewish organizations. The KGB leadership believed that these operations would undermine their anti-Soviet human rights movement and their assistance to the Soviet Zionist movement.

Yaakov Kedmi, who headed Nativ[6] from 1992 to 1999, has posited that, indeed, for the Soviet Union, the Zionist movement was a "key enemy," and

> the harsh anti-Jewish approach was shaped by Andropov more than anyone. The first reason for this approach was personal: Andropov was not one-quarter Jewish, one-third Jewish or half Jewish. He was Jewish, period. I heard it from senior KGB people. Andropov knew that the party's leadership was well aware of that, and some of them were infected with anti-Semitic racist attitudes. In order to prove that he was uninfluenced by his Jewish descent, and that he was genuinely pure when it came to that matter, he took the most radical line.[7]

In May 1967, Yurii Andropov was appointed head of the KGB, toughening anti-Jewish policies and launching domestic operations against Ukrainian nationalists and "Zionists." On 25 December 1970, supported by the Soviet Communist Party's Central Committee secretaries Mikhail Suslov and Ivan Kapitonov, Andropov issued a memorandum on limiting the receipt of foreign correspondence by Khrushchev who led the quiet life of a pensioner. One of the reasons for that was that Khrushchev received thousands of letters of support in which he was mistakenly portrayed and thanked as an "opponent of anti-Semitism."[8] To prevent potential criticisms from one of his former superiors and to silence the topic of state antisemitism, Andropov proposed the lustration of Khrushchev's correspondence to avoid the painful topic that could have potentially spilled from Khrushchev's home over into the public sphere. By the mid-1970s, Andropov significantly curtailed communication links, including phone calls, between Soviet Jews and their relatives abroad, and complicated Jewish emigration to Israel.

The prehistory of Stalin's anti-Jewish campaigns and the KGB's post-Stalin anti-Zionist campaign encouraged a group of young Kharkiv Jews to act. They realized that their cultural traditions, including their language, had been systematically erased through the Soviet anti-Jewish policies. Indeed, a significant decline of Yiddish speakers in the Soviet Union occurred between 1959 and 1970. Moreover, the 1970 census official statistics demonstrated that during this period one could observe an unprecedented drop in Jewish population. Among other reasons, fear of persecution and popular antisemitism drove Soviet Jews to conceal their Jewish identity.[9] In 1970 in Kharkiv, only 7.7 percent of the Jews identified Yiddish as their mother tongue; the majority of Jewish Kharkivites (92 percent) listed Russian as their mother tongue, and only 0.3 percent listed Ukrainian as their mother tongue.[10] According to the deputy chairman of the Council of Religious Affairs in the Soviet Union, of the 5,000 synagogues that existed in the USSR only 200 were functioning in 1976. Out of these 200, only ninety-two were officially registered as synagogues, forcing other 108 into the underground.[11] As a result, Kharkiv Jews, including writers, developed a "thin" (amorphous) Jewish culture and identity in the post-Stalin years.[12] Yet their national consciousness was stimulated by the 1967 Arab-Israeli war, "thickening" the Jewish aspect of their identity. They began to feel themselves Jewish. The Kharkiv critic Grigorii Gelfandbein's self-evaluation in 1967 was symptomatic of this trend: "For the first time, I feel proud to be Jewish."[13] Yet, Gelfandbein's suffering under Stalin's and Khrushchev's antisemitic campaigns taught him a lesson, and he revealed his thoughts only in a close circle of friends.[14] Nevertheless, these sentiments almost immediately became known to the KGB because of their agents' massive infiltration into the Kharkiv writers' circles.

Young poets and students of Kharkiv University, especially those who attended literary studios led by Gelfandbein and Chichibabin, were subjects of the KGB's surveillance. A gifted poet of Jewish origin Aleksandr Vernik, Chichibabin's student and an attendee of his literary studio, expressed his criticism of the Soviets' occupation of Czechoslovakia in 1968 in the company of his friends and among colleagues he trusted: "I hate everything here; if I had an automatic weapon, I would kill everyone here; if I were in Israel, at least I would [direct this hatred] and give my life for freedom."[15] The KGB received a report from an informer, whose identity remains unknown, about Vernik's escapade. Vernik was immediately placed under surveillance and was fortunate to avoid Soviet camps and emigrate to Israel a decade later, in 1978.[16]

In June 1969, the Kharkiv KGB uncovered a group of six individuals (one of Russian and five of Jewish origin) who were students of Kharkiv universities, including Kharkiv University's Philology Department. According to Vitalii Nikitchenko, KGB chairman in Ukraine, they allegedly planned to expand their group to a hundred people and change the regime in the Soviet Union through an armed rebellion, subsequently conducting economic and political reforms.[17] Anatolii Aushev, Mark Lotkin, Sofia Kats, Nonna Khait, Isaak Ganzman, and Boris Preshman were searching for people who would help them raise sufficient funds and establish the manufacturing of firearms to move forward with their ambitious plot. The group planned that their organization would be divided into smaller detachments of five people that, when the time was ripe, would take control over various strategic institutions, and composed lists of those who must be arrested first. In Kharkiv, for instance, they planned to hijack the headquarters of the Kharkiv *obkom*, the City Council of People's Deputies, the KGB and the militia headquarters (MVS), the radio and television centers, and the major newspapers' headquarters, and to arrest 25–30 party and KGB leaders of the Kharkiv oblast.[18] According to KGB operational materials, during their illegal meetings, the members of this anti-Soviet group discussed Soviet internal and foreign policies, particularly the issue of state antisemitism and Soviet nationalities policy. All six individuals were arrested and interrogated separately. During his interrogation, the leader of the group, Aushev, confessed that state antisemitism in the Soviet Union served as the foundation for their grievances and wishes to change the Soviet one-party regime.[19] Instead of emigrating, they wished to build a decent life in the Soviet Union, where Jews, Ukrainians, and other national minorities would have an opportunity to develop and nurture their cultural traditions. After lengthy interrogations of all members of the group, KGB associates claimed that all members of the group sincerely repented, which prompted the KGB leadership to avoid extremes, choosing "soft" punishments instead: the members of the group were expelled from the universities; in addition, the KGB informed their parents' employers about the transgressions and obliged them to hold meetings at their respective institutions about how to raise the Soviet youth.[20] The KGB attributed these anti-Soviet and "Zionist" tendencies to the successful work of "Zionist bourgeois centers" and their propaganda, and continued the surveillance of the alleged rebels.[21] The Kharkiv KGB leadership informed the KGB in Kyiv and Moscow about the "Jewish problem" in Kharkiv.

What inspired Aushev, an ethnic Russian, to join a group of frustrated Jews remains unclear. Possibly, beyond sharing political views, they all developed similar cultural and literary affinities, and Kharkiv literary studios established under the umbrella of the Writers' Union became those environments that nurtured not only their literary gifts but also their critical and independent thinking. Attended by people of various ethnic and cultural backgrounds, these clubs became a serious problem for the Kharkiv KGB, and the agency used the slightest pretext to shut them down.

Moreover, in the late 1960s and early 1970s, Kharkiv's Jewish activists, mostly the intelligentsia, strengthened their ties with Moscow Jews and systematically joined them in the capital, protesting Soviet emigration policies. Moreover, in winter and spring of 1973, a group of young Kharkiv Jews, including Leonid (Yona) Kolchinsky, known to the KGB as a young rebellious poet and troublemaker who "had spoken openly on behalf of Daniel and Siniavskii and publicly condemned Soviet intervention in Czechoslovakia,"[22] sent a letter to the *New York Times*, appealing for help to Henry Kissinger and to New York's mayor John Lindsay and denouncing Jewish emigration policies.[23] The Kharkiv KGB made Kolchinsky's high school leadership expel him and instructed the employers of other members of the group to fire them from their jobs for their political activism and revoke their visa applications to permanently emigrate to Israel. The gravity of punishment for local "Zionists," chosen by the KGB, varied, from "prophylactic talks" and "administrative detention" to forcible "treatment" in the Saburova Dacha and sentencing them to two and a half years of imprisonment under the "Ukrainian equivalent of Russian Article 190-1 (anti-Soviet slander)."[24] Often they were placed in city militia prisons for "hooliganism" for fifteen days. Some "veterans" served several terms there, but their militancy and persistence eventually bore fruit. All of them received emigration visas, after enduring hunger strikes, making public appeals, attending meetings in the KGB, and suffering beatings in the militia local departments.[25] Scholar and lawyer Leonard Schroeter believed that state antisemitism, discrimination, persecution, and harassment brought them "to the end of the line. They cease[d] calculating the personal risk. They [became] politically suicidal."[26]

The former Kharkivite and human rights activist Larisa Bogoraz, who spent four years in a labor camp in Siberia for participating in the Red Square demonstration against the Soviet invasion of Czechoslovakia in 1968, stated:

> I love life, and I valued freedom. I fully realized that I would be risking my freedom, and it was something I didn't want to lose. But I was faced with the choice of acting or remaining silent. Had I remained silent, it would have meant giving support to an action that I cannot condone. It would have amounted to the same thing as lying. I do not consider my course the only right one. But for me it was the only possible one.[27]

The dissident activities brought together a Jew, Bogoraz, and a Ukrainian, Anatoly Marchenko, the author of *My Testimony*. This book in which Marchenko told the truth about Soviet camps that did not disappear after Stalin's death was published in the West in 1969. For the international community, it became transparently clear that the change after Stalin was "mainly a quantitative one. While the prisoners under Stalin were numbered in millions, they are now numbered in tens (or hundreds?) of thousands."[28] Bogoraz was not only Marchenko's wife and the mother of their son, Pavel, but also his faithful supporter, his friend, and a like-minded person. After her return to Moscow from Siberia, she soon left the capital to be near exiled Anatoly. Despite the exceptionally difficult life Bogoraz chose for herself, she continued her political activities, participating in publishing and distributing *samizdat* and various dissident public actions, attracting attention from society and the authorities. In 1975, she wrote a letter to Andropov, demanding the opening of the KGB archive.[29] Marchenko spent twenty years in prison and died on 8 December 1986 after a three-month hunger strike in the Chistopol Prison, Tatarstan, RSFSR, two months before Gorbachev, on Andrei Sakharov's insistence, issued a decree, pardoning political prisoners. In February 1987, after Ronald Reagan and Margaret Thatcher intervened,

140 prisoners of conscience who had been sentenced for various terms in labor camps for conducting "anti-Soviet agitation and propaganda" were released, including the former Kharkivite psychiatrist Anatoly Koryagin, the religious dissident and Gulag survivor Aleksandr Ogorodnikov, and the *refusenik*, writer, and political activist Iosif Begun.[30] In December 1986, Larisa Bogoraz wrote:

> Anatoly Marchenko died in battle. For him, that battle had begun a quarter of a century earlier, and he had never—never—raised the white flag of truce. For twenty of those twenty-five years, his battle was waged in prison cells, camp barracks, internal exile. Anatoly could have lived free, but he deliberately chose prison. He chose prison so others would live in freedom.[31]

The late Kharkiv-Israeli writer and journalist Feliks Rakhlin identified the 1970s as the "years of timelessness" (*gody bezvremenia*), and the Kharkiv-Czech poet and journalist Mykola Shatylov—as the "cursed seventies" (*kliati simdesiaty*).[32] They lived through these times and left unforgettable accounts of literary Kharkiv under the thumb of the KGB. The Kharkiv literati were "managed" by KGB people, as one KGB officer stated, as they managed information and, ultimately, society. Discourses were so regimented and legal notions were so loosely defined that they were effectively employed by the *chekists* and functioned as tools of suppression and social control. The KGB's powers and its "overpowering presence in Soviet society" served as a societal straightjacket which was not challengeable, ensuring state stability.[33] The party encouraged and nurtured the KGB's sadism and cruelty, which became an overt tactic and strategy, helping the *chekists* maintain the Soviet system.

The KGB's "Helping Hands"

The Fifth Congress of Ukraine's Writers held on 16–20 November 1966 in Kyiv, the Dziuba "affair," publication of Oles Honchar's *Sobor* (The Cathedral) in January 1968, and a petition to Brezhnev, Kosygin, and Pidhornyi signed by 139 intellectuals, students, and workers protesting the trials of 1965–1966 in Ukraine provoked serious concerns among Moscow and Kyiv party and KGB officials. They realized that Ukraine's writers had no intentions of diluting the standards of Ukrainian literature and their cultural traditions.[34] The January 1970 plenary session of the Board of the Writers' Union held in Kyiv confirmed their fears: Pavlo Zahrebelnyi reported on the subversive status of the Ukrainian literary product, and called for closer ties with foreign writers and publishers, and for more translations of foreign works into Ukrainian.[35] To divert the writers' attention from this "progressive" thinking and to remind them about the foundational *partiinost* principle of Soviet literature to which the writers should adhere, the Central Committee suggested holding another plenary session of the Board of the Writers' Union in Kharkiv, under the Kharkiv KGB's watchful eye. The subject of this session was telling: "The Working Man in Soviet Ukrainian Literature." It was held on 18–19 November 1970, and led by the secretary of the Writers' Union Vasyl Kozachenko, a prose writer and a candidate for the Central Committee of the Communist Party of Ukraine who arrived from Kyiv. He stressed the significance of the notion of classes to literature and "warned against the illusion of 'creating a literature that stands above classes.'"[36] Boris Kotliarov, a poet and the secretary of the primary party cell of the Kharkiv chapter of the Writers' Union, enthusiastically supported the notion, and assured the Board that the Kharkiv chapter would work on the ideological growth of Kharkiv writers. Soon the editorial boards of the Kharkiv literary journal *Prapor* and its publishing house were restructured, and the KGB had serious conversations with their "assets" who were supposed to amplify their efforts and to accurately report on the atmosphere in the Writers' Union and the content of planned publications in *Prapor*.[37]

The professional activities of "Ukrainian nationalists" and "Zionists," the Union's members, were closely monitored, especially those who earned the reputation of "progressive thinkers" and "reformists." They were investigated (*razrabatyvalis*) by special groups and departments, since 1969—by the newly created Fifth Chief Directorate established to counter political dissidents. As mentioned earlier, the Fifth Chief Directorate was formed due to Andropov's initiative and included the elements of the Second Chief Directorate, the Ninth Department responsible for Soviet students, the Tenth Department responsible for the Soviet intelligentsia, and the Jewish Department. Each KGB operative from the Fifth Chief Directorate that surveilled the intelligentsia had on average from seven to ten informers who methodically listened to the writers' conversations in cultural institutions, the Writers' Union, and its literary sections, conveying their content to their handlers.[38]

On 10 March 1970, the head of Ukraine's KGB Vitalii Nikitchenko wrote a report to the Central Committee about the intelligentsia's reaction to a press conference for Soviet and foreign journalists on the situation in the Middle East.[39] The Soviet authorities used this conference as a platform for several representatives of the Jewish intelligentsia who were encouraged (likely forced into submission) to condemn the Israeli government and its Prime Minister Golda Meer for their interference in the Soviet Union's internal affairs and Jewish immigration policy. Boris Kotliarov was quoted in this report and presented to Shelest in a favorable light, in contrast to other Jews who identified this conference as an "act of shame and violence."[40] Kotliarov claimed that the press conference was a success, and the "entire world learned that the Jewish question as a political problem did not exist in the Soviet

Union. It is being imposed on us from outside, serving reactionary forces as a vehicle to provoke us."[41] As many of his colleagues suggested, Kotliarov seemed to be confused in terms of his identity, pushing his residual Jewish identity into the back of his mind. He did what he was told to do or what was consistent with the party line. According to many accounts, Kotliarov was successfully recruited by the KGB in the 1930s.[42] Having a Jewish mother, he felt vulnerable and settled for a calmer and easier life under the KGB's wing, which promised handsome incentives, such as professional promotions and publications in exchange for information about his colleagues' views. By the 1960s, Kotliarov was considered one of the Kharkiv celebrities and literary dignitaries, and even Mikhail Svetlov, a brilliant poet and uncompromised critic, published a panegyric in *Literaturnaia gazeta*, praising Kotliarov's mediocre poetry to the surprise of Kotliarov's colleagues.[43]

Kotliarov began his literary career in Kharkiv as a promising young poet before the Second World War, but his service as a secret agent (*seksot* or informer) destroyed his reputation and, apparently, his literary gift. Poetry connoisseurs complained that "it was impossible to read his poetry."[44] Kharkiv, and later Moscow, poet Zinovii Valshonok dedicated a poem to Kotliarov's mediocre books and his bifurcated identity. The poem began: "Remove your hats: the books have died . . ." and ended with the exclamation: "Oh, no, it's better to bite the dust from a heart attack than follow the hearse with untimely deceased books!"[45] Boris Chichibabin engraved Kotliarov's name in one of his poems, albeit as a code name but quite recognizable because of its phonetic similarity to Kotliarov's full name:

I was warming myself in the blizzards
from the flames of revolutionary bonfires.
And was routinely denounced
By Paris Zhuanych Kotelkov.

Ia grelsia v snezhnye zanosy
U Revoliutsii kostrov,
I na menia pisal donosy
Paris Zhuanych Kotelkov.[46]

Likely, Kotliarov read or heard Chichibabin's lines, and might have played a role in Chichibabin's persecution.

Kotliarov preserved his loyalty to the system to the very end. Even during the Thaw, he was extremely careful. In 1963, under the patronage of the Writers' Union and the nonofficial patronage of its party chief Kotliarov, the bookstore "Poeziia" in Pushkinska Street was opened, a store that has been mentioned in a dozen memoirs and accounts of Soviet writers, including

Eduard Limonov and Yevgenii Yevtushenko. The store's atmosphere nurtured by the Thaw quickly established its all-Soviet fame, popularity, and traditions. Public readings of unpublished poetry by well-established poets became one of its traditions. Arkadii Filatov, Aleksandr Cherevchenko, Marlena Rakhlina, Boris Chichibabin, Ushangi Rezhinashvili, Anatolii Zhitnitskii, David Samoilov, Viktor Urin, and Konstantin Vanshenkin read their poems for hours inside and outside the store in front of large crowds of people. At the peak of the Thaw, poetry evenings in Moscow's Polytechnical Institute became a routine, and the Kharkiv party and Komsomol *obkom*s allowed "Poeziia" to hold poetry evenings in the store.[47] In 1966, Yevtushenko visited Kharkiv and asked the girls working in the store about the tradition. They confirmed the "rumors." They agreed that he would come next day during their break and read his new poems. The store was rather small and could not hold all those who came the next day to listen to Yevtushenko's poems. He read them outside the store for five hours, and those who remember that day claim that there were nearly 10,000 people, passersby who stopped to listen the poet's declamations. Kotliarov who knew about the gathering in advance and understood its ramifications told the girls: "See, no one should know that I was here. I will be walking in the vicinity of the store with a woman: in case something happens, I will have a witness who can confirm that I was not here."[48]

The participation in "Poeziia's" evenings and the arrest of Yulii Daniel and Andrei Siniavskii in 1966 undermined the reputation of many Kharkivites who were close to Daniel. Mark Bogoslavskii, Arkadii Filatov, Marlena Rakhlina, and Boris Chichibabin, who wrote in Russian, were affected significantly by their friendship with Daniel. Publishers denied their publications, and the writers began to receive rejection letters from "thick" literary magazines. There is evidence to suggest that Kotliarov was guilty as charged: one of the editors of the Kyiv literary journal *Raduga*, published in Kyiv in Russian, secretly informed Rakhlina that Kotliarov who sat on *Raduga*'s board sent a letter to its editor-in-chief, denouncing Rakhlina, Chichibabin, and Bogoslavskii as friends of anti-Soviet Daniel, and thus publication of their poems in *Raduga* would be terribly inappropriate.[49] In 1999, one of the KGB lieutenants who worked for the KGB Fifth Directorate in Kharkiv confessed that his supervisor told him: "It's time to do something about this Jewish gang" (*zhidovskoie kodlo*).[50] The publication ban lasted approximately two decades, omitting their names from the official history of Soviet literary Kharkiv.

Functioning as KGB assets shaped the lives of several Kharkiv literati in a variety of ways. Throughout their careers, they lived under the shadow of the powerful and imperious agency, wandering through the labyrinths of guilt and self-justification, a Kafkian dilemma that might have tortured them by its insolvability. The difference between them and Kafka seemed to lay not only in the degree of their literary talents but also in their self-perception: Kafka, amid personal oppression and the domination of his abusive father, understood the time and place in which he lived, and his own role in them. However, creating masterpieces, Kafka doubted his talent.[51] Turning into literary dignitaries due to KGB connections, Kharkiv writers like Kotliarov developed delusion of grandeur, "shrinking" as writers. Living in their pasts and memories about their promising youth, their literary talents faded away with every denunciation, draining them morally and intellectually.

Literary Kharkiv during Late Socialism

By late 1971, the *samvydav* movement grew substantially in Ukraine, and in late December 1971, the Union's Central Committee issued a secret resolution to "silence dissent and quash the growing samizdat movement."[52] The Kremlin blamed Shelest and his leniency toward nationalists and made the decision to replace Ukrainians in key positions of power with people loyal to Moscow.[53] Leonid Brezhnev prepared the ground for Shelest's removal in advance. In July 1970, he appointed Vitalii Fedorchuk as head of Ukraine's KGB, replacing Vitalii Nikitchenko who had adopted Shelest's moderate approach to punishing dissent.[54] In June–July of 1972, Moscow blamed Shelest for supporting the Ukrainian intelligentsia and ultimately fomenting dissent, and replaced him with Shcherbytskyi who was considered more loyal to Moscow than Shelest.[55] In October 1972, the Central Committee in Moscow alerted all members of the Politburo and its candidates that over the last five years in various Soviet republics, including Ukraine, nearly 3,096 nationalist organized groups were identified and 13,602 members of these groups were reprimanded.[56] Immediately after replacing Shelest as the first party secretary of Ukraine, Shcherbytskyi positioned himself as a fighter against nationalists. In the fall of 1972, the crackdown on dissent in Ukraine intensified after Shcherbytskyi promoted Valentyn Malanchuk to ideological chief and secretary of the Central Committee.[57] Immediately after appointing Malanchuk, on 11 October 1972, Shcherbytskyi signed a top-secret resolution about the intensification of struggle against nationalism. The Malanchuk era is associated with the broad scope of repression and KGB operations designed to curb Ukrainian nationalism.[58] The apartments of many Kharkiv writers were searched, and many writers were questioned and subjected to extra-judicial forms of pressure.

Shelest was transferred to Moscow as one of the deputy chairmen of the USSR Council of Ministers, but in April 1973 was publicly humiliated and denounced for his idealization of the Ukrainian past and promoting nationalism in Ukraine. The Politburo forced him to retire, placing him under house arrest, and the KGB closely monitored his family's movements. Later, Brezhnev admitted to Shelest that Mikhail Suslov, a hard-liner on nationalities policy, was behind the campaign against Shelest, and his dismissal was implemented on Suslov's orders.[59] The KGB offensive of 1972–1973 in Ukraine resulted in hundreds of arrests among the intelligentsia. On 21 December 1972, in his keynote address at the celebration of the fiftieth anniversary of the establishment of the Soviet Union, Brezhnev declared that the nationality question in the Soviet Union "had been solved completely, definitely and irrevocably."[60]

However, the issue of human rights violations in the Soviet Union persisted, and Moscow dissidents established the Helsinki Group in May 1976, and six months later Ukrainian activists founded the Ukrainian Helsinki Group (UHH) in Kyiv to monitor the implementation of the 1975 Helsinki Accords. The two chapters effectively cooperated in publicizing the knowledge about violations of human rights in the Soviet Union, later overlapping with the Andrei Sakharov circle and establishing contacts abroad.[61] On 13 December 2001, on the jubilee of the UHH that was celebrated on 8–10 November 2001 in Kyiv, Inna Sukhorukova, member of the Kharkiv Group for Human Rights Protection, wrote:

> The journalists, mainly young people, were sitting in the hall side by side with old political prisoners. Some of them did prison terms counted in decades. The total prison term of 43 members of the UHH is more than 550 years. Such figures were unthinkable of in any other republic of the former Soviet Union. On the one hand, the reason was the extreme cruelty of the Ukrainian KGB, on the other hand—the intrepid courage and self-sacrifice of the UHH members. In fact the UHH members firmly knew that they would be arrested and convicted. Even those, who were ill and physically weak, for whom a prison term meant a death verdict—Marchenko, Stus, Tykhiy—entered the group without hesitation. They did it to inform the whole world that neither the freedom of speech, nor the freedom of public organizations, or the rights of national organizations existed in the USSR.[62]

The pressure of the Helsinki Groups in the Soviet Union, Amnesty International, and activists of the anti-Soviet human rights movement in the West forced the KGB to search for punishments other than imprisonment of dissidents. Hunger strikes, petitions, and literary works of political prisoners smuggled from prisons to the West attracted too much attention from the international community. Vladimir Bukovsky wrote that in the 1970s "the authorities preferred other means, from psychiatric confinement and defamatory campaigns ('compromising' people, as *chekists* called it) to expulsion abroad."[63]

The Kharkiv space of dissent was represented by official literary studios organized under the auspices of the Writers' Union and led by Mykola

Shapoval, Geldfandbein, and Chichibabin. Yet, there were other nonofficial literary "saloons"—kitchens of poets' private apartments. One such place was the apartment of Andrii Chernyshov who served as head of the prose department in the journal *Prapor* and later was the main aide of *Prapor*'s chief editor. The Kharkiv scholar, writer, and a member of Writers' Union Ihor Mykhailyn has noted that Chernyshov was a "reservoir of memory about the literary process of the preceding decades who deeply understood the essence and capabilities of the totalitarian regime, and its anti-Ukrainian vector."[64] What was unique about Chernyshov's place is that it attracted multiethnic young writers and talented poets from all over Ukraine. Among his frequent guests were Natalka Bilotserkivets, Mykhailo Shevchenko, Boris Chichibabin, Volodymyr Zatulyviter, Volodymyr Briuggen, and Natalka Nikulina.[65] The atmosphere of this place strengthened the links between Jews, Ukrainians, and Russians, oriented to experimentation and innovations. Yet publishing opportunities for these innovations were murky. Kharkiv censors thoroughly regimented them, marginalizing especially those who embraced national self-identification. Chernyshov was routinely ordered to make an appearance at the KGB headquarters for "prophylactic" talks.

For Robert Tretyakov, the 1970s and the suffocating atmosphere in *Prapor* deepened his inner crises. Forcible silence and poems dedicated to the International Workers' Day, 1 May, and other Soviet holidays, commissioned by the authorities, made Tretyakov's life unbearable. The local authorities and the Kharkiv *obkom* organized routine meetings, to which they invited the representatives of cultural institutions, newspapers, and journals. Tretyakov, as the secretary of the primary party cell in the journal *Prapor*, was a regular guest there and maintained close correspondence with local party chiefs.[66] Systematic reminders about the meetings scheduled by *obkom* functionaries that barely masked attempts at intimidation shaped his activities as an editor and as head of the poetry department in *Prapor*. He was supposed to thoroughly filter poems, in which there were themes alluding to drama, tragedy, Ukrainian patriotism, or Ukrainian identity. The authors who touched on those topics and who wanted to be published in *Prapor* received Tretyakov's rejection letters, polite in form and adamant in content.[67]

In contrast, the workers' themes were welcomed. The Kharkiv *obkom* leaders allocated additional funds for the Litfond that sponsored special meetings between the members of the Writers' Union and the workers of Kharkiv factories. In the view of *obkom*'s functionaries, this exchange was to be mutually beneficial: the workers were supposed to be inspired by optimistic poetry, and the writers were to draw inspiration for their creative work from observing the workers' successes. Interestingly, beyond ideological implications, these meetings became a source of survival for the writers. The opportunity to earn additional income by reading poetry was a form of co-optation from the local authorities who wanted little in exchange, the writers' obedient behavior. According to some interviews, the chief of the Kharkiv Litfond Yelena Lukashova who, according to several accounts, reported to the KGB, established distribution patterns consistent with the party's injunctions: the official writers were honored by the greatest number of trips locally and out of the republic; the "rebels" with ideologically questionable reputations received little from the Litfond.[68] Tretyakov's personal frustration caused by Lukashova's affiliation and her vulgar interpretation of the ideological value of each writer was occasionally revealed at home. His passionate monologues lasted approximately a minute: it took him that long to realize that the KGB might be listening. Only one of the oldest Ukrainian writers Ivan Bahmut could afford to publicly rebel against party orders and the system of the writers' co-optation that did not seem subtle to him at all. Bahmut systematically criticized the party demands to employ the workers' theme in the writers' work. "Do not force the writers to write on the workers' topic; let them come to it naturally."[69]

In the late 1960s and early 1970s, Tretyakov, together with his fellow writers, traveled regularly all over the Soviet Union, reading his poetry and meeting with the workers and the intelligentsia of other Soviet republics. At the peak of repressions in 1972, the Writers' Union sent him to Siberia to enlighten and to Sovietize the peoples of Yakutiia through patriotic poetry (Fig. 6.1). It is difficult to say whether the older generation of writers tried to protect Tretyakov from observing the repression of his colleagues and to keep him from the clutches of the KGB. Possibly, this initiative emanated from the *obkom* that planned to simply use him as a propaganda tool. Several attempts at establishing the source of this initiative failed, but what became clear is that Tretyakov's trip to Yakutsk, a Russian port city on the Lena River in east Siberia, triggered a cascade of personal crises for him. He did not or could not reject the offer and embarked on a physically challenging and lengthy trip to Siberia, which spatially and morally removed him from Ukraine at the peak of raging KGB repressions.

Upon his arrival home from Yakutsk, he was hospitalized in a Kharkiv psychiatric clinic, "Saburova Dacha," where the authorities typically isolated confused individuals and opponents of the regime.[70] Intense discussions about the terror against the Ukrainian intelligentsia with his colleagues during the trip, massive doses of alcohol, hallucinations, and fear of arrest resulted in a nervous breakdown. He continued to believe in socialist values, but his faith in the party was undermined by his recognition of the imperfections and lies that permeated the system. Tretyakov was characterized by his colleagues as a brave man, but his fears, chronically reinforced by Kharkiv party bosses and the KGB, generated a mental condition that could be treated only by specialists. Coincidentally, during his two stays in psychiatric clinics in

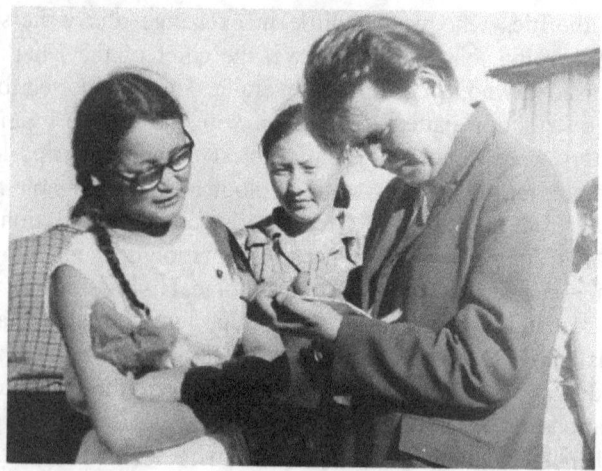

Figure 6.1 Robert Tretyakov Is Signing His Book. Yakutsk, 1972. *Source*: RTPA; a copy is located in the TsDAMLIMU, f. 712, op. 1, spr. 6, ark. 1.

1972 and 1979 where he was hospitalized with visual and hearing hallucinations, "*chekists* were crawling from all corners," as Tretyakov noted. The phantasmagoric plots, in which a KGB officer was trying to hit him with a metal pipe from behind and a group of other KGB lieutenants persistently following him, were very vivid, he stated. He understood that they were the fruits of his imagination, but his attempts to prevent the hallucinations on his own resulted in failure.[71] Tretyakov also realized that this was not only his "medical" problem. As he kept repeating, "Let's treat the dampness, not its result—the mold."[72] Polonskyi believed that Tretyakov's intellectual and mental crises resulted from his rejection of society's norms and rules, his family situation, and his internal perception that he was trapped by these circumstances and therefore finished as a writer.[73]

In the early 1970s, despite strong Cold War rhetoric and hostile attitudes toward the West and the United States in particular, the preceding Khrushchev era and détente generated a space in which cultural contacts among Soviet and Western intellectuals became possible, yet strictly regimented. The "enemy" (capitalists) had to be vigilantly observed, and at the same time their technological progress and cultural innovations were to be examined and emulated.[74] The cultural rapprochement between the United States and the USSR was gradual but cultural exchange opened the Soviet Union to information and ideas from the West, facilitating a dialogue between the two countries.[75] In August 1973, the Central Committee in Ukraine offered Tretyakov an opportunity to visit the United States as a member of the official delegation of Ukrainian writers in the format of cultural exchange. According to his wife Lidiya's diaries, he was approached by the leaders of the Kharkiv *obkom*, and this fact alone reveals the perceptions of the local party authorities about Tretyakov: apparently, after the "Siberian crisis," he managed to restore his reputation as a politically stable and reliable candidate for this mission.[76] Ironically, the economic situation of most Ukrainian writers in Kharkiv, conditioned by multiple state laws and stipulations that limited their ability to earn a decent living, made such a trip impossible for Tretyakov. Eager to see the United States, he simply could not afford the trip, although the party and the Writers' Union agreed to partially sponsor the mission. The attempt of the Tretyakov family to borrow the money necessary for the trip (800 rubles) ended in failure because his colleagues and relatives, equally impoverished, could hardly make ends meet.[77]

For the next three years, Tretyakov, like many other writers, continued to lead a turbulent existence, warning, when possible, his visitors at *Prapor*'s headquarters about KGB surveillance. To distract himself from gloomy realities, he decided to celebrate his fortieth birthday. On 26 February 1976, he arranged a big party in his new three-room apartment which he had received from the Writers' Union. The Tretyakov family moved from their two-room apartment in the Writers' House (*Budynok "Slovo"*) into a larger apartment downtown, which accommodated approximately fifty people on 26 February. Writers, actors, and artists came to congratulate him on his birthday. Lidiya was playing piano. The guests were relaxing and dancing. The KGB was working. His daughter who was only thirteen at the time received attention from an unknown man with dark eyes and salt-and-pepper hair who, in a playful manner, wanted to know about what topics she typically discussed with her father, and whether he brought friends home:

Man: Do they invite you to join their conversations?
Daughter: Sometimes.
Man: What are they talking about? You might be bored talking to adults?
Daughter: Not at all. They read poetry, and I enjoy it.
Man: They, probably, discuss some other interesting topics, don't they?
Daughter: Of course.
Man: Politics?
Daughter: Sometimes.

To the man's disappointment that he could hardly conceal, this conversation was interrupted by Radii Polonskyi, prose writer and Tretyakov's friend, who invited Tretyakov's daughter to dance. Polonskyi suggested to her that for the rest of the evening she should sit closer to her parents and avoid "interrogations."

In 1977, Tretyakov once again was named poet-laureate. He was awarded the Pavlo Tychyna Prize for his new collection of poetry *Merydiany kriz sertse* (Meridians through My Heart), and the local party leaders sent him congratulatory letters and telegrams.[78] But by 1979, he relapsed into alcohol abuse and hallucinations. His relationship with his wife and his children deteriorated.[79] His son confronted him about his alcohol abuse, and his daughter stopped speaking with him after he caught her in her room, secretly listening to the radio station *The Voice of America* which broadcast Nabokov's *Lolita*.[80] He took from her the radio "Rigonda," and stated that she might understand why when she grew up.[81]

Through translations of Western authors and cultural trips abroad, Kharkiv writers were introduced to Western narratives and cultural trends. Tretyakov's first trip outside the Soviet Union and his introduction to the West occurred in 1977, when, as part of the Ukrainian delegation, he traveled to Bulgaria to attend the Festival of Bulgarian and Soviet Friendship. Scholars who conducted research in the Stasi archive in Berlin discovered that there was an intense collaboration between the KGB and the Bulgarian and Hungarian secret services, "particularly with regard to the surveillance of citizens traveling to each other's countries." In this context, it is clear that Tretyakov's trip to Bulgaria was closely monitored.[82] The interaction between Ukrainian and Western intellectuals also became a reality in Kharkiv. Tretyakov's colleagues Yurii Stadnychenko and Volodymyr Briuggen broke the ice, translating from Polish, French, and English and publishing texts of Western authors in Ukraine and the Russian Federation. In 1978, Stadnychenko was allowed to invite the Polish writer Stanisław Supłatowicz to Kharkiv, known under his pen name Sat-Okh, whose autobiographical novels about the 1930's Shawnee in the Northwestern Territories Stadnychenko translated into Ukrainian and published in various Ukrainian publishing houses. Sat-Okh was born in Canada to a Polish mother and a Shawnee father, moving to Poland with his mother before the Second World War. Supłatowicz was a soldier in the Polish Resistance during the war and might have been an undesirable guest in the Soviet Union because of his potential knowledge and memories of what the Red Army, the NKVD, and the SMERSH did to Polish soldiers who were members of the resistance movement. Surveilled 24 hours per day, Sat-Okh spent some time in Kharkiv as a guest of the Writer's Union, and Stadnychenko's, Tretyakov's, and Polonskyi's close communications with Sat-Okh were tolerated (Fig. 6.2).

The content of the conversations that occurred among Tretyakov, Sat-Okh, and other Kharkiv writers is unknown but potentially damaging information about the regimentation of the writers' activities, total surveillance, arrests, and their financial difficulties in the "country of plenty" might have been discussed. Some scholars have argued that the "late-Soviet citizens enjoyed material improvements and more comfortable lifestyles, benefited from new spaces created for individual spiritual growth and self-perfection, and savored

Figure 6.2 Robert Tretyakov and the Polish Writer Stanisław Supłatowicz (Sat-Okh). Kharkiv, the Puppet Theater, 1978. *Source*: RTPA; a copy is located in the TsDAMLIMU, f. 712, op. 1, spr. 6, ark. 3.

new forms of entertainment."[83] For the majority of Kharkiv writers, with rare exception, this was not the case. Beyond political terror and intimidation, food shortages under Brezhnev devastated the majority of Ukrainian families who relied only on their legal income.[84] Tretyakov's material hardships were unceasing: he systematically borrowed money from the Litfond, and never could repay his debts in time.[85] His wife's diaries abound with descriptions about pure and simple starvation, when the family had no food on the table, and their two children were on strict rations.[86] Anatolii Makahonov, a Kharkiv journalist, has stated that financial instability and material hardships chased Tretyakov to his grave.[87] Some believe time heals all wounds. For Tretyakov, time could not heal anything; the time of late socialism became a disease in itself, lethal and inevitable.

In the early morning of 1 March 1979, the prominent Ukrainian poet Robert Tretyakov was found in his room at the Irpin's House of Creativity (*Budynok tvorchosti*) near Kyiv with his throat and wrists slashed.[88] He was still alive, rolling back and forth on the floor. He moaned and wheezed; his eyes were open but empty, expressing nothing. The signs of consciousness were absent, and it seemed he recognized no one among those who bustled around him. Two razor blades covered with blood were lying on the floor.[89] An examination of primary and secondary sources about this incident provides no clear answer to the question of whether Tretyakov attempted to commit suicide, whether he was forced to do so, or whether he fell victim to an attempted homicide. Much controversy surrounds the poet's silence about the motivations of the alleged suicide, and the fact that no investigation of the scene had been performed by the authorities. These circumstances seem to suggest a multidimensional interpretation of the tragedy. Some of his colleagues later claimed that this was an act of a morbid mind inflamed by alcohol; others suggested that it was a political protest against the authorities or a response to the KGB's demands to serve as a *seksot*. His friend poet Anatolii Miroshnychenko remembered a stranger in Tretyakov's room, with whom he was drinking all night. Tretyakov met the man on a local train, returning from Kyiv to Irpin that evening. The man approached Tretyakov, saying that he recognized him as a famous poet and that he appreciated his poetry. They began to talk and missed their stop. They got off the train at the next stop at twilight and eventually reached Irpin by foot. Miroshnychenko and another Kharkiv writer, Mykola Shapoval, met them, spoke a bit with Robert, and parted. Miroshnychenko had a bad premonition about the man, provoked by his "dark" visual appearance. The evil image of the man evoked in Miroshnychenko associations with the protagonist of Yesenin's poem "The Evil Man" (Chiornyi chelovek).[90]

That morning, Tretyakov was saved by Radii Polonskyi who, through the semi-opened doors to Tretyakov's room, accidentally heard Tretyakov, groaning and moaning. The stranger was gone, and for the rest of his life Tretyakov avoided discussions about the incident, even with his wife and children. The scenario of a suicide attempt was never challenged by either Polonskyi or Tretyakov himself. Someone in the *obkom* had uttered: "This intelligentsia cannot even properly kill itself."[91] Emile Durkheim might have been correct, arguing that the social and political environment kills people, preparing them for their final step into the abyss, a suicide. Moreover, many seem to be already dead, morally and intellectually, embodying a desolated place or a dry lifeless desert, and killing themselves is simply a technicality that had to be completed.[92] In Tretyakov's case, his individual personality and actions might be an important determinant of the social and political environment in which he existed for two decades, state violence and the KGB's sophisticated psychological torture that, in many respects, are comparable with other mnemonic markers in Ukraine's history, such as the Executed Renaissance of the 1920s, the Holodomor, the Great Terror, and the Second World War. What makes these events similar is not the number of the victims these calamities claimed (which differs) but rather the enormous cultural disruption that occurred in Ukraine as a result of these events.

Scholars have written extensively about the existence of the KGB Thirteenth Department that had been transformed into the Fifth Department which performed special operations, such as assassinations, kidnappings, preparations for sabotage, and the like.[93] Did the "evil man" work for the KGB, and did their friendly meeting in Irpin encouraged Tretyakov to commit suicide? The benevolent intentions of the person seem doubtful. He never revealed himself, even when he learned from the local press about what happened to the poet he admired so much. Mysteriously, Tretyakov's lips were sealed about the details of this day for the rest of his life, but he repeatedly expressed his gratitude to Polonskyi who accidentally passed by his room, ultimately saving his life.[94] Clearly, Tretyakov wanted to live.

The meaning of the incident that occurred in Irpin that day is complex and suggestive. Either scenario, a suicide or an attempted murder by the KGB, connotes Tretyakov's protest against the regime rather than productive collaboration with it. His inconsistent and at times erratic behavior contributed to his discord with the agency. In 1973, when the Writers' Union purged the Ukrainian poet Vasyl Borovyi and the Russian poet Boris Chichibabin from its ranks for their "anti-Soviet" stance,[95] Tretyakov was among the few who voted against the decision, which on the peak of repressions in Ukraine could be characterized as an act of civic gallantry. He never repudiated his friendship with Volodymyr Briuggen, Lev Galkin, or Vasyl Borovyi against the *obkom*'s advice to watch for those "cunning Jews" or "nationalistic *khokhly*."[96] The Kharkiv authorities seemed to have reminded Tretyakov several times about the danger of his behavior.

Thoroughly chosen by Moscow, the pro-Russian antisemitic cadres of the Kharkiv *obkom* and the KGB persistently tried to provincialize and Sovietize Kharkiv's cultural space that historically had been intellectually vigorous and ethnically diverse. In the vigor of the sixties' movement, in trepidation, the authorities observed the rejuvenation of the Ukrainian ethnos, culture, and language through Ukrainian poetry and prose which was cherished and promoted not only by the members of this ethnos but also by those who believed in being part of this ethnos. Tretyakov's use of the Ukrainian language continued to bother them tremendously. Walter Houston was right to suggest that ethnicity was never a matter of DNA and had never been defined only in genetic terms: "The fact is that an ethnos is defined in whatever way its members choose to define it."[97] An ethnic Russian, Tretyakov chose to be Ukrainian, affirming his choice and his cultural affiliation through his poetry. And that was exactly how the Kharkiv authorities perceived him, as a person who culturally, linguistically, and intellectually "polluted" the minds of Ukraine's citizens who were to be raised as Soviets, not as Ukrainians.

Throughout the period of the 1930s–1980s, cultural figures of various ethnicities were accused of Ukrainian nationalism only because they wrote in Ukrainian or were fully immersed in Ukrainian culture.[98] Like many Ukrainian *shistdesiatnyky*, Tretyakov embraced cultural nationalism.[99] Although he was fully bilingual, the Thaw and his hopes for Ukrainian cultural autonomy shaped him as a Ukrainian poet. His linguistic persistence appears to be a "compensatory response" to the authorities' pressure to Russify the republic. As his wife Lidiya characterized him, he was immensely stubborn when it came to his principles.[100]

The 1970s was the period of the KGB reign, when many writers were surviving rather than living. The headquarters of all Ukrainian chapters of the Writers' Union were bugged, and republican Congresses of the Writers' Union were thoroughly surveilled through a network of informants. Writers such as Radii Polonskyi from Kharkiv, Petro Skunts from Uzhorod, and Viktor Nekrasov from Kyiv were under careful scrutiny because of their human rights activism and "nationalistic stance."[101] For instance, at the Sixth Congress of the Writers' Union of Ukraine held on 18–21 May 1971 in Kyiv, out of 858 delegates of the Congress, fifty-seven KGB agents and twenty-three informers were registered as participants of the Congress, which means that every tenth participant worked for the KGB, writing detailed reports about the Congress's discussions and the content of private conversations among the writers.[102] In this atmosphere, Tretyakov's poetry seemed to stagnate.[103] He wrote little. "I cannot squeeze a line out of myself," Tretyakov told Mykola Shatylov.[104] He felt sequestered and isolated. The lyrical motifs became subdued and vague in his poems, while the social and ideological ones began to dominate.

Historiographically, the term "stagnation" that characterized the Brezhnev era has been used to define the developments, or rather their absence, in the political, economic, and social spheres in the Soviet Union.[105] Importantly, this term is equally applicable to the cultural transformations in the USSR, including Ukraine. The Kharkiv chapter of the Writers' Union had not increased its membership for decades, a symptom of the constrained and stagnated Ukrainian culture.[106] Apathy, anti-intellectualism, forcible Russification, problems with individual and national identity, and the legacies of Stalinism discouraged the writers from thinking and writing. In Tretyakov's world, the frustration with ideological constraints was exacerbated by his feeling of infinite loneliness inherent in many creative individuals and the constant need for self-adjustment to the demands of the party.[107] Literary critics identified this stage in his poetic career as the "weakening of his poetic muscle."[108]

Ideologically, Gorbachev's perestroika in early 1986 changed little, suffering from the inertia of Soviet bureaucrats who controlled cultural institutions. *Literaturna Ukraina* and other regional press still published reports about party committee meetings in various cultural institutions, where the directors of the Ukrainian publishing houses were chastised for their apolitical and anti-party approach in selecting literary works for publication. Similarly, the writers were admonished for their inability to reflect on the topics commissioned by the party and the publishing houses. "Poor thematic planning" and the importance of following the "party pulse" in literature were the key concepts that dominated the speeches of the local party bosses.[109] The February 1986 Twenty-Seventh Congress of the Communist Party of the USSR and the speeches delivered by the party leaders Mikhail Gorbachev, Volodymyr

Shcherbytskyi, and Boris Yeltsin, that emphasized the leading role of the Communist party in the democratization of society, largely continued to organize the minds of many writers around the idea of the party's vitality and resilience. The agony of the party was apparent to a few. Torn apart by internal contradictions, the Central Committee of the KPSS ingratiated itself with the Ukrainian party leaders and the local intelligentsia, searching for support. It issued a resolution to reward Kharkiv and the Kharkiv oblast with the Red Banner of the Central Committee of the Communist Party, the Council of Ministers of the USSR, the All-Union Central Council of Professional Unions, and the Central Committee of the All-Union Lenin Communist Union of Youth. At the meeting of the Kharkiv chapter of the Writers' Union, its head Borys Sylaev was reserved, reacting to Moscow's patronizing gesture with dignity. His brave remark about a lack of independent thought among the writers was the first sign of "deviation," inspired by perestroika. This was a transitional period when the intelligentsia, trained in the Communist traditions, simultaneously employed the terminology of the Brezhnev and Gorbachev eras, and newspapers articles were checkered with the rhetorical hodgepodge of the party bureaucratic slang which was entrenched and grew stronger under Brezhnev and Gorbachev's terms glasnost (openness), perestroika (restructuring), and uskorenie (acceleration).[110]

The April 1986 Chernobyl tragedy, when the fourth block of the Chernobyl nuclear power station exploded and Ukraine was immersed in a cloud of nuclear dust, undermined the trust of many Ukrainians in the Soviet government. For a week the authorities had covered up the scope and consequences of the tragedy which was later compared by many to the nuclear bombing of Hiroshima and Nagasaki.[111] Chernobyl provoked a public backlash against nuclear power and nuclear physicists,[112] and "played a key role in promoting the view of Ukraine as an exploited colony of Moscow."[113] Catherine Wanner has argued that Chernobyl "became a *cause célèbre* for the independence movement," and generated a great deal of anti-Soviet and pro-independent attitudes.[114] The two subsequent years were marked by remarkable transformations in the Kharkiv intellectual elite. The Kharkiv chapter of the Writers' Union headed by Radii Polonskyi further pushed for rehabilitation of the Kharkiv writers repressed under Stalin. Its secretary, the Ukrainian poet Anatolii Pererva, was especially active, helping the relatives of the Kharkiv writers who fell victim to Stalin's regime gain access to their criminal files located in the KGB archives.[115]

The Chernobyl experience seemed to liberate Tretyakov. He redefined and re-articulated himself: he was reborn as a poet and published a collection of brilliant poetry, emotional and intellectual at once. In his poem "My Chernobyl'" (*Mii Chornobyl*), he referred to his contemporaries as the "children of inquisition," with the individual inner moral Chernobyls that burned every Ukrainian from inside. Tretyakov grieved over the nation's and his own courage and heroism that had been buried voluntarily.[116] He realized his own guilt, and his heart was burning in tune with Chernobyl's flames: the civic and the personal became intertwined through a poetic metaphor. Tretyakov compared Ukrainians and himself with "voluntary Herostratuses."[117] An ancient Greek and arsonist, Herostratus committed a crime: he burned the temple built by the king of Lydia, a kingdom near ancient Ionia, to gain fame and to immortalize his name for eternity. The allegory was quite obvious. This was both a collective and personal indictment: for the national intelligentsia's guilty conscience and its desire to save themselves in Ukraine instead of saving Ukraine for future generations; and for his own crime of ruining his wife's hopes and love for the sake of poetry. Readers are left with the tragic reiteration depicting Ukraine as a place similar to Pompeii, buried under ashes and lies, without prospects for rejuvenation. This metaphor is polysemic and verbally distant from the socialist realism framework. The literary critic Volodymyr Briuggen has argued that it was not accidental that Tretyakov published a new collection of poetry entitled *Tobi* in 1991, the time of birth of independent Ukraine. This volume exemplified the rebirth of a unique poetic voice emblematic of the young Tretyakov: "He could have written only these late poems, which would be sufficient to characterize him as a great voice in Ukrainian literature," stated Briuggen.[118] Through these poems, Tretyakov hoped to make his last substantial contribution to Ukrainian poetry. He once asked the Kharkiv poet Leonid Toma: "Will they remember us?" In a moment, he answered himself: "Our poems will remind them of us . . . ."[119]

Rediscovering the voice of your youth and finding yourself in a new society free of censorship and lies often end in failure: lost poetic voices never entirely reemerge in their initial originality. Remembering the Ukrainian poet Ivan Vyrhan's last words on his death bed "Everything is a lie," Tretyakov searched for the truth after years of lies and semi-truths. His case seems to be rare. The authenticity and sincerity of his 1991 collection surpassed the personal by provoking in readers the recognition of their own pains and crises, together with the impossibility of recuperating from them or alleviating them. Hope for change, associated with the new beginning for Ukraine, helped him and several other Kharkiv writers liberate themselves from the pressure of the opaque Brezhnev era. Some of his colleagues are guilty of mythologizing Tretyakov's political bravery: they depicted him as an oppositionist to the regime.[120] His resistance manifested itself in preserving his Ukrainian language and in surviving every time when the KGB considered him dead. Most importantly, he survived the methodical slaughter of national cultures by the Soviets, reborn as a poet in independent Ukraine. Tretyakov's poetry in English translation was included in the anthology of Ukrainian poetry published in England as one of the most important reference points to *shistdesiatnytstvo* and its influence on Ukrainian literature and culture.[121] Memorably, as his colleagues have argued, he was a person of moral principles, courage, and conscience, and deeply suffered because of the political status quo.

Like many Kharkiv writers, Tretyakov was tamed by the party and intimidated by the KGB but was a "property" of neither one of them. Poet Vladimir Rodionov has suggested that "it would be easier to turn the river than to force Tretyakov to surrender his principles."[122] Poet Oleksa Marchenko, who was accused by the party and the KGB of Ukrainian nationalism for his poem that condemned Stalin's legacies and terror, remembered that Tretyakov was among a few (Ihor Muratov, Ivan Vyrhan, Vasyl Bondar, and Vasyl Borovyi) who supported him and continued to communicate with him despite the grave danger of being accused of Ukrainian nationalism and dissent. The KGB deprived Marchenko of the opportunity to write and work as a journalist. He was "exiled" to the Kharkiv Tractor Factory to earn a living as a worker.[123]

Some Kharkiv literati believed that apolitical behavior would lead to comfort and permit certain freedoms. Cultural provincialism could be tolerated, as long as the authorities left the writers alone. Soon they realized the impossibility of achieving this sort of transcendence: neither their art nor their lives were perceived by the *chekists* as apolitical, as long as they lived in Ukraine. Many identified Kharkiv of the Brezhnev era as a cultural province and prison. For Shatylov, surveilled by the KGB, *Budynok "Slovo"* was the "writers' ghetto," and the journal *Prapor* the "prison toilet" (*v'iaznychna parasha*). For some the "atmosphere of unrelieved moral squalor" and violence became unbearable.[124] Leonid Osmolovskyi attempted to hang himself but the rope broke. The former Kharkivite Hryhir Tiutiunnyk hung himself, suffocating from censorship and unable to tolerate lies.[125] To some extent, suicides became a national trend during the period of re-Stalinization. Like an animal hunted down by the system and the authorities, the Ukrainian artist Kateryna Bilokur, who charmed Pablo Picasso with her art, exclaimed in exasperation in January 1961, six months before her death: "What if I gather some strength and hang myself—and that's it!" Two decades later, in April 1981, the Ukrainian writer Viktor Blyznets committed suicide: he could no longer observe the desecration of artistic individuality under the Soviets. The spirit of the antisemitic and anti-Ukrainian authorities and their attempts to Russify and provincialize Kharkiv in the 1960s–1980s were dragged into the years of Ukrainian independence. Today the former "capital of arts" resembles a dinosaur whose tiny head, in the service of necessary progressive evolution, desperately tries to reduce its huge body of pernicious Soviet legacies that persist despite the collapse of the coercive system. The non-patriotic stance of the local authorities, persistent attempts at Russifying Ukrainian cultural institutions, and the harassment of political activists in Kharkiv recall memories of the Soviet times.[126]

At the end of his life, Tretyakov seemed to be liberated from his fears and political pressure. What had anchored him in the past was not the party or Leninist ideals, but the love he felt for his wife, a love which helped him regain his poetic voice.[127] Tretyakov recognized rather early the power of his words; they controlled his life. They could ruin him and his love, or they could sustain both, as long as he was careful with them. On his death bed, Tretyakov continued to read. His choice of *Begushchaia po volnam* (She Who Runs on the Waves) by Aleksandr Grin seems hardly accidental.[128] Some critics have argued that Grin's prose was nothing but fiction for adolescents. However, Grin's prose illuminates universal values, such as love, friendship, and faithfulness. Before his death, Tretyakov was eager to be absorbed by love, to reevaluate the simple and at the same time complex relationships between a woman and a man, and to internalize someone else's joyous consummation of dreams. Leonid Pliushch has suggested that Grin's subject is the same as Remarque's: simple human feelings and relations. Both reject everything that stands over man—ideology, the state, and God. Grin was the idol of Soviet youth for many years, and Scarlet Sails clubs, named after his most popular novel, were formed in many cities. For most young people a love for Grin is the first protest, whether conscious or not, against the falsehoods of adults. Grin represents for them a childhood miraculously transferred into adult life.[129] The Russian writer Grin, half Polish half Russian, seemed to help the Ukrainian poet Tretyakov, ethnic Russian, return to his youth, marked by purity and filled with hopes of a young romantic born out of the Thaw.

Kharkiv, a place of transcultural and transethnic encounters, expanded the intellectual and cultural worlds of Kharkivites, despite the efforts by the Kharkiv authorities and the KGB to homogenize post-Stalin Kharkiv. These transcultural communication links inspired the Kharkiv literati to appreciate national cultures, especially their own cultures, into which they were born. They realized that the Soviets and their "utopian socialist doctrines reduced to the level of popular slogans" greatly contributed to the century of *megadeath* and *metamyth*, using Zbigniew Brzezinski's terms, observing both phenomena in Ukraine on a massive scale.[130] A "coercive utopia" designed to stigmatize and eliminate nationalists, the Jews and the Ukrainians, as well as bourgeois capitalists as the "conspirators of evil," augmented the national and the creative among them. They created their own Kharkiv, secretly free, distinct, and rebellious.

Kharkiv was (and is) different for different people. For the Kyivite and *shistdesiatnyk* Dmytro Pavlychko, Kharkiv was a place, where "the spirit of the Ukrainian nation was born, where Ukrainian culture emerged, and where the idea of the Ukrainian statehood was revitalized, formulated by the great prophet of the [Ukrainian] state [Mykola] Mikhnovskyi."[131] "Kharkiv is not a child but rather the father of the Ukrainian nation!", Pavlychko argued.[132] For the chief editor of the Kharkiv literary magazine *Berezil* (former *Prapor*) from 1990 to 1999 and a Kharkivite Yurii Stadnychenko, Kharkiv was shaped by its cultural traditions of the 1920s and its Renaissance, executed in the 1930s but which had left Taras Shevchenko's monument for the Kharkivites, "smiling kindly" at them.[133] For Ihor Muratov, Kharkiv was associated with the Drobytskyi Yar, the extermination of Jews by the Nazis, and the "cliff" of Darwin Street downtown Kharkiv, from which one could observe the city's landscape.[134] The glimpse at the literary Kharkiv of the 1960s and 1970s and the individual histories of some of its writers demonstrate the centrality of the cultural dimension in Soviet history and the civic gallantry of Kharkiv intellectuals to transcend the ethnic and national boundaries established by the authorities. The "evil" constructed along ethnic lines by the KGB and the coercive utopia of erasing nationalist cultures and roots reinforced by Soviet propagandists corrupted and destroyed many writers. Yet the minds and the souls of a great many who went through and survived the labyrinths of timelessness being liberated from their coercion, thawed and flourished, never giving up their beliefs in their possible transformations.

NOTES

1. Alexander J. Motyl, *Will the Non-Russians Rebel? State, Ethnicity, and Stability in the USSR* (Ithaca and London: Cornell University Press, 1987), 137.

2. *Numerus clausus* ("closed number" in Latin) is a method used to limit the number of students who may study at a university.

3. Motyl, *Will the Non-Russians Rebel?*, 138; Leon Shapiro, "Soviet Jewry Since the Death of Stalin: A Twenty-five Year Perspective," *The American Jewish Year Book* 79 (1979): 80; also available at https://www.bjpa.org/content/upload/bjpa/sovi/Soviet%20Jewry%20stalin.pdf.

4. Odd Arne Westad, *The Cold War: A World History* (New York: Basic Books, 2019), 370; J. P. D. Dunbabin, *The Cold War: The Great Powers and Their Allies*, 2nd ed. (New York: Pearson Education Limited, 2008), 275; Carole K. Fink, *Cold War: An International History*, 2nd ed. (Boulder, CO: Western Press, 2017), 135.

5. Vladimir Semichastnyi, *Bespokoinoie serdtse* (Moskva: Vagrius, 2002), 446.

6. Nativ or Lishkat Hakesher (The Liaison Bureau) is an Israel governmental intelligence organization that maintained communication with East European Jews during the Cold War, encouraging immigration to Israel.

7. Quoted in Ronen Bergman, "The KGB's Middle East Files: The Fight against Zionism and World Jewry," 1 December 2016, https://www.ynetnews.com/articles/0,7340,L-4886594,00.html (accessed 8 November 2020).

8. See the text of Andropov's memorandum to the Central Committee in Sergei Khrushchev, ed., *Memoirs of Nikita Khrushchev: Reformer (1945–1964)*, vol. 2, trans. George Shriver and Stephen Shenfield (University Park, PA: The Pennsylvania State University Press, 2006), 662.

9. Shapiro, "Soviet Jewry Since the Death of Stalin," 80.

10. Zvi Gitelman, "The Social and Political Role of the Jews in Ukraine," in *Ukraine in the Seventies*, ed. Peter J. Potichnyj (Oakville, ON: Mosaic Press, 1975), 177.

11. Borys Lewytzkyj, *Politics and Society in Soviet Ukraine, 1953–1980* (Edmonton, Canada: Canadian Institute of Ukrainian Studies/University of Alberta, 1984), 198.

12. On Soviet Jews' "thin" Jewish culture, see Yaacov Ro'i, "The Move From Russia/the Soviet Union to Israel": A Transformation of Jewish Culture and Identity?" in *The New Jewish Diaspora: Russian-Speaking Immigrants in the United States, Israel, and Germany*, ed. Zvi Gitelman (New Brunswick, NJ and London: Rutgers University Press, 2016), 139–41.

13. Gelfandbein was quoted in a private conversation with Robert Tretyakov, 2 April 1994, Kharkiv, Ukraine.

14. On Khrushchev's antisemitism, see Martin McCauley, *The Khrushchev Era, 1953–1964* (London and New York: Longman, 1995), 13.

15. HDA SBU, f. 16, op. 1, spr. 979, ark. 377.

16. Aleksandr Vernik was born in Kharkiv in 1947. He graduated from Kharkiv University's Philology Department (Russian section) and began to publish his poetry only in immigration. His work has been published in journals *Dvadtsat dva* (Tel Aviv), *Vremia i my* (Tel Aviv and New York), *Kontinent* (Paris), *Novyi zhurnal* (New York), and *Znamia* (Moskva) among others.

17. HDA SBU, f. 16, op. 1, spr. 985, ark. 266.

18. HDA SBU, f. 16, op. 1, spr. 985, ark. 266–67.

19. HDA SBU, f. 16, op. 1, spr. 985, ark. 267.

20. HDA SBU, f. 16, op. 1, spr. 985, ark. 268.

21. On KGB analysts' assessment of the "Jewish question" in the USSR after 1967, see Vladislav Zubok, *Zhivago's Children: The Last Russian Intelligentsia* (Cambridge, MA: The Belknap Press of Harvard University Press, 2009), 255–57.

22. Leonard Schroeter, *The Last Exodus* (Seattle and London: University of Washington Press, 1974), 258.

23. Schroeter, *The Last Exodus*, 262.

24. Ibid.

25. Schroeter, *The Last Exodus*, 265.

26. Ibid., 383; also 407.

27. Quoted in Schroeter, *The Last Exodus*, 390.

28. Max Hayward, "Introduction," in *My Testimony* by Anatoly Marchenko, trans. Michael Scammell (New York: E. P. Dutton & Co. Inc., 1969), xi.

29. Jeremy Bransten, "Russia: Soviet Dissident Larisa Bogoraz Dead at 74," *RadioFreeEurope*, 7 April 2004, https://www.rferl.org/a/1052206.html (accessed 8 November 2020).

30. D. Mauritz Gustafson, "Soviet Human Rights under Gorbachev: Old Wine in a New Bottle," *The Denver Journal of International Law & Policy* 16, no. 1 (2020): 182.

31. Larisa Bogoraz, "Afterword," in *To Live Like Everyone* by Anatoly Marchenko (New York: Henry Holt and Company, 1989), 214.

32. Feliks Rakhlin, *O Borise Chichibabine o iego vremeni: Strochki iz zhizni* (Kharkov: Folio, 2004), 78.

33. Motyl, *Will the Non-Russians Rebel?*, 138.

34. Lewytszkyi, *Politics and Society in Soviet Ukraine*, 102–17; Simone Attilio Bellezza, *The Shore of Expectations: A Cultural Study of the Shistdesiatnyky* (Edmonton, Canada: CIUS, 2019), 220–38.

35. Lewytszkyi, *Politics and Society in Soviet Ukraine*, 121.

36. Ibid., 121–22.

37. Ibid., 122.

38. See the former lieutenant colonel Vladimir Popov (interview by Dmytro Gordon), *YouTube*, 28 July 2020, https://www.youtube.com/watch?v=oFcrn7w57TU (accessed 21 November 2020).

39. HDA SBU, f. 16, op. 1, spr. 994, ark. 92.

40. HDA SBU, f. 16, op. 1, spr. 994, ark. 95.

41. HDA SBU, f. 16, op. 1, spr. 994, ark. 93.

42. Private conversation with one of my former patients, a retired KGB officer who preferred to stay anonymous, 20 August 1999, Kharkiv, Ukraine.

43. Rakhlin, *O Borise Chichibabine*, 73.

44. Ibid.

45. Ibid.

46. Boris Chichibabin, *Stikhotvoreniia* (Kharkov: Ekskliuziv, 2003), 81. See also Rakhlin, 72. Kotliarov's full name was Boris Ivanovich Kotliarov.

47. Vitalii Orlov, "Akh, Zhenia, Zhenia, Zhenechka, s nim sluchai byl takoi . . ." *Elegant New York*, http://elegantnewyork.com/evtushenko-orlov/ (accessed 16 October 2020).

48. Orlov, "Akh, Zhenia."

49. Rakhlin, *O Borise Chichibabine*, 74.

50. Private conversation with a retired KGB officer who preferred to stay anonymous, 20 August 1999, Kharkiv, Ukraine.

51. On Kafka's labyrinths of guilt, see J. P. Stern, "Franz Kafka: The Labyrinths of Guilt," *Critical Quarterly* 7, no. 1 (1965): 35–48.

52. Kenneth C. Farmer, *Ukrainian Nationalism in the Post-Stalin Era* (The Hague/Boston/London: Matinus Nijhoff Publisher, 1980), 189; TsDAHOU, f. 1, op. 25, spr. 398, ark. 1–5, 8, 38.

53. Yaroslav Bilinsky, "The Communist Party of Ukraine after 1966," in *Ukraine in the Seventies*, edited by Peter J. Potichnyj (Oakville, ON: Mosaic Press, 1975), 239–55; Yurii Shapoval, ed., *Petro Shelest: "Spravshnii sud istorii shche poperedu": Spohady. Shchodennyky. Dokumenty. Materialy* (Kyiv: ADEF-Ukraina, 2011).

54. Jaroslaw Bilocerkowycz, *Soviet Ukrainian Dissent: A Study of Political Alienation* (Boulder, CO: Westview Press, 1988), 32.

55. Shapoval, *Petro Shelest*, 30–36.

56. See the copy of the document in Vladimir Bukovskii's private archive, http://www.bukovsky-archives.net/pdfs/sovter74/pb72-1.pdf (accessed 11 July 2020).

57. TsDAHOU, f. 1, op. 25, spr. 642, ark. 128.

58. Olga Bertelsen, "Political Affinities and Maneuvering of Soviet Ukrainian Political Elites: Heorhii Shevel and the Ministry of Strange Affairs in the 1970s," *Nationalities Papers: The Journal of Nationalism and Ethnicity* 47, no. 3 (2019): 394–411.

59. Bohdan Nahaylo and Victor Swoboda, *Soviet Disunion: A History of the Nationalities Problem in the USSR* (New York: The Free Press, 1998), 178.

60. L. I. Brezhnev, "O piatidesiatiletii Soiuza Sovetskikh Sotsialisticheskikh Respublik," *Pravda*, 22 December 1972, p. 2.

61. Yaroslav Bilinsky, "Political Relations Between Russians and Ukrainians in the USSR: The 1970s and Beyond," in *Ukraine and Russia in Their Historical Encounter*, eds. Peter J. Potichnyi, Marc Raeff, Jaroslaw Pelenski, and Gleb N. Zekulin (Edmonton, Canada: CIUS Press/University of Alberta, 1992), 172–73.

62. Inna Sukhorukova, "25 Years to the Ukrainian Helsinki Group," *The Kharkiv Human Rights Protection Group*, 13 December 2001, http://khpg.org/en/index.php?id=1008253233 (accessed 13 November 2020).

63. Vladimir Bukovsky, *Judgement in Moscow: Soviet Crimes and Western Complicity*, ed. Paul Boutin and trans. Alyona Kojevnikov (Ninth of November Press, 2019), 148.

64. Ihor Mykhailyn, *Literaturna Kharkivshchyna. Poeziia* (Kharkiv: Maidan, 2007), 225.

65. Mykhailyn, *Literaturna Kharkivshchyna*, 226.

66. TsDAMLIMU, f. 712, op. 1, spr. 11, ark. 1–2; TsDAMLIMU, f. 712, op. 1, spr. 15, ark. 2.

67. TsDAMLIMU, f. 712, op. 1, spr. 10, ark. 6, 7; TsDAMLIMU, f. 712, op. 1, spr. 11, ark. 3.

68. RTPA; interview with Yevdokiia Kudakova, the secretary of the Litfond, 15 July 2005, Kharkiv, Ukraine. Tretyakov also complained about the nepotism in the Union and Lukashova's biases in providing the best opportunities for trips to a certain group of establishment writers or her personal friends.

69. DAKhO, f. R-6165, op. 1, spr. 122, ark. 169.

70. On the Saburova Dacha and its use for punitive psychiatry during the 1960s–1980s, see chapter 4, and Olga Bertelsen, "Rethinking Psychiatric Terror against Nationalists in Ukraine," *Kyiv-Mohyla Arts and Humanities* 1 (2014): 27–76; for a discussion about punitive psychiatry in the Cold War context, see Robert van Voren, *Cold War in Psychiatry: Human Factors, Secret Actors* (Amsterdam and New York: Rodopi, 2010).

71. LTD, vol. 6; Mykola Shatylov, *Kliati simdesiati . . . : Na pam'iati stalo, na pam'iati staly* (Kharkiv: Vydavnytstvo "Apostrof," 2011), 162.

72. LTD, vol. 5.

73. Radii Polonskyi, "Nepoiasnymyi Robert," *Vechernii Kharkov*, 23 July 1998, p. 7.

74. Vladislav Zubok, *A Failed Empire: The Soviet Union in the Cold War from Stalin to Gorbachev* (Chapel Hill: University of North Carolina Press, 2007), 176; Sergei I. Zhuk, *Rock and Roll in the Rocket City: The West, Identity, and Ideology in Soviet Dniepropetrovsk, 1960–1985* (Baltimore, MD: Johns Hopkins University Press & Washington, DC: Woodrow Wilson Center Press, 2010).

75. On cultural exchange during the Cold War, see Yale Richmond, *Cultural Exchange and the Cold War: Raising the Iron Curtain* (University Park, PA: The Pennsylvania State University Press, 2003), 72.

76. LTD, vol. 10.

77. Ibid.

78. Robert Tretyakov, *Merydiany kriz sertse: Vybrane* (Kyiv: Dnipro, 1975). See the letter by the secretary of the Party Regional Committee (*raikom*) in Kharkiv M. Pobihailo in TsDAMLIMU, f. 712, op. 1, spr. 15, ark. 1–2.

79. LTD, vol. 10–11.

80. LTD, vol. 10. For a discussion about foreign radio stations and the KGB's efforts at monitoring their listeners in Dnipropetrovsk region, see Sergei I. Zhuk, "'Cultural Wars' in the Closed City of Soviet Ukraine, 1959–1982," in *Soviet Society in the Era of Late Socialism, 1964–1985*, eds. Neringa Klumbyte and Gulnaz Sharafutdinova (Lanham, MD: Lexington Books, 2014), 69–71. The year 1979 was marked by increased surveillance by the KGB and economic difficulties in the USSR. The Soviets invaded Afghanistan, and the entire country began to toil for the growing military-industrial complex. Food shortages during this time in Ukraine were notoriously famous.

81. "Rigonda" was the first Soviet lamp record player and radio that was produced in Riga (Latvia, the USSR) by the radio factory named after A. S. Popov from 1963 to 1977.

82. Van Voren, *Cold War in Psychiatry*, 159.

83. Neringa Klumbyte and Gulnaz Sharafutdinova, eds., *Soviet Society in the Era of Late Socialism, 1964–1985* (Lanham, MD: Lexington Books, 2014), 12.

84. For a discussion about economic difficulties in Ukraine, see David R. Marples, *Ukraine under Perestroika: Ecology, Economics and the Workers' Revolt* (New York: St. Martin's Press, 1991), 1–3, 5–7, 11–16. Marples has noted that the statistics released in April 1990 are a clear indication of the "continuing decline of the Ukrainian economy and the living standards of the population." Vasyl Sydorenko was once asked about his routinely sad eyes. His reply was laconic: "I am simply always hungry." See Iryna Zhylenko, *Homo Feriens: Spohady* (Kyiv: Smoloskyp, 2011), 114. Several months before his death, Tretyakov's daughter asked him: "Your refrigerator is empty. Do you eat enough?" Her father answered: "No. But I got used to it."

85. DAKhO, f. R-6164, op. 1, spr. 89, ark. 3, 5, 20; DAKhO, f. R-6164, op. 1, spr. 106, ark. 19.

86. LTD, vol. 4–10.

87. Anatolii Makahonov, "Prosti nas, Robert," *Vremia*, 9 November 1997, p. 2.

88. Houses of Creativity belonged to the Litfond (*Literaturnyi Fond*), an organization within the Writers' Union that supervised issues of the writers' welfare. The

Litfond built several resorts known as *Budynky tvorchosti* (Ukr.) or *Doma tvorchestva* (Rus.) in Crimea, the Baltic republics, Armenia, Azerbaijan, Kazakhstan, and Uzbekistan, including the famous village of Peredelkino near Moscow. These resorts were ultimately state properties and served as retreats for privileged writers, members of the Writers' Union, where they rested and at the same time worked on their new projects. The services provided there were heavily subsidized by the Litfond for the members of the Writers' Union and their close relatives. For details about the Litfond, see *Literaturnomu fondu SSSR 125 let* (Moskva: Vneshtorgizdat, 1984).

89. Radii Polonskyi, "Nepoiasnymyi Robert," *Vechernii Kharkov*, 23 July 1998, p. 7. For more details about this tragic night on 28 February–1 March 1979, see also Anatolii Miroshnichenko, "Zapiski inzhenera-poeta," *Slobozhanskyi kruh* 5 (2011): 76–77.

90. Miroshnichenko, "Zapiski inzhenera-poeta," 76.

91. Radii Polonskyi, "Nepoiasnymyi Robert," *Slobozhanskyi kruh* 5 (2011): 35–38.

92. See Emile Durkheim's study on suicide, *Suicide: A Study in Sociology*, ed. George Simpson, trans. John A. Spaulding and George Simpson (London: Routledge & Kegan Paul Ltd, 1968).

93. Christopher Andrew and Oleg Gordievsky, *KGB: The Inside Story of Its Foreign Operations from Lenin to Gorbachev* (New York: HarperCollins Publishers, 1990), 464–65; Herbert Romerstein and Stanislav Levchenko, *The KGB Against the "Main Enemy:" How the Soviet Intelligence Service Operates against the United States* (Toronto: Lexington Books, 1989), 312; John Barron, *KGB: The Secret Work of Soviet Secret Agents* (New York: Reader's Digest Press, 1974), 306–31.

94. LTD, vol. 11.

95. Anatolii Stozhuk, "Chervone sontse Kaerkana," *Literaturna Ukraina*, 12 September 2013, p. 15.

96. *Khokhly* is a derogatory term for Ukrainians, typically used in the Russian context. The word originated from the Ukrainian work *khokhol* or *oseledets*, a long lock of hair on the shaved head, signifying the Ukrainian Cossacks' military hairstyle.

97. Walter Houston, "A Diverse Collection of Peoples," *London Review of Books*, 4 July 2013, p. 4. Walter Houston was the Green Party candidate in Macclesfield Tytherington in the Cheshire East local election (United Kingdom).

98. Among them were Ivan Kaliannikov, Ivan Kulyk, and Boris Chichibabin. For a more detailed discussion, see Yohanan Petrovsky-Shtern, *The Anti-Imperial Choice: The Making of the Ukrainian Jew* (New Haven, CT: Yale University Press, 2009); Bertelsen, "The House of Writers in Ukraine, the 1930s."

99. For a discussion about the meaning of cultural nationalism, see Eleonora Narvselius, *Ukrainian Intelligentsia in Post-Soviet L'viv: Narratives, Identity, and Power* (New York: Lexington Books, 2012), 39.

100. LTD, vol. 5.

101. HDA SBU, f. 16, op. 1, spr. 1017, ark. 265.

102. HDA SBU, f. 16, op. 1, spr. 1017, ark. 266.

103. Vasyl Sokil, *Zdaleka do blyzkoho (spohady, rozdumy)* (Edmonton, CA: Kanadskyi instytut ukrainskykh studii, Albertskyi universytet, 1987), 276.

104. Shatylov, *Kliati simdesiati*, 165.

105. For various discussions of the Brezhnev era and stagnation, see Richard Sakwa, *The Rise and Fall of the Soviet Union, 1917–1991* (London and New York: Routledge, 1999); Robert Service, *A History of Modern Russia: From Tsarism to the Twenty-First Century*, 3rd ed. (Cambridge, MA: Harvard University Press, 2009); Gregory L. Freeze, "From Stalinism to Stagnation, 1953–1985," in *Russia: A History*, 2nd ed., ed. Gregory L. Freeze (New York: Oxford University Press, 2002), 347–82; Edwin Bacon and Mark Sandle, eds., *Brezhnev Reconsidered* (New York: Palgrave Macmillan, 2002); Philip Hanson, *The Rise and Fall of the Soviet Economy: An Economic History of the USSR from 1945* (London and New York: Longman, 2003).

106. Anonymous, "Poklykannia zobov'iazuie," *Literaturna Ukraina*, 27 February 1986, p. 3.

107. Mykhailo Naienko suggested that writers are the loneliest people in the world. The majority compensate for this feeling by constant literary work, creating texts, powerful and tense, that can truly be characterized as "high art." For details, see Mykhailo Naienko, "Samotnist dolaetsia slovom naimolodshykh," *Literaturna Ukraina*, 4 April 2013, p. 7.

108. Oleksandr Sharvarok, "Aktyvna pam'iat,'" *Literaturna Ukraina*, 11 December 1981, p. 3.

109. See, for instance, Yurii Tsekov's speech at the party committee meeting of the Kyiv chapter of the Writers' Union in *Literaturna Ukraina*, 27 February 1986, p. 4.

110. Anonymous, "Poklykannia zobov'iazuie," *Literaturna Ukraina*, 27 February 1986, p. 3.

111. For more details about the Chernobyl disaster, see Serhii Plokhy, *Chernobyl: The History of a Nuclear Catastrophe* (New York: Basic Books, 2020); Zubok, *A Failed Empire*, 288–94; V. G. Shkoda, ed., *Chernobyl: Dni ispytanii. Kniga svidetelstv* (Kiev: Radianskyi pysmennyk, 1988); David R. Marples, *Chernobyl and Nuclear Power in the USSR* (London, UK: Palgrave Macmillan, 1987).

112. Zubok, *Zhivago's Children*, 340–41.

113. Catherine Wanner, *Burden of Dreams: History and Identity in Post-Soviet Ukraine* (University Park, PA: The Pennsylvania State University Press, 1998), 27, 30, 31.

114. Ibid.

115. AU SBUKhO, spr. 014519, no page number (A. Pererva's request addressed to the head of the Ukrainian KGB in the Kharkiv oblast to grant permission to Zhanna Ovchinnikova to see the criminal file of her father, the Ukrainian writer Ivan Kallianykov). Kallianykov was sentenced to the VMN (the highest degree of punishment) as a Ukrainian nationalist. He was executed in Kyiv on August 15, 1937. See AU SBUKhO, spr. 014519, ark. 102.

116. Robert Tretyakov, *Tobi: poezii* (Kharkiv: Prapor, 1991), 44.

117. Tretyakov, *Tobi*, 45.

118. Private conversation with Volodymyr Briuggen, 4 July 2009, Kharkiv, Ukraine.

119. Private correspondence with Leonid Toma, 17 October 2013.

120. Valerii Zamesov, "Dlia nas vin buv klasykom: Spohady pro Roberta Tretyakova," *Berezil* 1–2 (2007): 164–68.

121. See a collection of Tretyakov's poetry in English translation by Gladys Evans in *Poetry of Soviet Ukraine's New World: An Anthology* (Woodchurch, Ashford, Kent, England: UNESCO; Paul Norbury Publications, 1986), 195–98, and in Zakhar Honcharuk, eds., *Anthology of Soviet Ukrainian Poetry* (Kiev: Dnipro Publishers, 1982), 392–96.

122. Volodymyr Rodionov, "Sribernyi kniaz Ukrainskoi poezii," *Literaturna Ukraina*, 23 February 2006, p. 7.

123. Viacheslav Romanovskyi, *Osiaiala natkhnenniam Slobozhan: Esei ta besidy* (Kharkiv: Vydavnytstvo Fedorko, 2013), 92.

124. The term which characterized the Soviet system came from Clive James, *Cultural Amnesia: Necessary Memories from History and the Arts* (New York: W. W. Norton & Company, 2007), 248.

125. Shatylov, *Kliati simdesiati*, 143, 155, 157–58, 171. For more details about Hryhir Tiutiunnyk, see his diaries, notes, and letters in Hryhir Tiutiunnyk, *Buty pysmennykom: Lysty. Shchodennyky. Zapysnyky*, ed. O. Nezhyvyi (Kyiv: Vydavnytstvo "Yaroslaviv Val," 2011); Natalia Lapina, "Zaliubleni v . . . Manuilivku," *Literaturna Ukraina*, 15 August 2013, p. 1, 5; and Zhylenko's diary (7 March 1980 entry) in her *Homo Feriens*, 672.

126. For a discussion about hostile attitudes of the pro-Russian Kharkiv local authorities toward Ukrainian culture, see Iryna Farion, "Polityka kriz tovshchu chasu, abo Pam'iat pro Sheveliova," *Literaturna Ukraina*, 12 September 2013, p. 3.

127. Private conversation with Tertyakov's friend Serhii Boltryk, 10 November 1996, Kharkiv, Ukraine.

128. Leonid Toma visited Tretyakov at the hospital, several days before he died on 9 November 1996, and saw the book near his bed. From personal correspondence with Toma, 12 October 2013.

129. Leonid Pliushch, *History's Carnival: A Dissident Autobiography*, trans. and ed. Marco Carynnyk (New York and London: A Helen and Kurt Wolff Book/ Harcourt Brace Jovanovich, 1979), 35.

130. Zbigniew Brzezinski, *Out of Control: Global Turmoil on the Eve of the Twenty-First Century* (New York: Macmillan Publishing Company, 1993), 19 (esp. 1–32).

131. Quoted in "Slobozhanskyi Velykden," in *Ukrainska diaspora* by Ivan Drach, ed. I. S. Riabchyi (Kharkiv: Folio, 2019), 267; on the Revolutionary Nationalist Declaration by Mikhnovskyi, see Zenon V. Wasyliw, "On a Revolutionary Nationalist Declaration: Mykola Mikhnovskyi's Samostiina Ukraina," *East European Quarterly* 33, no 3 (1999): 371–84. Wasyliw wrote:

> The end of the nineteenth and beginning of the twentieth centuries witnessed within the multinational Russian Empire the development of Ukrainian political activity with national goals. Despite the Tsarist government's restrictive policy of Russification, the

first Ukrainian political party, the Revolutionary Ukrainian party (RUP), was established in 1900 in the city of Kharkiv. The original membership, consisting primarily of university students, did not have a crystallized political or ideological platform. In their search for a possible program, the initiating members asked a young Ukrainian activist and lawyer, Mykola Mikhnovskyi, to write a tract for them. Mikhnovskyi produced a brochure entitled Samostiina Ukraina (Independent Ukraine), which was written in the form of a speech. The work was the first outward expression of Ukrainian aspirations for political autonomy based on national statehood within the Russian Empire. It presented highly charged demands based on historical and legal grounds. Though Samostiina Ukraina was later repudiated by the RUP membership for being too narrow and chauvinistic in its outlook, it nevertheless gave impetus to subsequent expressions of similar form within the scope of diverse political thought in the Ukrainian national movement.

132. Quoted in "Slobozhanskyi Velykden," in Drach, 267.

133. Yurii Stadnychenko, "Vesnianyi Kharkiv," in *Kharkiv, pisne moia*, ed. Yurii Stadnychenko (Kharkiv: Prapor, 1982), 78–79. One of Kharkiv's symbols is the monument to the outstanding Ukrainian poet, writer, and artist Taras Shevchenko (1814–1861). The monument is located downtown Kharkiv, in the garden named after Shevchenko—the Shevchenko Garden. It was erected on 24 March 1935, and Mykhail Semenko, a poet of the Executed Renaissance, took an active part in conceiving the ensemble.

134. Ihor Muratov, "Vohni," in Stadnychenko, 82–83.

Conclusion

The Kremlin's nationalities policy and violence against non-Russian ethnic groups foreshadowed the disintegration of the Soviet Union. In his book *The Last Empire: The Final Days of the Soviet Union*, Harvard professor Serhii Plokhy has suggested that the history of Russian-Ukrainian relations, particularly during the Soviet era, limited the possibility of consensus between the two largest Soviet republics, Ukraine and Russia, on preserving a unified state, ultimately shaping the last days of the Soviet empire.[1] Ukraine's multiethnic intelligentsia, whatever was left of it after systematic purges over seventy years of Soviet rule, played a key role in rejecting the idea of a shared future with the Russian Federation as one political entity. The claims of the vitality of communist ideology and Soviet ethnic stability were undermined by the political violence of the Soviet government directed primarily against Ukrainians and Jews residing in Ukraine who wanted simply to remain Ukrainians and Jews, "no more no less," as the Ukrainian poet and *shistdesiatnyk* Ivan Drach has stated.[2] It became quite obvious for them that the prospects of preserving their language and cultural traditions, as well as the potential for exercising their human rights, were murky under the Soviets.

Rapid re-Stalinization and persecution of the intelligentsia in the 1960s and 1970s encouraged many Soviet citizens, identified as "national minorities," to consider legal or illegal emigration from the Soviet Union. According to KGB statistics, from 1970 to 1975, in the territory of Ukraine, 217 people were arrested while attempting to illegally cross the Soviet border.[3] As under Stalin, they were considered "traitors to the Motherland." Ukraine's Jews were trying to leave the "socialist paradise" legally, applying for emigration visas to Israel, but, the Politburo under Khrushchev and under Brezhnev was reluctant to permit them to leave. Anatoly Dobrynin, Soviet ambassador to the United States who served in Washington, D.C. under six American presidents from 1962 to 1986 could never understand why the Soviet Union did not allow Jews to emigrate. In his memoirs, he wrote:

> By solving this question we could have ridden ourselves of a serious and permanent sources of irritation between us and the West, particularly the United States. Even the members of the Politburo under Khrushchev and Brezhnev could not provide a clear and convincing answer when asked in private to explain their views on emigration. Some were still under the influence of Stalin's view that emigrants were traitors. Others would claim that many Jews in the Soviet Union knew state secrets because of their work on military projects using science and technology or other sensitive work, or that Jewish emigrants would join noisy anti-Soviet campaigns abroad. Then there was our Middle East policy: the Arab countries were in permanent protest against Jewish emigration, which they thought would strengthen Israel by augmenting its population and skills.[4]

Zvi Gitelman has suggested that Brezhnev's speech at the 20 March 1973 Politburo meeting was an event that determined Soviet emigration policy. Brezhnev was against the "education tax" that forced emigrants to "repay" the USSR for their higher education received in the Soviet Union and reprimanded Andropov for delaying a decision on this urgent matter.[5] Yet, according to Dobrynin, the key reason behind the Soviet approach to Jewish emigration was the nature of the Soviet system. In closed societies, such as Soviet society, the authorities "are afraid of emigration in general (irrespective of nationality or religion)" because the freedom of movement seems to offer a "degree of liberalization that might destabilize the domestic situation."[6] Nevertheless, pressure from the West and domestic pressure forced the Soviet government to loosen emigration policies, and according to Brezhnev's claims shared with Dobrynin, 95.5 percent of applications for emigration to Israel were approved in 1972. Indeed, from 1971 to 1973, approximately 60,000 Soviet Jews left for Israel.[7] From 1971, Kharkiv began to lose its creative Jewish youth, including those who were part of Chichibabin's literary studio.

Those who chose Kharkiv over emigration experienced enormous pressure and controls imposed on them by the Kharkiv authorities. From the podiums of public events, Kharkiv party leaders proclaimed the "foundational principles" of the Soviet state—the "friendship of peoples" and "proletarian internationalism," but in their private conversation with writers, they incited ethnic hatred and mistrust toward Ukrainian and Jewish "nationalists." The writers' concerns for national traditions and language were labeled as "bourgeois nationalism," which reinforced prejudicial attitudes among the Kharkiv literati who were encouraged to believe that "certain nations [were] innately untrustworthy."[8] More than thirty years ago, the American scholar Alexander J. Motyl argued that "Ukrainian-Jewish relations are an excellent example of how this unfortunate dynamic works. Official anti-Zionism legitimizes Ukrainian anti-Semitism; official condemnation of 'Ukrainian bourgeois nationalism' reinforces Jewish Ukrainophobia."[9] KGB active measures, co-optation, and recruitment of the creative intelligentsia, silencing national historical narratives, and the Soviet cadre politics of nationality representation in the party, the government, and the army served to buttress ethnic boundaries. For party and KGB bureaucrats, it was exceedingly difficult to identify a degree of poetic talent, but they unmistakably defined on the subconscious level a degree of intellectualism and independent thought in an individual. Kharkiv officials ethnicized these faculties, and these definitions served as a "measuring stick" of potential danger that certain writers presented to the state. The objective was to raise a generation of Soviets, not Ukrainians or Jews. In the view of the former head of the KGB Fifth Chief Directorate Filipp Bobkov, silencing and isolating writers who inflamed "nationalistic moods" in Ukraine was absolutely necessary.[10]

The Soviet regime never again unleashed mass murder and terror similar to Stalin's genocides with their millions of victims, including the Holodomor. As many scholars have suggested, Stalin's mass killings and crimes against humanity "remained a unique episode in Soviet history."[11] Yet, as we have seen, in the 1960s and 1970s, the KGB designed a number of sophisticated techniques of psychological and physical torture imposed on intellectuals to prevent their unity, their anti-Soviet collective activities, and their individual critical thinking. These techniques included defamatory campaigns, deception, and forgeries that were designed to create a rift between Ukrainians and Jews and reinforce ethnic stereotypes and tensions between them. Among Kharkiv *shistdesiatnyky* were those who yielded to this pressure and those who actively and passively opposed it. The majority transcended the ethnic boundaries erected by the KGB, rejecting the oblique KGB games that ultimately failed to create a homogenous community of obedient Soviet propagandists in Kharkiv. More fundamentally, the Soviet government underestimated the effects of the political activism of Ukraine's young generation, including the Kharkiv literati who after their emigration enriched world literature and established mnemonic and emotional bridges between Soviet citizens and Western human rights activists, representatives of various ethnic diasporas. These transnational links further undermined Soviet authoritative discourse and Soviet historical narrative, instilling in the Kharkivites the pride of their spatial belonging and faith in their national survival. Through intimidation, however, the KGB managed to subdue the creativity of many Kharkiv writers. Only in the late 1980s, they abandoned writing panegyrics to the party and painting Lenin's portraits:[12] the Kharkivites again began to write love poems and paint Chagall-like blue cornflowers, mirroring the Kharkiv blue skies that they did not dare to observe in the 1960s and 1970s.

Kenneth C. Farmer has argued that "dissent at the periphery, away from foreign correspondents and under a more vigorous KGB, [was] more dangerous and difficult."[13] Then, who were they, those Kharkivites who avoided lengthy prison sentences during the period of three waves of post-Stalin repression in Ukraine? Silenced and withdrawn, were they perpetrators or victims of the Soviet regime? Lynne Viola suggests that "the identification of perpetrators and victims . . . is not always so clear-cut."[14] She argues that the factors that might be used as analytical tools to explain the behavior of perpetrators, such as fear, alcohol, duty, and ideology, were never stable, and were contingent on place, time, and circumstances in which people found themselves.[15] According to Viola, "perpetrators could easily become victims," and just the opposite, victims could become perpetrators.[16] This fluidity makes precise identification of Soviet citizens extremely difficult and even morally questionable. Labeling complex individuals, such as Briuggen, Muratov, or Tretyakov, would be of little value to understand them as human beings, or, on a macro-level, to understand the political and social system in which they existed.

Decades after Stalin's terror and repressions, this identification appears to be as problematic as during the first post-Stalin decade.[17] A glimpse into the lives of Kharkiv *shistdesiatnyky* suggests that they could not become perpetrators without first being victimized. In fact, they were always both, and they knew that. The intelligentsia, more than any other social group in Ukraine, was aware of the inquisitive and vindictive nature of the regime. The intrusive techniques of the KGB were well known, and obedience could not be a recipe for relative freedom. The system was insatiable. The literati were fully aware of how far to the left they might drift in their creative writing to be overlooked and tolerated. This political maneuvering and self-regulation seem on the surface rather cynical, although one should remember the extreme cynicism of the KGB that forcibly imposed this pattern of behavior on the literati through intimidation and blackmail.

Viola's advocacy of the analytical need for a discussion of the issue of perpetrators in Soviet studies invites an apt question about who might be at the base of this "pyramid of perpetrators." As Wendy Z. Goldman explains it,

> its imposing base is crowded with those who wrote denunciations, spoke against others at mass meetings, made fiery speeches about enemies, penned vicious critiques in newspapers, transformed accidents into "wrecking," and politicized technical, scientific, and cultural quarrels. They are joined by those who sought personal gain, promotions, and the property of their neighbors through the politics of terror.[18]

The majority of the Kharkiv literati mentioned in this narrative never participated in these sorts of activities and hardly used their position for personal gain. There is little question here about whether they, by their silence, perpetuated the status quo. In his short story "Iskuplenie" (Redemption), the former Kharkivite Yulii Daniel offered the definition of perpetrators: both those who were *seksots* and executioners, and those who refused to participate in the liberation movement and were innocent victims, perpetuated the status quo. Yet, Daniel has argued that there is a significant difference between those who committed the atrocities and those who were forcibly silenced by the regime. He seems to believe that in the final analysis a writer should be judged for his ultimate contribution to world literature, rather than in the context of the morality of his or her individual behavior.

For many Kharkiv writers, raised in the atmosphere of chronic intellectual abuse, artistic freedom remained an unattainable goal. For a few, their remarkable reincarnation mollified the loss of their potentially productive years when they were silenced. Briuggen's brilliant aphorisms that he began to publish in independent Ukraine illuminated painful memories of missed opportunities and loves, and of what he had lived through and suffered from. For Tretyakov, his new dazzlingly intellectual and emotional poetry might have been the last attempt of self-understanding before his physical death. For their readers, their disillusionment and belated repentance appear to be something much more than non-authoritative reflections of two men. Their ideas, identities, feelings, and emotions seem to be a mirror of the coercive Soviet era and the collective features of the entire generation of Ukraine's multicultural intelligentsia, shaped by the Khrushchev Thaw.

The story of their lives in authoritarian Kharkiv invites readers to revisit the pandemic features of oppressive regimes, such as fear. Fear permeated the depths of human subconsciousness. Fear was a migrating phenomenon that transcended spaces and places, shaping behavioral and communication patterns and rules among state officials and the intelligentsia. This idea is exemplified by a notoriously famous incident that occurred in 1966 in a courtroom. Present during the hearings, the Ukrainian poet Lina Kostenko threw a bouquet of flowers to the victims of the regime who were tried on this day for anti-Soviet propaganda. This innocent and spontaneous act of support and kindness induced the militia to drop on the floor in fear that a bomb had been thrown.[19] A sign of persistent subconscious fear that hijacked the minds of state officials materialized in their self-defensive reaction to the act of civic courage of a single individual, defending her human rights and entitlement to self-expression. Everyone's fear, however, was of a different nature. People like Leonid Pliushch feared the consequences of his own weakness, betrayal, and moral degradation under the KGB pressure; Tretyakov feared the state infringing on his poetic gift and treating his family as hostages to obtain his compliance; and the KGB feared nationalist uprisings and their supervisors who could take their privileged positions away from them, together with their benefits. Paraphrasing the Argentine poet Juan Gelman, fears, like words, belong to everyone, but their nature, etiology, and effects are what matters the most: they incite various human behaviors, from compassionate to genocidal.

Importantly, the brutality of the Soviet regime provokes questions about the moral stance of its leaders who claimed to be reformers. The semi-public acknowledgment of Stalin's crimes and the terror against "Ukrainian nationalists" and "Zionists" seem to be a reflection of Khrushchev's ambivalent personality. He had never expressed any remorse about the brutal treatment of his compatriots in Ukraine under his leadership.[20] Moreover, Khrushchev's and later Brezhnev's efforts at humanizing Stalinism failed to humanize the Soviet secret police. Because of its historical traditions, and ideological and structural foundations, the agency could not break from the Soviet system of coercion and violence. The KGB was willing to apply violence in any form, at any time, and on any occasion. The *chekists* created and perpetuated the system of violence, having never rescinded it even under Gorbachev's perestroika. The Australian literary critic Clive James has accurately characterized this system:

> They [the *chekists*] grew up in an atmosphere of unrelieved moral squalor. Through bad faith, they flourished; and good faith would have held them back. The system had been designed so that they always stood to benefit personally from the decay around them. If the whole thing had gone to dogs, they would have been all right. . . . Most men bend with the breeze: which is to say, they go with the prevailing power.[21]

Under Andropov, beyond imprisonment, the regime adopted sophisticated practices of torture, such as punitive psychiatry, that simply poisoned the everyday existence of the intelligentsia, anticipating the worst—a protracted torture by Soviet psychiatrists. The writers were daily reminded of the KGB's existence, were chastised in the press, and were routinely intimidated at party meetings and in the KGB headquarters. The party banned their works or forced the writers to revise them beyond recognition. The KGB, using their broad mandate, made many writers unemployable. These measures proved to be sufficient to break the spirit of some intellectuals, leading others to commit suicide.[22]

In 1962, in his emotional letter to Andrii Malyshko, Vasyl Stus shared his observations about the rapid process of Ukraine's denationalization and the interruption of its cultural traditions. He lamented about millions of assimilated Ukrainians indifferent to the lengthy martyrology list of fighters for the Ukrainian language and culture which the Soviet regime tried to erase.[23] Indeed, the political and structural organization of space in the Soviet Union reinforced in the peripheries a collective feeling that individuals truly existed in the cultural peripheries, stripped of national traditions. The writers' attempts at redefining this feeling in national terms were suppressed and subsequently punished. The KGB methodically erased people's historical memories, attempting to provincialize and denationalize the first capital of Ukraine, Kharkiv, by promoting and perpetuating the Kharkivites' cultural amnesia. The city had to be subordinate to Russian culture and be Russified. As a result, "much Soviet literature denied particularism—whether Ukrainian or Jewish," Myroslav Shkandrij has accurately noted.[24] Illogically, however, the *chekists* reinforced ethnic stereotypes and, under pressure, several Kharkiv writers buried their hopes for the resurrection of Kharkiv as a multiethnic and multicultural city, together with their authentic poetical voices. Briuggen was among a few who rejected the notion of Kharkiv as a cultural province: he preserved the feeling of "literature's centrality" inside him and the perception of literature as a way of life, perceptions that have little to do with geography but rather with the intimate inner core that helps writers insure their cultural and intellectual survival.[25] Similarly, the Ukrainian-American philologist of German origin and former Kharkivite Yurii Sheveliov has posited that the province should not be perceived as a geographical notion or a territory but rather as a psychological condition of one's soul and mind.[26]

A sketch of literary Kharkiv in the 1960s and 1970s revealed that despite the Kharkiv literati's inadequacies, their behavioral inconsistencies, and their conformism, their post-Khrushchev Thaw romanticism and new identities facilitated the emergence of a new transnational literature and a new literary community that placed Kharkiv on the map of world literature, offering readers not its truncated ethnic image but an image of a place where various ethnic groups could reside and cocreate without major conflicts and strife.

NOTES

1. Serhii Plokhy, *The Last Empire: The Final Days of the Soviet Union* (New York: Basic Books, 2015).

2. Ivan Drach, *Ukrainska diaspora,* ed. I. S. Riabchyi (Kharkiv: Folio, 2019), 118.

3. TsDAHOU, f. 1, op. 25, spr. 1399, ark. 105; see also Olga Bertelsen, "Political Affinities and Maneuvering of Soviet Ukrainian Political Elites: Heorhii Shevel and the Ministry of Strange Affairs in the 1970s," *Nationalities Papers: The Journal of Nationalism and Ethnicity* 47, no. 3 (2019): 401.

4. Anatoly Dobrynin, *In Confidence: Moscow's Ambassador to America's Six Cold War Presidents* (Seattle and London: University of Washington Press, 1995), 267.

5. On the three waves of emigration since 1970 in the Soviet Union, see Zvi Gitelman, "Native Land, Promised Land, Golden Land: Jewish Emigration from Russia and Ukraine," *Harvard Ukrainian Studies* 22, no. XII (1998): 140.

6. Dobrynin, *In Confidence*, 268.
7. Dobrynin, *In Confidence*, 269.
8. Alexander J. Motyl, *Will the Non-Russians Rebel? State, Ethnicity, and Stability in the USSR* (Ithaca and London: Cornell University Press, 1987), 153–54.
9. Motyl, *Will the Non-Russians Rebel?*, 154.
10. See Filipp Bobkov's memoirs *KGB i vlast* (Moskva: Izdatelstvo "Veteran MP," 1995), 318.
11. James Harris, *The Great Fear: Stalin's Terror of the 1930s* (Oxford, UK: Oxford University Press, 2016), 188.
12. On propaganda painting, see Alexei Yurchak, *Everything Was Forever, Until It Was No More: The Last Soviet Generation* (Princeton, NJ: Princeton University Press, 2006), 56.
13. Kenneth C. Farmer, *Ukrainian Nationalism in the Post-Stalin Era* (The Hague/Boston/London: Martinus Nijhoff Publishers, 1980), 161.
14. Lynne Viola, "The Question of the Perpetrator in Soviet History," *Slavic Review* 72, no. 1 (2013): 11.
15. Viola, "The Question of the Perpetrator in Soviet History," 12–13.
16. Ibid., 14, 18.
17. Miriam Dobson, *Khrushchev's Cold Summer: Gulag Returnees, Crime, and the Fate of Reform after Stalin* (Ithaca and London: Cornell University Press, 2009), 6. Miriam Dobson posited that during the de-Stalinization years "the task of defining who had the right to be called a victim proved just as difficult as identifying the perpetrators."
18. Wendy Z. Goldman, "Twin Pyramids—Perpetrators and Victims," *Slavic Review* 72, no. 1 (2013): 27.
19. Leonid Plyushch, *History's Carnival: A Dissident's Autobiography*, ed. and trans. Marco Carynnyk (New York & London: A Helen and Kurt Wolff Book/Harcourt Brace Jovanovich, 1979), 237.
20. Vladislav Zubok and Constantine Pleshakov, *Inside the Kremlin's Cold War: From Stalin to Khrushchev* (Cambridge, MA: Harvard University Press, 1996), 177; see also Khrushchev's memoirs "Memuary Nikity Sergeevicha Khrushcheva," *Voprosy istorii* 2–12 (1990); no. 1–12 (1991); no. 1–3, 6–9, 11–12 (1992); no. 2–12 (1993); no. 1–12 (1994); no. 1–6 (1995).
21. Clive James, *Cultural Amnesia: Necessary Memories from History and the Arts* (New York: W. W. Norton & Company, 2007), 248–49.
22. Oleksii Nezhyvyi, "Avtohrafy—ne tilky na paperi . . ." *Literaturna Ukraina*, 12 September 2013, p. 7.
23. Larysa Masenko, "Lyst Vasylia Stusa do Andriia Malyshka: Istoriia nezdiisnymoi sproby dialohu," *Literaturna Ukraina*, 12 September 2013, p. 6.
24. Myroslav Shkandrij, *Jews in Ukrainian Literature: Representation and Identity* (New Haven & London: Yale University Press, 2009), 231.
25. Private conversation with Volodymyr Briuggen, 8 August 2013, Kharkiv, Ukraine; Volodymyr Briuggen's interview with Yevhen Baran, "Ia rozumiiu literaturu peredusim iak sposib zhyttia," in *Liudy i knyhy: Statti i spohady* by Volodymyr Briuggen (Kharkiv: Maidan, 2006), 88–95.
26. Ihor Mykhailyn, "Yurii Sheveliov: Provintsiia—ne territoriia, a dusha," *Den*, 30 November–1 December 2012 (no. 219–220), p. 3.

Bibliography

Abramson, Henry. *A Prayer for the Government: Ukrainians and Jews in Revolutionary Times, 1917–1920*. Cambridge, MA: Harvard University Press, 1999.

Adamovych, Anthony. "The Non-Russians." In *Soviet Literature in the Sixties*, edited by Max Hayward and Edward L. Crowley, 100–29. London: Methuen & Co Ltd., 1964.

Afanas'ieva, E. S. et al., eds. *Apparat TsK KPSS i kultura, 1953–1957: Dokumenty*. Moskva: ROSSPEN, 2001.

Afiani, V. I., and N. G. Tomilina, eds. *"A za mnoiu shum pogoni..." Boris Pasternak i vlast': Dokumenty, 1956–1972*. Moskva: ROSSPEN, 2001.

Agursky, Mikhail. *Pepel Klaasa: Razryv*. Jerusalem: URA, 1996.

Aheieva, Vira. *Mystetstvo rivnovahy: Maksym Rylskyi na tli epokhy*. Kyiv: Vydavnytstvo "Knyha," 2012.

"Aleksandr Vernik." *Art in Process*. 2020. http://art-in-process.com/avtory/literatura/aleksandr-vernik/.

Alexeyeva, Ludmilla, and Paul Goldberg. *The Thaw Generation: Coming of Age in the Post-Stalin Era*. Boston: Little, Brown and Company, 1990.

Alexeyeva, Ludmilla. *Soviet Dissent: Contemporary Movements for National, Religious, and Human Rights*. Middletown, CT: Wesleyan University Press, 1985.

Altshuler, Mordechai. *Soviet Jewry on the Eve of the Holocaust: A Social and Demographic Profile*. Jerusalem: Maureen Mack, 1998.

Altunian, Genrikh. *Tsena svobody: Vospominaniia dissidenta*. Kharkov: Folio, 2000.

Amar, Tarik Cyril. *The Paradox of Ukrainian Lviv: A Borderland City between Stalinists, Nazis, and Nationalists*. Ithaca, NY: Cornell University Press, 2015.

"Amnesty International priznala triokh figurantov Bolotnogo dela uznikami sovesti." *Bolotnoe delo*. 3 October 2013. http://bolotnoedelo.info/news/3975/amnesty-international-priznala-trex-figurantov-bolotnogo-dela-uznikami-sovesti.

Amnesty International Publications. *A Chronicle of Current Events: Journal of the Human Rights Movement in the USSR*, 46 (1977). New York: Khronika Press, 1978.

Andrew, Christopher, and Oleg Gordievsky. *KGB: The Inside Story of Its Foreign Operations from Lenin to Gorbachev.* New York: Harper Collins Publishers, 1990.

Andrew, Christopher. *The Sword and the Shield: The Mitrokhin Archive and the Secret History of the KGB.* New York: Basic Books, 1999.

Andriewsky, Olga. "Towards a Decentered History: The Study of the Holodomor and Ukrainian Historiography." In *Contextualizing the Holodomor: The Impact of Thirty Years of Ukrainian Famine Studies,* edited by Andrij Makuch and Frank E. Sysyn, 14–48. Edmonton; Toronto: The Canadian Institute of Ukrainian Studies Press, 2015.

Andriichuk, Tamara. "Ananii Lebid' (1898–1937): trahediia liudyny i naukovtsia." In *Reabilitovani istoriieiu. Chernihivska oblast,* vol. 4, 202–12. Chernihiv: Vydavets Lozovyi V. M., 2012.

Andrusiv, Stefania. "Shistdesiatnytstvo yak iavyshche, yoho vytoky i naslidky." *Slovo i chas* 8 (1997): 50–52.

Antypova, Iryna. "Volodymyr Sosiura: Vriatovanyi bozhevilliam." *Druh Chytacha.* 25 June 2009. https://vsiknygy.net.ua/review/1011/.

Applebaum, Anne. *Red Famine: Stalin's War on Ukraine.* New York: Anchor, 2018.

"Arie Vudka." *Berkovich.* 2020. http://berkovich-zametki.com/Avtory/Vudka.htm.

Aristotle. *Rhetoric,* edited by C. D. C. Reeve. Indianapolis, IN: Hackett Publishing Company, Inc., 2018.

Artamonov, Nikolai. "Otshelnik s ulitsy Astronomicheskoi." *Kharkov–350: Gumanitarnyie resursy.* 2020. http://kharkovhumanit.narod.ru/Liki_kult.html.

Artress, Lauren. *Walking a Sacred Path: Rediscovering the Labyrinth as a Spiritual Tool.* New York: Riverhead Books, 1995.

Aster, Howard, and Peter J. Potichnyj. *Jewish-Ukrainian Relations: Two Solitudes.* Oakville, Ontario: Mosaic Press, 1983.

Babenko, Ivan. "Neskolko strok o bylom." In *Slobozhanskii krug,* edited by Pavel Gulakov et al., 31–41. Kharkov: TAL "Slobozhanshchyna," 2006.

Bachelard, Gaston. *The Poetics of Space: The Classic Look at How We Experience Intimate Places,* translated by Maria Jolas. Boston: Beacon Press, 1994.

Bacon, Edwin, and Mark Sandle, eds. *Brezhnev Reconsidered.* New York: Palgrave Macmillan, 2002.

Bahrianyi, Ivan. *Publitsystyka: Dopovidi, statti, pamflety, refleksii, ese,* 2nd ed., edited by Oleksii Konoval. Kyiv: Smoloskyp, 2006.

Baigell, Renee, and Matthew Baigell, eds. *Soviet Dissident Artists: Interviews After Perestroika* New Brunswick, NJ: Rutgers University Press, 1995.

Baran, Emily B., and Zoe Knox. "The 2002 Russian Anti-Extremism Law: An Introduction." *The Soviet and Post-Soviet Review* 46, no. 2 (2019): 97–104.

Baran, Yevhen. "Ya rozumiiu literaturu peredusim yak sposib zhyttia." in *Liudy i knyhy: Statti i spohady* by Volodymyr Briuggen, 88–95. Kharkiv: Maidan, 2006.

———. "Volodymyr Briuggen: Ya rozumiiu literaturu peredusim yak sposib zhyttia." *Kharkov–350: Gumanitarnyie resursy.* 2020. http://kharkovhumanit.narod.ru/Liki_kult.html.

———. "Zradlyva nizhnist 'Bloknotiv' Volodymyra Briuggena." *Berezil* 9–10 (2012): 156–63.

Barbakadze, M., ed. *Shestidesiatniki*. Moskva: Fond "Liberalnaia missiia," 2007.

Barber, John, Mark Harrison, Nikolai Simonov, and Boris Starkov. "The Structure and Development of the Soviet Defense-Industry Complex." In *The Soviet Defense-Industry Complex from Stalin to Khrushchev*, edited by John Barber and Mark Harrison, 3–32. London and Basingstoke: Macmillan, 2000.

Barnai, Samuel. "Social Trends Among Jews in the Post-Stalin Years." In *Revolution, Repression, and Revival: The Soviet Jewish Experience*, edited by Zvi Gitelman and Yaacov Roi, 131–52. New York: Rowman & Littlefield Publishers, Inc., 2007.

Baron, Nick. *Soviet Karelia: Politics, Planning and Terror in Stalin's Russia, 1920–39*. New York: Routledge, 2007.

Barron, John. *KGB: The Secret Work of Soviet Secret Agents*. New York: Reader's Digest Press, 1974.

Bazhan, O. H., and I. Z. Danyliuk. *Opozytsiia v Ukraini (druha polovyna 50-kh–80-ti rr. XX st.)*. Kyiv: NAN Ukrainy, Instytut istorii Ukrainy, Ridnyi krai, 2000.

Bazhan, O. H., and O. O. Kovalchuk. "Svitovyi Konhres Ukraintsiv" (Entsyklopediia istorii Ukrainy). *Instytut istorii Ukrainy, NANU*. http://www.history.org.ua/?termin =Svitovyj_Konhres.

Bazhan, O. H. "Diialnist klubiv tvorchoi molodi v Ukrainiv 1960-kh rokahk u ershodzherelakh." *Kraieznavstvo* 1–4 (2006): 80–82.

———. "Dysydentski (opozytsiini) rukhy 1960–1980-kh rokiv v Ukraini." In *Entsyklopediia istorii Ukrainy*, t. 2, edited by V. A. Smolii et al. Kyiv: Instytut Istorii Ukrainy NANU/"Naukova dumka," 2004.

Bazan, Oleh. "Do pytannia pro 'ukrainofilstvo' pershoho sekretaria TsK KPU Petra Shelesta." *Arkhiv Sluzhby Natsionalnoi Bezpeky Ukrainy*, http://dspace.nbuv.gov .ua/bitstream/handle/123456789/40456/14-Bazhan.pdf?sequence=1.

———. "Petro Shelest i protestnyi rukh v URSR u 1960–1970-kh rr." *Z arkiviv VUChK-GPU-NKVD-KGB*, 2, no. 43 (2014): 443–56.

———. "Petro Shelest: Shtrykhy politychnoho portreta." *Instytut Istorii Ukrainy, NANU*. 2021. http://resource.history.org.ua/cgi-bin/eiu/history.exe?I21DBN =EJRN&P21DBN=EJRN&S21REF=10&S21CNR=20&S21STN=1&S21FMT =ASP_meta&C21COM=S&2_S21P03=IDP=&2_S21STR=xxx_2011_16_152.

———. "Represyvni zakhody Radianskoi vlady shchodo hromadian yevreiskoi natsionalnosti v URSR (1960-ti–1980-ti rr.)." *Z arkiviv VUChK-GPU-NKVD-KGB* 22 (2004): 112–20.

Beckerman, Gal. *When They Come for Us, We'll Be Gone: The Epic Struggle to Save Soviet Jewry*. Boston/New York: Houghton Mifflin Harcourt, 2010.

Belleza, Simone Attilio. "Making Soviet Ukraine Ukrainian: The Debate on Ukrainian Statehood in the Journal Suchasnist (1961–1971)." *Nationalities Papers* 47, no. 3 (2019): 379–93.

Belleza, Simone Attilio. *The Shore of Expectations: A Cultural Study of the Shistdesiatnyky*. Edmonton/Toronto: Canadian Institute of Ukrainian Studies Press, 2019.

———. "Wings to Lift the Truth Up High: The Role of Language for the Shistdesiatnyky." *Harvard Ukrainian Studies* 35, no. 1–4 (2017–2018): 213–32.

Beliaieva (Gurina), Raisa. "Dom dlia druzei." In *Vsemu zhivomu ne chuzhoi: Boris Chichibabin v statiakh i vospominaniiakh*, edited by M. I. Bogoslavskii, L. S. Karas-Chichibabina, and B. Y. Ladenzon, 316–25. Kharkov: Folio, 1998.

Belov, Anatolii, and Andrei Shilkin. *Diversii bez dinamita*. Moskva: Izdatelstvo politicheskoi literatury, 1972.

Bergman, Ronen. "The KGB's Middle East Files: The Fight against Zionism and World Jewry." 1 December 2016. https://www.ynetnews.com/articles/0,7340,L-4886594,00.html.

Berenson, Bernard. *Rumour and Reflection: 1941: 1944*. London: Constable, 1952.

Berenson, Lazar. "'Napishut nashi imena.' Vospominaniia o Borise Chichibabine." *Sem iskustv* 2, no. 15 (February 2011). http://7iskusstv.com/2011/Nomer2/Berenson1.php.

Berlin, Isaiah. *Personal Impressions*, edited by Henry Hardy. New York: The Viking Press, 1980.

———. *The Soviet Mind: Russian Culture under Communism*, edited by Henry Hardy. Washington, DC: Brookings Institution Press, 2004.

Bernhard, Michael, and Jan Kubik, eds. *Twenty Years After Communism: The Politics of Memory and Commemoration*. New York: Oxford University Press, 2014.

Bertelsen, Dale A., and Olga Bertelsen. "Russian Hegemony in the Black Sea Basin: The 'Third Rome' in Contemporary Geopolitics." In *Revolution and War in Contemporary Ukraine: The Challenge of Change*, edited by Olga Bertelsen, 213–49. Stuttgart and New York: ibidem-Verlag/Columbia University Press, 2017.

Bertelsen, Olga, ed. *Russian Active Measures: Yesterday, Today, Tomorrow*. Stuttgart/New York: ibidem-Verlag/Columbia University Press, 2021.

Bertelsen, Olga, and Myroslav Shkandrij. "The Secret Police and the Campaign against Galicians in Soviet Ukraine, 1929–34." *Nationalities Papers: The Journal of Nationalism and Ethnicity* 42, no. 1 (2014): 37–62.

Bertelsen, Olga. "A Trial *in Absentia*: Purifying National Historical Narratives in Russia." *Kyiv-Mohyla Humanities Journal* 3 (2016): 57–87.

Bertelsen, Olga, ed. *Les Kurbas i teatr "Berezil": Arkhivni dokumenty (1927–1988)*. Kyiv: "Smoloskyp," 2016.

Bertelsen, Olga. "Political Affinities and Maneuvering of Soviet Political Elites: Heorhii Shevel and Ukraine's Ministry of Strange Affairs in the 1970s." *Nationalities Papers* 47, no. 3 (2019): 394–411.

———. "Rethinking Psychiatric Terror against Nationalists in Ukraine." *Kyiv-Mohyla Arts and Humanities* 1 (2014): 27–76.

———. "Robert Tretyakov – 'poet kokhannia'," *Literaturna Ukraina* 7 (5636), 25 (February 2016): 6–7.

———. "Starvation and Violence amid the Soviet Politics of Silence 1928–1929." *Genocide Studies International* 11, no. 1 (2018): 38–67.

———. "The House of Writers in Ukraine, the 1930s: Conceived, Lived, Perceived." *Carl Beck Papers* 2302 (August 2013): 4–72.

———. "Ukrainian and Jewish Émigrés as Targets of KGB Active Measures in the 1970s." *International Journal of Intelligence and Counterintelligence* 34, no. 2 (2021): 267–92.

_____. "Women at Sites of Mass Starvation: Ukraine, 1932–1933." In *Women and the Holodomor-Genocide: Victims, Survivors, Perpetrators*, edited by Victoria A. Malko, 33–49. Fresno, CA: The Press at California State University, 2019.

Bertelsen, Dale A. "Kenneth Burke and Multiculturalism: A Voice of Ethnocentrism and Apologia." *Qualitative Research Reports in Communication* 3, no. 4 (2002): 82–89.

Biletska-Muratova, Natalia. ". . . Ne smiiuchy skazaty: 'Vin pomer.'" In *Na krylakh Litany* by Ihor Muratov, 4–36. Kharkiv: Maidan, 2012.

Bilinsky, Yaroslav. "Political Relations Between Russians and Ukrainians in the USSR: The 1970s and Beyond." In *Ukraine and Russia in Their Historical Encounter*, edited by Peter J. Potichnyi, Marc Raeff, Jaroslaw Pelenski, and Gleb N. Zekulin, 165–98. Edmonton, Canada: CIUS Press/University of Alberta, 1992.

Bilinsky, Yaroslav. "The Communist Party of Ukraine after 1966." In *Ukraine in the Seventies*, edited by Peter J. Potichnyj, 239–55. Oakville, ON: Mosaic Press, 1975.

Bilocerkowycz, Jaroslaw. *Soviet Ukrainian Dissent: A Study of Political Alienation*. Boulder and London: Westview Press, 1988.

Bilokin, Serhii. *Masovyi teror yak zasib derzhavnoho upravlinnia v SRSR (1917–1941): dzhereloznavche doslidzhennia*. Kyiv: Fundatsiia "Volia," 1999.

Bitov, Andrei. "Pisatel sam ne p'iet . . ." *Moskovskie novosti*. 21 October 2011. http://www.mn.ru/friday/74757.

Bloch, Sidney, and Peter Reddaway. *Soviet Psychiatric Abuse: The Shadow over World Psychiatry*. Boulder, CO: Westview Press, 1985.

Bobkov, Filipp. *KGB i vlast*. Moskva: Izdatelstvo "Veteran MP," 1995.

Bogoraz, Larisa. "Afterword." In *To Live Like Everyone* by Anatoly Marchenko, 205–15. New York: Henry Holt and Company, 1989.

Bondarenko, Olena. "23 kvitnia 1920 narodyvsia ukrainskyi pysmennyk Hryhorii Tiutiunnyk." *Ridna kraina*. https://ridna.ua/2019/04/23-kvitnya-1920-roku-narodyvsya-ukrajinskyj-pysmennyk-hryhorij-tyutyunnyk/.

Bondarenko, Stanislav. "Odyn iz tvortsiv sprotyvu," *Literaturna Ukraina*, 18 October 2012, p. 5.

Borovsky, Victor. *Potsilunok satany: Spohady*. New York: Meta Publishing Company, 1981.

"Borovsky Tells Rutgers Students of Life Behind Iron Curtain." *The Ukrainian Weekly* 68, 23 March 1980, p. 5.

Borovyi, Vasyl (interview by Liutsyna Khvorost and Larysa Vyrovets). "Vasyl Borovyi: 'Mene blahoslovyv do druku Svidzinskyi.'" *Official site of Liutsyna Khvorost*. 14 March 2012. https://dobrolucina.wordpress.com/2012/03/14/василь-боровий-мене-благословив-до-д/.

_____. (interview by Serhii Shelkovyi). "No on-to darom sroka ne daiot . . ." *Kharkivska oblasna orhanizatsiia: Natsionalna spilka pysmennykiv Ukrainy*. 15 November 2014. http://kharkiv-nspu.org.ua/archives/3444.

Bourdieu, Pierre, and Richard Passeron. *Reproduction in Education, Society, and Culture*, 2nd ed. Translated by Richard Nice. Los Angeles, London, New Delhi, Singapore, and Washington, DC: Sage, 1990.

Bransten, Jeremy. "Russia: Soviet Dissident Larisa Bogoraz Dead at 74." *RadioFreeEurope.* 7 April 2004. https://www.rferl.org/a/1052206.html.
Brezhnev, L. I. "O piatidesiatiletii Soiuza Sovetskikh Sotsialisticheskikh Respublik." *Pravda,* 22 December 1972, p. 2.
Brikner, A. G. "Vskrytie chuzhykh pisem i depesh pri Ekaterine II (Perliustratsiia)." *Russkaia starina* 7, no. 1 (1873), *Bibliotekar.ru/Reprinty starinnykh knig.* 2021. http://www.bibliotekar.ru/reprint-133/.
Brintlinger, Angela, and Ilya Vinitsky, eds. *Madness and the Mad in Russian Culture.* Toronto: University of Toronto Press, 2007.
Briuggen, Vladimir. *Bloknoty: Kniga tret'ia.* Kharkov: Maidan 2010.
———. *Bloknoty.* Kharkov: Maidan, 2007.
Briuggen, Volodymyr (interview by Yurii Virchenko). *Slobozhanshchyna Slovo,* vyp. 6 (Robert Tretyakov). *YouTube.* 8 May 2012. https://www.youtube.com/watch?v =QIfMn_o0Ow0&t=419s.
Briuggen, V. O. *Liudyna tvoryt dobro: Literaturno-krytychni narysy.* Kyiv: Radianskyi pysmennyk, 1966.
Briuggen, Volodymyr. *Liudy i knyhy: Statti i spohady.* Kharkiv: Maidan, 2006.
———. "Znaiomyi i neznaiomyi Muratov." *Natsionalna spilka pysmennykiv Ukrainy/Kharkivska oblasna orhanizatsiia.* 20 September 2012. https://kharkiv -nspu.org.ua/archives/549#respond.
Briuggen, V. O. *Pro Ihoria Muratova: Literaturno-krytychni statti.* Kyiv: Radianskyi pysmennyk, 1972.
———. *Zemlia i liudy.* Kyiv: Radianskyi pysmennyk, 1973.
———. *Zvychainyi khlib mystetstva: Literaturno-krytychni statti.* Kyiv: Radianskyi pysmennyk, 1969.
Briukhovetskyi, Viacheslav. "Mykola Zerov." *Literaturna Ukraina* 32, no. 4441, 8 August 1991.
Browne, Michael, ed. *Ferment in the Ukraine: Documents by V. Chornovil, I. Kandyba, L. Lukyanenko, V. Moroz, and Others* with a foreword by Max Hayward. Woodhaven, NY: Crisis Press, 1973.
Bruce, Douglas R. "Silence, Rhetoric, and Freedom: Explicating Foucault through Augustine." In *Visions of Rhetoric: History, Theory and Criticism,* edited by Charles W. Kneupper, 157–68. Arlington, TX: Rhetoric Society of America, 1987.
Brusilovskii, Anatolii. *Studiia. Official site of Anatolii Brusilovskii.* 2021. https:// www.anatolbrusilov.com/тексты/книги/.
Brummett, Barry. "Towards a Theory of Silence as a Political Strategy." *Quarterly Journal of Speech* 66, no. 3 (1980): 289–303.
Brzezinski, Zbigniew. *Out of Control: Global Turmoil on the Eve of the Twenty-First Century.* New York: Macmillan Publishing Company, 1993.
Bukhtoiarova, Y. S. *Obraz UPA u svitskii presi ukrainskoi diaspory SShA (1950– 1980-ti rr.)* (unpublished thesis). Lviv: Ukrainskyi katolytskyi universytet, Lviv, 2014.
Bukovsky, Vladimir. *Judgement in Moscow: Soviet Crimes and Western Complicity,* translated by Alyona Kojevnikov and edited by Paul Boutin. Ninth of November Press, 2019.

———. *To Build a Castle – My Life as a Dissenter*. Translated by Michael Scammell. New York: The Viking Press, 1979.
Bulgakov, Mikhail. *The Master and Margarita*, translated by Diana Burgin and Katherine Tiernan O'Connor. New York: Vintage International, 1995.
Burdman, Mark. "British Documentary Exposes OSI Fraud in Demjanjuk Trial." *Executive Intelligence Review* 17, no. 24 (1990): 45–48.
Burke, Kenneth. *A Rhetoric of Motives*. New York: Prentice-Hall, 1950.
———. *Language as Symbolic Action: Essays on Life, Literature, and Method*. Berkeley: University of California Press, 1966.
Burns, Monique L. "Committee Rallies to Support Soviet Dissident Writer Moroz." *The Harvard Crimson*. 26 November 1974. http://www.thecrimson.com/article/1974/11/26/committee-rallies-to-support-soviet-dissident/.
Bushin, Vladimir. *Ya zhyl vo vremena Sovetov. Dnevniki*. Moskva: Algoritm, 2014.
Chalyi, Piotr. "Zemkiaki, ili Kharkovchanin iz moiei Rossoshi." *Den literatury*. 11 October 2016. https://denliteraturi.ru/article/2083.
Chamberlin, William Henry. *The Ukraine: A Submerged Nation*. New York: The Macmillan Company, 1944.
Chichibabin, B. A. *Ranneie i pozdneie*. Kharkov: Folio, 2002.
Chichibabin, Boris (interview with by Svetlana Dudar). "'Da budet volia tvoia, a ne moia, gospodi . . .'" *Official site of Boris Alekseevich Chichibabin*. 1993. http://chichibabin.narod.ru/interview.html.
———. *Stikhotvoreniia*. TO Ekskliuziv, 2003.
Chekhova, Tatiana. "Umer Eduard Siganevich. Literaturnyi dnevnik." *Proza.ru*. 18 November 2010. https://www.proza.ru/diary/mamlakat0256/2010-11-1.
Chepurna, O. V. "Obraz dytyny-dyvaka – kliuch do rozuminnia khudozhnioho svitu Hryhora Tiutiunnyka." *Visnyk Luhanskoho Natsionalnoho Universytetu imeni Tarasa Shevchenka* 3, no. 166 (February 2009): 91–100.
Cheremskyi, Kostyantyn. "'Spohady pro pochatok . . .'" *Spilka Ukrainskoi molodi*. 14 March 2013. http://cym.org.ua/2015.03/spogady-pro-pochatok/.
Cherevchenko, Aleksandr. "Bunt bessmyslennyi i besposhchadnyi?" *Press Latviia*. 6 February 2014. http://press.lv/post/bunt-bessmyslennyj-i-besposhhadnyj/.
Chernus, Ira. *General Eisenhower: Ideology and Discourse*. East Lansing, MI: Michigan State University Press, 2002.
Chornovil, Vyacheslav, ed. *The Chornovil Papers*. New York: McGraw-Hill, 1968.
Churchward, L. G. *The Soviet Intelligentsia: An Essay on the Social Structure and Roles of the Soviet Intellectuals during the 1960s*. London/Boston: Routledge & Kegan Paul, 1973.
Cohn, Norman. *The Pursuit of the Millennium*, rev. ed. Oxford, UK: Oxford University Press; 1970.
Conquest, Robert. *Harvest of Sorrow: Soviet Collectivization and the Terror-Famine*. New York: Oxford University Press, 1986.
———. *Inside Stalin's Secret Police: NKVD Politics, 1936–39*. London: Macmillan Press LTD, 1985.

Crankshaw, Edward. "Yury Andropov: Prisoner of His Country's Lies." In *Putting Up with the Russians: Commentary and Criticism, 1947–84*. New York: Elisabeth Sifton Books, Viking, 1984.

Danylenko, Vasyl, ed. *Politychni protesty i inakodumstvo v Ukraini (1960–1980)*. Kyiv: Smoloskyp, 2013.

_____. *Ukrainska intelihentsiia i vlada: Zvedennia sekretnoho viddilu DPU USSR, 1927–1929 rr*. Kyiv: Tempora, 2012.

Danylenko, V. M., ed. *Entsyklopedia istorii Ukrainy*, t. 1. Kyiv: NAN Ukrainy; Instytut istorii Ukrainy, "Naukova dumka," 2003.

Danylenko, V. M., L. L. Aulova, and V. V. Lavreniuk, eds. *Holodomor 1932–1933 rr. v Ukraini za dokumentamy HDA SBU: Anatovanyi dovidnyk*. Kyiv: Tsentr doslidzhen vyzvolnoho rukhu, 2010.

Dave, Nomi. "The Politics of Silence: Music, Violence and Protest in Guinea." *Ethnomusicology* 58, no. 1 (2014): 1–29.

Davies, R. W., Oleg V. Khlevniuk, and E. A. Rees, eds. *The Stalin-Kaganovich Correspondence: 1931–1936*. New Haven/London: Yale University Press, 2003.

Davies, Sarah, and James Harris, eds. *Stalin: A New History*. Cambridge, UK: Cambridge University Press, 2005.

d'Encausse, Helene Carrere. *Decline of An Empire: The Soviet Socialist Republics in Revolt*. Translated by Martin Sokolinsky and Henry A. La Farge. New York, NY: Newsweek Books, 1978.

de Saint-Exupéry, Antoine. *The Little Prince*. Translated by Katherine Woods. New York: Harcourt Brace Jovanovich, 1971.

"Deychakiwsky Orest." *Entsyklopedia Ukrainskoi Diaspory: Spolucheni Shtaty Ameryky*, vol. 1, kn. I, edited by Vasyl Markus and Dariia Markus, 224. New York and Chicago: Naukove Tovarystvo im. Shevchenka v Amerytsi, 2009.

Dillon, Millicent, and Michel Foucault. "Conversation with Michel Foucault." *The Threepenny Review* 1 (1980): 4–5.

Dingli, Sophia. "We Need to Talk about Silence: Re-examining Silence in International Relations Theory." *European Journal of International Relations* 21, no. 4 (2015): 721–42.

Dismukes, Donna E. *The Forced Repatriation of Soviet Citizens: A Study in Military Obedience*. Monterey, CA: Department of Defense/Naval Postgraduate School, 1996.

Diuk, Nadia, and Adrian Karatnycky. *The Hidden Nations: The People Challenge the Soviet Union*. New York: William Morrow and Company, Inc., 1990.

Dlaboha, Ihor. "Thousands Rally in New York To Commemorate Kremlin-Made Famine in Ukraine." *Svoboda: The Ukrainian Weekly*, 29 September 1973, pp. 1, 3.

Dobroszycki, Lucjan, and Jeffery S. Gurock, eds. *The Holocaust in the Soviet Union: Studies and Sources on the Destruction of Jews in the Nazi-occupied Territories of the USSR, 1941–1944*. New York: Routledge, 1994.

Dobrynin, Anatoly. *In Confidence: Moscow's Ambassador to America's Six Cold War Presidents*. Seattle and London: University of Washington Press, 1995.

Dobson, Miriam. *Khrushchev's Cold Summer: Gulag Returnees, Crime, and the Fate of Reform After Stalin*. Ithaca/London: Cornell University Press, 2009.

Drach, Ivan. *Ukrainska diaspora*, edited by I. S. Riabchyi. Kharkiv: Folio, 2019.

Dunbabin, J. P. D. *The Cold War: The Great Powers and Their Allies*, 2nd ed. New York: Pearson Education Limited, 2008.

Durkheim, Emile. *Suicide: A Study in Sociology*, edited by George Simpson, translated by John A. Spaulding and George Simpson. London: Routledge & Kegan Paul Ltd, 1968.

Dushnyck, Walter, ed. *Ukrainians and Jews: A Symposium*. New York, NY: The Ukrainian Congress Committee of America, Inc., 1966.

Dziuba, Ivan. *Internationalism or Russification? A Study in the Soviet Nationalities Problem*, 2nd ed. London: Weidenfeld and Nicolson, 1970.

_____. "Slovo sovisne i dobre." In *Vsemu zhivomu ne chuzhoi: Boris Chichibabin v stat'iakh i vospominaniiakh*, edited by M. I. Bogoslavskii, L. S. Karas-Chichibabina, and B. Y. Ladenzon, 200–208. Kharkov: Folio, 1998.

_____. *Z krynytsi lit*, vol. 1. Kyiv: Vydavnychyi dim "Kyievo-Mohylianska akademiia," 2006.

Edy, Jill A. "The Presence of the Past in Public Discourse." In *Politics, Discourse, and American Society*, edited by Roderick P. Hart and Bartholomew H. Sparrow, 53–70. New York: Rowman & Littlefield Publishers, Inc., 2001.

Edwards, Paul N. *The Closed World: Computers and the Politics of Discourse in Cold War America*. Cambridge, MA: The MIT Press, 1997.

Eghigian, Greg, ed. (with Gail Hornstein's contribution). *From Madness to Mental Health: Psychiatric Disorder and Its Treatment in Western Civilization*. New Brunswick, NJ: Rutgers University Press, 2010.

Eimermacher, Karl. "Predislovie." In *Apparat TsK KPSS i kultura. 1953–1957: Dokumenty*, edited by V. I. Afiani et al. Moskva: ROSSPEN, 2001.

Ellis, Mark S. "Purging the Past: The Current State of Lustration Laws in the Former Communist Bloc." *Law and Contemporary Problems* 59, no. 4 (1996): 181–96.

Emerson, R. W. *Basic Selections from Emerson: Essays, Poems, Apothegms*, edited by Eduard C. Lindeman. New York: Mentor Books, 1960.

Estraikh, Gennady. *In Harness: Yiddish Writers' Romance with Communism*. Syracuse, NY: Syracuse University Press, 2005.

_____. "Jewish Wards of the Soviet State: Fayvl Sito's *These Are Us*." In *Children and Yiddish Literature: From Early Modernity to Post-Modernity*, edited by Gennady Estraikh, Kerstin Hoge, and Mikhail Krutikov, 137–53. New York: Legenda, Studies in Yiddish, Modern Humanities Research Association and Routledge, 2016.

_____. "Literature versus Territory: Soviet Jewish Cultural Life in the 1950s." *East European Jewish Affairs* 33, no. 1 (2008): 30–48.

_____. "The Yiddish Kultur-Lige." In *Modernism in Kyiv: Jubilant Experimentation*, edited by Irena R. Makaryk and Virlana Tkacz, 197–217. Toronto: University of Toronto Press, 2010.

_____. *Yiddish in the Cold War*. London: Legenda, 2008.

Etkind, Alexander. *Internal Colonization: Russia's Imperial Experience*. Cambridge, UK: The Polity Press, 2011.

Etty, John. *Graphic Satire in the Soviet Union: Krokodil's Political Cartoons*, 1st ed. Jackson, MS: University Press of Mississippi, 2019.

Farion, Iryna. "Polityka kriz tovshchu chasu, abo pam'iat pro Sheveliova." *Literaturna Ukraina*, 12 September 2013, p. 3.

Farmer, Kenneth. *Ukrainian Nationalism in the Post-Stalin Era*. The Hague/Boston/London: Martinus Nijhoff, 1980.

Fedor, Julie. *Russia and the Cult of State Security*. New York: Routledge, 2011.

Fedynsky, Andrew. "Perspectives: Valentyn Moroz – 25 Years Later." *The Ukrainian Weekly* LXXII, no. 4 (25 January 2004). http://www.ukrweekly.com/old/archive/2004/040418.shtml.

Fernheimer, Janice W. "Confronting Kenneth Burke's Anti-Semitism." *Journal of Communication & Religion*, 39, no. 2 (2016): 36–53.

Figes, Orlando. *Whisperers: Private Life in Stalin's Russia*. New York: Metropolitan Books, 2007.

Filatov, Arkadii (interview with by Nikolai Artamonov). "Khrani tebia gospod." *Kharkovhumanit*. 2003. http://kharkovhumanit.narod.ru/Intervu.html.

_____. "Vdogonku." *Chichibabin.narod.ru*. 1995. http://chichibabin.narod.ru/filatov.html.

Fink, Carole K. *Cold War: An International History*, 2nd ed. Boulder, CO: Western Press, 2017.

Fireside, Harvey. *Soviet Psychoprisons*. New York: W. W. Norton & Co., 1979.

Fort, Jahmese M. "Politics of Silence: Theorizing Silence as Altered Participation." *Kinesis: Graduate Journal of Philosophy* 40, no. 2 (2015): 65–74.

Foucault, Michel. *Discipline and Punish: The Birth of the Prison*. New York: Vintage Books, 1995.

_____. *Madness and Civilization: A History of Insanity in the Age of Reason*. New York: Vintage Books, 1988.

_____. *Power Knowledge: Selected Interviews and Other Writings, 1972–1977*, edited by Colin Gordon, translated by Colin Gordon, Leo Marshall, John Mepham, and Kate Sopher. New York: Vintage, 1980.

_____. *The Archeology of Knowledge and the Discourse on Language*. Translated by A. M. Sheridan Smith. New York: Pantheon Books, 1972.

_____. *The Birth of the Clinic: An Archaeology of Medical Perception*. New York: Vintage Books, 1994.

_____. "The Order of Discourse." In *Untying the Text: A Post-Structuralist Reader*, edited by Robert Young, 51–78. Boston: Routledge, 1981.

Freedman, Jonathan L. *Crowding and Behavior*. San Francisco: W. H. Freeman and Company, 1975.

Freeze, Gregory L. "From Stalinism to Stagnation, 1953–1985." In *Russia: A History*, 2nd ed., edited by Gregory L. Freeze, 347–82. New York: Oxford University Press, 2002.

Fritzsche, Peter. "Comment: Making Perpetrators." *Slavic Review* 72, no. 1 (2013): 28–31.

Frukhtman, Lev. "Golos zhizni." *My zdes* 561 (14–24 January 2018), http://newswe.com/index.php?go=Pages&in=view&id=1724.

"Full Story of Massacre of Jews at Babi Yar Told by Soviet Writer." *Jewish Telegraphic Agency: Daily News Bulletin* XXXIII, no. 164 (26 August 1966): 2.

Gallii, Nikolai. *Organizovannyi golod v Ukraine 1932–1933*. Chicago and New York: Ukrainskii publitsysticheskii institut, 1968.

Garagozov, R. R. "Collective Memory and the Russian 'Schematic Narrative Template.'" *Journal of Russian and East European Psychology* 40, no. 5 (2002): 55–89.

Garrard, John and Carol. *Inside the Soviet Writers' Union*. New York: The Free Press, 1990.

Garros, Veronique, Natalia Korenevskaya, and Thomas Lahusen, eds. *Intimacy and Terror: Soviet Diaries of the 1930s*. Translated by Carol A. Flath. New York: The New Press, 1997.

Gerasimenko, Yurii. "Glaza v glaza," *Krasnoe znamia*, 18 February 1982, p. 3.

Gérin, Annie. *Devastation and Laughter: Satire, Power, and Culture in the Early Soviet State (1920s–1930s)*. Toronto: University of Toronto Press, 2018.

Getty, J. A., and Oleg V. N. *The Road to Terror: Stalin and the Self-Destruction of the Bolsheviks, 1932–1939*. New Haven/London: Yale University Press, 1999.

_____. *Yezhov: The Rise of Stalin's "Iron Fist."* New Haven and London: Yale University Press, 2008.

Gibney, Frank. *The Khrushchev Pattern*. New York: Duell, Sloan and Pearce, 1960.

Gilburd, Eleonory. *To See Paris and Die: The Soviet Lives of Western Culture*. Cambridge, MA and London, England: The Belknap Press of Harvard University Press, 2018.

Gitelman, Zvi. "Glasnost, Perestroika and Antisemitism." *Foreign Affairs*, 1 March 1991. pp. 141–59.

_____. "Native Land, Promised Land, Golden Land: Jewish Emigration from Russia and Ukraine." *Harvard Ukrainian Studies* 22, no. XII (1998): 137–63.

_____. "Soviet Jews: Creating a Cause and a Movement." In *A Second Exodus: The American Movement to Free Soviet Jews*, edited by M. Friedman and A. D. Chernin, 84–96. Hanover, NH: Brandeis University Press, 1999.

_____. "The Social and Political Role of the Jews in Ukraine." In *Ukraine in the Seventies*, edited by Peter J. Potichnyj, 167–86. Oakville, ON: Mosaic Press, 1975.

Glaser, Amelia M. "Jewish Alienation through a Ukrainian Looking Glass: Dovid Hofshteyn's Translations of Taras Shevchenko." *Prooftexts* 36, no. 1–2 (2017): 83–110.

Glenn, Cheryl. *Unspoken: A Rhetoric of Silence*. Carbondale: Southern Illinois UP, 2004.

Gluzman, Semen, and Robert van Voren (interview by Oleksii Bukhalo, RTB). *YouTube*. 11 June 2013. http://www.youtube.com/watch?v=iz04k1hWNgI.

_____. "Pro 'sovety.'" *Volyn Media*. 7 June 2013. http://www.youtube.com/watch?v=zjt8jQ-qies.

Gluzman, Semen (interview by Mikhail Gold). "V SSSR byli eshche odni yevrei – ukraintsy." *Lekhaim* 5772, no. 2 (238) (February 2012). https://lechaim.ru/ARHIV/238/gold.htm.

_____. "Mne stydno, chto ya grazhdanin Ukrainy." *Glavred*. 11 April 2012. http://glavred.info/archive/2012/04/11/084510-1.html.

Gluzman, S. F. *Risunki po pamiati, ili vospominaniia otsidenta*. Kiev: Izdatelskii dom Dmitriia Burago, 2012.

Goble, Paul A. "Readers, Writers, and Republics: The Structural Basis of Non-Russian Literary Politics." In *The Nationalities Factors in Soviet Politics and Society*, edited by Lubomyr Hajda and Mark Beissinger, 131–47. Boulder, San Francisco, and Oxford: Westview Press, 1990.

Goldman, Wendy Z. *Inventing the Enemy: Denunciations and Terror in Stalin's Russia*. New York: Cambridge University Press, 2011.

———. "Comment: Twin Pyramids—Perpetrators and Victims." *Slavic Review* 72, no. 1 (2013): 24–27.

Gorenburg, Dmitry. "Soviet Nationalities Policy and Assimilation." In *Rebounding Identities: The Politics of Identity in Russia and Ukraine*, edited by Dominique Arel and Blair A. Ruble, 273–303. Washington, DC: Woodrow Wilson Center Press, 2006.

Gorham, Michael. *After Newspeak: Language Culture and Politics in Russia from Gorbachev to Putin*. Ithaca and London: Cornell University Press, 2014.

———. *Speaking in Soviet Tongues: Language Culture and the Politics of Voice in Revolutionary Russia*. DeKalb, IL: Northern Illinois University Press, 2003.

Gorovskii, F. I. et al. *Ievrei Ukrainy (kratkii ocherk istorii)*, part II. Kiev: Ukrainsko-finskii institut menedzhmenta i biznesa, 1999.

Graziosi, Andrea, and Frank E. Sysyn, eds. *Communism and Hunger: The Ukrainian, Chinese, Kazakh, and Soviet Famines in Comparative Perspective*. Edmonton and Toronto: CIUS Press, 2016.

Grigorenko, Petro G. *Memoirs*. Translated by Thomas P. Whitney. New York & London: W.W. Norton and Company, 1982.

Grigorenko, Petro. "Zvychaina psykholikarnia." In *Potsilunok Satany: Spohady* by Victor Borovsky, 5–6. New York: Meta Publishing Company, 1981.

Grossman, Vasilii, and Il'ia Erenburg, eds. *Neizvestnaia chiornaia kniga*. Moskva: Izdatelstvo ACT, 1993.

Gulko, Boris, Vladimir Popov, Yuri Felshtinsky, and Viktor Kortschnoi. *The KGB Plays Chess: The Soviet Secret Police and the Fight for the World Chess Crown*. Milford, CT: Russell Enterprises, Inc., 2010.

Gustafson, D. Mauritz. "Soviet Human Rights under Gorbachev: Old Wine in a New Bottle." *The Denver Journal of International Law & Policy* 16, no. 1 (2020): 177–89.

Hagen, Mark Von. "Wartime Occupation and Peacetime Alien Rule: 'Notes and Materials' toward a(n) (Anti-) (Post-) Colonial History of Ukraine." In *The Future of the Past: New Perspectives on Ukrainian History*, edited by Serhii Plokhy, 143–84. Cambridge, MA: Ukrainian Research Institute, Harvard University, Harvard University Press, 2016.

Halfin, Igal. *Language and Revolution: Making Modern Political Identities*. London: Routledge, 2004.

Halfin, Igal. *Stalinist Confessions: Messianism and Terror at the Leningrad Communist University*. Pittsburgh, PA: University of Pittsburgh Press, 2009.

Hall, Edward T. *The Hidden Dimension*. New York: Anchor Books/Doubleday, 1990.

Hanson, Philip. *The Rise and Fall of the Soviet Economy: An Economic History of the USSR from 1945.* London and New York: Longman, 2003.
Harlow, William Forrest. "The Rhetoric of Silence and the Collapse of the Soviet Empire." *American Communication Journal* 16, no. 2 (2014): 52–66.
Harris, James. *The Great Fear: Stalin's Terror of the 1930s.* Oxford, UK: Oxford University Press, 2016.
Harrison, Mark. "Secrecy, Fear, and Transaction Costs: The Business of Soviet Forced Labour in the Early Cold War." *University of Warwick, U.K.* 8 October 2010. https://www.academia.edu/2864919/Secrecy_Fear_and_Transaction_Costs_The_Business_of_Soviet_Forced_Labour_in_the_Early_Cold_War.
_____. "Why Secrets? The Uses of Secrecy in Stalin's Command Economy." *University of Warwick, U.K.* 10 October 2003. https://www.academia.edu/2865010/Why_secrets_The_uses_of_secrecy_in_Stalin_s_command_economy.
Harris, Sarah, and James Harris. "Joseph Stalin: Power and Ideas." In *Stalin: A New History*, edited by Sarah Davies and James Harris, 1–17. Cambridge, UK: Cambridge University Press, 2005.
Hayward, Max. "Introduction." In *My Testimony* by Anatoly Marchenko, translated by Michael Scammell, ix–xix. New York: E. P. Dutton & Co. Inc., 1969.
Hayward, Max, and Edward L. Crowley, eds. *Soviet Literature in the Sixties: An International Symposium.* New York: Frederick A. Praeger, Publisher, 1964.
Healey, Dan. "Russian and Soviet Forensic Psychiatry: Troubled and Troubling." *International Journal of Law and Psychiatry* 37, no. 1 (2014): 71–81.
Heidegger, Martin. *Being and Time.* Translated by John Macquarrie and Edward Robinson. New York: Harper and Row, 1962.
Heiman, Leo. "Ukrainians and the Jews." In *Ukrainians and Jews: A Symposium*, 57–64. New York: The Ukrainian Congress Committee of America, Inc., 1966.
Hel, Ivan. *Vyklyk systemi: Ukrainskyi vyzvolnyi rukh druhoi polovyny XX stolittia*, edited by I. Iezerska. Lviv: Chasopys, 2013.
Herasymiuk, Olena. *Rozstrilnyi calendar.* Kharkiv: Klub simeinoho dozvillia, 2017.
Himka, John-Paul. "Interventions: Challenging the Myths of Twentieth-Century Ukrainian History." In *Convolutions of Historical Politics*, edited by Alexei Miller and Maria Lipman, 211–38. Budapest: Central European University Press, 2012.
_____. "Leonid Plyushch: The Ukrainian Marxist Resurgent." *Journal of Ukrainian Studies* 9 (1980): 61–79.
_____. "The Lviv Pogrom of 1941: The Germans, Ukrainian Nationalists, and the Carnival Crow." *Canadian Slavonic Papers* LII, nos. 2–4 (2011): 209–43.
_____. "Ukrainian Memories of the Holocaust: The Destruction of Jews as Reflected in Memoirs Collected in 1947," *Canadian Slavonic Papers* LIV, nos. 3–4 (2012): 427–42.
Hladkykh, Oleksandr. "My podolaly strakh," *Literaturna Ukraina*, 13 June 2013, pp. 13–14.
Hoffmann, David L. *Cultivating the Masses: Modern State Practices and Soviet Socialism, 1914–1939.* Ithaca, NY: Cornell University Press, 2011.

Hollander, Paul. "Leading Specialists in 'State Security' (Political Police)." In *Political Will and Personal Belief: The Decline and Fall of Soviet Communism* by Paul Hollander, 209–74. New Haven and London, 1999.

———. *Political Will and Personal Belief: The Decline and Fall of Soviet Communism*. New Haven/London: Yale University Press, 1999.

"Holodomor: What is the Kremlin Afraid Of?" *The Kharkiv Human Rights Protection Group*. 4 July 2012. http://khpg.org/en/index.php?id=1341237033&w=holodomor.

Holquist, Peter. "'Information Is the Alpha and Omega of Our Work': Bolshevik Surveillance in Its Pan-European Context." *The Journal of Modern History* 69, no. 3 (1997): 415–50.

Honcharuk, Zakhar, eds. *Anthology of Soviet Ukrainian Poetry*. Kiev: Dnipro Publishers, 1982.

Horelov, Denis. "Vplyv orhanizatsii ukrainskoi diaspory na rozvytok hromadianskoho suspilstva v Ukraini." *Stratehichni priorytety* 3, no. 20 (2011): 32–38.

Horovyi, Vasyl. "Ia prahnu v svit . . ." *Leninskyi shliakh*, 16 November 1971, p. 3.

Horyn, Bohdan. *Ne tilky pro sebe: Knyha druha (1965–1985)*. Kyiv: Pulsary, 2008.

Houston, Walter. "A Diverse Collection of Peoples." *London Review of Books*, 4 July 2013, p. 4.

Hrytsak, Yaroslav. "Khto i koly vpershe vzhyv slovo "Holodomor?" *Ukraina Moderna*. 24 November 2017. https://uamoderna.com/blogy/yaroslav-griczak/etymology-holodomor.

Hrynevych, Liudmyla. *Khronika kolektyvizatsii ta Holodomoru v Ukraini: 1927–1933* (all volumes). Kyiv: Krytyka, 2008–2012.

Hrynevych, Vladyslav, and Paul Robert Magosci, eds. *Babyn Yar: Istoriia i pam'iat*. Kyiv: Dukh i litera, 2016.

Hrytsiak, Yevhen. *Korotkyi zapys spohadiv: Norylske povstannia. Pislia povstannia*. Kyiv: "Smoloskyp," 2013.

Ilnytskyi, Mykola. *Na perekhrestiakh viku*, vol. II. Kyiv: KMA, 2008.

Inin, A. Ia., and L. V. Osadchuk. *V ozhidanii chuda*. Moskva: Iskusstvo, 1985.

Inin, Arkadii (interview by Grigorii Kroshin). "'Vybiraiu sovetskuiu vlast . . .'" *Partner* 5 (188), 2013. https://www.partner-inform.de/partner/detail/2013/5/237/5959/arkadij-inin-vybiraju-sovetskuju-vlast?lang=ru.

———. (interview by Konstantin Kevorkian). "'Vsia Ukraina – russkoiazychnaia.'" *Ukraina.ru*. 22 August 2020. https://ukraina.ru/interview/20200822/1028627200.html?fbclid=IwAR3pxpW3y7OTEwqVqyMZigv53si1vb_bwAwnPukcmlFBNFMXaeMJA5es4N4.

Ioffe, Aleksandr (interview by Yulii Kosharovskii). *Kosharovskii*. 29 April 2004. http://kosharovsky.com/интервью/александр-иоффе/.

"Iosif Goldenberg." *Sviaz vremen*. 2020. http://www.thetimejoint.com/taxonomy/term/3893.

Isajiw, Christina. *Negotiating Human Rights: In Defence of Dissidents during the Soviet Era*. Edmonton and Toronto: Canadian Institute of Ukrainian Studies, 2014.

Ivanenko, V. V. "'Mala vidlyha' P. I. Shelesta: mif chy realnist?" *Hrani* 8 (136) (2016): 180–89.

Jackson, Nigel. "John Demjanjuk: The Man More Sinned Against." *Inconvenient History* 4, no. 2 (2012). https://codoh.com/library/document/3177/?lang=en.
James, Clive. *Cultural Amnesia: Necessary Memories from History and the Arts.* New York: W. W. Norton & Company, 2007.
"Jews." *Encyclopedia of Ukraine*, vol. II, edited by Volodymyr Kubijovyc, 385–93. Toronto: University of Toronto Press, 1988.
Jones, Lesya, and Bohdan Yasen. "Preface." In *Dissent in Ukraine: The Ukrainian Herald: An Underground Journal from Soviet Ukraine*, translated by Lesya Jones and Bohdan Yasen, 5–12. Baltimore/Paris/Toronto: Smoloskyp Publisher, 1977.
Kalugin, Oleg. *Spymaster: My Thirty-Two Years in Intelligence and Espionage Against the West* New York: Basic Books, 2009.
Kalynychenko, Volodymyr. "Volodymyr Pasichnyk – poet-protestant, borets-orhanizator." In *Zona*, no. 27, edited by Oleksa Riznykiv. Odesa: Simeks-prynt, 2011.
Karas-Chichibabina, Liliia. "Ty i sama b do smerti ne zabyla." In *Vsemu zhivomu ne chuzhoi: Boris Chichibabin v stat'iakh i vospominaniiakh*, edited by M. I. Bogoslavskii, L. S. Karas-Chichibabina, and B. Y. Ladenzon, 127–48. Kharkov: Folio, 1998.
Kas'ianov, Heorhii. *Nezhodni: Ukrainska intelihentsiia v rusi oporu 1960–80-kh rokiv.* Kyiv: Lybid, 1995.
Kats, Elena M. "The Literary Development of Yekhiel Shraybman: A Jewish Writer in Soviet Clothing." *East European Jewish Affairs* 38, no. 3 (2008): 281–301.
Khanin, Vladimir. "Introduction." In *Documents on Ukrainian-Jewish Identity and Emigration, 1944–1990*, ed. Vladimir Khanin, 1–37. New York: Frank Cass Publishers, 2003.
Khanin, Vladimir (Zeev). "The Jewish National Movement and the Struggle for Community in the Late Soviet Period." In *Revolution, Repression, and Revival: The Soviet Jewish Experience*, edited by Zvi Gitelman and Yaacov Roi, 221–38. New York: Rowman & Littlefield Publishers, Inc., 2007.
_____. "The Refusenik Community in Moscow: Social Networks and Models of Identification." *East European Jewish Affairs* 41, nos. 1–2 (2011): 75–88.
"Kharkiv." *YIVO Encyclopedia of Jews in Eastern Europe.* 2020. https://yivoencyclopedia.org/article.aspx/Kharkiv.
"Kharkovskiie filologi otlichaiutsia chuvstvom iumora i priamotoi." *Vechernii Kharkov.* 23 April 2012. https://vecherniy.kharkov.ua/news/62847/.
Kheifets, Mikhail. *Ukrainskiie siluety.* Kyiv: Ukrainska pres-hrupa, 2014.
Khiterer, Viktoria. *Dokumenty po ievreiskoi istorii XVI-XX vekov v Kievskikh arkhivakh.* Kyiv: Institut Yudaiki, and Moscow: Mosty kultury, 2001.
Khodorovich, Tatyana, ed. *The Case of Leonid Plyushch*, translated by Marite Sapiets, Peter Reddaway and Caryl Emerson. Boulder, CO: Westview Press, 1976.
Khrushchev, Sergei, ed. *Memoirs of Nikita Khrushchev: Reformer (1945–1964)*, vol. 2. Translated by George Shriver and Stephen Shenfield. University Park, PA: The Pennsylvania State University Press, 2006.
_____. *Khrushchev in Power: Unfinished Reforms, 1961–1964.* Translated by George Shriver. Boulder, CO: Lynne Rienner Publishers, 2014.

Klein, Peter, ed. *Die Einsatzgruppen in der besetzten Sowjetunion, 1941/42: Die Tätigkeitsund Lageberichte des Chefs der Scicherheitspolizei und des SD.* Berlin: Edition Hentrich, 1997.

Klid, Bohdan, and Alexander J. Motyl, eds. *The Holodomor Reader: A Sourcebook on the Famine of 1932–1933 in Ukraine.* Edmonton and Toronto: CIUS Press, 2012.

Klumbyte, Neringa, and Gulnaz Sharafutdinova, eds. *Soviet Society in the Era of Late Socialism, 1964–1985.* New York: Lexington Books, 2013.

Knight, Amy. *Beria: Stalin's First Lieutenant.* Princeton, NJ: Princeton University Press, 1993.

Knysh, Zynovii. *"Yevrei" chy "zhydy."* Toronto: Sribna Surma, 1984.

Koenker, Diane P., and Ronald D. Bachman, eds. *Revelations from the Russian Archives: Documents in English Translation.* Washington, DC: Library of Congress, 1997.

Kolomiiets, Lada. *Ukrainskyi khudozhnii pereklad ta perekladachi 1920–30-kh rokiv.* Vinnytsia: Nova Knyha, 2015.

Kolstø, Pål. "Faulted for the Wrong Reasons: Soviet Institutionalization of Ethnic Diversity and Western (Mis)interpretations." In *Institutional Legacies of Communism: Change and Continuities in Minority Protection*, edited by Karl Cordell, Timofey Agarin, and Alexander Osipov, 31–44. New York: Routledge, 2013.

Koryagin, Anatolii. "Autobiographical Notes." In *Koryagin: A Man Struggling for Human Dignity*, edited by Robert van Voren, 14–25. Amsterdam: Second World Press, Vladimir Bukovsky Foundation, 1987.

———. "Unwilling Patients." *The Lancet*, 11 April 1981, pp. 821–24.

Koryagin, Anatoliy. "Compulsion in Psychiatry: Blessing or Curse?" *Psychiatric Bulletin* 14 (1990): 394–98.

Kornblatt, Judith Deutsch. *Doubly Chosen: Jewish Identity, the Soviet Intelligentsia, and the Russian Orthodox Church.* Madison: The University of Wisconsin Press, 2004.

Korotenko, A., and N. Alikina. *Sovetskaia psikhiatriia: Zabluzhdeniia i umysel.* Kiev: Sphera, 2002.

Korotich, Vitalii. *Zhili-byli—eli-pili.* Kharkov: Folio, 2005.

Kostyrchenko, Gennadii. *Stalin protiv "kosmopolitov": Vlast i yevreiskaia intelligentsia v SSSR.* Moskva: Rosspen, 2010.

Kotkin, Stephen. *Magnetic Mountain: Stalinism as a Civilization.* Los Angeles/London: University of California Press Berkeley, 1995.

Kozak, Mykola. "Maister pershoi ruky." *Gonta Project.* 25 April 2006. http://virchi.narod.ru/poeziya/muratov-biograf2.htm.

Kozlov, Denis. *The Readers of Novyi Mir: Coming to Terms with the Stalinist Past.* Cambridge, MA: Harvard University Press, 2013.

Kravchenko, Volodymyr. "Stolytsia dlia Ukrainy." In *Ukraina, Imperiia, Rosiia: Vybrani statti z modernoi istorii ta istoriohrafii*, edited by Volodymyr Kravchenko, 45–85. Kyiv: Krytyka, 2011.

Kravchenko, Yaroslav. "Okhrim Kravchenko. Kriz zhyttia. Virnist tradytsiiam shkoly Mykhaila Boichuka." *Tekst i obraz: Aktualni problemy istorii mystetstva* 1 (2017): 39–54.

Krishnan, Armin. "The Neglected Dimension of Ideology in Russia's Political Warfare Against the West." *Global Security and Intelligence Studies* 4, no. 2 (2019): 25–46.

Krivin, Feliks. "Druz'ia moi, prekrasen nash soiuz!" In *Vsemu zhivomu ne chuzhoi: Boris Chichibabin v stat'iakh i vospominaniiakh*, edited by M. I. Bogoslavskii, L. S. Karas-Chichibabina, and B. Y. Ladenzon, 151–59. Kharkov: Folio, 1998.

Krotov, Nikolai. "Gonka na zolotykh teltsakh." *Neprikosnovennyi zapas* 2, no. 52 (2007). http://magazines.russ.ru/nz/2007/2/kro13.html.

Kruglashov, Anatoliy. "Chernivtsi: A City with Mysterious Flavor of Tolerance." *Eurolimes* 19 (2015): 139–58.

Kryvcheniuk, Valentyna. "Stanislav Shumytskyi ta ioho seredovyshche." *Official site of Liubotynska miska rada*. 20 March 2015. http://lubotin.kharkov.ua/main/5669-do-dnya-narodzhennya-s-shumickogo.html.

Kubik, Jan, and Michael Bernhard. "A Theory of the Politics of Memory." In *Twenty Years After Communism: The Politics of Memory and Commemoration*, edited by Jan Kubik and Michael Bernhard, 7–34. New York: Oxford University Press, 2014.

Kubiiovych, V., and V. Markus. "Emihratsiia." In *Entsyklopediia Ukrainoznavstva*, T. 2, edited by V. Kubiiovych, 629–37. Paris/New York: "Molode zhyttia," 1955–1957.

Kulchytskyi, Stanislav. *Chervonyi vyklyk: Istoriia komunizmu v Ukraini vid ioho narodzhennia do zahybeli*, vol. 3. Kyiv: Tempora, 2013.

Kulchytsky, Stanislav. *The Famine of 1932–1933 in Ukraine: An Anatomy of the Holodomor*. Translated by Ali Kinsella. Edmonton and Toronto: CIUS Press, 2018.

Kupchinsky, Roman. "Nazi War Criminals: The Role of Soviet Disinformation." In *Ukraine During World War II: History and its Aftermath*, edited by Yury Boshyk. Edmonton: Canadian Institute of Ukrainian Studies Press, 1986.

Kurokhta, Leonid. "Chomu ia vybrav novu zemliu." *Proza.ru*. 2013.https://proza.ru/2013/04/21/1969?fbclid=IwAR3GDCxjnsl0N8XZ4WxUDKwabEVZQUrnVjSqP_50NWlyiNdzWuiXAWzh850.

Kuromiya, Hiroaki. "Political Leadership and Ukrainian Nationalism, 1938–1989: The Burden of History." *Problems of Post-Communism* 52, no. 1 (2005): 39–48.

———. *The Voices of the Dead: Stalin's Great Terror in the 1930s*. New Haven: Yale University Press, 2007.

Kuropas, Myron B. "Fighting Moscow from Afar: Ukrainian Americans and the Evil Empire." In *Anti-Communist Minorities in the U.S.: Political Activism of Ethnic Refugees*, edited by Ieva Zake, 43–66. New York: Palgrave Macmillan, 2009.

———. *Lesia and I: A Progress Report and a Ukrainian-American Love Story*. Bloomington, IN: Xlibris, 2014.

———. *Scourging of a Nation: CBS and the Defamation of Ukraine*. Kingston and Kyiv: The Kashtan Press, 1995.

———. "Ukrainian Americans and the Search for War Criminals." In *Ukraine During World War II: History and Its Aftermath*, edited by Yury Boshyk. Edmonton: Canadian Institute of Ukrainian Studies Press, 1986.

———. *Ukrainian-American Citadel: The First One Hundred Years of the Ukrainian National Association.* Boulder, CO: East European Monographs, 1996.

Kuzio, Taras, and Andrew Wilson. *Ukraine: Perestroika to Independence.* New York: Palgrave Macmillan, 1994.

Kuzio, Taras. *Putin's War Against Ukraine: Revolution, Nationalism, and Crime.* Toronto: University of Toronto, CreateSpace, 2017.

———. "The Soviet Roots of Anti-Fascism and Antisemitism." *New Eastern Europe* 6 (2016): 93–100.

Kuznetsov, Eduard. "Poet krutogo zamesa: Zinoviiu Valshonku – 85." *NG Ex Libris.* 7 March 2019. https://www.ng.ru/ng_exlibris/2019-03-07/13_973_poet.html.

Kychko, T. K. *Iudaism bez prykras.* Kyiv: V-vo Akademii Nauk URSR, 1963.

———. *Iudeiska relihiia: ii pokhodzhennia i sut.* Kyiv: Radianska Ukraina, 1957.

Laing, R. D. *The Divided Self: An Existential Study of Sanity and Madness.* New York: Penguin Books, 1990.

Lanovyk, B. D., M. V. Traf'iak, R. M. Mateiko, and Z. M. Matysiakevych. *Ukrainska emihratsiia vid mynuvshchyny do siohodennia.* Ternopil: Charivnytsia, 1999.

Lapidus, Rina. *Young Jewish Poets Who Fell as Soviet Soldiers in the Second World War.* London/New York: Routledge, 2014.

Lay, Paul. "Norman Cohn." *The Guardian.* 8 August 2007. https://www.theguardian.com/news/2007/aug/09/guardianobituaries.obituaries.

Lazin, Fred A. *The Struggle for Soviet Jewry in American Politics.* New York: Lexington Books, 2005.

Lefebvre, Henri. *The Production of Space.* Translated by Donald Nicholson-Smith. Malden, MA: Blackwell Publishing, 1991.

Legget, George. *The Cheka: Lenin's Political Police.* Oxford, UK: Clarendon Press, 1981.

Lenin, V. I. *Polnoie sobraniie sochinenii*, vol. 45. Moskva: Izdatelstvo politicheskoi literatury, 1970.

Lepore, Jill. "Just the Facts, Ma'am: Fake Memoirs, Factual Fictions, and the History of History." *The New Yorker*, 24 March 2008, pp. 79–83.

Levanon, Nehemiah. "Israel's Role in the Campaign." In *A Second Exodus: The American Movement to Free Soviet Jews*, edited by M. Friedman and A. D. Chernin, 70–83. Hanover, NH: Brandeis University Press, 1999.

Levina, Khana. *Ridne.* Kharkiv: Prapor, 1967.

Levin, Vadim. *Kuda uiekhal tsirk.* Kharkiv: Folio, 2001.

Levytska, Vita. "Andrii Holovko: Ubyvtsi – Shevchenkivsku premiiu." *Druh Chytacha.* 7 July 2008. https://vsiknygy.net.ua/person/424/.

Lewytzkyi, Borys. *Politics and Society in Soviet Ukraine, 1953–1980.* Edmonton, Canada: CIUS/University of Alberta, 1984.

Liakhovitskii, Yurii M. *Poprannaia mezuza: Kniga Drobitskogo Yara*, vol. 1. Kharkiv: Osnova, 1991.

Liber, George O. "The Thaw." In *Alexander Dovzhenko: A Life in Soviet Film* by George O. Liber, 246–74. London: British Film Institute Publishing, 2002.

Lim, Jie-Hyun, Barbara Walker, and Peter Lambert, eds. *Mass Dictatorship and Memory as Ever Present Past*. New York: Palgrave Macmillan, 2014.

Limonov, Eduard. *Molodoi negodiai*. Kostroma: Zhurnal "Glagol," 1992.

———. *U nas byla velikaia epokha; Podrostok Savenko*. Moscow: Literaturno-khudozhestvennyi zhurnal "Glagol," 1994.

Literaturnomu fondu SSSR 125 let. Moskva: Vneshtorgizdat, 1984.

Logachiova, Tamara. "Dialog s pisatelem: realnyi i myslennyi." *Kharkov–350: Gumanitarnyie resursy*. 2020. http://kharkovhumanit.narod.ru/Liki_kult.html.

———. *Rozhdionnaia v SSSR*. Kharkov: Maidan, 2012.

Lotman, Y. M. *Stat'ii po semiotike kultury i iskusstva*, edited by R. G. Grigor'ieva. Moskva: Akademicheskii proekt, 2002.

Lysiak-Rudnytskyi, Ivan. "Politychna dumka ukrainskykh pidradianskykh dysydentiv." In *Istorychni ese*, vol. 2, by Ivan Lysiak-Rudnytskyi, 477–88. Kyiv: Osnovy, 1994.

Luckyj, George S. N. "Polarity in Ukrainian Intellectual Dissent." *Canadian Slavonic Papers* 14, no. 2 (1972): 269–79.

———. "The Ukrainian Literary Scene Today." *Slavic Review* 31, no. 4 (1972): 863–69.

Luk'ianenko, Levko. "Do istorii Ukrainskoi Helsinskoi Spilky." In *Ukrainska Helsinska Spilka u spohadakh i dokumentakh*, edited by Oles Shevchenko, 7–70. Kyiv: "Iaroslaviv Val," 2012.

———. *Neznyshchennist*. Kyiv: Diokor, 2003.

Lygo, Emily. "The Need for New Voices: Writers' Union Policy towards Young Writers, 1953–1964." In *The Dilemmas of De-Stalinization: Negotiating Cultural and Social Change in the Khrushchev Era*, edited by Polly Jones, 193–208. London: Routledge, 2006.

Mace, James E., and Leonid Heretz, eds. *Investigation of the Ukrainian famine, 1932–1933: Oral History Project of the Commission on the Ukraine Famine*. Washington, DC: United States Government Printing Office, 1990.

Mace, James E. *Communism and the Dilemmas of National Liberation: National Communism in Soviet Ukraine, 1918–1933*. Cambridge, MA: Harvard University Press, 1983.

Magocsi, Paul Robert. *A History of Ukraine*. Seattle: University of Washington Press, 1998.

Magocsi, Paul Robert, and Yohanan Petrovsky-Shtern. *Jews and Ukrainians: A Millennium of Co-Existence*. Toronto: University of Toronto Press, 2016.

Magocsi, Paul Robert. *The Roots of Ukrainian Nationalism: Galicia as Ukraine's Piedmont*. Toronto: University of Toronto Press, 2002.

Maistrenko, Ivan. *Natsionalnaia politika KPSS*. Munich: Suchasnist, 1978.

Makahonov, Anatolii. "Prosti nas, Robert." *Vremia*, 9 November 1997, p. 2.

Makuch, Andrij, and Frank E. Sysyn, eds. *Contextualizing the Holodomor: The Impact of Thirty Years of Ukrainian Famine Studies*. Edmonton and Toronto: CIUS Press, 2015.

Malis, Aleksandr. "Nash 'Robertino.'" *Sloboda*, 20 May 1997, p. 2.

Malko, Victoria A., ed. *Women and the Holodomor-Genocide: Victims, Survivors, Perpetrators*. Fresno, CA: The Press of California State University, 2019.

———. "Russian (Dis)information Warfare vis-à-vis the Holodomor-Genocide." In *Russian Active Measures: Yesterday, Today, Tomorrow*, edited by Olga Bertelsen, 215–62. Stuttgart and New York: ibidem-Verlag/Columbia University Press, 2021.

Marochko, Vasyl. "Holodomor – henotsyd." In *Entsyklopediia Holodomoru 1932–1933 rokiv v Ukraïni*, 91–93. Drohobych: "Kolo," 2018.

———. "'Russkii Mir' u Feodosii: zaborona slova pro Holodomor." *Istorychna Pravda*. 28 January 2015. http://www.istpravda.com.ua/columns/2015/01/28/146975/.

Marples, David R. *Chernobyl and Nuclear Power in the USSR*. London, UK: Palgrave Macmillan, 1987.

———. *Ukraine under Perestroika: Ecology, Economics and the Workers' Revolt*. New York: St. Martin's Press, 1991.

Martin, Douglas. "Norman Cohn, Historian, Dies at 92." *The New York Times*. 27 August 2007. https://www.nytimes.com/2007/08/27/world/europe/27cohn.html.

Masenko, Larysa. "Lyst Vasylia Stusa do Andriia Malyshka: Istoriia nezdiisnymoi sproby dialohu." *Literaturna Ukraina*, 12 September 2013, p. 6.

Matviichuk, O., and N. Struk, eds. *Kyivskyi natsionalnyi universytet imeni Tarasa Shevchenka: Nezabutni postati*. Kyiv: Svit uspikhu, 2005.

Mccauley, Martin. *The Khrushchev Era, 1953–1964*. London: Routledge, 1995.

McDermott, Kevin, and Matthew Stibbe, eds. *Stalinist Terror in Eastern Europe: Elite Purges and Mass Repression*. Manchester and New York: Manchester University Press, 2010.

McDonough, Richard. "Wittgenstein's and Borges' Labyrinth-Imagery." *Athens Journal of Humanities & Arts* 5, no. 4 (2018): 425–46.

Medhurst, Martin J., Robert L. Ivie, Philip Wander, and Robert L. Scott. *Cold War Rhetoric: Strategy, Metaphor, and Ideology*. East Lansing, MI: Michigan State University Press, 1997.

Medvedeva, Galina. "'Sushchestvovan'ia svetloe usilie' (Yulii Daniel)." *Znamia* 2 (2001). *Zhurnalnyi zal*. 2021. http://magazines.russ.ru/znamia/2001/2/medvedeva.html.

Melnykiv, Rostyslav. *Literaturni 1920-ti: Postati (Narysy, obrazky, etiudy)*. Kharkiv: Maidan, 2013.

Menand, Louis. "Woke Up This Morning: Why Do We read Diaries?" *The New Yorker*, 10 December 2007, pp. 106–112.

Mileke, Bob. "Rhetoric and Ideology in the Nuclear Test Documentary." *Film Quarterly; Berkeley* 58, no. 3 (2005): 28–37.

Miloslavskii, Yurii, and Konstantin Skoblinskii. "Skazy." In *Antologiia noveishei russkoi poezii "U goluboi laguny,"* edited by Konstantin K. Kuzminskii and Grigorii L. Kovalev, vol. 3a, 102–06. Newtonville, MA: Oriental Research Partners, 1980–1986.

Minakov, Stanislav. "Dom dlia druzei." *Nezavisimaia gazeta*. 26 February 2020. https://www.ng.ru/ng_exlibris/2009-02-26/5_home.html.

Miroshnichenko, Anatolii. "Zapiski inzhenera-poeta." *Slobozhanskyi kruh* 5 (2011): 75–77.

Mitsel, Mikhail (interview by Mikhail Gold). "Zasluzhennyi antisemit. Kak Trofim Kichko zvezdoi stal." *Hadashot.* 4 April 2020. http://hadashot.kiev.ua/content/zasluzhennyy-antisemit-kak-trofim-kichko-zvezdoy-antisionizma-stal.

Mlechin, Leonid. *Brezhnev.* Moskva: Molodaia gvardiia, 2011.

———. "Pochti ezhednevno . . ." *Novaia gazeta,* 18 October 2013, pp. 16–17.

"Moloda literatura v Ukraini." *Smoloskyp,* January/February 1962, p. 8.

Morgan, Daniel. *Merchants of Grain: The Power and Profits of the Five Giant Companies at the Center of the World's Food Supply.* New York: Viking Adult, 1979.

Moroz, Valentyn. "Moses and Dathan," translated by Olenka Hanushevska. *Smoloskyp* 1, no. 1 (1978): 1–12.

Moroz, V. *Esei, lysty, dokumenty.* Miunkhen: Suchasnist, 1975.

Moshkovich, Itskhak. "Dissidenty i otkazniki." *World.lib.ru.* 26 October 2004. http://world.lib.ru/m/moshkowich_i/dissidentsrefusniks.shtml.

Motyl, Alexander J. "Ukraine, Europe, and Bandera." *The Cicero Foundation Great Debate Paper* 10, no. 5 (2010): 1–14.

———. *Ukraine vs. Russia.* Washington, DC: Westphalia Press, 2017.

———. *Will the Non-Russians Rebel? State, Ethnicity, and Stability in the USSR.* Ithaca and London: Cornell University Press, 1987.

Muratov, Ihor. *Na krylakh Litany.* Kharkiv: Maidan, 2012.

———. *Tvory.* Kyiv: Dnipro, 1983.

Murav, Harriet. *Music from a Speeding Train: Soviet Yiddish and Russian-Jewish Literature of the Twentieth Century.* Stanford, CA: Stanford University Press, 2011.

Mykhailyn, Ihor. *Literaturna Kharkivshchyna. Poeziia.* Kharkiv: "Maidan," 2007.

———. "Yurii Sheveliov: Provintsiia—ne territoriia, a dusha." *Den,* 30 November–1 December 2012 (no. 219–220), p. 3.

Nahaylo, Bohdan, and Victor Swoboda. *Soviet Disunion: A History of the Nationalities Problem in the USSR.* New York: The Free Press, 1989.

Naienko, Mykhailo. "Samotnist dolaetsia slovom naimolodshykh." *Literaturna Ukraina,* 4 April 2013, p. 7.

———. "Shistdesiatnyky." In *Khudozhnia literatura Ukrainy: Vid mifiv do modernoi realnosti* by Mykhailo Naienko, 1002–1040. Kyiv: Vydavnychyi tsentr "Prosvita," 2008.

Naimark, Norman M. *Stalin's Genocides.* Princeton, NJ: Princeton University Press, 2010.

Narvselius, Eleonora. *Ukrainian Intelligentsia in Post-Soviet L'viv: Narratives, Identity, and Power.* New York: Lexington Books, 2012.

Navalna, Maryna, ed. *Vydatni osobystosti z ukrainskoho movoznavstva. Khrestomatiia.* Pereiaslav-Khmelnytskyi: V-vo KSV, 2016.

Nezhyvyi, O. *Hryhir Tiutiunnyk: tekstolohichna ta dzhereloznavcha problematyka zhyttia i tvorchosti.* Luhansk: Vyd-vo "Luhanskyi natsionalnyi universytet imeni Tarasa Shevchenka," 2010.

Nezhyvyi, Oleksii. "Avtohrafy—ne til'ky na paperi . . ." *Literaturna Ukraina*, 12 September 2013, p. 7.

Novotny, Donald J. (interview by Allan Mustard). *The Association for Diplomatic Studies and Training* (Foreign Affairs Oral History Project). 1 April 2009. https://www.adst.org/OH%20TOCs/Novotny,%20Donald.toc.pdf, 10.

Obertas, Oles. *Ukrainskyi samvydav: Literaturna krytyka ta publitsystyka (1960-i – pochatok 1970-kh rokiv)*. Kyiv: Smoloskyp, 2010.

Oleszczuk, Thomas A. *Political Justice in the USSR: Dissent and Repression in Lithuania, 1969–1987*. New York: Columbia University Press, 1988.

Oliinyk, Borys. "Robertu Tretyakovu – 50." *Literaturna Ukraina*, 27 February 1986, p. 5.

Omelchenko, Vasilii. *Smutnyie gody (zapiski ochevidtsa)*. Kharkiv: Maidan, 2013.

———. "Tam zhili poety . . ." *Prostranstvo literatury*. 5 May 2016. www.kpi.kharkov.ua - /archive/Conferences/Пространство литературы, искусства и образования – путь к миру, согласию и сотрудничеству между славянскими народами/2013/.

Orlov, Vitalii. "Akh, Zhenia, Zhenia, Zhenechka, s nim sluchai byl takoi . . ." *Elegant New York*. 27 January 2017. http://elegantnewyork.com/evtushenko-orlov/.

"Osherowitch Mendel." *Entsyklopediia Ukrainskoi diaspory: Spolucheni Shtaty Ameryky*, vol. 1, kn. 2, edited by Vasyl Markus and Dariia Markus, 222. New York and Chicago: Naukove Tovarystvo im. Shevchenka v Amerytsi, 2012.

Osherowitch, Mendel. *How People Live in Soviet Russia: Impressions from a Journey*, edited by Lubomyr Y. Luciuk, translated from the original Yiddish edition by Sharon Power. Kingston, Ontario: Kashtan Press, 2020.

———. *Shtet un shtetlekh in Ukraine*. New York: The M. Osherowitch Jubillee-Committee, 1948.

———. "The Fear of the GPU across the Country." In Mendel Osherowitch, *How People Live in Soviet Russia: Impressions from a Journey*, edited by Lubomyr Y. Luciuk, translated by Sharon Power, 187–96. Toronto: University of Toronto/Chair of Ukrainian Studies/Kashtan Press, 2020.

Ovsiienko, Vasyl. "Druha khvylia areshtiv, 1972–73 rr." *Kharkivska pravozakhysna hrupa*. 1 November 2006. http://museum.khpg.org/index.php?id=1162386564.

———. *Svitlo liudei: Memuary ta publitsystyka*, 2 vol. Kharkiv: Kharkivska pravozakhysna hrupa, 2005.

———. *Svitlo liudei: Memuary ta publitsystyka*, 2 ed., 1 vol. Kharkiv: "Prava liudyny," 2007.

———. "Vidkrytyi lyst dysydenta Ovsiienka dysydentu (i fantazeru) Sapeliaku." *Istorychna Pravda*. 29 August 2011. https://www.istpravda.com.ua/articles/2011/08/29/53451/.

———. "Z pryvodu procesu nad Pohruzhalskym." *Dysydentskyi rukh v Ukraini/Kharkivska pravozakhysna hrupa*. 6 November 2006. http://museum.khpg.org/index.php?id=1162802785.

Pakhliovska, Oksana. "Poeziia liubovi i strazhdannia." *Literaturna Ukraina*, 11 December 1981, p. 4.

Panchenko, Volodymyr. *Kiltsia na drevi*. Kyiv: TOV "Vydavnytstvo 'Klio,'" 2015.

Paradzhanov, Sergei. "Kak ia zavidoval Fellini." In *Kollazh na fone avtoportreta: Zhyzn – igra*, edited by K. D. Tsereteli, 96. Nizhnii Novgorod: Dekom, 2005.
Pasternak, Boris. *Izbrannoe v dvukh tomakh: Stikhotvoreniia i poemy*. Moscow: Khudozhestvennaia literatura, 1985.
Pavlyshyn, Marko. "Martyrology and Literary Scholarship: The Case of Vasyl Stus." *The Slavic and East European Journal* 54, no. 4 (2010): 585–606.
"Psych Ward Verdict for Russian Protester 'A Return to Soviet Psychiatric Persecution of Dissidents.'" *CCHR InternationalThe Mental Health Watchdog* (by Agence France-Presse). 10 October 2013. https://www.cchrint.org/2013/10/11/psych-ward-verdict-for-russian-protester-a-return-to-soviet-psychiatric-persecution-of-dissidents/.
Pechatnov, Vladimir O., and C. Earl Edmondson. "The Russian Perspective." In *Debating the Origins of the Cold War: American and Russian Perspective*, edited by Ralph B. Levering et al., 85–151. New York: Rowman & Littlefield Publishers, Inc., 2001.
Peleshenko, Natalia. "Dukhovnyi podvyh kniaziv Borysa i Hliba v ukrainskii literaturi XX st. (na materiali poezii Borysa Chychybabina)." *Ukrainska Mohylianska akademiia*. 2020. http://ekmair.ukma.edu.ua/bitstream/handle/123456789/11556/Peleshenko_Dukhovnyi_podvyh_kniaziv.pdf?sequence=1&isAllowed=y.
Perepeliak, Ivan (interview by Ihor Mykhailyn). "Poet v optytsi svoho chasu." *Official site of the Kharkiv chapter of the Writers' Union (NSPU)*. 2013. https://kharkiv-nspu.org.ua/archives/2644.
Pererva, Anatolii, ed. *Natsionalna spilka pysmennykiv Ukrainy: 75 rokiv*. Kharkiv: Maidan, 2009.
Petrovsky-Shtern, Yohanan. *The Anti-Imperial Choice: The Making of the Ukrainian Jew*. New Haven & London: Yale University Press, 2009.
———. "Being for the Victims: Leonid Pervomais'kyi's Ethical Responses to Violence." In *The Anti-Imperial Choice: The Making of the Ukrainian Jew*, edited by Yohanan Petrovsky-Shtern, 165–227. New Haven & London: Yale University Press, 2009.
———. "Reconceptualizing the Alien: Jews in Modern Ukrainian Thought." *Ab Imperio* 4 (2003): 519–80.
Pinsky, Anatoly. "The Diatristic Form and Subjectivity under Khrushchev." *Slavic Review* 73, no. 4 (2014): 805–27.
Pipes, Richard. *The Formation of the Soviet Union: Communism and Nationalism, 1917–1923*. New York: Harvard University Press/Atheneum, 1968.
Plakhotniuk, Mykola. *Kolovorot: Statti, spohady, dokumenty*. Kyiv: Smoloskyp, 2012.
Plyushch, Leonid. *History's Carnival: A Dissident's Autobiography*. Translated and edited by Marco Carynnyk. New York and London: A Helen and Kurt Wolff Book/Harcourt Brace Jovanovich, 1979.
———. *Na karnavale istorii*. Overseas Publications Interchange Ltd., 1979.
———. *U karnavali istorii: Svidchennia*. Kyiv: Fakt, 2002.
Plokhy, Serhii. *Chernobyl: The History of a Nuclear Catastrophe*. New York: Basic Books, 2020.

———. *Lost Kingdom: The Quest for Empire and the Making of the Russian Nation.* New York: Basic Books, 2017.
Plokhii, Serhii. "Quo Vadis Ukrainian History?" *Harvard Ukrainian Studies* 34, no. 1–4 (2015–2016): 11–34.
Poetry of Soviet Ukraine's New World: An Anthology. Woodchurch, Ashford, Kent, England: UNESCO; Paul Norbury Publications, 1986.
Podorozhnii, Maks. "Pam'iati Petra Cheremskoho (1942–2006)." *Spilka Ukrainskoi molodi.* 10 July 2016. http://cym.org.ua/2016.07/pam-yati-petra-cheremskogo-1942-2006/.
Podrabinek, Alexander. *Punitive Medicine*, 1st ed. Ann Arbor: Karoma Publishers, Inc., 1980.
Polonskyi, Radii. "Nepoiasnymyi Robert." *Slobozhanskyi kruh* 5 (2011): 35–38.
———. "Nepoiasnymyi Robert." *Vechernii Kharkov*, 18 July 1998, p. 3.
———. "Nepoiasnymyi Robert." *Vechernii Kharkov*, 23 July 1998, p. 7.
Pomerantsev, Peter. "Diary." *London Review of Books,* 5 December 2013, p. 42.
Pomerants, Grigorii. "Without Repentance." *Russian Studies in Literature* 34, no. 3 (1998): 72–43.
"Pomer Volodymyr Briuggen" (a eulogy). *Natsionalna spilka pysmennykiv Ukrainy: Kharkivska oblasna orhanizatsiia.* 19 July 2018. https://kharkiv-nspu.org.ua/archives/5969.
Popov, Vladimir (interview by Dmytro Gordon). *YouTube.* 28 July 2020. https://www.youtube.com/watch?v=oFcrn7w57TU.
Potichnyi, Peter J., ed. *Ukraine in the Seventies.* Oakville, ON: Mosaic Press, 1975.
Priestland, David. "Stalin as Bolshevik Romantic: Ideology and Mobilization, 1917–1939." In *Stalin: A New History*, edited by Sarah Davies and James Harris, 181–201. Cambridge, UK: Cambridge University Press, 2005.
Prizel, Ilya. *National Identity and Foreign Policy: Nationalism and Leadership in Poland, Russia, and Ukraine.* Cambridge, UK: Cambridge University Press, 1998.
Procyk, Anna. "Dissent in Ukraine Through the Prism of Amnesty International." *Human Rights in Ukraine*: *The Kharkiv Human Rights Protection Group.* 1 November 2012. http://khpg.org/en/index.php?id=1326302237.
———, ed. *Two Worlds. One Idea.* New York/Kyiv: Smoloskyp Publisher, 2013.
Prusin, Alexander V. "A 'Zone of Violence': The Anti-Jewish Pogroms in Eastern Galicia in 1914–1915 and 1941." In *Shatterzone of Empires: Coexistence and Violence in the German, Habsburg, Russian, and Ottoman Borderlands*, edited by Omer Bartov and Eric D. Weitz, 362–77. Bloomington and Indianapolis, IN: Indiana University Press, 2013.
Prystaiko, V. I., and Yu. I. Shapoval. *Sprava "Spilky Vyzvolennia Ukrainy": nevidomi dokumenty i fakty.* Kyiv: Intel, 1995.
Pyanov, Aleksey, ed. *Soviet Humor: The Best of Krokodil.* Kansas City/New York: Andrews and McMeel/A University Press Syndicate Company, 1989.
Rafalsky, Viktor. "Reportazh niotkuda." In *Sovetskaia psikhiatriia: Zabluzhdeniia i umysel*, edited by A. Korotenko and N. Alikina, 219–50. Kyiv: Sfera, 2002.
Rakhlina, Marlena. *Chto bylo—vidali . . .* Kharkiv: "Prava liudyny," 2006.
Rakhlin, David, and Feliks Rakhlin. *Rukopis.* Kharkov: "Prava liudyny," 2007.

Rakhlin, Feliks. *O Borise Chichibabine i iego vremeni: Strochka iz zhizni.* Kharkov: Folio, 2004.

Ramsey, Ramsey Eric. "Listening to Heidegger on Rhetoric." *Philosophy and Rhetoric* 26, no. 4 (1993): 266–76.

Ranciere, Jacques. "Ten Theses on Politics." *Theory & Event* 5, no. 3 (2001): 1–16.

Reblitschek, Immo. "Lessons from the Terror: Soviet Prosecutors and Police Violence in Molotov Province, 1942 to 1949." *Slavic Review* 78, no. 3 (2019): 738–57.

Reddaway, Peter. "Soviet Policies toward Dissent, 1953–1986." *Journal of Interdisciplinary Studies* 24, nos. 1–2 (2012): 57–82.

Redlich, Shimon. *Together and Apart in Brzezany: Poles, Jews, and Ukrainians, 1919–1945.* Bloomington and Indianapolis, IN: Indiana University Press, 2002.

Reich, Rebecca. *State of Madness: Psychiatry, Literature, and Dissent After Stalin.* DeKalb, IL: Northern Illinois University Press, 2018.

Remennick, Larissa I. *Russian Jews on Three Continents: Identity, Integration, and Conflict* New Brunswick, NJ: Transaction, 2007.

Reva, Iryna. *Po toi bik sebe: sotsialno-psyholohichni i kulturni naslidky Holodomoru ta stalinskykh represii.* Dnipro: A. L. Svidler, 2013.

Reznik, Shaul. "Zhydobanderovtsy, Pokoleniie 1.0." *Lekhaim* 271 (30 October 2014). http://old.lechaim.ru/2461.

Riabchuk, Mykola. "Vid VChK do SBU: Tiahlist i modyfikatsiia 'antynatsional-istychnykh' dyskursiv i polityk." *Historians.* 14 March 2013. http://www.historians.in.ua/index.php/en/dyskusiya/618-mykola-riabchuk-vid-vchk-do-sbu-tiahlist-ta-modyfikatsiia-antynatsionalistychnykh-dyskursiv-i-polityk.

Richmond, Yale. *Cultural Exchange and the Cold War: Raising the Iron Curtain.* University Park, PA: The Pennsylvania State University Press, 2003.

Rid, Thomas. *Active Measures: The Secret History of Disinformation and Political Warfare.* New York: Farrar, Straus, and Giroux, 2020.

Risch, William Jay. *The Ukrainian West: Culture and the Fate of Empire in Soviet Lviv.* Cambridge, MA: Harvard University Press, 2011.

Robins, James. "Can Historians Be Traumatized by History?" *TNR/The New Republic.* 16 February 2021. https://newrepublic.com/article/161127/can-historians-traumatized-history?fbclid=IwAR1WhvBHwTgnrwQGyENXztkoxrGCtHN5caBfNxS11EIHuhQ-OEmxt5gF0-g.

Rodionov, Volodymyr. "Sribernyi kniaz Ukrainskoi poezii." *Literaturna Ukraina*, 23 February 2006, p. 7.

Roginskii, Arsenii. "KGB reformirovat nevozmozhno." *Radio Svoboda.* 18 December 2017. https://www.svoboda.org/a/28924835.html.

Ro'i, Yaacov. "'The Move From Russia/the Soviet Union to Israel': A Transformation of Jewish Culture and Identity?" In *The New Jewish Diaspora: Russian-Speaking Immigrants in the United States, Israel, and Germany*, edited by Zvi Gitelman, 139–55. New Brunswick, NJ and London: Rutgers University Press, 2016.

⸻. "Union of Soviet Socialist Republics." *The YIVO Encyclopedia of Jews in Eastern Europe.* 2020. http://www.yivoencyclopedia.org/article.aspx/Union_of_Soviet_Socialist_Republics.

Romanovskyi, Viacheslav. *Osiaiala natkhnenniam Slobozhan: Esei ta besidy*. Kharkiv: Vydavnytstvo Fedorko, 2013.

Romerstein, Herbert, and Stanislav Levchenko. *The KGB Against the "Main Enemy:" How the Soviet Intelligence Service Operates against the United States*. Toronto: Lexington Books, 1989.

Rosenberg, Victor. "Refugee Status for Soviet Jewish Immigrants to the United States." *Touro Law Review* 19, no. 2, Art. 22 (2014): 419–50.

Rosenfeldt, Niels Erik. *The "Special" World*, 1 and 2 vols. Copenhagen, Denmark: Museum Tusculanum Press/University of Copenhagen, 2009.

Rossetti, Livio. "'If We Link the Essence of Rhetoric with Deception': Vincenzo on Socrates and Rhetoric." *Philosophy and Rhetoric* 26, no. 4 (1993): 311–21.

Rubenstein, Joshua. *Soviet Dissidents: Their Struggle for Human Rights*. Boston: Beacon Press, 1980.

Ruby, Walter. "The Role of Non-establishment Groups." In *A Second Exodus: The American Movement to Free Soviet Jews*, edited by M. Friedman and A. D. Chernin, 200–223. Hanover, NH: Brandeis University Press, 1999.

Rudenko, Raisa, ed. *Mykola Rudenko: "Naibilshe dyvo – zhyttia." Spohady*. Kyiv: Smoloskyp, 2013.

Rudiachenko, Oleksandr. "Leonid Bykov: Prybulets, shcho vidbuv." *Ukrinform*. 12 December 2018. https://www.ukrinform.ua/rubric-culture/2598839-leonid-bikov-pribulec-so-pisov.html.

Rudnytskyi, Ivan L. "Comments on Professor Zvi Gitelman: The Social and Political Role of the Jews in Ukraine." In *Ukraine in the Seventies*, edited by Peter J. Potichnyi Oakville, 187–93. Oakville, ON: Mosaic Press, 1975.

———. "The Political Thought of Soviet Ukrainian Dissidents." In *Essays in Modern Ukrainian History*, edited by Peter L. Rudnytsky, 477–89. Edmonton: Canadian Institute of Ukrainian Studies, 1987.

Rudnytskyi, Omelian, Nataliia Levchuk, Oleh Wolowyna, Pavlo Shevchuk, and Alla Kovbasiuk. "Demography of a Man-Made Human Catastrophe: The Case of Massive Famine in Ukraine 1932–1933." *Canadian Studies in Population* 42, no. 1–2 (2015): 53–80.

Rusnachenko, A. *Natsionalno-vyzvolnyi rukh v Ukraini: seredyna 1950–kh–pochatok 1990-kh rokiv*. Kyiv: V-vo imeni Oleny Telihy, 1998.

Sakwa, Richard. *The Rise and Fall of the Soviet Union, 1917–1991*. London and New York: Routledge, 1999.

Sarnov, Benedikt. *Skuki ne bylo. Vtoraia kniga vospominanii*. https://www.e-reading.club/bookreader.php/1053492/Sarnov_Skuki_ne_bylo._Vtoraya_kniga_vospominaniy.html.

Satzewich, Vic. *The Ukrainian Diaspora*. London and New York: Routledge, 2003.

Schroeter, Leonard. *The Last Exodus*. Seattle and London: University of Washington Press, 1974.

Schuman, Tomas. *Black Is Beautiful. Communism Is Not*. Los Angeles, CA: Almanac, 1985.

Seelye, Katharine Q. "Sergei Khrushchev, Son of Former Soviet Premier, Dies at 84." *The New York Times*. 24 June 2020. https://www.nytimes.com/2020/06/24/us/sergei-khrushchev-dead.html.

Seko, Yaroslav. "Rozvytok ukrainskoho shistdesiatnytsva u 1965–1971 rr." In *Naukovi zapysky Ternopilskoho natsionalnoho pedahohichnoho universytetu imeni Volodymyra Hnatiuka,* vyp. 2, ch. 1, 128–34. Ternopil: Vyd-vo TNPU im. V. Hnatiuka, 2014.

Semichastnyi, Vladimir. *Bespokoinoie serdtse.* Moskva: Vagrius, 2002.

Senderovich, Sasha. "Scenes of Encounter: The 'Soviet Jew' in Fiction by Russian Jewish Writers in America." *Prooftexts* 35, no. 1 (2015): 98–132.

Sergeyev, Sergei, comp. *Zionism – Enemy of Peace and Social Progress.* Translated by Barry Jones. Moscow: Progress Publishers, 1984.

Service, Robert. *A History of Modern Russia: From Tsarism to the Twenty-First Century,* 3rd ed. Cambridge, MA: Harvard University Press, 2009.

Sicking, J.M.J. "Judaism and Literature in Carry van Bruggen and Jacob Israël de Haan." *Studia Rosenthaliana* (Proceedings of the Seventh International Symposium on the History and Culture of the Jews in the Netherlands) 30, no. 1 (1996): 99–108.

Shain, Yossi, and Aharon Barth. "Diasporas and International Relations Theory." *International Organization* 57, no. 3 (2003): 449–79.

Shanes, Joshua, and Yohanan Petrovsky-Shtern. "An Unlikely Alliance: The 1907 Ukrainian–Jewish Electoral Coalition." *Nations and Nationalism* 15, no. 3 (2009): 483–505.

Shankowsky, Lew. "Russia, the Jews and the Ukrainian Liberation Movement." In *Ukrainians and Jews: A Symposium,* 65–96. New York: The Ukrainian Congress Committee of America, Inc. 1966.

Shapiro, Leon. "Soviet Jewry Since the Death of Stalin: A Twenty-five Year Perspective." *The American Jewish Year Book* 79 (1979): 77–103; also available at https://www.bjpa.org/content/upload/bjpa/sovi/Soviet%20Jewry%20stalin.pdf.

Shapoval, Yurii, and Hiroaki Kuromiya, eds. *Ukraina v dobu "Velykoho Teroru": 1936–1938 roky.* Kyiv: Lybid, 2009.

Shapoval, Yurii, and Vadym Zolotariov. "Yevrei v kerivnytstvi orhaniv DPU-NKVS USRR-URSR u 1920-1930-kh rr." *Z arkhiviv VUChK-GPU-NKVD-KGB* 1 (2010): 53–93.

Shapoval, Yu., and V. Panchenko, eds. *Poliuvannia na Valdshnepa: Rozsekrechenyi Mykola Khvyliovyi.* Kyiv: Tempora, 2009.

Shapoval, Yurii, ed. *Petro Shelest: 'Spravzhnii sud istorii shche poperedu . . .' Spohady, shchodennyky, dokumenty, materialy.* Kyiv: Heneza, 2003.

Shapoval, Yurii. "Ideolog natsionalisticheskikh elementov respubliki . . ." *Gazeta ZN,UA.* 22 July 2011. http://gazeta.zn.ua/SOCIETY/ideolog_natsionalisticheskih _elementov_respubliki_.html.

_____. "Petro Shelest u konteksti politychnoi istorii Ukrainy XX stolittia." *Bakhmutskyi shliakh* 1–2 (2008): 101–12.

_____. "Petro Shelest u konteksti politychnoi istorii Ukrainy XX stolittia." *Ukrainskyi istorychnyi zhurnal* 3 (2008): 134–49.

_____. "Petro Shelest: zhyttia ta politychna dolia." In *Petro Shelest: "Spravzhnii sud istorii shche poperedu,"* edited by Yurii Shapoval, 19–44. Kyiv: ADEF-Ukraina, 2011.

———. "Sprava Ivana Dziuby." *Z arkhiviv VUChK/GPU/NKVD/KGB* 1, no. 36 (2011): 259–94.

Shapoval, Yurii, Volodymyr Prystaiko, and Vadym Zolotariov. *ChK-GPU-NKVD v Ukraini: Osoby, Fakty, Dokumenty*. Kyiv: Abris, 1997.

Sharova, T. M. "Vasyl Bondar: Osoblyvosti biohrafichnoi prozy ta ideino-khudozhni poshuky pysmennyka." *Visnyk Luhanskoho Natsionalnoho Universytetu imeni Tarasa Shevchenka* 3, no. 166 (2009): 179–85.

Sharvarok, Oleksandr. "Aktyvna pam'iat.'" *Literaturna Ukraina*, 11 December 1981, p. 3.

Shatylov, Mykola. *Kliati simdesiati . . . Na pam'iati stalo, na pam'iati staly*. Kharkiv: Vydavnytstvo "Apostrof," 2011.

———. (interview by Liutsyna Khvorost). "Kozhen mii virsh – shchodennykovyi zapys . . ." *Vsesvit*. 2020. http://www.vsesvit-journal.com/old/content/view/1028/41/.

Shcherbak, Yurii. *Ukraina v zoni turbulentnosti: demony mynuloho i tryvohy XXI stolittia*. Kyiv: Ukrainskyi pysmennyk, 2010.

Sheftel, Yoram. *The Demjanjuk Affair: The Rise and Fall of a Show-Trial*, revised ed. London: Victor Gollancz, 1994.

Sheiko, Konstantin, and Stephen Brown. *History as Therapy: Alternative History and Nationalist Imaginings in Russia, 1991–2014*. Stuttgart: ibidem-Verlag/Columbia University Press, 2014.

Shevchenko, Oles, ed. *Ukrainska Helsinska Spilka u spohadakh i dokumentakh*. Kyiv: "Yaroslaviv Val," 2012.

Shevel, Oxana. "Memories of the Past and Visions of the Future Remembering the Soviet Era and Its End in Ukraine." In *Twenty Years After Communism: The Politics of Memory and Commemoration*, edited by Michael Bernhard and Jan Kubik, 146–67. New York: Oxford University Press, 2014.

Sheveliov, Yurii (Yurii Sherekh). *Ia, meni, mene (i dovkruhy). Spohady*. Kharkiv and New York: Vydavnytstvo M. P. Kots, 2001.

Shkandrij, Myroslav, and Olga Bertelsen. "The Soviet Regime's National Operations in Ukraine, 1929–1934." *Canadian Slavonic Papers* LV, nos. 3–4 (2013): 417–47.

Shkandrij, Myroslav. *Jews in Ukrainian Literature: Representation and Identity*. New Haven and London, Yale University Press, 2009.

———. "Poet of Dissent: Vasyl Stus." In *Russia and Ukraine: Literature and Discourse of Empire from Napoleonic to Postcolonial Times*, 249–58. London: McGill-Queen's University Press, 2001.

———. *Russia and Ukraine: Literature and the Discourse of Empire from Napoleonic to Postcolonial Times*. Montreal & Kingston: McGill-Queen's University Press, 2001.

Shkoda, V. G., ed. *Chernobyl: Dni ispytanii. Kniga svidetelstv*. Kiev: Radianskyi pysmennyk, 1988.

Shmerkin, Genrikh. "Boris Chichibabin i russkaia drama." *Sem iskusstv* 11, no. 12 (November 2010). http://7iskusstv.com/2010/Nomer11/Shmerkin1.php.

Shternshis, Anna. *Soviet and Kosher: Jewish Popular Culture in the Soviet Union, 1923–1929*. Bloomington: Indiana University Press, 2013.

Shtohrin, Iryna. "Yak vyvozyly ostanky Stusa, Lytvyna, i Tykhoho z Gulagu." *Radio Svoboda*, 19 November 2019. https://www.radiosvoboda.org/a/perepohovannya-stusa-lytvyna-tyhoho/30278986.html.

Shultz, Richard H., and Roy Godson. *Dezinformatsia: The Strategy of Soviet Disinformation*. New York: Berkley Books, 1986.

Shvets, Yuri (interview by Dmytro Gordon). *YouTube*. 2 March 2019. https://www.youtube.com/watch?v=M4YFeXr031E; *YouTube*. 18 August 2020. https://www.youtube.com/watch?v=wjMJIUZLJVs.

Sicher, Efraim. *Jews in Russian Literature after the October Revolution: Writers and Artists Between Hope and Apostasy*. Cambridge: Cambridge University Press, 1995.

Slezkine, Yuri. *The Jewish Century*. Princeton, NJ: Princeton University press, 2004.

Slonim, Marc. *Soviet Russian Literature: Writers and Problems, 1917–1977*, 2nd ed. New York: Oxford University Press, 1977.

Slutskii, Boris. *Sovremennyie istorii*. Moskva: Molodaiia gvardiia, 1969.

Smith, T. C., and T. A. Oleszczuk. *No asylum: State Psychiatric Repression in the Former USSR*. New York: New York University Press, 1996.

Snyder, Sarah B. "'Promising Everything Under the Sun': Helsinki Activism and Human Rights in Eastern Europe." In *The Establishment Responds: Power, Politics, and Protest since 1945*, edited by Kathrin Fahlenbrach, Martin Klimke, Joachim Scharloth, and Laura Wong, 91–102. New York: Palgrave Macmillan, 2012.

Snyder, Timothy. *Bloodlands: Europe Between Hitler and Stalin*. New York: Basic Books: 2012.

Sokil, Vasyl. *Zdaleka do blyzkoho: spohady, rozdumy*. Edmonton: Canadian Institute of Ukrainian Studies, 1987.

Solodko, Pavlo. "Yak pysaty pro Holodomor." *Istorychna Pravda*. 26 November 2012. http://www.istpravda.com.ua/artefacts/2012/11/26/101572/.

Sosin, I. K. "Dva goda is dvukh stoletii . . ." *Novosti Ukrainskoi psikhiatrii*. 2003. http://www.psychiatry.ua/books/saburka/paper034.htm.

"Spysok osib, yaki pidpadaiut pid zakon o dekomunizatsii." *Ukrainskyi Instytut natsionalnoi pam'iati*. http://www.memory.gov.ua/publication/spisok-osib-yaki-pidpadayut-pid-zakon-pro-dekomunizatsiyu.

Stadnychenko, Yurii. "Vesnianyi Kharkiv." In *Kharkiv, pisne moia*, edited by Yurii Stadnychenko, 78–79. Kharkiv: Prapor, 1982.

Stern, August, ed. *The USSR vs. Dr. Mikhail Stern: The Only Tape Recording of a Trial Smuggled Out of the Soviet Union*. Translated by Marko Carynnyk. New York: Urizen Books, 1977.

Stern, J. P. "Franz Kafka: The Labyrinths of Guilt." *Critical Quarterly* 7, no. 1 (1965): 35–48.

Stradnyk, Petro. *Pravda pro sovetsku vladu v Ukraini*. Kyiv: Tsentr navchalnoi literatury, 2019.

Stozhuk, Anatolii. "Chervone sontse Kaerkana." *Literaturna Ukraina*, 12 September 2013, p. 15.

Sverstiuk, Yevhen. "My obraly zhyttia." In *Bunt pokolinnia: rozmovy z ukrainskymy intelektualamy*, edited by Bogumila Berdykhovska and Olia Hnatiuk, translated by Roksana Kharchuk. Kyiv: Dukh i litera, 2004.

———. *Na poli chesti: Nevzhe to ia?*, edited by Oleksii Sinchenko (knyha I). Kyiv: TOV "Vydavnytstvo 'Klio,'" 2015.

Szporluk, Roman. "Russians in Ukraine and Problems of Ukrainian Identity in the USSR." In *Ukraine in the Seventies*, edited by Peter J. Potichnyj, 195–217. Oakville, ON: Mosaic Press, 1975.

———. "The Press and Soviet Nationalities: The Party Resolution of 1975 and Its Implementation." In *Russia, Ukraine, and the Breakup of the Soviet Union* by Roman Szporluk, 277–97. Stanford, CA: Hoover Institution Press, 2000.

Stradnyk, Petro. *Pravda pro sovetsku vladu v Ukraini*. Kyiv: Tsentr navchalnoi literatury, 2019.

Sukhorukova, Inna. "25 Years to the Ukrainian Helsinki Group." *The Kharkiv Human Rights Protection Group*. 13 December 2001. http://khpg.org/en/index.php?id =1008253233.

Szasz, Thomas S. *Ideology and Insanity: Essays on the Psychiatric Dehumanization of Man*. New York: Anchor Books, 1970.

———. *The Myth of Mental Illness: Foundations of a Theory of Personal Conduct*. New York: Happer & Row, Publishers, 1974

Taitslin, V. I. "O Saburovoi Dache." *Novosti Ukrainskoi psikhiatrii*. 2003. http://www.psychiatry.ua/books/saburka/paper038.htm.

Taniuk, Les. *Talan i talant Lesia Kurbasa*. Kyiv: Derzhavnyi tsentr teatralnoho mystetstva imeni Lesia Kurbasa, 2007.

Tarnashynska, L. B. "Ivan Drach: 'Narodzhuite sebe, dopoky svitu . . .'" In *Ivan Drach: Literatura. Kinematohraf. Polityka*, 5–32. Kyiv: Natsionalna parlamentska biblioteka Ukrainy, 2011.

Tarnashynska, Liudmyla. *Ukrainske shistdesiatnytstvo: profili na tli pokolinnia (Istoryko-literaturnyi ta poetykalnyi aspekty)*. Kyiv: "Smoloskyp," 2010.

Tarsis, Valeriy. *Ward 7: An Autobiographical Novel*. Translated by Katya Brown. New York: E. P. Dutton & Co., Inc., 1966.

Tatarchenko, Ksenia. "Calculating a Showcase: Mikhail Lavrentiev, the Politics of Expertise, and the International Life of the Siberian Science-City." *Historical Studies in the Natural Sciences* 46, no. 5 (2016): 592–632.

Terelya, Josyp (with Michael H. Brown). *Witness to Apparitions and Persecution in the USSR: An Autobiography*. Milford, OH: Faith Publishing Company, 1991.

The Royal College of Psychiatrists. "Dr. Alexander Voloshanovich: A Critic of the Political Misuse of Psychiatry in the USSR." *The Psychiatric Bulletin* 4 (1980): 70–71. http://pb.rcpsych.org/content/4/5/70.full.pdf.

Thompson, Ewa M. *Imperial Knowledge: Russian Literature and Colonialism*, 1st ed. Westport, CT: Greenwood Press, 2000.

Thorne, Ludmilla. "Three Years of Repression in the Soviet Union: A Statistical Study." *Freedom Appeals* 9 (March–April 1981): 29–31.

Tietge, David James. *Post-World War II Rhetoric of Science and Its Impact on Civic Ideology in a Nuclear Age*. Carbondale: IL: Southern Illinois University; ProQuest Dissertations Publishing, 1997.

Tillett, Lowell. *The Great Friendship: Soviet Historians on the Non-Russian Nationalities*. Chapel Hill: University of North Carolina Press, 1969.

———. "Ukrainian Nationalism and the Fall of Shelest." *Slavic Review* 34, no. 4 (1975): 752–768.

Tiutiunnyk, Hryhir. *Buty pysmennykom: shchodennyky, zapysnyky, lysty*, edited by O. Nezhyvyi. Kyiv: Yaroslaviv Val, 2011.

Toma, Leonid. "Ty uiavy sobi . . ." *Slobozhanskyi kruh* 5 (2011): 60–62.

Torbakov, Igor. "Ukraine and Russia: Entangled Histories, Contested Identities, and a War of Narratives." In *Revolution and War in Contemporary Ukraine: The Challenge of Change*, edited by Olga Bertelsen, 89–119. Stuttgart/New York: ibidem-Verlag/Columbia University Press, 2017.

Totska, Liudmyla. "Na perekhrestiakh doli. Ivan Kozub." *Trudova slava* 37–40 (16 March 2018). Also available at Boryspilska raionna derzhavna administratsiia Kyivskoi oblasti, http://raybori.gov.ua/2018/03/16/na-perehrestyah-doli-ivan-kozub/.

Tretyakov, Robert. *Merydiany kriz sertse: Vybrane*. Kyiv: Dnipro, 1975.

———. *Palitra: Virshi*. Kharkiv: Vydavnytstvo "Prapor," 1965.

———. *Portrety*. Kharkiv: Vydavnytstvo "Prapor," 1967.

———. *Tobi: poezii*. Kharkiv: Prapor, 1991.

———. *Zorianist: Poezii*. Kharkiv: Kharkivske knyzhkove vydavnytstvo, 1961.

Tromly, Benjamin. "An Unlikely National Revival: Soviet Higher Learning and the Ukrainian 'Sixtiers,' 1953–1965." *Russian Review* 68, no. 4 (2009): 607–22.

———. *Making the Soviet Intelligentsia: Universities and Intellectual Life under Stalin and Khrushchev*. Cambridge, UK: Cambridge University Press, 2014.

Tucker, Robert C., ed. *Stalinism: Essays in Historical Interpretation*. New York: W. W. Norton & Company, Inc., 1977.

———. *The Soviet Political Mind*. London: George Allen and Unwin, 1972.

Ulam, Adam B. "What Is "Soviet"—Is "Russian"? In *End of Empire: The Demise of the Soviet Union*, edited by G. R. Urban, 155–77. Washington, DC: The American University Press, 1993.

"Umerla Marlena Rakhlina" (Feliks Rakhlin). *Memorial*. 5 June 2010. http://old.memo.ru/2010/06/06/marlena_rakhlina.htm.

Umland, Andreas. "Ofitsialnyi sovetskii antisemitism poslestalinskogo perioda." *Pro et Contra* 7, no. 2 (2002): 158–68.

United States Citizenship and Immigration Services (USCIS). www.uscis.gov› foia › PRD2014000534-John_Demjanjuk.

Usoltsev, Vladimir (interview by Andrei Sharogradskii). *Radio Svoboda*. 11 November 2003. https://www.svoboda.org/a/24187711.html.

Van Voren, Robert. *Cold War in Psychiatry: Human Factors, Secret Actors*. Amsterdam and New York: Rodopi, 2010.

———. *On Dissidents and Madness: From the Soviet Union of Leonid Brezhnev to the "Soviet Union" of Vladimir Putin*. New York: Rodopi, 2009.

Vasylenko, Volodymyr, and Myroslava Antonovych, eds. *Holodomor 1932–1933 rokiv v Ukraini yak zlochyn henotsydu zhidno z mizhnarodnym pravom*, 4th ed. Kyiv: Kyievo-Mohylianska akademiia, 2016.

Vedenieiev, Dmytro. "Nezakonni politychni represii 1920–1980-kh rokiv v Ukraini ta problemy formuvannia natsionalnoi pam'iati." *Istorychna Pravda*. 26 December 2012. https://www.istpravda.com.ua/research/50db659307b77/.

Veidlinger, Jeffrey. *In the Shadow of the Shtetl: Small Town Jewish Life in Soviet Ukraine*. Bloomington: Indiana University Press, 2013.

Velikanova, Olga. *Popular Perceptions of Soviet Politics in the 1920s: Disenchantment of the Dreamers*. New York: Palgrave Macmillan, 2013.

Vernik, Aleksandr. "Boris A. Chichibabin." In *The Blue Lagoon: Anthology of Modern Russian Poetry*, edited by Konstantin Kuzminsky and Grigorii Kovalev. Newtonville, MA: Oriental Research Partners, 1982.

Veselova, O. M., V. I. Marochko, and O. M. Movchan, eds. *Holodomory v Ukraini. 1921–1923, 1932–1933, 1946–1947: Zlochyny proty narodu*. Kyiv: Vyd-vo MP Kots, 2000.

V'iatrovych, Volodymyr. "Operatsiia 'Blok.' Diia persha." In *Istoriia z hryfom "Sekretno"* by Volodymyr V'iatrovych, 204–12. Lviv/Kyiv: Tsentr doslidzhen vyzvolnoho rukhu, 2011.

Viola, Lynne. *Stalinist Perpetrators on Trial: Scenes from the Great Terror in Ukraine*. Oxford, UK: Oxford University Press, 2017.

⸻. "The Question of the Perpetrator in Soviet History." *Slavic Review* 72, no. 1 (2013): 1–23.

Voss, D. Stephen. "The Story of the Two Ivans: Portrait of a Government Conspiracy." *University of Kentucky*. 2020. http://www.uky.edu/~dsvoss/docs/ps101/twoivans.htm.

Vsia Moskva: Adresnaia i spravochnaia kniga na 1914 god. Moskva: T-vo A. V. Suvorina "Novoie Vriemia"/Gorodskaia Tipografiia, 1914. *Gosudarstvennaia publichnaia biblioteka Rossii*. 2020. http://elib.shpl.ru/ru/nodes/2923-na-1914-god-m-1914#mode/inspect/page/1541/zoom/4.

"Vynos tela Stalina iz Mavzoleia." *YouTube*. 1 January 2012. http://www.youtube.com/watch?v=YR9o6A3Nfl0.

Walker, Barbara. "Pollution and Purification in the Moscow Human Rights Networks of the 1960s and 1970s." *Slavic Review* 68, no. 2 (2009): 376–95.

Wanner, Catherine. *Burden of Dreams: History and Identity in Post-Soviet Ukraine*. University Park, PA: The Pennsylvania State University Press, 1998.

Wasyliw, Zenon V. "On a Revolutionary Nationalist Declaration: Mykola Mikhnovskyi's Samostiina Ukraina." *East European Quarterly* 33, no. 3 (1999): 371–84.

Westad, Odd Arne. *The Cold War: A World History*. New York: Basic Books, 2019.

Westrate, Michael T. *Living Soviet in Ukraine from Stalin to Maidan: Under the Falling Red Star in Kharkiv*. Lanham/Boulder/New York/London: 2016.

Wilson, Andrew. *The Ukrainians: Unexpected Nation*, 2nd ed. New Haven and London: Yale University Press, 2002.

⸻. *Ukrainian Nationalism in the 1990s: A Minority Faith*. Cambridge: Cambridge University Press, 1997.

Wojnowski, Zbigniew. *The Near Abroad: Socialist Eastern Europe and Soviet Patriotism in Ukraine, 1956–1985*. Toronto: University of Toronto Press, 2017.

Wolfe, Thomas C. *Governing Soviet Journalism: The Press and the Socialist Person after Stalin*. Bloomington and Indianapolis: Indiana University Press, 2005.
Wood, Michael. "Report from the Interior." *London Review of Books*, 9 January 2014, p. 30.
Yakimov, I. "Chtoby pisma shli bystreet." *Krasnoe znamia*, 25 February 1971, p. 4.
Yang, Michelle Murray. "President Nixon's Speeches and Toasts during His 1972 Trip to China: A Study in Diplomatic Rhetoric." *Rhetoric and Public Affairs* 14, no. 1 (2011): 1–44.
Yarova, V. S. "Shevchenkivska tema v drukovanii hrafitsi Kharkova 1960-kh rokiv." *Visnyk Lvivskoi natsionalnoi akademii mystetstv* 25 (2014): 228–37.
Yekelchyk, Serhy. *Stalin's Empire of Memory: Russian-Ukrainian Relations in the Soviet Historical Imaginations*. Toronto: University of Toronto Press, 2004.
———. "The Early 1960s as a Cultural Space: A Microhistory of Ukraine's Generation of Cultural Rebels." *Nationalities Papers* 43, no. 1 (2015): 45–62.
"Yevreiskaia tragediia Voznesenskogo." *IsraLove*. 2020. https://isralove.org/load/14-1-0-1462.
"Yevtushenko i Kharkov." *Kharkovskiie Izvestiia*. 7 April 2017. http://izvestia.kharkov.ua/on-line/18/1237277.html.
Yevtushenko, Yevgenii. "Igra v poddavki: Istoriia odnoi verbovki." *Sovershenno Sekretno* 4, no. 51 (April 2012): 20.
Yonah, Yossi. "Reclaiming Diaspora: The Israeli State, Migration, and Ethnonationalism in the Global Era." *Diaspora: A Journal of Transnational Studies* 16, no. 1/2 (2007): 190–228.
Yovenko, Svitlana. "'Omanlyvist velykykh istyn' Volodymyra Briuggena" (a foreword). In *Bloknoty*, edited by Vladimir Briuggen, 4–7. Kharkov: Maidan, 2007.
Yurchak, Alexei. *Everything Was Forever, Until It Was No More: The Last Soviet Generation*. Princeton, NJ: Princeton University Press, 2006.
Zabila, Natalia. "Pro Zhyttia i tvorchist Ihoria Muratova" (a foreword). In *Veselo, soniachno, druzhno*, edited by Ihor Muratov, 3–6. Kyiv: Derzhavne vydavnytstvo dytiachoi literatury URSR, 1960.
Zabushko, Oksana. *Khroniky vid Fortinbrasa: Vybrana eseistyka*. Kyiv: Fakt, 2006.
———. *Z mapy knyh i liudei*. Kamianets-Podilskyi: Meridian Czernowits, 2012.
———. "Z neznyshchennoho." In *Na poli chesti: Nash suchasnyk Yevhen Sverstiuk* (knyha II), edited by Vasyl Ovsiienko, 140–58. Kyiv: TOV "Vydavnytstvo 'Klio,'" 2015.
Zakharov, B. *Narys istorii dysydentskoho rukhu v Ukraini (1956–1987)*. Kharkiv: Folio, 2003.
Zakharkov, Yevhen (interview by Mykola Kniazhytskyi). "Yak reformuvaty sudovu systemu" (Kharkivska pravozakhysna hrupa). *Espreso*. 24 July 2016. http://espreso.tv/article/2016/07/24/zakharov.
Zalkalns, Lilita. *Back to the Motherland: Repatriation and Latvian Émigrés 1955–1958*. Stockholm, Sweden: Stockholm University, 2014.
Zamesov, Valerii. "Dlia nas vin buv klasykom: Spohady pro Roberta Tretyakova." *Berezil* 1–2 (2007): 164–68.

Zashko, Olena. *Pidtrymka uv'iaznenykh dysydentiv diasporoiu SShA (za materialamy vydan "Ameryka" ta "Svoboda")* (unpublished thesis). Lviv: Ukrainskyi katolytskyi universytet, 2017.

Zaitsev, Yurii. "Polska oposytsiia 1970–1980-kh rokiv pro zasady ukrainsko-polskoho porozuminnia." In *Deportatsii ukraintsiv ta poliakiv: kinets 1939–pochatok 50-kh rokiv*, edited by Yurii Slyvka. Lviv: NAN Ukrainy, Instytut ukrainoznavstva im. Krypiakevycha, 1998.

"Zbigniew Brzezinski . . ." *Telegraph*. 27 May 2017. https://www.telegraph.co.uk/news/2017/05/27/zbigniew-brzezinski-jimmy-carters-national-security-adviser/.

Zhabotinskii, Vladimir (Zeev). "O 'yevreiakh i russkoi literature'" (an excerpt from *Izbrannoe*, Jerusalem: Biblioteka-Alia, 1978). *YouTube* (read and posted by Mikhail Polskii). 4 May 2019. https://www.youtube.com/watch?v=Li-I0NWdHp0&t=795s.

Zhuk, Sergei I. "'Cultural Wars' in the Closed City of Soviet Ukraine, 1959–1982." In *Soviet Society in the Era of Late Socialism, 1964–1985*, edited by Neringa Klumbyte and Gulnaz Sharafutdinova, 68–89. New York: Lexington Books, 2013.

———. *Rock and Roll in the Rocket City: The West, Identity, and Ideology in Soviet Dniepropetrovsk, 1960–1985*. Washington, DC/Baltimore: Woodrow Wilson Center Press/The Johns Hopkins University Press, 2010.

———. *Nikolai Bolkhovitinov and American Studies in the USSR: People's Diplomacy in the Cold War*. New York: Lexington Books, 2017.

Zhulynskyi, Mykola. *Natsiia. Kultura. Literatura: Natsionalno-kulturni mify ta ideino-estetychni poshuky Ukrainskoi literatury*. Kyiv: Naukova dumka, 2011.

Zhurzhenko, Tatiana. *Borderlands into Bordered Lands: Geopolitics of Identity in Post-Soviet Ukraine*. Stuttgart: ibidem-Verlag, 2010.

———. "'Capital of Despair': Holodomor Memory and Political Conflicts in Kharkiv after the Orange Revolution." *East European Politics and Societies* 25, no. 3 (2011): 597–639.

Zhvanetskii, Mikhail (interview by Dmitrii Gordon). *Bulvar Gordona*. 14 November 2006. http://bulvar.com.ua/gazeta/archive/s46_5398/2859.html.

Zhylenko, Iryna. *Homo Feriens: Spohady*. Kyiv: Smoloskyp, 2011.

Zinkevych, Osyp, ed. *Ukrainska Helsinska Hrupa, 1978–1982: Dokumenty i materiialy*. Toronto: V. Symonenko Smoloskyp Publishers, 1983.

———. "Rozhrom molodoi literatury v Ukraini." *Dysydentskyi rukh v Ukraini*. 4 March 2016. http://archive.khpg.org/index.php?id=1457121207.

———, ed. *Rukh oporu v Ukraini: Entsyklopedychnyi dovidnyk*. Kyiv: Smoloskyp, 2010.

"Zinovii Valshonok." *Sem iskusstv*, no. 46, edited by Yevgenii Berkovich. 2021. http://7iskusstv.com/Avtory/Valshonok.php.

"Zionists Appeal for Soviet Jews." *The New York Times*, 14 September 1959, p. 6.

Žižek, Slavoj. *Violence: Six Sideways Reflections*. New York: Picador, 2008.

Zolotariov, V. A., and Y. I. Shapoval. "'Kolyvan u provedenni linii partii ne bulo' (Storinky biohrafii K. M. Karlsona)." *Ukrainskyi istorychnyi zhurnal* 1 (1996): 91–105.

Zolotariov, Vadym. *ChK-DPU-NKVS na Kharkivshchyni: liudy ta doli. 1919–1941*. Kharkiv: Folio, 2003.

Zolotariov, Vadym, and Valerii Stepkin. *Chk-GPU-NKVD v Donbasse: 1919–1941*. Donetsk: Aleks, 2010.

Zolotariov, Vadym. "Kerivnyi sklad NKVS URSR pid chas 'velykoho teroru' (1936–1938 rr.): sotsialno-statystychnyi analiz." *Z arkhiviv VUChK-GPU-NKVD-KGB* 2 (2009): 86–115.

———. "Nachalnytskyi sklad NKVS USRR naperedodni 'yezhovshchyny': sotaialno-statystychnyi analiz." In *Ukraina v dobu "Velykoho teroru", 1936–1938 rr.*, edited by S. Bohunov et al., 60–83. Kyiv: Lybid, 2009.

———. *Sekretno-politychnyi viddil DPU USRR: Spavy ta liudy*. Kharkiv: Folio, 2007.

Zolotonosov, Mikhail. "Kak pisateli borolis s p'ianstvom . . ." *812 Online*. 30 December 2010. http://www.online812.ru/2010/12/29/003/.

Zubok, Vladislav, and Constantine Pleshakov. *Inside the Kremlin's Cold War: From Stalin to Khrushchev*. Cambridge, MA: Harvard University Press, 1996.

Zubok, Vladislav M. *A Failed Empire: The Soviet Union in the Cold War from Stalin to Gorbachev*. Chapel Hill: The University of North Carolina Press, 2007.

Zubok, Vladislav. *Zhivago's Children: The Last Russian Intelligentsia*. Cambridge, MA: The Belknap Press of Harvard University Press, 2009.

Zysels, Iosyp (interview by Mykhailo Shterngel). "Prymyrennia ne pochynaietsia zi spyskiv vzaiemnykh zvynuvachen.'" *Ukrainska Helsinska Spilka z prav liudyny*. 27 December 2009.

———. "Ukrainski ta yevreiski dysydenty: vid spilnoi borotby do samorealizatsii v natsionalnykh derzhavakh." *Madan*. 6 October 2017. http://madan.org.il/ru/news/iosif-zisels-ob-ukrainskih-i-evreyskih-dissidentah.

INTERVIEWS

A retired KGB officer (anonymous), 20 August 1999, Kharkiv, Ukraine.

Boltryk, Serhii. 10 November 1996, Kharkiv, Ukraine; 11 November 1996, Kharkiv, Ukraine.

Briuggen, Volodymyr. 4 July 2009, Kharkiv, Ukraine; 2 July 2011, Kharkiv, Ukraine; 15 July 2011, Kharkiv, Ukraine; 27 July 2011, Kharkiv, Ukraine; 8 August 2013, Kharkiv, Ukraine; 9 August 2013, Kharkiv, Ukraine; 10 August 2013, Kharkiv, Ukraine; 16 July 2015, Kharkiv, Ukraine.

Filatov, Arkadii. 14 July 2005, Kharkiv, Ukraine.

Kasha, Aleksandr. 5 July 1985, Kharkiv, Ukraine; 27 July 1989, Kharkiv, Ukraine.

Kudakova, Yevdokiia. 15 July 2005, Kharkiv, Ukraine.

Marchenko, Oleksa. 19 July 2004, Kharkiv, Ukraine.

Osadchuk, Leonid. 20 November 1996, Kharkiv, Ukraine.

Polonskyi, Radii. 16 May 1988, Kharkiv, Ukraine.

Stadnychenko, Yurii. 3 July 2007, Kharkiv, Ukraine.

Starodub, Anatolii. 12 August 2008, Kharkiv, Ukraine.

Tretyakova, Lidiya. 19 July 2005, Kharkiv, Ukraine; 8 September 2013, Bloomsburg, PA, U.S.A.

Tretyakov, Robert. 27 June 1982, Kharkiv, Ukraine; 2 July 1986, Kharkiv, Ukraine; 2 April 1994, Kharkiv, Ukraine; 17 June 1996, Kharkiv, Ukraine; 17 July 1996, Kharkiv, Ukraine; 25 July 1996, Kharkiv, Ukraine.

Yevtushenko, Yevgenii. 6 May 1988, Kharkiv, Ukraine; 27 May 1989, Kharkiv, Ukraine.

Zisels, Iosyp. 3 October 2017, Sleepy Hollow, NY, USA.

Zulim, Maria. 12 October 2013 (via telephone).

ARCHIVES

AU SBUKhO (*Arkhiv Upravlinnia Sluzhby Bezpeky Ukrainy Kharkivskoi Oblasti*), the Archive of the Security Service of Ukraine of Kharkiv Oblast. Files: 017800 (Yurii Vukhnal's criminal case); 014519 (Ivan Kallianykov's criminal case).

DAKhO (*Derzhavnyi Arkhiv Kharkivskoi Oblasti*), State Archive of Kharkiv Oblast. Fondy: R-846; R-6164; R-6165.

HDA SBU (*Haluzevyi Derzhavnyi Arkhiv Sluzhby Bezpeky Ukrainy*), the Sectoral State Archive of Security Services in Ukraine. Fondy: 6; 16.

HDAMVSU (*Haluzevyi derzhavnyi arkhiv MVS Ukrainy*), the Sectoral State Archive of the Ministry of Internal Affairs in Ukraine. Fondy: 54.

LTPA, Lidiya Tretyakova's Private Archive.

RTPA, Robert Tretyakov's Private Archive.

The Aleksandr N. Yakovlev Archive, https://www.alexanderyakovlev.org/.

The Central Intelligence Agency (CIA) Archive, https://www.cia.gov/readingroom/historical-collections.

"A New Freeze: A Collection of Material on Recent Developments in Ukrainian Soviet Literature." 28 August 1963 (declassified and released in 2007). https://www.cia.gov/library/readingroom/docs/AERODYNAMIC%20%20%20VOL.%2026%20%20%28OPERATIONS%29_0071.pdf.

"On Occasion of Pohruzhalsky's Trial." 1964 (declassified in 2007). https://www.cia.gov/library/readingroom/docs/AERODYNAMIC%20%20%20VOL.%2030%20%20(OPERATIONS)_0029.pdf.

"Project Action: QRDYNAMIC." 5 April 1973 (declassified and released in 2007). https://www.cia.gov/library/readingroom/docs/QRPLUMB%20%20%20VOL.%202%20%20(DEVELOPMENT%20AND%20PLANS,%201970-78)_0018.pdf.

The Vladimir Bukovsky Archive (VBA), https://bukovsky-archives.net/.

"About Psychiatric Care in the USSR." 18 February 1972. http://www.bukovsky-archives.net/pdfs/psychiat/psy-rus.html.

"The 22 January 1970 Decree of the Politburo TsK KPSS about identifying and isolating mentally ill individuals with terrorist and politically harmful inclinations." http://www.bukovsky-archives.net/pdfs/psychiat/psy-rus.html.

TsDAHOU (*Tsentralnyi Derzhavnyi Arkhiv Hromadskykh Ob'iednan Ukrainy*), Central State Archive of Civic Organizations of Ukraine. Fondy: 1.

TsDAMLIMU (*Tsentralnyi Derzhavnyi Arkhiv-Muzei Literatury i Mystetstva Ukrainy*), the Central State Archive-Museum of Literature and Art in Ukraine, Kyiv, Ukraine. Fondy: 290, 500, 712, 781, 783, 816, 840.

DIARIES

LTD, Lidiya Tretyakova's diary Volumes: 2, 4–11.

PRIVATE CORRESPONDENCE

Brusilovskii, Anatolii. 2 September 2017.
Muratova, Olha. 13 August 2017.
Toma, Leonid. 12 October 2013; 17 October 2013.
Ulishchenko, Olha. 25 April 2019.
Valshonok, Zinovii. 23 July 2020; 7 February 2021; 8 February 2021; 9 February 2021.

DOCUMENTARIES

Kniazev, Sergei. *A genii –sushchii diavol!* (1995, Moscow Studio "Chelovek i vremia"). Available: *Facebook* (placed by Liudmila Osokina). 30 January 2018. https://www.facebook.com/vlodowa/videos/1582318815184098/.

Nowytskj, Slavko, and Yurij Luhovy. *Harvest of Despair: The Man-Made Famine of 1932–1933 in Ukraine* (1985, Toronto, ON, Canada). Available: *Ukrainian Canadian Research and Documentation Center*, http://www.ucrdc.org/Film-Harvest_of_Despair.html.

Index

Abram, Morris B., 63
Abrams, Elliot, 132, 133
Akademgorodok, 136, 154
Adamovych, Anthony, 75
Administration of the Preservation of State Secrets, 26
Afghanistan, 184, 269
Africa, 226
agitation, 24, 52, 117, 124, 133
agricultural, 46
Aheieva, Vira, 6
Akhmadulina, Bella, 13
Akhmatova, Anna, 88
Aksionov, Vasilii, 58, 91
alcohol/alcoholism, 25, 27, 28, 48, 87, 256, 258, 278
Alikina, Nataliia, 172
All-Union Society of Psychiatrists, 186
Altunian, Genrikh, 31, 50, 133–37, 153, 181
America: North, xvi, 114, 118, 120, 131, 150, 205, 222, 224; Northwestern Territories, 256; South America, 150, 226
American/s, 227, 238, 239, 275; commercial trade, 227; Continental Grain Company, 226; Jewish Committee (AJC), 63, 130, 145; Jewish Committee in Chicago, 130
Americans for Human Rights in the Ukraine, 132
Americans in Defense of Human Rights in Ukraine, 117, 132
American-Soviet relations, 132, 226
Amnesty International, 127, 128, 132, 200, 251; Madison Avenue Group, 128; Riverside Group, 128; Washington Center, 128
anarchist, 64
Andievska, Emma, 200
Andriivka, 65
Andropov, Yurii, 26, 70, 115, 140, 168, 179, 180, 186, 187, 221, 237, 241, 242, 245, 276, 280
anticolonial, 2, 7, 8
anti-communist, 46
anti-intellectualism, 260
anti-Jewish, 73, 83, 91, 93, 94, 113, 120, 141, 242
anti-Judaic, xviii
anti-Russian, 67
antisemite/antisemites, 64, 65, 123, 125, 221
antisemitism, xvi, xviii, xxiii, 10, 26, 58–60, 63, 64, 73–75, 79, 80, 88, 91–93, 98, 108, 113, 119, 120, 122, 145, 242, 244, 245, 266, 277; antisemitic, 22, 55, 59, 62, 63, 65, 66, 78, 79, 86,

321

92, 94, 113, 122, 137, 139, 145, 221, 237, 242, 243, 259, 263
antisovetchik, 58, 137, 143, 198
anti-Sovietism, 27; anti-Soviet, 30, 37, 42, 46, 56, 63, 69, 71, 85, 103, 116–19, 125, 126, 133, 135, 138–41, 143, 144, 169, 181, 214, 220, 223, 224, 244, 245, 259, 276, 277 ; activities, 35, 115, 123, 182, 199, 210, 219; agitation/propaganda, 24, 32, 146, 147, 154, 174, 176, 182, 188, 196, 198, 208, 220, 223, 246, 279; attitudes, 24, 211
anti-Ukrainian, 31, 58, 83, 122, 182, 228, 252, 263; anti-Ukrainianism, xvi, xviii, 10
anti-Zionism, 26, 98, 277; anti-Zionist, xvii, 73, 86, 99, 113, 241, 242
Antokolskii, Pavel, 78
Antoniuk, Zinovii, 35
apparatchik, or *apparatchiki* (pl.), 38
Arab-Israeli Six-Day War, 26, 70, 71, 80, 95, 126, 127, 243
Argentina, 118, 227
Armenia, 129, 182, 270; Armenian, 133; Armenians, 6, 64, 92, 95
Artress, Lauren, xxv
Arzhak, Nikolay, 136
Association to Perpetuate the Memory of Ukrainian Jews, 118
Aster, Howard, 120
Aushev, Anatolii, 243, 244
Australia, 118, 150, 226, 227
authoritarianism, xxi, xxiii, 187; authoritarian, 56, 118, 187
Azerbaijan/is, 6, 270

Babii Yar (Babyn Yar), xxv, 88, 97
Babusenko, 143
Bachelard, Gaston, 93
Bahalii, Dmytro, 138, 155
Bahmut, Ivan, 18, 84, 87, 253
Bahrianyi, Ivan, 119, 120
Baklanov, Grigorii, 13
Bakunin, Mikhail, 64

Balakliia, 157
Baltics, 79, 137, 168, 270; Baltic region, 102, 131
Balytskyi, Vsevolod, 210, 215
Bandera, Stepan, 41
banderovtsy, or banderite(s), 7, 24
Barabash, Yurii, 85, 93
Baran, Yevhen, 72
Basiuk, Aleksandr, 28
Bavaria, 107
Bazhan, Mykola, 215
BBC, 116
Begun, Iosif, 246
Belarus, 129, 136; Belorussian, 176
Beliaieva (Gurina), Raisa, 89
Belleza, Simone Attilio, 9
Benenson, Peter, 127
Benjamin, Walter, 191
"Berezil", 27, 192, 203, 210, 230
Berezil, 47, 72, 265
Berlin, 82, 107, 256
Berlin, Isaiah, 64
Bertelsen, Dale A., 74
Beryslavskyi, Mykola, 31
Bezuhly, Anatoly, 178
Biletskyi, Oleksandr, 15
Bilinsky, Yaroslav, 149
Bilokur, Kateryna, 263
Bilotserkivets, Natalka, 252
Bitov, Andrei, 27
Block, Sidney, 166, 167, 169
Blok, Aleksandr, 90
Blyznets, Viktor, 263
Bobkov, Filipp, 277
Bohodukhivskyi district, 52
Bogoraz, Larisa, 134–36, 245, 246
Bogoslavskii, Mark, 66, 136, 249
Boichuk, Mykhailo, 213, 214
Boleslavskii, Lev, 143, 144
Bolsheviks, 204; Bolshevik Party, 22
Boltryk, Serhii, xxv, 27, 49, 272
Bondar, Valerii, 144
Bondar, Vasyl, 24, 28, 29, 33, 34, 38, 68, 86, 87, 108, 263
Bondarev, Yurii, 13

Bonner, Yelena, 146
Borges, Jorge Luis, 69, 184
Borovsky, Victor, 162, 163, 166, 175–86, 189, 192, 198, 200
Borovyi, Vasyl, 20–22, 47, 144, 158, 216, 217, 236, 259, 263
Borysenko, Mykola, 230
Boussenard, Louis Henri, 68
Bratun, Rostyslav, 9
Brazil, 118
Brezhnev, Leonid, xiv, 2, 11, 22, 23, 26, 33, 66, 87, 93–95, 108, 118, 180, 186, 223, 226, 241, 246, 250, 251, 257, 261–63, 271, 275, 276, 280; coup, 25
Briggen, Aleksandr Fiodorovich, 67
Briuggen, Volodymyr, xiii, xxiv, xxv, 16, 34, 38, 52, 53, 67–74, 76, 78–81, 84, 85, 90, 101, 102, 104, 105, 107, 110, 111, 143, 146, 208, 221, 234, 237, 252, 256, 259, 262, 278, 279, 281, 282
Brodsky, Joseph, 74
Bruggen, A., 67
Brusilovskii, Anatolii, 60, 89
Brusilovskii, Rafail, 60, 89
Brzezinski, Zbigniew, 128, 264
Bukovsky, Vladimir, 166, 177, 186, 192, 194, 251
Bulakhovskyi, Leonid, 15
Bulgakov, Mikhail, 33
Bulgaria, 129, 256; Bulgarians, 64
Bunchukov, Revolt, 94, 135
Burke, Kenneth, 74, 209
Bushin, Vladimir, 79
Bykov, Leonid, 203, 230
Byron, Lord, 156

Cambridge, MA, 156
Canada, 117, 118, 120, 121, 140, 184, 204, 225–27, 256; Canadian, 238
Carter, Jimmy, 128
Carynnyk, Vsevolod, 236
Catherine II, 33
Caucasus, 215

CBS, 145
censorship, 32, 35, 59, 72, 91, 114, 181
Central Asia, 79
Chagall, Marc, 278
Chase, James Hadley, 68
chauvinism, 64, 92; chauvinist/chauvinistic, 22, 113
Cheka, xxv
chekist/chekists (pl.), or *chekizatsiia*, xv, xx, xxii, xxiii, xxv, 35, 50, 139–42, 168, 171, 178, 179, 183, 191, 195, 203–16, 221, 222, 224, 226, 227, 229–32, 234, 246, 251, 254, 263, 280
Cherchenko, Natalia, 35
Cherednychenko, Yevhen, 219–21
Cheremskyi, Andrii, 144
Cheremskyi, Petro, 144
Cherevchenko, Aleksandr (Oleksandr), 16, 86, 89, 95, 142, 158, 249
Cherkasy, 65
Cherniakov, Mark, 92
Chernihiv, 221
Chernivtsi, 239
Chernobyl, 183, 261, 271
Chernyshov, Andrii, 22, 47, 79, 252
Chicago, 117, 130, 131
Chichibabin, Boris, xx, 27, 30, 49, 66, 67, 78, 79, 81, 88–96, 109, 133, 134, 136–38, 143, 144, 154, 157, 158, 243, 248, 249, 252, 259, 270, 276
Chistopol Prison, 245
Chomsky, Noam, 11
Chornovil, Viacheslav, 26, 31, 35, 113, 128, 183
Christie, Agatha, 68
CIA, 4, 36, 227, 238; operation "Project QRDYNAMIC", 36, 53
Civil War, 51
Cohn, Norman, xxii, xxiii, xxvi
Cold War, 36, 112, 114, 116, 123, 127, 205, 206, 212, 216, 222, 225, 226, 228, 254
collectivization, 210, 211, 214–16, 218
colonization: colonial, 224; cultural, 70, 71; internal, 103

Columbia University, 156, 200
Commission on Security and
  Cooperation in Europe (CSCE), 129,
  130, 132, 152
Commission on Ukraine Famine, 228
Committee for the Defense of Soviet
  Political Prisoners, 117
communism, 75, 105, 122; national, 57,
  96
communist parties, 63
Communist Party (KPSS), xiii, 1, 9,
  20, 21, 25, 37, 43, 51, 61, 63, 83,
  87, 88, 93, 115, 166, 183, 189, 241,
  242, 261; Central Committee, 11,
  19, 26, 55, 115, 123, 124, 139, 140,
  157, 166, 183, 193, 199, 223, 224,
  228, 242, 247, 250, 261; Politburo,
  xxiv, 26, 93, 94, 224, 250, 275, 276;
  Twentieth Party Congress, 1, 13, 20,
  38, 44, 55; Twenty-Second Party
  Congress, 21; Twenty-Third Party
  Congress, 23; Twenty-Seventh Party
  Congress, 260
compromat, 142, 221
Conquest, Robert, 204
co-optation, 22, 141, 252
cosmopolitanism, 88
counterintelligence, 30, 140, 226, 228,
  236; Department No. 2 of the School
  of Advanced Studies of the KGB,
  168
Crankshaw, Edward, 186, 187, 201
Crimea, 37, 101, 102, 137, 221, 227,
  270; Crimean Biological Station, 67,
  101, 102; Crimean Tatars, 31, 92,
  137; Karadag Nature Reserve, 101,
  102
Criminal Code of the UkrSSR, 24, 31
Cross, Gary, xxiv
Cuba, 226
cultural amnesia, 281
cultural provincialism, 263
cultural stagnation, 260
Czechoslovakia, 19, 71, 91, 186, 243–
  45; Czechoslovak, 129

Dachau, 28, 29, 33, 83, 107
Daedalus, 68
Damaskin, Volodymyr, 20, 46
Daniel, Yulii, 22, 23, 47, 134–36, 154,
  244, 249, 279
Dante, 156
Datskiv, Mykhailo, 210
death penalty, 21
d'Encausse, Helene Carrere, xxv
dehumanization, 188
de Saint-Exupéry, Antoine, 19
Decemberist, 67
de-communization laws, 62
Deineko, Viktor, 30
dekady (art festivals), 13, 68
de La Bruyère, Jean, 73
Demjanjuk, John, 122–24, 131, 149,
  150
de-Russification, 67
de-Stalinization, xvii, 1, 8, 9, 13, 19, 21,
  55, 75, 95, 282
Detroit, 117
Deychakiwsky, Orest, 129
Dialohy, 121
diaspora, xvi, 56, 114–19, 122–25,
  128–31, 133, 205, 222, 226, 228;
  organizations and NGOs, 117, 118,
  122, 222, 223
Didenko, Vasyl, 14
Dilo, 232
discrimination, 65, 71, 137, 139, 245
disinformation, 94, 122, 123, 212,
  218
displacement, 118; DPs (displaced
  persons), 29, 108
dissident movement, 3, 13, 47, 55, 56,
  114, 135, 137, 168, 218; dissident/
  dissidents, 7, 13, 30, 31, 36, 52, 61,
  71, 92–95, 113, 115–18, 121, 123,
  125, 126, 128, 129, 131–33, 136–39,
  144–46, 154, 163, 166, 168–70, 173,
  175, 176, 179, 180, 183, 187, 188,
  190, 192, 198, 200, 245
Dmitrieva, Tatiana, 167
Dnipro, 15

Dnipropetrovsk, 32, 169, 176, 227; special psychiatric clinic, 181
Dobroszycki, Lucjan, 77
Dobrovolskii, Aleksei, 136
Dobrovolskii, Vladimir, 28, 29
Dobrynin, Anatoly, 275, 276
Dobson, Miriam, xxv, 282
Donbas, 221
Donchyk, Vitalii, 72
Dontsov, Dmytro, 120
Dostoyevsky, Fyodor, xxiv
Drach, Ivan, 7, 13, 18, 37, 52, 275
Drai-Khmara, Mykhailo, 215
Drobytskyi Yar, 77, 138, 265
Drozd, Volodymyr, 18
Druzhba narodov, 77
Dubrava, G. I., 142
Duchy of Courland and Semigallia, 68
Dudintsev, Vladimir, 13
Durkheim, Emile, 258
Dziuba, Ivan, 6, 8, 13, 23, 26, 32, 35, 36, 52, 59, 72, 74, 113, 136, 137, 141, 217, 246
Dzvon, 72

Egypt, 26, 127
Ehrlich, Paul, 156
Eimermacher, Karl, 13
Ellis, Mark S., 189
Elton, Geoffrey, xxiv
Emerson, Ralph Waldo, 185, 186
emigration, 62, 71, 72, 94, 95, 116, 118, 121, 122, 127, 130, 133, 137, 144, 151, 152, 242–44, 275, 276, 281
England, 140, 263; English, 68, 81, 124, 256
Epelman-Sterkis, Nelli, 90, 93
Erenburg, Il'ia, 134
Estonia: Estonian, 133; Estonians, 6
ethnic, 67, 85, 86, 91, 116, 120, 136, 230, 259, 275; belonging/identity, 60, 99; boundaries, 265, 277; groups, 7, 55, 58, 74, 99, 120, 132, 139, 205, 281; hatred, 140; politics, 55
ethnicity, 60, 61, 64, 74, 87, 92, 185

ethnicization, 91
ethnocentrism, 73, 74
Europe, 82, 116, 118, 128, 150, 230; Central, 9, 130; Eastern, xxii, 119, 130, 132, 189; Western, 118, 203, 222
Executed Renaissance (*Rozstriliane vidrodzhennia*), xiv, 7, 209, 258, 273

Fainberg, Viktor, 128, 133, 194
Fallet, René, 68
famines, 209, 225, 226, 229, 232
Farmer, Kenneth C., xxv, 169, 278
fascism, 137, 215; fascist, 211–15
Fedorchuk, Vitalii, 27, 33, 35, 93, 139–42, 186, 220, 221, 223, 224, 227, 238, 250
fifth column, 132, 218
Filatov, Arkadii, 16, 23, 89, 107, 136, 138, 157, 249
Finkelshtein, Yurii, 90
Fireside, Harvey, 166
Firsova, Nadiia, xi, 41
First World War, 102
Fishbein, Moisei, 200
Fisheleva, Anna, 80
Flagellants, xxiii
Flekenshtein, Yevgenia, 237
For Return to the Motherland, 82
Foucault, Michel, 164, 172, 190, 207, 218, 222
François VI, Duc de La Rochefoucauld, 73
Franko, Ivan, 138, 156
Franko, Zinoviia, 141
France, 140; French, 68, 81, 256
Freud, Sigmund, 207
Frukhtman, Lev, 71
Fylypovych, Pavlo, 211, 215

Galanskov, Yurii, 136
Galich, Aleksandr, 203
Galicia, 24
Galician/Galicians, 24, 48, 68; intelligentsia, 24

Galkin, Lev, 76, 85, 87, 88, 92, 259
Gallii, Nikolai, 223
Ganzman, Isaak, 243
Garagozov, Rauf R., xxiii, xxvi
Gelfandbein, Grigorii, 75, 84, 85, 88, 92, 94, 144, 243, 252, 266
Gelman, Juan, 145, 159, 280
Gender & History, 204
General Secretary, 22, 26
genocide, 8, 74, 88, 205, 224, 228, 229, 277; genocidal practices, xxiii, 169, 204, 218, 223, 230
Georgia, 79, 129, 182; Georgian, 133; Georgians, 6, 64
Gerasimenko, Yurii, 93
German, 68, 79, 81, 82; concentration camps, 82, 107, 122; Empire, 102; peasants, xxiii
Germany, 29, 89, 90, 93, 102, 107, 123, 140, 155, 156, 198, 212; East, 129; West, 226
Gestapo, 63, 201
Gibadulov, N. G., 183, 199
Gibney, Frank, 46
Giedroyc, Jersy, 41
Ginzburg, Aleksandr, 129, 136
Ginzburg, Yevgeniia, 58
Gitelman, Zvi, 276
Gluzman, Semen, 113, 166, 172, 176, 189, 197
Goethe, Johann Wolfgang, 156
Goldenberg, Iosif, 136
Goldesgeim (Goldes), Oizer, 59, 80, 81
Goldman, Wendy Z., 278
Gorbachev, Mikhail, 144, 183, 188, 200, 220, 228, 245, 260, 261, 280; glasnost, 79, 228; perestroika, 49, 79, 144, 158, 183, 188, 220, 260, 261, 280; uskorenie, 261
Gorbacheva, Raisa, 184, 200
Gorbanevskaia, Natalia, 194
Gorenburg, Dmitry, 188
gorkom, 11, 22, 174
GPU, xxiv, 156, 205, 210–15
Great Terror, 126, 156, 221, 258

Grigorenko (Hryhorenko), Petro (Piotr), 113, 133, 134, 137, 153, 166, 186, 194, 201
Grigorenko, Zinaida, 134
Grin, Aleksandr, 264
Gulag, 7, 12, 20, 21, 31, 36, 41, 44, 82, 93, 114, 120, 135, 138, 152–54, 220, 246
Gurock, Jeffrey S., 77

Hall, Edward, xxv
Hallandale Beach, Florida, 176
Harvard University, 156; Harvard University Committee for the Defense of Soviet Political Prisoners, 117
Healey, Dan, 166
Hebrew, 95, 127
Heine, Charlotte, 82
Heine, Heinrich, 82
Hel, Ivan, 26, 35, 113
Helsinki, 116, 126, 251, 252
Helsinki Accords, 130, 182, 195, 251
Helsinki Final Act, 130, 132
Helsinki Group (Moscow), 168, 195, 251
Hemingway, Leicester, 68
Herostratus, 262
Hevrych, Yaroslav, 176
Hickman, D., 227
Hirniak, Yosyp, 210
Hiroshima, 261
Hitler, Adolf, 60
Hnatiuk, Volodymyr, 68
Hofshteyn, Dovid, 76
Hollander, Paul, xix, xxvi
Holocaust, xxii, xxiii, 29, 59, 63, 74, 82, 91–93, 122, 136
Holodomor, xxiii, 8, 20, 192, 203–9, 216, 217, 219–22, 224–26, 228–32, 234, 238, 258, 277; *holodomornyky*, 208, 212, 221, 234
Holovanivskyi, Savva, 86
Holovko, Andrii, 184
Holovlit, 26

Holushko, Mykola, 183
Honchar, Oles, 18, 37, 182, 246
Hordievsky, Ihor, 200
Horska, Alla, 117
Horyn, Bohdan, 24, 26, 183
Horyn, Mykhailo, 24, 26, 183
House of Writers (Budynok "Slovo"), 21, 30, 60, 255, 263
Houston, Walter, 259
Hrymailo, Yaroslav, 80, 81
Hrynevych, Vladislav, xxv
Hrytsenko, Liubov, 180, 181
Hrytsiak, Yevhen, 44
Hubanov, Volodymyr, 20, 46
Hugo, Victor, 156
humanism, 96, 183
human rights, 9, 31, 36, 52, 56, 111, 112, 114–19, 121, 125–30, 132, 133, 135, 144, 146, 151, 169, 173, 179, 182, 184, 195, 217, 222, 242, 251, 260, 275, 277; Human Rights Commission (HRC), 119; Initiative Group on Human Rights in the USSR, 153
Hungary, 2, 19, 63, 129, 187; revolution, 46; Soviet invasion, 2
Hutsalo, Yevhen, 7, 18
Huzhva, Valerii, 14

ideology, 43, 58, 72, 82, 96, 125, 137, 173, 206, 209, 218, 228, 229, 278; Ideological Commission, 114; ideological sabotage, 30
Ilchenko, Viktor, 66
Iliichiov, Leonid, 63, 114
Illienko, Yurii, 65
Ilnytskyi, Mykola, 72
imperialism, 46, 56, 112, 119, 126; imperial culture, 60; imperialists, 62
Independent Psychiatric Association of Russia, 201
Inin, Arkadii, 90, 93, 161, 162, 192
intellectualism, 8

intelligence, 140, 141, 143, 236; American, 36; Bulgarian, 256; Hungarian, 256; Soviet, 82, 140, 207; Stasi, 217, 256
internationalism, 37, 58, 63, 91, 92, 137, 276
Irchan, Myroslav, 210
Iron Curtain, 36, 62, 115, 117, 121, 127, 228
Irpin, 258; Irpin's House of Creativity, 257
Isajiw, Christina, 132
Israel, 26, 71, 72, 76, 79, 81, 89–91, 93–95, 116, 120, 122, 123, 127, 128, 130, 137, 141, 142, 144, 151, 183, 242–44, 275, 276; Israeli government, 122, 127, 247; Israeli Jewish leaders, 120; Israeli visas, 118
Italy, 19, 156
Ivano-Frankivsk, 91, 177
Ivanov, Boris, 63
Ivanychuk, Roman, 9
Ivinskaia, Olga, 46, 50
Izvestiia, 63

James, Clive, 280
Jameson, Frederic, 190
Jersey City, NJ, 131
Jewdophilia, 81, 91, 109, 138
Jewish, xvii, 7, 10, 27, 56, 58, 63, 66, 67, 71, 74–79, 81–83, 85, 88, 91, 92, 94, 95, 114, 116–22, 125–27, 129, 142, 151, 161, 184, 221, 242, 243, 247, 249, 276, 277; Anti-Fascist Committee, 58; community, 58, 59, 71, 74, 93, 115, 116, 123–27, 131, 132, 142; consciousness, 127; culture, 26, 66, 75, 81, 97, 243, 266; dissent, 63; history, 57, 121; identity, 91, 104, 137, 242, 243, 248; institutions/organizations, 59, 66, 130, 140, 141, 242; intelligentsia/ intellectuals, 55, 56, 58, 59, 64, 71, 74, 88, 89, 91, 94, 95, 97,

110, 113, 116, 136, 137, 139–41, 154, 244, 247; nationalism, 26; nationalists, 26, 93, 105, 121, 139, 141–43, 276; national movement, 70; question, 55, 60, 66, 74, 79, 80, 139, 241, 244, 247, 266; revival, 57; sixtiers/*shistdesiatnytstvo*, 56, 74, 76, 82, 94; youth, 26, 94, 276
Jewishness, 96, 161
Jewish-Ukrainian cooperation, 118
Jewry, 71, 116, 119, 127–33, 241–45, 259, 265; Soviet Jewry movement, 119
Jews, xv, xvi, xviii, xxiii, 6, 16, 26, 28, 38, 55–65, 67, 68, 70–75, 77, 79–81, 84–89, 91–95, 97, 98, 103, 107, 110–20, 122–27, 137–40, 142–45, 151, 152, 182, 185, 186, 188, 221, 222, 247, 264, 275–77, 281
John Hopkins University, 156
Jordan, 26, 127
Journalists' Union, 34
Judaism, 62, 63, 88

Kachurovsky, Ihor, 200
Kafka, Franz, 184, 249, 250
Kagan, Donald, xxiv
Kaliannikov, Ivan, 270, 271
Kalinovskii, Aleksandr, 133, 153
Kallistratova, Sofia, 134
Kalugin, Oleg, 238
Kalynets, Ihor, 35, 52
Kalynets, Iryna, 35, 52
Kamenetska, Ella, 181
Kaniv, 61
Kapitonov, Ivan, 242
Kaplun, Irina, 196
Kaplun, Yevhen, 64
Kapto, Aleksandr, 65
Karas, Lilia, 67, 93, 133
Karasik, Sofiia, 133, 153
Karavan, 52
Karavanskyi, Sviatoslav, 26, 66, 113, 128
Kartsev, Roman, 66

Kas'ianov, Heorhii, xxv, 5
Kasha, Aleksandr, 30, 49, 192, 237
Kats, Sofia, 243
Kats, Zelman, 76, 85, 86, 90, 92–94, 143
Kazakhstan, 270; Kazakh, 6
Kazakov, Yasha, 91
Kazarin, V. P., 142
Kedmi, Yaakov, 242
Kennedy, John F., 128, 226
KGB, xiv–xvi, xviii–xiii, xxvi, 2–4, 7, 9, 11, 12, 17, 19–36, 38, 47, 50, 52, 55, 56, 60, 61, 63, 70, 77, 78, 80, 82, 85–88, 91, 93–95, 103, 108, 111–14, 116, 121–27, 133–46, 149, 153, 157, 161–66, 168–74, 176–80, 183, 185, 186, 189–91, 195, 198–200, 204–6, 217–29, 237, 238, 241–56, 258–66, 271, 275, 277–81; active measures, xvi, 12, 224, 228, 229, 238, 277; Counterintelligence Department No. 2 of the School of Advanced Studies of the KGB, 168; Fifth Directorate, 30, 115, 121, 142, 247, 249, 277; First Directorate, 149, 241; Ninth Department, 247; operation "Blok", xvii, 10, 30, 141, 219; operation "Retribution" or "Payback" (Vozmezdiie), 63, 123, 149; operations of ideological subversion, 99, 141, 205, 212; recruitment operations, 221; Second Directorate, 241, 247; Tenth Department, 247; Thirteenth Department, 258
Khaet (first name is unknown), 213
Khait, Nonna, 243
Kharkiv, xiii, xv–xvii, xx, xxi, xxv, 2, 3, 5, 10, 12, 14–16, 19, 21–23, 25, 27, 29, 30, 32, 34, 35, 38, 47, 48, 51, 55, 58–61, 67–70, 74–83, 87–95, 109, 111, 114, 127, 133–36, 138–40, 142–44, 155, 156, 161, 162, 175, 177, 183, 185, 189, 203, 209, 215–17, 221, 227, 239, 242–44, 246–50, 256, 259–61, 263–65, 272,

273, 276, 277, 279, 281; bookstore "Poeziia", 248, 249; City Council of People's Deputies, 243; factory "Serp i Molot", 64, 88; Group for Human Rights Protection, 251; Institute of Arts, 203, 230; Institute of Commerce, 156; Institute of Law, 137; intelligentsia, xxii, 3, 30, 60, 146; Korolenko State Scientific Library, 41; literati, xvi, xxii, 3, 14, 20, 30, 32, 33, 36, 48, 79, 80, 82, 83, 86, 88, 89, 92, 93, 111, 112, 136, 142, 162, 184, 243, 246, 247, 249, 250, 254, 256, 257, 261–64, 276, 277, 279, 281; Military Academy, 22, 31; Ministry of Internal Affairs (MVS), 31, 34, 243; Palace of Culture, 89; Palace of Pioneers, 90; Park of Victory, 89; Pedagogical Institute, 156; Poetry Square, 49, 68; Polytechnical Institute, 68, 156, 161; Private Narcology Center "Avitsenna", 189, 202; Prosecutor's Office, 31 (Regional Prosecutor General, 174); psychiatric hospital (Saburova Dacha), 145, 162, 171, 172, 174–76, 179–81, 183–85, 187, 189, 191, 245, 253 (Psycho-Neurological Clinic, 174); Puppet Theater, 88, 257; Shevchenko Garden, 273; Shevchenko Ukrainian Drama Theater, 203; sixtiers/*shistdesiatnyky*, xiii, 81, 93; State University, 25, 30, 68, 77, 87, 88, 133, 134, 136–38, 155, 156, 161, 191, 192, 243, 266 (Philology Department, 77, 88, 133, 134, 136, 137, 155, 161, 191, 192, 243, 266; School of Journalism, 68); Tractor Factory, 29, 263

Kharkiv/Kharkivska oblast, 65, 68, 139, 155, 157, 180, 183, 185, 244, 261

Khazin, Aleksandr, 80

Kheifets, Mikhail, 71, 114

khokhly, 259, 270

Kholodnyi, Mykola, 141

Khristichev, Ivan, 19, 45

Khrushchev, Nikita, xv, xvi, xviii, 1, 2, 4, 9, 11, 13, 14, 19, 20, 22, 25, 26, 46, 55, 57, 58, 61, 66, 76, 77, 88, 91, 93, 96, 98, 114, 241, 242, 254, 276, 280; Secret Speech, 21, 38, 55, 59, 61–63

Khrushchev, Sergei, 61, 99

Khvyliovyi, Mykola, 176, 210, 214

Kirgiz, 6, 176

Kirov, 153

Kissinger, Henry, 244

Kochevskyi, Viktor, 80, 81

Kohut, Zenon, 120

Koktebel, 37, 79, 101

Kolchinsky, Leonid, 244

kolhosp, or *kolhospy* (pl.), or *kolkhozy* (Rus.), 44, 46

Kolomiets, Tamara, 14

Kolomiets, Volodymyr, 14

Kolomyia, 52

Komashka, Antin, 19, 45

Komi ARSR, 113

Komsomol, 20, 21, 178, 249; Prize, 23

Kontinent, 90, 135, 154

Kopshtein, Aron, 82, 107

Koptylov, Viktor, 79

Koriagin, Anatoly (Koryagin, Anatoly), 166, 171, 174, 187, 189, 196, 246

Kornilov, Lev, 133, 153

Korotenko, Ada, 172

Korotych, Vitalii, 163

Kosenko, Mikhail, 185, 200, 201

Kosior, Stanislav, 210

Kosiv, Mykhailo, 24

Kostenko, Lina, 13, 74, 82, 279

Kostrov, Vladimir, 91

Kosygin, Aleksei, 2, 246

Kotkin, Stephen, 12

Kotliar, Iosif, 71

Kotliarov, Boris, 88, 94, 157, 247–50

Kotsiubynska, Mykhailyna, 219–21

Kovaliov, Ivan, 146

Kozachenko, Vasyl, 247

Index

Kozub, Ivan, 211
Krasivskyj, Zenovii, 128, 152, 155
Krasnoie znamia, 37, 88
Kravchenko, Bohdan, 114
Kravchenko, Okhrim, 214, 235
Kravtsiv, Ihor, 133
Kravtsov, Aleksandr, 85
Kremlin, xviii, 2, 12, 25, 57, 65, 113, 116, 136, 205, 212, 219, 232, 241, 250, 275
Krivin, Feliks, 144
Krokodil, 161, 191
Krushelnytskyi, Mar'ian, 203
Kuban, 223
Kudlyk, Roman, 9
Kulchyncky, Mykola, 176
Kulyk, Ivan, 270
Kupchinsky, Roman, 123
Kurbas, Oleksandr (Les), 203, 210, 211
Kurokhta, Leonid, 79
Kuropas, Myron, 130–32
Kursin, Mykola, 19, 45
Kurskii, Dmitrii, 239
Kuzmin, Mikhail, 239
Kuznets, Simon, 138, 156
Kuznetsov, Eduard, 113
Kwitkowskyi, Denys, 120
Kychko, Trokhym, 62, 63
Kyiv, 64
Kyiv/Kyiv oblast, xix, 2, 9, 13–15, 18, 21, 23–25, 27, 29, 31, 48, 52, 59, 61, 65, 66, 72, 86, 88, 92–94, 97, 112, 113, 123, 127, 134, 142, 177, 182, 198, 203, 209, 215, 239, 244, 246, 247, 249, 251, 257, 258, 260; Art Institute, 214; intelligentsia, xxii, 209; Public Library of the Academy of Science, 204; Shevchenko State University, 13–15, 20, 68, 92 (School of Journalism, 13–15, 20, 68)
Kyseliov, Leonid, 6
Kyshyntsi, Ukraine, 214

Ladenzon, Boris, 133
Lainé, Pascal, 68

Laing, Ronald David, 177
Landau, Lev, 138, 156
Landau, Yakov, 173
Landman, Olga, 90
Lashkova, Vera, 136
Latvia, 102; Latvian, 133
Lavrynenko, Yurii, 41
Lebid, Anannii, 211, 214–16
Lena River, 253
Lenin, Vladimir, 59, 229, 239, 277; Komsomol Award, 86
Leningrad, xviii, 13, 65
leninism, 8; Leninist ideals, 264; Leninist rhetoric, 37
Leninska zmina, 15
Lepore, Jill, xiii, xxiv
Lesnikova, Aleksandra, 136
Levin, Arkadii, 31, 133, 153
Levin, Grigorii, 134
Levin, Roman, 27, 85, 86, 94, 139
Levin, Vadim, 76, 85, 86, 90, 108
Levina, Hana, 59, 80–82, 90
Lewytzkyi (Levytsky), Borys, xxv, 7, 200
Liber, George O., 7
liberal: reforms, 57
Lifshitz, Yevgenii, 156
Limonov (Savenko), Eduard, 59, 60, 89, 91–93, 249
Lindsay, John, 244
Literaturnaia gazeta, xviii, 59, 248
Literaturna Ukraina, 33, 260
Litfond, 21, 77, 81, 85, 87, 252, 253, 257, 266, 270
Lithuania, 102, 129, 182; Lithuanian nationalists, 197; Lithuanians, 92
Liubotyn, 52
London, 140
Lotkin, Mark, 243
Lotman, Yurii, 27
Lozova, 175, 179
Luciuk, Lubomyr Y., xxvi
Luckyj, George S. N., 7, 8
Luhovy, Yurij, 228
Lukash, Mykola, 72
Lukashova, Olena, 85

Lukashova, Yelena, 253
Luk'ianenko, Levko, 145, 183
Luk'ianivka, 15
Lunts, Daniil, 172, 194
Lupynis, Anatoly, 197
Lutsk, 221
Lviv, 2, 9, 27, 41, 66, 84, 103, 108, 112, 156, 213, 221, 232
Lypynskyi, Viacheslav, 120
Lysiak-Rudnytsky, Ivan (Rudnytskyi, Ivan L.), 7, 120
Lytvyn, Yurii (Yurko), 182, 198

Mace, James, 204
Magadan, 142
"Magistral," 134
Magocsi, Paul Robert, xxv, 120
Mahomet, Iosyp, 15
Maistrenko, Ivan, 200
Makahonov, Anatolii, 257
Makhnenko, Yurii, 2
Maksimov, Vladimir, 90, 154
Makukha, Vasyl, 31
Malamud, Bernard, 68
Malanchuk, Valentyn, 32, 35, 51, 124, 250
Malko, Victoria A., 236, 239
Malynkovych, Volodomyr, 182
Malyshko, Andrii, 16, 280
Mandelshtam, Osip, 139
Maoist, 124
Mar'ian, Borys, 20, 46
Marchenko, Anatoly, 245, 246
Marchenko, Oleksa, 16, 33, 49, 68, 263
Marchenko, Valerii, 182, 251
Mariengof, Anatolii, 70
Mariupol Metallurgical Institute, 65
Marochko, Vasyl, 232
Marshak, Samuil, 134
Marxism, 8; Marxist, 46
Masenko, Larysa, 24
Mashtalier, Mykola, 103
mass culture, 7
mass media, 125, 190
Mausoleum, 21
Mayakovskii, Vladimir, 13

Mccauley, Martin, xxv
Mechnikov, Il'ia, 138, 156
Medvedev, Zhores, 194
Meer, Golda, 247
Meiman, Naum, 134
Mekhed, Akim, 214
Melnyk, Mykhailo, 182
Memorial, 94
memorycide, 204, 205
Menand, Louis, xxvi
Merkulov, Anatolii, 124
MGB, 62, 82, 205, 217, 236
Mickiewicz, Adam, 156
Middle East, 230, 247, 276
Mikhnovskyi, Mykola, 265, 273
Miloslavskii, Yurii, 71, 76, 88–94
Ministry of Health, 163, 166
Ministry of Internal Affairs (MVD), 166
Minotaur, 69
Mirabeau, 194
Miroshnychenko, Anatolii, 258
Mlechin, Leonid, 195
modernism, 7
modernity, 8
Moldova, 79, 129
Molotov-Ribbentrop Pact, 91
Montaigne, 73
Montreal, 140
Mordovia, 46; Mordovian, 113, 198
Moroz, Valentyn, 26, 32, 52, 117, 129, 147, 148, 152
Morozov, Georgy, 168, 172, 194
Moscow, xviii, xxii, 1, 2, 7, 13, 23, 26, 30, 33, 36, 44, 45, 49, 51, 56, 57, 60, 67, 68, 75, 78, 80, 89–91, 93, 112, 113, 117, 120, 128, 134–37, 139, 140, 142, 154, 156, 162, 163, 165, 167, 168, 171, 176, 182, 192, 211–13, 215, 223, 224, 229, 241, 244–46, 248, 250, 261; ideologues, 25; intelligentsia, xxii, 79; Polytechnical Institute, 249
Moshkovich, Itskhak, 31
Motrich, Vladimir, 28
Motyl, Alexander J., 241, 277
Movchan, Mykola, 184, 200

Mukha, Stepan, 182, 183, 225, 226, 228
Munich, 107
Muratov, Ihor, 18, 74, 80–84, 86, 90, 92, 95, 106, 263, 265, 278
Muratov, Levant Maksudovych, 82
Muratova, Olha, 106
Murmansk, xviii
Muzhutska, Olha, 35
Mykhailenko, Anna, 200
Mykhailyn, Ihor, 252
Mykhalchuk, Vil'iamin, 176
Myliukha, Volodymyr, 203, 204
Mysnychenko, V. P., 199
Mysyk, Vasyl, 18, 20, 21, 84, 86, 87
Mytkevych, Leonid, 211

Nabokov, Vladimir, 256
Nagasaki, 261
Nahaylo, Bohdan, xxv, xxvi
Naienko, Mykhailo, 6, 271
national: communists, 57; consciousness, 95; exceptionalism, 139, 169; identity, 13, 55, 137; minorities, 31, 57, 71, 228, 244, 275; Security Council, 132
nationalism, 7, 36, 64, 66, 74, 93, 95, 105, 114, 121, 126, 176, 190, 212, 221, 276; nationalist/nationalists, 23, 124, 140, 144, 176, 177, 190, 223, 264 (movements, 57, 228)
Nativ, 242, 265
Nazi/Nazis, 29, 44, 57, 63, 77, 91, 92, 97, 107, 122–24, 136, 138, 179, 212, 216, 217, 221, 265; nazism, 92
Nechyporivna, Vira, 220
Nedobora, Vladislav, 31, 133, 153
Nekrasov, Viktor, 177, 198, 260
neo-sentimentalism, 45
nepotism, 28
Netherlands, 67
News from Ukraine, 124
New York City, 60, 140, 156, 175, 184, 198, 200
New Yorker, xiii
New York Times, 62, 244

Nikitchenko, Vitalii, 93, 186, 243, 247, 250
Nikitin, G. A., 180, 183
Nikulina, Natalka, 252
Nixon, Richard, 171
NKVD, 44, 178, 205, 256
Nobel Prize, 43, 68, 138, 156
nomenklatura, 88, 171
Norilsk, 44, 217
Norilsk rebellion, 12, 44, 236
Nova Ukraina, 216, 236
Novosibirsk, 136, 154
Novotny, Donald J., 227
Novyi Mir, 1, 13, 77, 78, 108, 134, 158
Nowytskyj, Slavko, 228
Nudel, Ida, 129

obkom, xv, 3, 4, 19, 21, 22, 35, 37, 38, 47, 69, 77, 78, 82, 86–88, 134, 144, 174, 199, 203, 204, 243, 249, 252, 253, 255, 258, 259
October Revolution, 21
Odesa, 58, 66, 127, 156, 239; Spiritual Seminary, 179
O'Donohue, John, 56
Office of Special Investigations (OSI), 123, 131, 149, 150
Ogoniok, 77, 163
Ogorodnikov, Aleksandr, 246
Okudzhava, Bulat, 13, 154, 158
Oleszczuk, Thomas, 166, 176
Oliinyk, Borys, 13, 14, 182
Oliver, Spencer, 132
Olshanivskyi, Ihor, 117
Omelchenko, Vasilii, 27
Omskaia oblast, 15
Organization of Ukrainian Nationalists (OUN), 140, 141
Orlov, Yurii, 129
Osadchuk, Bohdan, 200
Osadchyi, Mykhailo, 24, 26, 35
Osherowitch, Mendel, xxiii, xxiv, xxvi, 118
Osipova, Tatiana, 146

Osmolovskyi (Osadchuk), Leonid, ix, 16, 28, 76, 85, 87, 90, 161, 162, 184, 185, 188, 191, 192, 263
Ottawa, 226
Ovsiienko, Vasyl, 146

Palamarchuk, Luka, 63
Palestine, 64
Panasuk, Larry, 227
Panchenko, Volodymyr, 6
Paradzhanov, Sergei, 14, 23, 65
Paris, 82, 90, 106, 135, 154, 156, 213
Paritskii, Aleksandr, 31
parochialism, 8
partiinost, 246
Pascal, Blaise, 73
Pasichnyk, Volodymyr, 133, 136, 137, 144
Pasternak, Boris, 19, 20, 45, 46, 50, 64, 88, 89, 163
Pasteur, Louis, 156
Patolichev, Nikolai, 239
Pavlovskii, Gleb, 113, 146
Pavlychko, Dmytro, 52, 264
Pavlyshyn, Marko, 7
Peive, Yan, 66
People's Movement of Ukraine (Rukh), 144
Peredelkino (Moscow), 270
Perepeliak, Ivan, 108
Pererva, Anatolii, 261
Perets, 112, 219
Perlustration, 33, 51
Perm, 14, 146
Perse, Saint-John, 68
Pervomaiskyi, Leonid, 7, 86, 113
petliurite, or *petliurites*, 214, 218
Petrov, Volodymyr, 22
Petrovska, T., 72
Petrovsky, Boris, 180
Petrovsky-Shtern, Yohanan, 7, 112, 119, 120
piatidesiatnik, 58
Picasso, Pablo, 136, 263
Pidhornyi, Mykola, 22, 47, 61, 246

Pipes, Richard, 132
Piven (Huk), Lidiia, 176
Plakhotniuk, Mykola, 35, 181, 199
Pliushch, Leonid, 13, 25, 31, 35, 44, 113, 166, 169, 170, 186, 194, 200, 263, 279
Plokhy, Serhii, 275
Podrabinek, Alexander, 133, 134, 171, 172, 188, 197
Pohribnyi, Anatolii, 217
Pohruzhalskyi, Viktor, 51, 204
Poland, 19, 102, 122, 213, 256; Poles, 74, 122; Polish, 81, 129, 220, 256; Polish-Lithuanian Commonwealth, 102; Polish Public Self-Defense Committee, 129; Polish Resistance, 256
Polianetskyi, Viktor, 44
Polikarpov, Dmitrii, 20, 46
political/punitive psychiatry, 128, 146, 166–68, 171, 175, 176, 178, 184–89, 199, 280
Polonskyi, Radii, 18, 24, 27, 32, 34, 37, 49, 51, 95, 139, 254–56, 258–61
Poltava, 221; Poltava psychiatric clinic, 184
Pomerantsev, Peter, 175
Pomerantsev, Vladimir, 1, 38
Ponomariov, Vladimir, 133, 153
Popov, Vladimir, 231, 237
populism, 8
postmodernism, xiii
Postyshev, Pavlo, 210, 215
Potebnia, Oleksandr, 138, 155
Potichnyj, Peter, 120
Pozdniakov, M., 26
Pozhenian, Grigorii, 158
Prague, 71, 213; Prague Spring, 91
Prapor, 2, 3, 21, 26, 27, 35–37, 47, 68–70, 82, 84, 175, 247, 252, 255, 263, 265
Pravda, 63
Pravda Ukrainy, 86
Preshman, Boris, 243
Pritsak, Omeljan, 120

Privedyonnaya, Yulia, 201
Procyk, Anna, 128
propaganda, 9, 46, 52, 71, 80, 113–17, 119, 122, 124–26, 137, 139, 141, 176, 184, 190, 191, 218, 219, 244
prophylactic talks/meetings, 22, 26, 38, 204, 245, 252
pro-Soviet, 27
Prosvita, 155
Proudhon, Pierre-Joseph, 64
Public Committee for Jewish-Ukrainian Cooperation, 130
Pugachiov, Leonid, 136
Putin, Vladimir, 185, 200
Pylypenko, Borys, 211

Quasimodo, Salvatore, 12, 43

racist, 64
Radio Liberty (Svoboda), 116, 123, 184, 198, 200
Raduga, 77, 249
Radygin, Anatolii, 128
Rafalsky, Viktor, 170, 183, 189, 195
raikom, 21
Rakhlin, Feliks, 4, 91, 246
Rakhlina, Marlena, 60, 66, 67, 76, 90–93, 133–36, 143, 144, 249
Rapoport (first name unknown), 211
Ravensbrück, 83, 107
Reagan, Ronald, 245
Red Army, 14, 156, 256
Reddaway, Peter, 166, 167, 169
Redlich, Shimon, 122
Red Renaissance, xiv, 58, 209
Red Square, 245
refusenik, 116, 121, 127, 129, 130, 146, 241, 246
rehabilitation, xviii, 20, 58, 65, 212; Rehabilitation Commission, 65
Remarque, Erich Maria, 264
Renard, Pierre-Jules, 73
Repin, Il'ia, 45
re-Stalinization, xvii, xx, 1, 9, 12, 19, 21, 55, 59, 68, 90, 91, 93, 95, 111, 126, 203, 241, 263, 275

returnees, 21, 76, 182
Revolutionary Ukrainian Party (RUP), 272, 273
Revolution of Poets, 1, 2
Rezhinashvili, Ushangi, 249
Risch, William Jay, 9
Rivne, 221
Robins, James, xiv, xxiv
Rochester, 117
Rodionov, Vladimir, 263
Roginskii, Arsenii, 94
Romania, 129
Romm, Mikhail, 59, 97
Rosenbaum, Yevheniia Iosypivna, 82
Rossiia, 110
Roth, David, 130, 132
Rozanov, Vasilii, 73
Rozhdestvenskii, Robert, 13
RSFSR, xviii, 14, 57, 58, 136, 137, 216, 245; Criminal Code, 196
Ruban, Petro, 200
Rubinshtein, Anna, 93
Rudenko, Mykola, 129, 136, 137, 154, 155, 179, 180, 198, 219–21
Russia, xxiii, 46, 67, 79, 91, 98, 129, 136, 154, 156, 167, 185, 189, 195, 206, 208, 217, 223, 232, 275; imperial, 33, 211
Russian/s, xv, xvi, xviii, xxiii, 6, 7, 10, 16, 19, 22, 23, 27, 28, 38, 64, 65, 68, 72–75, 80, 81, 84, 85, 92, 95, 96, 111, 113, 114, 117, 133–35, 138–40, 154, 185, 230, 243, 244, 252; Association of Independent Psychiatrists, 167; Association of Psychiatrists, 167; culture, 59, 67, 281; Duma (Parliament), 201, 230; émigré literature, 91; Empire, 102, 272, 273; Federation, 52, 76, 146, 206, 208, 256, 275; intelligentsia/intellectuals, 10, 95, 136, 139; language, 37, 59, 76–78, 80, 81, 89, 136, 137, 156, 177, 178, 181, 200, 242, 249; military, 188; nationalism, 59
Russian-Ukrainian relations, 275

Russification, 6, 7, 23, 31, 35, 80, 116, 137, 138, 176, 177, 188, 210, 222, 259, 260, 263, 272, 281
Russo-centric, xviii
Russo-Finish war, 82
Russophilism, 67
Russophone/russophones, 22, 24
Ruvinskaia, Irina, 93
Rybak, Natan, 75
Rylskyi, Maksym, 15, 16, 214–16

Safer, Morley, 145
Sahaidachnyi, Petro, 236
Sakharov, Andrei, 31, 133, 134, 146, 245, 251
Samoilov, David, 78, 249
Samvydav/samizdat, 7, 8, 11, 13, 23, 26, 31, 32, 41, 52, 70, 117, 125–28, 139, 143, 144, 218, 245, 250
Sapeliak, Stepan, 133, 144, 199
Sapir, Edward, xv
Saratov, 52
Savvina, Iia, 51
Schiller, Friedrich, 156
Schindler's List, 74
schizophrenia, 167–69, 187, 196, 201
Schroeter, Leonard, 245
Second World War, 14, 22, 29, 63, 68, 88, 118, 122, 124, 126, 156, 169, 217, 248, 256, 258
seksot/seksoty, 30, 50, 220, 248, 258, 279
Seleznenko, Leonid, 141
Semenko, Mykhail,' 273
Semichastnyi, Vladimir, 241
Sentinel, 131
Serbsky Scientific Research Institute of Forensic Psychiatry, 128, 166–69, 171–73, 181, 193, 200, 201
Serbyn, Roman, 205, 231
Serhienko, Oleksandr, 35
Shabatura, Stefaniia, 35
Shakespeare, William, 156
Shankowsky, Lew, 67
Shapoval, Mykola, 252, 258
Sharanskii, Natan, 129

Shatylov, Mykola, xv, xxv, 36, 61, 246, 260, 263
Shawnee, 256
Shazar, Zalman, 127, 151
Shcherbak, Yurii, 202
Shcherbytskyi, Volodymyr, xiv, 32, 33, 140, 142, 182, 186, 199, 219, 220, 225, 227, 250, 260
Shchipachiov, Stepan, 78
Shelepin, Aleksandr, 50
Shelest, Petro, xiv, xxiv, 33, 51, 55–58, 61–66, 70, 93–96, 118, 186, 247, 250, 251; era, 74
Shepilov, Dmitrii, 20
Sheptystky, Andrey, 213
Sherement, Mykola, 113
shestidesiatnik, xviii
Shevchenko, Mykhailo, 252
Shevchenko, Mykola, 180, 181
Shevchenko, Taras, 8, 12, 61, 65, 76, 137, 177, 265, 273; Literary Award, 84, 217
Shevel, Heorhii, 124, 125, 150
Shevelov, George (Sheveliov, Yurii), 138, 156, 281
Shifrin, Avraam, 113
shistdesiatnytstvo, or *shistdesiatnyky*, or sixties movement, 2, 4–10, 12–14, 55, 58, 68, 75, 77, 78, 89, 90, 112, 140, 169, 204, 259, 263, 275, 277, 278
Shkandrij, Myroslav, 7, 281
Shklovskii, Viktor, 134
Shliakh Peremohy, 225
Shmerkin, Genrikh, 76, 90, 93
Shorokh, Sasha, 64
Shostakovich, Dmitrii, 59
Shovkoplias, Yurii, 22, 84, 87
Shumuk, Danylo, 35
Shumytskyi, Stanislav, 16, 25, 28, 34, 35, 38, 51, 52, 87, 108
Shvets, Ivan, 20
Shvets, Yuri, 221
Siberia, 15, 68, 128, 245, 253; Siberian, 113
Siganevich, Eduard, 76, 90

Silaiev, Boris, 135, 154
Silver Age, 19
Simferopol, 239
Siniavskii, Andrei, 23, 47, 136, 244, 249
Siroshtan, Mykola Antonovych, 22, 47, 87
sixties generation (*shistdesiatnyky*), 2–10, 22, 24, 52
Skaba, Andrii, 22, 47
Skliarov, Yurii, 37
Skoblinskii, Konstantin, 90
Skochuk, Pavlo, 183
Skovoroda, Hyrhorii, 73, 138, 155
Skovorodynivka, 138
Skryprnyk, Mykola, 213, 214
Skunts, Petro, 18, 260
Skvyra, 15
Sloboda, 24, 48
Slobozhany, 24, 48
Slonim, Marc, 38
Sloviansk Pedagogical Institute, 175
Sloviansk psychiatric hospital, 175, 178, 179, 181
Sluch River, 15
Slutskii, Boris, 95, 134
Smena, 77
SMERSH, 256
Smila, 15
Smith, Teresa, 166
Smorodinsky, S., 194
Snezhnevsky, Andrei, 167, 172, 187, 194
socialism, 105, 219; late, 41, 191, 225, 250, 257
socialist/realism, 59, 97, 134
Society for the Propaganda of Political and Scientific Knowledge, 62
Sokulskyi, Ivan, 32, 176
Solidarity, 144, 159
Solzhenitsyn, Aleksandr, 13, 31, 139, 177
Som, Mykola, 14
Soroka, Petro, 72
Sosin, Ivan, 174, 180, 181, 189, 196, 202
Sosiura, Volodymyr, 184

Sovetish Heymland, 75, 77, 80
Sovetskii ekran, 77
Soviet: Army, 46; citizens, 21, 41, 62, 78, 82, 94, 95, 107, 141, 143, 145, 153, 163, 184, 206, 218, 226, 275, 278; cultural politics/cultural trends, 7, 218, 229; empire, 275; era, xiv, 11, 36, 43, 51, 73, 77, 172, 196, 206, 208, 212, 229, 279; gold trade, 239; hegemony, 24; history, xviii, xxi, 10, 61, 205, 265, 277; identity, 58; institutions, 103, 121, 218, 226, 260; intelligentsia, 11, 19; nationalities policy/policies, 10, 23, 57, 59, 65, 71, 125, 188, 218; repression, 36, 116, 184, 224; Russia, xxiv; secret police, xxv, 103; Ukraine, xiii, xiv, xx, xxiii, 2, 3, 8, 60, 98, 120, 141, 164, 195, 205, 206, 209, 213, 229; Union, xx, 1, 5, 9, 19, 20, 31, 33, 36, 48, 56, 62, 63, 67, 70, 71, 75, 79, 82, 91, 93, 94, 98, 104, 113, 115–19, 121–25, 128, 130, 132, 133, 136, 137, 139, 144, 151, 152, 161–63, 165–68, 176, 179, 180, 183–87, 190, 191, 194, 201, 206, 208, 218, 224–26, 242–44, 247, 248, 251, 253, 254, 256, 260, 275, 276
sovok, 98
spatial belonging, 61
spetskor, 86
Spielberg, Steven, 74
SS, xxii
Stadnychenko, Yurii, 22, 47, 192, 256, 265
Stalin, Josef, xiv, xviii, xxi, 11, 21, 22, 46, 55, 57, 60, 62, 65, 82, 91, 93, 105, 126, 137, 205, 245, 261, 275–77; camps, 20; command economy, 225; crimes, 9; cult, 58; era, 3, 4, 57, 178, 212, 216, 235; legacies, 263; Prize, 15, 28, 82; repression (mass repression), xviii, 11, 21; terror, 2, 7, 59, 65, 93, 96, 122, 263, 278

Stalinism, xviii, xxi, 20, 57, 177, 187, 241, 260, 280
Stalinist, 2, 9, 76, 79; era, 26, 225; methods of governing, 26; rhetoric, 19; traditions, 13, 20
Stanislaviv, 91
Starodub, Anatolii, 28, 49, 108
Stebun, Illia, 86
Stern, Mikhail, 122, 150
Stradnyk, Petro, 223
Strokata-Karavanska, Nina, 35
Stus, Vasyl, 7, 35, 113, 114, 146, 182, 198, 251, 280
Subtelny, Orest, 120
Suchasnist, 121, 144
Suk, Ivan, 218
Sukhorukov, Boris, 80
Sukhorukova, Inna, 251
Sumtsov, Mykola, 138, 155
Sumy, 146
Supłatowicz, Stanisław (Sat-Okh), 74, 256, 257
Support Committee for Ukrainian Jews, 118
Surkov, Aleksei, 12, 43
surveillance, 26, 30, 33, 50, 51, 95, 115, 142, 181, 243, 244, 255, 256
Suslenskii, Yakov, 130–32, 145
Suslov, Mikhail, 20, 26, 65, 70, 93, 242, 251
Sverstiuk, Yevhen, 35, 59, 113, 183, 204
Svetlov, Mikhail, 248
Svirskii, Vitalii, 88
Svitlychna, Nadiia, 35, 200
Svitlychnyi, Ivan, 6, 24, 26, 35, 59, 72, 183, 204
Svoboda, 224, 225
Swoboda, Victor, xxv, xxvi
Sylaev, Borys, 261
Symonenko, Vasyl, 13, 14
synagogues, 59, 94, 243
Synhaiivskyi, Mykola, 18
Syria, 26, 127
Syvokin, Hyrhorii, 72

Szporluk, Roman, 7

Taitslin, V. I., 172
Tajik, 6, 176
Talmud, 77
Taranenko, I. V., 199
Tarkovskii, Arsenii, 78
Tarnapolskii, Yurii, 31
Tarnashynska, Liudmyla, 5
Tarsis, Valery, 166
Tashkent, 153
Tatars, 6, 64, 95
Tatarstan, 245
Telniuk, Stanislav, 37
Terekhin, N. M., 142
Terelya, Josyp, 197
Tertz, Abram, 136
Thatcher, Margaret, 245
Thaw, xvii, xx, xxii, 2, 4–6, 8–10, 12, 13, 25, 58, 59, 61, 75–78, 90, 94, 95, 126, 165, 241, 249, 259, 264, 279
Theseus, 69, 184
Tikhonov, Nikolai, 26
Tiumen, 68
Tiutiunnyk, Hryhir, 87, 107, 161, 191, 263
Tiutiunnyk, Hryhorii, 84, 107
Tiutiunnyk, Yevhen, 15
Toma, Leonid, 262, 272
Toronto, 132, 224
Treblinka, 122
Tretyakov, Robert, xxiv, 12, 14–25, 30, 31, 33–36, 38, 44, 45, 47, 51, 68, 70, 74, 78, 81, 84–86, 90, 92, 95, 107, 144, 161, 175, 176, 184, 185, 197, 203, 230, 252–64, 266, 272, 278, 279
Tretyakova, Lidiya, 19–21, 44, 49, 51, 254, 255, 259
trials: Bolotnoe delo, 185; Daniel-Siniavskii, 136; Koryagin, 196; Moroz-Ivashchenko, 136; Pohruzhalskyi, 204; Stern, 122, 150
Trick, Alan, 227
Tromly, Benjamin, 8
Troy, New York, 117

Trufanova, Lidiya, 15
Tsvetaieva, Marina, 89
Turkmen, 6
Tvardovskii, Aleksandr, 13, 78, 143
Tychyna, Pavlo, 16; Pavlo Tychyna Prize, 255
Tykhyi, Oleksa, 129, 179, 182, 198, 251

Ukraine, xvii, xviii, xix, xxv, 1, 2, 6–8, 10–12, 14, 15, 18, 20, 23, 24, 26, 29, 31–33, 35, 36, 38, 47–49, 51, 55–60, 62, 65–68, 70, 72, 76, 79, 82, 91–96, 98, 114, 116–18, 123–30, 136, 137, 139–42, 144–46, 162, 164, 167–69, 175–77, 182–86, 188–98, 203–5, 208, 210–13, 215, 216, 218, 220, 222–25, 227–30, 243, 246, 250, 252, 253, 256, 258–63, 275, 277–81; Eastern, 32, 35, 168; Southern, 32; Western, 24, 41, 48, 156, 168
Ukrainian-Jewish encounter/encounters /relations/friendship, xvi, 119, 120, 122, 129, 131, 132, 145, 277
Ukrainianness, 6, 38, 185
Ukrainian, xv, xvi, xvii, xviii, xxiii, 5–8, 10–12, 15, 16, 26–28, 38, 55, 56, 60, 61, 63, 65, 72, 73, 75, 80, 81, 83–86, 88, 92, 93, 95, 96, 111–23, 125–28, 130, 131, 133, 135, 137–40, 144, 145, 150, 168, 176, 177, 185, 186, 188, 197, 204, 211, 213, 219–23, 229, 241, 244, 250, 252, 259, 261, 262, 264, 275, 277, 280, 281; Academy of Arts and Science, New York, 118; Academy of Sciences, Kyiv, 124, 155, 220, 226 (Institute of History, 124; Institute of Literature, 220); Autocephalous Orthodox Church, 124; Canadian Research & Documentation Center, 228; Communist Party (KPU), xiv, 55, 63, 94, 124, 157, 199, 247; Congress Committee of America (UKKA), 223, 224, 238; consciousness, 65; Criminal Code, 176, 196; culture, 5, 8, 15, 23, 32, 57, 63, 65, 68, 139, 157, 176, 188, 204, 259, 260, 263, 264, 272, 275; Democratic Movement, 131; diplomats, 124; famine, xxiii, 20, 169, 204, 205, 208–16, 218–26, 228, 229, 231; Famine Commission, 132; Famine Research Committee, 228; government, 74; Greek Catholic Church, 213; Helsinki Group (UHH), 128, 182, 198, 199, 251; Helsinki Human Rights Union, 144; Helsinki Union, 182, 183; history, 57, 120, 121, 157, 258; identity, 9, 176, 252, 260; Institute of Doctors' Advancement, 189 (Narcology Department, 189); intelligentsia/ intellectuals, xvii, xviii, 12–14, 22–27, 30, 31, 35, 36, 48, 56, 60, 61, 64, 66, 74, 91, 93, 95, 96, 113, 116, 126, 136, 139–41, 182, 188, 207–9, 212, 214–16, 219, 224, 225, 250, 251, 253, 254, 261, 275, 278; language, 5, 19, 22, 23, 32, 34–36, 38, 65, 66, 68, 76, 80, 81, 89, 108, 113, 124, 137, 155, 156, 175–79, 181, 200, 204, 205, 220, 232, 242, 246, 256, 259, 262, 280; Military Organization, 210; Ministry of Foreign Affairs, 124, 125, 226; Ministry of Health, 189; Ministry of Internal Affairs (MVS), 126; multicultural, 65, 96 (distinctiveness, 57); National Association (UNA), 130, 131, 152; National Committee (UNK), 103; National Front (UNF), 128, 155; nationalism, xvi, 21, 22, 25, 32, 37, 50, 56, 57, 60, 113, 120, 121, 137, 141, 182, 183, 198, 207, 208, 210, 211, 214, 218, 219, 241, 250, 259, 263, 277; nationalist/ nationalists, 20, 24, 26, 30, 32, 33, 38, 47, 74, 93, 94, 111, 112, 123–25, 131, 136, 137, 139–41, 169, 175, 177, 179, 182, 183, 197,

205, 207, 208, 211–13, 218, 222–25, 232, 242, 247, 250, 271, 276, 280 (Movement of Ukrainian Nationalists (PUN), 120); national liberation, 24 (movement, 12, 67, 94, 182, 273); National Women's League of America (UNWLA), 117; Psychiatric Association, 189; Research Institute at Harvard University (HURI), 120; revival, 57; sovereignty, 188, 208, 213; Soviet Socialist Republic (SSR), xiv, xxiv, 114; statehood, 264; World Congress, 132
Ukrainian Weekly, 131
Ukrainka, Lesia, 37
Ukrainophilia, 65
Ukrainophobia, 277
Ulishchenko, Olha, 192
ulpany, 127
UNESCO, 117
Union of Councils for Soviet Jews (UCSJ), 119
Union of Ukrainian Youth (SUM), 144
United Nations (UN), 63, 117; UN Committee on Human Rights, 127; UN Secretariat, 124
United States, 72, 79, 89, 93, 99, 117–23, 127, 128, 131, 140, 141, 151, 152, 156, 175, 184, 223, 225–27, 230, 239, 254, 255, 275; Commission on Ukraine Famine, 228; Congress, 117, 123; Department of Agriculture, 227 (Foreign Agriculture Service, 227; Grain Division Office, 227); Department of Justice, 123, 131; Department of State, 133; Embassy in Moscow, 227; Federal Government, 130, 226, 227; foreign food aid programs, 227; Helsinki Commission, 152; Immigration and Naturalization Service, 123
universalism, 8
University of Pennsylvania, 156

Urals, 113
Urin, Viktor, 249
Usoltsev, Vladimir, 142
USSR, 10, 20, 26, 36, 43, 46, 47, 59, 61–63, 65, 72, 79, 82, 90, 94, 112, 115, 116, 118, 121, 127, 130–32, 141, 144, 166, 168, 171, 176, 179, 184–86, 204, 208, 209, 212, 213, 215, 216, 222, 224–27, 241, 254, 260, 261, 266; Council of Ministers, 2, 250, 261; Council of Religious Affairs, 242; Ministry of State Security, 236
Uzbekistan, 270; Uzbek, 6, 176
Uzhorod, 144, 260

Valkivskyi district, 52
Valshonok, Zinovii, 16, 76–79, 93, 142, 248
van Bruggen, Adolph Cornelis, 67
van Bruggen, Kees, 67, 101
Vanshenkin, Konstantin, 249
van Voren, Robert, 166–68, 171, 189, 195
Vashchenko, Hyrhorii, xv
Vatican Radio, 116
Velikanova, Natalia, 134
Verne, Jules Gabriel, 68
Vernik, Aleksandr, 71, 76, 90, 93, 243, 266
ViatLag, 134, 153
Viazemskii, Terentii, 102
Vienna, xxii, 61, 213
Vinhranovskyi, Mykola, 13, 18
Vinnytsia, 65, 239
Vinogradov, Igor, 154
Viola, Lynne, 278
Virchenko, Yurii, xxiv
Vishnevskii, David, 66, 84, 87
Visti z Ukrainy, 124
Vitchyzna, 72
Vladimir Prison, 117
Vladivostok, xviii
Vlodov, Yurii, 95, 96, 110
Voice of America, 116, 135, 153

The Voice of America, 256
Volga River, 52
Voloshanovich, Aleksandr, 166, 173, 174, 196
von Bruggen, Baron, 68
Voronko, Platon, 16
Voronyi, Marko, 211, 215
Voronyi, Mykola, 215
Voznesenskii, Andrei, 13, 91
Vudka, Ar'ie, 113
Vukhnal, Yurii, 41
Vvedenskyi, Andrii, 15
Vyrhan, Ivan, 18, 20, 21, 36, 84, 86, 87, 262, 263

Walesa, Lech, 159
Wanner, Catherine, 261
war criminals, 123
Warsaw, Poland, 220
Warsaw Pact, 159
White Guard, 56
Whorf, Benjamin Lee, xv
Wilson, Andrew, 7, 13
Wittgenstein, Ludwig, 184, 185
Wood, Michael, 190
Working Commission to Investigate the Use of Psychiatry for Political Purposes, 173, 174, 196
World Congress of Free Ukrainians (WCFU), 132, 223, 238
World Psychiatric Association, 186
Writers' Union, 9, 12, 16, 18, 21, 23, 27–32, 34–37, 43, 45, 46, 49, 66, 72, 77, 80, 81, 84–89, 92, 93, 98, 111, 114, 135–40, 143, 144, 154, 158, 203, 217, 221, 246–48, 251, 252, 255, 256, 259–61, 266, 270

Yakutiia, 253
Yakutsk, 253, 254
Yanovskyi, Yurii, 215
Yekelchyk, Serhy, 8
Yelchenko, Yurii, 124
Yeltsin, Boris, 261
Yemel'ianova, Irina, 46
Yesenin, Sergei, 19, 70, 90, 258
Yevtushenko, Yevgenii, xviii, xxv, 3, 13, 49, 59, 88, 91, 97, 158, 249
Yezhenkova, Valentina, 90
Yiddish, xv, xvi, 59, 77, 242; culture, 59; institutions, 58, 59, 67; language, 59, 67, 75, 76, 80–82, 105, 113; writers, 76
Yovenko, Svitlana, 73
Yukhvid, Leonid, 75

Zabuzhko, Oksana, 13, 35, 36
Zahrebelnyi, Pavlo, 246
Zakharov, Yefim, 133
Zakharov, Yevhen, 144
Zalygin, Sergei, 158
Zalyvakha, Panas, 24
Zaporizhzhia, 221, 227, 239
Zatulyviter, Volodymyr, 252
Zbanatskyi, Yurii, 29
Zdorovyi, Anatolii, 133
Zelinskii, Valerii, 112
Zelman, Hryhorii, 103
Zelman, Oleksii, 103
Zeltman, Yadya, 128
Zerov, Mykola, 211, 214–16
Zhabotinskii, Vladimir, 81
Zheludkov, Sergei, 134
Zhitnitskii, Anatolii, 249
Zhuk, Sergei I, xxv, 8
Zhulynskyi, Mykola, 5, 217
Zhuravsky, Arkady, 178, 179, 181, 198
Zhvanetskii, Mikhail, 66
Zhyhalko, Serhii, 211, 216
Zhylenko, Iryna, 25
Zhytomyr, 221
Zionism, xvi, 46, 56, 60, 62, 63, 71, 77, 91, 95, 121, 151
Zionists, xviii, 20, 46, 56, 60, 62, 63, 70, 71, 74, 77, 78, 88, 89, 91, 94, 95, 111, 112, 121, 123, 124, 131, 138, 142, 151, 242, 244, 247, 280;

movement, 242; Organization of America, 62
Zisels, Iosif (Zysels, Iosyp), 113, 146, 151
Žižek, Slavoj, 11, 14, 170, 187

Znam'ianka, Ukraine, 203
Zubarev, Oleksandr, 23
Zulim, Maria, 200
Zvezda, 77

About the Author

Olga Bertelsen is associate professor of global security and intelligence at Tiffin University, Ohio. Educated at the Medical State University (Ukraine), Bloomsburg University of Pennsylvania, Penn State University, and the University of Nottingham, she is published widely on state violence in the USSR and the methods and traditions of the Soviet/Russian secret police. She is the author of *The House of Writers in Ukraine, the 1930s: Conceived, Lived, Perceived* (2013), and the editor of anthologies of archival KGB documents on persecutions of Jews (2011) and Ukrainian intellectuals in the Soviet Union (2016), *Revolution and War in Contemporary Ukraine: The Challenge of Change* (2017), and *Russian Active Measures: Yesterday, Today, Tomorrow* (2021).

www.ingramcontent.com/pod-product-compliance
Lightning Source LLC
Chambersburg PA
CBHW071358300426
44114CB00016B/2106